Y0-DYF-476

2000
America's
Top-Rated Cities:
A Statistical Handbook

Volume 1: Southern Region

Grey House
Publishing

LAKEVILLE, CT 06039

HA
214
.A43
1999
V.1

PUBLISHER: Leslie Mackenzie
EDITOR: David Garoogian
EDITORIAL DIRECTOR: Laura Mars
EDITORIAL ASSISTANT: Robin Williams
PRODUCTION MANAGER: Timothy Cushman
MARKET RESEARCH: Jessica Moody
GRAPHIC DESIGNER: Deb Fletcher

Grey House Publishing, Inc.
Pocket Knife Square
Lakeville, CT 06039
860.435.0868
FAX 860.435.6613
http://www.greyhouse.com

While every effort has been made to ensure the reliability of the information presented in this publication, Grey House Publishing neither guarantees the accuracy of the data contained herein nor assumes any responsibility for errors, omissions or discrepancies. Grey House accepts no payment for listing; inclusion in the publication of any organization, agency, institution, publication, service or individual does not imply endorsement of the editors or publisher.

Errors brought to the attention of the publisher and verified to the satisfaction of the publisher will be corrected in future editions.

Except by express prior written permission of the Copyright Proprietor no part of this work may be copied by any means of publication or communication now known or developed hereafter including, but not limited to, use in any directory of compilation or other print publication, in any information storage and retrieval system, in any other electronic device, or in any visual or audio-visual device or product.

This publication is an original and creative work, copyrighted by Grey House Publishing, Inc. and is fully protected by all applicable copyright laws, as well as by laws covering misappropriation, trade secrets and unfair competition.

Grey House has added value to the underlying factual material through one or more of the following efforts: unique and original selection; expression; arrangement; coordination; and classification.

Grey House Publishing, Inc. will defend its rights in this publication.

Copyright© 1999 Grey House Publishing
All rights reserved

First edition published 1992
Seventh edition published 1999

Printed in the USA

Library of Congress Cataloging in Publication Data available

4-Volume Set	ISBN 1-891482-50-5
Volume 1	**ISBN 1-891482-51-3**
Volume 2	ISBN 1-891482-52-1
Volume 3	ISBN 1-891482-53-X
Volume 4	ISBN 1-891482-54-8

Table of Contents

Atlanta, Georgia

Background 1

General Rankings and Evaluative Comments 2

Business Environment

STATE ECONOMY 4

IMPORTS/EXPORTS 4

CITY FINANCES 4

POPULATION 5

INCOME 6

EMPLOYMENT 7

TAXES 9

COMMERCIAL REAL ESTATE 10

COMMERCIAL UTILITIES 11

TRANSPORTATION 11

BUSINESSES 12

HOTELS & MOTELS 14

CONVENTION CENTERS 14

Living Environment

COST OF LIVING 15

HOUSING 15

RESIDENTIAL UTILITIES 15

HEALTH CARE 15

EDUCATION 16

MAJOR EMPLOYERS 17

PUBLIC SAFETY 18

RECREATION 18

MEDIA 18

CLIMATE 20

AIR & WATER QUALITY 20

Austin, Texas

Background 21

General Rankings and Evaluative Comments 22

Business Environment

STATE ECONOMY 24

IMPORTS/EXPORTS 24

CITY FINANCES 24

POPULATION 25

INCOME 26

EMPLOYMENT 27

TAXES 29

COMMERCIAL REAL ESTATE 29

COMMERCIAL UTILITIES 30

TRANSPORTATION 31

BUSINESSES 31

HOTELS & MOTELS 32

CONVENTION CENTERS 33

Living Environment

COST OF LIVING 34

HOUSING 34

RESIDENTIAL UTILITIES 34

HEALTH CARE 34

EDUCATION 35

MAJOR EMPLOYERS 36

PUBLIC SAFETY 36

RECREATION 36

MEDIA 37

CLIMATE 38

AIR & WATER QUALITY 38

Birmingham, Alabama

Background 41

General Rankings and Evaluative Comments 42

Business Environment

STATE ECONOMY 43
IMPORTS/EXPORTS 43
CITY FINANCES 43
POPULATION 44
INCOME 45
EMPLOYMENT 46
TAXES 48
COMMERCIAL REAL ESTATE 49
COMMERCIAL UTILITIES 49
TRANSPORTATION 50
BUSINESSES 50
HOTELS & MOTELS 51
CONVENTION CENTERS 51

Living Environment

COST OF LIVING 52
HOUSING 52
RESIDENTIAL UTILITIES 52
HEALTH CARE 53
EDUCATION 53
MAJOR EMPLOYERS 54
PUBLIC SAFETY 55
RECREATION 55
MEDIA 55
CLIMATE 56
AIR & WATER QUALITY 57

Chattanooga, Tennessee

Background 59

General Rankings and Evaluative Comments 60

Business Environment

STATE ECONOMY 61
IMPORTS/EXPORTS 61
CITY FINANCES 61
POPULATION 62
INCOME 63
EMPLOYMENT 64
TAXES 66
COMMERCIAL REAL ESTATE 66
COMMERCIAL UTILITIES 67
TRANSPORTATION 67
BUSINESSES 68
HOTELS & MOTELS 68
CONVENTION CENTERS 68

Living Environment

COST OF LIVING 69
HOUSING 69
RESIDENTIAL UTILITIES 69
HEALTH CARE 69
EDUCATION 70
MAJOR EMPLOYERS 71
PUBLIC SAFETY 71
RECREATION 71
MEDIA 72
CLIMATE 73
AIR & WATER QUALITY 73

Columbia, South Carolina

Background 75

General Rankings and Evaluative Comments 76

Business Environment

STATE ECONOMY 77
IMPORTS/EXPORTS 77
CITY FINANCES. 77
POPULATION. 78
INCOME 79
EMPLOYMENT. 80
TAXES 82
COMMERCIAL REAL ESTATE. 83
COMMERCIAL UTILITIES 83
TRANSPORTATION 84
BUSINESSES. 84
HOTELS & MOTELS 85
CONVENTION CENTERS 85

Living Environment

COST OF LIVING 86
HOUSING 86
RESIDENTIAL UTILITIES 86
HEALTH CARE 86
EDUCATION 87
MAJOR EMPLOYERS. 88
PUBLIC SAFETY. 88
RECREATION 88
MEDIA 89
CLIMATE 90
AIR & WATER QUALITY 91

Dallas, Texas

Background 93

General Rankings and Evaluative Comments 94

Business Environment

STATE ECONOMY 96
IMPORTS/EXPORTS 96
CITY FINANCES. 96
POPULATION. 97
INCOME 98
EMPLOYMENT. 99
TAXES 101
COMMERCIAL REAL ESTATE. 101
COMMERCIAL UTILITIES 102
TRANSPORTATION 103
BUSINESSES. 103
HOTELS & MOTELS 105
CONVENTION CENTERS 105

Living Environment

COST OF LIVING 106
HOUSING 106
RESIDENTIAL UTILITIES 106
HEALTH CARE 107
EDUCATION 107
MAJOR EMPLOYERS. 108
PUBLIC SAFETY. 109
RECREATION 109
MEDIA 109
CLIMATE 111
AIR & WATER QUALITY 111

Fort Lauderdale, Florida

Background 113

General Rankings and Evaluative Comments 114

Business Environment

STATE ECONOMY 115
IMPORTS/EXPORTS 115
CITY FINANCES 115
POPULATION 116
INCOME 117
EMPLOYMENT 118
TAXES 120
COMMERCIAL REAL ESTATE 120
COMMERCIAL UTILITIES 121
TRANSPORTATION 122
BUSINESSES 122
HOTELS & MOTELS 123
CONVENTION CENTERS 123

Living Environment

COST OF LIVING 124
HOUSING 124
RESIDENTIAL UTILITIES 124
HEALTH CARE 125
EDUCATION 125
MAJOR EMPLOYERS 126
PUBLIC SAFETY 126
RECREATION 127
MEDIA 127
CLIMATE 128
AIR & WATER QUALITY 128

Fort Worth, Texas

Background 129

General Rankings and Evaluative Comments 130

Business Environment

STATE ECONOMY 131
IMPORTS/EXPORTS 131
CITY FINANCES 131
POPULATION 132
INCOME 133
EMPLOYMENT 134
TAXES 136
COMMERCIAL REAL ESTATE 136
COMMERCIAL UTILITIES 137
TRANSPORTATION 138
BUSINESSES 138
HOTELS & MOTELS 139
CONVENTION CENTERS 139

Living Environment

COST OF LIVING 140
HOUSING 140
RESIDENTIAL UTILITIES 140
HEALTH CARE 140
EDUCATION 141
MAJOR EMPLOYERS 142
PUBLIC SAFETY 142
RECREATION 142
MEDIA 143
CLIMATE 144
AIR & WATER QUALITY 144

Houston, Texas

Background 145

General Rankings and Evaluative Comments 146

Business Environment

STATE ECONOMY	148
IMPORTS/EXPORTS	148
CITY FINANCES	148
POPULATION	149
INCOME	150
EMPLOYMENT	151
TAXES	153
COMMERCIAL REAL ESTATE	154
COMMERCIAL UTILITIES	155
TRANSPORTATION	155
BUSINESSES	156
HOTELS & MOTELS	158
CONVENTION CENTERS	158

Living Environment

COST OF LIVING	159
HOUSING	159
RESIDENTIAL UTILITIES	159
HEALTH CARE	160
EDUCATION	160
MAJOR EMPLOYERS	162
PUBLIC SAFETY	162
RECREATION	162
MEDIA	162
CLIMATE	164
AIR & WATER QUALITY	165

Jackson, Mississippi

Background 167

General Rankings and Evaluative Comments 168

Business Environment

STATE ECONOMY	169
IMPORTS/EXPORTS	169
CITY FINANCES	169
POPULATION	170
INCOME	171
EMPLOYMENT	172
TAXES	174
COMMERCIAL REAL ESTATE	175
COMMERCIAL UTILITIES	175
TRANSPORTATION	176
BUSINESSES	176
HOTELS & MOTELS	176
CONVENTION CENTERS	177

Living Environment

COST OF LIVING	178
HOUSING	178
RESIDENTIAL UTILITIES	178
HEALTH CARE	178
EDUCATION	179
MAJOR EMPLOYERS	180
PUBLIC SAFETY	180
RECREATION	180
MEDIA	181
CLIMATE	182
AIR & WATER QUALITY	183

Jacksonville, Florida

Background 185

General Rankings and Evaluative Comments 186

Business Environment

STATE ECONOMY 188
IMPORTS/EXPORTS 188
CITY FINANCES 188
POPULATION 189
INCOME 190
EMPLOYMENT 191
TAXES 193
COMMERCIAL REAL ESTATE 194
COMMERCIAL UTILITIES 195
TRANSPORTATION 195
BUSINESSES 195
HOTELS & MOTELS 196
CONVENTION CENTERS 197

Living Environment

COST OF LIVING 198
HOUSING 198
RESIDENTIAL UTILITIES 198
HEALTH CARE 198
EDUCATION 199
MAJOR EMPLOYERS 200
PUBLIC SAFETY 200
RECREATION 200
MEDIA 201
CLIMATE 202
AIR & WATER QUALITY 203

Knoxville, Tennessee

Background 205

General Rankings and Evaluative Comments 206

Business Environment

STATE ECONOMY 207
IMPORTS/EXPORTS 207
CITY FINANCES 207
POPULATION 208
INCOME 209
EMPLOYMENT 210
TAXES 212
COMMERCIAL REAL ESTATE 212
COMMERCIAL UTILITIES 213
TRANSPORTATION 213
BUSINESSES 214
HOTELS & MOTELS 214
CONVENTION CENTERS 214

Living Environment

COST OF LIVING 215
HOUSING 215
RESIDENTIAL UTILITIES 215
HEALTH CARE 215
EDUCATION 216
MAJOR EMPLOYERS 217
PUBLIC SAFETY 217
RECREATION 217
MEDIA 218
CLIMATE 219
AIR & WATER QUALITY 219

Memphis, Tennessee

Background 221

General Rankings and Evaluative Comments 222

Business Environment

STATE ECONOMY 223
IMPORTS/EXPORTS 223
CITY FINANCES 223
POPULATION 224
INCOME 225
EMPLOYMENT 226
TAXES 228
COMMERCIAL REAL ESTATE 229
COMMERCIAL UTILITIES 229
TRANSPORTATION 230
BUSINESSES 230
HOTELS & MOTELS 231
CONVENTION CENTERS 231

Living Environment

COST OF LIVING 232
HOUSING 232
RESIDENTIAL UTILITIES 232
HEALTH CARE 232
EDUCATION 233
MAJOR EMPLOYERS 234
PUBLIC SAFETY 234
RECREATION 234
MEDIA 235
CLIMATE 236
AIR & WATER QUALITY 236

Miami, Florida

Background 239

General Rankings and Evaluative Comments 240

Business Environment

STATE ECONOMY 242
IMPORTS/EXPORTS 242
CITY FINANCES 242
POPULATION 243
INCOME 244
EMPLOYMENT 245
TAXES 247
COMMERCIAL REAL ESTATE 248
COMMERCIAL UTILITIES 249
TRANSPORTATION 249
BUSINESSES 249
HOTELS & MOTELS 251
CONVENTION CENTERS 251

Living Environment

COST OF LIVING 252
HOUSING 252
RESIDENTIAL UTILITIES 252
HEALTH CARE 253
EDUCATION 253
MAJOR EMPLOYERS 254
PUBLIC SAFETY 254
RECREATION 255
MEDIA 255
CLIMATE 256
AIR & WATER QUALITY 257

Nashville, Tennessee

Background 259

General Rankings and Evaluative Comments 260

Business Environment

STATE ECONOMY 262
IMPORTS/EXPORTS 262
CITY FINANCES 262
POPULATION 263
INCOME 264
EMPLOYMENT 265
TAXES 267
COMMERCIAL REAL ESTATE 268
COMMERCIAL UTILITIES 269
TRANSPORTATION 269
BUSINESSES 269
HOTELS & MOTELS 270
CONVENTION CENTERS 271

Living Environment

COST OF LIVING 272
HOUSING 272
RESIDENTIAL UTILITIES 272
HEALTH CARE 272
EDUCATION 273
MAJOR EMPLOYERS 274
PUBLIC SAFETY 274
RECREATION 274
MEDIA 275
CLIMATE 276
AIR & WATER QUALITY 277

New Orleans, Louisiana

Background 279

General Rankings and Evaluative Comments 280

Business Environment

STATE ECONOMY 282
IMPORTS/EXPORTS 282
CITY FINANCES 282
POPULATION 283
INCOME 284
EMPLOYMENT 285
TAXES 287
COMMERCIAL REAL ESTATE 288
COMMERCIAL UTILITIES 288
TRANSPORTATION 289
BUSINESSES 289
HOTELS & MOTELS 290
CONVENTION CENTERS 290

Living Environment

COST OF LIVING 291
HOUSING 291
RESIDENTIAL UTILITIES 291
HEALTH CARE 291
EDUCATION 292
MAJOR EMPLOYERS 293
PUBLIC SAFETY 293
RECREATION 293
MEDIA 294
CLIMATE 295
AIR & WATER QUALITY 295

Orlando, Florida

Background 297

General Rankings and Evaluative Comments 298

Business Environment

STATE ECONOMY 300
IMPORTS/EXPORTS 300
CITY FINANCES. 300
POPULATION. 301
INCOME 302
EMPLOYMENT. 303
TAXES 305
COMMERCIAL REAL ESTATE. 305
COMMERCIAL UTILITIES 306
TRANSPORTATION 307
BUSINESSES. 307
HOTELS & MOTELS 308
CONVENTION CENTERS 309

Living Environment

COST OF LIVING 310
HOUSING 310
RESIDENTIAL UTILITIES 310
HEALTH CARE 310
EDUCATION 311
MAJOR EMPLOYERS. 312
PUBLIC SAFETY. 312
RECREATION 312
MEDIA 313
CLIMATE 314
AIR & WATER QUALITY 314

San Antonio, Texas

Background 317

General Rankings and Evaluative Comments 318

Business Environment

STATE ECONOMY 320
IMPORTS/EXPORTS 320
CITY FINANCES. 320
POPULATION. 321
INCOME 322
EMPLOYMENT. 323
TAXES 325
COMMERCIAL REAL ESTATE. 326
COMMERCIAL UTILITIES 326
TRANSPORTATION 327
BUSINESSES. 327
HOTELS & MOTELS 328
CONVENTION CENTERS 329

Living Environment

COST OF LIVING 330
HOUSING 330
RESIDENTIAL UTILITIES 330
HEALTH CARE 330
EDUCATION 331
MAJOR EMPLOYERS. 332
PUBLIC SAFETY. 332
RECREATION 333
MEDIA 333
CLIMATE 334
AIR & WATER QUALITY 335

Tampa, Florida

Background 337

General Rankings and Evaluative Comments............................. 338

Business Environment

    STATE ECONOMY 340

    IMPORTS/EXPORTS 340

    CITY FINANCES........................... 340

    POPULATION 341

    INCOME 342

    EMPLOYMENT............................. 343

    TAXES................................... 345

    COMMERCIAL REAL ESTATE................ 345

    COMMERCIAL UTILITIES 346

    TRANSPORTATION 347

    BUSINESSES............................. 347

    HOTELS & MOTELS........................ 348

    CONVENTION CENTERS 348

Living Environment

    COST OF LIVING 349

    HOUSING 349

    RESIDENTIAL UTILITIES 349

    HEALTH CARE 349

    EDUCATION 350

    MAJOR EMPLOYERS....................... 351

    PUBLIC SAFETY........................... 351

    RECREATION 351

    MEDIA 352

    CLIMATE 353

    AIR & WATER QUALITY 353

APPENDIX A - Comparative Statistics 355

APPENDIX B - Metropolitan Statistical Areas 383

APPENDIX C - Chambers of Commerce 385

APPENDIX D - State Departments of Labor 387

Introduction

Welcome to *America's Top-Rated Cities, A Statistical Handbook, 2000,* a current and concise statistical profile of 76 cities that have received high marks for their business and living environment. This 7th edition of *ATRC*, previously published by Universal Reference Publications, incorporates information from hundreds of resources into one, easy-to-use format. It combines magazine rankings (*Money, Fortune, Entrepreneur, Sales & Marketing Management, Working Woman,* etc.) latest Federal, state and local statistics, published newspaper and magazine reports, and web site data to fill more than 60 charts and tables for each city.

Each of the four volumes is approximately 400 pages, and comprises a different region of the country – Southern, Western, Central and Eastern, and each region includes 19 cities, all with populations over 100,000.

Every year, our editors review hundreds of sources to develop the list of top cities in each region, invariably dropping some and adding others. This year's edition has 17 new cities not included last year – five Southern (**Birmingham, Chattanooga, Columbia, Jackson, Memphis**), five Eastern (**Akron, Louisville, Manchester, Providence, Rochester**), four Central (**Gary, Lansing, Omaha, Wichita**), and three Western (**Albuquerque, Reno, Spokane**). Plus, the cities from last year that made this year's cut have been revised and refreshed with new and updated data.

Within each volume, city chapters are arranged alphabetically, and each is divided into two sections: Business Environment and Living Environment. Each chapter begins with a background about the city, and narrative comments about changes in its environmental, political, or employment atmosphere that occurred in the past year. You'll learn, for example, that Las Vegas is cleaning up its image, how Chicago's mayor – an avid cyclist – supports his fellow riders, and the Y2K-ready measures the cities are taking.

There is data on cost of living, finances, taxes, population, employment and earnings, commercial real estate, education, major employers, media, crime, climate, professional sports teams and more. In most cases, you'll find comparisons between Metropolitan Statistical Areas (MSA) and U.S. census figures.

In addition to the comprehensive chapters, each volume contains four appendices: **Appendix A, Comparative Statistics:** City by city comparison of more than 50 categories that gives not just an overview of the city, but a broad profile of each geographic region of the country.

Appendix B, Metropolitan Statistical Areas (MSA): Includes the counties (and in some cases, state) that combine to form each city's MSA – an official designation used to define the area in terms of population, finance, economy, etc.

Appendix C, Chambers of Commerce and Economic Development Organizations: Includes address, phone numbers and fax numbers of these additional resources to help the readers to get further, more detailed information on each city.

Appendix D, State Departments of Labor and Employment: Another source of additional, more specific economic and employment data for each city, with address and phone numbers for easy access.

As in all previous editions, the material provided by public and private agencies and organizations was supplemented by numerous library sources and Internet sites. The editors thank everyone who responded to our requests for information, especially the Chambers of Commerce, Economic Development Organizations and Labor Market Information groups.

America's Top-Rated Cities is designed for a wide range of readers: private individuals considering relocating a residence or business; professionals considering expanding their business or changing careers; corporations considering relocation, opening up additional offices or creating new divisions; government agencies; general and market researchers; real estate consultants; human resource personnel; urban planners; investors; and urban government students.

Grey House Publishing has also acquired from Universal Reference Publications the following titles: *America's Top-Rated Smaller Cities, Health & Environment in America's Top-Rated Cities* and *Crime in America's Top-Rated Cities*, developed in the spirit of offering a series of comprehensive statistical reference books about America's top cities. Grey House is revising and updating each of these and will offer the *Smaller Cities* and *Crime* titles in the Spring of 2000, and *Environment* in the Fall of that year.

As always, we welcome your comments and suggestions for continuous improvement.

Atlanta, Georgia

Background

When you think of the South, you may imagine antebellum gentility. Atlanta, however, was borne of a rough and tumble past: first as a natural outgrowth of a thriving railroad network in the 1840s; and second, as a resilient go-getter that proudly rose again above the rubble of the Civil War.

Blanketed over the rolling hills of the Piedmont Plateau, at the foot of the Blue Ridge Mountains, Georgia's capital stands 1,000 miles above sea level. Atlanta is located in the northwest corner of Georgia where the terrain is rolling to hilly, and slopes downward to the east, west, and south.

Atlanta proper begins at the "terminus," or zero mile mark, of the now defunct Western and Atlantic Railroad Line. However its metropolitan area, comprised of twenty counties that include Fulton, DeKalb, and Clayton, extends as far as 30 miles from its origin. Atlanta's Chamber of Commerce calls its city, "The City Without Limits."

Atlanta's diversified economy allows for employment in a variety of sectors such as manufacturing (transportation, equipment, and textiles), retail, and the government. More than 700 of the Fortune 1,000 companies have operations in Atlanta, with 25 of them headquartered there, including Cable News Network, Coca-Cola, The Center for Disease Control and Vanstar.

These accomplishments are the result of an involved city government that seeks to work closely with its business community. This may be largely due to a change in its Charter in 1974, when greater administrative powers were vested in the Mayoral Office, and when the city inaugurated its first black mayor.

Atlanta, after the 1996 Olympics, is facing the complex issue of where it plans to move as an urban center in light of the conflict between the city and its surroundings. Middle-class residents, both white and black have increasingly moved to the suburbs separating themselves from Atlanta's old downtown and possibly any sense of responsibility for its future. *New York Times, 6/23/96*

While schools in the city remain predominantly black, and schools in its suburbs predominantly white, Atlanta can still boast of a racially progressive climate. The Martin Luther King, Jr. Historic District, Auburn Avenue, a street of black middle-class enterprises, and a consortium of black colleges that includes Morehouse College and the Interdenominational Theological Center testify to the city's appreciation for a people who have always been one-third of Atlanta's population.

The Appalachian chain of mountains, the Gulf of Mexico, and the Atlantic Ocean influence Atlanta's climate. Temperatures are moderate throughout the year. Prolonged periods of hot weather are unusual and 100-degree heat is rarely experienced. Atlanta winters are mild with a few, short-lived cold spells. Summers can be humid.

General Rankings and Evaluative Comments

- Atlanta was ranked #6 out of 19 large, southern metropolitan areas in *Money's* 1998 survey of "The Best Places to Live in America." The survey was conducted by first contacting 512 representative households nationwide and asking them to rank 37 quality-of-life factors on a scale of 1 to 10. Next, a demographic profile was compiled on the 300 largest metropolitan statistical areas in the U.S. The numbers were crunched together to arrive at an overall ranking (things Americans consider most important, like clean air and water, low crime and good schools, received extra weight). Unlike previous years, the 1998 rankings were broken down by region (northeast, midwest, south, west) and population size (100,000 to 249,999; 250,000 to 999,999; 1 million plus). The city had a nationwide ranking of #159 out of 300 in 1997 and #115 out of 300 in 1996. *Money, July 1998; Money, July 1997; Money, September 1996*

- Atlanta appeared on *Fortune's* list of "The Best Cities for Business." Rank: #8 out of 10. One hundred and sixty cities worldwide were analyzed by Arthur Andersen's Business Location Service. The North American research focused on cities creating new wealth and opportunities. *Fortune* made the final selection of the top 10 cities in the U.S. *Fortune, November 1998*

- *Ladies Home Journal* ranked America's 200 largest cities based on the qualities women care about most. Atlanta ranked #62 out of 200. Criteria: low crime rate, well-paying jobs, quality health and child care, good public schools, the presence of women in government, size of the gender wage gap, number of sexual-harassment and discrimination complaints filed, unemployment and divorce rates, commute times, population density, number of houses of worship, parks and cultural offerings, number of women's health specialists, how well a community's women cared for themselves, complexion kindness index based on UV radiation levels, odds of finding affordable fashions, rental rates for romance movies, champagne sales and other matters of the heart. *Ladies Home Journal, November 1998*

- Zero Population Growth ranked 229 cities in terms of children's health, safety, and economic well-being. Atlanta was ranked #21 out of 25 major cities (main city in a metro area with population of greater than 2 million) and was given a grade of D. Criteria: total population, percent of population under 18 years of age, household language, percent population change, percent of births to teens, infant mortality rate, percent of low birth weights, dropout rate, enrollment in preprimary school, violent and property crime rates, unemployment rate, percent of children in poverty, percent of owner occupied units, number of bad air days, percent of public transportation commuters, and average travel time to work. *Zero Population Growth, Children's Environmental Index, Fall 1999*

- Atlanta was ranked #2 out of 59 metro areas in *The Regional Economist's* "Rational Livability Ranking of 59 Large Metro Areas." The rankings were based on the metro area's total population change over the period 1990-97 divided by the number of people moving in from elsewhere in the United States (net domestic in-migration). *St. Louis Federal Reserve Bank of St. Louis, The Regional Economist, April 1999*

- Atlanta appeared on *Travel & Leisure's* list of the world's 100 best cities. It was ranked #30 in the U.S. and #88 in the world. Criteria: activities/attractions, culture/arts, people, restaurants/food, and value. *Travel & Leisure, 1998 World's Best Awards*

- Atlanta was selected by *Yahoo! Internet Life* as one of "America's Most Wired Cities & Towns." The city ranked #9 out of 50. Criteria: home and work net use, domain density, hosts per capita, directory density and content quality. *Yahoo! Internet Life, March 1999*

- Cognetics studied 273 metro areas in the United States, ranking them by entrepreneurial activity. Atlanta was ranked #4 out of the 50 largest metro areas. Criteria: Significant Starts (firms started in the last 10 years that still employ at least 5 people) and Young Growers (percent of firms 10 years old or less that grew significantly during the last 4 years). *Cognetics, "Entrepreneurial Hot Spots: The Best Places in America to Start and Grow a Company," 1998*

- Atlanta appeared on *Forbes* list of "Best Places for Business Growth." Rank: #10 out of 162 metro areas. Criteria: average wage and salary increases, job growth rates, number of technology clusters (measures business activity in 13 different technology areas), overall concentration of technology activity relative to national average and technology output growth. *Forbes, May 31, 1999*

- Atlanta was included among *Entrepreneur* magazine's listing of the "20 Best Cities for Small Business." It was ranked #4 among large metro areas and #3 among southern metro areas. Criteria: entrepreneurial activity, small-business growth, economic growth, and risk of failure. *Entrepreneur, October 1999*

- Atlanta was selected as one of the "Best American Cities to Start a Business" by *Point of View* magazine. Criteria: coolness, quality-of-life, and business concerns. The city was ranked #9 out of 75. *Point of View, November 1998*

- Atlanta appeared on *Sales & Marketing Management's* list of the "20 Hottest Cities for Selling." Rank: #6 out of 20. *S&MM* editors looked at Metropolitan Statistical Areas with populations of more than 150,000. The areas were ranked based on population increases, retail sales increases, effective buying income, increase in both residential and commercial building permits issued, unemployment rates, job growth, mix of industries, tax rates, number of corporate relocations, and the number of new corporations.
Sales & Marketing Management, April 1999

- *Computerworld* selected the best markets for IT job seekers based on their annual salary, skills, and hiring surveys. Atlanta ranked #3 out of 10. *Computerworld, January 11, 1999*

- Reliastar Financial Corp. ranked the 125 largest metropolitan areas according to the general financial security of residents. Atlanta was ranked #6 out of 125 with a score of 14.6. The score indicates the percentage a metropolitan area is above or below the metropolitan norm. A metro area with a score of 10.6 is 10.6% above the metro average. Criteria: Earnings and Wealth Potential (household income, education, net assets, cost of living); Safety Net (health insurance, retirement savings, life insurance, income support programs); Personal Threats (unemployment rate, low-income households, crime rate); Community Economic Vitality (cost of community services, job quality, job creation, housing costs).
Reliastar Financial Corp., "The Best Cities to Earn and Save Money," 1999 Edition

Business Environment

STATE ECONOMY

State Economic Profile

"Georgia came out of the 1991-92 recession with a bang and has been on a roll ever since. By almost any measure of strength, GA has outpaced the nation by a considerable degree. Such a rate of growth is not sustainable for too much longer. Growth in employment and Gross State Product (GSP), while still expected to outpace the nation, will likely slow in the years ahead.

The Georgia economy can be called the Atlanta economy. More than 80% of GSP growth is occurring within the Atlanta metro area. Atlanta is also the magnet for the vast majority of migrates to GA, which account for 60% of the state's population growth. To some extent Atlanta's gains have been at the expense of the rest of GA. Educated workers in the rest of the state have been, on net, moving to Atlanta, leaving a shortage of skilled labor in the rest of GA.

For most of the 1990s, GA's growth in per capita income outpaced the nation. In recent years, while still strong, per capita income growth has lagged the nation. This trend should continue as much of GA's job growth is taking place in lower paying service sector jobs, particularly temporary help services. Wage growth in the smaller metros continues to lag Atlanta by a considerable amount.

Atlanta's housing boom seems to be never-ending. 1998 witnessed a 19% increase in single-family permits and a 15% increase in multifamily permits. In spite of a large amount of construction in the pipeline, home price appreciation in 1998 exceeded the nation's and should do so in 1999. Current efforts at controlling growth, such as building moratoria, and a lack of infrastructure in some areas make it likely that price appreciation will remain robust in the inner suburbs, although construction will continue at the fringe." *National Association of Realtors, Economic Profiles: The Fifty States and the District of Columbia, http://nar.realtor.com/databank/profiles.htm*

IMPORTS/EXPORTS

Total Export Sales

Area	1994 ($000)	1995 ($000)	1996 ($000)	1997 ($000)	% Chg. 1994-97	% Chg. 1996-97
MSA[1]	4,739,124	5,811,439	5,891,451	6,604,616	39.4	12.1
U.S.	512,415,609	583,030,524	622,827,063	687,597,999	34.2	10.4

Note: (1) Metropolitan Statistical Area - see Appendix A for areas included
Source: U.S. Department of Commerce, International Trade Association, Metropolitan Area Exports: An Export Performance Report on Over 250 U.S. Cities, November 10, 1998

CITY FINANCES

City Government Finances

Component	FY92 ($000)	FY92 (per capita $)
Revenue	810,963	2,045.85
Expenditure	766,514	1,933.71
Debt Outstanding	1,433,054	3,615.22
Cash & Securities	1,874,189	4,728.08

Source: U.S. Bureau of the Census, City Government Finances: 1991-92

City Government Revenue by Source

Source	FY92 ($000)	FY92 (per capita $)	FY92 (%)
From Federal Government	55,486	139.98	6.8
From State Governments	9,683	24.43	1.2
From Local Governments	72,714	183.44	9.0
Property Taxes	122,556	309.18	15.1
General Sales Taxes	0	0.00	0.0
Selective Sales Taxes	68,136	171.89	8.4
Income Taxes	0	0.00	0.0
Current Charges	209,484	528.47	25.8
Utility/Liquor Store	60,911	153.66	7.5
Employee Retirement[1]	55,397	139.75	6.8
Other	156,596	395.05	19.3

Note: (1) Excludes "city contributions," classified as "nonrevenue," intragovernmental transfers.
Source: U.S. Bureau of the Census, City Government Finances: 1991-92

City Government Expenditures by Function

Function	FY92 ($000)	FY92 (per capita $)	FY92 (%)
Educational Services	18,757	47.32	2.4
Employee Retirement[1]	60,929	153.71	7.9
Environment/Housing	141,995	358.22	18.5
Government Administration	54,684	137.95	7.1
Interest on General Debt	96,468	243.36	12.6
Public Safety	129,441	326.55	16.9
Social Services	437	1.10	0.1
Transportation	136,428	344.17	17.8
Utility/Liquor Store	81,845	206.47	10.7
Other	45,530	114.86	5.9

Note: (1) Payments to beneficiaries including withdrawal of contributions.
Source: U.S. Bureau of the Census, City Government Finances: 1991-92

Municipal Bond Ratings

Area	Moody's	S & P
Atlanta	Aa3	n/a

Note: n/a not available; n/r not rated
Source: Moody's Bond Record, 6/99

POPULATION

Population Growth

Area	1980	1990	% Chg. 1980-90	July 1998 Estimate	% Chg. 1990-98
City	425,022	394,017	-7.3	403,819	2.5
MSA[1]	2,138,231	2,833,511	32.5	3,735,140	31.8
U.S.	226,545,805	248,765,170	9.8	270,299,000	8.7

Note: (1) Metropolitan Statistical Area - see Appendix A for areas included;
July 1998 MSA population estimate was calculated by the editors
Source: 1980/1990 Census of Housing and Population, Summary Tape File 3C;
Census Bureau Population Estimates 1998

Population Characteristics

Race	City 1980 Population	%	City 1990 Population	%	% Chg. 1980-90	MSA[1] 1990 Population	%
White	138,235	32.5	122,363	31.1	-11.5	2,021,586	71.3
Black	283,158	66.6	264,213	67.1	-6.7	735,477	26.0
Amer Indian/Esk/Aleut	610	0.1	626	0.2	2.6	6,176	0.2
Asian/Pacific Islander	2,001	0.5	3,327	0.8	66.3	49,965	1.8
Other	1,018	0.2	3,488	0.9	242.6	20,307	0.7
Hispanic Origin[2]	5,842	1.4	7,640	1.9	30.8	54,318	1.9

Note: (1) Metropolitan Statistical Area - see Appendix A for areas included;
(2) people of Hispanic origin can be of any race
Source: 1980/1990 Census of Housing and Population, Summary Tape File 3C

Ancestry

Area	German	Irish	English	Italian	U.S.	French	Polish	Dutch
City	6.2	5.3	8.1	1.0	4.3	1.5	0.8	0.5
MSA[1]	15.1	15.5	15.8	2.5	9.5	2.9	1.6	1.9
U.S.	23.3	15.6	13.1	5.9	5.3	4.2	3.8	2.5

Note: Figures are percentages and include persons that reported multiple ancestry (eg. if a person reported being Irish and Italian, they were included in both columns); (1) Metropolitan Statistical Area - see Appendix A for areas included
Source: 1990 Census of Population and Housing, Summary Tape File 3C

Age

Area	Median Age (Years)	Age Distribution (%) Under 5	Under 18	18-24	25-44	45-64	65+	80+
City	31.4	7.6	24.1	13.0	34.7	16.8	11.3	2.9
MSA[1]	31.4	7.7	25.9	10.7	37.8	17.7	7.9	1.6
U.S.	32.9	7.3	25.6	10.5	32.6	18.7	12.5	2.8

Note: (1) Metropolitan Statistical Area - see Appendix A for areas included
Source: 1990 Census of Population and Housing, Summary Tape File 3C

Male/Female Ratio

Area	Number of males per 100 females (all ages)	Number of males per 100 females (18 years old+)
City	91.0	87.8
MSA[1]	94.7	91.5
U.S.	95.0	91.9

Note: (1) Metropolitan Statistical Area - see Appendix A for areas included
Source: 1990 Census of Population, General Population Characteristics

INCOME

Per Capita/Median/Average Income

Area	Per Capita ($)	Median Household ($)	Average Household ($)
City	15,279	22,275	37,882
MSA[1]	16,897	36,051	44,968
U.S.	14,420	30,056	38,453

Note: All figures are for 1989; (1) Metropolitan Statistical Area - see Appendix A for areas included
Source: 1990 Census of Population and Housing, Summary Tape File 3C

Household Income Distribution by Race

Income ($)	City (%)					U.S. (%)				
	Total	White	Black	Other	Hisp.[1]	Total	White	Black	Other	Hisp.[1]
Less than 5,000	14.8	5.7	20.7	18.3	13.3	6.2	4.8	15.2	8.6	8.8
5,000 - 9,999	11.6	7.2	14.5	11.5	10.7	9.3	8.6	14.2	9.9	11.1
10,000 - 14,999	9.9	7.0	11.7	13.0	11.1	8.8	8.5	11.0	9.8	11.0
15,000 - 24,999	17.8	14.9	19.7	17.3	20.4	17.5	17.3	18.9	18.5	20.5
25,000 - 34,999	13.1	13.1	13.2	10.7	13.9	15.8	16.1	14.2	15.4	16.4
35,000 - 49,999	12.5	15.1	10.8	15.2	14.6	17.9	18.6	13.3	16.1	16.0
50,000 - 74,999	10.1	15.1	6.8	8.5	6.9	15.0	15.8	9.3	13.4	11.1
75,000 - 99,999	3.9	7.1	1.7	2.2	2.4	5.1	5.5	2.6	4.7	3.1
100,000+	6.3	14.7	0.9	3.3	6.7	4.4	4.8	1.3	3.7	1.9

Note: All figures are for 1989; (1) people of Hispanic origin can be of any race
Source: 1990 Census of Population and Housing, Summary Tape File 3C

Effective Buying Income

Area	Per Capita ($)	Median Household ($)	Average Household ($)
City	17,521	27,204	44,150
MSA[1]	18,461	39,355	49,367
U.S.	16,803	34,536	45,243

Note: Data as of 1/1/99; (1) Metropolitan Statistical Area - see Appendix A for areas included
Source: Standard Rate & Data Service, Newspaper Advertising Source, 9/99

Effective Household Buying Income Distribution

Area	% of Households Earning						
	$10,000 -$19,999	$20,000 -$34,999	$35,000 -$49,999	$50,000 -$74,999	$75,000 -$99,000	$100,000 -$124,999	$125,000 and up
City	17.6	21.7	13.6	12.6	5.7	2.5	5.0
MSA[1]	12.4	22.3	19.9	21.8	8.4	2.8	3.1
U.S.	16.0	22.6	18.2	18.9	7.2	2.4	2.7

Note: Data as of 1/1/99; (1) Metropolitan Statistical Area - see Appendix A for areas included
Source: Standard Rate & Data Service, Newspaper Advertising Source, 9/99

Poverty Rates by Race and Age

Area	Total (%)	By Race (%)				By Age (%)		
		White	Black	Other	Hisp.[2]	Under 5 years old	Under 18 years old	65 years and over
City	27.3	9.8	35.0	35.5	30.5	47.1	42.9	25.1
MSA[1]	10.0	5.4	22.4	14.4	16.2	15.5	13.9	14.3
U.S.	13.1	9.8	29.5	23.1	25.3	20.1	18.3	12.8

Note: Figures show the percent of people living below the poverty line in 1989. The average poverty threshold was $12,674 for a family of four in 1989; (1) Metropolitan Statistical Area - see Appendix A for areas included; (2) people of Hispanic origin can be of any race
Source: 1990 Census of Population and Housing, Summary Tape File 3C

EMPLOYMENT

Labor Force and Employment

Area	Civilian Labor Force			Workers Employed		
	Jun. 1998	Jun. 1999	% Chg.	Jun. 1998	Jun. 1999	% Chg.
City	222,446	220,622	-0.8	208,028	208,425	0.2
MSA[1]	2,133,463	2,126,262	-0.3	2,052,330	2,056,258	0.2
U.S.	138,798,000	140,666,000	1.3	132,265,000	134,395,000	1.6

Note: Data is not seasonally adjusted and covers workers 16 years of age and older; (1) Metropolitan Statistical Area - see Appendix A for areas included
Source: Bureau of Labor Statistics, http://stats.bls.gov

Unemployment Rate

Area	1998						1999					
	Jul.	Aug.	Sep.	Oct.	Nov.	Dec.	Jan.	Feb.	Mar.	Apr.	May.	Jun.
City	6.3	5.7	5.7	5.6	5.1	4.9	4.8	5.5	5.5	4.8	4.7	5.5
MSA[1]	3.9	3.3	3.5	3.3	3.0	2.8	2.9	3.2	3.4	2.8	2.8	3.3
U.S.	4.7	4.5	4.4	4.2	4.1	4.0	4.8	4.7	4.4	4.1	4.0	4.5

Note: Data is not seasonally adjusted and covers workers 16 years of age and older; all figures are percentages; (1) Metropolitan Statistical Area - see Appendix A for areas included
Source: Bureau of Labor Statistics, http://stats.bls.gov

Employment by Industry

Sector	MSA[1]		U.S.
	Number of Employees	Percent of Total	Percent of Total
Services	646,000	30.6	30.4
Retail Trade	372,400	17.6	17.7
Government	260,000	12.3	15.6
Manufacturing	221,100	10.5	14.3
Finance/Insurance/Real Estate	141,400	6.7	5.9
Wholesale Trade	177,800	8.4	5.4
Transportation/Public Utilities	182,200	8.6	5.3
Construction	108,900	5.2	5.0
Mining	1,600	0.1	0.4

Note: Figures cover non-farm employment as of 6/99 and are not seasonally adjusted;
(1) Metropolitan Statistical Area - see Appendix A for areas included
Source: Bureau of Labor Statistics, http://stats.bls.gov

Employment by Occupation

Occupation Category	City (%)	MSA[1] (%)	U.S. (%)
White Collar	60.2	65.7	58.1
Executive/Admin./Management	12.8	15.6	12.3
Professional	16.0	13.6	14.1
Technical & Related Support	3.6	4.0	3.7
Sales	11.5	13.9	11.8
Administrative Support/Clerical	16.2	18.5	16.3
Blue Collar	20.7	22.4	26.2
Precision Production/Craft/Repair	6.8	10.2	11.3
Machine Operators/Assem./Insp.	4.9	4.8	6.8
Transportation/Material Movers	4.2	3.8	4.1
Cleaners/Helpers/Laborers	4.7	3.7	3.9
Services	17.9	10.9	13.2
Farming/Forestry/Fishing	1.2	1.1	2.5

Note: Figures cover employed persons 16 years old and over;
(1) Metropolitan Statistical Area - see Appendix A for areas included
Source: 1990 Census of Population and Housing, Summary Tape File 3C

Occupational Employment Projections: 1996 - 2006

Occupations Expected to Have the Largest Job Growth (ranked by numerical growth)	Fast-Growing Occupations[1] (ranked by percent growth)
1. General managers & top executives	1. Medical assistants
2. Cashiers	2. Physical therapy assistants and aides
3. Salespersons, retail	3. Occupational therapists
4. Child care workers, private household	4. Home health aides
5. Truck drivers, light	5. Occupational therapy assistants
6. General office clerks	6. Personal and home care aides
7. Systems analysts	7. Paralegals
8. Registered nurses	8. Respiratory therapists
9. Marketing & sales, supervisors	9. Customer service representatives
10. Receptionists and information clerks	10. Child care workers, private household

Note: Projections cover Georgia; (1) Excludes occupations with total job growth less than 300
Source: U.S. Department of Labor, Employment and Training Administration, America's Labor Market Information System (ALMIS)

TAXES

Major State and Local Tax Rates

State Corp. Income (%)	State Personal Income (%)	Residential Property (effective rate per $100)	Sales & Use		State Gasoline (cents/ gallon)	State Cigarette (cents/ pack)
			State (%)	Local (%)		
6.0	1.0 - 6.0	2.05	4.0	3.0	7.5	12.0

Note: Personal/corporate income, sales, gasoline and cigarette tax rates as of January 1999. Property tax rates as of 1997.
Source: Federation of Tax Administrators, www.taxadmin.org; Washington D.C. Department of Finance and Revenue, Tax Rates and Tax Burdens in the District of Columbia: A Nationwide Comparison, July 1998; Chamber of Commerce, 1999

Total Taxes Per Capita and as a Percent of Income

Area	Per Capita Income ($)	Per Capita Taxes ($)			Percent of Income (%)		
		Total	Federal	State/ Local	Total	Federal	State/ Local
Georgia	26,398	9,313	6,277	3,036	35.3	23.8	11.5
U.S.	27,876	9,881	6,690	3,191	35.4	24.0	11.4

Note: Figures are for 1998
Source: Tax Foundation, www.taxfoundation.org

Estimated Tax Burden

Area	State Income	Local Income	Property	Sales	Total
Atlanta	3,040	0	4,000	585	7,625

Note: The numbers are estimates of taxes paid by a married couple with two children and annual earnings of $75,000. Sales tax estimates assume they spend average amounts on food, clothing, household goods and gasoline. Property tax estimates assume they live in a $250,000 home.
Source: Kiplinger's Personal Finance Magazine, October 1998

**COMMERCIAL
REAL ESTATE**

Office Market

Class/Location	Total Space (sq. ft.)	Vacant Space (sq. ft.)	Vac. Rate (%)	Under Constr. (sq. ft.)	Net Absorp. (sq. ft.)	Rental Rates ($/sq.ft./yr.)
Class A						
CBD	14,097,198	1,614,450	11.5	306,000	n/a	16.25-28.31
Outside CBD	30,243,196	1,929,784	6.4	2,483,046	n/a	18.00-32.50
Class B						
CBD	3,066,019	557,896	18.2	0	n/a	15.00-22.50
Outside CBD	24,016,648	2,403,310	10.0	1,431,184	n/a	12.00-27.00

*Note: Data as of 10/98 and covers Atlanta; CBD = Central Business District; n/a not available;
Source: Society of Industrial and Office Realtors, 1999 Comparative Statistics of Industrial and Office
Real Estate Markets*

"Atlanta will solidify its position as the Southeast's regional hub with its strong infrastructure network, concentration of headquarters operations, and relatively low housing costs. Speculative development is centered around six sub-markets—Buckhead, North Fulton, Northeast, Northwest, Peachtree Corners, and Perimeter Central—totaling more than 2.5 million sq. ft. of Class A space and 1.4 million sq. ft. of Class B. Preleasing remains an important component, with current figures indicating approximately 18 percent of new construction to be preleased. The probability that the rate of proposed starts will diminish over time appears likely as concern for overbuilding intensifies. According to SIOR's reporter, the abundance of new space will not drive down rents. The Southeast has all the right ingredients necessary for a prosperous future into the 21st century." *Society of Industrial and Office Realtors, 1999 Comparative Statistics of Industrial and Office Real Estate Markets*

Industrial Market

Location	Total Space (sq. ft.)	Vacant Space (sq. ft.)	Vac. Rate (%)	Under Constr. (sq. ft.)	Net Absorp. (sq. ft.)	Lease ($/sq.ft./yr.)
Central City	30,490,661	2,657,031	8.7	47,200	470,859	2.00-4.75
Suburban	298,893,606	21,394,184	7.2	10,220,676	11,783,009	2.40-6.50

*Note: Data as of 10/98 and covers Atlanta; n/a not available
Source: Society of Industrial and Office Realtors, 1999 Comparative Statistics of Industrial and Office
Real Estate Markets*

"Steady growth is expected for the Georgia economy. Overall vacancy rates could increase in 1999 with the bulk sector especially vulnerable. Sales prices may weaken due to a general slowing of the economy and an expected increase in building inventory. Additionally, REITs have started to sell their properties, bringing more square footage to the investment market. Speculative development while decreasing, will still supply the market with ample new product. Developers will continue to watch the bulk market closely to determine if the trend toward construction of 'big block' space can continue at its current levels. The northern suburbs will see continued development of smaller, multi-tenanted spaces. Expansion of local business continues to be the driving positive force in Atlanta's net absorption." *Society of Industrial and Office Realtors, 1999 Comparative Statistics of Industrial and Office Real Estate Markets*

Retail Market

Shopping Center Inventory (sq. ft.)	Shopping Center Construction (sq. ft.)	Construction as a Percent of Inventory (%)	Torto Wheaton Rent Index[1] ($/sq. ft.)
76,638,000	1,303,000	1.7	14.43

*Note: Data as of 1997 and covers the Metropolitan Statistical Area - see Appendix A for areas
included; (1) Index is based on a model that predicts what the average rent should be for leases with
certain characteristics, in certain locations during certain years.
Source: National Association of Realtors, 1997-1998 Market Conditions Report*

"An estimated 1.5 million visitors to the Summer Olympics spent over $1.2 billion at Atlanta hotels, restaurants, and retail shops. Now that the Games are over, people are watching the Atlanta retail market. The area's retail rent index increased nearly 6% in 1997 and is above the South's average of $13.79 per square foot. The area's population growth is expected to average 1.7% per year through 1998. The Buckhead and northern retail markets should benefit from the continued growth. Strong net absorption is likely to persist since new centers are mostly pre-leased." *National Association of Realtors, 1997-1998 Market Conditions Report*

COMMERCIAL UTILITIES

Typical Monthly Electric Bills

Area	Commercial Service ($/month)		Industrial Service ($/month)	
	12 kW demand 1,500 kWh	100 kW demand 30,000 kWh	1,000 kW demand 400,000 kWh	20,000 kW demand 10,000,000 kWh
City	175	2,152	23,993	358,567
U.S.	150	2,174	23,995	508,569

Note: Based on rates in effect January 1, 1999
Source: Edison Electric Institute, Typical Residential, Commercial and Industrial Bills, Winter 1999

TRANSPORTATION

Transportation Statistics

Average minutes to work	24.2
Interstate highways	I-20; I-75; I-85
Bus lines	
In-city	Metropolitan Atlanta Rapid Transit Authority, 704 vehicles
Inter-city	1
Passenger air service	
Airport	Hartsfield Atlanta International
Airlines	33
Aircraft departures	345,512 (1996)
Enplaned passengers	30,371,772 (1996)
Rail service	Amtrak
Motor freight carriers	95
Major waterways/ports	None

Source: Editor & Publisher Market Guide, 1999; FAA Airport Activity Statistics, 1997; Amtrak National Time Table, Northeast Timetable, Spring/Summer 1999; 1990 Census of Population and Housing, STF 3C; Chamber of Commerce/Economic Development 1999; Jane's Urban Transport Systems 1999-2000

Means of Transportation to Work

Area	Car/Truck/Van		Public Transportation			Bicycle	Walked	Other Means	Worked at Home
	Drove Alone	Car-pooled	Bus	Subway	Railroad				
City	61.2	11.6	16.7	2.9	0.1	0.3	3.8	1.2	2.4
MSA[1]	78.0	12.7	3.5	1.0	0.1	0.1	1.5	1.0	2.2
U.S.	73.2	13.4	3.0	1.5	0.5	0.4	3.9	1.2	3.0

Note: Figures shown are percentages and only include workers 16 years old and over;
(1) Metropolitan Statistical Area - see Appendix A for areas included
Source: 1990 Census of Population and Housing, Summary Tape File 3C

BUSINESSES

Major Business Headquarters

Company Name	1999 Rankings	
	Fortune 500	Forbes 500
Bellsouth	52	-
Coca-Cola	73	-
Coca-Cola Enterprises	119	-
Cox Enterprises	-	38
Delta Air Lines	111	-
First Data	316	-
Genuine Parts	252	-
Georgia-Pacific	122	-
Home Depot	32	-
National Distributing	-	190
Printpack	-	264
RTM Restaurant Group	-	427
Riverwood International	-	160
Simmons	-	408
Southern	148	-
Suntrust Banks	227	-
United Parcel Service	46	3
Watkins Associated Industries	-	282

Note: Companies listed are located in the city; dashes indicate no ranking
Fortune 500: Companies that produce a 10-K are ranked 1 to 500 based on 1998 revenue
Forbes 500: Private companies are ranked 1 to 500 based on 1997 revenue
Source: Forbes, November 30, 1998; Fortune, April 26, 1999

Best Companies to Work For

Interface (commercial carpeting), headquartered in Atlanta, is among the "100 Best Companies to Work for in America." Criteria: trust in management, pride in work/company, camaraderie, company responses to the Hewitt People Practices Inventory, and employee responses to their Great Place to Work survey. The companies also had to be at least 10 years old and have a minimum of 500 employees. *Fortune, January 11, 1999*

Turner Broadcasting System, headquartered in Atlanta, is among the "100 Best Companies for Working Mothers." Criteria: fair wages, opportunities for women to advance, support for child care, flexible work schedules, family-friendly benefits, and work/life supports. *Working Mother, October 1998*

The Home Depot (retail) and Norrell Corp. (professional services), headquartered in Atlanta, are among the "100 Best Places to Work in IS." Criteria: compensation, turnover and training. *Computerworld, May 25, 1998*

Chapter 11 Books (discount bookseller), Gensler (design firm), Home Box Office and NationsBank, headquartered in Atlanta, are among the best companies for women. Criteria: salary, benefits, opportunities for advancement and work/family policies. *www.womenswire.com*

Fast-Growing Businesses

According to *Inc.*, Atlanta is home to one of America's 100 fastest-growing private companies: Tactics. Criteria for inclusion: must be an independent, privately-held, U.S. corporation, proprietorship or partnership; sales of at least $200,000 in 1995; five-year operating/sales history; increase in 1999 sales over 1998 sales; holding companies, regulated banks, and utilities were excluded. *Inc. 500, 1999*

Atlanta is home to three of *Business Week's* "hot growth" companies: LHS Group, Advanced Technical Products and Automobile Protection. Criteria: increase in sales and profits, return on capital and stock price. *Business Week, 5/31/99*

According to *Fortune*, Atlanta is home to two of America's 100 fastest-growing companies: Profit Recovery Group and Premier Bancshares. Companies were ranked based on earnings-per-share growth, revenue growth and total return over the previous three years. Criteria for inclusion: public companies with sales of least $50 million. Companies that lost money in the most recent quarter, or ended in the red for the past four quarters as a whole, were not eligible. Limited partnerships and REITs were also not considered. *Fortune, "America's Fastest-Growing Companies," 1999*

According to Deloitte & Touche LLP, Atlanta is home to one of America's 100 fastest-growing high-technology companies: Premiere Technologies. Companies are ranked by percentage growth in revenue over a five-year period. Criteria for inclusion: must be a U.S. company developing and/or providing technology products or services; company must have been in business for five years with 1993 revenues of at least $50,000. *Deloitte & Touche LLP, November 17, 1998*

Women-Owned Firms: Number, Employment and Sales

Area	Number of Firms	Employ-ment	Sales ($000)	Rank[2]
MSA[1]	138,700	331,800	50,206,800	12

Note: (1) Metropolitan Statistical Area - see Appendix A for areas included;
(2) Calculated on an averaging of the number of businesses, employment and sales
Source: The National Foundation for Women Business Owners, 1999 Facts on Women-Owned Businesses: Trends in the Top 50 Metropolitan Areas

Women-Owned Firms: Growth

Area	% change from 1992 to 1999			Rank[2]
	Number of Firms	Employ-ment	Sales	
MSA[1]	53.9	110.3	150.3	16

Note: (1) Metropolitan Statistical Area - see Appendix A for areas included; (2) Calculated on an averaging of the percent growth of number of businesses, employment and sales
Source: The National Foundation for Women Business Owners, 1999 Facts on Women-Owned Businesses: Trends in the Top 50 Metropolitan Areas

Minority Business Opportunity

Atlanta is home to two companies which are on the Black Enterprise Industrial/Service 100 list (largest based on gross sales): H.J. Russell & Co. (construction, property mgmt., airport concessions, real estate devel.); Gourmet Companies Inc. (food services, golf course mgmt.) . Criteria: operational in previous calendar year, at least 51% black-owned and manufactures/owns the product it sells or provides industrial or consumer services. Brokerages, real estate firms and firms that provide professional services are not eligible. *Black Enterprise, www.blackenterprise.com*

Four of the 500 largest Hispanic-owned companies in the U.S. are located in Atlanta. *Hispanic Business, June 1999*

Small Business Opportunity

According to *Forbes*, Atlanta is home to three of America's 200 best small companies: Aaron Rents, Automobile Protection and K&G Men's Center. Criteria: companies included must be publicly traded since November 1997 with a stock price of at least $5 per share and an average daily float of 1,000 shares. The company's latest 12-month sales must be between $5 and $350 million, return on equity (ROE) must be a minimum of 12% for both the past 5 years and the most recent four quarters, and five-year sales and EPS growth must average at least 10%. Companies with declining sales or earnings during the past year were dropped as well as businesses with debt/equity ratios over 1.25. Companies with negative operating cash flow in each of the past two years were also excluded. *Forbes, November 2, 1998*

HOTELS & MOTELS

Hotels/Motels

Area	Hotels/ Motels	Rooms	Luxury-Level Hotels/Motels		Average Minimum Rates ($)		
			♦♦♦♦	♦♦♦♦♦	♦♦	♦♦♦	♦♦♦♦
City	117	26,920	4	2	91	124	185
Airport	35	6,756	0	0	n/a	n/a	n/a
Suburbs	107	12,527	0	0	n/a	n/a	n/a
Total	259	46,203	4	2	n/a	n/a	n/a

Note: n/a not available; classifications range from one diamond (budget properties with basic amenities) to five diamond (luxury properties with the finest service, rooms and facilities).
Source: OAG, Business Travel Planner, Winter 1998-99

CONVENTION CENTERS

Major Convention Centers

Center Name	Meeting Rooms	Exhibit Space (sq. ft.)
Atlanta Exposition Center	5	160,000
Atlanta Hilton & Towers	87	41,000
Atlanta Market Center/INFORUM	41	376,000
Cobb Galleria Center	n/a	n/a
Emory Conference Center Hotel	20	30,000
Georgia International Convention Center	35	329,000
Georgia World Congress Center	76	950,000
Hyatt Regency Atlanta	38	66,500
Lakewood Exhibit Center	n/a	114,000
Omni Hotel at CNN Center	n/a	40,000
Sheraton Gateway Hotel	25	125,000
Southern Conference Center at Colony Square Hotel	14	36,000
Westin Peachtree Plaza	41	55,000

Note: n/a not available
Source: Trade Shows Worldwide, 1998; Meetings & Conventions, 4/15/99;
Sucessful Meetings, 3/31/98

Living Environment

COST OF LIVING

Cost of Living Index

Composite Index	Groceries	Housing	Utilities	Trans-portation	Health Care	Misc. Goods/ Services
103.3	103.3	102.9	102.3	101.5	118.5	102.0

Note: U.S. = 100
Source: ACCRA, Cost of Living Index, 1st Quarter 1999

HOUSING

Median Home Prices and Housing Affordability

Area	Median Price[2] 1st Qtr. 1999 ($)	HOI[3] 1st Qtr. 1999	Afford-ability Rank[4]
MSA[1]	130,000	80.7	47
U.S.	134,000	69.6	–

Note: (1) Metropolitan Statistical Area - see Appendix A for areas included; (2) U.S. figures calculated from the sales of 524,324 new and existing homes in 181 markets; (3) Housing Opportunity Index - percent of homes sold that were within the reach of the median income household at the prevailing mortgage interest rate; (4) Rank is from 1-181 with 1 being most affordable
Source: National Association of Home Builders, Housing Opportunity Index, 1st Quarter 1999

Median Home Price Projection

It is projected that the median price of existing single-family homes in the metro area will increase by 5.3% in 1999. Nationwide, home prices are projected to increase 3.8%.
Kiplinger's Personal Finance Magazine, January 1999

Average New Home Price

Area	Price ($)
City	144,634
U.S.	142,735

Note: Figures are based on a new home with 1,800 sq. ft. of living area on an 8,000 sq. ft. lot.
Source: ACCRA, Cost of Living Index, 1st Quarter 1999

Average Apartment Rent

Area	Rent ($/mth)
City	728
U.S.	601

Note: Figures are based on an unfurnished two bedroom, 1-1/2 or 2 bath apartment, approximately 950 sq. ft. in size, excluding all utilities except water
Source: ACCRA, Cost of Living Index, 1st Quarter 1999

RESIDENTIAL UTILITIES

Average Residential Utility Costs

Area	All Electric ($/mth)	Part Electric ($/mth)	Other Energy ($/mth)	Phone ($/mth)
City	99.60	–	–	22.75
U.S.	100.02	55.73	43.33	19.71

Source: ACCRA, Cost of Living Index, 1st Quarter 1999

HEALTH CARE

Average Health Care Costs

Area	Hospital ($/day)	Doctor ($/visit)	Dentist ($/visit)
City	340.10	70.62	87.21
U.S.	430.43	52.45	66.35

Note: Hospital—based on a semi-private room; Doctor—based on a general practitioner's routine exam of an established patient; Dentist—based on adult teeth cleaning and periodic oral exam.
Source: ACCRA, Cost of Living Index, 1st Quarter 1999

Distribution of Office-Based Physicians

Area	Family/Gen. Practitioners	Specialists		
		Medical	Surgical	Other
MSA[1]	557	2,223	1,784	1,727

Note: Data as of 12/31/97; (1) Metropolitan Statistical Area - see Appendix A for areas included
Source: American Medical Assn., Physician Characteristics & Distribution in the U.S., 1999

Hospitals

Atlanta has 1 general medical and surgical hospital, 5 psychiatric, 1 rehabilitation, 1 alcoholism and other chemical dependency, 2 other specialty, 1 children's general, 1 children's psychiatric, 1 children's other specialty. *AHA Guide to the Healthcare Field, 1998-99*

According to *U.S. News and World Report,* Atlanta has 2 of the best hospitals in the U.S.: **Emory University Hospital**, noted for cancer, cardiology, gastroenterology, geriatrics, gynecology, neurology, ophthalmology, orthopedics, otolaryngology, urology; **Crawford Long Hospital at Emory University**, noted for endocrinology. *U.S. News Online, "America's Best Hospitals," 10th Edition, www.usnews.com*

EDUCATION

Public School District Statistics

District Name	Num. Sch.	Enroll.	Classroom Teachers	Pupils per Teacher	Minority Pupils (%)	Current Exp.[1] ($/pupil)
Atlanta City School District	98	60,024	3,635	16.5	93.4	6,969
Fulton County School District	63	62,798	3,944	15.9	49.4	6,120

Note: Data covers the 1997-1998 school year unless otherwise noted; (1) Data covers fiscal year 1996; SD = School District; ISD = Independent School District; n/a not available
Source: National Center for Education Statistics, Common Core of Data Public Education Agency Universe 1997-98; National Center for Education Statistics, Characteristics of the 100 Largest Public Elementary and Secondary School Districts in the United States: 1997-98, July 1999

Educational Quality

School District	Education Quotient[1]	Graduate Outcome[2]	Community Index[3]	Resource Index[4]
Atlanta City	82.0	51.0	119.0	135.0

Note: Nearly 1,000 secondary school districts were rated in terms of educational quality. The scores range from a low of 50 to a high of 150; (1) Average of the Graduate Outcome, Community and Resource indexes; (2) Based on graduation rates and college board scores (SAT/ACT); (3) Based on the surrounding community's average level of education and the area's average income level; (4) Based on teacher salaries, per-pupil expenditures and student-teacher ratios.
Source: Expansion Management, Ratings Issue, 1998

Educational Attainment by Race

Area	High School Graduate (%)					Bachelor's Degree (%)				
	Total	White	Black	Other	Hisp.[2]	Total	White	Black	Other	Hisp.[2]
City	69.9	86.7	59.8	62.1	54.4	26.6	51.9	11.1	34.6	21.7
MSA[1]	79.5	82.6	70.3	72.7	69.8	26.8	29.7	16.6	32.3	24.5
U.S.	75.2	77.9	63.1	60.4	49.8	20.3	21.5	11.4	19.4	9.2

Note: Figures shown cover persons 25 years old and over; (1) Metropolitan Statistical Area - see Appendix A for areas included; (2) people of Hispanic origin can be of any race
Source: 1990 Census of Population and Housing, Summary Tape File 3C

School Enrollment by Type

Area	Preprimary				Elementary/High School			
	Public		Private		Public		Private	
	Enrollment	%	Enrollment	%	Enrollment	%	Enrollment	%
City	3,898	59.8	2,621	40.2	55,393	90.3	5,935	9.7
MSA[1]	28,793	49.6	29,303	50.4	437,891	92.0	37,989	8.0
U.S.	2,679,029	59.5	1,824,256	40.5	38,379,689	90.2	4,187,099	9.8

Note: Figures shown cover persons 3 years old and over;
(1) Metropolitan Statistical Area - see Appendix A for areas included
Source: 1990 Census of Population and Housing, Summary Tape File 3C

School Enrollment by Race

Area	Preprimary (%)				Elementary/High School (%)			
	White	Black	Other	Hisp.[1]	White	Black	Other	Hisp.[1]
City	26.6	71.9	1.5	1.5	13.8	84.6	1.6	1.9
MSA[2]	72.8	25.3	1.9	1.5	64.8	32.0	3.2	2.0
U.S.	80.4	12.5	7.1	7.8	74.1	15.6	10.3	12.5

Note: Figures shown cover persons 3 years old and over; (1) people of Hispanic origin can be of any
race; (2) Metropolitan Statistical Area - see Appendix A for areas included
Source: 1990 Census of Population and Housing, Summary Tape File 3C

Classroom Teacher Salaries in Public Schools

District	B.A. Degree		M.A. Degree		Maximum	
	Min. ($)	Rank[1]	Max. ($)	Rank[1]	Max. ($)	Rank[1]
Atlanta	31,080	12	50,331	21	62,012	6
Average	26,980	-	46,065	-	51,435	-

Note: Salaries are for 1997-1998; (1) Rank ranges from 1 to 100
Source: American Federation of Teachers, Survey & Analysis of Salary Trends, 1998

Higher Education

Two-Year Colleges		Four-Year Colleges		Medical Schools	Law Schools	Voc/ Tech
Public	Private	Public	Private			
2	2	2	10	2	3	23

Source: College Blue Book, Occupational Education, 1997; Medical School Admission Requirements,
1999-2000; Peterson's Guide to Two-Year Colleges, 1999; Peterson's Guide to Four-Year Colleges,
2000; Barron's Guide to Law Schools, 1999

MAJOR EMPLOYERS

Major Employers

BellSouth Telecommunications	Coca-Cola
Delta Air Lines	Equifax (credit reporting)
Fulton DeKalb Hospital Authority	Georgia Power
Home Depot	Piedmont Hospital
ESR Children's Health Care System	Turner Broadcasting
United Parcel Service	Georgia-Pacific Corp.

Note: Companies listed are located in the city
Source: Dun's Business Rankings, 1999; Ward's Business Directory, 1998

PUBLIC SAFETY

Crime Rate

Area	All Crimes	Violent Crimes				Property Crimes		
		Murder	Forcible Rape	Robbery	Aggrav. Assault	Burglary	Larceny -Theft	Motor Vehicle Theft
City	13,921.6	35.6	87.0	1,128.9	1,797.0	2,181.9	6,821.4	1,869.7
Suburbs[1]	5,737.1	4.9	28.6	183.7	224.7	1,045.9	3,511.4	737.9
MSA[2]	6,711.5	8.6	35.5	296.2	411.9	1,181.2	3,905.5	872.6
U.S.	4,922.7	6.8	35.9	186.1	382.0	919.6	2,886.5	505.8

Note: Crime rate is the number of crimes per 100,000 pop.; (1) defined as all areas within the MSA but located outside the central city; (2) Metropolitan Statistical Area - see Appendix A for areas incl. Source: FBI Uniform Crime Reports, 1997

RECREATION

Culture and Recreation

Museums	Symphony Orchestras	Opera Companies	Dance Companies	Professional Theatres	Zoos	Pro Sports Teams
20	4	0	2	9	1	3

Source: International Directory of the Performing Arts, 1997; Official Museum Directory, 1999; Stern's Performing Arts Directory, 1997; USA Today Four Sport Stadium Guide, 1997; Chamber of Commerce/Economic Development, 1999

Library System

The Atlanta-Fulton Public Library has 32 branches, holdings of 1,904,614 volumes, and a budget of $17,989,124 (1996-1997). *American Library Directory, 1998-1999*

MEDIA

Newspapers

Name	Type	Freq.	Distribution	Circulation
Atlanta Constitution	General	7x/wk	State	313,990
The Atlanta Inquirer	Black	1x/wk	Area	61,082
Atlanta Journal	General	7x/wk	Area	115,447
Atlanta Voice	Black	1x/wk	Area	133,000
The Decatur-De Kalb Neighbor	General	1x/wk	Local	47,250
Mid-De Kalb Neighbor	General	1x/wk	Local	60,000
The Sandy Springs Neighbor	General	1x/wk	Local	27,475
The Stone Mountain-De Kalb Neighbor	General	1x/wk	Local	60,000

Note: Includes newspapers with circulations of 25,000 or more located in the city; Source: Burrelle's Media Directory, 1999 Edition

Television Stations

Name	Ch.	Affiliation	Type	Owner
WSB	n/a	ABCT	Commercial	Cox Enterprises Inc.
WAGA	n/a	FBC	Commercial	New World Communications
WGTV	n/a	PBS	Public	Georgia Public Broadcasting
WXIA	11	NBCT	Commercial	Gannett Broadcasting
WTBS	17	n/a	Commercial	Turner Broadcasting System Inc.
WPBA	30	PBS	Commercial	Atlanta Board of Education
WATL	36	WB	Commercial	Qwest Broadcasting
WGNX	46	CBST	Commercial	Meredith Corporation
WUPA	69	UPN	Commercial	VSC Communications

Note: Stations included broadcast in the Atlanta metro area; n/a not available Source: Burrelle's Media Directory, 1999 Edition

AM Radio Stations

Call Letters	Freq. (kHz)	Target Audience	Station Format	Music Format
WDWD	590	General	M/N	n/a
WGST	640	General	N/T	n/a
WCNN	680	General	N/T	n/a
WSB	750	General	N/T	n/a
WQXI	790	General	S/T	n/a
WAEC	860	Religious	M/T	Christian
WNIV	970	G/S	N/S/T	n/a
WGKA	1190	General	M	Adult Standards/Big Band/Classic Rock/Classical/Country/Jazz/Oldies/R&B
WFOM	1230	General	N/T	n/a
WTJH	1260	General	M	Gospel
WXLL	1310	Religious	M/N/T	Christian
WALR	1340	General	M	Gospel
WAOK	1380	Black	M/N/S	Gospel
WLTA	1400	General	N/T	n/a
WAZX	1550	Hispanic	M/N/S/T	Latin
WSSA	1570	G/R/W	M/N/S	Christian/Country

Note: Stations included broadcast in the Atlanta metro area; n/a not available
Target Audience: A=Asian; B=Black; C=Christian; E=Ethnic; F=French; G=General; H=Hispanic; M=Men; N=Native American; R=Religious; S=Senior Citizen; W=Women; Y=Young Adult; Z=Children
Station Format: E=Educational; M=Music; N=News; S=Sports; T=Talk
Source: Burrelle's Media Directory, 1999 Edition

FM Radio Stations

Call Letters	Freq. (mHz)	Target Audience	Station Format	Music Format
WJSP	88.1	General	M/N/T	Classical/Jazz
WPPR	88.3	General	M/N/T	Classical/Jazz
WRAS	88.5	General	M/N/S	Alternative
WRFG	89.3	Black	E/M/T	Jazz/Latin/R&B/Urban Contemporary
WDCO	89.7	General	M/N/T	Classical/Jazz
WABE	90.1	General	M/N	Classical/Jazz
WXVS	90.1	General	M/N/T	Classical
WJWV	90.9	General	M/N/T	Classical/Jazz
WREK	91.1	General	E/M/N/S/T	Alternative/Big Band/Blues/Classic Rock/Classical/Country/Jazz/Oldies/Reggae/R&B/Urban Contemp.
WABR	91.1	General	M/N/T	Classical
WWET	91.7	General	M/N/T	Classical
WUNV	91.7	General	M/N/T	Classical/Jazz
WCLK	91.9	General	M/S/T	Jazz
WZGC	92.9	General	M/N/S	Classic Rock
WSTR	94.1	General	M	n/a
WPCH	94.9	Women	M/N	Adult Contemporary
WKLS	96.1	General	M/N/S	AOR
WFOX	97.1	General	M	Oldies
WHTA	97.5	General	M	R&B/Urban Contemporary
WSB	98.5	General	M/N	Adult Contemporary
WNNX	99.7	General	M/N/S	Alternative
WKHX	101.5	General	M/N/S	Country
WVEE	103.3	General	M/N/S	Urban Contemporary
WALR	104.7	General	M/N/S	R&B
WGST	105.7	Men	N/T	n/a
WYAY	106.7	General	M	Country
WAMJ	107.5	General	M	Oldies/R&B

Note: Stations included broadcast in the Atlanta metro area; n/a not available
Station Format: E=Educational; M=Music; N=News; S=Sports; T=Talk
Target Audience: A=Asian; B=Black; C=Christian; E=Ethnic; F=French; G=General; H=Hispanic; M=Men; N=Native American; R=Religious; S=Senior Citizen; W=Women; Y=Young Adult; Z=Children
Music Format: AOR=Album Oriented Rock; MOR=Middle-of-the-Road
Source: Burrelle's Media Directory, 1999 Edition

CLIMATE

Average and Extreme Temperatures

Temperature	Jan	Feb	Mar	Apr	May	Jun	Jul	Aug	Sep	Oct	Nov	Dec	Yr.
Extreme High (°F)	79	80	85	93	95	101	105	102	98	95	84	77	105
Average High (°F)	52	56	64	73	80	86	88	88	82	73	63	54	72
Average Temp. (°F)	43	46	53	62	70	77	79	79	73	63	53	45	62
Average Low (°F)	33	36	42	51	59	66	70	69	64	52	42	35	52
Extreme Low (°F)	-8	5	10	26	37	46	53	55	36	28	3	0	-8

Note: Figures cover the years 1945-1990
Source: National Climatic Data Center, International Station Meteorological Climate Summary, 3/95

Average Precipitation/Snowfall/Humidity

Precip./Humidity	Jan	Feb	Mar	Apr	May	Jun	Jul	Aug	Sep	Oct	Nov	Dec	Yr.
Avg. Precip. (in.)	4.7	4.6	5.7	4.3	4.0	3.5	5.1	3.6	3.4	2.8	3.8	4.2	49.8
Avg. Snowfall (in.)	1	1	Tr	Tr	0	0	0	0	0	0	Tr	Tr	2
Avg. Rel. Hum. 7am (%)	79	77	78	78	82	83	88	89	88	84	81	79	82
Avg. Rel. Hum. 4pm (%)	56	50	48	45	49	52	57	56	56	51	52	55	52

Note: Figures cover the years 1945-1990; Tr = Trace amounts (<0.05 in. of rain; <0.5 in. of snow)
Source: National Climatic Data Center, International Station Meteorological Climate Summary, 3/95

Weather Conditions

Temperature			Daytime Sky			Precipitation		
10°F & below	32°F & below	90°F & above	Clear	Partly cloudy	Cloudy	0.01 inch or more precip.	0.1 inch or more snow/ice	Thunder-storms
1	49	38	98	147	120	116	3	48

Note: Figures are average number of days per year and covers the years 1945-1990
Source: National Climatic Data Center, International Station Meteorological Climate Summary, 3/95

AIR & WATER QUALITY

Maximum Pollutant Concentrations

	Particulate Matter (ug/m³)	Carbon Monoxide (ppm)	Sulfur Dioxide (ppm)	Nitrogen Dioxide (ppm)	Ozone (ppm)	Lead (ug/m³)
MSA[1] Level	75	4	0.027	0.025	0.14	0.34
NAAQS[2]	150	9	0.140	0.053	0.12	1.50
Met NAAQS?	Yes	Yes	Yes	Yes	No	Yes

Note: (1) Metropolitan Statistical Area - see Appendix A for areas included; (2) National Ambient Air Quality Standards; ppm = parts per million; ug/m³ = micrograms per cubic meter; n/a not available
Source: EPA, National Air Quality and Emissions Trends Report, 1997

Pollutant Standards Index

In the Atlanta MSA (see Appendix A for areas included), the Pollutant Standards Index (PSI) exceeded 100 on 36 days in 1997. A PSI value greater than 100 indicates that air quality would be in the unhealthful range on that day. *EPA, National Air Quality and Emissions Trends Report, 1997*

Drinking Water

Water System Name	Pop. Served	Primary Water Source Type	Number of Violations in 1998	Type of Violation/ Contaminants
Atlanta	649,836	Surface	None	None

Note: Data as of July 10, 1999
Source: EPA, Office of Ground Water and Drinking Water, Safe Drinking Water Information System

Atlanta tap water is neutral, soft.
Editor & Publisher Market Guide, 1999

Austin, Texas

Background

Austin is the legacy of bloody raids, dusty stampedes, and charging bayonets in the glaring sun of the territorial expansion age of the United States. Starting out in 1730 as a peaceful Spanish mission on the north bank of the Colorado River in south central Texas, it soon engaged in an imbroglio of territorial wars, beginning when the "Father of Texas," Stephen F. Austin, annexed the territory from Mexico in 1833 as his own. Later, the Republic of Texas named the territory Austin in honor of the colonizer, and conferred state capital status. Challenges to this decision ensued, ranging from an invasion by the Mexican government to reclaim its land, to Sam Houston's call that the capital ought to move from Austin to Houston.

During peaceful times, however, Austin has been called the "City of the Violet Crown." Coined by the short story writer, William Sydney Porter, or O'Henry, the name refers to the purple mist that circles the surrounding hills of the Colorado River Valley.

Because of its desirable location along the Colorado River, many recreational activities and public facilities center around water. Austin boasts of being one of the first cities to operate its own hydroelectric plant. It shouldn't be surprising, then, that a city of such technological innovation is home to a strong computer and aerospace industry.

Austin's high-tech focus continues to strengthen with numerous high-tech companies having recently undergone major expansions. Solectron, Applied Materials, Tokyo Electron, and Dell Computer have all expanded their facilities. 3M is adding a new customer center to its research and development complex, and Austin recently landed Samsung Electronics' $1.3 billion computer chip plant. And the number of software firms alone has ballooned from 177 in 1989 to over 600 by the end of 1998.

Austin is Texas' third-largest air cargo market and a new 20 million air cargo facility opened in 1997 at Austin-Bergstrom International, which is now ready for passenger traffic.

With this growth has come the problem of increased traffic, especially on Interstate 35, the main highway linking the U.S. and Mexico. Despite these growing pains, Austinites still see their city as special, and individuals and corporate executives still think of relocating there.

In addition to its technological orientation, Austin seeks to be a well-rounded leader in cultural activities. As the hard-fought capital of Texas, Austin takes pride in its support of its cultural institutions.

The climate of Austin is humid subtropical with hot summers. Winters are mild, with below-freezing temperatures occurring on an average of 25 days a year. Cold spells are short, seldom lasting more than two days. Daytime temperatures in summer are hot, while summer nights are usually pleasant.

General Rankings and Evaluative Comments

■ Austin was ranked #14 out of 19 large, southern metropolitan areas in *Money's* 1998 survey of "The Best Places to Live in America." The survey was conducted by first contacting 512 representative households nationwide and asking them to rank 37 quality-of-life factors on a scale of 1 to 10. Next, a demographic profile was compiled on the 300 largest metropolitan statistical areas in the U.S. The numbers were crunched together to arrive at an overall ranking (things Americans consider most important, like clean air and water, low crime and good schools, received extra weight). Unlike previous years, the 1998 rankings were broken down by region (northeast, midwest, south, west) and population size (100,000 to 249,999; 250,000 to 999,999; 1 million plus). The city had a nationwide ranking of #44 out of 300 in 1997 and #8 out of 300 in 1996. *Money, July 1998; Money, July 1997; Money, September 1996*

■ Austin appeared on *Fortune's* list of "The Best Cities for Business." Rank: #1 out of 10. One hundred and sixty cities worldwide were analyzed by Arthur Andersen's Business Location Service. The North American research focused on cities creating new wealth and opportunities. *Fortune* made the final selection of the top 10 cities in the U.S.

"It's the homebase for Dell Computer, now the region's largest private employer, who adds a staggering 100 to 200 jobs each week. The number of Austin-based software firms alone has ballooned from 177 in 1989 to over 600 by the end of last year." *Fortune, November 1998*

■ *Ladies Home Journal* ranked America's 200 largest cities based on the qualities women care about most. Austin ranked #70 out of 200. Criteria: low crime rate, well-paying jobs, quality health and child care, good public schools, the presence of women in government, size of the gender wage gap, number of sexual-harassment and discrimination complaints filed, unemployment and divorce rates, commute times, population density, number of houses of worship, parks and cultural offerings, number of women's health specialists, how well a community's women cared for themselves, complexion kindness index based on UV radiation levels, odds of finding affordable fashions, rental rates for romance movies, champagne sales and other matters of the heart. *Ladies Home Journal, November 1998*

■ Zero Population Growth ranked 229 cities in terms of children's health, safety, and economic well-being. Austin was ranked #41 out of 112 independent cities (cities with populations greater than 100,000 which were neither Major Cities nor Suburbs/Outer Cities) and was given a grade of C+. Criteria: total population, percent of population under 18 years of age, household language, percent population change, percent of births to teens, infant mortality rate, percent of low birth weights, dropout rate, enrollment in preprimary school, violent and property crime rates, unemployment rate, percent of children in poverty, percent of owner occupied units, number of bad air days, percent of public transportation commuters, and average travel time to work. *Zero Population Growth, Children's Environmental Index, Fall 1999*

■ Austin was ranked #4 out of 59 metro areas in *The Regional Economist's* "Rational Livability Ranking of 59 Large Metro Areas." The rankings were based on the metro area's total population change over the period 1990-97 divided by the number of people moving in from elsewhere in the United States (net domestic in-migration). *St. Louis Federal Reserve Bank of St. Louis, The Regional Economist, April 1999*

■ Austin appeared on *Travel & Leisure's* list of the world's 100 best cities. It was ranked #26 in the U.S. and #84 in the world. Criteria: activities/attractions, culture/arts, people, restaurants/food, and value. *Travel & Leisure, 1998 World's Best Awards*

■ *Conde Nast Traveler* polled 37,293 readers for travel satisfaction. Cities were ranked based on the following criteria: people/friendliness, environment/ambiance, cultural enrichment, restaurants and fun/energy. Austin appeared in the top 25, ranking number 21, with an overall rating of 58.9 out of 100. *Conde Nast Traveler, Readers' Choice Poll 1998*

■ Austin was selected by *Yahoo! Internet Life* as one of "America's Most Wired Cities & Towns." The city ranked #2 out of 50. Criteria: home and work net use, domain density, hosts per capita, directory density and content quality. *Yahoo! Internet Life, March 1999*

- Austin was chosen as one of "America's 10 Best Bike Towns." Rank: #6 out of 10. Criteria: marked bike lanes, municipal bike racks, bicycle access to bridges and public transportation, employment of a local government bicycle coordinator, area cycling advocacy efforts, bike-safety programs, budget for cycling programs, and local cycling culture. *Bicycling, March 1999*

- Cognetics studied 273 metro areas in the United States, ranking them by entrepreneurial activity. Austin was ranked #3 out of 134 smaller metro areas. Criteria: Significant Starts (firms started in the last 10 years that still employ at least 5 people) and Young Growers (percent of firms 10 years old or less that grew significantly during the last 4 years). *Cognetics, "Entrepreneurial Hot Spots: The Best Places in America to Start and Grow a Company," 1998*

- Austin appeared on *Forbes* list of "Best Places for Business Growth." Rank: #2 out of 162 metro areas. Criteria: average wage and salary increases, job growth rates, number of technology clusters (measures business activity in 13 different technology areas), overall concentration of technology activity relative to national average and technology output growth. *Forbes, May 31, 1999*

- Austin was included among *Entrepreneur* magazine's listing of the "20 Best Cities for Small Business." It was ranked #19 among large metro areas and #5 among central metro areas. Criteria: entrepreneurial activity, small-business growth, economic growth, and risk of failure. *Entrepreneur, October 1999*

- Austin was selected as one of the "Best American Cities to Start a Business" by *Point of View* magazine. Criteria: coolness, quality-of-life, and business concerns. The city was ranked #2 out of 75. *Point of View, November 1998*

- Austin appeared on *Sales & Marketing Management's* list of the "20 Hottest Cities for Selling." Rank: #1 out of 20. *S&MM* editors looked at Metropolitan Statistical Areas with populations of more than 150,000. The areas were ranked based on population increases, retail sales increases, effective buying income, increase in both residential and commercial building permits issued, unemployment rates, job growth, mix of industries, tax rates, number of corporate relocations, and the number of new corporations.

  "Austin's effective buying income between 1997 and 2000 will increase by 46 percent, and retail sales will increase by 45 percent; both of those figures are more than twice the national average." *Sales & Marketing Management, April 1999*

- *Computerworld* selected the best markets for IT job seekers based on their annual salary, skills, and hiring surveys. Austin ranked #10 out of 10. *Computerworld, January 11, 1999*

- Reliastar Financial Corp. ranked the 125 largest metropolitan areas according to the general financial security of residents. Austin was ranked #42 (tie) out of 125 with a score of 5.0. The score indicates the percentage a metropolitan area is above or below the metropolitan norm. A metro area with a score of 10.6 is 10.6% above the metro average. Criteria: Earnings and Wealth Potential (household income, education, net assets, cost of living); Safety Net (health insurance, retirement savings, life insurance, income support programs); Personal Threats (unemployment rate, low-income households, crime rate); Community Economic Vitality (cost of community services, job quality, job creation, housing costs). *Reliastar Financial Corp., "The Best Cities to Earn and Save Money," 1999 Edition*

Business Environment

STATE ECONOMY

State Economic Profile

"Economic growth in Texas has slowed as both its new and old economies are under pressure. Weak commodity prices and over-capacity have hurt TX's old economic powers, agriculture and oil. Soft global demand has slowed TX's new economic powers, semiconductors and computer sales. A slowing US economy in 1999 will also place a drag on TX's biotech and software companies. Despite the current slowdown, TX's long-term outlook is extremely bright, and its current problems will last no more than two years.

Weak commodity prices, over-capacity and soft foreign demand have all coincided to undermine TX's oil and farm sector. Despite OPEC cutbacks, the TX oil industry remains vulnerable because of its high costs, high inventories and high capacity. TX's farm sector is similarly positioned; commodity prices are expected to continue their long-term downward trend.

The TX economy is more diversified today than ever before. Growth in services and hi-tech employment have more than offset declines in TX's resource economy. Services employment in 1998 grew at 3.8%, adding some 93,000 jobs, while construction employment grew 4.9%, adding 22,700 jobs. Construction employment, along with home sales and starts, should contract in 1999 and 2000. TX's demographic situation is positive; the state continues to attract educated, young households. However, the current weakness in the state's semiconductor and computer industry has slowed job growth from its previous feverish pace. In the near-term, TX's growth should slow along with the US economy. Its long-term prospects are bright given its business friendly atmosphere and central location." *National Association of Realtors, Economic Profiles: The Fifty States and the District of Columbia, http://nar.realtor.com/databank/profiles.htm*

IMPORTS/EXPORTS

Total Export Sales

Area	1994 ($000)	1995 ($000)	1996 ($000)	1997 ($000)	% Chg. 1994-97	% Chg. 1996-97
MSA[1]	2,128,774	2,929,208	2,743,135	3,354,809	57.6	22.3
U.S.	512,415,609	583,030,524	622,827,063	687,597,999	34.2	10.4

Note: (1) Metropolitan Statistical Area - see Appendix A for areas included
Source: U.S. Department of Commerce, International Trade Association, Metropolitan Area Exports: An Export Performance Report on Over 250 U.S. Cities, November 10, 1998

CITY FINANCES

City Government Finances

Component	FY92 ($000)	FY92 (per capita $)
Revenue	1,130,427	2,261.65
Expenditure	1,112,679	2,226.14
Debt Outstanding	3,189,676	6,381.59
Cash & Securities	1,541,196	3,083.47

Source: U.S. Bureau of the Census, City Government Finances: 1991-92

City Government Revenue by Source

Source	FY92 ($000)	FY92 (per capita $)	FY92 (%)
From Federal Government	8,470	16.95	0.7
From State Governments	22,018	44.05	1.9
From Local Governments	3,768	7.54	0.3
Property Taxes	98,147	196.36	8.7
General Sales Taxes	55,401	110.84	4.9
Selective Sales Taxes	18,466	36.94	1.6
Income Taxes	0	0.00	0.0
Current Charges	232,264	464.69	20.5
Utility/Liquor Store	500,130	1,000.61	44.2
Employee Retirement[1]	69,967	139.98	6.2
Other	121,796	243.68	10.8

Note: (1) Excludes "city contributions," classified as "nonrevenue," intragovernmental transfers.
Source: U.S. Bureau of the Census, City Government Finances: 1991-92

City Government Expenditures by Function

Function	FY92 ($000)	FY92 (per capita $)	FY92 (%)
Educational Services	8,188	16.38	0.7
Employee Retirement[1]	22,975	45.97	2.1
Environment/Housing	179,041	358.21	16.1
Government Administration	20,629	41.27	1.9
Interest on General Debt	99,995	200.06	9.0
Public Safety	88,567	177.20	8.0
Social Services	142,961	286.02	12.8
Transportation	37,281	74.59	3.4
Utility/Liquor Store	478,325	956.98	43.0
Other	34,717	69.46	3.1

Note: (1) Payments to beneficiaries including withdrawal of contributions.
Source: U.S. Bureau of the Census, City Government Finances: 1991-92

Municipal Bond Ratings

Area	Moody's	S & P
Austin	Aaa	n/a

Note: n/a not available; n/r not rated
Source: Moody's Bond Record, 6/99

POPULATION

Population Growth

Area	1980	1990	% Chg. 1980-90	July 1998 Estimate	% Chg. 1990-98
City	345,544	465,577	34.7	552,434	18.7
MSA[1]	536,688	781,572	45.6	1,106,364	41.6
U.S.	226,545,805	248,765,170	9.8	270,299,000	8.7

Note: (1) Metropolitan Statistical Area - see Appendix A for areas included;
July 1998 MSA population estimate was calculated by the editors
Source: 1980/1990 Census of Housing and Population, Summary Tape File 3C;
Census Bureau Population Estimates 1998

Population Characteristics

Race	City 1980 Population	%	City 1990 Population	%	% Chg. 1980-90	MSA[1] 1990 Population	%
White	263,618	76.3	329,309	70.7	24.9	601,163	76.9
Black	42,108	12.2	57,675	12.4	37.0	71,959	9.2
Amer Indian/Esk/Aleut	1,516	0.4	1,768	0.4	16.6	2,906	0.4
Asian/Pacific Islander	4,127	1.2	13,939	3.0	237.8	18,341	2.3
Other	34,175	9.9	62,886	13.5	84.0	87,203	11.2
Hispanic Origin[2]	64,766	18.7	105,162	22.6	62.4	157,866	20.2

Note: (1) Metropolitan Statistical Area - see Appendix A for areas included;
(2) people of Hispanic origin can be of any race
Source: 1980/1990 Census of Housing and Population, Summary Tape File 3C

Ancestry

Area	German	Irish	English	Italian	U.S.	French	Polish	Dutch
City	20.7	12.6	13.7	2.3	2.7	3.6	1.6	1.5
MSA[1]	23.7	14.2	14.7	2.3	3.3	3.9	1.7	1.7
U.S.	23.3	15.6	13.1	5.9	5.3	4.2	3.8	2.5

Note: Figures are percentages and include persons that reported multiple ancestry (eg. if a person reported being Irish and Italian, they were included in both columns); (1) Metropolitan Statistical Area - see Appendix A for areas included
Source: 1990 Census of Population and Housing, Summary Tape File 3C

Age

Area	Median Age (Years)	Age Distribution (%) Under 5	Under 18	18-24	25-44	45-64	65+	80+
City	28.9	7.5	23.1	17.2	38.7	13.6	7.4	1.8
MSA[1]	29.4	7.7	25.3	14.9	38.1	14.4	7.3	1.7
U.S.	32.9	7.3	25.6	10.5	32.6	18.7	12.5	2.8

Note: (1) Metropolitan Statistical Area - see Appendix A for areas included
Source: 1990 Census of Population and Housing, Summary Tape File 3C

Male/Female Ratio

Area	Number of males per 100 females (all ages)	Number of males per 100 females (18 years old+)
City	99.9	98.4
MSA[1]	99.8	97.8
U.S.	95.0	91.9

Note: (1) Metropolitan Statistical Area - see Appendix A for areas included
Source: 1990 Census of Population, General Population Characteristics

INCOME

Per Capita/Median/Average Income

Area	Per Capita ($)	Median Household ($)	Average Household ($)
City	14,295	25,414	33,947
MSA[1]	14,521	28,474	36,754
U.S.	14,420	30,056	38,453

Note: All figures are for 1989; (1) Metropolitan Statistical Area - see Appendix A for areas included
Source: 1990 Census of Population and Housing, Summary Tape File 3C

Household Income Distribution by Race

Income ($)	City (%)					U.S. (%)				
	Total	White	Black	Other	Hisp.[1]	Total	White	Black	Other	Hisp.[1]
Less than 5,000	8.9	7.4	14.8	13.4	10.2	6.2	4.8	15.2	8.6	8.8
5,000 - 9,999	9.5	8.5	12.4	12.5	11.5	9.3	8.6	14.2	9.9	11.1
10,000 - 14,999	10.6	9.5	12.9	14.7	13.6	8.8	8.5	11.0	9.8	11.0
15,000 - 24,999	20.3	19.3	23.6	23.2	23.7	17.5	17.3	18.9	18.5	20.5
25,000 - 34,999	16.1	16.2	16.4	15.2	16.7	15.8	16.1	14.2	15.4	16.4
35,000 - 49,999	15.6	16.7	10.8	12.9	14.2	17.9	18.6	13.3	16.1	16.0
50,000 - 74,999	11.6	13.2	6.9	6.3	7.9	15.0	15.8	9.3	13.4	11.1
75,000 - 99,999	4.0	4.9	1.3	1.2	1.4	5.1	5.5	2.6	4.7	3.1
100,000+	3.5	4.4	1.0	0.6	0.8	4.4	4.8	1.3	3.7	1.9

Note: All figures are for 1989; (1) people of Hispanic origin can be of any race
Source: 1990 Census of Population and Housing, Summary Tape File 3C

Effective Buying Income

Area	Per Capita ($)	Median Household ($)	Average Household ($)
City	18,999	33,690	45,417
MSA[1]	19,332	36,486	49,623
U.S.	16,803	34,536	45,243

Note: Data as of 1/1/99; (1) Metropolitan Statistical Area - see Appendix A for areas included
Source: Standard Rate & Data Service, Newspaper Advertising Source, 9/99

Effective Household Buying Income Distribution

Area	% of Households Earning						
	$10,000 -$19,999	$20,000 -$34,999	$35,000 -$49,999	$50,000 -$74,999	$75,000 -$99,000	$100,000 -$124,999	$125,000 and up
City	15.7	23.0	16.8	17.1	7.4	3.1	3.6
MSA[1]	14.8	21.5	17.1	19.2	8.7	3.2	3.5
U.S.	16.0	22.6	18.2	18.9	7.2	2.4	2.7

Note: Data as of 1/1/99; (1) Metropolitan Statistical Area - see Appendix A for areas included
Source: Standard Rate & Data Service, Newspaper Advertising Source, 9/99

Poverty Rates by Race and Age

Area	Total (%)	By Race (%)				By Age (%)		
		White	Black	Other	Hisp.[2]	Under 5 years old	Under 18 years old	65 years and over
City	17.9	13.5	26.5	30.2	27.4	23.4	21.5	11.7
MSA[1]	15.3	11.8	26.2	27.7	26.3	19.1	17.4	13.0
U.S.	13.1	9.8	29.5	23.1	25.3	20.1	18.3	12.8

Note: Figures show the percent of people living below the poverty line in 1989. The average poverty threshold was $12,674 for a family of four in 1989; (1) Metropolitan Statistical Area - see Appendix A for areas included; (2) people of Hispanic origin can be of any race
Source: 1990 Census of Population and Housing, Summary Tape File 3C

EMPLOYMENT

Labor Force and Employment

Area	Civilian Labor Force			Workers Employed		
	Jun. 1998	Jun. 1999	% Chg.	Jun. 1998	Jun. 1999	% Chg.
City	369,091	381,934	3.5	356,377	371,152	4.1
MSA[1]	683,165	707,903	3.6	661,832	689,270	4.1
U.S.	138,798,000	140,666,000	1.3	132,265,000	134,395,000	1.6

Note: Data is not seasonally adjusted and covers workers 16 years of age and older; (1) Metropolitan Statistical Area - see Appendix A for areas included
Source: Bureau of Labor Statistics, http://stats.bls.gov

Unemployment Rate

Area	1998						1999					
	Jul.	Aug.	Sep.	Oct.	Nov.	Dec.	Jan.	Feb.	Mar.	Apr.	May.	Jun.
City	3.2	3.1	3.1	2.7	2.7	2.6	2.9	2.6	2.3	2.2	2.4	2.8
MSA[1]	2.9	2.8	2.7	2.4	2.5	2.3	2.7	2.4	2.1	2.0	2.2	2.6
U.S.	4.7	4.5	4.4	4.2	4.1	4.0	4.8	4.7	4.4	4.1	4.0	4.5

Note: Data is not seasonally adjusted and covers workers 16 years of age and older; all figures are percentages; (1) Metropolitan Statistical Area - see Appendix A for areas included
Source: Bureau of Labor Statistics, http://stats.bls.gov

Employment by Industry

Sector	MSA[1]		U.S.
	Number of Employees	Percent of Total	Percent of Total
Services	183,300	29.5	30.4
Retail Trade	107,800	17.4	17.7
Government	126,100	20.3	15.6
Manufacturing	84,300	13.6	14.3
Finance/Insurance/Real Estate	32,700	5.3	5.9
Wholesale Trade	28,100	4.5	5.4
Transportation/Public Utilities	21,000	3.4	5.3
Construction	36,600	5.9	5.0
Mining	1,300	0.2	0.4

Note: Figures cover non-farm employment as of 6/99 and are not seasonally adjusted; (1) Metropolitan Statistical Area - see Appendix A for areas included
Source: Bureau of Labor Statistics, http://stats.bls.gov

Employment by Occupation

Occupation Category	City (%)	MSA[1] (%)	U.S. (%)
White Collar	69.3	68.4	58.1
Executive/Admin./Management	15.3	15.6	12.3
Professional	19.0	17.9	14.1
Technical & Related Support	5.5	5.3	3.7
Sales	11.4	11.6	11.8
Administrative Support/Clerical	18.1	18.0	16.3
Blue Collar	15.9	17.5	26.2
Precision Production/Craft/Repair	7.5	8.5	11.3
Machine Operators/Assem./Insp.	3.4	3.8	6.8
Transportation/Material Movers	2.3	2.5	4.1
Cleaners/Helpers/Laborers	2.6	2.7	3.9
Services	13.8	12.7	13.2
Farming/Forestry/Fishing	1.0	1.4	2.5

Note: Figures cover employed persons 16 years old and over; (1) Metropolitan Statistical Area - see Appendix A for areas included
Source: 1990 Census of Population and Housing, Summary Tape File 3C

Occupational Employment Projections: 1996 - 2006

Occupations Expected to Have the Largest Job Growth (ranked by numerical growth)	Fast-Growing Occupations[1] (ranked by percent growth)
1. Cashiers	1. Desktop publishers
2. Salespersons, retail	2. Systems analysts
3. General managers & top executives	3. Customer service representatives
4. Truck drivers, light	4. Physical therapy assistants and aides
5. Child care workers, private household	5. Computer engineers
6. General office clerks	6. Emergency medical technicians
7. Systems analysts	7. Medical assistants
8. Food preparation workers	8. Respiratory therapists
9. Food service workers	9. Telephone & cable TV line install & repair
10. Registered nurses	10. Physical therapists

Note: Projections cover Texas; (1) Excludes occupations with total job growth less than 300
Source: U.S. Department of Labor, Employment and Training Administration, America's Labor Market Information System (ALMIS)

TAXES

Major State and Local Tax Rates

State Corp. Income (%)	State Personal Income (%)	Residential Property (effective rate per $100)	Sales & Use		State Gasoline (cents/ gallon)	State Cigarette (cents/ pack)
			State (%)	Local (%)		
None[a]	None	n/a	6.25	2.0	20.0	41.0

Note: Personal/corporate income, sales, gasoline and cigarette tax rates as of January 1999. Property tax rates as of 1997; (a) Texas imposes a franchise tax of 4.5% of earned surplus
Source: Federation of Tax Administrators, www.taxadmin.org; Washington D.C. Department of Finance and Revenue, Tax Rates and Tax Burdens in the District of Columbia: A Nationwide Comparison, July 1998; Chamber of Commerce, 1999

Total Taxes Per Capita and as a Percent of Income

Area	Per Capita Income ($)	Per Capita Taxes ($)			Percent of Income (%)		
		Total	Federal	State/ Local	Total	Federal	State/ Local
Texas	25,563	8,741	6,051	2,690	34.2	23.7	10.5
U.S.	27,876	9,881	6,690	3,191	35.4	24.0	11.4

Note: Figures are for 1998
Source: Tax Foundation, www.taxfoundation.org

COMMERCIAL REAL ESTATE

Office Market

Class/ Location	Total Space (sq. ft.)	Vacant Space (sq. ft.)	Vac. Rate (%)	Under Constr. (sq. ft.)	Net Absorp. (sq. ft.)	Rental Rates ($/sq.ft./yr.)
Class A						
CBD	3,941,681	218,874	5.6	n/a	625,778	23.15-27.13
Outside CBD	5,742,452	225,942	3.9	683,927	779,909	20.00-28.50
Class B						
CBD	2,968,637	262,368	8.8	n/a	-431,721	14.00-22.75
Outside CBD	9,368,464	394,408	4.2	n/a	-183,584	12.00-24.00

Note: Data as of 10/98 and covers Austin; CBD = Central Business District; n/a not available;
Source: Society of Industrial and Office Realtors, 1999 Comparative Statistics of Industrial and Office Real Estate Markets

"The semiconductor industry has seen a downturn, but because Austin's office market is based more on computer software technology, its growth has not been seriously affected so far. Austin's most critical need is for additional space. Despite tight money, SIOR's reporters expect new construction to rise five percent in 1999. Two 400,000 sq. ft. buildings with completion dates in the first or second quarter of the year 2000 are under construction in Austin's CBD. Some corporate users are also consolidating into single-campus locations, a trend which could cause a temporary vacancy increase. Since REITs have backed off of this market and available space will be limited, most other indicators, including the sales and leasing volume, will probably drop by one to five percent." *Society of Industrial and Office Realtors, 1999 Comparative Statistics of Industrial and Office Real Estate Markets*

Industrial Market

Location	Total Space (sq. ft.)	Vacant Space (sq. ft.)	Vac. Rate (%)	Under Constr. (sq. ft.)	Net Absorp. (sq. ft.)	Net Lease ($/sq.ft./yr.)
Central City	n/a	n/a	n/a	n/a	n/a	n/a
Suburban	21,055,655	1,557,639	7.4	1,630,160	1,019,416	4.20-5.40

Note: Data as of 10/98 and covers Austin; n/a not available
Source: Society of Industrial and Office Realtors, 1999 Comparative Statistics of Industrial and Office Real Estate Markets

"The amount of warehouse/manufacturing space proposed for Austin has decreased, even though vacancies in some high-demand sectors are at one to four percent. A basic question for 1999 is how significant changes in the financial markets will affect future development projects. Continuing reasonable demand and low vacancy rates are probable for 1999. However, SIOR's reporter foresees a downturn of six to 10 percent in absorption construction, and the dollar volume of sales and leases. The only exception may be in the high tech/R&D sector. A considerable amount of high tech/R&D space is already under construction. The opening of the Austin Bergstrom International Airport, scheduled for mid-1999, may also provide a boost to industrial development in the southeast sector. Development in the popular north central market close to Austin's dense base of high-technology companies may be somewhat limited since infill sites are in limited supply." *Society of Industrial and Office Realtors, 1999 Comparative Statistics of Industrial and Office Real Estate Markets*

Retail Market

Shopping Center Inventory (sq. ft.)	Shopping Center Construction (sq. ft.)	Construction as a Percent of Inventory (%)	Torto Wheaton Rent Index[1] ($/sq. ft.)
19,509,000	630,000	3.2	15.90

Note: Data as of 1997 and covers the Metropolitan Statistical Area - see Appendix A for areas included; (1) Index is based on a model that predicts what the average rent should be for leases with certain characteristics, in certain locations during certain years.
Source: National Association of Realtors, 1997-1998 Market Conditions Report

"Between 1994 and 1996, Austin registered a blistering 6.0% average annual rate of employment growth, which slowed somewhat in 1997. Nonetheless, such strong employment and population growth have caused vacancy rates to drop and the rent index to soar 56% since 1994. A large amount of retail activity has been centered in the Golden Triangle area near Research Boulevard, Loop 360, and North MoPac Expressway. Development has also been found in the IH-35 area. Expect population and real income growth to decelerate somewhat over the next few years, which will likely put downward pressure on the retail rent index." *National Association of Realtors, 1997-1998 Market Conditions Report*

COMMERCIAL UTILITIES

Typical Monthly Electric Bills

Area	Commercial Service ($/month)		Industrial Service ($/month)	
	12 kW demand 1,500 kWh	100 kW demand 30,000 kWh	1,000 kW demand 400,000 kWh	20,000 kW demand 10,000,000 kWh
City[1]	97	2,494[a]	22,798	527,400
U.S.[2]	150	2,174	23,995	508,569

Note: (1) Based on rates in effect January 1, 1998; (2) Based on rates in effect January 1, 1999; (a) Based on 120 kW demand and 30,000 kWh usage.
Source: Memphis Light, Gas and Water, 1998 Utility Bill Comparisons for Selected U.S. Cities; Edison Electric Institute, Typical Residential, Commercial and Industrial Bills, Winter 1999

TRANSPORTATION

Transportation Statistics

Average minutes to work	19.1
Interstate highways	I-35
Bus lines	
In-city	Capital Metro TA, 462 vehicles
Inter-city	2
Passenger air service	
Airport	Robert Mueller Austin Municipal
Airlines	21
Aircraft departures	40,647 (1996)
Enplaned passengers	2,829,581 (1996)
Rail service	Amtrak
Motor freight carriers	20
Major waterways/ports	None

Source: Editor & Publisher Market Guide, 1999; FAA Airport Activity Statistics, 1997; Amtrak National Time Table, Northeast Timetable, Spring/Summer 1999; 1990 Census of Population and Housing, STF 3C; Chamber of Commerce/Economic Development 1999; Jane's Urban Transport Systems 1999-2000

Means of Transportation to Work

Area	Car/Truck/Van		Public Transportation			Bicycle	Walked	Other Means	Worked at Home
	Drove Alone	Car-pooled	Bus	Subway	Railroad				
City	73.6	13.3	4.8	0.0	0.0	0.8	3.3	1.3	2.8
MSA[1]	75.3	13.9	3.2	0.0	0.0	0.5	2.9	1.2	3.0
U.S.	73.2	13.4	3.0	1.5	0.5	0.4	3.9	1.2	3.0

Note: Figures shown are percentages and only include workers 16 years old and over;
(1) Metropolitan Statistical Area - see Appendix A for areas included
Source: 1990 Census of Population and Housing, Summary Tape File 3C

BUSINESSES

Major Business Headquarters

Company Name	1999 Rankings	
	Fortune 500	Forbes 500

No companies listed.

Note: Companies listed are located in the city; dashes indicate no ranking
Fortune 500: Companies that produce a 10-K are ranked 1 to 500 based on 1998 revenue
Forbes 500: Private companies are ranked 1 to 500 based on 1997 revenue
Source: Forbes, November 30, 1998; Fortune, April 26, 1999

Best Companies to Work For

Whole Foods Market (natural foods supermarket), headquartered in Austin, is among the " 100 Best Companies to Work for in America." Criteria: trust in management, pride in work/company, camaraderie, company responses to the Hewitt People Practices Inventory, and employee responses to their Great Place to Work survey. The companies also had to be at least 10 years old and have a minimum of 500 employees. *Fortune, January 11, 1999*

Fast-Growing Businesses

According to *Inc.*, Austin is home to two of America's 100 fastest-growing private companies: Sunset Direct and InfoEdge Technology. Criteria for inclusion: must be an independent, privately-held, U.S. corporation, proprietorship or partnership; sales of at least $200,000 in 1995; five-year operating/sales history; increase in 1999 sales over 1998 sales; holding companies, regulated banks, and utilities were excluded. *Inc. 500, 1999*

According to Deloitte & Touche LLP, Austin is home to one of America's 100 fastest-growing high-technology companies: Metrowerks. Companies are ranked by percentage growth in revenue over a five-year period. Criteria for inclusion: must be a U.S. company developing and/or providing technology products or services; company must have been in business for five years with 1993 revenues of at least $50,000. *Deloitte & Touche LLP, November 17, 1998*

Women-Owned Firms: Number, Employment and Sales

Area	Number of Firms	Employ-ment	Sales ($000)	Rank[2]
MSA[1]	40,200	74,100	9,601,700	50

Note: (1) Metropolitan Statistical Area - see Appendix A for areas included;
(2) Calculated on an averaging of the number of businesses, employment and sales
Source: The National Foundation for Women Business Owners, 1999 Facts on Women-Owned Businesses: Trends in the Top 50 Metropolitan Areas

Women-Owned Firms: Growth

Area	% change from 1992 to 1999			Rank[2]
	Number of Firms	Employ-ment	Sales	
MSA[1]	42.8	102.8	128.5	30

Note: (1) Metropolitan Statistical Area - see Appendix A for areas included; (2) Calculated on an averaging of the percent growth of number of businesses, employment and sales
Source: The National Foundation for Women Business Owners, 1999 Facts on Women-Owned Businesses: Trends in the Top 50 Metropolitan Areas

Minority Business Opportunity

Austin is home to one company which is on the Black Enterprise Auto Dealer 100 list (largest based on gross sales): Pavilion Lincoln-Mercury/JMC Auto Group (Lincoln-Mercury) . Criteria: 1) operational in previous calendar year; 2) at least 51% black-owned. *Black Enterprise, www.blackenterprise.com*

Three of the 500 largest Hispanic-owned companies in the U.S. are located in Austin. *Hispanic Business, June 1999*

Small Business Opportunity

According to *Forbes*, Austin is home to two of America's 200 best small companies: National Instruments and Travis Boats & Motors. Criteria: companies included must be publicly traded since November 1997 with a stock price of at least $5 per share and an average daily float of 1,000 shares. The company's latest 12-month sales must be between $5 and $350 million, return on equity (ROE) must be a minimum of 12% for both the past 5 years and the most recent four quarters, and five-year sales and EPS growth must average at least 10%. Companies with declining sales or earnings during the past year were dropped as well as businesses with debt/equity ratios over 1.25. Companies with negative operating cash flow in each of the past two years were also excluded. *Forbes, November 2, 1998*

HOTELS & MOTELS

Hotels/Motels

Area	Hotels/ Motels	Rooms	Luxury-Level Hotels/Motels		Average Minimum Rates ($)		
			♦♦♦♦	♦♦♦♦♦	♦♦	♦♦♦	♦♦♦♦
City	81	11,951	2	0	71	133	186
Airport	5	906	0	0	n/a	n/a	n/a
Suburbs	6	411	0	0	n/a	n/a	n/a
Total	92	13,268	2	0	n/a	n/a	n/a

Note: n/a not available; classifications range from one diamond (budget properties with basic amenities) to five diamond (luxury properties with the finest service, rooms and facilities).
Source: OAG, Business Travel Planner, Winter 1998-99

CONVENTION CENTERS

Major Convention Centers

Center Name	Meeting Rooms	Exhibit Space (sq. ft.)
Austin Convention Center	29	400,000
City Coliseum	2	30,000
Lakeway Inn	10	n/a
Palmer Auditorium	13	60,000

Note: n/a not available
Source: Trade Shows Worldwide, 1998; Meetings & Conventions, 4/15/99;
Sucessful Meetings, 3/31/98

Living Environment

COST OF LIVING

Cost of Living Index

Composite Index	Groceries	Housing	Utilities	Trans-portation	Health Care	Misc. Goods/ Services
98.4	92.9	89.0	90.7	100.3	105.6	109.1

Note: U.S. = 100
Source: ACCRA, Cost of Living Index, 1st Quarter 1999

HOUSING

Median Home Prices and Housing Affordability

Area	Median Price[2] 1st Qtr. 1999 ($)	HOI[3] 1st Qtr. 1999	Afford-ability Rank[4]
MSA[1]	137,000	66.9	132
U.S.	134,000	69.6	—

Note: (1) Metropolitan Statistical Area - see Appendix A for areas included; (2) U.S. figures calculated from the sales of 524,324 new and existing homes in 181 markets; (3) Housing Opportunity Index - percent of homes sold that were within the reach of the median income household at the prevailing mortgage interest rate; (4) Rank is from 1-181 with 1 being most affordable
Source: National Association of Home Builders, Housing Opportunity Index, 1st Quarter 1999

Median Home Price Projection

It is projected that the median price of existing single-family homes in the metro area will increase by 5.7% in 1999. Nationwide, home prices are projected to increase 3.8%.
Kiplinger's Personal Finance Magazine, January 1999

Average New Home Price

Area	Price ($)
City	110,500
U.S.	142,735

Note: Figures are based on a new home with 1,800 sq. ft. of living area on an 8,000 sq. ft. lot.
Source: ACCRA, Cost of Living Index, 1st Quarter 1999

Average Apartment Rent

Area	Rent ($/mth)
City	872
U.S.	601

Note: Figures are based on an unfurnished two bedroom, 1-1/2 or 2 bath apartment, approximately 950 sq. ft. in size, excluding all utilities except water
Source: ACCRA, Cost of Living Index, 1st Quarter 1999

RESIDENTIAL UTILITIES

Average Residential Utility Costs

Area	All Electric ($/mth)	Part Electric ($/mth)	Other Energy ($/mth)	Phone ($/mth)
City	–	63.49	28.32	15.62
U.S.	100.02	55.73	43.33	19.71

Source: ACCRA, Cost of Living Index, 1st Quarter 1999

HEALTH CARE

Average Health Care Costs

Area	Hospital ($/day)	Doctor ($/visit)	Dentist ($/visit)
City	423.33	53.80	76.00
U.S.	430.43	52.45	66.35

Note: Hospital—based on a semi-private room; Doctor—based on a general practitioner's routine exam of an established patient; Dentist—based on adult teeth cleaning and periodic oral exam.
Source: ACCRA, Cost of Living Index, 1st Quarter 1999

Distribution of Office-Based Physicians

| Area | Family/Gen. Practitioners | Specialists | | |
		Medical	Surgical	Other
MSA[1]	296	513	456	482

Note: Data as of 12/31/97; (1) Metropolitan Statistical Area - see Appendix A for areas included
Source: American Medical Assn., Physician Characteristics & Distribution in the U.S., 1999

Hospitals

Austin has 5 general medical and surgical hospitals, 5 psychiatric, 3 rehabilitation, 2 other specialty. *AHA Guide to the Healthcare Field, 1998-99*

EDUCATION

Public School District Statistics

District Name	Num. Sch.	Enroll.	Classroom Teachers	Pupils per Teacher	Minority Pupils (%)	Current Exp.[1] ($/pupil)
American Institute For Learnin	1	155	10	15.5	n/a	n/a
Austin ISD	101	76,606	4,561	16.8	63.3	4,830
Eanes ISD	9	7,184	525	13.7	n/a	n/a
Lake Travis ISD	4	3,197	247	12.9	n/a	n/a
Texas Academy of Excellence	1	77	6	12.8	n/a	n/a

Note: Data covers the 1997-1998 school year unless otherwise noted; (1) Data covers fiscal year 1996; SD = School District; ISD = Independent School District; n/a not available
Source: National Center for Education Statistics, Common Core of Data Public Education Agency Universe 1997-98; National Center for Education Statistics, Characteristics of the 100 Largest Public Elementary and Secondary School Districts in the United States: 1997-98, July 1999

Educational Quality

School District	Education Quotient[1]	Graduate Outcome[2]	Community Index[3]	Resource Index[4]
Austin ISD	93.0	108.0	119.0	58.0

Note: Nearly 1,000 secondary school districts were rated in terms of educational quality. The scores range from a low of 50 to a high of 150; (1) Average of the Graduate Outcome, Community and Resource indexes; (2) Based on graduation rates and college board scores (SAT/ACT); (3) Based on the surrounding community's average level of education and the area's average income level; (4) Based on teacher salaries, per-pupil expenditures and student-teacher ratios.
Source: Expansion Management, Ratings Issue, 1998

Educational Attainment by Race

| Area | High School Graduate (%) | | | | | Bachelor's Degree (%) | | | | |
	Total	White	Black	Other	Hisp.[2]	Total	White	Black	Other	Hisp.[2]
City	82.3	88.7	69.6	58.4	57.9	34.4	40.0	16.5	18.4	13.8
MSA[1]	82.5	87.3	70.0	58.5	56.8	32.2	35.9	16.9	17.8	13.1
U.S.	75.2	77.9	63.1	60.4	49.8	20.3	21.5	11.4	19.4	9.2

Note: Figures shown cover persons 25 years old and over; (1) Metropolitan Statistical Area - see Appendix A for areas included; (2) people of Hispanic origin can be of any race
Source: 1990 Census of Population and Housing, Summary Tape File 3C

School Enrollment by Type

| Area | Preprimary | | | | Elementary/High School | | | |
| | Public | | Private | | Public | | Private | |
	Enrollment	%	Enrollment	%	Enrollment	%	Enrollment	%
City	4,815	52.7	4,328	47.3	62,838	93.4	4,472	6.6
MSA[1]	8,688	52.4	7,888	47.6	119,826	94.2	7,318	5.8
U.S.	2,679,029	59.5	1,824,256	40.5	38,379,689	90.2	4,187,099	9.8

Note: Figures shown cover persons 3 years old and over;
(1) Metropolitan Statistical Area - see Appendix A for areas included
Source: 1990 Census of Population and Housing, Summary Tape File 3C

School Enrollment by Race

Area	Preprimary (%)				Elementary/High School (%)			
	White	Black	Other	Hisp.[1]	White	Black	Other	Hisp.[1]
City	73.9	11.0	15.1	20.9	58.1	18.2	23.8	33.8
MSA[2]	80.3	7.7	12.0	18.3	69.7	12.2	18.2	28.3
U.S.	80.4	12.5	7.1	7.8	74.1	15.6	10.3	12.5

Note: Figures shown cover persons 3 years old and over; (1) people of Hispanic origin can be of any race; (2) Metropolitan Statistical Area - see Appendix A for areas included
Source: 1990 Census of Population and Housing, Summary Tape File 3C

Classroom Teacher Salaries in Public Schools

District	B.A. Degree		M.A. Degree		Maximum	
	Min. ($)	Rank[1]	Max. ($)	Rank[1]	Max. ($)	Rank[1]
Austin	25,840	54	42,100	79	42,100	93
Average	26,980	-	46,065	-	51,435	-

Note: Salaries are for 1997-1998; (1) Rank ranges from 1 to 100
Source: American Federation of Teachers, Survey & Analysis of Salary Trends, 1998

Higher Education

Two-Year Colleges		Four-Year Colleges		Medical Schools	Law Schools	Voc/ Tech
Public	Private	Public	Private			
1	2	0	4	0	1	6

Source: College Blue Book, Occupational Education, 1997; Medical School Admission Requirements, 1999-2000; Peterson's Guide to Two-Year Colleges, 1999; Peterson's Guide to Four-Year Colleges, 2000; Barron's Guide to Law Schools, 1999

MAJOR EMPLOYERS

Major Employers

Austin State Hospital	Temple-Inland Financial Services
Crystal Semiconductor	Samsung Austin Semiconductor
St. David's Health Care System	Commemorative Brands (jewelery mfg.)
Whole Foods Market Southwest	Solectron Texas (electronics)
Daughters of Charity Health System	North Austin Medical Center

Note: Companies listed are located in the city
Source: Dun's Business Rankings, 1999; Ward's Business Directory, 1998

PUBLIC SAFETY

Crime Rate

Area	All Crimes	Violent Crimes				Property Crimes		
		Murder	Forcible Rape	Robbery	Aggrav. Assault	Burglary	Larceny -Theft	Motor Vehicle Theft
City	7,870.0	7.3	51.8	235.1	351.5	1,375.1	5,031.8	817.4
Suburbs[1]	3,637.9	4.0	38.7	39.5	230.1	835.7	2,323.7	166.3
MSA[2]	5,905.2	5.8	45.7	144.3	295.1	1,124.7	3,774.5	515.1
U.S.	4,922.7	6.8	35.9	186.1	382.0	919.6	2,886.5	505.8

Note: Crime rate is the number of crimes per 100,000 pop.; (1) defined as all areas within the MSA but located outside the central city; (2) Metropolitan Statistical Area - see Appendix A for areas incl.
Source: FBI Uniform Crime Reports, 1997

RECREATION

Culture and Recreation

Museums	Symphony Orchestras	Opera Companies	Dance Companies	Professional Theatres	Zoos	Pro Sports Teams
13	1	1	4	3	0	0

Source: International Directory of the Performing Arts, 1997; Official Museum Directory, 1999; Stern's Performing Arts Directory, 1997; USA Today Four Sport Stadium Guide, 1997; Chamber of Commerce/Economic Development, 1999

Library System

The Austin Public Library has 20 branches, holdings of 1,538,929 volumes, and a budget of $11,857,168 (1996-1997). *American Library Directory, 1998-1999*

MEDIA

Newspapers

Name	Type	Freq.	Distribution	Circulation
Austin American-Statesman	General	7x/wk	Area	175,000
The Daily Texan	n/a	5x/wk	Camp/Comm	30,000
El Mundo	General	1x/wk	Area	20,000
Lake and Country Living	General	1x/wk	Local	15,000

Note: Includes newspapers with circulations of 10,000 or more located in the city; n/a not available
Source: Burrelle's Media Directory, 1999 Edition

Television Stations

Name	Ch.	Affiliation	Type	Owner
KTBC	n/a	FBC	Commercial	Fox Television Stations Inc.
KXAM	14	NBCT	Commercial	Lin Broadcasting
KLRU	18	PBS	Public	Capital of Texas Public Telecommunications
KVUE	24	ABCT	Commercial	A.H. Belo Corporation
KXAN	36	NBCT	Commercial	Lin Broadcasting
KEYE	42	CBST	Commercial	Granite Broadcasting Corporation
KNVA	54	n/a	Commercial	54 Broadcasting Inc.

Note: Stations included broadcast in the Austin metro area; n/a not available
Source: Burrelle's Media Directory, 1999 Edition

FM Radio Stations

Call Letters	Freq. (mHz)	Target Audience	Station Format	Music Format
KNLE	88.1	n/a	M/N/S	Adult Contemporary/Alternative/Christian
KAZI	88.7	B/R	E/M/N/S/T	Christian/Jazz/Latin/Oldies/R&B/Urban Contemp.
KMFA	89.5	n/a	E/M	Classical
KUTX	90.1	General	E/M/N/T	Classical/Jazz
KUT	90.5	General	E/M/N	Blues/Classical/Jazz/R&B/World Music
KOOP	91.7	G/H	E/M/N/T	n/a
KVRX	91.7	General	E/M/N/S/T	Alternative/Classical/Country/Jazz/Latin
KKLB	92.5	Hispanic	M	Latin
KLNC	93.3	General	M	Adult Contemporary/Country
KLBJ	93.7	General	M/N/S	AOR
KAMX	94.7	General	M	Adult Contemporary/Alternative
KKMJ	95.5	General	M	Adult Contemporary
KHFI	96.7	General	M	n/a
KVET	98.1	General	M/N/S	Country
KJFK	98.9	Men	T	n/a
KASE	100.7	General	M	Country
KROX	101.5	Young Adult	M/T	Alternative
KPEZ	102.3	General	M/S	Classic Rock
KEYI	103.5	General	M	Oldies
KQBT	104.3	General	M/N/S/T	Adult Top 40
KFMK	105.9	General	M	Oldies
KGSR	107.1	General	M	Alternative

Note: Stations included broadcast in the Austin metro area; n/a not available
Station Format: E=Educational; M=Music; N=News; S=Sports; T=Talk
Target Audience: A=Asian; B=Black; C=Christian; E=Ethnic; F=French; G=General; H=Hispanic; M=Men; N=Native American; R=Religious; S=Senior Citizen; W=Women; Y=Young Adult; Z=Children
Music Format: AOR=Album Oriented Rock; MOR=Middle-of-the-Road
Source: Burrelle's Media Directory, 1999 Edition

AM Radio Stations

Call Letters	Freq. (kHz)	Target Audience	Station Format	Music Format
KLBJ	590	General	N/S/T	n/a
KIXL	970	Religious	E/M/N/T	Christian
KFIT	1060	B/H	M/N/T	Christian/Latin
KVET	1300	General	S	n/a
KJCE	1370	General	M	R&B
KELG	1440	Hispanic	M	n/a
KFON	1490	General	S	n/a
KTXZ	1560	Hispanic	M	n/a

Note: Stations included broadcast in the Austin metro area; n/a not available
Target Audience: A=Asian; B=Black; C=Christian; E=Ethnic; F=French; G=General; H=Hispanic; M=Men; N=Native American; R=Religious; S=Senior Citizen; W=Women; Y=Young Adult; Z=Children
Station Format: E=Educational; M=Music; N=News; S=Sports; T=Talk
Source: Burrelle's Media Directory, 1999 Edition

CLIMATE

Average and Extreme Temperatures

Temperature	Jan	Feb	Mar	Apr	May	Jun	Jul	Aug	Sep	Oct	Nov	Dec	Yr.
Extreme High (°F)	90	97	98	98	100	105	109	106	104	98	91	90	109
Average High (°F)	60	64	72	79	85	91	95	96	90	81	70	63	79
Average Temp. (°F)	50	53	61	69	75	82	85	85	80	70	60	52	69
Average Low (°F)	39	43	50	58	65	72	74	74	69	59	49	41	58
Extreme Low (°F)	-2	7	18	35	43	53	64	61	47	32	20	4	-2

Note: Figures cover the years 1948-1990
Source: National Climatic Data Center, International Station Meteorological Climate Summary, 3/95

Average Precipitation/Snowfall/Humidity

Precip./Humidity	Jan	Feb	Mar	Apr	May	Jun	Jul	Aug	Sep	Oct	Nov	Dec	Yr.
Avg. Precip. (in.)	1.6	2.3	1.8	2.9	4.3	3.5	1.9	1.9	3.3	3.5	2.1	1.9	31.1
Avg. Snowfall (in.)	1	Tr	Tr	0	0	0	0	0	0	0	Tr	Tr	1
Avg. Rel. Hum. 6am (%)	79	80	79	83	88	89	88	87	86	84	81	79	84
Avg. Rel. Hum. 3pm (%)	53	51	47	50	53	49	43	42	47	47	49	51	48

Note: Figures cover the years 1948-1990; Tr = Trace amounts (<0.05 in. of rain; <0.5 in. of snow)
Source: National Climatic Data Center, International Station Meteorological Climate Summary, 3/95

Weather Conditions

Temperature			Daytime Sky			Precipitation		
10°F & below	32°F & below	90°F & above	Clear	Partly cloudy	Cloudy	0.01 inch or more precip.	0.1 inch or more snow/ice	Thunder-storms
< 1	20	111	105	148	112	83	1	41

Note: Figures are average number of days per year and covers the years 1948-1990
Source: National Climatic Data Center, International Station Meteorological Climate Summary, 3/95

AIR & WATER QUALITY

Maximum Pollutant Concentrations

	Particulate Matter (ug/m³)	Carbon Monoxide (ppm)	Sulfur Dioxide (ppm)	Nitrogen Dioxide (ppm)	Ozone (ppm)	Lead (ug/m³)
MSA[1] Level	n/a	1	n/a	n/a	0.11	n/a
NAAQS[2]	150	9	0.140	0.053	0.12	1.50
Met NAAQS?	n/a	Yes	n/a	n/a	Yes	n/a

Note: (1) Metropolitan Statistical Area - see Appendix A for areas included; (2) National Ambient Air Quality Standards; ppm = parts per million; ug/m³ = micrograms per cubic meter; n/a not available
Source: EPA, National Air Quality and Emissions Trends Report, 1997

Pollutant Standards Index

In the Austin MSA (see Appendix A for areas included), the Pollutant Standards Index (PSI) exceeded 100 on 6 days in 1997. A PSI value greater than 100 indicates that air quality would be in the unhealthful range on that day. *EPA, National Air Quality and Emissions Trends Report, 1997*

Drinking Water

Water System Name	Pop. Served	Primary Water Source Type	Number of Violations in 1998	Type of Violation/ Contaminants
Austin Water & Wastewater	609,571	Surface	None	None

Note: Data as of July 10, 1999
Source: EPA, Office of Ground Water and Drinking Water, Safe Drinking Water Information System

Austin tap water is alkaline, soft and fluoridated.
Editor & Publisher Market Guide, 1999

Birmingham, Alabama

Background

Lying in the South's Appalachian Ridge and Valley, Birmingham's founding reaches back to 1813 and was it later named after the industrial city of England. During the Civil War, a small iron factory was developed. Realizing the potential of an area rich in iron ore and coal, businessmen in later years founded the city in 1871. The city expanded but tragedy struck when a cholera epidemic and the economic depression of 1873 simultaneously hit Birmingham. The city nearly collapsed.

A change in fortunes occurred in 1880 when the state's first blast furnace began spewing out iron. The decade of the 1880s saw great demands for iron, which helped expand the city's manufacturing base. Population rose so miraculously, from a few thousand in 1880 to over 100,000 in 1910, that Birmingham earned the sobriquet, the Magic City. In the early 1960s the city was the scene of dramatic developments in the civil rights movement, as the police commissioner sicked attack dogs on protesters. However, race relations have improved remarkably since those dark days, as the city's electorate in 1979 chose Richard Arrington, Jr., as its first African American mayor, and the black middle class has expanded in recent years.

The city's economic foundation was built of course, on iron, due to its location in the mineral rich Jones Valley. Birmingham became the most important steel and iron manufacturing site in the South in the late nineteenth century and through much of the twentieth. Atop Red Mountain to the south, as a dedication to the importance of the industry, stands a cast-iron statue, the largest in the world, of the Roman deity Vulcan, patron of ironsmiths.

Now eighty-five percent of employees work in businesses other than manufacturing. The second largest employer in Birmingham is the telecommunications industry; South Central Bell and Bell South have located their headquarters there. The remaining employees are in 850 factories, producing such items as chemicals, transportation equipment, and pipe, all this in addition to the still important manufacture of steel and iron.

In recent decades the construction industry has grown in Birmingham. Workers expanded the Birmingham Municipal Airport in 1973. In 1976 builders finished the Birmingham-Jefferson Civic Center, which advanced the arts and sport.

There are many opportunities for higher education, principal of which is the local campus of the University of Alabama, the city's largest employer. The university opened the Medical Center in 1945. It experienced a great expansion in the late 1970s and early 1980s. The city offers advantages to businesses wanting to start operations there, with building costs nearly twenty percent below the national average. Birmingham enjoys the lowest per capita property tax in the country. Alabama also offers newcomers a tax credit for long-term capital investment.

The metropolitan area possesses a mild climate. It endures less rain than some other parts of the state, seeing on average fifty-four inches of rain a year. Summers tend to hot and humid, as to be expected in the Deep South, with temperatures averaging in the low eighty-degree range. Because of its location on the edge of the Appalachian Range, however, Birmingham's winters are cooler than one would expect in a subtropical region, with temperatures ranging from the low thirties to the middle sixties.

General Rankings and Evaluative Comments

- Birmingham was ranked #24 out of 44 mid-sized, southern metropolitan areas in *Money's* 1998 survey of "The Best Places to Live in America." The survey was conducted by first contacting 512 representative households nationwide and asking them to rank 37 quality-of-life factors on a scale of 1 to 10. Next, a demographic profile was compiled on the 300 largest metropolitan statistical areas in the U.S. The numbers were crunched together to arrive at an overall ranking (things Americans consider most important, like clean air and water, low crime and good schools, received extra weight). Unlike previous years, the 1998 rankings were broken down by region (northeast, midwest, south, west) and population size (100,000 to 249,999; 250,000 to 999,999; 1 million plus). The city had a nationwide ranking of #274 out of 300 in 1997 and #237 out of 300 in 1996. *Money, July 1998; Money, July 1997; Money, September 1996*

- *Ladies Home Journal* ranked America's 200 largest cities based on the qualities women care about most. Birmingham ranked #108 out of 200. Criteria: low crime rate, well-paying jobs, quality health and child care, good public schools, the presence of women in government, size of the gender wage gap, number of sexual-harassment and discrimination complaints filed, unemployment and divorce rates, commute times, population density, number of houses of worship, parks and cultural offerings, number of women's health specialists, how well a community's women cared for themselves, complexion kindness index based on UV radiation levels, odds of finding affordable fashions, rental rates for romance movies, champagne sales and other matters of the heart. *Ladies Home Journal, November 1998*

- Zero Population Growth ranked 229 cities in terms of children's health, safety, and economic well-being. Birmingham was ranked #105 out of 112 independent cities (cities with populations greater than 100,000 which were neither Major Cities nor Suburbs/Outer Cities) and was given a grade of F. Criteria: total population, percent of population under 18 years of age, household language, percent population change, percent of births to teens, infant mortality rate, percent of low birth weights, dropout rate, enrollment in preprimary school, violent and property crime rates, unemployment rate, percent of children in poverty, percent of owner occupied units, number of bad air days, percent of public transportation commuters, and average travel time to work. *Zero Population Growth, Children's Environmental Index, Fall 1999*

- Cognetics studied 273 metro areas in the United States, ranking them by entrepreneurial activity. Birmingham was ranked #15 out of the 50 largest metro areas. Criteria: Significant Starts (firms started in the last 10 years that still employ at least 5 people) and Young Growers (percent of firms 10 years old or less that grew significantly during the last 4 years). *Cognetics, "Entrepreneurial Hot Spots: The Best Places in America to Start and Grow a Company," 1998*

- Birmingham was selected as one of the "Best American Cities to Start a Business" by *Point of View* magazine. Criteria: coolness, quality-of-life, and business concerns. The city was ranked #53 out of 75. *Point of View, November 1998*

- Reliastar Financial Corp. ranked the 125 largest metropolitan areas according to the general financial security of residents. Birmingham was ranked #42 (tie) out of 125 with a score of 5.0. The score indicates the percentage a metropolitan area is above or below the metropolitan norm. A metro area with a score of 10.6 is 10.6% above the metro average. Criteria: Earnings and Wealth Potential (household income, education, net assets, cost of living); Safety Net (health insurance, retirement savings, life insurance, income support programs); Personal Threats (unemployment rate, low-income households, crime rate); Community Economic Vitality (cost of community services, job quality, job creation, housing costs). *Reliastar Financial Corp., "The Best Cities to Earn and Save Money," 1999 Edition*

Business Environment

STATE ECONOMY

State Economic Profile

"After several years of strong growth during the early 1990s, Alabama has begun to lag the nation slightly in terms of economic and employment growth. However, long-term employment prospects look positive as Birmingham is well positioned to serve as a low-cost alternative to Atlanta. The immediate near term will see some softening in real estate markets as existing home sales weaken and much of the current construction comes onto the market.

Employment in Alabama's traditional heavy industry has witnessed considerable losses in recent years. The apparel and textile industries lost some 5,000 jobs in the last year alone. Alabama's tire and rubber industries have also seen considerable losses, especially with the closure of Gadsden's Goodyear plant. While some analysts predict a rebounding of Alabama manufacturing employment after the current retrenchment, such predictions are speculative at best.

The construction sector has added considerable strength to both Alabama's economic and employment growth in recent years. Single family permits were up over 20% in the last year. Multifamily and commercial activity have shown similar strength, albeit at a slightly lower rate. The office markets of Birmingham and Huntsville have been characterized by low vacancy and strong rents over the last year.

These office markets should weaken slightly from current conditions as new space becomes available.

The Alabama economic outlook is one of both pluses and minuses. The cost of doing business is still relatively attractive in Alabama, even compared to its southern neighbors. However, population growth among the 'typical buyers' of housing will be negative over the next several years." *National Association of Realtors, Economic Profiles: The Fifty States and the District of Columbia, http://nar.realtor.com/databank/profiles.htm*

IMPORTS/EXPORTS

Total Export Sales

Area	1994 ($000)	1995 ($000)	1996 ($000)	1997 ($000)	% Chg. 1994-97	% Chg. 1996-97
MSA[1]	453,848	550,543	625,776	941,394	107.4	50.4
U.S.	512,415,609	583,030,524	622,827,063	687,597,999	34.2	10.4

Note: (1) Metropolitan Statistical Area - see Appendix A for areas included
Source: U.S. Department of Commerce, International Trade Association, Metropolitan Area Exports: An Export Performance Report on Over 250 U.S. Cities, November 10, 1998

CITY FINANCES

City Government Finances

Component	FY92 ($000)	FY92 (per capita $)
Revenue	325,889	1,234.87
Expenditure	329,042	1,246.82
Debt Outstanding	807,341	3,059.21
Cash & Securities	1,083,490	4,105.61

Source: U.S. Bureau of the Census, City Government Finances: 1991-92

City Government Revenue by Source

Source	FY92 ($000)	FY92 (per capita $)	FY92 (%)
From Federal Government	13,446	50.95	4.1
From State Governments	8,091	30.66	2.5
From Local Governments	7,995	30.29	2.5
Property Taxes	27,650	104.77	8.5
General Sales Taxes	56,272	213.23	17.3
Selective Sales Taxes	68	0.26	0.0
Income Taxes	38,491	145.85	11.8
Current Charges	28,709	108.79	8.8
Utility/Liquor Store	0	0.00	0.0
Employee Retirement[1]	48,717	184.60	14.9
Other	96,450	365.47	29.6

Note: (1) Excludes "city contributions," classified as "nonrevenue," intragovernmental transfers.
Source: U.S. Bureau of the Census, City Government Finances: 1991-92

City Government Expenditures by Function

Function	FY92 ($000)	FY92 (per capita $)	FY92 (%)
Educational Services	13,452	50.97	4.1
Employee Retirement[1]	19,901	75.41	6.0
Environment/Housing	64,698	245.16	19.7
Government Administration	23,876	90.47	7.3
Interest on General Debt	55,855	211.65	17.0
Public Safety	72,178	273.50	21.9
Social Services	3,445	13.05	1.0
Transportation	67,717	256.60	20.6
Utility/Liquor Store	0	0.00	0.0
Other	7,920	30.01	2.4

Note: (1) Payments to beneficiaries including withdrawal of contributions.
Source: U.S. Bureau of the Census, City Government Finances: 1991-92

Municipal Bond Ratings

Area	Moody's	S & P
Birmingham	Aaa	n/a

Note: n/a not available; n/r not rated
Source: Moody's Bond Record, 6/99

POPULATION

Population Growth

Area	1980	1990	% Chg. 1980-90	July 1998 Estimate	% Chg. 1990-98
City	284,413	265,852	-6.5	252,997	-4.8
MSA[1]	883,946	907,810	2.7	912,956	0.6
U.S.	226,545,805	248,765,170	9.8	270,299,000	8.7

Note: (1) Metropolitan Statistical Area - see Appendix A for areas included;
July 1998 MSA population estimate was calculated by the editors
Source: 1980/1990 Census of Housing and Population, Summary Tape File 3C;
Census Bureau Population Estimates 1998

Population Characteristics

Race	City 1980 Population	%	1990 Population	%	% Chg. 1980-90	MSA[1] 1990 Population	%
White	124,767	43.9	94,988	35.7	-23.9	655,153	72.2
Black	158,200	55.6	168,464	63.4	6.5	245,260	27.0
Amer Indian/Esk/Aleut	220	0.1	431	0.2	95.9	2,050	0.2
Asian/Pacific Islander	933	0.3	1,734	0.7	85.9	4,440	0.5
Other	293	0.1	235	0.1	-19.8	907	0.1
Hispanic Origin[2]	2,054	0.7	1,175	0.4	-42.8	3,699	0.4

Note: (1) Metropolitan Statistical Area - see Appendix A for areas included;
(2) people of Hispanic origin can be of any race
Source: 1980/1990 Census of Housing and Population, Summary Tape File 3C

Ancestry

Area	German	Irish	English	Italian	U.S.	French	Polish	Dutch
City	5.5	7.7	7.3	1.3	7.0	1.4	0.4	0.9
MSA[1]	10.7	15.0	13.1	2.1	15.0	2.3	0.6	2.1
U.S.	23.3	15.6	13.1	5.9	5.3	4.2	3.8	2.5

Note: Figures are percentages and include persons that reported multiple ancestry (eg. if a person reported being Irish and Italian, they were included in both columns); (1) Metropolitan Statistical Area - see Appendix A for areas included
Source: 1990 Census of Population and Housing, Summary Tape File 3C

Age

Area	Median Age (Years)	Under 5	Under 18	18-24	25-44	45-64	65+	80+
City	32.9	7.4	25.4	10.5	32.2	17.0	14.8	3.7
MSA[1]	33.8	7.0	25.4	9.8	32.4	19.2	13.2	3.0
U.S.	32.9	7.3	25.6	10.5	32.6	18.7	12.5	2.8

Note: (1) Metropolitan Statistical Area - see Appendix A for areas included
Source: 1990 Census of Population and Housing, Summary Tape File 3C

Male/Female Ratio

Area	Number of males per 100 females (all ages)	Number of males per 100 females (18 years old+)
City	83.2	78.8
MSA[1]	89.7	85.6
U.S.	95.0	91.9

Note: (1) Metropolitan Statistical Area - see Appendix A for areas included
Source: 1990 Census of Population, General Population Characteristics

INCOME

Per Capita/Median/Average Income

Area	Per Capita ($)	Median Household ($)	Average Household ($)
City	10,127	19,193	25,313
MSA[1]	13,082	26,151	34,240
U.S.	14,420	30,056	38,453

Note: All figures are for 1989; (1) Metropolitan Statistical Area - see Appendix A for areas included
Source: 1990 Census of Population and Housing, Summary Tape File 3C

Household Income Distribution by Race

Income ($)	City (%)					U.S. (%)				
	Total	White	Black	Other	Hisp.[1]	Total	White	Black	Other	Hisp.[1]
Less than 5,000	13.6	7.2	18.2	20.2	10.9	6.2	4.8	15.2	8.6	8.8
5,000 - 9,999	14.6	11.3	17.2	4.1	9.8	9.3	8.6	14.2	9.9	11.1
10,000 - 14,999	12.1	10.1	13.6	13.9	19.3	8.8	8.5	11.0	9.8	11.0
15,000 - 24,999	20.7	21.4	20.1	22.4	16.8	17.5	17.3	18.9	18.5	20.5
25,000 - 34,999	15.3	17.5	13.7	16.3	16.2	15.8	16.1	14.2	15.4	16.4
35,000 - 49,999	12.5	15.1	10.6	15.4	10.3	17.9	18.6	13.3	16.1	16.0
50,000 - 74,999	7.9	11.4	5.3	4.7	9.4	15.0	15.8	9.3	13.4	11.1
75,000 - 99,999	1.8	3.1	0.9	1.6	2.6	5.1	5.5	2.6	4.7	3.1
100,000+	1.4	3.0	0.3	1.5	4.6	4.4	4.8	1.3	3.7	1.9

Note: All figures are for 1989; (1) people of Hispanic origin can be of any race
Source: 1990 Census of Population and Housing, Summary Tape File 3C

Effective Buying Income

Area	Per Capita ($)	Median Household ($)	Average Household ($)
City	13,125	24,971	32,690
MSA[1]	17,533	33,719	45,282
U.S.	16,803	34,536	45,243

Note: Data as of 1/1/99; (1) Metropolitan Statistical Area - see Appendix A for areas included
Source: Standard Rate & Data Service, Newspaper Advertising Source, 9/99

Effective Household Buying Income Distribution

Area	% of Households Earning						
	$10,000 -$19,999	$20,000 -$34,999	$35,000 -$49,999	$50,000 -$74,999	$75,000 -$99,000	$100,000 -$124,999	$125,000 and up
City	20.5	24.1	15.3	12.9	4.2	1.2	1.2
MSA[1]	16.0	21.9	17.3	18.3	7.4	2.4	2.8
U.S.	16.0	22.6	18.2	18.9	7.2	2.4	2.7

Note: Data as of 1/1/99; (1) Metropolitan Statistical Area - see Appendix A for areas included
Source: Standard Rate & Data Service, Newspaper Advertising Source, 9/99

Poverty Rates by Race and Age

Area	Total (%)	By Race (%)				By Age (%)		
		White	Black	Other	Hisp.[2]	Under 5 years old	Under 18 years old	65 years and over
City	24.8	11.4	32.2	22.8	21.0	38.3	35.9	22.2
MSA[1]	15.3	9.2	31.4	18.4	16.2	21.7	20.4	18.3
U.S.	13.1	9.8	29.5	23.1	25.3	20.1	18.3	12.8

Note: Figures show the percent of people living below the poverty line in 1989. The average poverty threshold was $12,674 for a family of four in 1989; (1) Metropolitan Statistical Area - see Appendix A for areas included; (2) people of Hispanic origin can be of any race
Source: 1990 Census of Population and Housing, Summary Tape File 3C

EMPLOYMENT

Labor Force and Employment

Area	Civilian Labor Force			Workers Employed		
	Jun. 1998	Jun. 1999	% Chg.	Jun. 1998	Jun. 1999	% Chg.
City	133,369	134,573	0.9	126,198	127,314	0.9
MSA[1]	478,093	482,423	0.9	461,747	465,830	0.9
U.S.	138,798,000	140,666,000	1.3	132,265,000	134,395,000	1.6

Note: Data is not seasonally adjusted and covers workers 16 years of age and older; (1) Metropolitan Statistical Area - see Appendix A for areas included
Source: Bureau of Labor Statistics, http://stats.bls.gov

Unemployment Rate

Area	1998						1999					
	Jul.	Aug.	Sep.	Oct.	Nov.	Dec.	Jan.	Feb.	Mar.	Apr.	May.	Jun.
City	4.8	4.9	4.6	4.8	4.2	3.5	3.7	4.1	3.9	4.4	4.4	5.4
MSA[1]	3.0	3.1	2.9	3.1	2.6	2.2	2.4	2.7	2.5	2.9	2.8	3.4
U.S.	4.7	4.5	4.4	4.2	4.1	4.0	4.8	4.7	4.4	4.1	4.0	4.5

Note: Data is not seasonally adjusted and covers workers 16 years of age and older; all figures are percentages; (1) Metropolitan Statistical Area - see Appendix A for areas included
Source: Bureau of Labor Statistics, http://stats.bls.gov

Employment by Industry

Sector	MSA[1]		U.S.
	Number of Employees	Percent of Total	Percent of Total
Services	143,500	29.7	30.4
Retail Trade	83,900	17.4	17.7
Government	67,300	13.9	15.6
Manufacturing	52,700	10.9	14.3
Finance/Insurance/Real Estate	36,900	7.6	5.9
Wholesale Trade	33,900	7.0	5.4
Transportation/Public Utilities	31,700	6.6	5.3
Construction	30,400	6.3	5.0
Mining	2,700	0.6	0.4

Note: Figures cover non-farm employment as of 6/99 and are not seasonally adjusted;
(1) Metropolitan Statistical Area - see Appendix A for areas included
Source: Bureau of Labor Statistics, http://stats.bls.gov

Employment by Occupation

Occupation Category	City (%)	MSA[1] (%)	U.S. (%)
White Collar	56.4	60.3	58.1
Executive/Admin./Management	9.2	12.0	12.3
Professional	13.6	13.6	14.1
Technical & Related Support	4.7	3.9	3.7
Sales	11.4	13.6	11.8
Administrative Support/Clerical	17.5	17.2	16.3
Blue Collar	24.3	26.7	26.2
Precision Production/Craft/Repair	8.6	11.7	11.3
Machine Operators/Assem./Insp.	6.3	6.1	6.8
Transportation/Material Movers	4.4	4.6	4.1
Cleaners/Helpers/Laborers	5.0	4.2	3.9
Services	18.1	11.7	13.2
Farming/Forestry/Fishing	1.2	1.4	2.5

Note: Figures cover employed persons 16 years old and over;
(1) Metropolitan Statistical Area - see Appendix A for areas included
Source: 1990 Census of Population and Housing, Summary Tape File 3C

Occupational Employment Projections: 1996 - 2006

Occupations Expected to Have the Largest Job Growth (ranked by numerical growth)	Fast-Growing Occupations[1] (ranked by percent growth)
1. Cashiers	1. Computer engineers
2. Teachers, secondary school	2. Personal and home care aides
3. Truck drivers, light	3. Database administrators
4. General managers & top executives	4. Occupational therapists
5. Nursing aides/orderlies/attendants	5. Systems analysts
6. Janitors/cleaners/maids, ex. priv. hshld.	6. Home health aides
7. Registered nurses	7. Physical therapy assistants and aides
8. Home health aides	8. Medical assistants
9. Marketing & sales, supervisors	9. Teachers, special education
10. Systems analysts	10. Physical therapists

Note: Projections cover Alabama; (1) Excludes occupations with total job growth less than 300
Source: U.S. Department of Labor, Employment and Training Administration, America's Labor Market Information System (ALMIS)

TAXES

Major State and Local Tax Rates

| State Corp. Income (%) | State Personal Income (%) | Residential Property (effective rate per $100) | Sales & Use | | State Gasoline (cents/ gallon) | State Cigarette (cents/ pack) |
			State (%)	Local (%)		
5.0	2.0 - 5.0	0.79	4.0	4.0	18.0[a]	16.5[b]

Note: Personal/corporate income, sales, gasoline and cigarette tax rates as of January 1999.
Property tax rates as of 1997; (a) Rate is comprised of 16 cents excise plus 2 cents motor carrier tax.
Rate does not include 1 - 3 cents local option tax; (b) Counties and cities may impose an additional tax of 1 - 6 cents per pack
Source: Federation of Tax Administrators, www.taxadmin.org; Washington D.C. Department of Finance and Revenue, Tax Rates and Tax Burdens in the District of Columbia: A Nationwide Comparison, July 1998; Chamber of Commerce, 1999

Total Taxes Per Capita and as a Percent of Income

| Area | Per Capita Income ($) | Per Capita Taxes ($) | | | Percent of Income (%) | | |
		Total	Federal	State/ Local	Total	Federal	State/ Local
Alabama	22,670	7,468	5,322	2,146	32.9	23.5	9.5
U.S.	27,876	9,881	6,690	3,191	35.4	24.0	11.4

Note: Figures are for 1998
Source: Tax Foundation, www.taxfoundation.org

Estimated Tax Burden

Area	State Income	Local Income	Property	Sales	Total
Birmingham	2,311	750	1,750	1,196	6,007

Note: The numbers are estimates of taxes paid by a married couple with two children and annual earnings of $75,000. Sales tax estimates assume they spend average amounts on food, clothing, household goods and gasoline. Property tax estimates assume they live in a $250,000 home.
Source: Kiplinger's Personal Finance Magazine, October 1998

COMMERCIAL
REAL ESTATE

Office Market

Class/ Location	Total Space (sq. ft.)	Vacant Space (sq. ft.)	Vac. Rate (%)	Under Constr. (sq. ft.)	Net Absorp. (sq. ft.)	Rental Rates ($/sq.ft./yr.)
Class A						
CBD	2,867,862	115,300	4.0	120,000	149,700	16.00-20.50
Outside CBD	9,248,125	206,900	2.2	329,000	306,600	16.00-21.00
Class B						
CBD	2,043,500	402,838	19.7	n/a	119,162	10.00-14.50
Outside CBD	2,698,633	283,242	10.5	n/a	-79,871	11.00-15.00

Note: Data as of 10/98 and covers Birmingham; CBD = Central Business District; n/a not available;
Source: Society of Industrial and Office Realtors, 1999 Comparative Statistics of Industrial and Office
Real Estate Markets

"There are six new office projects, totaling 700,000 sq. ft. currently under construction for delivery in 1999. Much of the new speculative development will have a positive effect on the local economy, allowing local businesses to expand and hopefully attract new businesses from outside the area. Local economic development officials have targeted service sector firms to stay competitive with regional markets such as Charlotte, North Carolina and Nashville, Tennessee. The health care industry is an important element in the local economy. Medical offices and insurance companies account for a large part of demand. The outlook for the Birmingham metropolitan area is favorable with rental rates rising by roughly 10 percent this year, as anticipated by SIOR's reporters." *Society of Industrial and Office Realtors, 1999 Comparative Statistics of Industrial and Office Real Estate Markets*

Industrial Market

Location	Total Space (sq. ft.)	Vacant Space (sq. ft.)	Vac. Rate (%)	Under Constr. (sq. ft.)	Net Absorp. (sq. ft.)	Lease ($/sq.ft./yr.)
Central City	18,177,418	1,562,740	8.6	0	348,963	2.00-4.00
Suburban	67,341,854	1,835,421	2.7	209,000	482,673	3.20-6.25

Note: Data as of 10/98 and covers Birmingham (Central, Irondale, Oxmoor, Perimeter Highway, Pinson); n/a not available
Source: Society of Industrial and Office Realtors, 1999 Comparative Statistics of Industrial and Office
Real Estate Markets

"The planning pipeline remains relatively empty, with two speculative projects in the Oxmoor submarket underway totaling 225,000 sq. ft. Birmingham has created a special niche as a center for medical care and research, based at the University of Alabama at Birmingham. UAB has a medical school, and it is the largest employer in Alabama. In fact, the university is the financial engine that drives the community, with an estimated annual economic impact of $1.6 billion. As a result, the manufacturing sector in Birmingham contributes a great deal to producing pharmaceutical and other specialty end-use products. Continued diversification into health research and services will help bolster growth in 1999." *Society of Industrial and Office Realtors, 1999 Comparative Statistics of Industrial and Office Real Estate Markets*

COMMERCIAL UTILITIES

Typical Monthly Electric Bills

Area	Commercial Service ($/month)		Industrial Service ($/month)	
	12 kW demand 1,500 kWh	100 kW demand 30,000 kWh	1,000 kW demand 400,000 kWh	20,000 kW demand 10,000,000 kWh
City	146	2,170	18,302	302,607
U.S.	150	2,174	23,995	508,569

Note: Based on rates in effect January 1, 1999
Source: Edison Electric Institute, Typical Residential, Commercial and Industrial Bills, Winter 1999

TRANSPORTATION

Transportation Statistics

Average minutes to work	20.4
Interstate highways	I-65; I-59; I-20
Bus lines	
In-city	Birminghan-Jefferson Co. TA, 143 Vehicles
Inter-city	1
Passenger air service	
Airport	Birmingham International
Airlines	11
Aircraft departures	23,060 (1996)
Enplaned passengers	1,312,897 (1996)
Rail service	Amtrak
Motor freight carriers	20
Major waterways/ports	None

Source: Editor & Publisher Market Guide, 1999; FAA Airport Activity Statistics, 1997; Amtrak National Time Table, Northeast Timetable, Spring/Summer 1999; 1990 Census of Population and Housing, STF 3C; Chamber of Commerce/Economic Development 1999; Jane's Urban Transport Systems 1999-2000

Means of Transportation to Work

Area	Car/Truck/Van		Public Transportation			Bicycle	Walked	Other Means	Worked at Home
	Drove Alone	Car-pooled	Bus	Subway	Railroad				
City	76.2	16.1	3.5	0.0	0.0	0.2	2.3	0.8	1.0
MSA[1]	81.2	14.0	1.2	0.0	0.0	0.1	1.4	0.6	1.6
U.S.	73.2	13.4	3.0	1.5	0.5	0.4	3.9	1.2	3.0

Note: Figures shown are percentages and only include workers 16 years old and over; (1) Metropolitan Statistical Area - see Appendix A for areas included
Source: 1990 Census of Population and Housing, Summary Tape File 3C

BUSINESSES

Major Business Headquarters

Company Name	1999 Rankings	
	Fortune 500	Forbes 500
American Cast Iron Pipe	-	467
BE&K	-	180
Brasfield & Gorrie	-	492
Drummond	-	307
Ebsco Industries	-	197
HealthSouth	383	-
McWane	-	397
Medpartners	241	-
O'Neal Steel	-	299
Regions Financial	476	-
Saks	267	-
Sonat	409	-
Southtrust Corp.	493	-

Note: Companies listed are located in the city; dashes indicate no ranking
Fortune 500: Companies that produce a 10-K are ranked 1 to 500 based on 1998 revenue
Forbes 500: Private companies are ranked 1 to 500 based on 1997 revenue
Source: Forbes, November 30, 1998; Fortune, April 26, 1999

Best Companies to Work For

BE&K (engineering and construction), Alagasco (natural gas) and Acipco (foundry), headquartered in Birmingham, are among the " 100 Best Companies to Work for in America." Criteria: trust in management, pride in work/company, camaraderie, company responses to the Hewitt People Practices Inventory, and employee responses to their Great Place to Work survey. The companies also had to be at least 10 years old and have a minimum of 500 employees. *Fortune, January 11, 1999*

Healthsouth Corp. (healthcare), headquartered in Birmingham, is among the "100 Best Places to Work in IS." Criteria: compensation, turnover and training. *Computerworld, May 25, 1998*

Small Business Opportunity

According to *Forbes*, Birmingham is home to two of America's 200 best small companies: Hibbett Sporting Goods and Medical Assurance. Criteria: companies included must be publicly traded since November 1997 with a stock price of at least $5 per share and an average daily float of 1,000 shares. The company's latest 12-month sales must be between $5 and $350 million, return on equity (ROE) must be a minimum of 12% for both the past 5 years and the most recent four quarters, and five-year sales and EPS growth must average at least 10%. Companies with declining sales or earnings during the past year were dropped as well as businesses with debt/equity ratios over 1.25. Companies with negative operating cash flow in each of the past two years were also excluded. *Forbes, November 2, 1998*

HOTELS & MOTELS

Hotels/Motels

Area	Hotels/Motels	Rooms	Luxury-Level Hotels/Motels		Average Minimum Rates ($)		
			♦♦♦♦	♦♦♦♦♦	♦♦	♦♦♦	♦♦♦♦
City	34	5,646	1	0	n/a	n/a	n/a
Airport	3	556	0	0	n/a	n/a	n/a
Suburbs	15	1,572	0	0	n/a	n/a	n/a
Total	52	7,774	1	0	n/a	n/a	n/a

Note: n/a not available; classifications range from one diamond (budget properties with basic amenities) to five diamond (luxury properties with the finest service, rooms and facilities).
Source: OAG, Business Travel Planner, Winter 1998-99

CONVENTION CENTERS

Major Convention Centers

Center Name	Meeting Rooms	Exhibit Space (sq. ft.)
Birmingham Jefferson Civic Center	64	220,000
Birmingham Jefferson Civic Center	64	220,000
Boutwell Auditorium & Exhibition Hall	3	30,000

Source: Trade Shows Worldwide, 1998; Meetings & Conventions, 4/15/99; Sucessful Meetings, 3/31/98

Living Environment

COST OF LIVING

Cost of Living Index

Composite Index	Groceries	Housing	Utilities	Trans-portation	Health Care	Misc. Goods/ Services
97.8	98.2	94.5	101.8	97.5	95.1	99.8

Note: U.S. = 100; Figures are for the Metropolitan Statistical Area - see Appendix A for areas included
Source: ACCRA, Cost of Living Index, 1st Quarter 1999

HOUSING

Median Home Prices and Housing Affordability

Area	Median Price[2] 1st Qtr. 1999 ($)	HOI[3] 1st Qtr. 1999	Afford-ability Rank[4]
MSA[1]	105,000	79.6	60
U.S.	134,000	69.6	—

Note: (1) Metropolitan Statistical Area - see Appendix A for areas included; (2) U.S. figures calculated from the sales of 524,324 new and existing homes in 181 markets; (3) Housing Opportunity Index - percent of homes sold that were within the reach of the median income household at the prevailing mortgage interest rate; (4) Rank is from 1-181 with 1 being most affordable
Source: National Association of Home Builders, Housing Opportunity Index, 1st Quarter 1999

Median Home Price Projection

It is projected that the median price of existing single-family homes in the metro area will increase by 3.0% in 1999. Nationwide, home prices are projected to increase 3.8%.
Kiplinger's Personal Finance Magazine, January 1999

Average New Home Price

Area	Price ($)
MSA[1]	134,895
U.S.	142,735

Note: Figures are based on a new home with 1,800 sq. ft. of living area on an 8,000 sq. ft. lot; (1) Metropolitan Statistical Area - see Appendix A for areas included
Source: ACCRA, Cost of Living Index, 1st Quarter 1999

Average Apartment Rent

Area	Rent ($/mth)
MSA[1]	573
U.S.	601

Note: Figures are based on an unfurnished two bedroom, 1-1/2 or 2 bath apartment, approximately 950 sq. ft. in size, excluding all utilities except water; (1) Metropolitan Statistical Area - see Appendix A for areas included
Source: ACCRA, Cost of Living Index, 1st Quarter 1999

RESIDENTIAL UTILITIES

Average Residential Utility Costs

Area	All Electric ($/mth)	Part Electric ($/mth)	Other Energy ($/mth)	Phone ($/mth)
MSA[1]	—	57.94	40.89	22.98
U.S.	100.02	55.73	43.33	19.71

Note: (1) (1) Metropolitan Statistical Area - see Appendix A for areas included
Source: ACCRA, Cost of Living Index, 1st Quarter 1999

HEALTH CARE

Average Health Care Costs

Area	Hospital ($/day)	Doctor ($/visit)	Dentist ($/visit)
MSA[1]	467.00	53.00	55.40
U.S.	430.43	52.45	66.35

Note: Hospital—based on a semi-private room; Doctor—based on a general practitioner's routine exam of an established patient; Dentist—based on adult teeth cleaning and periodic oral exam; (1) Metropolitan Statistical Area - see Appendix A for areas included
Source: ACCRA, Cost of Living Index, 1st Quarter 1999

Distribution of Office-Based Physicians

Area	Family/Gen. Practitioners	Specialists		
		Medical	Surgical	Other
MSA[1]	172	793	601	557

Note: Data as of 12/31/97; (1) Metropolitan Statistical Area - see Appendix A for areas included
Source: American Medical Assn., Physician Characteristics & Distribution in the U.S., 1999

Hospitals

Birmingham has 9 general medical and surgical hospitals, 1 psychiatric, 1 eye, ear, nose and throat, 1 rehabilitation, 1 alcoholism and other chemical dependency, 1 children's general.
AHA Guide to the Healthcare Field, 1998-99

According to *U.S. News and World Report,* Birmingham has 1 of the best hospitals in the U.S.:
University of Alabama Hospital at Birmingham, noted for cardiology, gynecology, neurology, otolaryngology, pulmonology, rheumatology. *U.S. News Online, "America's Best Hospitals," 10th Edition, www.usnews.com*

EDUCATION

Public School District Statistics

District Name	Num. Sch.	Enroll.	Classroom Teachers	Pupils per Teacher	Minority Pupils (%)	Current Exp.[1] ($/pupil)
Birmingham City Sch Dist	93	39,831	2,455	16.2	n/a	n/a
Jefferson County Sch Dist	62	42,228	2,658	15.9	n/a	n/a
Tarrant City Sch Dist	3	1,385	95	14.6	n/a	n/a
Vestavia Hills City Sch Dist	5	4,283	258	16.6	n/a	n/a

Note: Data covers the 1997-1998 school year unless otherwise noted; (1) Data covers fiscal year 1996; SD = School District; ISD = Independent School District; n/a not available
Source: National Center for Education Statistics, Common Core of Data Public Education Agency Universe 1997-98; National Center for Education Statistics, Characteristics of the 100 Largest Public Elementary and Secondary School Districts in the United States: 1997-98, July 1999

Educational Quality

School District	Education Quotient[1]	Graduate Outcome[2]	Community Index[3]	Resource Index[4]
Birmingham City	58.0	58.0	78.0	54.0

Note: Nearly 1,000 secondary school districts were rated in terms of educational quality. The scores range from a low of 50 to a high of 150; (1) Average of the Graduate Outcome, Community and Resource indexes; (2) Based on graduation rates and college board scores (SAT/ACT); (3) Based on the surrounding community's average level of education and the area's average income level; (4) Based on teacher salaries, per-pupil expenditures and student-teacher ratios.
Source: Expansion Management, Ratings Issue, 1998

Educational Attainment by Race

Area	High School Graduate (%)					Bachelor's Degree (%)				
	Total	White	Black	Other	Hisp.[2]	Total	White	Black	Other	Hisp.[2]
City	69.3	76.7	63.9	73.8	79.9	16.2	23.2	10.7	43.1	32.2
MSA[1]	71.7	74.5	63.1	74.1	77.3	18.7	21.0	11.1	36.1	27.2
U.S.	75.2	77.9	63.1	60.4	49.8	20.3	21.5	11.4	19.4	9.2

Note: Figures shown cover persons 25 years old and over; (1) Metropolitan Statistical Area - see Appendix A for areas included; (2) people of Hispanic origin can be of any race
Source: 1990 Census of Population and Housing, Summary Tape File 3C

School Enrollment by Type

Area	Preprimary				Elementary/High School			
	Public		Private		Public		Private	
	Enrollment	%	Enrollment	%	Enrollment	%	Enrollment	%
City	2,439	64.8	1,323	35.2	41,586	90.5	4,349	9.5
MSA[1]	7,796	52.9	6,946	47.1	143,764	91.0	14,224	9.0
U.S.	2,679,029	59.5	1,824,256	40.5	38,379,689	90.2	4,187,099	9.8

Note: Figures shown cover persons 3 years old and over;
(1) Metropolitan Statistical Area - see Appendix A for areas included
Source: 1990 Census of Population and Housing, Summary Tape File 3C

School Enrollment by Race

Area	Preprimary (%)				Elementary/High School (%)			
	White	Black	Other	Hisp.[1]	White	Black	Other	Hisp.[1]
City	27.5	71.2	1.3	0.9	19.0	80.3	0.7	0.3
MSA[2]	70.7	28.0	1.3	0.7	64.7	34.4	0.9	0.4
U.S.	80.4	12.5	7.1	7.8	74.1	15.6	10.3	12.5

Note: Figures shown cover persons 3 years old and over; (1) people of Hispanic origin can be of any race; (2) Metropolitan Statistical Area - see Appendix A for areas included
Source: 1990 Census of Population and Housing, Summary Tape File 3C

Classroom Teacher Salaries in Public Schools

District	B.A. Degree		M.A. Degree		Maximum	
	Min. ($)	Rank[1]	Max. ($)	Rank[1]	Max. ($)	Rank[1]
Birmingham	26,235	51	36,564	92	42,301	91
Average	26,980	-	46,065	-	51,435	-

Note: Salaries are for 1997-1998; (1) Rank ranges from 1 to 100
Source: American Federation of Teachers, Survey & Analysis of Salary Trends, 1998

Higher Education

Two-Year Colleges		Four-Year Colleges		Medical Schools	Law Schools	Voc/Tech
Public	Private	Public	Private			
2	3	1	4	1	0	5

Source: College Blue Book, Occupational Education, 1997; Medical School Admission Requirements, 1999-2000; Peterson's Guide to Two-Year Colleges, 1999; Peterson's Guide to Four-Year Colleges, 2000; Barron's Guide to Law Schools, 1999

MAJOR EMPLOYERS

Major Employers

AmSouth Bank
Blue Cross & Blue Shield of Alabama
Carraway Methodist Health Systems
Alabama Staff (help supply)
St. Vincent's Hospital

American Cast Iron Pipe
Children's Hospital of Alabama
Tacala North (eating places)
Southern Co. Services (engineering services)
Alabama Power

Note: Companies listed are located in the city
Source: Dun's Business Rankings, 1999; Ward's Business Directory, 1998

PUBLIC SAFETY

Crime Rate

Area	All Crimes	Violent Crimes				Property Crimes		
		Murder	Forcible Rape	Robbery	Aggrav. Assault	Burglary	Larceny -Theft	Motor Vehicle Theft
City	9,590.0	39.2	80.7	485.8	769.5	1,884.2	5,110.9	1,219.7
Suburbs[1]	3,883.9	6.1	23.7	132.6	244.3	680.9	2,444.6	351.7
MSA[2]	5,639.6	16.3	41.3	241.2	405.9	1,051.2	3,265.0	618.8
U.S.	4,922.7	6.8	35.9	186.1	382.0	919.6	2,886.5	505.8

Note: Crime rate is the number of crimes per 100,000 pop.; (1) defined as all areas within the MSA but located outside the central city; (2) Metropolitan Statistical Area - see Appendix A for areas incl.
Source: FBI Uniform Crime Reports, 1997

RECREATION

Culture and Recreation

Museums	Symphony Orchestras	Opera Companies	Dance Companies	Professional Theatres	Zoos	Pro Sports Teams
4	1	1	2	1	1	0

Source: International Directory of the Performing Arts, 1997; Official Museum Directory, 1999; Stern's Performing Arts Directory, 1997; USA Today Four Sport Stadium Guide, 1997; Chamber of Commerce/Economic Development, 1999

Library System

The Birmingham Public Library has 19 branches, holdings of 973,936 volumes, and a budget of $11,494,337 (1996-1997). *American Library Directory, 1998-1999*

MEDIA

Newspapers

Name	Type	Freq.	Distribution	Circulation
The Birmingham News	General	7x/wk	Area	150,346
Birmingham Post-Herald	General	6x/wk	Area	33,683
Birmingham Times	Black	1x/wk	Local	26,500
Birmingham World	Black	1x/wk	State	12,600
Community Shopper	General	1x/mo	Local	32,000
One Voice	Religious	1x/wk	Area	17,000
Over the Mountain Journal	General	26x/yr	Local	40,700

Note: Includes newspapers with circulations of 1,000 or more located in the city;
Source: Burrelle's Media Directory, 1999 Edition

Television Stations

Name	Ch.	Affiliation	Type	Owner
WDIQ	n/a	PBS	Public	Alabama ETV Commission
WBRC	n/a	FBC	Commercial	Fox Television Stations Inc.
WCIQ	n/a	PBS	Public	Alabama ETV Commission
WBIQ	10	PBS	Public	Alabama ETV Commission
WVTM	13	NBCT	Commercial	General Electric Corporation
WTTO	21	FBC/WB	Non-comm.	Sinclair Communications Inc.
WHIQ	25	PBS	Public	Alabama ETV Commission
WAIQ	26	PBS	Public	Alabama ETV Commission
WFIQ	36	PBS	Public	Alabama ETV Commission
WIIQ	41	PBS	Public	Alabama ETV Commission
WEIQ	42	PBS	Public	Alabama ETV Commission
WIAT	42	CBST	Commercial	Media General Inc.
WGIQ	43	PBS	Public	Alabama ETV Commission
WPXH	44	CBST	Commercial	Paxson Communications Corporation
WAQF	51	n/a	n/a	Fant Broadcasting Company
WBMA	58	ABCT	Commercial	Allbritton Communications Company
WABM	68	UPN	Commercial	Glen-Kairin Ltd.

Note: Stations included broadcast in the Birmingham metro area; n/a not available
Source: Burrelle's Media Directory, 1999 Edition

AM Radio Stations

Call Letters	Freq. (kHz)	Target Audience	Station Format	Music Format
WAGG	610	General	M/N/T	Gospel
WEZN	610	General	M/N/S	Country
WJOX	690	G/M	S	n/a
WYDE	850	General	M	n/a
WATV	900	General	M	Urban Contemporary
WERC	960	General	N/T	n/a
WAPI	1070	General	N/T	n/a
WAYE	1220	Black	M/N	Christian
WDJC	1260	Religious	M/T	Christian
WJLD	1400	Black	E/M/N/T	Christian/Jazz/R&B
WLPH	1480	General	M/N	Christian/Gospel

Note: Stations included broadcast in the Birmingham metro area; n/a not available
Target Audience: A=Asian; B=Black; C=Christian; E=Ethnic; F=French; G=General; H=Hispanic;
M=Men; N=Native American; R=Religious; S=Senior Citizen; W=Women; Y=Young Adult; Z=Children
Station Format: E=Educational; M=Music; N=News; S=Sports; T=Talk
Source: Burrelle's Media Directory, 1999 Edition

FM Radio Stations

Call Letters	Freq. (mHz)	Target Audience	Station Format	Music Format
WBFR	89.5	n/a	E/M/N/T	Christian
WBHM	90.3	General	M/N	Classical
WVSU	91.1	General	M	n/a
WGIB	91.9	Religious	M/T	Christian
WZJT	92.5	General	M	n/a
WDJC	93.7	General	M	Christian
WYSF	94.5	General	M	Adult Contemporary
WBHJ	95.7	Young Adult	M	Urban Contemporary
WMJJ	96.5	General	M	Adult Contemporary
WBHK	98.7	General	M	Urban Contemporary
WZRR	99.5	General	M	Classic Rock
WOWC	102.5	General	n/a	n/a
WZZK	104.7	General	M/N/S	Country
WENN	105.9	General	M	Urban Contemporary
WODL	106.9	General	M/N/S	Oldies
WRAX	107.7	General	M	Alternative/Modern Rock

Note: Stations included broadcast in the Birmingham metro area; n/a not available
Station Format: E=Educational; M=Music; N=News; S=Sports; T=Talk
Target Audience: A=Asian; B=Black; C=Christian; E=Ethnic; F=French; G=General; H=Hispanic;
M=Men; N=Native American; R=Religious; S=Senior Citizen; W=Women; Y=Young Adult; Z=Children
Source: Burrelle's Media Directory, 1999 Edition

CLIMATE

Average and Extreme Temperatures

Temperature	Jan	Feb	Mar	Apr	May	Jun	Jul	Aug	Sep	Oct	Nov	Dec	Yr.
Extreme High (°F)	81	83	89	92	99	102	106	103	100	94	84	80	106
Average High (°F)	53	58	66	75	82	88	90	90	84	75	64	56	73
Average Temp. (°F)	43	47	54	63	70	77	80	80	74	63	53	46	63
Average Low (°F)	33	36	42	50	58	66	70	69	63	51	41	35	51
Extreme Low (°F)	-6	3	11	26	36	42	51	53	37	27	5	1	-6

Note: Figures cover the years 1948-1990
Source: National Climatic Data Center, International Station Meteorological Climate Summary, 3/95

Average Precipitation/Snowfall/Humidity

Precip./Humidity	Jan	Feb	Mar	Apr	May	Jun	Jul	Aug	Sep	Oct	Nov	Dec	Yr.
Avg. Precip. (in.)	5.1	4.9	6.1	4.7	4.4	3.7	5.2	3.8	4.0	2.8	4.2	4.9	53.6
Avg. Snowfall (in.)	1	Tr	Tr	Tr	0	0	0	0	0	0	Tr	Tr	1
Avg. Rel. Hum. 6am (%)	81	80	80	83	85	85	87	89	87	86	84	81	84
Avg. Rel. Hum. 3pm (%)	57	52	47	45	50	53	57	55	54	49	51	56	52

Note: Figures cover the years 1948-1990; Tr = Trace amounts (<0.05 in. of rain; <0.5 in. of snow)
Source: National Climatic Data Center, International Station Meteorological Climate Summary, 3/95

Weather Conditions

Temperature			Daytime Sky			Precipitation		
0°F & below	32°F & below	65°F & above	Clear	Partly cloudy	Cloudy	0.01 inch or more precip.	0.1 inch or more snow/ice	Thunder-storms
< 1	57	261	92	157	116	116	3	57

Note: Figures are average number of days per year and covers the years 1948-1990
Source: National Climatic Data Center, International Station Meteorological Climate Summary, 3/95

AIR & WATER QUALITY

Maximum Pollutant Concentrations

	Particulate Matter (ug/m^3)	Carbon Monoxide (ppm)	Sulfur Dioxide (ppm)	Nitrogen Dioxide (ppm)	Ozone (ppm)	Lead (ug/m^3)
MSA[1] Level	111	6	0.018	0.010	0.12	n/a
NAAQS[2]	150	9	0.140	0.053	0.12	1.50
Met NAAQS?	Yes	Yes	Yes	Yes	Yes	n/a

Note: (1) Metropolitan Statistical Area - see Appendix A for areas included; (2) National Ambient Air Quality Standards; ppm = parts per million; ug/m^3 = micrograms per cubic meter; n/a not available
Source: EPA, National Air Quality and Emissions Trends Report, 1997

Pollutant Standards Index

In the Birmingham MSA (see Appendix A for areas included), the Pollutant Standards Index (PSI) exceeded 100 on 8 days in 1997. A PSI value greater than 100 indicates that air quality would be in the unhealthful range on that day. *EPA, National Air Quality and Emissions Trends Report, 1997*

Drinking Water

Water System Name	Pop. Served	Primary Water Source Type	Number of Violations in 1998	Type of Violation/ Contaminants
Birmingham Water Board	600,000	Surface	None	None

Note: Data as of July 10, 1999
Source: EPA, Office of Ground Water and Drinking Water, Safe Drinking Water Information System

Birmingham tap water is alkaline, soft.
Editor & Publisher Market Guide, 1999

Chattanooga, Tennessee

Background

Cannons still look down upon Chattanooga from Lookout Mountain, site of a famous Civil War battle. But the guns have long since been silenced, and the city is now a bustling hub of commerce.

The Chickamauga, a tribe of the Cherokee nation, originally lived in the area. A Cherokee chief, John Ross, established a trading post and ferry crossing, Ross' Landing, in the early nineteenth century. In 1838, after the Cherokee were forcibly removed to the West along the Trail of Tears, white settlers changed the name of the settlement to Chattanooga, a Cherokee word describing the sharp summit of Lookout Mountain. By the eve of the Civil War, the city was a critical railroad hub for the Southeast. Chattanooga and its environs were in 1863 the scene of important battles of the war.

After the strife ended in 1865, veterans from the Confederacy and the Union moved to the city. An early reconciliation took place, and many of the problems of Reconstruction were avoided. Commerce and industry flourished in the second half of the nineteenth century and it became known as the Dynamo of Dixie. In 1899, Coca-Cola was first bottled there. Insurance and textiles also became important industries in the community. The Tennessee Valley Authority of the 1930s also helped the city, providing a cheap source of energy, controlling floods, and upgrading navigation on the Tennessee River.

Several hundred factories are in Chattanooga, producing a wide array of useful items such as chemicals, metals, clothing, textiles and clay products. Nearly a quarter of the population is engaged in manufacturing. The city is an integral part of the TVA, with the company's electric utility headquarters located there.

It has maintained its role as a vital transportation hub for nearly a century-and-a-half. The crossroads of three major interstates, the city is only a day by road from a third of the major markets in the nation. Two railroad companies, Norfolk Southern and CSX, have lines that run through the city.

Chattanooga is also an important center for the insurance industry. Its Provident Life and Accident Insurance Company has been listed in the Fortune 500 and Forbes 500. There are many programs on the federal, state, and local level offering incentives and financial help for businesses. On the local level, the Business Development Center offers much assistance to many kinds of new, non-retail companies, and has been nationally recognized for excellence.

Higher education is a significant part of the city's scene, with opportunities afforded by a branch of the University of Tennessee and the Chattanooga State Technical Community College.

Wedged between the Cumberland Mountains to the west and the Appalachians to the east, the metropolitan area's climate is mild, with warm summers and cool winters. Summer temperatures range from the low sixties to the upper eighties, while winters can see the thermometer's mercury dip to the upper twenties and rise to the lower sixties. Chattanooga sees about fifty-three inches of precipitation annually (forty percent of which occurs in the winter months), and about four inches of snow.

General Rankings and Evaluative Comments

■ Chattanooga was ranked #18 out of 44 mid-sized, southern metropolitan areas in *Money's* 1998 survey of "The Best Places to Live in America." The survey was conducted by first contacting 512 representative households nationwide and asking them to rank 37 quality-of-life factors on a scale of 1 to 10. Next, a demographic profile was compiled on the 300 largest metropolitan statistical areas in the U.S. The numbers were crunched together to arrive at an overall ranking (things Americans consider most important, like clean air and water, low crime and good schools, received extra weight). Unlike previous years, the 1998 rankings were broken down by region (northeast, midwest, south, west) and population size (100,000 to 249,999; 250,000 to 999,999; 1 million plus). The city had a nationwide ranking of #213 out of 300 in 1997 and #248 out of 300 in 1996. *Money, July 1998; Money, July 1997; Money, September 1996*

■ *Ladies Home Journal* ranked America's 200 largest cities based on the qualities women care about most. Chattanooga ranked #149 out of 200. Criteria: low crime rate, well-paying jobs, quality health and child care, good public schools, the presence of women in government, size of the gender wage gap, number of sexual-harassment and discrimination complaints filed, unemployment and divorce rates, commute times, population density, number of houses of worship, parks and cultural offerings, number of women's health specialists, how well a community's women cared for themselves, complexion kindness index based on UV radiation levels, odds of finding affordable fashions, rental rates for romance movies, champagne sales and other matters of the heart. *Ladies Home Journal, November 1998*

■ Zero Population Growth ranked 229 cities in terms of children's health, safety, and economic well-being. Chattanooga was ranked #85 out of 112 independent cities (cities with populations greater than 100,000 which were neither Major Cities nor Suburbs/Outer Cities) and was given a grade of D. Criteria: total population, percent of population under 18 years of age, household language, percent population change, percent of births to teens, infant mortality rate, percent of low birth weights, dropout rate, enrollment in preprimary school, violent and property crime rates, unemployment rate, percent of children in poverty, percent of owner occupied units, number of bad air days, percent of public transportation commuters, and average travel time to work. *Zero Population Growth, Children's Environmental Index, Fall 1999*

■ Cognetics studied 273 metro areas in the United States, ranking them by entrepreneurial activity. Chattanooga was ranked #63 out of 134 smaller metro areas. Criteria: Significant Starts (firms started in the last 10 years that still employ at least 5 people) and Young Growers (percent of firms 10 years old or less that grew significantly during the last 4 years). *Cognetics, "Entrepreneurial Hot Spots: The Best Places in America to Start and Grow a Company," 1998*

■ Reliastar Financial Corp. ranked the 125 largest metropolitan areas according to the general financial security of residents. Chattanooga was ranked #98 out of 125 with a score of -5.2. The score indicates the percentage a metropolitan area is above or below the metropolitan norm. A metro area with a score of 10.6 is 10.6% above the metro average. Criteria: Earnings and Wealth Potential (household income, education, net assets, cost of living); Safety Net (health insurance, retirement savings, life insurance, income support programs); Personal Threats (unemployment rate, low-income households, crime rate); Community Economic Vitality (cost of community services, job quality, job creation, housing costs). *Reliastar Financial Corp., "The Best Cities to Earn and Save Money," 1999 Edition*

Business Environment

STATE ECONOMY

State Economic Profile

"Tennessee's economy has been decelerating for almost three years now, a trend that should continue into 1999 and 2000. TN continues to shed jobs in its manufacturing sector, specifically textiles and apparels. In previous years, growth in other sectors was enough to offset these losses. Now growth in these other sectors has slowed. TN's demographics are still strong, and TN continues to have one of the lowest business costs in the country. The TN outlook is one of moderating growth.

TN's manufacturing employment shed some 11,500 jobs in 1998, a decline of 2.2%. Weak export demand and a strong dollar have undermined the apparel industry's competitive position. Soft commodity prices have also hurt TN's metals industry. Neither of these situations will reverse in 1999.

Job growth across TN has been mixed. Declines in manufacturing have hit central and eastern TN harder than the west. Memphis' distribution and transportation sectors, located along the Mississippi, have continued to provide job growth even as the manufacturing sector stumbles. Federal Express and United Parcel Service continue to expand operations. A slowing of the US economy in 1999 and 2000 will weaken the demand for distribution services, although less so than in most industries.

Nashville's economic outlook is less bright. Almost half of 1998's employment gains were in the construction industry. The city's tourism and convention industry remain strong, although it appears likely that commercial construction, especially hotel, has outpaced demand. Construction employment should contract in 1999. The slowing US economy will also place a drag on tourism." *National Association of Realtors, Economic Profiles: The Fifty States and the District of Columbia, http://nar.realtor.com/databank/profiles.htm*

IMPORTS/EXPORTS

Total Export Sales

Area	1994 ($000)	1995 ($000)	1996 ($000)	1997 ($000)	% Chg. 1994-97	% Chg. 1996-97
MSA[1]	237,267	301,012	273,466	331,361	39.7	21.2
U.S.	512,415,609	583,030,524	622,827,063	687,597,999	34.2	10.4

Note: (1) Metropolitan Statistical Area - see Appendix A for areas included
Source: U.S. Department of Commerce, International Trade Association, Metropolitan Area Exports: An Export Performance Report on Over 250 U.S. Cities, November 10, 1998

CITY FINANCES

City Government Finances

Component	FY92 ($000)	FY92 (per capita $)
Revenue	514,831	3,395.02
Expenditure	556,744	3,671.41
Debt Outstanding	194,194	1,280.60
Cash & Securities	234,247	1,544.73

Source: U.S. Bureau of the Census, City Government Finances: 1991-92

City Government Revenue by Source

Source	FY92 ($000)	FY92 (per capita $)	FY92 (%)
From Federal Government	21,316	140.57	4.1
From State Governments	46,327	305.50	9.0
From Local Governments	47,167	311.04	9.2
Property Taxes	53,839	355.04	10.5
General Sales Taxes	0	0.00	0.0
Selective Sales Taxes	6,630	43.72	1.3
Income Taxes	0	0.00	0.0
Current Charges	32,544	214.61	6.3
Utility/Liquor Store	279,483	1,843.03	54.3
Employee Retirement[1]	9,037	59.59	1.8
Other	18,488	121.92	3.6

Note: (1) Excludes "city contributions," classified as "nonrevenue," intragovernmental transfers.
Source: U.S. Bureau of the Census, City Government Finances: 1991-92

City Government Expenditures by Function

Function	FY92 ($000)	FY92 (per capita $)	FY92 (%)
Educational Services	90,511	596.87	16.3
Employee Retirement[1]	4,491	29.62	0.8
Environment/Housing	47,874	315.70	8.6
Government Administration	8,206	54.11	1.5
Interest on General Debt	12,009	79.19	2.2
Public Safety	29,035	191.47	5.2
Social Services	10,364	68.34	1.9
Transportation	10,154	66.96	1.8
Utility/Liquor Store	307,432	2,027.34	55.2
Other	36,668	241.80	6.6

Note: (1) Payments to beneficiaries including withdrawal of contributions.
Source: U.S. Bureau of the Census, City Government Finances: 1991-92

Municipal Bond Ratings

Area	Moody's	S & P
Chattanooga	Aa3	n/a

Note: n/a not available; n/r not rated
Source: Moody's Bond Record, 6/99

POPULATION

Population Growth

Area	1980	1990	% Chg. 1980-90	July 1998 Estimate	% Chg. 1990-98
City	169,550	152,488	-10.1	147,790	-3.1
MSA[1]	426,540	433,210	1.6	453,346	4.6
U.S.	226,545,805	248,765,170	9.8	270,299,000	8.7

Note: (1) Metropolitan Statistical Area - see Appendix A for areas included;
July 1998 MSA population estimate was calculated by the editors
Source: 1980/1990 Census of Housing and Population, Summary Tape File 3C;
Census Bureau Population Estimates 1998

Population Characteristics

Race	City 1980 Population	%	City 1990 Population	%	% Chg. 1980-90	MSA[1] 1990 Population	%
White	114,523	67.5	98,960	64.9	-13.6	370,628	85.6
Black	53,792	31.7	51,360	33.7	-4.5	57,998	13.4
Amer Indian/Esk/Aleut	277	0.2	534	0.4	92.8	1,160	0.3
Asian/Pacific Islander	765	0.5	1,374	0.9	79.6	2,740	0.6
Other	193	0.1	260	0.2	34.7	684	0.2
Hispanic Origin[2]	1,274	0.8	925	0.6	-27.4	2,412	0.6

Note: (1) Metropolitan Statistical Area - see Appendix A for areas included;
(2) people of Hispanic origin can be of any race
Source: 1980/1990 Census of Housing and Population, Summary Tape File 3C

Ancestry

Area	German	Irish	English	Italian	U.S.	French	Polish	Dutch
City	13.4	15.6	12.6	1.2	9.8	2.2	0.5	2.2
MSA[1]	15.3	19.6	14.7	1.2	14.0	2.2	0.6	3.2
U.S.	23.3	15.6	13.1	5.9	5.3	4.2	3.8	2.5

Note: Figures are percentages and include persons that reported multiple ancestry (eg. if a person reported being Irish and Italian, they were included in both columns); (1) Metropolitan Statistical Area - see Appendix A for areas included
Source: 1990 Census of Population and Housing, Summary Tape File 3C

Age

Area	Median Age (Years)	Age Distribution (%) Under 5	Under 18	18-24	25-44	45-64	65+	80+
City	34.6	6.8	23.3	10.8	30.6	20.1	15.2	3.9
MSA[1]	34.5	6.6	24.8	10.0	31.4	20.9	13.0	2.9
U.S.	32.9	7.3	25.6	10.5	32.6	18.7	12.5	2.8

Note: (1) Metropolitan Statistical Area - see Appendix A for areas included
Source: 1990 Census of Population and Housing, Summary Tape File 3C

Male/Female Ratio

Area	Number of males per 100 females (all ages)	Number of males per 100 females (18 years old+)
City	85.2	81.1
MSA[1]	90.9	86.8
U.S.	95.0	91.9

Note: (1) Metropolitan Statistical Area - see Appendix A for areas included
Source: 1990 Census of Population, General Population Characteristics

INCOME

Per Capita/Median/Average Income

Area	Per Capita ($)	Median Household ($)	Average Household ($)
City	12,332	22,197	29,933
MSA[1]	12,493	25,475	32,334
U.S.	14,420	30,056	38,453

Note: All figures are for 1989; (1) Metropolitan Statistical Area - see Appendix A for areas included
Source: 1990 Census of Population and Housing, Summary Tape File 3C

...

Household Income Distribution by Race

Income ($)	City (%)					U.S. (%)				
	Total	White	Black	Other	Hisp.[1]	Total	White	Black	Other	Hisp.[1]
Less than 5,000	10.6	6.2	20.6	9.7	10.6	6.2	4.8	15.2	8.6	8.8
5,000 - 9,999	12.9	11.5	16.4	7.1	3.8	9.3	8.6	14.2	9.9	11.1
10,000 - 14,999	11.2	10.5	12.9	9.4	10.6	8.8	8.5	11.0	9.8	11.0
15,000 - 24,999	20.2	20.2	20.5	10.7	35.1	17.5	17.3	18.9	18.5	20.5
25,000 - 34,999	15.7	16.5	13.8	18.3	10.9	15.8	16.1	14.2	15.4	16.4
35,000 - 49,999	14.1	15.7	10.3	17.1	4.7	17.9	18.6	13.3	16.1	16.0
50,000 - 74,999	10.1	12.4	4.4	21.6	15.9	15.0	15.8	9.3	13.4	11.1
75,000 - 99,999	2.6	3.4	0.8	4.2	0.0	5.1	5.5	2.6	4.7	3.1
100,000+	2.7	3.7	0.4	1.9	8.3	4.4	4.8	1.3	3.7	1.9

Note: All figures are for 1989; (1) people of Hispanic origin can be of any race
Source: 1990 Census of Population and Housing, Summary Tape File 3C

Effective Buying Income

Area	Per Capita ($)	Median Household ($)	Average Household ($)
City	15,943	28,919	38,764
MSA[1]	16,163	30,705	41,414
U.S.	16,803	34,536	45,243

Note: Data as of 1/1/99; (1) Metropolitan Statistical Area - see Appendix A for areas included
Source: Standard Rate & Data Service, Newspaper Advertising Source, 9/99

Effective Household Buying Income Distribution

Area	% of Households Earning						
	$10,000 -$19,999	$20,000 -$34,999	$35,000 -$49,999	$50,000 -$74,999	$75,000 -$99,000	$100,000 -$124,999	$125,000 and up
City	18.6	23.4	16.2	14.8	5.7	1.9	2.5
MSA[1]	18.1	23.8	17.7	16.2	5.8	1.8	2.3
U.S.	16.0	22.6	18.2	18.9	7.2	2.4	2.7

Note: Data as of 1/1/99; (1) Metropolitan Statistical Area - see Appendix A for areas included
Source: Standard Rate & Data Service, Newspaper Advertising Source, 9/99

Poverty Rates by Race and Age

Area	Total (%)	By Race (%)				By Age (%)		
		White	Black	Other	Hisp.[2]	Under 5 years old	Under 18 years old	65 years and over
City	18.2	11.0	32.2	12.5	11.5	33.1	28.1	17.5
MSA[1]	13.6	10.8	31.3	12.3	14.2	21.5	18.3	17.5
U.S.	13.1	9.8	29.5	23.1	25.3	20.1	18.3	12.8

Note: Figures show the percent of people living below the poverty line in 1989. The average poverty threshold was $12,674 for a family of four in 1989; (1) Metropolitan Statistical Area - see Appendix A for areas included; (2) people of Hispanic origin can be of any race
Source: 1990 Census of Population and Housing, Summary Tape File 3C

EMPLOYMENT

Labor Force and Employment

Area	Civilian Labor Force			Workers Employed		
	Jun. 1998	Jun. 1999	% Chg.	Jun. 1998	Jun. 1999	% Chg.
City	74,836	74,814	-0.0	71,020	71,813	1.1
MSA[1]	222,203	219,205	-1.3	211,901	211,387	-0.2
U.S.	138,798,000	140,666,000	1.3	132,265,000	134,395,000	1.6

Note: Data is not seasonally adjusted and covers workers 16 years of age and older;
(1) Metropolitan Statistical Area - see Appendix A for areas included
Source: Bureau of Labor Statistics, http://stats.bls.gov

Unemployment Rate

Area	1998						1999					
	Jul.	Aug.	Sep.	Oct.	Nov.	Dec.	Jan.	Feb.	Mar.	Apr.	May.	Jun.
City	4.3	4.5	4.1	3.9	4.0	3.4	4.4	4.3	4.1	3.9	3.7	4.0
MSA[1]	4.0	4.0	3.7	3.6	3.4	3.0	3.9	3.9	3.7	3.3	3.2	3.6
U.S.	4.7	4.5	4.4	4.2	4.1	4.0	4.8	4.7	4.4	4.1	4.0	4.5

Note: Data is not seasonally adjusted and covers workers 16 years of age and older; all figures are percentages; (1) Metropolitan Statistical Area - see Appendix A for areas included
Source: Bureau of Labor Statistics, http://stats.bls.gov

Employment by Industry

Sector	MSA[1]		U.S.
	Number of Employees	Percent of Total	Percent of Total
Services	57,500	26.3	30.4
Retail Trade	38,500	17.6	17.7
Government	31,500	14.4	15.6
Manufacturing	44,200	20.2	14.3
Finance/Insurance/Real Estate	15,900	7.3	5.9
Wholesale Trade	9,900	4.5	5.4
Transportation/Public Utilities	11,700	5.3	5.3
Construction	n/a	n/a	5.0
Mining	n/a	n/a	0.4

Note: Figures cover non-farm employment as of 6/99 and are not seasonally adjusted; (1) Metropolitan Statistical Area - see Appendix A for areas included; n/a not available
Source: Bureau of Labor Statistics, http://stats.bls.gov

Employment by Occupation

Occupation Category	City (%)	MSA[1] (%)	U.S. (%)
White Collar	56.9	54.0	58.1
Executive/Admin./Management	10.8	10.4	12.3
Professional	13.9	12.4	14.1
Technical & Related Support	3.5	3.2	3.7
Sales	12.8	12.4	11.8
Administrative Support/Clerical	15.9	15.5	16.3
Blue Collar	26.3	32.5	26.2
Precision Production/Craft/Repair	9.1	12.1	11.3
Machine Operators/Assem./Insp.	8.6	10.7	6.8
Transportation/Material Movers	4.3	5.2	4.1
Cleaners/Helpers/Laborers	4.4	4.5	3.9
Services	15.9	12.2	13.2
Farming/Forestry/Fishing	0.9	1.3	2.5

Note: Figures cover employed persons 16 years old and over; (1) Metropolitan Statistical Area - see Appendix A for areas included
Source: 1990 Census of Population and Housing, Summary Tape File 3C

Occupational Employment Projections: 1996 - 2006

Occupations Expected to Have the Largest Job Growth (ranked by numerical growth)	Fast-Growing Occupations[1] (ranked by percent growth)
1. Salespersons, retail	1. Personal and home care aides
2. Truck drivers, light	2. Systems analysts
3. Cashiers	3. Paralegals
4. General managers & top executives	4. Respiratory therapists
5. Janitors/cleaners/maids, ex. priv. hshld.	5. Home health aides
6. Food service workers	6. Directors, religious activities & educ.
7. Child care workers, private household	7. Computer engineers
8. Cooks, fast food and short order	8. Child care workers, private household
9. Registered nurses	9. Corrections officers & jailers
10. Waiters & waitresses	10. Emergency medical technicians

Note: Projections cover Tennessee; (1) Excludes occupations with total job growth less than 300
Source: U.S. Department of Labor, Employment and Training Administration, America's Labor Market Information System (ALMIS)

TAXES

Major State and Local Tax Rates

State Corp. Income (%)	State Personal Income (%)	Residential Property (effective rate per $100)	Sales & Use State (%)	Sales & Use Local (%)	State Gasoline (cents/gallon)	State Cigarette (cents/pack)
6.0	6.0[a]	n/a	6.0	2.25	21.0[b]	13.0[c]

Note: Personal/corporate income, sales, gasoline and cigarette tax rates as of January 1999. Property tax rates as of 1997; (a) Applies to interest and dividend income only; (b) Rate is comprised of 20 cents excise and 1 cent motor carrier tax. Does not include a 1 cent local option tax; (c) Counties and cities may impose an additional tax of 1 cent per pack. Dealers pay a additional enforcement and admin. fee of 0.05 cent per pack
Source: Federation of Tax Administrators, www.taxadmin.org; Washington D.C. Department of Finance and Revenue, Tax Rates and Tax Burdens in the District of Columbia: A Nationwide Comparison, July 1998; Chamber of Commerce, 1999

Total Taxes Per Capita and as a Percent of Income

Area	Per Capita Income ($)	Per Capita Taxes ($) Total	Per Capita Taxes ($) Federal	Per Capita Taxes ($) State/Local	Percent of Income (%) Total	Percent of Income (%) Federal	Percent of Income (%) State/Local
Tennessee	24,591	8,048	5,930	2,118	32.7	24.1	8.6
U.S.	27,876	9,881	6,690	3,191	35.4	24.0	11.4

Note: Figures are for 1998
Source: Tax Foundation, www.taxfoundation.org

COMMERCIAL REAL ESTATE

Office Market

Class/Location	Total Space (sq. ft.)	Vacant Space (sq. ft.)	Vac. Rate (%)	Under Constr. (sq. ft.)	Net Absorp. (sq. ft.)	Rental Rates ($/sq.ft./yr.)
Class A						
CBD	1,340,824	50,000	3.7	0	20,000	13.50-18.00
Outside CBD	917,850	10,000	1.1	0	20,050	11.00-18.00
Class B						
CBD	1,033,200	121,265	11.7	0	9,085	10.00-14.00
Outside CBD	926,826	50,000	5.4	0	10,940	6.00-10.00

Note: Data as of 10/98 and covers Chattanooga; CBD = Central Business District; n/a not available; Source: Society of Industrial and Office Realtors, 1999 Comparative Statistics of Industrial and Office Real Estate Markets

"Continued expansions of local industries will remain the major factor in Chattanooga's economic scene. There are proposed plans for attractive new commercial developments as well as an expansion of the Trade Center. Included in the list of proposed developments is a 100,000 sq. ft. office project on a CBD central block and a 200,000 sq. ft. suburban office project. Our SIOR reporter forecasts increased demand, rental rates, and sales prices for Chattanooga. Development groups are supporting the promotion of Chattanooga as a strategic link to the resources of east Tennessee's Technology Corridor and area educational institutions. Sustainable growth and a commitment to economic development will continue to be the mantra of Chattanooga in 1999." *Society of Industrial and Office Realtors, 1999 Comparative Statistics of Industrial and Office Real Estate Markets*

Industrial Market

Location	Total Space (sq. ft.)	Vacant Space (sq. ft.)	Vac. Rate (%)	Under Constr. (sq. ft.)	Net Absorp. (sq. ft.)	Gross Lease ($/sq.ft./yr.)
Central City	27,625,000	2,000,000	7.2	0	-1,425,000	2.50-3.65
Suburban	6,500,000	100,000	1.5	0	100,000	2.75-5.25

Note: Data as of 10/98 and covers Chattanooga; n/a not available
Source: Society of Industrial and Office Realtors, 1999 Comparative Statistics of Industrial and Office Real Estate Markets

"In 1998, there was only one small speculative project underway. This 60-acre tract lies in the northeast quadrant and has access to all utilities. Opportunities exist in the build-to-suit market and for smaller, prime industrial complexes. The textile industry is expected to see further challenges created by NAFTA opening up trade to Mexico. A public/private economic development group continues in its efforts to invigorate the market. The dollar volume of sales is expected to increase moderately over the next year. Moderate absorption of warehouse/distribution space and manufacturing space is predicted in spite of unexpected forth quarter vacancies in 1998. The addition of the 20,000 seat football stadium and the announcement of plans to develop a new baseball stadium in the north-end are expected to help the market and increase Chattanooga's draw as an industrial business location." *Society of Industrial and Office Realtors, 1999 Comparative Statistics of Industrial and Office Real Estate Markets*

COMMERCIAL UTILITIES

Typical Monthly Electric Bills

Area	Commercial Service ($/month)		Industrial Service ($/month)	
	12 kW demand 1,500 kWh	100 kW demand 30,000 kWh	1,000 kW demand 400,000 kWh	20,000 kW demand 10,000,000 kWh
City	n/a	n/a	n/a	n/a
U.S.	150	2,174	23,995	508,569

Note: Based on rates in effect January 1, 1999; n/a not available
Source: Edison Electric Institute, Typical Residential, Commercial and Industrial Bills, Winter 1999

TRANSPORTATION

Transportation Statistics

Average minutes to work	19.1
Interstate highways	I-24; I-59; I-75
Bus lines	
In-city	CARTA
Inter-city	1
Passenger air service	
Airport	Chattanooga Metropolitan (Lovell Field)
Airlines	4
Aircraft departures	n/a
Enplaned passengers	n/a
Rail service	No Amtrak Service
Motor freight carriers	96
Major waterways/ports	Tennessee River

Source: Editor & Publisher Market Guide, 1999; FAA Airport Activity Statistics, 1997; Amtrak National Time Table, Northeast Timetable, Spring/Summer 1999; 1990 Census of Population and Housing, STF 3C; Chamber of Commerce/Economic Development 1999; Jane's Urban Transport Systems 1999-2000

Means of Transportation to Work

Area	Car/Truck/Van		Public Transportation			Bicycle	Walked	Other Means	Worked at Home
	Drove Alone	Car-pooled	Bus	Subway	Railroad				
City	78.0	13.4	2.9	0.0	0.0	0.0	2.6	1.3	1.7
MSA[1]	79.4	14.7	1.2	0.0	0.0	0.0	1.9	0.9	1.9
U.S.	73.2	13.4	3.0	1.5	0.5	0.4	3.9	1.2	3.0

Note: Figures shown are percentages and only include workers 16 years old and over;
(1) Metropolitan Statistical Area - see Appendix A for areas included
Source: 1990 Census of Population and Housing, Summary Tape File 3C

BUSINESSES

Major Business Headquarters

Company Name	1999 Rankings	
	Fortune 500	Forbes 500
Provident Cos.	393	-

Note: Companies listed are located in the city; dashes indicate no ranking
Fortune 500: Companies that produce a 10-K are ranked 1 to 500 based on 1998 revenue
Forbes 500: Private companies are ranked 1 to 500 based on 1997 revenue
Source: Forbes, November 30, 1998; Fortune, April 26, 1999

Small Business Opportunity

According to *Forbes*, Chattanooga is home to one of America's 200 best small companies: Covenant Transport. Criteria: companies included must be publicly traded since November 1997 with a stock price of at least $5 per share and an average daily float of 1,000 shares. The company's latest 12-month sales must be between $5 and $350 million, return on equity (ROE) must be a minimum of 12% for both the past 5 years and the most recent four quarters, and five-year sales and EPS growth must average at least 10%. Companies with declining sales or earnings during the past year were dropped as well as businesses with debt/equity ratios over 1.25. Companies with negative operating cash flow in each of the past two years were also excluded. *Forbes, November 2, 1998*

HOTELS & MOTELS

Hotels/Motels

Area	Hotels/ Motels	Rooms	Luxury-Level Hotels/Motels		Average Minimum Rates ($)		
			♦♦♦♦	♦♦♦♦♦	♦♦	♦♦♦	♦♦♦♦
City	29	3,253	0	0	55	95	n/a
Airport	8	703	0	0	n/a	n/a	n/a
Total	37	3,956	0	0	n/a	n/a	n/a

Note: n/a not available; classifications range from one diamond (budget properties with basic amenities) to five diamond (luxury properties with the finest service, rooms and facilities).
Source: OAG, Business Travel Planner, Winter 1998-99

CONVENTION CENTERS

Major Convention Centers

Center Name	Meeting Rooms	Exhibit Space (sq. ft.)
Chattanooga Marriott	n/a	15,112
Chattanooga-Hamilton Co. Convention & Trade Center	5	60,000
Soldiers & Sailors Memorial Auditorium	4	10,000

Note: n/a not available
Source: Trade Shows Worldwide, 1998; Meetings & Conventions, 4/15/99;
Sucessful Meetings, 3/31/98

Living Environment

COST OF LIVING

Cost of Living Index

Composite Index	Groceries	Housing	Utilities	Trans- portation	Health Care	Misc. Goods/ Services
97.1	98.7	95.7	90.7	91.1	92.9	101.4

Note: U.S. = 100
Source: ACCRA, Cost of Living Index, 1st Quarter 1999

HOUSING

Median Home Prices and Housing Affordability

Area	Median Price[2] 1st Qtr. 1999 ($)	HOI[3] 1st Qtr. 1999	Afford- ability Rank[4]
MSA[1]	n/a	n/a	n/a
U.S.	134,000	69.6	–

Note: (1) Metropolitan Statistical Area - see Appendix A for areas included; (2) U.S. figures calculated from the sales of 524,324 new and existing homes in 181 markets; (3) Housing Opportunity Index - percent of homes sold that were within the reach of the median income household at the prevailing mortgage interest rate; (4) Rank is from 1-181 with 1 being most affordable; n/a not available
Source: National Association of Home Builders, Housing Opportunity Index, 1st Quarter 1999

Median Home Price Projection

It is projected that the median price of existing single-family homes in the metro area will decrease by -1.0% in 1999. Nationwide, home prices are projected to increase 3.8%. Kiplinger's Personal Finance Magazine, January 1999

Average New Home Price

Area	Price ($)
City	136,520
U.S.	142,735

Note: Figures are based on a new home with 1,800 sq. ft. of living area on an 8,000 sq. ft. lot.
Source: ACCRA, Cost of Living Index, 1st Quarter 1999

Average Apartment Rent

Area	Rent ($/mth)
City	605
U.S.	601

Note: Figures are based on an unfurnished two bedroom, 1-1/2 or 2 bath apartment, approximately 950 sq. ft. in size, excluding all utilities except water
Source: ACCRA, Cost of Living Index, 1st Quarter 1999

RESIDENTIAL UTILITIES

Average Residential Utility Costs

Area	All Electric ($/mth)	Part Electric ($/mth)	Other Energy ($/mth)	Phone ($/mth)
City	–	48.84	39.03	20.74
U.S.	100.02	55.73	43.33	19.71

Source: ACCRA, Cost of Living Index, 1st Quarter 1999

HEALTH CARE

Average Health Care Costs

Area	Hospital ($/day)	Doctor ($/visit)	Dentist ($/visit)
City	371.00	53.00	58.20
U.S.	430.43	52.45	66.35

Note: Hospital—based on a semi-private room; Doctor—based on a general practitioner's routine exam of an established patient; Dentist—based on adult teeth cleaning and periodic oral exam.
Source: ACCRA, Cost of Living Index, 1st Quarter 1999

Distribution of Office-Based Physicians

Area	Family/Gen. Practitioners	Specialists		
		Medical	Surgical	Other
MSA[1]	89	269	249	217

Note: Data as of 12/31/97; (1) Metropolitan Statistical Area - see Appendix A for areas included
Source: American Medical Assn., Physician Characteristics & Distribution in the U.S., 1999

Hospitals

Chattanooga has 4 general medical and surgical hospitals, 1 psychiatric, 2 rehabilitation, 1 other specialty. *AHA Guide to the Healthcare Field, 1998-99*

EDUCATION

Public School District Statistics

District Name	Num. Sch.	Enroll.	Classroom Teachers	Pupils per Teacher	Minority Pupils (%)	Current Exp.[1] ($/pupil)
Chattanooga City School Dist	n/a	n/a	n/a	n/a	n/a	n/a
Hamilton County School Distrct	80	42,701	n/a	n/a	n/a	n/a

Note: Data covers the 1997-1998 school year unless otherwise noted; (1) Data covers fiscal year 1996; SD = School District; ISD = Independent School District; n/a not available
Source: National Center for Education Statistics, Common Core of Data Public Education Agency Universe 1997-98; National Center for Education Statistics, Characteristics of the 100 Largest Public Elementary and Secondary School Districts in the United States: 1997-98, July 1999

Educational Quality

School District	Education Quotient[1]	Graduate Outcome[2]	Community Index[3]	Resource Index[4]
Chattanooga City	92.0	88.0	60.0	107.0

Note: Nearly 1,000 secondary school districts were rated in terms of educational quality. The scores range from a low of 50 to a high of 150; (1) Average of the Graduate Outcome, Community and Resource indexes; (2) Based on graduation rates and college board scores (SAT/ACT); (3) Based on the surrounding community's average level of education and the area's average income level; (4) Based on teacher salaries, per-pupil expenditures and student-teacher ratios.
Source: Expansion Management, Ratings Issue, 1998

Educational Attainment by Race

Area	High School Graduate (%)					Bachelor's Degree (%)				
	Total	White	Black	Other	Hisp.[2]	Total	White	Black	Other	Hisp.[2]
City	69.0	73.6	57.6	76.6	79.7	18.2	22.0	8.6	37.9	28.9
MSA[1]	67.7	69.0	57.9	72.5	76.4	15.7	16.5	9.1	32.2	23.0
U.S.	75.2	77.9	63.1	60.4	49.8	20.3	21.5	11.4	19.4	9.2

Note: Figures shown cover persons 25 years old and over; (1) Metropolitan Statistical Area - see Appendix A for areas included; (2) people of Hispanic origin can be of any race
Source: 1990 Census of Population and Housing, Summary Tape File 3C

School Enrollment by Type

Area	Preprimary				Elementary/High School			
	Public		Private		Public		Private	
	Enrollment	%	Enrollment	%	Enrollment	%	Enrollment	%
City	1,244	53.9	1,065	46.1	20,393	86.5	3,185	13.5
MSA[1]	3,872	59.6	2,625	40.4	64,955	88.9	8,140	11.1
U.S.	2,679,029	59.5	1,824,256	40.5	38,379,689	90.2	4,187,099	9.8

Note: Figures shown cover persons 3 years old and over;
(1) Metropolitan Statistical Area - see Appendix A for areas included
Source: 1990 Census of Population and Housing, Summary Tape File 3C

School Enrollment by Race

Area	Preprimary (%)				Elementary/High School (%)			
	White	Black	Other	Hisp.[1]	White	Black	Other	Hisp.[1]
City	59.5	39.2	1.3	0.2	51.0	47.0	2.0	0.8
MSA[2]	83.9	14.9	1.2	0.3	81.4	17.2	1.5	0.7
U.S.	80.4	12.5	7.1	7.8	74.1	15.6	10.3	12.5

Note: Figures shown cover persons 3 years old and over; (1) people of Hispanic origin can be of any race; (2) Metropolitan Statistical Area - see Appendix A for areas included
Source: 1990 Census of Population and Housing, Summary Tape File 3C

Classroom Teacher Salaries in Public Schools

District	B.A. Degree		M.A. Degree		Maximum	
	Min. ($)	Rank[1]	Max. ($)	Rank[1]	Max. ($)	Rank[1]
	n/a	n/a	n/a	n/a	n/a	n/a
Average	26,980	-	46,065	-	51,435	-

Note: Salaries are for 1997-1998; (1) Rank ranges from 1 to 100; n/a not available
Source: American Federation of Teachers, Survey & Analysis of Salary Trends, 1998

Higher Education

Two-Year Colleges		Four-Year Colleges		Medical Schools	Law Schools	Voc/ Tech
Public	Private	Public	Private			
1	0	1	1	0	0	3

Source: College Blue Book, Occupational Education, 1997; Medical School Admission Requirements, 1999-2000; Peterson's Guide to Two-Year Colleges, 1999; Peterson's Guide to Four-Year Colleges, 2000; Barron's Guide to Law Schools, 1999

MAJOR EMPLOYERS

Major Employers

Erlanger Health System	Chattanooga Hospital & Medical Service Assn.
Provident Companies	HealthSource Provident Insurance
Provident Life & Accident	Seaboard Farms of Chattanooga
Parkridge Hospital	Astec Inc. (construction machinery)
Covenant Transport	Brach & Brock Confections

Note: Companies listed are located in the city
Source: Dun's Business Rankings, 1999; Ward's Business Directory, 1998

PUBLIC SAFETY

Crime Rate

Area	All Crimes	Violent Crimes				Property Crimes		
		Murder	Forcible Rape	Robbery	Aggrav. Assault	Burglary	Larceny -Theft	Motor Vehicle Theft
City	9,836.3	22.8	54.5	379.3	1,218.9	1,765.9	5,558.6	836.4
Suburbs[1]	n/a	n/a	n/a	n/a	n/a	n/a	n/a	n/a
MSA[2]	n/a	n/a	n/a	n/a	n/a	n/a	n/a	n/a
U.S.	4,922.7	6.8	35.9	186.1	382.0	919.6	2,886.5	505.8

Note: Crime rate is the number of crimes per 100,000 pop.; (1) defined as all areas within the MSA but located outside the central city; (2) Metropolitan Statistical Area - see Appendix A for areas incl.
Source: FBI Uniform Crime Reports, 1997

RECREATION

Culture and Recreation

Museums	Symphony Orchestras	Opera Companies	Dance Companies	Professional Theatres	Zoos	Pro Sports Teams
8	1	1	1	0	1	0

Source: International Directory of the Performing Arts, 1997; Official Museum Directory, 1999; Stern's Performing Arts Directory, 1997; USA Today Four Sport Stadium Guide, 1997; Chamber of Commerce/Economic Development, 1999

Library System

The Chattanooga-Hamilton Co. Bicentennial Library has four branches, holdings of 404,597 volumes, and a budget of $4,731,107 (1997-1998). *American Library Directory, 1998-1999*

MEDIA

Newspapers

Name	Type	Freq.	Distribution	Circulation
Chattanooga Shofar	Religious	10x/yr	Area	1,000
The Chattanooga Times & The Chattanooga Free Press	General	6x/wk	Area	42,000

Note: Includes newspapers with circulations of 1,000 or more located in the city;
Source: Burrelle's Media Directory, 1999 Edition

Television Stations

Name	Ch.	Affiliation	Type	Owner
WRCB	n/a	NBCT	Commercial	Sarkes Tarzian Inc.
WTVC	n/a	ABCT	Commercial	Freedom Communications Inc.
WDEF	12	CBST	Commercial	Media General Inc.
WTCI	45	PBS	Public	Greater Chattanooga Public TV Corp.
WFLI	53	UPN	Commercial	Ying Benns
WDSI	61	FBC	Commercial	Pegasus Broadcast Television Inc.

Note: Stations included broadcast in the Chattanooga metro area; n/a not available
Source: Burrelle's Media Directory, 1999 Edition

AM Radio Stations

Call Letters	Freq. (kHz)	Target Audience	Station Format	Music Format
WLMX	980	General	M/N/T	Adult Contemporary
WFLI	1070	G/R	M/N/S/T	Gospel
WGOW	1150	General	N/T	n/a
WNOO	1260	B/C	M	Christian/Gospel
WDOD	1310	General	M	Adult Standards
WDEF	1370	General	S	n/a

Note: Stations included broadcast in the Chattanooga metro area; n/a not available
Target Audience: A=Asian; B=Black; C=Christian; E=Ethnic; F=French; G=General; H=Hispanic; M=Men; N=Native American; R=Religious; S=Senior Citizen; W=Women; Y=Young Adult; Z=Children
Station Format: E=Educational; M=Music; N=News; S=Sports; T=Talk
Source: Burrelle's Media Directory, 1999 Edition

FM Radio Stations

Call Letters	Freq. (mHz)	Target Audience	Station Format	Music Format
WUTC	88.1	General	M/N	Adult Contemporary/Alternative/Jazz
WMBW	88.9	Religious	E/M/N/T	Christian
WDYN	89.7	General	E/M/T	Christian/Easy Listening
WDEF	92.3	General	M	Adult Contemporary
WMPZ	93.7	n/a	M/N/S	Urban Contemporary
WJTT	94.3	General	M	Urban Contemporary
WDOD	96.5	General	M	AOR
WKXJ	97.3	General	M/N/S/T	Top 40
WLOV	98.1	General	M/N/T	Oldies/R&B
WUSY	100.7	General	M/N/T	Country
WLMX	105.5	General	M/N/T	Adult Contemporary
WSKZ	106.5	General	M/N/S	Adult Contemporary/Classic Rock
WOGT	107.9	General	M/N/T	Oldies

Note: Stations included broadcast in the Chattanooga metro area; n/a not available
Station Format: E=Educational; M=Music; N=News; S=Sports; T=Talk
Target Audience: A=Asian; B=Black; C=Christian; E=Ethnic; F=French; G=General; H=Hispanic; M=Men; N=Native American; R=Religious; S=Senior Citizen; W=Women; Y=Young Adult; Z=Children
Music Format: AOR=Album Oriented Rock; MOR=Middle-of-the-Road
Source: Burrelle's Media Directory, 1999 Edition

CLIMATE

Average and Extreme Temperatures

Temperature	Jan	Feb	Mar	Apr	May	Jun	Jul	Aug	Sep	Oct	Nov	Dec	Yr.
Extreme High (°F)	78	79	87	92	97	104	106	104	102	94	84	78	106
Average High (°F)	49	53	62	72	80	87	90	89	83	72	61	51	71
Average Temp. (°F)	39	43	51	60	68	76	79	78	72	61	50	42	60
Average Low (°F)	29	32	39	47	56	64	68	68	61	48	38	32	49
Extreme Low (°F)	-10	1	8	26	34	41	51	53	36	22	4	-2	-10

Note: Figures cover the years 1948-1990
Source: National Climatic Data Center, International Station Meteorological Climate Summary, 3/95

Average Precipitation/Snowfall/Humidity

Precip./Humidity	Jan	Feb	Mar	Apr	May	Jun	Jul	Aug	Sep	Oct	Nov	Dec	Yr.
Avg. Precip. (in.)	5.3	5.0	5.9	4.3	4.1	3.6	4.8	3.5	4.2	3.2	4.5	5.1	53.3
Avg. Snowfall (in.)	2	1	Tr	Tr	0	0	0	0	0	Tr	Tr	1	4
Avg. Rel. Hum. 7am (%)	81	81	81	83	88	89	90	92	92	91	86	83	86
Avg. Rel. Hum. 4pm (%)	58	53	48	44	50	52	55	55	55	50	52	57	52

Note: Figures cover the years 1948-1990; Tr = Trace amounts (<0.05 in. of rain; <0.5 in. of snow)
Source: National Climatic Data Center, International Station Meteorological Climate Summary, 3/95

Weather Conditions

Temperature			Daytime Sky			Precipitation		
10°F & below	32°F & below	90°F & above	Clear	Partly cloudy	Cloudy	0.01 inch or more precip.	0.1 inch or more snow/ice	Thunder-storms
2	73	48	88	141	136	120	3	55

Note: Figures are average number of days per year and covers the years 1948-1990
Source: National Climatic Data Center, International Station Meteorological Climate Summary, 3/95

AIR & WATER QUALITY

Maximum Pollutant Concentrations

	Particulate Matter (ug/m^3)	Carbon Monoxide (ppm)	Sulfur Dioxide (ppm)	Nitrogen Dioxide (ppm)	Ozone (ppm)	Lead (ug/m^3)
MSA[1] Level	63	n/a	n/a	n/a	0.11	n/a
NAAQS[2]	150	9	0.140	0.053	0.12	1.50
Met NAAQS?	Yes	n/a	n/a	n/a	Yes	n/a

Note: (1) Metropolitan Statistical Area - see Appendix A for areas included; (2) National Ambient Air Quality Standards; ppm = parts per million; ug/m^3 = micrograms per cubic meter; n/a not available
Source: EPA, National Air Quality and Emissions Trends Report, 1997

Drinking Water

Water System Name	Pop. Served	Primary Water Source Type	Number of Violations in 1998	Type of Violation/ Contaminants
Tenn.-American Water Co.	169,922	Surface	None	None

Note: Data as of July 10, 1999
Source: EPA, Office of Ground Water and Drinking Water, Safe Drinking Water Information System

Chattanooga tap water is slightly alkaline, moderately hard and fluoridated.
Editor & Publisher Market Guide, 1999

Columbia, South Carolina

Background

Having long since arisen, Phoenix-like, from the ashes of the Civil War, Columbia is now the largest city in South Carolina. The Congaree inhabited what would later become Columbia until the early eighteenth century, before moving to the north. In the middle of the century whites built a fort in the area, and soon a settlement appeared on the other side of the Congaree River. After the American Revolution, an argument between residents of the Tidewater and the Piedmont led, in 1786, to the relocation of the state capital from Charleston to the further inland. Founders named the new capital Columbia, which poets had sometimes called the new nation. During the nineteenth century, as railroads linked the city not only with Charleston, but with other parts of the South, Columbia expanded rapidly in population. Cotton mills became a dominant industry in the area.

The Civil War was a disastrous time for the city. Refugees, in flight before the armies of Union General William Tecumseh Sherman, huddled within the city. Northern troops marched into the city on February 17, 1865, torching most of it, although the state capitol survived.

Columbians rebuilt the city, and by the 1880s it was thriving again. Textile mills became an important part of the local economy. In the mid-twentieth century, the issue of civil rights, so troublesome in other areas of the South, was less so in Columbia, due to cooperation between white and African Americans.

As might be expected in South Carolina's capital, state government is the largest employer in the city, with local government the second largest. Both levels offer a low tax rate and incentives to assist commerce. Fort Jackson is another significant part of the local economy.

In the private sector, Columbia is an important Southern market. It is in the center of a web of five interstates, which run through or close to the city, giving it easy access to the rest of the South and much of the country. The State Farmers Market, a thriving site for the selling and buying of farm produce in the South, is located in Columbia.

Industry also plays a role in the city's economy. The manufacturers of textiles and clay products, which have been part of the city's commercial fabric for many years, are still of importance. Other industries include the production of cameras, chemicals, electronics, fertilizer, concrete, foodstuffs, and boats. In recent years software and fiber optics have also become vital to the area's commerce, as has finance. The city is the hub for the state's banking and insurance concerns.

There are numerous post-secondary educational institutions in the city. The most important is the University of South Carolina, but there are also business colleges and a few sectarian institutions.

Columbia enjoys a moderate climate. Although the summers are long and hot, as to be expected in the Deep South, winters are short and mild. Temperatures average about eighty-one degrees in the summer, and range from the thirties to the sixties in the winter. Rainfall per year usually amounts to around forty-five inches, and there is very little snow in the metropolitan area.

General Rankings and Evaluative Comments

- Columbia was ranked #21 out of 44 mid-sized, southern metropolitan areas in *Money's* 1998 survey of "The Best Places to Live in America." The survey was conducted by first contacting 512 representative households nationwide and asking them to rank 37 quality-of-life factors on a scale of 1 to 10. Next, a demographic profile was compiled on the 300 largest metropolitan statistical areas in the U.S. The numbers were crunched together to arrive at an overall ranking (things Americans consider most important, like clean air and water, low crime and good schools, received extra weight). Unlike previous years, the 1998 rankings were broken down by region (northeast, midwest, south, west) and population size (100,000 to 249,999; 250,000 to 999,999; 1 million plus). The city had a nationwide ranking of #203 out of 300 in 1997 and #209 out of 300 in 1996. *Money, July 1998; Money, July 1997; Money, September 1996*

- *Ladies Home Journal* ranked America's 200 largest cities based on the qualities women care about most. Columbia ranked #55 out of 200. Criteria: low crime rate, well-paying jobs, quality health and child care, good public schools, the presence of women in government, size of the gender wage gap, number of sexual-harassment and discrimination complaints filed, unemployment and divorce rates, commute times, population density, number of houses of worship, parks and cultural offerings, number of women's health specialists, how well a community's women cared for themselves, complexion kindness index based on UV radiation levels, odds of finding affordable fashions, rental rates for romance movies, champagne sales and other matters of the heart. *Ladies Home Journal, November 1998*

- Zero Population Growth ranked 229 cities in terms of children's health, safety, and economic well-being. Columbia was ranked #65 out of 112 independent cities (cities with populations greater than 100,000 which were neither Major Cities nor Suburbs/Outer Cities) and was given a grade of C. Criteria: total population, percent of population under 18 years of age, household language, percent population change, percent of births to teens, infant mortality rate, percent of low birth weights, dropout rate, enrollment in preprimary school, violent and property crime rates, unemployment rate, percent of children in poverty, percent of owner occupied units, number of bad air days, percent of public transportation commuters, and average travel time to work. *Zero Population Growth, Children's Environmental Index, Fall 1999*

- Cognetics studied 273 metro areas in the United States, ranking them by entrepreneurial activity. Columbia was ranked #28 out of 134 smaller metro areas. Criteria: Significant Starts (firms started in the last 10 years that still employ at least 5 people) and Young Growers (percent of firms 10 years old or less that grew significantly during the last 4 years). *Cognetics, "Entrepreneurial Hot Spots: The Best Places in America to Start and Grow a Company," 1998*

- Reliastar Financial Corp. ranked the 125 largest metropolitan areas according to the general financial security of residents. Columbia was ranked #16 out of 125 with a score of 9.6. The score indicates the percentage a metropolitan area is above or below the metropolitan norm. A metro area with a score of 10.6 is 10.6% above the metro average. Criteria: Earnings and Wealth Potential (household income, education, net assets, cost of living); Safety Net (health insurance, retirement savings, life insurance, income support programs); Personal Threats (unemployment rate, low-income households, crime rate); Community Economic Vitality (cost of community services, job quality, job creation, housing costs). *Reliastar Financial Corp., "The Best Cities to Earn and Save Money," 1999 Edition*

Business Environment

STATE ECONOMY

State Economic Profile

"South Carolina has been on a roll and is expected to continue that trend. SC's friendly business environment and high quality of life have attracted an amazing number of businesses and residents. Both the construction and housing markets have been booming. As the US economy cools in 1999, its feverish growth will slow; however, SC will remain one of the nation's fastest growing states.

SC non-farm employment grew by 4.0% in 1998. Although manufacturing employment growth slowed to 0.2%, service jobs expanded at 6.1%. Many of these service jobs are in the tourism industry, which benefited in 1998 from the strong US expansion. Other important gains took place in the financial and business services sectors.

SC construction employment grew by 9.8% in 1998, with residential permits growing by 8% and home sales growing by almost 17%. The continued expansion of the Port of Charleston and the strong Charlotte-Gastonia-Rock Hill commercial markets brought a wave of new commercial construction in 1998. Home sales and construction activity are expected to slow in 1999 and 2000, although still remain strong by national standards.

Unlike many states, SC's strength is spread across the state. Expanding port facilities, fueled by the auto industry, are helping drive job growth in Charleston. Columbia added jobs at a rate of 3% in 1998, below the state average but still high above the national. Employment gains were also strong along the I-85 corridor. The state's real strength has been its ability to attract new residents, both in the form of new workers and retirees. SC's affordable living and pleasant climate will assure continued strong positive migration." *National Association of Realtors, Economic Profiles: The Fifty States and the District of Columbia, http://nar.realtor.com/databank/profiles.htm*

IMPORTS/EXPORTS

Total Export Sales

Area	1994 ($000)	1995 ($000)	1996 ($000)	1997 ($000)	% Chg. 1994-97	% Chg. 1996-97
MSA[1]	300,390	343,311	310,848	328,546	9.4	5.7
U.S.	512,415,609	583,030,524	622,827,063	687,597,999	34.2	10.4

Note: (1) Metropolitan Statistical Area - see Appendix A for areas included
Source: U.S. Department of Commerce, International Trade Association, Metropolitan Area Exports: An Export Performance Report on Over 250 U.S. Cities, November 10, 1998

CITY FINANCES

City Government Finances

Component	FY92 ($000)	FY92 (per capita $)
Revenue	94,592	847.65
Expenditure	117,614	1,053.95
Debt Outstanding	177,337	1,589.14
Cash & Securities	104,099	932.85

Source: U.S. Bureau of the Census, City Government Finances: 1991-92

City Government Revenue by Source

Source	FY92 ($000)	FY92 (per capita $)	FY92 (%)
From Federal Government	2,897	25.96	3.1
From State Governments	3,537	31.70	3.7
From Local Governments	3,036	27.21	3.2
Property Taxes	20,489	183.60	21.7
General Sales Taxes	0	0.00	0.0
Selective Sales Taxes	3,429	30.73	3.6
Income Taxes	0	0.00	0.0
Current Charges	28,944	259.37	30.6
Utility/Liquor Store	18,300	163.99	19.3
Employee Retirement[1]	0	0.00	0.0
Other	13,960	125.10	14.8

Note: (1) Excludes "city contributions," classified as "nonrevenue," intragovernmental transfers.
Source: U.S. Bureau of the Census, City Government Finances: 1991-92

City Government Expenditures by Function

Function	FY92 ($000)	FY92 (per capita $)	FY92 (%)
Educational Services	0	0.00	0.0
Employee Retirement[1]	0	0.00	0.0
Environment/Housing	33,114	296.74	28.2
Government Administration	6,819	61.11	5.8
Interest on General Debt	2,217	19.87	1.9
Public Safety	24,388	218.54	20.7
Social Services	425	3.81	0.4
Transportation	6,185	55.42	5.3
Utility/Liquor Store	41,226	369.43	35.1
Other	3,240	29.03	2.8

Note: (1) Payments to beneficiaries including withdrawal of contributions.
Source: U.S. Bureau of the Census, City Government Finances: 1991-92

Municipal Bond Ratings

Area	Moody's	S & P
Columbia	Aa3	n/a

Note: n/a not available; n/r not rated
Source: Moody's Bond Record, 6/99

POPULATION

Population Growth

Area	1980	1990	% Chg. 1980-90	July 1998 Estimate	% Chg. 1990-98
City	101,208	98,052	-3.1	110,840	13.0
MSA[1]	410,088	453,331	10.5	499,633	10.2
U.S.	226,545,805	248,765,170	9.8	270,299,000	8.7

Note: (1) Metropolitan Statistical Area - see Appendix A for areas included;
July 1998 MSA population estimate was calculated by the editors
Source: 1980/1990 Census of Housing and Population, Summary Tape File 3C;
Census Bureau Population Estimates 1998

Population Characteristics

Race	City 1980 Population	%	City 1990 Population	%	% Chg. 1980-90	MSA[1] 1990 Population	%
White	58,664	58.0	52,785	53.8	-10.0	307,723	67.9
Black	40,762	40.3	42,757	43.6	4.9	137,835	30.4
Amer Indian/Esk/Aleut	134	0.1	268	0.3	100.0	1,039	0.2
Asian/Pacific Islander	721	0.7	1,368	1.4	89.7	4,496	1.0
Other	927	0.9	874	0.9	-5.7	2,238	0.5
Hispanic Origin[2]	2,202	2.2	2,033	2.1	-7.7	5,740	1.3

Note: (1) Metropolitan Statistical Area - see Appendix A for areas included;
(2) people of Hispanic origin can be of any race
Source: 1980/1990 Census of Housing and Population, Summary Tape File 3C

Ancestry

Area	German	Irish	English	Italian	U.S.	French	Polish	Dutch
City	13.0	9.4	12.1	2.0	5.0	2.7	0.8	1.2
MSA[1]	20.1	13.6	13.3	2.0	7.2	3.0	1.0	1.8
U.S.	23.3	15.6	13.1	5.9	5.3	4.2	3.8	2.5

Note: Figures are percentages and include persons that reported multiple ancestry (eg. if a person reported being Irish and Italian, they were included in both columns); (1) Metropolitan Statistical Area - see Appendix A for areas included
Source: 1990 Census of Population and Housing, Summary Tape File 3C

Age

Area	Median Age (Years)	Age Distribution (%) Under 5	Under 18	18-24	25-44	45-64	65+	80+
City	28.5	6.1	19.9	22.7	32.9	12.9	11.6	2.9
MSA[1]	31.2	7.0	25.0	13.0	35.3	17.6	9.2	1.7
U.S.	32.9	7.3	25.6	10.5	32.6	18.7	12.5	2.8

Note: (1) Metropolitan Statistical Area - see Appendix A for areas included
Source: 1990 Census of Population and Housing, Summary Tape File 3C

Male/Female Ratio

Area	Number of males per 100 females (all ages)	Number of males per 100 females (18 years old+)
City	95.4	93.7
MSA[1]	94.4	91.7
U.S.	95.0	91.9

Note: (1) Metropolitan Statistical Area - see Appendix A for areas included
Source: 1990 Census of Population, General Population Characteristics

INCOME

Per Capita/Median/Average Income

Area	Per Capita ($)	Median Household ($)	Average Household ($)
City	12,210	23,216	31,826
MSA[1]	13,618	30,474	36,727
U.S.	14,420	30,056	38,453

Note: All figures are for 1989; (1) Metropolitan Statistical Area - see Appendix A for areas included
Source: 1990 Census of Population and Housing, Summary Tape File 3C

Household Income Distribution by Race

Income ($)	City (%)					U.S. (%)				
	Total	White	Black	Other	Hisp.[1]	Total	White	Black	Other	Hisp.[1]
Less than 5,000	10.1	6.0	16.7	17.3	15.3	6.2	4.8	15.2	8.6	8.8
5,000 - 9,999	11.6	9.4	15.1	15.6	14.1	9.3	8.6	14.2	9.9	11.1
10,000 - 14,999	11.3	8.3	16.2	11.7	6.3	8.8	8.5	11.0	9.8	11.0
15,000 - 24,999	20.0	18.9	21.9	18.6	25.4	17.5	17.3	18.9	18.5	20.5
25,000 - 34,999	15.7	16.4	14.7	13.9	23.1	15.8	16.1	14.2	15.4	16.4
35,000 - 49,999	13.9	16.5	9.5	15.2	10.8	17.9	18.6	13.3	16.1	16.0
50,000 - 74,999	10.3	13.8	4.7	4.8	0.8	15.0	15.8	9.3	13.4	11.1
75,000 - 99,999	3.3	4.8	0.8	3.0	2.8	5.1	5.5	2.6	4.7	3.1
100,000+	3.8	5.8	0.4	0.0	1.5	4.4	4.8	1.3	3.7	1.9

Note: All figures are for 1989; (1) people of Hispanic origin can be of any race
Source: 1990 Census of Population and Housing, Summary Tape File 3C

Effective Buying Income

Area	Per Capita ($)	Median Household ($)	Average Household ($)
City	14,489	27,766	41,283
MSA[1]	16,106	34,476	43,549
U.S.	16,803	34,536	45,243

Note: Data as of 1/1/99; (1) Metropolitan Statistical Area - see Appendix A for areas included
Source: Standard Rate & Data Service, Newspaper Advertising Source, 9/99

Effective Household Buying Income Distribution

Area	% of Households Earning						
	$10,000 -$19,999	$20,000 -$34,999	$35,000 -$49,999	$50,000 -$74,999	$75,000 -$99,000	$100,000 -$124,999	$125,000 and up
City	19.5	24.5	15.5	13.8	5.1	2.0	2.5
MSA[1]	15.6	24.6	20.0	19.3	6.3	1.8	1.7
U.S.	16.0	22.6	18.2	18.9	7.2	2.4	2.7

Note: Data as of 1/1/99; (1) Metropolitan Statistical Area - see Appendix A for areas included
Source: Standard Rate & Data Service, Newspaper Advertising Source, 9/99

Poverty Rates by Race and Age

Area	Total (%)	By Race (%)				By Age (%)		
		White	Black	Other	Hisp.[2]	Under 5 years old	Under 18 years old	65 years and over
City	21.2	11.8	32.4	26.3	22.5	29.9	28.7	16.7
MSA[1]	11.7	6.9	22.6	17.0	13.3	16.8	15.3	14.8
U.S.	13.1	9.8	29.5	23.1	25.3	20.1	18.3	12.8

Note: Figures show the percent of people living below the poverty line in 1989. The average poverty threshold was $12,674 for a family of four in 1989; (1) Metropolitan Statistical Area - see Appendix A for areas included; (2) people of Hispanic origin can be of any race
Source: 1990 Census of Population and Housing, Summary Tape File 3C

EMPLOYMENT

Labor Force and Employment

Area	Civilian Labor Force			Workers Employed		
	Jun. 1998	Jun. 1999	% Chg.	Jun. 1998	Jun. 1999	% Chg.
City	48,970	50,878	3.9	47,221	48,941	3.6
MSA[1]	283,326	293,735	3.7	276,484	286,555	3.6
U.S.	138,798,000	140,666,000	1.3	132,265,000	134,395,000	1.6

Note: Data is not seasonally adjusted and covers workers 16 years of age and older; (1) Metropolitan Statistical Area - see Appendix A for areas included
Source: Bureau of Labor Statistics, http://stats.bls.gov

Unemployment Rate

Area	1998						1999					
	Jul.	Aug.	Sep.	Oct.	Nov.	Dec.	Jan.	Feb.	Mar.	Apr.	May.	Jun.
City	3.8	3.1	3.3	3.3	2.7	2.6	3.0	3.4	3.0	2.8	3.3	3.8
MSA[1]	2.5	2.1	2.2	2.2	1.8	1.7	2.0	2.2	1.8	1.8	2.2	2.4
U.S.	4.7	4.5	4.4	4.2	4.1	4.0	4.8	4.7	4.4	4.1	4.0	4.5

Note: Data is not seasonally adjusted and covers workers 16 years of age and older; all figures are percentages; (1) Metropolitan Statistical Area - see Appendix A for areas included
Source: Bureau of Labor Statistics, http://stats.bls.gov

Employment by Industry

Sector	MSA[1]		U.S.
	Number of Employees	Percent of Total	Percent of Total
Services	77,900	25.6	30.4
Retail Trade	52,400	17.2	17.7
Government	76,200	25.0	15.6
Manufacturing	26,700	8.8	14.3
Finance/Insurance/Real Estate	22,800	7.5	5.9
Wholesale Trade	16,700	5.5	5.4
Transportation/Public Utilities	13,800	4.5	5.3
Construction	n/a	n/a	5.0
Mining	n/a	n/a	0.4

Note: Figures cover non-farm employment as of 6/99 and are not seasonally adjusted; (1) Metropolitan Statistical Area - see Appendix A for areas included; n/a not available
Source: Bureau of Labor Statistics, http://stats.bls.gov

Employment by Occupation

Occupation Category	City (%)	MSA[1] (%)	U.S. (%)
White Collar	66.6	63.7	58.1
Executive/Admin./Management	12.6	13.7	12.3
Professional	21.1	15.8	14.1
Technical & Related Support	4.6	4.4	3.7
Sales	11.2	12.4	11.8
Administrative Support/Clerical	17.0	17.5	16.3
Blue Collar	15.8	22.0	26.2
Precision Production/Craft/Repair	6.6	10.4	11.3
Machine Operators/Assem./Insp.	3.4	5.2	6.8
Transportation/Material Movers	2.5	3.4	4.1
Cleaners/Helpers/Laborers	3.3	3.1	3.9
Services	16.5	12.9	13.2
Farming/Forestry/Fishing	1.2	1.3	2.5

Note: Figures cover employed persons 16 years old and over; (1) Metropolitan Statistical Area - see Appendix A for areas included
Source: 1990 Census of Population and Housing, Summary Tape File 3C

Occupational Employment Projections: 1996 - 2006

Occupations Expected to Have the Largest Job Growth (ranked by numerical growth)	Fast-Growing Occupations[1] (ranked by percent growth)
1. Cashiers	1. Desktop publishers
2. Salespersons, retail	2. Database administrators
3. General managers & top executives	3. Computer engineers
4. Marketing & sales, supervisors	4. Paralegals
5. Food preparation workers	5. Systems analysts
6. Truck drivers, light	6. Personal and home care aides
7. Cooks, fast food and short order	7. Medical assistants
8. Food service workers	8. Physical therapy assistants and aides
9. Waiters & waitresses	9. Respiratory therapists
10. Food service and lodging managers	10. Data processing equipment repairers

Note: Projections cover South Carolina; (1) Excludes occupations with total job growth less than 300
Source: U.S. Department of Labor, Employment and Training Administration, America's Labor Market Information System (ALMIS)

TAXES

Major State and Local Tax Rates

State Corp. Income (%)	State Personal Income (%)	Residential Property (effective rate per $100)	Sales & Use		State Gasoline (cents/gallon)	State Cigarette (cents/pack)
			State (%)	Local (%)		
5.0	2.5 - 7.0	1.42	5.0	None	16.0	7.0

Note: Personal/corporate income, sales, gasoline and cigarette tax rates as of January 1999. Property tax rates as of 1997.
Source: Federation of Tax Administrators, www.taxadmin.org; Washington D.C. Department of Finance and Revenue, Tax Rates and Tax Burdens in the District of Columbia: A Nationwide Comparison, July 1998; Chamber of Commerce, 1999

Total Taxes Per Capita and as a Percent of Income

Area	Per Capita Income ($)	Per Capita Taxes ($)			Percent of Income (%)		
		Total	Federal	State/Local	Total	Federal	State/Local
South Carolina	22,624	7,937	5,333	2,604	35.1	23.6	11.5
U.S.	27,876	9,881	6,690	3,191	35.4	24.0	11.4

Note: Figures are for 1998
Source: Tax Foundation, www.taxfoundation.org

Estimated Tax Burden

Area	State Income	Local Income	Property	Sales	Total
Columbia	3,334	0	3,250	748	7,332

Note: The numbers are estimates of taxes paid by a married couple with two children and annual earnings of $75,000. Sales tax estimates assume they spend average amounts on food, clothing, household goods and gasoline. Property tax estimates assume they live in a $250,000 home.
Source: Kiplinger's Personal Finance Magazine, October 1998

COMMERCIAL REAL ESTATE

Office Market

Class/ Location	Total Space (sq. ft.)	Vacant Space (sq. ft.)	Vac. Rate (%)	Under Constr. (sq. ft.)	Net Absorp. (sq. ft.)	Rental Rates ($/sq.ft./yr.)
Class A						
CBD	4,000,000	320,000	8.0	305,000	160,000	15.50-18.50
Outside CBD	1,640,000	98,400	6.0	0	32,801	15.00-16.75
Class B						
CBD	2,420,000	193,600	8.0	0	72,600	12.50-15.00
Outside CBD	1,895,000	227,400	12.0	0	94,750	14.00-16.00

Note: Data as of 10/98 and covers Columbia; CBD = Central Business District; n/a not available;
Source: Society of Industrial and Office Realtors, 1999 Comparative Statistics of Industrial and Office Real Estate Markets

"Three new buildings in the central business district and Congaree Vista areas will come on line in 1999 for a total of 305,000 sq. ft. of space. Two additional buildings are planned for the suburbs. Two of the buildings are anchored by small banks, and two by law firms. Those openings will bring a combined total of 150,000 sq. ft. of speculative space to the market. However, with vacancy rates down to 8.4 percent, it would not be surprising to see speculative announcements sometime during 1999. The market should have no trouble with newly constructed space. The labor market is extremely tight as a result of several customer service firms entering the market. The shortage could potentially constrain future growth, both in the office and service sectors." *Society of Industrial and Office Realtors, 1999 Comparative Statistics of Industrial and Office Real Estate Markets*

Industrial Market

Location	Total Space (sq. ft.)	Vacant Space (sq. ft.)	Vac. Rate (%)	Under Constr. (sq. ft.)	Net Absorp. (sq. ft.)	Lease ($/sq.ft./yr.)
Central City	4,300,000	300,000	7.0	0	0	2.50-4.00
Suburban	21,200,000	750,000	3.5	800,000	850,000	2.50-4.25

Note: Data as of 10/98 and covers Columbia; n/a not available
Source: Society of Industrial and Office Realtors, 1999 Comparative Statistics of Industrial and Office Real Estate Markets

"Two things are occurring in the region that will directly affect the industrial market as well as the local economy. The high-technology sector is a golden opportunity. Local economic development officials have set up the South Carolina Technology Alliance, a public-private group whose goal is to lure high-technology business to the state through financial incentives and educational reforms. Firms already established include NCR, Intel, and Solectron Corp. Also, South Carolina recently unveiled a plan to slowly phase in electric competition through 2003. The big winner is Carolina Power & Light (CP&L), which earns roughly $450 million annually from its 170,000 South Carolina customers. The outlook for the industrial market is good, with construction, absorption, and lease prices increasing by up to five percent in warehouses and distribution facilities." *Society of Industrial and Office Realtors, 1999 Comparative Statistics of Industrial and Office Real Estate Markets*

COMMERCIAL UTILITIES

Typical Monthly Electric Bills

Area	Commercial Service ($/month)		Industrial Service ($/month)	
	12 kW demand 1,500 kWh	100 kW demand 30,000 kWh	1,000 kW demand 400,000 kWh	20,000 kW demand 10,000,000 kWh
City	n/a	n/a	n/a	n/a
U.S.	150	2,174	23,995	508,569

Note: Based on rates in effect January 1, 1999; n/a not available
Source: Edison Electric Institute, Typical Residential, Commercial and Industrial Bills, Winter 1999

TRANSPORTATION

Transportation Statistics

Average minutes to work	15.7
Interstate highways	I-20; I-26; I-77
Bus lines	
In-city	n/a
Inter-city	2
Passenger air service	
Airport	Columbia Metropolitan
Airlines	4
Aircraft departures	11,721 (1996)
Enplaned passengers	512,326 (1996)
Rail service	Amtrak
Motor freight carriers	47
Major waterways/ports	Congaree River

Source: Editor & Publisher Market Guide, 1999; FAA Airport Activity Statistics, 1997; Amtrak National Time Table, Northeast Timetable, Spring/Summer 1999; 1990 Census of Population and Housing, STF 3C; Chamber of Commerce/Economic Development 1999; Jane's Urban Transport Systems 1999-2000

Means of Transportation to Work

Area	Car/Truck/Van		Public Transportation			Bicycle	Walked	Other Means	Worked at Home
	Drove Alone	Car-pooled	Bus	Subway	Railroad				
City	61.5	11.8	4.6	0.0	0.0	0.8	17.8	1.9	1.7
MSA[1]	76.4	14.3	1.6	0.0	0.0	0.2	4.6	1.1	1.8
U.S.	73.2	13.4	3.0	1.5	0.5	0.4	3.9	1.2	3.0

Note: Figures shown are percentages and only include workers 16 years old and over;
(1) Metropolitan Statistical Area - see Appendix A for areas included
Source: 1990 Census of Population and Housing, Summary Tape File 3C

BUSINESSES

Major Business Headquarters

Company Name	1999 Rankings	
	Fortune 500	Forbes 500

No companies listed.

Note: Companies listed are located in the city; dashes indicate no ranking
Fortune 500: Companies that produce a 10-K are ranked 1 to 500 based on 1998 revenue
Forbes 500: Private companies are ranked 1 to 500 based on 1997 revenue
Source: Forbes, November 30, 1998; Fortune, April 26, 1999

Small Business Opportunity

According to *Forbes*, Columbia is home to one of America's 200 best small companies: Resource Bancshares Mortgage. Criteria: companies included must be publicly traded since November 1997 with a stock price of at least $5 per share and an average daily float of 1,000 shares. The company's latest 12-month sales must be between $5 and $350 million, return on equity (ROE) must be a minimum of 12% for both the past 5 years and the most recent four quarters, and five-year sales and EPS growth must average at least 10%. Companies with declining sales or earnings during the past year were dropped as well as businesses with debt/equity ratios over 1.25. Companies with negative operating cash flow in each of the past two years were also excluded. *Forbes, November 2, 1998*

HOTELS & MOTELS

Hotels/Motels

Area	Hotels/ Motels	Rooms	Luxury-Level Hotels/Motels		Average Minimum Rates ($)		
			♦♦♦♦	♦♦♦♦♦	♦♦	♦♦♦	♦♦♦♦
City	41	4,540	0	0	58	85	n/a
Airport	1	88	0	0	n/a	n/a	n/a
Total	42	4,628	0	0	n/a	n/a	n/a

Note: n/a not available; classifications range from one diamond (budget properties with basic amenities) to five diamond (luxury properties with the finest service, rooms and facilities).
Source: OAG, Business Travel Planner, Winter 1998-99

CONVENTION CENTERS

Major Convention Centers

Center Name	Meeting Rooms	Exhibit Space (sq. ft.)
Carolina Coliseum	2	50,000
South Carolina State Fairgrounds	1	115,000
The Township	2	8,000

Source: Trade Shows Worldwide, 1998; Meetings & Conventions, 4/15/99; Sucessful Meetings, 3/31/98

Living Environment

COST OF LIVING

Cost of Living Index

Composite Index	Groceries	Housing	Utilities	Trans-portation	Health Care	Misc. Goods/ Services
97.3	98.5	90.3	121.8	87.1	94.1	100.2

Note: U.S. = 100
Source: ACCRA, Cost of Living Index, 1st Quarter 1999

HOUSING

Median Home Prices and Housing Affordability

Area	Median Price[2] 1st Qtr. 1999 ($)	HOI[3] 1st Qtr. 1999	Afford-ability Rank[4]
MSA[1]	105,000	80.5	50
U.S.	134,000	69.6	—

Note: (1) Metropolitan Statistical Area - see Appendix A for areas included; (2) U.S. figures calculated from the sales of 524,324 new and existing homes in 181 markets; (3) Housing Opportunity Index - percent of homes sold that were within the reach of the median income household at the prevailing mortgage interest rate; (4) Rank is from 1-181 with 1 being most affordable
Source: National Association of Home Builders, Housing Opportunity Index, 1st Quarter 1999

Median Home Price Projection

It is projected that the median price of existing single-family homes in the metro area will increase by 4.9% in 1999. Nationwide, home prices are projected to increase 3.8%.
Kiplinger's Personal Finance Magazine, January 1999

Average New Home Price

Area	Price ($)
City	127,197
U.S.	142,735

Note: Figures are based on a new home with 1,800 sq. ft. of living area on an 8,000 sq. ft. lot.
Source: ACCRA, Cost of Living Index, 1st Quarter 1999

Average Apartment Rent

Area	Rent ($/mth)
City	617
U.S.	601

Note: Figures are based on an unfurnished two bedroom, 1-1/2 or 2 bath apartment, approximately 950 sq. ft. in size, excluding all utilities except water
Source: ACCRA, Cost of Living Index, 1st Quarter 1999

RESIDENTIAL UTILITIES

Average Residential Utility Costs

Area	All Electric ($/mth)	Part Electric ($/mth)	Other Energy ($/mth)	Phone ($/mth)
City	121.38	–	–	23.50
U.S.	100.02	55.73	43.33	19.71

Source: ACCRA, Cost of Living Index, 1st Quarter 1999

HEALTH CARE

Average Health Care Costs

Area	Hospital ($/day)	Doctor ($/visit)	Dentist ($/visit)
City	374.75	55.80	58.20
U.S.	430.43	52.45	66.35

Note: Hospital—based on a semi-private room; Doctor—based on a general practitioner's routine exam of an established patient; Dentist—based on adult teeth cleaning and periodic oral exam.
Source: ACCRA, Cost of Living Index, 1st Quarter 1999

Distribution of Office-Based Physicians

Area	Family/Gen. Practitioners	Specialists		
		Medical	Surgical	Other
MSA[1]	138	292	274	300

Note: Data as of 12/31/97; (1) Metropolitan Statistical Area - see Appendix A for areas included
Source: American Medical Assn., Physician Characteristics & Distribution in the U.S., 1999

Hospitals

Columbia has 4 general medical and surgical hospitals, 3 psychiatric, 1 rehabilitation, 1 other specialty. *AHA Guide to the Healthcare Field, 1998-99*

EDUCATION

Public School District Statistics

District Name	Num. Sch.	Enroll.	Classroom Teachers	Pupils per Teacher	Minority Pupils (%)	Current Exp.[1] ($/pupil)
Juvenile Justice	4	1,423	126	11.3	n/a	n/a
Palmetto Unified School Dist	15	647	94	6.9	n/a	n/a
Richland School District 01	51	27,263	1,953	14.0	n/a	n/a
Richland School District 02	17	15,483	1,026	15.1	n/a	n/a

Note: Data covers the 1997-1998 school year unless otherwise noted; (1) Data covers fiscal year 1996; SD = School District; ISD = Independent School District; n/a not available
Source: National Center for Education Statistics, Common Core of Data Public Education Agency Universe 1997-98; National Center for Education Statistics, Characteristics of the 100 Largest Public Elementary and Secondary School Districts in the United States: 1997-98, July 1999

Educational Quality

School District	Education Quotient[1]	Graduate Outcome[2]	Community Index[3]	Resource Index[4]
Richland County	79.0	65.0	112.0	99.0

Note: Nearly 1,000 secondary school districts were rated in terms of educational quality. The scores range from a low of 50 to a high of 150; (1) Average of the Graduate Outcome, Community and Resource indexes; (2) Based on graduation rates and college board scores (SAT/ACT); (3) Based on the surrounding community's average level of education and the area's average income level; (4) Based on teacher salaries, per-pupil expenditures and student-teacher ratios.
Source: Expansion Management, Ratings Issue, 1998

Educational Attainment by Race

Area	High School Graduate (%)					Bachelor's Degree (%)				
	Total	White	Black	Other	Hisp.[2]	Total	White	Black	Other	Hisp.[2]
City	76.0	86.2	61.0	89.0	80.7	31.7	45.1	11.4	53.9	29.6
MSA[1]	78.6	83.0	66.8	80.5	77.9	25.3	29.7	13.2	35.6	22.2
U.S.	75.2	77.9	63.1	60.4	49.8	20.3	21.5	11.4	19.4	9.2

Note: Figures shown cover persons 25 years old and over; (1) Metropolitan Statistical Area - see Appendix A for areas included; (2) people of Hispanic origin can be of any race
Source: 1990 Census of Population and Housing, Summary Tape File 3C

School Enrollment by Type

Area	Preprimary				Elementary/High School			
	Public		Private		Public		Private	
	Enrollment	%	Enrollment	%	Enrollment	%	Enrollment	%
City	742	52.0	684	48.0	11,931	89.9	1,334	10.1
MSA[1]	4,221	53.5	3,664	46.5	73,368	93.4	5,155	6.6
U.S.	2,679,029	59.5	1,824,256	40.5	38,379,689	90.2	4,187,099	9.8

Note: Figures shown cover persons 3 years old and over;
(1) Metropolitan Statistical Area - see Appendix A for areas included
Source: 1990 Census of Population and Housing, Summary Tape File 3C

School Enrollment by Race

Area	Preprimary (%)				Elementary/High School (%)			
	White	Black	Other	Hisp.[1]	White	Black	Other	Hisp.[1]
City	40.2	59.0	0.8	0.9	32.9	64.8	2.2	2.3
MSA[2]	63.6	35.1	1.3	1.2	59.0	39.5	1.5	1.4
U.S.	80.4	12.5	7.1	7.8	74.1	15.6	10.3	12.5

Note: Figures shown cover persons 3 years old and over; (1) people of Hispanic origin can be of any race; (2) Metropolitan Statistical Area - see Appendix A for areas included
Source: 1990 Census of Population and Housing, Summary Tape File 3C

Classroom Teacher Salaries in Public Schools

District	B.A. Degree		M.A. Degree		Maximum	
	Min. ($)	Rank[1]	Max. ($)	Rank[1]	Max. ($)	Rank[1]
	n/a	n/a	n/a	n/a	n/a	n/a
Average	26,980	-	46,065	-	51,435	-

Note: Salaries are for 1997-1998; (1) Rank ranges from 1 to 100; n/a not available
Source: American Federation of Teachers, Survey & Analysis of Salary Trends, 1998

Higher Education

Two-Year Colleges		Four-Year Colleges		Medical Schools	Law Schools	Voc/ Tech
Public	Private	Public	Private			
1	1	1	3	1	1	7

Source: College Blue Book, Occupational Education, 1997; Medical School Admission Requirements, 1999-2000; Peterson's Guide to Two-Year Colleges, 1999; Peterson's Guide to Four-Year Colleges, 2000; Barron's Guide to Law Schools, 1999

MAJOR EMPLOYERS

Major Employers

Blue Cross & Blue Shield of South Carolina	Colonial Life & Accident Insurance
South Carolina Electric & Gas	South Carolina Dept. of Transportation
State-Record Co.	SMI-Owen Steel
Southeastern Freight Lines	Wachovia Bank of South Carolina
NationsBank of South Carolina	Fleet Mortgage Group

Note: Companies listed are located in the city
Source: Dun's Business Rankings, 1999; Ward's Business Directory, 1998

PUBLIC SAFETY

Crime Rate

Area	All Crimes	Violent Crimes				Property Crimes		
		Murder	Forcible Rape	Robbery	Aggrav. Assault	Burglary	Larceny -Theft	Motor Vehicle Theft
City	11,291.2	11.2	59.7	473.0	1,009.5	1,514.3	7,450.0	773.5
Suburbs[1]	5,474.5	6.6	53.7	190.7	596.6	1,115.4	3,105.5	405.9
MSA[2]	6,721.7	7.6	55.0	251.3	685.2	1,200.9	4,037.0	484.7
U.S.	4,922.7	6.8	35.9	186.1	382.0	919.6	2,886.5	505.8

Note: Crime rate is the number of crimes per 100,000 pop.; (1) defined as all areas within the MSA but located outside the central city; (2) Metropolitan Statistical Area - see Appendix A for areas incl.
Source: FBI Uniform Crime Reports, 1997

RECREATION

Culture and Recreation

Museums	Symphony Orchestras	Opera Companies	Dance Companies	Professional Theatres	Zoos	Pro Sports Teams
7	2	0	1	1	1	0

Source: International Directory of the Performing Arts, 1997; Official Museum Directory, 1999; Stern's Performing Arts Directory, 1997; USA Today Four Sport Stadium Guide, 1997; Chamber of Commerce/Economic Development, 1999

Library System

The Richland County Public Library has nine branches, holdings of 906,329 volumes, and a budget of $9,839,252 (1997-1998). *American Library Directory, 1998-1999*

MEDIA

Newspapers

Name	Type	Freq.	Distribution	Circulation
Carolina Panorama	n/a	1x/wk	n/a	16,000
Point	Alternative	1x/mo	Local	20,000
The State	General	7x/wk	State	126,000

Note: Includes newspapers with circulations of 500 or more located in the city; n/a not available
Source: Burrelle's Media Directory, 1999 Edition

Television Stations

Name	Ch.	Affiliation	Type	Owner
WITV	n/a	n/a	Public	S. Carolina Educational Television Commission
WIS	10	NBCT	Commercial	Cosmos Broadcasting Corporation
WEBA	14	PBS	Public	S. Carolina Educational Television Commission
WJWJ	16	PBS	Public	S. Carolina Educational Television Commission
WLTX	19	CBST	Commercial	Gannett Broadcasting
WHMC	23	PBS	Public	S. Carolina Educational Television Commission
WOLO	25	ABCT	Commercial	Bahakel Communications Inc.
WRJA	27	PBS	Public	S. Carolina Educational Television Commission
WNTV	29	PBS	Public	S. Carolina Educational Television Commission
WNSC	30	PBS	Public	S. Carolina Educational Television Commission
WJPM	33	PBS	Public	S. Carolina Educational Television Commission
WRLK	35	PBS	Public	S. Carolina Educational Television Commission
WNEH	38	PBS	Public	S. Carolina Educational Television Commission
WRET	49	PBS	Public	S. Carolina Educational Television Commission
WACH	57	n/a	Commercial	Raycom Media Inc.

Note: Stations included broadcast in the Columbia metro area; n/a not available
Source: Burrelle's Media Directory, 1999 Edition

AM Radio Stations

Call Letters	Freq. (kHz)	Target Audience	Station Format	Music Format
WVOC	560	General	N/S/T	n/a
WOIC	1230	General	M/T	Urban Contemporary
WISW	1320	General	N	n/a
WCOS	1400	General	S/T	n/a
WQXL	1470	Religious	M/N/S	Christian

Note: Stations included broadcast in the Columbia metro area; n/a not available
Target Audience: A=Asian; B=Black; C=Christian; E=Ethnic; F=French; G=General; H=Hispanic; M=Men; N=Native American; R=Religious; S=Senior Citizen; W=Women; Y=Young Adult; Z=Children
Station Format: E=Educational; M=Music; N=News; S=Sports; T=Talk
Source: Burrelle's Media Directory, 1999 Edition

FM Radio Stations

Call Letters	Freq. (mHz)	Target Audience	Station Format	Music Format
WRJA	88.1	General	M/N	Classical/Jazz
WNSC	88.9	General	E/M/N	Classical/Jazz
WLJK	89.1	General	M/N	Classical/Jazz
WSCI	89.3	General	E/M	Classical
WMHK	89.7	Religious	E/M/N/S	Adult Contemporary
WJWJ	89.9	General	E/M/N	Classical
WEPR	90.1	General	M/N/S	Classical/Jazz
WHMC	90.1	General	M/N	Big Band/Classical/Jazz
WUSC	90.5	General	E/M/N/S/T	n/a
WLTR	91.3	General	M/N	Classical/Jazz
WARQ	93.5	Alternative	M	Alternative/Modern Rock
WFMV	95.3	B/R	M	Christian/Gospel
WHKZ	96.7	General	M/N	Country
WCOS	97.5	General	M	Country
WSCQ	100.1	General	M/N/T	Adult Standards
WWDM	101.3	General	M	Urban Contemporary
WMFX	102.3	G/M	M	AOR/Classic Rock
WOMG	103.1	General	M	Oldies
WNOK	104.7	General	M	Adult Top 40/Top 40
WTCB	106.7	General	M/N/T	Adult Contemporary

Note: Stations included broadcast in the Columbia metro area; n/a not available
Station Format: E=Educational; M=Music; N=News; S=Sports; T=Talk
Target Audience: A=Asian; B=Black; C=Christian; E=Ethnic; F=French; G=General; H=Hispanic;
M=Men; N=Native American; R=Religious; S=Senior Citizen; W=Women; Y=Young Adult; Z=Children
Music Format: AOR=Album Oriented Rock; MOR=Middle-of-the-Road
Source: Burrelle's Media Directory, 1999 Edition

CLIMATE

Average and Extreme Temperatures

Temperature	Jan	Feb	Mar	Apr	May	Jun	Jul	Aug	Sep	Oct	Nov	Dec	Yr.
Extreme High (°F)	84	84	91	94	101	107	107	107	101	101	90	83	107
Average High (°F)	56	60	67	77	84	90	92	91	85	77	67	59	75
Average Temp. (°F)	45	48	55	64	72	78	82	80	75	64	54	47	64
Average Low (°F)	33	35	42	50	59	66	70	69	64	51	41	35	51
Extreme Low (°F)	-1	5	4	26	34	44	54	53	40	23	12	4	-1

Note: Figures cover the years 1948-1990
Source: National Climatic Data Center, International Station Meteorological Climate Summary, 3/95

Average Precipitation/Snowfall/Humidity

Precip./Humidity	Jan	Feb	Mar	Apr	May	Jun	Jul	Aug	Sep	Oct	Nov	Dec	Yr.
Avg. Precip. (in.)	4.0	4.0	4.7	3.4	3.6	4.2	5.5	5.9	4.0	2.9	2.7	3.4	48.3
Avg. Snowfall (in.)	1	1	Tr	0	0	0	0	0	0	0	Tr	Tr	2
Avg. Rel. Hum. 7am (%)	83	83	84	82	84	85	88	91	91	90	88	84	86
Avg. Rel. Hum. 4pm (%)	51	47	44	41	46	50	54	56	54	49	48	51	49

Note: Figures cover the years 1948-1990; Tr = Trace amounts (<0.05 in. of rain; <0.5 in. of snow)
Source: National Climatic Data Center, International Station Meteorological Climate Summary, 3/95

Weather Conditions

Temperature			Daytime Sky			Precipitation		
10°F & below	32°F & below	90°F & above	Clear	Partly cloudy	Cloudy	0.01 inch or more precip.	0.1 inch or more snow/ice	Thunder-storms
< 1	58	77	97	149	119	110	1	53

Note: Figures are average number of days per year and covers the years 1948-1990
Source: National Climatic Data Center, International Station Meteorological Climate Summary, 3/95

AIR & WATER QUALITY

Maximum Pollutant Concentrations

	Particulate Matter (ug/m^3)	Carbon Monoxide (ppm)	Sulfur Dioxide (ppm)	Nitrogen Dioxide (ppm)	Ozone (ppm)	Lead (ug/m^3)
MSA[1] Level	130	3	0.020	0.011	0.11	0.01
NAAQS[2]	150	9	0.140	0.053	0.12	1.50
Met NAAQS?	Yes	Yes	Yes	Yes	Yes	Yes

Note: (1) Metropolitan Statistical Area - see Appendix A for areas included; (2) National Ambient Air Quality Standards; ppm = parts per million; ug/m^3 = micrograms per cubic meter; n/a not available
Source: EPA, National Air Quality and Emissions Trends Report, 1997

Drinking Water

Water System Name	Pop. Served	Primary Water Source Type	Number of Violations in 1998	Type of Violation/ Contaminants
City of Columbia	259,293	Surface	None	None

Note: Data as of July 10, 1999
Source: EPA, Office of Ground Water and Drinking Water, Safe Drinking Water Information System

Columbia tap water is alkaline, very soft and fluoridated.
Editor & Publisher Market Guide, 1999

Dallas, Texas

Background

Dallas is one of those cities that offers everything. Founded in 1841 by Tennessee lawyer and trader, John Neely Bryan, Dallas has come to symbolize in modern times, all that is big, exciting, and affluent.

Originally one of the largest markets for cotton in the U.S., Dallas moved on to become one of the largest markets for oil in the country. In the 1930s, oil was struck on the eastern fields of Texas. As a result of that discovery, millionaires and oil companies were made. The face we now associate with Dallas, and the state of Texas, had emerged.

Today, oil still plays a dominant role in the Dallas economy. Outside of Alaska, Texas holds 75 percent of the U.S. oil reserves. For that reason, more oil companies choose to headquarter themselves in the silver skyscrapers of Dallas, than in any other U.S. city.

In addition to many employment opportunities in the oil industry, the Dallas branch of the Federal Reserve Bank, and a host of other banks and investment firms clustering around the Federal Reserve hub employ many. Other opportunities are offered in the aircraft, advertising, motion picture, and publishing industries. From 1994 to 1997 the Dallas/Fort Worth area added between 80,000 and 100,000 each year. And 500,000 more new jobs are projected from 1997 to 2005.

The Dallas Convention Center, with more than two million square feet of space, is the largest convention center in Texas with 800,000 sq. ft. of exhibit space, and plans to add another 200,000 sq. ft. by 2002.

Dallas also offers a busy cultural calendar. A host of independent theatre groups is sponsored by Southern Methodist University. The Museum of Fine Arts houses an excellent collection of modern art, especially American paintings, and the Dallas Civic Opera, has showcased Maria Callas, Joan Sutherland, and Monserrat Caballé. There are also many historical districts, such as the Swiss Avenue District, and elegant buildings, such as the City Hall Building designed by I.M. Pei to investigate.

The climate of Dallas is generally temperate. Periods of extreme cold that occasionally occur are short lived and extremely high temperatures that sometimes occur in summer usually do not last for extended periods of time.

General Rankings and Evaluative Comments

- Dallas was ranked #10 out of 19 large, southern metropolitan areas in *Money's* 1998 survey of "The Best Places to Live in America." The survey was conducted by first contacting 512 representative households nationwide and asking them to rank 37 quality-of-life factors on a scale of 1 to 10. Next, a demographic profile was compiled on the 300 largest metropolitan statistical areas in the U.S. The numbers were crunched together to arrive at an overall ranking (things Americans consider most important, like clean air and water, low crime and good schools, received extra weight). Unlike previous years, the 1998 rankings were broken down by region (northeast, midwest, south, west) and population size (100,000 to 249,999; 250,000 to 999,999; 1 million plus). The city had a nationwide ranking of #40 out of 300 in 1997 and #65 out of 300 in 1996. *Money, July 1998; Money, July 1997; Money, September 1996*

- *Ladies Home Journal* ranked America's 200 largest cities based on the qualities women care about most. Dallas ranked #129 out of 200. Criteria: low crime rate, well-paying jobs, quality health and child care, good public schools, the presence of women in government, size of the gender wage gap, number of sexual-harassment and discrimination complaints filed, unemployment and divorce rates, commute times, population density, number of houses of worship, parks and cultural offerings, number of women's health specialists, how well a community's women cared for themselves, complexion kindness index based on UV radiation levels, odds of finding affordable fashions, rental rates for romance movies, champagne sales and other matters of the heart. *Ladies Home Journal, November 1998*

- Zero Population Growth ranked 229 cities in terms of children's health, safety, and economic well-being. Dallas was ranked #14 out of 25 major cities (main city in a metro area with population of greater than 2 million) and was given a grade of C. Criteria: total population, percent of population under 18 years of age, household language, percent population change, percent of births to teens, infant mortality rate, percent of low birth weights, dropout rate, enrollment in preprimary school, violent and property crime rates, unemployment rate, percent of children in poverty, percent of owner occupied units, number of bad air days, percent of public transportation commuters, and average travel time to work. *Zero Population Growth, Children's Environmental Index, Fall 1999*

- Dallas was ranked #19 out of 59 metro areas in *The Regional Economist's* "Rational Livability Ranking of 59 Large Metro Areas." The rankings were based on the metro area's total population change over the period 1990-97 divided by the number of people moving in from elsewhere in the United States (net domestic in-migration). *St. Louis Federal Reserve Bank of St. Louis, The Regional Economist, April 1999*

- Dallas appeared on *Travel & Leisure's* list of the world's 100 best cities. It was ranked #29 in the U.S. and #87 in the world. Criteria: activities/attractions, culture/arts, people, restaurants/food, and value. *Travel & Leisure, 1998 World's Best Awards*

- Dallas was selected by *Yahoo! Internet Life* as one of "America's Most Wired Cities & Towns." The city ranked #10 out of 50. Criteria: home and work net use, domain density, hosts per capita, directory density and content quality. *Yahoo! Internet Life, March 1999*

- Cognetics studied 273 metro areas in the United States, ranking them by entrepreneurial activity. Dallas was ranked #8 out of the 50 largest metro areas. Criteria: Significant Starts (firms started in the last 10 years that still employ at least 5 people) and Young Growers (percent of firms 10 years old or less that grew significantly during the last 4 years). *Cognetics, "Entrepreneurial Hot Spots: The Best Places in America to Start and Grow a Company," 1998*

- Dallas appeared on *Forbes* list of "Best Places for Business Growth." Rank: #3 out of 162 metro areas. Criteria: average wage and salary increases, job growth rates, number of technology clusters (measures business activity in 13 different technology areas), overall concentration of technology activity relative to national average and technology output growth. *Forbes, May 31, 1999*

- Dallas was included among *Entrepreneur* magazine's listing of the "20 Best Cities for Small Business." It was ranked #13 among large metro areas and #2 among central metro areas. Criteria: entrepreneurial activity, small-business growth, economic growth, and risk of failure. *Entrepreneur, October 1999*

- Dallas was selected as one of the "Best American Cities to Start a Business" by *Point of View* magazine. Criteria: coolness, quality-of-life, and business concerns. The city was ranked #12 out of 75. *Point of View, November 1998*

- Dallas appeared on *Sales & Marketing Management's* list of the "20 Hottest Cities for Selling." Rank: #11 out of 20. *S&MM* editors looked at Metropolitan Statistical Areas with populations of more than 150,000. The areas were ranked based on population increases, retail sales increases, effective buying income, increase in both residential and commercial building permits issued, unemployment rates, job growth, mix of industries, tax rates, number of corporate relocations, and the number of new corporations. *Sales & Marketing Management, April 1999*

- Reliastar Financial Corp. ranked the 125 largest metropolitan areas according to the general financial security of residents. Dallas was ranked #10 out of 125 with a score of 11.7. The score indicates the percentage a metropolitan area is above or below the metropolitan norm. A metro area with a score of 10.6 is 10.6% above the metro average. Criteria: Earnings and Wealth Potential (household income, education, net assets, cost of living); Safety Net (health insurance, retirement savings, life insurance, income support programs); Personal Threats (unemployment rate, low-income households, crime rate); Community Economic Vitality (cost of community services, job quality, job creation, housing costs). *Reliastar Financial Corp., "The Best Cities to Earn and Save Money," 1999 Edition*

Business Environment

STATE ECONOMY

State Economic Profile

"Economic growth in Texas has slowed as both its new and old economies are under pressure. Weak commodity prices and over-capacity have hurt TX's old economic powers, agriculture and oil. Soft global demand has slowed TX's new economic powers, semiconductors and computer sales. A slowing US economy in 1999 will also place a drag on TX's biotech and software companies. Despite the current slowdown, TX's long-term outlook is extremely bright, and its current problems will last no more than two years.

Weak commodity prices, over-capacity and soft foreign demand have all coincided to undermine TX's oil and farm sector. Despite OPEC cutbacks, the TX oil industry remains vulnerable because of its high costs, high inventories and high capacity. TX's farm sector is similarly positioned; commodity prices are expected to continue their long-term downward trend.

The TX economy is more diversified today than ever before. Growth in services and hi-tech employment have more than offset declines in TX's resource economy. Services employment in 1998 grew at 3.8%, adding some 93,000 jobs, while construction employment grew 4.9%, adding 22,700 jobs. Construction employment, along with home sales and starts, should contract in 1999 and 2000. TX's demographic situation is positive; the state continues to attract educated, young households. However, the current weakness in the state's semiconductor and computer industry has slowed job growth from its previous feverish pace. In the near-term, TX's growth should slow along with the US economy. Its long-term prospects are bright given its business friendly atmosphere and central location." *National Association of Realtors, Economic Profiles: The Fifty States and the District of Columbia, http://nar.realtor.com/databank/profiles.htm*

IMPORTS/EXPORTS

Total Export Sales

Area	1994 ($000)	1995 ($000)	1996 ($000)	1997 ($000)	% Chg. 1994-97	% Chg. 1996-97
MSA[1]	5,679,711	6,870,414	7,096,879	8,645,861	52.2	21.8
U.S.	512,415,609	583,030,524	622,827,063	687,597,999	34.2	10.4

Note: (1) Metropolitan Statistical Area - see Appendix A for areas included
Source: U.S. Department of Commerce, International Trade Association, Metropolitan Area Exports: An Export Performance Report on Over 250 U.S. Cities, November 10, 1998

CITY FINANCES

City Government Finances

Component	FY94 ($000)	FY94 (per capita $)
Revenue	1,561,799	1,495.75
Expenditure	1,537,863	1,472.82
Debt Outstanding	3,875,959	3,712.03
Cash & Securities	3,018,488	2,890.83

Source: U.S. Bureau of the Census, City Government Finances: 1993-94

City Government Revenue by Source

Source	FY94 ($000)	FY94 (per capita $)	FY94 (%)
From Federal Government	56,274	53.89	3.6
From State Governments	12,419	11.89	0.8
From Local Governments	4,526	4.33	0.3
Property Taxes	284,809	272.76	18.2
General Sales Taxes	120,027	114.95	7.7
Selective Sales Taxes	86,724	83.06	5.6
Income Taxes	0	0.00	0.0
Current Charges	440,806	422.16	28.2
Utility/Liquor Store	139,559	133.66	8.9
Employee Retirement[1]	277,619	265.88	17.8
Other	139,036	133.16	8.9

Note: (1) Excludes "city contributions," classified as "nonrevenue," intragovernmental transfers.
Source: U.S. Bureau of the Census, City Government Finances: 1993-94

City Government Expenditures by Function

Function	FY94 ($000)	FY94 (per capita $)	FY94 (%)
Educational Services	14,896	14.27	1.0
Employee Retirement[1]	106,174	101.68	6.9
Environment/Housing	269,766	258.36	17.5
Government Administration	68,854	65.94	4.5
Interest on General Debt	210,004	201.12	13.7
Public Safety	260,647	249.62	16.9
Social Services	18,397	17.62	1.2
Transportation	382,748	366.56	24.9
Utility/Liquor Store	171,390	164.14	11.1
Other	34,987	33.51	2.3

Note: (1) Payments to beneficiaries including withdrawal of contributions.
Source: U.S. Bureau of the Census, City Government Finances: 1993-94

Municipal Bond Ratings

Area	Moody's	S & P
Dallas	Aaa	n/a

Note: n/a not available; n/r not rated
Source: Moody's Bond Record, 6/99

POPULATION

Population Growth

Area	1980	1990	% Chg. 1980-90	July 1998 Estimate	% Chg. 1990-98
City	904,074	1,006,831	11.4	1,075,894	6.9
MSA[1]	1,957,378	2,553,362	30.4	3,171,895	24.2
U.S.	226,545,805	248,765,170	9.8	270,299,000	8.7

Note: (1) Metropolitan Statistical Area - see Appendix A for areas included;
July 1998 MSA population estimate was calculated by the editors
Source: 1980/1990 Census of Housing and Population, Summary Tape File 3C;
Census Bureau Population Estimates 1998

Population Characteristics

Race	City 1980 Population	%	City 1990 Population	%	% Chg. 1980-90	MSA[1] 1990 Population	%
White	558,443	61.8	557,957	55.4	-0.1	1,856,119	72.7
Black	265,105	29.3	297,018	29.5	12.0	410,458	16.1
Amer Indian/Esk/Aleut	3,878	0.4	4,646	0.5	19.8	13,378	0.5
Asian/Pacific Islander	9,163	1.0	21,543	2.1	135.1	66,097	2.6
Other	67,485	7.5	125,667	12.5	86.2	207,310	8.1
Hispanic Origin[2]	111,083	12.3	204,712	20.3	84.3	359,484	14.1

Note: (1) Metropolitan Statistical Area - see Appendix A for areas included;
(2) people of Hispanic origin can be of any race
Source: 1980/1990 Census of Housing and Population, Summary Tape File 3C

Ancestry

Area	German	Irish	English	Italian	U.S.	French	Polish	Dutch
City	12.4	10.4	11.1	1.7	3.7	2.7	1.3	1.4
MSA[1]	18.4	15.5	14.4	2.3	5.7	3.5	1.5	2.2
U.S.	23.3	15.6	13.1	5.9	5.3	4.2	3.8	2.5

Note: Figures are percentages and include persons that reported multiple ancestry (eg. if a person reported being Irish and Italian, they were included in both columns); (1) Metropolitan Statistical Area - see Appendix A for areas included
Source: 1990 Census of Population and Housing, Summary Tape File 3C

Age

Area	Median Age (Years)	Age Distribution (%) Under 5	Under 18	18-24	25-44	45-64	65+	80+
City	30.5	8.0	25.0	11.4	37.6	16.4	9.7	2.2
MSA[1]	30.4	8.4	27.2	10.7	37.7	16.7	7.7	1.7
U.S.	32.9	7.3	25.6	10.5	32.6	18.7	12.5	2.8

Note: (1) Metropolitan Statistical Area - see Appendix A for areas included
Source: 1990 Census of Population and Housing, Summary Tape File 3C

Male/Female Ratio

Area	Number of males per 100 females (all ages)	Number of males per 100 females (18 years old+)
City	97.0	94.5
MSA[1]	97.2	94.5
U.S.	95.0	91.9

Note: (1) Metropolitan Statistical Area - see Appendix A for areas included
Source: 1990 Census of Population, General Population Characteristics

INCOME

Per Capita/Median/Average Income

Area	Per Capita ($)	Median Household ($)	Average Household ($)
City	16,300	27,489	40,299
MSA[1]	16,455	33,277	43,582
U.S.	14,420	30,056	38,453

Note: All figures are for 1989; (1) Metropolitan Statistical Area - see Appendix A for areas included
Source: 1990 Census of Population and Housing, Summary Tape File 3C

Household Income Distribution by Race

Income ($)	City (%)					U.S. (%)				
	Total	White	Black	Other	Hisp.[1]	Total	White	Black	Other	Hisp.[1]
Less than 5,000	7.3	4.1	14.8	8.4	7.4	6.2	4.8	15.2	8.6	8.8
5,000 - 9,999	8.2	6.5	12.5	8.7	9.2	9.3	8.6	14.2	9.9	11.1
10,000 - 14,999	9.2	7.6	12.1	12.2	12.4	8.8	8.5	11.0	9.8	11.0
15,000 - 24,999	20.2	18.4	22.7	25.8	27.1	17.5	17.3	18.9	18.5	20.5
25,000 - 34,999	16.7	16.9	15.4	18.3	18.2	15.8	16.1	14.2	15.4	16.4
35,000 - 49,999	15.7	16.9	12.8	15.8	15.4	17.9	18.6	13.3	16.1	16.0
50,000 - 74,999	11.8	14.2	7.4	7.5	7.7	15.0	15.8	9.3	13.4	11.1
75,000 - 99,999	4.6	6.3	1.6	1.9	1.6	5.1	5.5	2.6	4.7	3.1
100,000+	6.2	9.1	0.7	1.4	1.0	4.4	4.8	1.3	3.7	1.9

Note: All figures are for 1989; (1) people of Hispanic origin can be of any race
Source: 1990 Census of Population and Housing, Summary Tape File 3C

Effective Buying Income

Area	Per Capita ($)	Median Household ($)	Average Household ($)
City	19,949	34,730	50,071
MSA[1]	20,448	41,000	54,713
U.S.	16,803	34,536	45,243

Note: Data as of 1/1/99; (1) Metropolitan Statistical Area - see Appendix A for areas included
Source: Standard Rate & Data Service, Newspaper Advertising Source, 9/99

Effective Household Buying Income Distribution

Area	% of Households Earning						
	$10,000 -$19,999	$20,000 -$34,999	$35,000 -$49,999	$50,000 -$74,999	$75,000 -$99,000	$100,000 -$124,999	$125,000 and up
City	14.8	24.0	17.2	16.3	7.2	3.4	5.6
MSA[1]	12.4	21.0	18.0	21.1	9.9	3.8	4.6
U.S.	16.0	22.6	18.2	18.9	7.2	2.4	2.7

Note: Data as of 1/1/99; (1) Metropolitan Statistical Area - see Appendix A for areas included
Source: Standard Rate & Data Service, Newspaper Advertising Source, 9/99

Poverty Rates by Race and Age

Area	Total (%)	By Race (%)				By Age (%)		
		White	Black	Other	Hisp.[2]	Under 5 years old	Under 18 years old	65 years and over
City	18.0	9.5	29.1	27.2	27.8	27.8	27.3	14.6
MSA[1]	12.0	7.2	26.7	22.7	24.0	17.2	16.2	13.1
U.S.	13.1	9.8	29.5	23.1	25.3	20.1	18.3	12.8

Note: Figures show the percent of people living below the poverty line in 1989. The average poverty threshold was $12,674 for a family of four in 1989; (1) Metropolitan Statistical Area - see Appendix A for areas included; (2) people of Hispanic origin can be of any race
Source: 1990 Census of Population and Housing, Summary Tape File 3C

EMPLOYMENT

Labor Force and Employment

Area	Civilian Labor Force			Workers Employed		
	Jun. 1998	Jun. 1999	% Chg.	Jun. 1998	Jun. 1999	% Chg.
City	671,346	688,777	2.6	637,052	656,954	3.1
MSA[1]	1,896,137	1,948,107	2.7	1,821,731	1,878,643	3.1
U.S.	138,798,000	140,666,000	1.3	132,265,000	134,395,000	1.6

Note: Data is not seasonally adjusted and covers workers 16 years of age and older;
(1) Metropolitan Statistical Area - see Appendix A for areas included
Source: Bureau of Labor Statistics, http://stats.bls.gov

Unemployment Rate

Area	1998						1999					
	Jul.	Aug.	Sep.	Oct.	Nov.	Dec.	Jan.	Feb.	Mar.	Apr.	May.	Jun.
City	4.6	4.4	4.2	3.9	4.0	3.6	4.2	3.9	3.6	3.6	3.9	4.6
MSA[1]	3.5	3.3	3.2	2.9	3.0	2.7	3.2	3.0	2.8	2.8	3.0	3.6
U.S.	4.7	4.5	4.4	4.2	4.1	4.0	4.8	4.7	4.4	4.1	4.0	4.5

Note: Data is not seasonally adjusted and covers workers 16 years of age and older; all figures are percentages; (1) Metropolitan Statistical Area - see Appendix A for areas included
Source: Bureau of Labor Statistics, http://stats.bls.gov

Employment by Industry

Sector	MSA[1]		U.S.
	Number of Employees	Percent of Total	Percent of Total
Services	587,500	30.9	30.4
Retail Trade	307,700	16.2	17.7
Government	202,500	10.7	15.6
Manufacturing	255,300	13.4	14.3
Finance/Insurance/Real Estate	158,000	8.3	5.9
Wholesale Trade	150,000	7.9	5.4
Transportation/Public Utilities	130,200	6.8	5.3
Construction	97,900	5.2	5.0
Mining	11,800	0.6	0.4

Note: Figures cover non-farm employment as of 6/99 and are not seasonally adjusted;
(1) Metropolitan Statistical Area - see Appendix A for areas included
Source: Bureau of Labor Statistics, http://stats.bls.gov

Employment by Occupation

Occupation Category	City (%)	MSA[1] (%)	U.S. (%)
White Collar	62.3	65.3	58.1
Executive/Admin./Management	14.4	15.3	12.3
Professional	13.9	13.9	14.1
Technical & Related Support	3.5	4.2	3.7
Sales	13.1	13.6	11.8
Administrative Support/Clerical	17.3	18.3	16.3
Blue Collar	22.0	21.7	26.2
Precision Production/Craft/Repair	8.4	9.7	11.3
Machine Operators/Assem./Insp.	6.0	5.3	6.8
Transportation/Material Movers	3.4	3.3	4.1
Cleaners/Helpers/Laborers	4.3	3.5	3.9
Services	14.5	11.8	13.2
Farming/Forestry/Fishing	1.2	1.2	2.5

Note: Figures cover employed persons 16 years old and over;
(1) Metropolitan Statistical Area - see Appendix A for areas included
Source: 1990 Census of Population and Housing, Summary Tape File 3C

Occupational Employment Projections: 1996 - 2006

Occupations Expected to Have the Largest Job Growth (ranked by numerical growth)	Fast-Growing Occupations[1] (ranked by percent growth)
1. Cashiers	1. Desktop publishers
2. Salespersons, retail	2. Systems analysts
3. General managers & top executives	3. Customer service representatives
4. Truck drivers, light	4. Physical therapy assistants and aides
5. Child care workers, private household	5. Computer engineers
6. General office clerks	6. Emergency medical technicians
7. Systems analysts	7. Medical assistants
8. Food preparation workers	8. Respiratory therapists
9. Food service workers	9. Telephone & cable TV line install & repair
10. Registered nurses	10. Physical therapists

Note: Projections cover Texas; (1) Excludes occupations with total job growth less than 300
Source: U.S. Department of Labor, Employment and Training Administration, America's Labor Market
Information System (ALMIS)

TAXES

Major State and Local Tax Rates

State Corp. Income (%)	State Personal Income (%)	Residential Property (effective rate per $100)	Sales & Use		State Gasoline (cents/ gallon)	State Cigarette (cents/ pack)
			State (%)	Local (%)		
None[a]	None	n/a	6.25	2.0	20.0	41.0

Note: Personal/corporate income, sales, gasoline and cigarette tax rates as of January 1999.
Property tax rates as of 1997; (a) Texas imposes a franchise tax of 4.5% of earned surplus
Source: Federation of Tax Administrators, www.taxadmin.org; Washington D.C. Department of
Finance and Revenue, Tax Rates and Tax Burdens in the District of Columbia: A Nationwide
Comparison, July 1998; Chamber of Commerce, 1999

Total Taxes Per Capita and as a Percent of Income

Area	Per Capita Income ($)	Per Capita Taxes ($)			Percent of Income (%)		
		Total	Federal	State/ Local	Total	Federal	State/ Local
Texas	25,563	8,741	6,051	2,690	34.2	23.7	10.5
U.S.	27,876	9,881	6,690	3,191	35.4	24.0	11.4

Note: Figures are for 1998
Source: Tax Foundation, www.taxfoundation.org

COMMERCIAL REAL ESTATE

Office Market

Class/ Location	Total Space (sq. ft.)	Vacant Space (sq. ft.)	Vac. Rate (%)	Under Constr. (sq. ft.)	Net Absorp. (sq. ft.)	Rental Rates ($/sq.ft./yr.)
Class A						
CBD	18,352,751	2,937,697	16.0	0	764,681	16.50-29.50
Outside CBD	54,837,829	5,162,762	9.4	7,971,849	1,279,690	13.00-37.50
Class B						
CBD	6,350,195	2,805,478	44.2	0	-48,200	10.00-21.50
Outside CBD	55,323,239	6,722,910	12.2	4,198,930	5,010,480	7.00-29.50

Note: Data as of 10/98 and covers Dallas; CBD = Central Business District; n/a not available;
Source: Society of Industrial and Office Realtors, 1999 Comparative Statistics of Industrial and Office
Real Estate Markets

"Record prices were paid for Dallas office buildings in 1998, including a high of $155 per sq. ft. in the CBD and $157 per sq. ft. in the suburbs. Since REITs have tended to pay the highest prices for office product and their activity has been curtailed, 1999 sales prices could decrease by 11 to 15 percent. Although Dallas' diversified economy should remain strong in 1999, global economic woes and a potential scarcity of workers could moderate its growth somewhat. The huge amount of new construction will also cause vacancy to rise, and landlords of existing space will be forced to make more concessions to attract tenants. Service industries, which expanded by 32,400 employees last year, will continue to lead Metroplex growth in 1999." *Society of Industrial and Office Realtors, 1999 Comparative Statistics of Industrial and Office Real Estate Markets*

Industrial Market

Location	Total Space (sq. ft.)	Vacant Space (sq. ft.)	Vac. Rate (%)	Under Constr. (sq. ft.)	Net Absorp. (sq. ft.)	Lease ($/sq.ft./yr.)
Central City	n/a	n/a	n/a	n/a	n/a	n/a
Suburban	296,000,000	23,680,000	8.0	9,500,000	14,220,000	3.15-4.50

Note: Data as of 10/98 and covers Dallas; n/a not available
Source: Society of Industrial and Office Realtors, 1999 Comparative Statistics of Industrial and Office Real Estate Markets

"Approximately 101,000 jobs were created in Dallas/Fort Worth during 1998, and the economy of the Metroplex remains among the nation's strongest. Even though there has also been a substantial increase in vacancy over the past year, the absorption of space should continue at a steady rate during 1999. The biggest market constraint could be the lack of available funds for new development. Insurance companies and commercial banks will be supplying most of the money for new development, and they have not forgotten the overbuilding of the late 1980s. Speculative construction will probably slow in 1999, even though site prices are expected to drop and 10 million sq. ft. are still on the drawing board. SIOR's reporters also anticipate a one to five percent drop in the dollar volume of sales and leases during 1999. Otherwise, 1998 market conditions should prevail." *Society of Industrial and Office Realtors, 1999 Comparative Statistics of Industrial and Office Real Estate Markets*

Retail Market

Shopping Center Inventory (sq. ft.)	Shopping Center Construction (sq. ft.)	Construction as a Percent of Inventory (%)	Torto Wheaton Rent Index[1] ($/sq. ft.)
57,368,000	1,180,000	2.1	14.41

Note: Data as of 1997 and covers the Metropolitan Statistical Area - see Appendix A for areas included; (1) Index is based on a model that predicts what the average rent should be for leases with certain characteristics, in certain locations during certain years.
Source: National Association of Realtors, 1997-1998 Market Conditions Report

"The Dallas retail market has improved since 1994, with the retail rent index climbing 39%. The area's economy expanded at a 3.8% pace last year, pouring nearly 60,000 jobs into the MSA. Much of this strong growth is centered in areas north of Dallas. Two new shopping malls are proposed for North Dallas including the 1.2 million square foot Stonebriar Mall at the intersection of the Dallas North Tollway and State Highway 121 (opening spring 1999), and a high-end fashion mall by Taubman Centers Inc. Competition is fierce among the area's malls, and the additions may doom any struggling retail centers in North Dallas." *National Association of Realtors, 1997-1998 Market Conditions Report*

COMMERCIAL UTILITIES

Typical Monthly Electric Bills

Area	Commercial Service ($/month)		Industrial Service ($/month)	
	12 kW demand 1,500 kWh	100 kW demand 30,000 kWh	1,000 kW demand 400,000 kWh	20,000 kW demand 10,000,000 kWh
City	151	2,142	23,072	383,469
U.S.	150	2,174	23,995	508,569

Note: Based on rates in effect January 1, 1999
Source: Edison Electric Institute, Typical Residential, Commercial and Industrial Bills, Winter 1999

TRANSPORTATION

Transportation Statistics

Average minutes to work	24.0
Interstate highways	I-20; I-30; I-35E; I-45
Bus lines	
In-city	Dallas Area Rapid Transit, 1,021 vehicles
Inter-city	4
Passenger air service	
Airport	Dallas/Ft. Worth International; Love Field
Airlines	31
Aircraft departures	421,977 (1996)
Enplaned passengers	30,162,820 (1996)
Rail service	Amtrak; Dallas Area Rapid Transit (light rail)
Motor freight carriers	120
Major waterways/ports	None

Source: Editor & Publisher Market Guide, 1999; FAA Airport Activity Statistics, 1997; Amtrak National Time Table, Northeast Timetable, Spring/Summer 1999; 1990 Census of Population and Housing, STF 3C; Chamber of Commerce/Economic Development 1999; Jane's Urban Transport Systems 1999-2000

Means of Transportation to Work

Area	Car/Truck/Van		Public Transportation			Bicycle	Walked	Other Means	Worked at Home
	Drove Alone	Car-pooled	Bus	Subway	Railroad				
City	72.5	15.2	6.4	0.0	0.0	0.2	2.4	1.2	2.2
MSA[1]	77.6	14.0	3.1	0.0	0.0	0.1	1.9	1.0	2.3
U.S.	73.2	13.4	3.0	1.5	0.5	0.4	3.9	1.2	3.0

Note: Figures shown are percentages and only include workers 16 years old and over;
(1) Metropolitan Statistical Area - see Appendix A for areas included
Source: 1990 Census of Population and Housing, Summary Tape File 3C

BUSINESSES

Major Business Headquarters

Company Name	1999 Rankings	
	Fortune 500	Forbes 500
Austin Industries	-	366
Beck Group	-	456
Ben E Keith	-	339
Centex	385	-
Central & South West	299	-
Club Corporation International	-	261
CompUSA	307	-
Glazer's Wholesale Distributors	-	311
Halliburton	85	-
Hunt Consolidated/Hunt Oil	-	329
Lincoln Property	-	151
Marcus Cable	-	489
Mary Kay	-	171
Perot Systems	-	288
Sammons Enterprises	-	104
Southern Foods Group	-	309
Southwest Airlines	371	-
Suiza Foods	443	-
Texas Instruments	191	-
Texas Utilities	105	-
Union Pacific	154	-

Note: Companies listed are located in the city; dashes indicate no ranking
Fortune 500: Companies that produce a 10-K are ranked 1 to 500 based on 1998 revenue
Forbes 500: Private companies are ranked 1 to 500 based on 1997 revenue
Source: Forbes, November 30, 1998; Fortune, April 26, 1999

Best Companies to Work For

TD Industries (plumbing and A/C contracting) and Southwest Airlines, headquartered in Dallas, are among the "100 Best Companies to Work for in America." Criteria: trust in management, pride in work/company, camaraderie, company responses to the Hewitt People Practices Inventory, and employee responses to their Great Place to Work survey. The companies also had to be at least 10 years old and have a minimum of 500 employees. *Fortune, January 11, 1999*

Texas Instruments, headquartered in Dallas, is among the "100 Best Companies for Working Mothers." Criteria: fair wages, opportunities for women to advance, support for child care, flexible work schedules, family-friendly benefits, and work/life supports. *Working Mother, October 1998*

Texas Instruments (computers/electronics), headquartered in Dallas, is among the "100 Best Places to Work in IS." Criteria: compensation, turnover and training. *Computerworld, May 25, 1998*

Fast-Growing Businesses

According to *Inc.*, Dallas is home to four of America's 100 fastest-growing private companies: CapRock Communications, Inteq Group, TXCC and ObjectSpace. Criteria for inclusion: must be an independent, privately-held, U.S. corporation, proprietorship or partnership; sales of at least $200,000 in 1995; five-year operating/sales history; increase in 1999 sales over 1998 sales; holding companies, regulated banks, and utilities were excluded. *Inc. 500, 1999*

Dallas is home to one of *Business Week's* "hot growth" companies: Centex Construction Products. Criteria: increase in sales and profits, return on capital and stock price. *Business Week, 5/31/99*

According to *Fortune*, Dallas is home to one of America's 100 fastest-growing companies: FYI. Companies were ranked based on earnings-per-share growth, revenue growth and total return over the previous three years. Criteria for inclusion: public companies with sales of least $50 million. Companies that lost money in the most recent quarter, or ended in the red for the past four quarters as a whole, were not eligible. Limited partnerships and REITs were also not considered. Fortune, "America's Fastest-Growing Companies," 1999

Women-Owned Firms: Number, Employment and Sales

Area	Number of Firms	Employ-ment	Sales ($000)	Rank[2]
MSA[1]	123,900	431,900	63,114,900	8

Note: (1) Metropolitan Statistical Area - see Appendix A for areas included;
(2) Calculated on an averaging of the number of businesses, employment and sales
Source: The National Foundation for Women Business Owners, 1999 Facts on Women-Owned Businesses: Trends in the Top 50 Metropolitan Areas

Women-Owned Firms: Growth

Area	% change from 1992 to 1999			Rank[2]
	Number of Firms	Employ-ment	Sales	
MSA[1]	40.9	180.0	192.6	8

Note: (1) Metropolitan Statistical Area - see Appendix A for areas included; (2) Calculated on an averaging of the percent growth of number of businesses, employment and sales
Source: The National Foundation for Women Business Owners, 1999 Facts on Women-Owned Businesses: Trends in the Top 50 Metropolitan Areas

Minority Business Opportunity

Dallas is home to one company which is on the Black Enterprise Industrial/Service 100 list (largest based on gross sales): Pro-Line Corp. (hair care products mfg. and distrib.) . Criteria: operational in previous calendar year, at least 51% black-owned and manufactures/owns the product it sells or provides industrial or consumer services. Brokerages, real estate firms and firms that provide professional services are not eligible. *Black Enterprise, www.blackenterprise.com*

Dallas is home to two companies which are on the Black Enterprise Auto Dealer 100 list (largest based on gross sales): Village Auto Plaza Inc. (Ford); Davis Automotive Inc. (GMC, Honda, Hyundai, Buick, Oldsmobile) . Criteria: 1) operational in previous calendar year; 2) at least 51% black-owned. *Black Enterprise, www.blackenterprise.com*

Four of the 500 largest Hispanic-owned companies in the U.S. are located in Dallas. *Hispanic Business, June 1999*

Small Business Opportunity

According to *Forbes*, Dallas is home to five of America's 200 best small companies: EW Blanch Holdings, Centex Construction Products, FYI, Silverleaf Resorts and Southwest Securities Group. Criteria: companies included must be publicly traded since November 1997 with a stock price of at least $5 per share and an average daily float of 1,000 shares. The company's latest 12-month sales must be between $5 and $350 million, return on equity (ROE) must be a minimum of 12% for both the past 5 years and the most recent four quarters, and five-year sales and EPS growth must average at least 10%. Companies with declining sales or earnings during the past year were dropped as well as businesses with debt/equity ratios over 1.25. Companies with negative operating cash flow in each of the past two years were also excluded. *Forbes, November 2, 1998*

HOTELS & MOTELS

Hotels/Motels

Area	Hotels/ Motels	Rooms	Luxury-Level Hotels/Motels		Average Minimum Rates ($)		
			♦♦♦♦	♦♦♦♦♦	♦♦	♦♦♦	♦♦♦♦
City	101	20,953	4	3	81	129	174
Airport	61	11,119	2	0	n/a	n/a	n/a
Suburbs	68	7,581	0	0	n/a	n/a	n/a
Total	230	39,653	6	3	n/a	n/a	n/a

Note: n/a not available; classifications range from one diamond (budget properties with basic amenities) to five diamond (luxury properties with the finest service, rooms and facilities). Source: OAG, Business Travel Planner, Winter 1998-99

Dallas is home to one of the top 100 hotels in the world according to *Travel & Leisure*: Mansion on Turtle Creek (#24) . Criteria: value, rooms/ambience, location, facilities/activities and service. *Travel & Leisure, 1998 World's Best Awards, Best Hotels and Resorts*

CONVENTION CENTERS

Major Convention Centers

Center Name	Meeting Rooms	Exhibit Space (sq. ft.)
Dallas Apparel Mart	3	1,000,000
Dallas Convention Center	105	807,000
Dallas Market Center	318	313,000
Fair Park	n/a	747,180
Fairmont Hotel of Dallas	24	n/a
Infomart	30	300,000

Note: n/a not available
Source: Trade Shows Worldwide, 1998; Meetings & Conventions, 4/15/99; Sucessful Meetings, 3/31/98

Living Environment

COST OF LIVING

Cost of Living Index

Composite Index	Groceries	Housing	Utilities	Trans-portation	Health Care	Misc. Goods/ Services
100.4	98.5	95.2	101.8	105.1	109.6	102.5

Note: U.S. = 100; Figures are for the Metropolitan Statistical Area - see Appendix A for areas included
Source: ACCRA, Cost of Living Index, 1st Quarter 1999

HOUSING

Median Home Prices and Housing Affordability

Area	Median Price[2] 1st Qtr. 1999 ($)	HOI[3] 1st Qtr. 1999	Afford-ability Rank[4]
MSA[1]	135,000	68.5	125
U.S.	134,000	69.6	–

Note: (1) Metropolitan Statistical Area - see Appendix A for areas included; (2) U.S. figures calculated from the sales of 524,324 new and existing homes in 181 markets; (3) Housing Opportunity Index - percent of homes sold that were within the reach of the median income household at the prevailing mortgage interest rate; (4) Rank is from 1-181 with 1 being most affordable
Source: National Association of Home Builders, Housing Opportunity Index, 1st Quarter 1999

Median Home Price Projection

It is projected that the median price of existing single-family homes in the metro area will increase by 5.0% in 1999. Nationwide, home prices are projected to increase 3.8%.
Kiplinger's Personal Finance Magazine, January 1999

Average New Home Price

Area	Price ($)
MSA[1]	125,580
U.S.	142,735

Note: Figures are based on a new home with 1,800 sq. ft. of living area on an 8,000 sq. ft. lot;
(1) Metropolitan Statistical Area - see Appendix A for areas included
Source: ACCRA, Cost of Living Index, 1st Quarter 1999

Average Apartment Rent

Area	Rent ($/mth)
MSA[1]	799
U.S.	601

Note: Figures are based on an unfurnished two bedroom, 1-1/2 or 2 bath apartment, approximately 950 sq. ft. in size, excluding all utilities except water; (1) Metropolitan Statistical Area - see Appendix A for areas included
Source: ACCRA, Cost of Living Index, 1st Quarter 1999

RESIDENTIAL UTILITIES

Average Residential Utility Costs

Area	All Electric ($/mth)	Part Electric ($/mth)	Other Energy ($/mth)	Phone ($/mth)
MSA[1]	–	75.66	28.38	16.33
U.S.	100.02	55.73	43.33	19.71

Note: (1) (1) Metropolitan Statistical Area - see Appendix A for areas included
Source: ACCRA, Cost of Living Index, 1st Quarter 1999

HEALTH CARE

Average Health Care Costs

Area	Hospital ($/day)	Doctor ($/visit)	Dentist ($/visit)
MSA[1]	503.00	52.50	76.91
U.S.	430.43	52.45	66.35

Note: Hospital—based on a semi-private room; Doctor—based on a general practitioner's routine exam of an established patient; Dentist—based on adult teeth cleaning and periodic oral exam; (1) Metropolitan Statistical Area - see Appendix A for areas included
Source: ACCRA, Cost of Living Index, 1st Quarter 1999

Distribution of Office-Based Physicians

Area	Family/Gen. Practitioners	Specialists		
		Medical	Surgical	Other
MSA[1]	514	1,545	1,402	1,461

Note: Data as of 12/31/97; (1) Metropolitan Statistical Area - see Appendix A for areas included
Source: American Medical Assn., Physician Characteristics & Distribution in the U.S., 1999

Hospitals

Dallas has 1 general medical and surgical hospital, 2 psychiatric, 3 rehabilitation, 1 other specialty, 2 children's general, 1 children's orthopedic. *AHA Guide to the Healthcare Field, 1998-99*

According to *U.S. News and World Report,* Dallas has 3 of the best hospitals in the U.S.: **Baylor University Medical Center**, noted for cancer, endocrinology, gastroenterology, geriatrics, gynecology, neurology, orthopedics, otolaryngology, pulmonology, rheumatology, urology; **Parkland Memorial Hospital**, noted for rheumatology; **Methodist Medical Center**, noted for endocrinology, urology. *U.S. News Online, "America's Best Hospitals," 10th Edition, www.usnews.com*

EDUCATION

Public School District Statistics

District Name	Num. Sch.	Enroll.	Classroom Teachers	Pupils per Teacher	Minority Pupils (%)	Current Exp.[1] ($/pupil)
Dallas Can Academy Charter	1	565	24	23.5	n/a	n/a
Dallas ISD	220	157,622	9,413	16.7	89.8	5,146
Highland Park ISD	7	5,695	418	13.6	n/a	n/a
Pegasus Charter School	1	106	5	21.2	n/a	n/a
Wilmer-Hutchins ISD	7	3,495	185	18.9	n/a	n/a

Note: Data covers the 1997-1998 school year unless otherwise noted; (1) Data covers fiscal year 1996; SD = School District; ISD = Independent School District; n/a not available
Source: National Center for Education Statistics, Common Core of Data Public Education Agency Universe 1997-98; National Center for Education Statistics, Characteristics of the 100 Largest Public Elementary and Secondary School Districts in the United States: 1997-98, July 1999

Educational Quality

School District	Education Quotient[1]	Graduate Outcome[2]	Community Index[3]	Resource Index[4]
Dallas ISD	62.0	55.0	109.0	66.0

Note: Nearly 1,000 secondary school districts were rated in terms of educational quality. The scores range from a low of 50 to a high of 150; (1) Average of the Graduate Outcome, Community and Resource indexes; (2) Based on graduation rates and college board scores (SAT/ACT); (3) Based on the surrounding community's average level of education and the area's average income level; (4) Based on teacher salaries, per-pupil expenditures and student-teacher ratios.
Source: Expansion Management, Ratings Issue, 1998

Educational Attainment by Race

Area	High School Graduate (%)					Bachelor's Degree (%)				
	Total	White	Black	Other	Hisp.[2]	Total	White	Black	Other	Hisp.[2]
City	73.5	82.5	67.2	38.6	33.9	27.1	36.9	10.9	10.9	7.0
MSA[1]	79.0	84.1	70.1	50.0	41.7	27.6	31.5	13.5	16.5	8.9
U.S.	75.2	77.9	63.1	60.4	49.8	20.3	21.5	11.4	19.4	9.2

Note: Figures shown cover persons 25 years old and over; (1) Metropolitan Statistical Area - see Appendix A for areas included; (2) people of Hispanic origin can be of any race
Source: 1990 Census of Population and Housing, Summary Tape File 3C

School Enrollment by Type

Area	Preprimary				Elementary/High School			
	Public		Private		Public		Private	
	Enrollment	%	Enrollment	%	Enrollment	%	Enrollment	%
City	8,029	52.2	7,349	47.8	147,967	90.2	16,105	9.8
MSA[1]	24,235	49.1	25,151	50.9	413,238	92.3	34,313	7.7
U.S.	2,679,029	59.5	1,824,256	40.5	38,379,689	90.2	4,187,099	9.8

Note: Figures shown cover persons 3 years old and over;
(1) Metropolitan Statistical Area - see Appendix A for areas included
Source: 1990 Census of Population and Housing, Summary Tape File 3C

School Enrollment by Race

Area	Preprimary (%)				Elementary/High School (%)			
	White	Black	Other	Hisp.[1]	White	Black	Other	Hisp.[1]
City	56.1	31.5	12.4	16.8	38.2	39.7	22.2	30.3
MSA[2]	76.1	15.8	8.2	10.6	64.7	20.3	15.0	19.3
U.S.	80.4	12.5	7.1	7.8	74.1	15.6	10.3	12.5

Note: Figures shown cover persons 3 years old and over; (1) people of Hispanic origin can be of any race; (2) Metropolitan Statistical Area - see Appendix A for areas included
Source: 1990 Census of Population and Housing, Summary Tape File 3C

Classroom Teacher Salaries in Public Schools

District	B.A. Degree		M.A. Degree		Maximum	
	Min. ($)	Rank[1]	Max. ($)	Rank[1]	Max. ($)	Rank[1]
Dallas	27,000	40	46,808	38	47,920	67
Average	26,980	-	46,065	-	51,435	-

Note: Salaries are for 1997-1998; (1) Rank ranges from 1 to 100
Source: American Federation of Teachers, Survey & Analysis of Salary Trends, 1998

Higher Education

Two-Year Colleges		Four-Year Colleges		Medical Schools	Law Schools	Voc/ Tech
Public	Private	Public	Private			
5	4	1	6	1	1	23

Source: College Blue Book, Occupational Education, 1997; Medical School Admission Requirements, 1999-2000; Peterson's Guide to Two-Year Colleges, 1999; Peterson's Guide to Four-Year Colleges, 2000; Barron's Guide to Law Schools, 1999

MAJOR EMPLOYERS

Major Employers

Baylor University Medical Center	Dallas County Hospital District
PSC Energy Corp.	International Brotherhood of Electrical Workers
Nationsbank of Texas	Presbyterian Hospital of Dallas
Southwest Airlines	Perot Systems Corp.
Texas Instruments	Centex Homes

Note: Companies listed are located in the city
Source: Dun's Business Rankings, 1999; Ward's Business Directory, 1998

PUBLIC SAFETY

Crime Rate

Area	All Crimes	Violent Crimes				Property Crimes		
		Murder	Forcible Rape	Robbery	Aggrav. Assault	Burglary	Larceny -Theft	Motor Vehicle Theft
City	9,335.8	19.4	69.0	522.0	773.4	1,647.3	4,693.3	1,611.4
Suburbs[1]	4,384.4	3.3	29.9	65.8	236.9	801.7	2,911.7	335.1
MSA[2]	6,188.3	9.2	44.1	232.0	432.4	1,109.8	3,560.8	800.1
U.S.	4,922.7	6.8	35.9	186.1	382.0	919.6	2,886.5	505.8

Note: Crime rate is the number of crimes per 100,000 pop.; (1) defined as all areas within the MSA but located outside the central city; (2) Metropolitan Statistical Area - see Appendix A for areas incl.
Source: FBI Uniform Crime Reports, 1997

RECREATION

Culture and Recreation

Museums	Symphony Orchestras	Opera Companies	Dance Companies	Professional Theatres	Zoos	Pro Sports Teams
12	2	2	3	10	1	3

Source: International Directory of the Performing Arts, 1997; Official Museum Directory, 1999; Stern's Performing Arts Directory, 1997; USA Today Four Sport Stadium Guide, 1997; Chamber of Commerce/Economic Development, 1999

Library System

The Dallas Public Library has 22 branches, holdings of 2,552,832 volumes, and a budget of $16,827,753 (1996-1997). *American Library Directory, 1998-1999*

MEDIA

Newspapers

Name	Type	Freq.	Distribution	Circulation
The Dallas Morning News	General	7x/wk	Regional	521,162
Novedades News	Hispanic	2x/wk	Local	32,000
Texas Catholic	Religious	2x/mo	Local	45,200
United Methodist Reporter	Religious	1x/wk	U.S./Int'l.	400,000

Note: Includes newspapers with circulations of 25,000 or more located in the city;
Source: Burrelle's Media Directory, 1999 Edition

Television Stations

Name	Ch.	Affiliation	Type	Owner
KDTN	n/a	PBS	Public	North Texas Public Broadcasting Inc.
KDFW	n/a	FBC	Commercial	Fox Television Stations Inc.
WFAA	n/a	ABCT	Commercial	A.H. Belo Corporation
KERA	13	PBS	Public	North Texas Public Broadcasting Inc.
KTXA	21	UPN	Commercial	Paramount Communications Inc.
KUVN	23	UNIN	Commercial	Perenchio Television Inc.
KDFI	27	n/a	Commercial	Dallas Media Investors
KDAF	33	WB	Commercial	Tribune Broadcasting Company
KXTX	39	n/a	Commercial	LIN Television
KHSX	49	n/a	Commercial	n/a
KFWD	52	TMUN	Commercial	Interspan Communications Ltd.
KDTX	58	n/a	Non-comm.	Trinity Broadcasting Network
KPXD	68	n/a	n/a	Paxson Communications Corporation

Note: Stations included broadcast in the Dallas metro area; n/a not available
Source: Burrelle's Media Directory, 1999 Edition

AM Radio Stations

Call Letters	Freq. (kHz)	Target Audience	Station Format	Music Format
KLIF	570	Men	S/T	n/a
KSKY	660	H/R	M/S/T	Christian
KKDA	730	Black	M	R&B
KPBC	770	Religious	E/M/T	n/a
KHVN	970	Black	M	Christian
KGGR	1040	B/R	M/N/S	Christian/Gospel
KRLD	1080	General	N/S/T	n/a
KDMM	1150	General	N	n/a
KESS	1270	Hispanic	E/M/N/S/T	Latin
KTCK	1310	General	S/T	n/a
KGVL	1400	General	M/N/S	Country/Oldies
KDXX	1480	Hispanic	M/N/T	Latin
KEGG	1560	Religious	M/N/T	Christian
KRVA	1600	Hispanic	M/N/S	Adult Contemporary

Note: Stations included broadcast in the Dallas metro area; n/a not available
Target Audience: A=Asian; B=Black; C=Christian; E=Ethnic; F=French; G=General; H=Hispanic; M=Men; N=Native American; R=Religious; S=Senior Citizen; W=Women; Y=Young Adult; Z=Children
Station Format: E=Educational; M=Music; N=News; S=Sports; T=Talk
Source: Burrelle's Media Directory, 1999 Edition

FM Radio Stations

Call Letters	Freq. (mHz)	Target Audience	Station Format	Music Format
KEOM	88.5	General	E/M/N/S	Oldies
KNON	89.3	Z/G	M/T	n/a
KERA	90.1	B/C	E/M/N/T	Alternative
KCBI	90.9	G/R	M/N/S	Christian
KVTT	91.7	General	E/M/T	Christian
KZPS	92.5	General	M/N/S/T	Classic Rock
KKZN	93.3	General	M/N	Alternative
KIKT	93.5	General	M	Country
KLTY	94.1	General	M	Christian
KDGE	94.5	Young Adult	M/N/T	Alternative
KEGL	97.1	General	M/T	Classic Rock
KBFB	97.9	General	M/N/T	Adult Contemporary
KLUV	98.7	General	M/N/T	Oldies
KHCK	99.1	G/H	M	Latin
KPLX	99.5	General	M	Country
KRBV	100.3	Black	M/N/T	R&B
WRR	101.1	General	M/N/T	Classical
KTXQ	102.1	General	M/N/T	Adult Contemporary/Classic Rock
KDMX	102.9	Women	M/N/T	Adult Contemporary
KVIL	103.7	General	M	Adult Contemporary
KKDA	104.5	Black	M	Urban Contemporary
KTCY	104.9	Religious	M/N/T	Christian
KYNG	105.3	General	M	Country
KRNB	105.7	General	M/N/S	R&B
KHKS	106.1	General	M/N/T	Top 40
KMRT	106.7	G/H	n/a	n/a
KZDF	106.9	Hispanic	M/N/S	Latin
KZDL	107.1	Hispanic	M/N/S	Latin
KOAI	107.5	General	M/N/T	Adult Contemporary/Jazz/R&B
KICI	107.9	Hispanic	M/N/S/T	Latin

Note: Stations included broadcast in the Dallas metro area; n/a not available
Station Format: E=Educational; M=Music; N=News; S=Sports; T=Talk
Target Audience: A=Asian; B=Black; C=Christian; E=Ethnic; F=French; G=General; H=Hispanic; M=Men; N=Native American; R=Religious; S=Senior Citizen; W=Women; Y=Young Adult; Z=Children
Source: Burrelle's Media Directory, 1999 Edition

CLIMATE

Average and Extreme Temperatures

Temperature	Jan	Feb	Mar	Apr	May	Jun	Jul	Aug	Sep	Oct	Nov	Dec	Yr.
Extreme High (°F)	85	90	100	100	101	112	111	109	107	101	91	87	112
Average High (°F)	55	60	68	76	84	92	96	96	89	79	67	58	77
Average Temp. (°F)	45	50	57	66	74	82	86	86	79	68	56	48	67
Average Low (°F)	35	39	47	56	64	72	76	75	68	57	46	38	56
Extreme Low (°F)	-2	9	12	30	39	53	58	58	42	24	16	0	-2

Note: Figures cover the years 1945-1993
Source: National Climatic Data Center, International Station Meteorological Climate Summary, 3/95

Average Precipitation/Snowfall/Humidity

Precip./Humidity	Jan	Feb	Mar	Apr	May	Jun	Jul	Aug	Sep	Oct	Nov	Dec	Yr.
Avg. Precip. (in.)	1.9	2.3	2.6	3.8	4.9	3.4	2.1	2.3	2.9	3.3	2.3	2.1	33.9
Avg. Snowfall (in.)	1	1	Tr	Tr	0	0	0	0	0	Tr	Tr	Tr	3
Avg. Rel. Hum. 6am (%)	78	77	75	77	82	81	77	76	80	79	78	77	78
Avg. Rel. Hum. 3pm (%)	53	51	47	49	51	48	43	41	46	46	48	51	48

Note: Figures cover the years 1945-1993; Tr = Trace amounts (<0.05 in. of rain; <0.5 in. of snow)
Source: National Climatic Data Center, International Station Meteorological Climate Summary, 3/95

Weather Conditions

Temperature			Daytime Sky			Precipitation		
10°F & below	32°F & below	90°F & above	Clear	Partly cloudy	Cloudy	0.01 inch or more precip.	0.1 inch or more snow/ice	Thunder-storms
1	34	102	108	160	97	78	2	49

Note: Figures are average number of days per year and covers the years 1945-1993
Source: National Climatic Data Center, International Station Meteorological Climate Summary, 3/95

AIR & WATER QUALITY

Maximum Pollutant Concentrations

	Particulate Matter (ug/m³)	Carbon Monoxide (ppm)	Sulfur Dioxide (ppm)	Nitrogen Dioxide (ppm)	Ozone (ppm)	Lead (ug/m³)
MSA[1] Level	104	5	0.022	0.018	0.14	0.04
NAAQS[2]	150	9	0.140	0.053	0.12	1.50
Met NAAQS?	Yes	Yes	Yes	Yes	No	Yes

Note: (1) Metropolitan Statistical Area - see Appendix A for areas included; (2) National Ambient Air Quality Standards; ppm = parts per million; ug/m³ = micrograms per cubic meter; n/a not available
Source: EPA, National Air Quality and Emissions Trends Report, 1997

Pollutant Standards Index

In the Dallas MSA (see Appendix A for areas included), the Pollutant Standards Index (PSI) exceeded 100 on 32 days in 1997. A PSI value greater than 100 indicates that air quality would be in the unhealthful range on that day. *EPA, National Air Quality and Emissions Trends Report, 1997*

Drinking Water

Water System Name	Pop. Served	Primary Water Source Type	Number of Violations in 1998	Type of Violation/ Contaminants
Dallas Water Utility	1,003,150	Surface	None	None

Note: Data as of July 10, 1999
Source: EPA, Office of Ground Water and Drinking Water, Safe Drinking Water Information System

Dallas tap water is moderately hard and fluoridated.
Editor & Publisher Market Guide, 1999

Fort Lauderdale, Florida

Background

Located on the Atlantic Ocean in southeast Florida, Fort Lauderdale is a city of tiny residential islands, canals, and yacht basins, and is called the "Venice of America."

Originally built as a fortification in 1837 for the Seminole War, Fort Lauderdale eased into more peaceful times as a top tourist spot. Photos of students on Spring Break, cars cruising "The Strip," and tan young men and women on the beach stimulated the imagination of people around the world.

Today, Fort Lauderdale remains a popular tourist spot, and is host to many attractions: Fashionable Las Olas Boulevard, the main artery of downtown, is full of shops and restaurants and a quaint street on which to stroll; the Museum of Art is a handsome modern edifice that showcases 19th and 20th century paintings and Japanese objects d'art, and is noted as having the largest U.S. collection of artwork from Copenhagen, Brussels, and Amsterdam; the Museum of Discovery and Science includes the Blockbuster IMAX Theater, compliments of the multi-corporation mogul Wayne Huizenga, and is fascinating to children of all ages; and the Broward Center for Performing Arts hosts Broadway plays and other major cultural events.

As home to one of the biggest yacht basins in the country, Fort Lauderdale's second largest industry is boating products. And, because of its largely residential character, the home improvement industry—concrete, air-conditioning, and roofing—lays a large claim to the economy as well.

Fort Lauderdale's climate is primarily subtropical marine which produces a long, warm summer with abundant rainfall, followed by a mild, dry winter. Hurricanes occasionally affect the area, with most occurring in September and October. Funnel clouds and waterspouts are occasionally sighted during the summer months but neither cause significant damage. Strong, and sometimes spectacular, lightening events occur most often during June, July, and August.

General Rankings and Evaluative Comments

■ Fort Lauderdale was ranked #8 out of 19 large, southern metropolitan areas in *Money's* 1998 survey of "The Best Places to Live in America." The survey was conducted by first contacting 512 representative households nationwide and asking them to rank 37 quality-of-life factors on a scale of 1 to 10. Next, a demographic profile was compiled on the 300 largest metropolitan statistical areas in the U.S. The numbers were crunched together to arrive at an overall ranking (things Americans consider most important, like clean air and water, low crime and good schools, received extra weight). Unlike previous years, the 1998 rankings were broken down by region (northeast, midwest, south, west) and population size (100,000 to 249,999; 250,000 to 999,999; 1 million plus). The city had a nationwide ranking of #15 out of 300 in 1997 and #4 out of 300 in 1996. *Money, July 1998; Money, July 1997; Money, September 1996*

■ *Ladies Home Journal* ranked America's 200 largest cities based on the qualities women care about most. Fort Lauderdale ranked #151 out of 200. Criteria: low crime rate, well-paying jobs, quality health and child care, good public schools, the presence of women in government, size of the gender wage gap, number of sexual-harassment and discrimination complaints filed, unemployment and divorce rates, commute times, population density, number of houses of worship, parks and cultural offerings, number of women's health specialists, how well a community's women cared for themselves, complexion kindness index based on UV radiation levels, odds of finding affordable fashions, rental rates for romance movies, champagne sales and other matters of the heart. *Ladies Home Journal, Nov. 1998*

■ Zero Population Growth ranked 229 cities in terms of children's health, safety, and economic well-being. Fort Lauderdale was ranked #82 out of 92 suburbs and outer cities (incorporated areas of more than 100,000 within the MSA of a major city) and was given a grade of D. Criteria: total population, percent of population under 18 years of age, household language, percent population change, percent of births to teens, infant mortality rate, percent of low birth weights, dropout rate, enrollment in preprimary school, violent and property crime rates, unemployment rate, percent of children in poverty, percent of owner occupied units, number of bad air days, percent of public transportation commuters, and average travel time to work. *Zero Population Growth, Children's Environmental Index, Fall 1999*

■ Fort Lauderdale was ranked #8 out of 59 metro areas in *The Regional Economist's* "Rational Livability Ranking of 59 Large Metro Areas." The rankings were based on the metro area's total population change over the period 1990-97 divided by the number of people moving in from elsewhere in the United States (net domestic in-migration). *St. Louis Federal Reserve Bank of St. Louis, The Regional Economist, April 1999*

■ Cognetics studied 273 metro areas in the United States, ranking them by entrepreneurial activity. Fort Lauderdale was ranked #25 out of the 50 largest metro areas. Criteria: Significant Starts (firms started in the last 10 years that still employ at least 5 people) and Young Growers (percent of firms 10 years old or less that grew significantly during the last 4 years). *Cognetics, "Entrepreneurial Hot Spots: The Best Places in America to Start and Grow a Company," 1998*

■ Fort Lauderdale was included among *Entrepreneur* magazine's listing of the "20 Best Cities for Small Business." It was ranked #15 among large metro areas. Criteria: entrepreneurial activity, small-business growth, economic growth, and risk of failure. *Entrepreneur, Oct. 1999*

■ Reliastar Financial Corp. ranked the 125 largest metropolitan areas according to the general financial security of residents. Fort Lauderdale was ranked #91 (tie) out of 125 with a score of -3.1. The score indicates the percentage a metropolitan area is above or below the metropolitan norm. A metro area with a score of 10.6 is 10.6% above the metro average. Criteria: Earnings and Wealth Potential (household income, education, net assets, cost of living); Safety Net (health insurance, retirement savings, life insurance, income support programs); Personal Threats (unemployment rate, low-income households, crime rate); Community Economic Vitality (cost of community services, job quality, job creation, housing costs). *Reliastar Financial Corp., "The Best Cities to Earn and Save Money," 1999 Edition*

Business Environment

STATE ECONOMY

State Economic Profile

"Florida's economy has been among the nation's strongest in recent years. Job growth has outpaced the nation by a considerable amount since 1992.

While Florida has been able to avoid any significant fallout from the Asian crisis, the weakening of economies in Latin American will dampen both tourism and international trade. 1998 saw the decline in Latin tourism more than offset by domestic visitors. Domestic tourism is projected to soften as US growth cools in 1999, offering no offset against the expected decline in Latin tourism. Weaker tourism and trade with Latin American will slow growth in 1999; FL will still outpace the nation in job growth as Gross State Product growth (GSP) slows.

Over half of FL's 230,000 new jobs created in 1998 were in the services sector, which grew at 5.2%, more than offsetting a minor decline in manufacturing employment. Much of this growth is taking place in the finance and business services sector.

In spite of strong home sales and a slowing construction market, FL's price appreciation continued to lag the nation. Although residential permits per 1,000 residents stands at 5.1, well above the national average, this number is only slightly up from 1997 and will decline in 1999.

Growth in FL, while strong throughout, has been hottest in the Naples, Ft. Myers and Orlando areas. Construction and employment in the construction industry has begun to slow in South Florida. Projected employment and housing gains will be concentrated in Northern and Central Florida during 1999. Growing diversification of the economy into financial and business services promises a strong outlook for the years ahead." *National Association of Realtors, Economic Profiles: The Fifty States and the District of Columbia, http://nar.realtor.com/databank/profiles.htm*

IMPORTS/EXPORTS

Total Export Sales

Area	1994 ($000)	1995 ($000)	1996 ($000)	1997 ($000)	% Chg. 1994-97	% Chg. 1996-97
MSA[1]	1,506,662	1,774,654	1,864,518	2,143,001	42.2	14.9
U.S.	512,415,609	583,030,524	622,827,063	687,597,999	34.2	10.4

Note: (1) Metropolitan Statistical Area - see Appendix A for areas included
Source: U.S. Department of Commerce, International Trade Association, Metropolitan Area Exports: An Export Performance Report on Over 250 U.S. Cities, November 10, 1998

CITY FINANCES

City Government Finances

Component	FY92 ($000)	FY92 (per capita $)
Revenue	271,657	1,805.02
Expenditure	247,353	1,643.53
Debt Outstanding	110,999	737.53
Cash & Securities	381,498	2,534.85

Source: U.S. Bureau of the Census, City Government Finances: 1991-92

City Government Revenue by Source

Source	FY92 ($000)	FY92 (per capita $)	FY92 (%)
From Federal Government	9,475	62.96	3.5
From State Governments	22,201	147.51	8.2
From Local Governments	5,701	37.88	2.1
Property Taxes	44,418	295.13	16.4
General Sales Taxes	0	0.00	0.0
Selective Sales Taxes	32,808	217.99	12.1
Income Taxes	0	0.00	0.0
Current Charges	28,945	192.32	10.7
Utility/Liquor Store	39,592	263.07	14.6
Employee Retirement[1]	53,282	354.03	19.6
Other	35,235	234.12	13.0

Note: (1) Excludes "city contributions," classified as "nonrevenue," intragovernmental transfers.
Source: U.S. Bureau of the Census, City Government Finances: 1991-92

City Government Expenditures by Function

Function	FY92 ($000)	FY92 (per capita $)	FY92 (%)
Educational Services	0	0.00	0.0
Employee Retirement[1]	12,945	86.01	5.2
Environment/Housing	77,621	515.75	31.4
Government Administration	11,453	76.10	4.6
Interest on General Debt	5,915	39.30	2.4
Public Safety	62,686	416.52	25.3
Social Services	0	0.00	0.0
Transportation	22,076	146.68	8.9
Utility/Liquor Store	41,059	272.82	16.6
Other	13,598	90.35	5.5

Note: (1) Payments to beneficiaries including withdrawal of contributions.
Source: U.S. Bureau of the Census, City Government Finances: 1991-92

Municipal Bond Ratings

Area	Moody's	S & P
Fort Lauderdale	Aa3	n/a

Note: n/a not available; n/r not rated
Source: Moody's Bond Record, 6/99

POPULATION

Population Growth

Area	1980	1990	% Chg. 1980-90	July 1998 Estimate	% Chg. 1990-98
City	153,279	149,377	-2.5	153,728	2.9
MSA[1]	1,018,200	1,255,488	23.3	1,499,128	19.4
U.S.	226,545,805	248,765,170	9.8	270,299,000	8.7

Note: (1) Metropolitan Statistical Area - see Appendix A for areas included;
July 1998 MSA population estimate was calculated by the editors
Source: 1980/1990 Census of Housing and Population, Summary Tape File 3C;
Census Bureau Population Estimates 1998

Population Characteristics

Race	City 1980 Population	%	City 1990 Population	%	% Chg. 1980-90	MSA[1] 1990 Population	%
White	119,327	77.8	104,015	69.6	-12.8	1,027,465	81.8
Black	32,222	21.0	41,997	28.1	30.3	193,360	15.4
Amer Indian/Esk/Aleut	246	0.2	383	0.3	55.7	2,907	0.2
Asian/Pacific Islander	685	0.4	1,125	0.8	64.2	16,499	1.3
Other	799	0.5	1,857	1.2	132.4	15,257	1.2
Hispanic Origin[2]	6,402	4.2	10,574	7.1	65.2	105,668	8.4

Note: (1) Metropolitan Statistical Area - see Appendix A for areas included;
(2) people of Hispanic origin can be of any race
Source: 1980/1990 Census of Housing and Population, Summary Tape File 3C

Ancestry

Area	German	Irish	English	Italian	U.S.	French	Polish	Dutch
City	16.5	13.1	12.8	7.6	3.3	3.9	3.3	1.7
MSA[1]	16.3	13.4	10.1	11.2	4.1	3.4	5.8	1.4
U.S.	23.3	15.6	13.1	5.9	5.3	4.2	3.8	2.5

Note: Figures are percentages and include persons that reported multiple ancestry (eg. if a person reported being Irish and Italian, they were included in both columns); (1) Metropolitan Statistical Area - see Appendix A for areas included
Source: 1990 Census of Population and Housing, Summary Tape File 3C

Age

Area	Median Age (Years)	Under 5	Under 18	18-24	25-44	45-64	65+	80+
City	37.1	6.0	18.8	8.1	34.8	20.4	17.9	5.0
MSA[1]	37.6	6.2	20.4	8.0	32.0	18.9	20.7	5.1
U.S.	32.9	7.3	25.6	10.5	32.6	18.7	12.5	2.8

Note: (1) Metropolitan Statistical Area - see Appendix A for areas included
Source: 1990 Census of Population and Housing, Summary Tape File 3C

Male/Female Ratio

Area	Number of males per 100 females (all ages)	Number of males per 100 females (18 years old+)
City	100.9	101.6
MSA[1]	91.7	88.8
U.S.	95.0	91.9

Note: (1) Metropolitan Statistical Area - see Appendix A for areas included
Source: 1990 Census of Population, General Population Characteristics

INCOME

Per Capita/Median/Average Income

Area	Per Capita ($)	Median Household ($)	Average Household ($)
City	19,814	27,239	43,756
MSA[1]	16,883	30,571	39,823
U.S.	14,420	30,056	38,453

Note: All figures are for 1989; (1) Metropolitan Statistical Area - see Appendix A for areas included
Source: 1990 Census of Population and Housing, Summary Tape File 3C

Household Income Distribution by Race

Income ($)	City (%)					U.S. (%)				
	Total	White	Black	Other	Hisp.[1]	Total	White	Black	Other	Hisp.[1]
Less than 5,000	7.5	5.1	17.7	10.6	10.2	6.2	4.8	15.2	8.6	8.8
5,000 - 9,999	8.9	7.3	15.4	9.2	8.3	9.3	8.6	14.2	9.9	11.1
10,000 - 14,999	9.7	8.8	13.1	12.5	11.2	8.8	8.5	11.0	9.8	11.0
15,000 - 24,999	19.9	18.6	25.2	22.4	22.3	17.5	17.3	18.9	18.5	20.5
25,000 - 34,999	14.9	15.4	13.0	11.2	16.2	15.8	16.1	14.2	15.4	16.4
35,000 - 49,999	14.7	15.8	10.1	18.5	17.1	17.9	18.6	13.3	16.1	16.0
50,000 - 74,999	12.7	14.8	4.0	7.3	7.8	15.0	15.8	9.3	13.4	11.1
75,000 - 99,999	4.6	5.5	1.1	4.0	2.5	5.1	5.5	2.6	4.7	3.1
100,000+	7.1	8.7	0.4	4.2	4.5	4.4	4.8	1.3	3.7	1.9

Note: All figures are for 1989; (1) people of Hispanic origin can be of any race
Source: 1990 Census of Population and Housing, Summary Tape File 3C

Effective Buying Income

Area	Per Capita ($)	Median Household ($)	Average Household ($)
City	21,311	29,969	47,958
MSA[1]	19,008	33,637	45,067
U.S.	16,803	34,536	45,243

Note: Data as of 1/1/99; (1) Metropolitan Statistical Area - see Appendix A for areas included
Source: Standard Rate & Data Service, Newspaper Advertising Source, 9/99

Effective Household Buying Income Distribution

Area	% of Households Earning						
	$10,000 -$19,999	$20,000 -$34,999	$35,000 -$49,999	$50,000 -$74,999	$75,000 -$99,000	$100,000 -$124,999	$125,000 and up
City	17.8	24.1	15.3	14.9	5.9	2.7	5.1
MSA[1]	16.8	23.7	17.9	18.1	6.8	2.4	2.9
U.S.	16.0	22.6	18.2	18.9	7.2	2.4	2.7

Note: Data as of 1/1/99; (1) Metropolitan Statistical Area - see Appendix A for areas included
Source: Standard Rate & Data Service, Newspaper Advertising Source, 9/99

Poverty Rates by Race and Age

Area	Total (%)	By Race (%)				By Age (%)		
		White	Black	Other	Hisp.[2]	Under 5 years old	Under 18 years old	65 years and over
City	17.1	8.8	38.1	17.3	21.0	33.2	31.0	10.8
MSA[1]	10.2	7.0	26.8	13.2	13.7	15.5	15.0	9.0
U.S.	13.1	9.8	29.5	23.1	25.3	20.1	18.3	12.8

Note: Figures show the percent of people living below the poverty line in 1989. The average poverty threshold was $12,674 for a family of four in 1989; (1) Metropolitan Statistical Area - see Appendix A for areas included; (2) people of Hispanic origin can be of any race
Source: 1990 Census of Population and Housing, Summary Tape File 3C

EMPLOYMENT

Labor Force and Employment

Area	Civilian Labor Force			Workers Employed		
	Jun. 1998	Jun. 1999	% Chg.	Jun. 1998	Jun. 1999	% Chg.
City	93,747	95,911	2.3	88,170	90,732	2.9
MSA[1]	763,483	782,027	2.4	727,176	748,309	2.9
U.S.	138,798,000	140,666,000	1.3	132,265,000	134,395,000	1.6

Note: Data is not seasonally adjusted and covers workers 16 years of age and older; (1) Metropolitan Statistical Area - see Appendix A for areas included
Source: Bureau of Labor Statistics, http://stats.bls.gov

Unemployment Rate

Area	1998						1999					
	Jul.	Aug.	Sep.	Oct.	Nov.	Dec.	Jan.	Feb.	Mar.	Apr.	May.	Jun.
City	5.4	5.3	5.5	5.5	5.6	5.2	6.1	5.5	5.4	5.7	5.6	5.4
MSA[1]	4.3	4.3	4.4	4.4	4.5	4.1	4.9	4.4	4.3	4.6	4.5	4.3
U.S.	4.7	4.5	4.4	4.2	4.1	4.0	4.8	4.7	4.4	4.1	4.0	4.5

Note: Data is not seasonally adjusted and covers workers 16 years of age and older; all figures are percentages; (1) Metropolitan Statistical Area - see Appendix A for areas included
Source: Bureau of Labor Statistics, http://stats.bls.gov

Employment by Industry

Sector	MSA[1]		U.S.
	Number of Employees	Percent of Total	Percent of Total
Services	232,900	35.2	30.4
Retail Trade	143,600	21.7	17.7
Government	86,800	13.1	15.6
Manufacturing	39,400	5.9	14.3
Finance/Insurance/Real Estate	50,200	7.6	5.9
Wholesale Trade	42,200	6.4	5.4
Transportation/Public Utilities	30,800	4.6	5.3
Construction	36,500	5.5	5.0
Mining	100	<0.1	0.4

Note: Figures cover non-farm employment as of 6/99 and are not seasonally adjusted;
(1) Metropolitan Statistical Area - see Appendix A for areas included
Source: Bureau of Labor Statistics, http://stats.bls.gov

Employment by Occupation

Occupation Category	City (%)	MSA[1] (%)	U.S. (%)
White Collar	57.8	62.4	58.1
Executive/Admin./Management	13.5	14.0	12.3
Professional	12.3	12.2	14.1
Technical & Related Support	2.9	3.7	3.7
Sales	14.9	15.5	11.8
Administrative Support/Clerical	14.1	17.0	16.3
Blue Collar	21.3	21.2	26.2
Precision Production/Craft/Repair	10.1	11.7	11.3
Machine Operators/Assem./Insp.	3.6	3.1	6.8
Transportation/Material Movers	3.9	3.1	4.1
Cleaners/Helpers/Laborers	3.7	3.2	3.9
Services	19.2	14.8	13.2
Farming/Forestry/Fishing	1.7	1.6	2.5

Note: Figures cover employed persons 16 years old and over;
(1) Metropolitan Statistical Area - see Appendix A for areas included
Source: 1990 Census of Population and Housing, Summary Tape File 3C

Occupational Employment Projections: 1996 - 2006

Occupations Expected to Have the Largest Job Growth (ranked by numerical growth)	Fast-Growing Occupations[1] (ranked by percent growth)
1. Cashiers	1. Systems analysts
2. Salespersons, retail	2. Physical therapy assistants and aides
3. General managers & top executives	3. Desktop publishers
4. Registered nurses	4. Home health aides
5. Waiters & waitresses	5. Computer engineers
6. Marketing & sales, supervisors	6. Medical assistants
7. Janitors/cleaners/maids, ex. priv. hshld.	7. Physical therapists
8. General office clerks	8. Paralegals
9. Food preparation workers	9. Emergency medical technicians
10. Hand packers & packagers	10. Occupational therapists

Note: Projections cover Florida; (1) Excludes occupations with total job growth less than 300
Source: U.S. Department of Labor, Employment and Training Administration, America's Labor Market Information System (ALMIS)

TAXES

Major State and Local Tax Rates

State Corp. Income (%)	State Personal Income (%)	Residential Property (effective rate per $100)	Sales & Use State (%)	Sales & Use Local (%)	State Gasoline (cents/ gallon)	State Cigarette (cents/ pack)
5.5[a]	None	n/a	6.0	None	13.1[b]	33.9

Note: Personal/corporate income, sales, gasoline and cigarette tax rates as of January 1999.
Property tax rates as of 1997; (a) 3.3% Alternative Minimum Tax. An exemption of $5,000 is allowed;
(b) Rate is comprised of 4 cents excise and 9.1 cents motor carrier tax
Source: Federation of Tax Administrators, www.taxadmin.org; Washington D.C. Department of Finance and Revenue, Tax Rates and Tax Burdens in the District of Columbia: A Nationwide Comparison, July 1998; Chamber of Commerce, 1999

Total Taxes Per Capita and as a Percent of Income

Area	Per Capita Income ($)	Per Capita Taxes ($) Total	Federal	State/ Local	Percent of Income (%) Total	Federal	State/ Local
Florida	27,655	9,768	6,824	2,944	35.3	24.7	10.6
U.S.	27,876	9,881	6,690	3,191	35.4	24.0	11.4

Note: Figures are for 1998
Source: Tax Foundation, www.taxfoundation.org

COMMERCIAL REAL ESTATE

Office Market

Class/ Location	Total Space (sq. ft.)	Vacant Space (sq. ft.)	Vac. Rate (%)	Under Constr. (sq. ft.)	Net Absorp. (sq. ft.)	Rental Rates ($/sq.ft./yr.)
Class A						
CBD	1,589,427	70,568	4.4	238,753	n/a	24.00-33.98
Outside CBD	3,234,444	315,293	9.7	739,176	294,162	17.00-26.25
Class B						
CBD	1,499,904	208,781	13.9	0	249,307	13.50-32.00
Outside CBD	8,969,352	1,001,405	11.2	280,094	675,480	10.00-24.42

Note: Data as of 10/98 and covers Ft. Lauderdale/Broward County; CBD = Central Business District; n/a not available;
Source: Society of Industrial and Office Realtors, 1999 Comparative Statistics of Industrial and Office Real Estate Markets

"New development will continue to concentrate toward West Broward. This development will be cautious. Priority on construction will be given to pre-leased and build-to-suit space. The need for quality space and the availability of financing will continue to strengthen Florida's markets. As new development comes to market within the next few years, vacancy rates will increase. However, over 1999 vacancy rates are still expected to decrease by up to five percent. According to our SIOR reporter, absorption is expected to increase slightly while construction is expected to increase between six and 10 percent. Rental rates are expected to remain level over the next year. Sales prices for Class A properties will be stable while sales prices for Class B properties will decrease slightly." *Society of Industrial and Office Realtors, 1999 Comparative Statistics of Industrial and Office Real Estate Markets*

Industrial Market

Location	Total Space (sq. ft.)	Vacant Space (sq. ft.)	Vac. Rate (%)	Under Constr. (sq. ft.)	Net Absorp. (sq. ft.)	Net Lease ($/sq.ft./yr.)
Central City	48,300,000	1,932,000	4.0	1,000,000	1,000,000	4.00-5.25
Suburban	20,000,000	800,000	4.0	500,000	500,000	4.00-5.75

Note: Data as of 10/98 and covers Fort Lauderdale/Broward County; n/a not available
Source: Society of Industrial and Office Realtors, 1999 Comparative Statistics of Industrial and Office Real Estate Markets

"Demand for build-to-suit space is high, and shortages exists in all size categories. Sales prices for all categories are expected to increase by up to ten percent. This is also true of lease prices and site prices. Absorption of all types of space is also anticipated to increase by six to 10 percent. This will be matched with an equal percentage change in absorption. The demand for space will be partially met with the ample supply of inventory already in the planning or construction phases. There is currently more than six million sq. ft. planned. Most of the space that will be constructed in 1999 will be pre-leased and within the 50,000 to 60,000 sq. ft. size range. Some of the area's large companies will downsize which will have some mild impact on the market." Society of Industrial and Office Realtors, 1999 Comparative Statistics of Industrial and Office Real Estate Markets

Retail Market

Shopping Center Inventory (sq. ft.)	Shopping Center Construction (sq. ft.)	Construction as a Percent of Inventory (%)	Torto Wheaton Rent Index[1] ($/sq. ft.)
42,661,000	862,000	2.0	13.88

Note: Data as of 1997 and covers the Metropolitan Statistical Area - see Appendix A for areas included; (1) Index is based on a model that predicts what the average rent should be for leases with certain characteristics, in certain locations during certain years.
Source: National Association of Realtors, 1997-1998 Market Conditions Report

"Fort Lauderdale's retail market is on the rise, as higher rates of absorption from a year ago helped the retail rent index jump 12.7% in 1997. The opening of the 290,000 square foot Pembroke Crossing shopping center contributed to the increase in demand. Considerable shopping center space was filled with entertainment-oriented and nontraditional tenants. Seven new shopping centers are currently under construction in Broward County, which should add an estimated 900,000 square feet of retail space by the spring of next year. The retail rent index is expected to increase another 9.0% in 1998." *National Association of Realtors, 1997-1998 Market Conditions Report*

COMMERCIAL UTILITIES ## Typical Monthly Electric Bills

Area	Commercial Service ($/month)		Industrial Service ($/month)	
	12 kW demand 1,500 kWh	100 kW demand 30,000 kWh	1,000 kW demand 400,000 kWh	20,000 kW demand 10,000,000 kWh
City	118	1,993	23,247	387,510
U.S.	150	2,174	23,995	508,569

Note: Based on rates in effect January 1, 1999
Source: Edison Electric Institute, Typical Residential, Commercial and Industrial Bills, Winter 1999

TRANSPORTATION

Transportation Statistics

Average minutes to work	20.6
Interstate highways	I-95
Bus lines	
In-city	Broward County Transit System
Inter-city	3
Passenger air service	
Airport	Ft. Lauderdale-Hollywood International Airport
Airlines	24
Aircraft departures	49,502 (1996)
Enplaned passengers	4,847,608 (1996)
Rail service	Amtrak; Tri-Rail
Motor freight carriers	33
Major waterways/ports	Intracoastal Waterway; Port Everglades

Source: Editor & Publisher Market Guide, 1999; FAA Airport Activity Statistics, 1997; Amtrak National Time Table, Northeast Timetable, Spring/Summer 1999; 1990 Census of Population and Housing, STF 3C; Chamber of Commerce/Economic Development 1999; Jane's Urban Transport Systems 1999-2000

Means of Transportation to Work

Area	Car/Truck/Van		Public Transportation			Bicycle	Walked	Other Means	Worked at Home
	Drove Alone	Car-pooled	Bus	Subway	Railroad				
City	73.6	13.3	4.4	0.0	0.2	1.1	3.3	1.6	2.6
MSA[1]	79.7	12.8	1.8	0.0	0.1	0.7	1.8	1.2	1.9
U.S.	73.2	13.4	3.0	1.5	0.5	0.4	3.9	1.2	3.0

Note: Figures shown are percentages and only include workers 16 years old and over; (1) Metropolitan Statistical Area - see Appendix A for areas included
Source: 1990 Census of Population and Housing, Summary Tape File 3C

BUSINESSES

Major Business Headquarters

Company Name	1999 Rankings	
	Fortune 500	Forbes 500
Ed Morse Automotive Group	-	86
Republic Industries	83	-

Note: Companies listed are located in the city; dashes indicate no ranking
Fortune 500: Companies that produce a 10-K are ranked 1 to 500 based on 1998 revenue
Forbes 500: Private companies are ranked 1 to 500 based on 1997 revenue
Source: Forbes, November 30, 1998; Fortune, April 26, 1999

Fast-Growing Businesses

Fort Lauderdale is home to one of *Business Week's* "hot growth" companies: Citrix Systems. Criteria: increase in sales and profits, return on capital and stock price. *Business Week, 5/31/99*

According to *Fortune*, Fort Lauderdale is home to three of America's 100 fastest-growing companies: Citrix Systems, Extended Stay America and AutoNation. Companies were ranked based on earnings-per-share growth, revenue growth and total return over the previous three years. Criteria for inclusion: public companies with sales of least $50 million. Companies that lost money in the most recent quarter, or ended in the red for the past four quarters as a whole, were not eligible. Limited partnerships and REITs were also not considered. *Fortune, "America's Fastest-Growing Companies," 1999*

Women-Owned Firms: Number, Employment and Sales

Area	Number of Firms	Employment	Sales ($000)	Rank[2]
MSA[1]	67,300	189,100	31,679,700	26

Note: (1) Metropolitan Statistical Area - see Appendix A for areas included;
(2) Calculated on an averaging of the number of businesses, employment and sales
Source: The National Foundation for Women Business Owners, 1999 Facts on Women-Owned Businesses: Trends in the Top 50 Metropolitan Areas

Women-Owned Firms: Growth

Area	% change from 1992 to 1999			Rank[2]
	Number of Firms	Employment	Sales	
MSA[1]	52.8	107.5	165.3	14

Note: (1) Metropolitan Statistical Area - see Appendix A for areas included; (2) Calculated on an averaging of the percent growth of number of businesses, employment and sales
Source: The National Foundation for Women Business Owners, 1999 Facts on Women-Owned Businesses: Trends in the Top 50 Metropolitan Areas

Small Business Opportunity

According to *Forbes*, Fort Lauderdale is home to one of America's 200 best small companies: Pediatrix Medical Group. Criteria: companies included must be publicly traded since November 1997 with a stock price of at least $5 per share and an average daily float of 1,000 shares. The company's latest 12-month sales must be between $5 and $350 million, return on equity (ROE) must be a minimum of 12% for both the past 5 years and the most recent four quarters, and five-year sales and EPS growth must average at least 10%. Companies with declining sales or earnings during the past year were dropped as well as businesses with debt/equity ratios over 1.25. Companies with negative operating cash flow in each of the past two years were also excluded. *Forbes, November 2, 1998*

HOTELS & MOTELS

Hotels/Motels

Area	Hotels/ Motels	Rooms	Luxury-Level Hotels/Motels		Average Minimum Rates ($)		
			♦♦♦♦	♦♦♦♦♦	♦♦	♦♦♦	♦♦♦♦
City	53	9,504	2	0	85	128	174
Airport	18	2,984	0	0	n/a	n/a	n/a
Suburbs	61	6,219	0	0	n/a	n/a	n/a
Total	132	18,707	2	0	n/a	n/a	n/a

Note: n/a not available; classifications range from one diamond (budget properties with basic amenities) to five diamond (luxury properties with the finest service, rooms and facilities).
Source: OAG, Business Travel Planner, Winter 1998-99

CONVENTION CENTERS

Major Convention Centers

Center Name	Meeting Rooms	Exhibit Space (sq. ft.)
Bonaventure Resort & Spa	25	83,000
Broward County Convention Center	28	300,000
The Inverrary Golf Resort & Conference Center	15	14,000
War Memorial Auditorium (Fort Lauderdale)	1	20,000

Source: Trade Shows Worldwide, 1998; Meetings & Conventions, 4/15/99; Sucessful Meetings, 3/31/98

Living Environment

COST OF LIVING

Cost of Living Index

Composite Index	Groceries	Housing	Utilities	Trans-portation	Health Care	Misc. Goods/ Services
107.7	104.2	112.0	109.0	99.8	111.8	107.3

Note: U.S. = 100; Figures are for the Metropolitan Statistical Area - see Appendix A for areas included
Source: ACCRA, Cost of Living Index, 4th Quarter 1998

HOUSING

Median Home Prices and Housing Affordability

Area	Median Price[2] 1st Qtr. 1999 ($)	HOI[3] 1st Qtr. 1999	Afford-ability Rank[4]
MSA[1]	113,000	79.2	63
U.S.	134,000	69.6	–

Note: (1) Metropolitan Statistical Area - see Appendix A for areas included; (2) U.S. figures calculated from the sales of 524,324 new and existing homes in 181 markets; (3) Housing Opportunity Index - percent of homes sold that were within the reach of the median income household at the prevailing mortgage interest rate; (4) Rank is from 1-181 with 1 being most affordable
Source: National Association of Home Builders, Housing Opportunity Index, 1st Quarter 1999

Median Home Price Projection

It is projected that the median price of existing single-family homes in the metro area will increase by 4.5% in 1999. Nationwide, home prices are projected to increase 3.8%.
Kiplinger's Personal Finance Magazine, January 1999

Average New Home Price

Area	Price ($)
MSA[1]	149,400
U.S.	141,438

Note: Figures are based on a new home with 1,800 sq. ft. of living area on an 8,000 sq. ft. lot; (1) Metropolitan Statistical Area - see Appendix A for areas included
Source: ACCRA, Cost of Living Index, 4th Quarter 1998

Average Apartment Rent

Area	Rent ($/mth)
MSA[1]	921
U.S.	593

Note: Figures are based on an unfurnished two bedroom, 1-1/2 or 2 bath apartment, approximately 950 sq. ft. in size, excluding all utilities except water; (1) Metropolitan Statistical Area - see Appendix A for areas included
Source: ACCRA, Cost of Living Index, 4th Quarter 1998

RESIDENTIAL UTILITIES

Average Residential Utility Costs

Area	All Electric ($/mth)	Part Electric ($/mth)	Other Energy ($/mth)	Phone ($/mth)
MSA[1]	112.24	–	–	17.22
U.S.	101.64	55.45	43.56	19.81

Note: (1) (1) Metropolitan Statistical Area - see Appendix A for areas included
Source: ACCRA, Cost of Living Index, 4th Quarter 1998

HEALTH CARE

Average Health Care Costs

Area	Hospital ($/day)	Doctor ($/visit)	Dentist ($/visit)
MSA[1]	405.00	60.00	73.40
U.S.	417.46	51.94	64.89

Note: Hospital—based on a semi-private room; Doctor—based on a general practitioner's routine exam of an established patient; Dentist—based on adult teeth cleaning and periodic oral exam; (1) Metropolitan Statistical Area - see Appendix A for areas included
Source: ACCRA, Cost of Living Index, 4th Quarter 1998

Distribution of Office-Based Physicians

Area	Family/Gen. Practitioners	Specialists Medical	Surgical	Other
MSA[1]	245	1,116	703	632

Note: Data as of 12/31/97; (1) Metropolitan Statistical Area - see Appendix A for areas included
Source: American Medical Assn., Physician Characteristics & Distribution in the U.S., 1999

Hospitals

Fort Lauderdale has 7 general medical and surgical hospitals, 2 psychiatric, 1 rehabilitation.
AHA Guide to the Healthcare Field, 1998-99

EDUCATION

Public School District Statistics

District Name	Num. Sch.	Enroll.	Classroom Teachers	Pupils per Teacher	Minority Pupils (%)	Current Exp.[1] ($/pupil)
Broward County Sch Dist	197	224,799	10,765	20.9	54.0	5,178

Note: Data covers the 1997-1998 school year unless otherwise noted; (1) Data covers fiscal year 1996; SD = School District; ISD = Independent School District; n/a not available
Source: National Center for Education Statistics, Common Core of Data Public Education Agency Universe 1997-98; National Center for Education Statistics, Characteristics of the 100 Largest Public Elementary and Secondary School Districts in the United States: 1997-98, July 1999

Educational Quality

School District	Education Quotient[1]	Graduate Outcome[2]	Community Index[3]	Resource Index[4]
Broward County	103.0	97.0	84.0	118.0

Note: Nearly 1,000 secondary school districts were rated in terms of educational quality. The scores range from a low of 50 to a high of 150; (1) Average of the Graduate Outcome, Community and Resource indexes; (2) Based on graduation rates and college board scores (SAT/ACT); (3) Based on the surrounding community's average level of education and the area's average income level; (4) Based on teacher salaries, per-pupil expenditures and student-teacher ratios.
Source: Expansion Management, Ratings Issue, 1998

Educational Attainment by Race

Area	High School Graduate (%) Total	White	Black	Other	Hisp.[2]	Bachelor's Degree (%) Total	White	Black	Other	Hisp.[2]
City	74.2	83.1	41.6	68.0	61.3	21.9	26.5	4.7	21.2	14.6
MSA[1]	76.8	79.9	55.5	71.5	68.2	18.8	19.9	10.1	21.4	15.7
U.S.	75.2	77.9	63.1	60.4	49.8	20.3	21.5	11.4	19.4	9.2

Note: Figures shown cover persons 25 years old and over; (1) Metropolitan Statistical Area - see Appendix A for areas included; (2) people of Hispanic origin can be of any race
Source: 1990 Census of Population and Housing, Summary Tape File 3C

School Enrollment by Type

Area	Preprimary Public Enrollment	%	Preprimary Private Enrollment	%	Elementary/High School Public Enrollment	%	Elementary/High School Private Enrollment	%
City	946	46.1	1,108	53.9	15,660	84.4	2,903	15.6
MSA[1]	9,740	43.6	12,606	56.4	146,453	87.1	21,625	12.9
U.S.	2,679,029	59.5	1,824,256	40.5	38,379,689	90.2	4,187,099	9.8

Note: Figures shown cover persons 3 years old and over;
(1) Metropolitan Statistical Area - see Appendix A for areas included
Source: 1990 Census of Population and Housing, Summary Tape File 3C

School Enrollment by Race

Area	Preprimary (%) White	Black	Other	Hisp.[1]	Elementary/High School (%) White	Black	Other	Hisp.[1]
City	59.2	39.5	1.3	3.0	41.2	55.4	3.4	8.8
MSA[2]	77.7	19.9	2.4	7.8	67.7	28.3	4.0	11.4
U.S.	80.4	12.5	7.1	7.8	74.1	15.6	10.3	12.5

Note: Figures shown cover persons 3 years old and over; (1) people of Hispanic origin can be of any
race; (2) Metropolitan Statistical Area - see Appendix A for areas included
Source: 1990 Census of Population and Housing, Summary Tape File 3C

Classroom Teacher Salaries in Public Schools

District	B.A. Degree Min. ($)	Rank[1]	M.A. Degree Max. ($)	Rank[1]	Maximum Max. ($)	Rank[1]
	n/a	n/a	n/a	n/a	n/a	n/a
Average	26,980	-	46,065	-	51,435	-

Note: Salaries are for 1997-1998; (1) Rank ranges from 1 to 100; n/a not available
Source: American Federation of Teachers, Survey & Analysis of Salary Trends, 1998

Higher Education

Two-Year Colleges Public	Private	Four-Year Colleges Public	Private	Medical Schools	Law Schools	Voc/ Tech
1	3	0	3	0	1	10

Source: College Blue Book, Occupational Education, 1997; Medical School Admission Requirements,
1999-2000; Peterson's Guide to Two-Year Colleges, 1999; Peterson's Guide to Four-Year Colleges,
2000; Barron's Guide to Law Schools, 1999

MAJOR EMPLOYERS

Major Employers

Beneficial Payroll Services
Columbia Hospital Corp. of S. Broward
Vacation Break USA
Holy Cross Hospital
University Hospital

Vacation Break Management
Hospital Development & Service Corp.
Florida Medical Center
All Around Travel Club
Kemper National Services (health services)

Note: Companies listed are located in the city
Source: Dun's Business Rankings, 1999; Ward's Business Directory, 1998

PUBLIC SAFETY

Crime Rate

Area	All Crimes	Violent Crimes Murder	Forcible Rape	Robbery	Aggrav. Assault	Property Crimes Burglary	Larceny -Theft	Motor Vehicle Theft
City	12,084.3	9.9	58.5	760.7	635.6	2,297.9	6,236.6	2,085.1
Suburbs[1]	6,655.5	3.9	31.6	225.4	431.2	1,253.7	3,885.5	824.2
MSA[2]	7,294.7	4.6	34.8	288.4	455.2	1,376.6	4,162.4	972.7
U.S.	4,922.7	6.8	35.9	186.1	382.0	919.6	2,886.5	505.8

Note: Crime rate is the number of crimes per 100,000 pop.; (1) defined as all areas within the MSA but
located outside the central city; (2) Metropolitan Statistical Area - see Appendix A for areas incl.
Source: FBI Uniform Crime Reports, 1997

RECREATION

Culture and Recreation

Museums	Symphony Orchestras	Opera Companies	Dance Companies	Professional Theatres	Zoos	Pro Sports Teams
6	1	1	0	1	0	0

Source: International Directory of the Performing Arts, 1997; Official Museum Directory, 1999; Stern's Performing Arts Directory, 1997; USA Today Four Sport Stadium Guide, 1997; Chamber of Commerce/Economic Development, 1999

Library System

The Broward County Library has 29 branches, holdings of 2,044,766 volumes, and a budget of $28,291,900 (1996-1997). *American Library Directory, 1998-1999*

MEDIA

Newspapers

Name	Type	Freq.	Distribution	Circulation
Jewish Journal Palm Beach South	Religious	1x/wk	Area	808,000
Sun-Sentinel	General	7x/wk	Area	272,258
Westside Gazette	Black	1x/wk	Area	35,000

Note: Includes newspapers with circulations of 500 or more located in the city;
Source: Burrelle's Media Directory, 1999 Edition

Television Stations

Name	Ch.	Affiliation	Type	Owner
WBZL	39	WB	Commercial	Tribune Broadcasting Company
WHFT	45	n/a	Non-comm.	Trinity Broadcasting Network

Note: Stations included broadcast in the Fort Lauderdale metro area; n/a not available
Source: Burrelle's Media Directory, 1999 Edition

AM Radio Stations

Call Letters	Freq. (kHz)	Target Audience	Station Format	Music Format
WQAM	560	G/M	S	n/a
WAVS	1170	Black	E/M/N/S/T	Christian/R&B/Urban Contemporary
WEXY	1520	G/R	M	n/a
WSRF	1580	General	M/N/S/T	Adult Standards/Big Band/Classic Rock/Classical/ Jazz/Oldies/Reggae/R&B/Top 40/Urban Contemp.

Note: Stations included broadcast in the Fort Lauderdale metro area; n/a not available
Target Audience: A=Asian; B=Black; C=Christian; E=Ethnic; F=French; G=General; H=Hispanic; M=Men; N=Native American; R=Religious; S=Senior Citizen; W=Women; Y=Young Adult; Z=Children
Station Format: E=Educational; M=Music; N=News; S=Sports; T=Talk
Source: Burrelle's Media Directory, 1999 Edition

FM Radio Stations

Call Letters	Freq. (mHz)	Target Audience	Station Format	Music Format
WKPX	88.5	General	E/M/N/S	Alternative
WAFG	90.3	G/R	E/M/T	Christian
WFLC	97.3	General	M/N	Adult Contemporary
WKIS	99.9	General	M/N/S	Country
WHYI	100.7	General	M/N	Adult Contemporary
WPLL	103.5	General	M	Adult Contemporary
WHQT	105.1	General	M	Urban Contemporary

Note: Stations included broadcast in the Fort Lauderdale metro area
Station Format: E=Educational; M=Music; N=News; S=Sports; T=Talk
Target Audience: A=Asian; B=Black; C=Christian; E=Ethnic; F=French; G=General; H=Hispanic; M=Men; N=Native American; R=Religious; S=Senior Citizen; W=Women; Y=Young Adult; Z=Children
Source: Burrelle's Media Directory, 1999 Edition

CLIMATE

Average and Extreme Temperatures

Temperature	Jan	Feb	Mar	Apr	May	Jun	Jul	Aug	Sep	Oct	Nov	Dec	Yr.
Extreme High (°F)	88	89	92	96	95	98	98	98	97	95	89	87	98
Average High (°F)	75	77	79	82	85	88	89	90	88	85	80	77	83
Average Temp. (°F)	68	69	72	75	79	82	83	83	82	78	73	69	76
Average Low (°F)	59	60	64	68	72	75	76	76	76	72	66	61	69
Extreme Low (°F)	30	35	32	42	55	60	69	68	68	53	39	30	30

Note: Figures cover the years 1948-1990
Source: National Climatic Data Center, International Station Meteorological Climate Summary, 3/95

Average Precipitation/Snowfall/Humidity

Precip./Humidity	Jan	Feb	Mar	Apr	May	Jun	Jul	Aug	Sep	Oct	Nov	Dec	Yr.
Avg. Precip. (in.)	1.9	2.0	2.3	3.0	6.2	8.7	6.1	7.5	8.2	6.6	2.7	1.8	57.1
Avg. Snowfall (in.)	0	0	0	0	0	0	0	0	0	0	0	0	0
Avg. Rel. Hum. 7am (%)	84	84	82	80	81	84	84	86	88	87	85	84	84
Avg. Rel. Hum. 4pm (%)	59	57	57	57	62	68	66	67	69	65	63	60	63

Note: Figures cover the years 1948-1990; Tr = Trace amounts (<0.05 in. of rain; <0.5 in. of snow)
Source: National Climatic Data Center, International Station Meteorological Climate Summary, 3/95

Weather Conditions

Temperature			Daytime Sky			Precipitation		
32°F & below	45°F & below	90°F & above	Clear	Partly cloudy	Cloudy	0.01 inch or more precip.	0.1 inch or more snow/ice	Thunder-storms
< 1	7	55	48	263	54	128	0	74

Note: Figures are average number of days per year and covers the years 1948-1990
Source: National Climatic Data Center, International Station Meteorological Climate Summary, 3/95

AIR & WATER QUALITY

Maximum Pollutant Concentrations

	Particulate Matter (ug/m3)	Carbon Monoxide (ppm)	Sulfur Dioxide (ppm)	Nitrogen Dioxide (ppm)	Ozone (ppm)	Lead (ug/m3)
MSA[1] Level	39	5	0.011	0.010	0.09	0.04
NAAQS[2]	150	9	0.140	0.053	0.12	1.50
Met NAAQS?	Yes	Yes	Yes	Yes	Yes	Yes

Note: (1) Metropolitan Statistical Area - see Appendix A for areas included; (2) National Ambient Air Quality Standards; ppm = parts per million; ug/m3 = micrograms per cubic meter; n/a not available
Source: EPA, National Air Quality and Emissions Trends Report, 1997

Pollutant Standards Index

In the Fort Lauderdale MSA (see Appendix A for areas included), the Pollutant Standards Index (PSI) exceeded 100 on 0 days in 1997. A PSI value greater than 100 indicates that air quality would be in the unhealthful range on that day. *EPA, National Air Quality and Emissions Trends Report, 1997*

Drinking Water

Water System Name	Pop. Served	Primary Water Source Type	Number of Violations in 1998	Type of Violation/ Contaminants
City of Ft. Lauderdale	172,680	Ground	1	(1)

Note: Data as of July 10, 1999; (1) System collected or speciated some but not all follow-up samples for compliance period under the total coliform rule (1 time in 1998).
Source: EPA, Office of Ground Water and Drinking Water, Safe Drinking Water Information System

Fort Lauderdale tap water is alkaline, very soft and fluoridated.
Editor & Publisher Market Guide, 1999

Fort Worth, Texas

Background

Fort Worth lies in north central Texas near the headwaters of the Trinity River. Despite its modern skyscrapers, multiple freeways, shopping malls, and extensive industry, the city is known for its easy-going, western atmosphere.

The area has seen many travelers. Nomadic Native Americans of the Plains rode through on horses bred from those brought by Spanish explorers. The 1840s saw American-Anglos settle in the region. On June 6, 1849 Major Ripley A. Arnold and his U.S. Cavalry troop established an outpost on the Trinity River to protect settlers moving westward. The fort was named for General William J. Worth, Commander of the U.S. Army's Texas department. When the fort was abandoned in 1853, settlers moved in and converted the vacant barracks into trading establishments and homes and stole the county seat from Birdville (an act made legal in the 1860 election).

In the 1860s Fort Worth, which was close to the Chisholm Trail, became an oasis for cowboys travelling to and from Kansas.

Although the town's growth virtually stopped during the Civil War, Fort Worth was incorporated as a city in 1873. In a race against time, the final 26 miles of the Texas & Pacific Line were completed and Fort Worth survived to be a part of the West Texas oil boom in 1917.

Real prosperity followed at the end of World War II, when the city became a center for a number of military installations. Aviation has been the city's principal source of economic growth. Among the city's leading industries are the manufacture of aircraft, automobiles, machinery, containers, food processing, and brewing.

Winter temperatures and rainfall are both modified by the northeast-northwest mountain barrier which prevents shallow cold air masses from crossing over from the west. Summer temperatures vary with the cloud and shower activity, but are generally mild. Summer precipitation is largely from local thunderstorms and varies from year to year. Damaging rains are infrequent. Hurricanes have produced heavy rainfall, but are usually not accompanied by destructive winds.

General Rankings and Evaluative Comments

- Fort Worth was ranked #9 out of 19 large, southern metropolitan areas in *Money's* 1998 survey of "The Best Places to Live in America." The survey was conducted by first contacting 512 representative households nationwide and asking them to rank 37 quality-of-life factors on a scale of 1 to 10. Next, a demographic profile was compiled on the 300 largest metropolitan statistical areas in the U.S. The numbers were crunched together to arrive at an overall ranking (things Americans consider most important, like clean air and water, low crime and good schools, received extra weight). Unlike previous years, the 1998 rankings were broken down by region (northeast, midwest, south, west) and population size (100,000 to 249,999; 250,000 to 999,999; 1 million plus). The city had a nationwide ranking of #57 out of 300 in 1997 and #55 out of 300 in 1996. *Money, July 1998; Money, July 1997; Money, September 1996*

- *Ladies Home Journal* ranked America's 200 largest cities based on the qualities women care about most. Fort Worth ranked #121 out of 200. Criteria: low crime rate, well-paying jobs, quality health and child care, good public schools, the presence of women in government, size of the gender wage gap, number of sexual-harassment and discrimination complaints filed, unemployment and divorce rates, commute times, population density, number of houses of worship, parks and cultural offerings, number of women's health specialists, how well a community's women cared for themselves, complexion kindness index based on UV radiation levels, odds of finding affordable fashions, rental rates for romance movies, champagne sales and other matters of the heart. *Ladies Home Journal, November 1998*

- Zero Population Growth ranked 229 cities in terms of children's health, safety, and economic well-being. Fort Worth was ranked #11 out of 25 major cities (main city in a metro area with population of greater than 2 million) and was given a grade of C+. Criteria: total population, percent of population under 18 years of age, household language, percent population change, percent of births to teens, infant mortality rate, percent of low birth weights, dropout rate, enrollment in preprimary school, violent and property crime rates, unemployment rate, percent of children in poverty, percent of owner occupied units, number of bad air days, percent of public transportation commuters, and average travel time to work. *Zero Population Growth, Children's Environmental Index, Fall 1999*

- Fort Worth was ranked #19 out of 59 metro areas in *The Regional Economist's* "Rational Livability Ranking of 59 Large Metro Areas." The rankings were based on the metro area's total population change over the period 1990-97 divided by the number of people moving in from elsewhere in the United States (net domestic in-migration). *St. Louis Federal Reserve Bank of St. Louis, The Regional Economist, April 1999*

- Cognetics studied 273 metro areas in the United States, ranking them by entrepreneurial activity. Fort Worth was ranked #8 out of the 50 largest metro areas. Criteria: Significant Starts (firms started in the last 10 years that still employ at least 5 people) and Young Growers (percent of firms 10 years old or less that grew significantly during the last 4 years). *Cognetics, "Entrepreneurial Hot Spots: The Best Places in America to Start and Grow a Company," 1998*

- Fort Worth was selected as one of the "Best American Cities to Start a Business" by *Point of View* magazine. Criteria: coolness, quality-of-life, and business concerns. The city was ranked #12 out of 75. *Point of View, November 1998*

- Reliastar Financial Corp. ranked the 125 largest metropolitan areas according to the general financial security of residents. Fort Worth was ranked #26 out of 125 with a score of 6.8. The score indicates the percentage a metropolitan area is above or below the metropolitan norm. A metro area with a score of 10.6 is 10.6% above the metro average. Criteria: Earnings and Wealth Potential (household income, education, net assets, cost of living); Safety Net (health insurance, retirement savings, life insurance, income support programs); Personal Threats (unemployment rate, low-income households, crime rate); Community Economic Vitality (cost of community services, job quality, job creation, housing costs). *Reliastar Financial Corp., "The Best Cities to Earn and Save Money," 1999 Edition*

Business Environment

STATE ECONOMY

State Economic Profile

"Economic growth in Texas has slowed as both its new and old economies are under pressure. Weak commodity prices and over-capacity have hurt TX's old economic powers, agriculture and oil. Soft global demand has slowed TX's new economic powers, semiconductors and computer sales. A slowing US economy in 1999 will also place a drag on TX's biotech and software companies. Despite the current slowdown, TX's long-term outlook is extremely bright, and its current problems will last no more than two years.

Weak commodity prices, over-capacity and soft foreign demand have all coincided to undermine TX's oil and farm sector. Despite OPEC cutbacks, the TX oil industry remains vulnerable because of its high costs, high inventories and high capacity. TX's farm sector is similarly positioned; commodity prices are expected to continue their long-term downward trend.

The TX economy is more diversified today than ever before. Growth in services and hi-tech employment have more than offset declines in TX's resource economy. Services employment in 1998 grew at 3.8%, adding some 93,000 jobs, while construction employment grew 4.9%, adding 22,700 jobs. Construction employment, along with home sales and starts, should contract in 1999 and 2000. TX's demographic situation is positive; the state continues to attract educated, young households. However, the current weakness in the state's semiconductor and computer industry has slowed job growth from its previous feverish pace. In the near-term, TX's growth should slow along with the US economy. Its long-term prospects are bright given its business friendly atmosphere and central location." *National Association of Realtors, Economic Profiles: The Fifty States and the District of Columbia, http://nar.realtor.com/databank/profiles.htm*

IMPORTS/EXPORTS

Total Export Sales

Area	1994 ($000)	1995 ($000)	1996 ($000)	1997 ($000)	% Chg. 1994-97	% Chg. 1996-97
MSA[1]	2,052,001	1,915,014	2,372,703	3,045,861	48.4	28.4
U.S.	512,415,609	583,030,524	622,827,063	687,597,999	34.2	10.4

Note: (1) Metropolitan Statistical Area - see Appendix A for areas included
Source: U.S. Department of Commerce, International Trade Association, Metropolitan Area Exports: An Export Performance Report on Over 250 U.S. Cities, November 10, 1998

CITY FINANCES

City Government Finances

Component	FY92 ($000)	FY92 (per capita $)
Revenue	500,619	1,085.38
Expenditure	522,690	1,133.23
Debt Outstanding	934,606	2,026.29
Cash & Securities	1,028,431	2,229.71

Source: U.S. Bureau of the Census, City Government Finances: 1991-92

City Government Revenue by Source

Source	FY92 ($000)	FY92 (per capita $)	FY92 (%)
From Federal Government	19,343	41.94	3.9
From State Governments	19,018	41.23	3.8
From Local Governments	3,652	7.92	0.7
Property Taxes	130,086	282.04	26.0
General Sales Taxes	39,809	86.31	8.0
Selective Sales Taxes	21,651	46.94	4.3
Income Taxes	0	0.00	0.0
Current Charges	69,168	149.96	13.8
Utility/Liquor Store	64,998	140.92	13.0
Employee Retirement[1]	54,901	119.03	11.0
Other	77,993	169.09	15.6

Note: (1) Excludes "city contributions," classified as "nonrevenue," intragovernmental transfers.
Source: U.S. Bureau of the Census, City Government Finances: 1991-92

City Government Expenditures by Function

Function	FY92 ($000)	FY92 (per capita $)	FY92 (%)
Educational Services	7,530	16.33	1.4
Employee Retirement[1]	21,869	47.41	4.2
Environment/Housing	144,587	313.48	27.7
Government Administration	23,988	52.01	4.6
Interest on General Debt	54,655	118.50	10.5
Public Safety	87,841	190.45	16.8
Social Services	10,583	22.94	2.0
Transportation	81,269	176.20	15.5
Utility/Liquor Store	64,559	139.97	12.4
Other	25,809	55.96	4.9

Note: (1) Payments to beneficiaries including withdrawal of contributions.
Source: U.S. Bureau of the Census, City Government Finances: 1991-92

Municipal Bond Ratings

Area	Moody's	S & P
Fort Worth	Aa2	n/a

Note: n/a not available; n/r not rated
Source: Moody's Bond Record, 6/99

POPULATION

Population Growth

Area	1980	1990	% Chg. 1980-90	July 1998 Estimate	% Chg. 1990-98
City	385,166	447,619	16.2	491,801	9.9
MSA[1]	n/a	1,332,053	n/a	1,581,760	18.7
U.S.	226,545,805	248,765,170	9.8	270,299,000	8.7

Note: (1) Metropolitan Statistical Area - see Appendix A for areas included;
July 1998 MSA population estimate was calculated by the editors
Source: 1980/1990 Census of Housing and Population, Summary Tape File 3C;
Census Bureau Population Estimates 1998

Population Characteristics

Race	City 1980 Population	%	City 1990 Population	%	% Chg. 1980-90	MSA[1] 1990 Population	%
White	266,638	69.2	286,072	63.9	7.3	1,070,993	80.4
Black	87,635	22.8	98,679	22.0	12.6	143,824	10.8
Amer Indian/Esk/Aleut	1,841	0.5	1,990	0.4	8.1	6,554	0.5
Asian/Pacific Islander	2,954	0.8	8,465	1.9	186.6	29,728	2.2
Other	26,098	6.8	52,413	11.7	100.8	80,954	6.1
Hispanic Origin[2]	48,568	12.6	85,835	19.2	76.7	146,143	11.0

Note: (1) Metropolitan Statistical Area - see Appendix A for areas included;
(2) people of Hispanic origin can be of any race
Source: 1980/1990 Census of Housing and Population, Summary Tape File 3C

Ancestry

Area	German	Irish	English	Italian	U.S.	French	Polish	Dutch
City	14.8	13.2	12.3	1.5	4.9	3.0	1.1	1.9
MSA[1]	20.9	18.2	15.5	2.2	6.8	3.9	1.5	2.7
U.S.	23.3	15.6	13.1	5.9	5.3	4.2	3.8	2.5

Note: Figures are percentages and include persons that reported multiple ancestry (eg. if a person reported being Irish and Italian, they were included in both columns); (1) Metropolitan Statistical Area - see Appendix A for areas included
Source: 1990 Census of Population and Housing, Summary Tape File 3C

Age

Area	Median Age (Years)	Age Distribution (%) Under 5	Under 18	18-24	25-44	45-64	65+	80+
City	30.3	8.6	26.6	11.7	34.7	15.9	11.2	2.6
MSA[1]	30.6	8.4	27.3	10.7	36.3	17.1	8.6	1.8
U.S.	32.9	7.3	25.6	10.5	32.6	18.7	12.5	2.8

Note: (1) Metropolitan Statistical Area - see Appendix A for areas included
Source: 1990 Census of Population and Housing, Summary Tape File 3C

Male/Female Ratio

Area	Number of males per 100 females (all ages)	Number of males per 100 females (18 years old+)
City	96.3	94.3
MSA[1]	97.8	95.4
U.S.	95.0	91.9

Note: (1) Metropolitan Statistical Area - see Appendix A for areas included
Source: 1990 Census of Population, General Population Characteristics

INCOME

Per Capita/Median/Average Income

Area	Per Capita ($)	Median Household ($)	Average Household ($)
City	13,162	26,547	34,359
MSA[1]	14,842	32,121	39,560
U.S.	14,420	30,056	38,453

Note: All figures are for 1989; (1) Metropolitan Statistical Area - see Appendix A for areas included
Source: 1990 Census of Population and Housing, Summary Tape File 3C

Household Income Distribution by Race

Income ($)	City (%)					U.S. (%)				
	Total	White	Black	Other	Hisp.[1]	Total	White	Black	Other	Hisp.[1]
Less than 5,000	7.7	5.0	17.1	7.9	7.9	6.2	4.8	15.2	8.6	8.8
5,000 - 9,999	9.4	8.1	14.0	10.0	10.0	9.3	8.6	14.2	9.9	11.1
10,000 - 14,999	10.1	9.1	13.2	11.2	11.7	8.8	8.5	11.0	9.8	11.0
15,000 - 24,999	19.7	18.8	20.9	24.1	24.3	17.5	17.3	18.9	18.5	20.5
25,000 - 34,999	17.1	17.5	14.1	20.2	20.3	15.8	16.1	14.2	15.4	16.4
35,000 - 49,999	16.7	18.2	11.7	15.5	15.0	17.9	18.6	13.3	16.1	16.0
50,000 - 74,999	12.5	14.6	7.1	8.5	8.3	15.0	15.8	9.3	13.4	11.1
75,000 - 99,999	3.6	4.5	1.3	1.6	2.1	5.1	5.5	2.6	4.7	3.1
100,000+	3.2	4.3	0.5	0.9	0.3	4.4	4.8	1.3	3.7	1.9

Note: All figures are for 1989; (1) people of Hispanic origin can be of any race
Source: 1990 Census of Population and Housing, Summary Tape File 3C

Effective Buying Income

Area	Per Capita ($)	Median Household ($)	Average Household ($)
City	15,833	32,448	42,121
MSA[1]	18,447	39,080	49,289
U.S.	16,803	34,536	45,243

Note: Data as of 1/1/99; (1) Metropolitan Statistical Area - see Appendix A for areas included
Source: Standard Rate & Data Service, Newspaper Advertising Source, 9/99

Effective Household Buying Income Distribution

Area	% of Households Earning						
	$10,000 -$19,999	$20,000 -$34,999	$35,000 -$49,999	$50,000 -$74,999	$75,000 -$99,000	$100,000 -$124,999	$125,000 and up
City	16.7	23.8	17.7	17.1	6.7	2.1	2.6
MSA[1]	13.6	21.8	18.6	21.1	9.3	3.2	3.0
U.S.	16.0	22.6	18.2	18.9	7.2	2.4	2.7

Note: Data as of 1/1/99; (1) Metropolitan Statistical Area - see Appendix A for areas included
Source: Standard Rate & Data Service, Newspaper Advertising Source, 9/99

Poverty Rates by Race and Age

Area	Total (%)	By Race (%)				By Age (%)		
		White	Black	Other	Hisp.[2]	Under 5 years old	Under 18 years old	65 years and over
City	17.4	10.8	31.3	25.4	25.9	26.0	24.9	14.4
MSA[1]	11.0	7.7	27.0	21.8	22.2	16.5	14.7	12.2
U.S.	13.1	9.8	29.5	23.1	25.3	20.1	18.3	12.8

Note: Figures show the percent of people living below the poverty line in 1989. The average poverty threshold was $12,674 for a family of four in 1989; (1) Metropolitan Statistical Area - see Appendix A for areas included; (2) people of Hispanic origin can be of any race
Source: 1990 Census of Population and Housing, Summary Tape File 3C

EMPLOYMENT

Labor Force and Employment

Area	Civilian Labor Force			Workers Employed		
	Jun. 1998	Jun. 1999	% Chg.	Jun. 1998	Jun. 1999	% Chg.
City	271,479	279,786	3.1	257,658	266,665	3.5
MSA[1]	893,824	922,233	3.2	859,054	889,085	3.5
U.S.	138,798,000	140,666,000	1.3	132,265,000	134,395,000	1.6

Note: Data is not seasonally adjusted and covers workers 16 years of age and older; (1) Metropolitan Statistical Area - see Appendix A for areas included
Source: Bureau of Labor Statistics, http://stats.bls.gov

Unemployment Rate

Area	1998						1999					
	Jul.	Aug.	Sep.	Oct.	Nov.	Dec.	Jan.	Feb.	Mar.	Apr.	May.	Jun.
City	5.4	4.4	4.3	3.9	4.0	3.6	4.5	4.1	3.8	3.7	4.0	4.7
MSA[1]	4.1	3.3	3.3	3.0	3.0	2.7	3.4	3.1	2.9	2.8	3.1	3.6
U.S.	4.7	4.5	4.4	4.2	4.1	4.0	4.8	4.7	4.4	4.1	4.0	4.5

Note: Data is not seasonally adjusted and covers workers 16 years of age and older; all figures are percentages; (1) Metropolitan Statistical Area - see Appendix A for areas included
Source: Bureau of Labor Statistics, http://stats.bls.gov

Employment by Industry

Sector	MSA[1]		U.S.
	Number of Employees	Percent of Total	Percent of Total
Services	211,800	27.5	30.4
Retail Trade	150,300	19.5	17.7
Government	94,700	12.3	15.6
Manufacturing	113,200	14.7	14.3
Finance/Insurance/Real Estate	36,300	4.7	5.9
Wholesale Trade	42,000	5.5	5.4
Transportation/Public Utilities	73,200	9.5	5.3
Construction	42,900	5.6	5.0
Mining	4,600	0.6	0.4

Note: Figures cover non-farm employment as of 6/99 and are not seasonally adjusted; (1) Metropolitan Statistical Area - see Appendix A for areas included
Source: Bureau of Labor Statistics, http://stats.bls.gov

Employment by Occupation

Occupation Category	City (%)	MSA[1] (%)	U.S. (%)
White Collar	57.0	62.0	58.1
Executive/Admin./Management	11.0	13.4	12.3
Professional	14.6	13.8	14.1
Technical & Related Support	3.6	4.3	3.7
Sales	11.5	13.0	11.8
Administrative Support/Clerical	16.2	17.6	16.3
Blue Collar	27.9	25.1	26.2
Precision Production/Craft/Repair	11.5	11.8	11.3
Machine Operators/Assem./Insp.	8.5	6.3	6.8
Transportation/Material Movers	3.4	3.5	4.1
Cleaners/Helpers/Laborers	4.6	3.6	3.9
Services	13.9	11.7	13.2
Farming/Forestry/Fishing	1.3	1.1	2.5

Note: Figures cover employed persons 16 years old and over; (1) Metropolitan Statistical Area - see Appendix A for areas included
Source: 1990 Census of Population and Housing, Summary Tape File 3C

Occupational Employment Projections: 1996 - 2006

Occupations Expected to Have the Largest Job Growth (ranked by numerical growth)	Fast-Growing Occupations[1] (ranked by percent growth)
1. Cashiers	1. Desktop publishers
2. Salespersons, retail	2. Systems analysts
3. General managers & top executives	3. Customer service representatives
4. Truck drivers, light	4. Physical therapy assistants and aides
5. Child care workers, private household	5. Computer engineers
6. General office clerks	6. Emergency medical technicians
7. Systems analysts	7. Medical assistants
8. Food preparation workers	8. Respiratory therapists
9. Food service workers	9. Telephone & cable TV line install & repair
10. Registered nurses	10. Physical therapists

Note: Projections cover Texas; (1) Excludes occupations with total job growth less than 300
Source: U.S. Department of Labor, Employment and Training Administration, America's Labor Market Information System (ALMIS)

TAXES

Major State and Local Tax Rates

State Corp. Income (%)	State Personal Income (%)	Residential Property (effective rate per $100)	Sales & Use State (%)	Sales & Use Local (%)	State Gasoline (cents/gallon)	State Cigarette (cents/pack)
None[a]	None	n/a	6.25	2.0	20.0	41.0

Note: Personal/corporate income, sales, gasoline and cigarette tax rates as of January 1999. Property tax rates as of 1997; (a) Texas imposes a franchise tax of 4.5% of earned surplus
Source: Federation of Tax Administrators, www.taxadmin.org; Washington D.C. Department of Finance and Revenue, Tax Rates and Tax Burdens in the District of Columbia: A Nationwide Comparison, July 1998; Chamber of Commerce, 1999

Total Taxes Per Capita and as a Percent of Income

Area	Per Capita Income ($)	Per Capita Taxes ($) Total	Federal	State/Local	Percent of Income (%) Total	Federal	State/Local
Texas	25,563	8,741	6,051	2,690	34.2	23.7	10.5
U.S.	27,876	9,881	6,690	3,191	35.4	24.0	11.4

Note: Figures are for 1998
Source: Tax Foundation, www.taxfoundation.org

COMMERCIAL REAL ESTATE

Office Market

Class/Location	Total Space (sq. ft.)	Vacant Space (sq. ft.)	Vac. Rate (%)	Under Constr. (sq. ft.)	Net Absorp. (sq. ft.)	Rental Rates ($/sq.ft./yr.)
Class A						
CBD	4,935,115	629,068	12.7	0	139,747	13.00-18.50
Outside CBD	6,929,724	413,883	6.0	365,000	-72,467	11.00-25.00
Class B						
CBD	1,993,283	542,943	27.2	0	21,448	10.00-14.00
Outside CBD	4,574,963	608,830	13.3	0	-47,785	8.00-19.00

Note: Data as of 10/98 and covers Ft. Worth/Tarrant County; CBD = Central Business District; n/a not available;
Source: Society of Industrial and Office Realtors, 1999 Comparative Statistics of Industrial and Office Real Estate Markets

"Little speculative office construction is expected in 1999. Absorption is low; the money supply is tight, and despite a strong economy, the prevailing attitude among developers is 'wait and see.' Northeast Tarrant County is most likely to see new development. The largest proposed project is Fidelity Investment's 600,000 sq. ft. corporate campus in Westlake. Southlake's Town Center, currently under construction, and development around Alliance Airport may also bring office tenants to this area. The Arlington market can probably expect office development as well, since only 65,400 sq. ft., or 2.9 percent of its Class A space is available. In addition, SIOR's reporter expects building sales to drop somewhat in 1999. Slowly decreasing vacancy rates will keep upward pressure on rental rates." Society of Industrial and Office Realtors, 1999 Comparative Statistics of Industrial and Office Real Estate Markets

Industrial Market

Location	Total Space (sq. ft.)	Vacant Space (sq. ft.)	Vac. Rate (%)	Under Constr. (sq. ft.)	Net Absorp. (sq. ft.)	Net Lease ($/sq.ft./yr.)
Central City	n/a	n/a	n/a	n/a	n/a	n/a
Suburban	154,146,196	12,926,451	8.4	3,200,000	9,393,471	3.25-4.75

Note: Data as of 10/98 and covers Fort Worth/Tarrant County; n/a not available
Source: Society of Industrial and Office Realtors, 1999 Comparative Statistics of Industrial and Office Real Estate Markets

"Speculative construction should slow down in the Fort Worth area during 1999 for several reasons: REITs are out of the market; capital sources have dried up; bulk warehouse space is overbuilt; and rental rates are becoming softer. Approximately two to three million sq. ft. will likely be built in 1999. North Fort Worth, the Alliance Development and the Dallas/Fort Worth Airport area will continue to develop the most new space. During 1999 the manufacturing segment of the Fort Worth market will probably see a decrease of one to five percent in sales prices, lease prices, and construction. All other areas will flatten out and remain the same as in 1998, as everyone takes a 'wait and see' attitude. The Dallas/Fort Worth economy is expected to remain strong, but low unemployment of 3.4 percent could negatively affect companies desiring to expand." *Society of Industrial and Office Realtors, 1999 Comparative Statistics of Industrial and Office Real Estate Markets*

Retail Market

Shopping Center Inventory (sq. ft.)	Shopping Center Construction (sq. ft.)	Construction as a Percent of Inventory (%)	Torto Wheaton Rent Index[1] ($/sq. ft.)
38,755,000	904,000	2.3	13.33

Note: Data as of 1997 and covers the Metropolitan Statistical Area - see Appendix A for areas included; (1) Index is based on a model that predicts what the average rent should be for leases with certain characteristics, in certain locations during certain years.
Source: National Association of Realtors, 1997-1998 Market Conditions Report

"Fort Worth has come a long way since Dallasites called it the 'Panther City', claiming that the city was so sedate that a large panther could sleep peacefully in its downtown streets. Indeed, healthy population growth has buoyed the retail sector, which has added jobs at a staggering rate. Robust growth has caused the area's unemployment rate to fall to 3.9%, the lowest rate in more than a decade. Fort Worth's retail rent index has jumped 53% since 1995, and should continue to rise over the next few years amid the area's burgeoning economy." *National Association of Realtors, 1997-1998 Market Conditions Report*

COMMERCIAL UTILITIES

Typical Monthly Electric Bills

Area	Commercial Service ($/month)		Industrial Service ($/month)	
	12 kW demand 1,500 kWh	100 kW demand 30,000 kWh	1,000 kW demand 400,000 kWh	20,000 kW demand 10,000,000 kWh
City	151	2,142	23,072	383,469
U.S.	150	2,174	23,995	508,569

Note: Based on rates in effect January 1, 1999
Source: Edison Electric Institute, Typical Residential, Commercial and Industrial Bills, Winter 1999

TRANSPORTATION

Transportation Statistics

Average minutes to work	21.0
Interstate highways	I-20; I-35W; I-30
Bus lines	
In-city	The T (The Ft. Worth TA), 184 vehicles
Inter-city	2
Passenger air service	
Airport	Dallas/Ft. Worth International Airport; Love Field
Airlines	14
Aircraft departures	421,977 (1996)
Enplaned passengers	30,162,820 (1996)
Rail service	Amtrak; Light Rail
Motor freight carriers	45
Major waterways/ports	None

Source: Editor & Publisher Market Guide, 1999; FAA Airport Activity Statistics, 1997; Amtrak National Time Table, Northeast Timetable, Spring/Summer 1999; 1990 Census of Population and Housing, STF 3C; Chamber of Commerce/Economic Development 1999; Jane's Urban Transport Systems 1999-2000

Means of Transportation to Work

Area	Car/Truck/Van		Public Transportation			Bicycle	Walked	Other Means	Worked at Home
	Drove Alone	Car-pooled	Bus	Subway	Railroad				
City	76.7	16.3	1.6	0.0	0.0	0.2	2.3	1.2	1.8
MSA[1]	80.9	13.5	0.6	0.0	0.0	0.1	1.7	0.9	2.2
U.S.	73.2	13.4	3.0	1.5	0.5	0.4	3.9	1.2	3.0

Note: Figures shown are percentages and only include workers 16 years old and over;
(1) Metropolitan Statistical Area - see Appendix A for areas included
Source: 1990 Census of Population and Housing, Summary Tape File 3C

BUSINESSES

Major Business Headquarters

Company Name	1999 Rankings	
	Fortune 500	Forbes 500
AMR	71	-
Burlington Northern Santa Fe	178	-
Tandy	330	-
Williamson-Dickie Manufacturing	-	461

Note: Companies listed are located in the city; dashes indicate no ranking
Fortune 500: Companies that produce a 10-K are ranked 1 to 500 based on 1998 revenue
Forbes 500: Private companies are ranked 1 to 500 based on 1997 revenue
Source: Forbes, November 30, 1998; Fortune, April 26, 1999

Best Companies to Work For

Alcon Laboratories (eye-care products) and Union Pacific Resources (oil and gas driller), headquartered in Fort Worth, are among the "100 Best Companies to Work for in America." Criteria: trust in management, pride in work/company, camaraderie, company responses to the Hewitt People Practices Inventory, and employee responses to their Great Place to Work survey. The companies also had to be at least 10 years old and have a minimum of 500 employees. *Fortune, January 11, 1999*

Union Pacific Resources Group (oil and gas exploration), headquartered in Fort Worth, is among the "100 Best Companies for Working Mothers." Criteria: fair wages, opportunities for women to advance, support for child care, flexible work schedules, family-friendly benefits, and work/life supports. *Working Mother, October 1998*

Women-Owned Firms: Number, Employment and Sales

Area	Number of Firms	Employ-ment	Sales ($000)	Rank[2]
MSA[1]	54,200	74,900	14,192,200	43

Note: (1) Metropolitan Statistical Area - see Appendix A for areas included;
(2) Calculated on an averaging of the number of businesses, employment and sales
Source: The National Foundation for Women Business Owners, 1999 Facts on Women-Owned Businesses: Trends in the Top 50 Metropolitan Areas

Women-Owned Firms: Growth

Area	% change from 1992 to 1999			Rank[2]
	Number of Firms	Employ-ment	Sales	
MSA[1]	41.0	79.4	137.2	38

Note: (1) Metropolitan Statistical Area - see Appendix A for areas included; (2) Calculated on an averaging of the percent growth of number of businesses, employment and sales
Source: The National Foundation for Women Business Owners, 1999 Facts on Women-Owned Businesses: Trends in the Top 50 Metropolitan Areas

Minority Business Opportunity

Fort Worth is home to one company which is on the Black Enterprise Auto Dealer 100 list (largest based on gross sales): Alan Young Buick-GMC Truck Inc. (GMC, Buick) . Criteria: 1) operational in previous calendar year; 2) at least 51% black-owned. *Black Enterprise, www.blackenterprise.com*

Two of the 500 largest Hispanic-owned companies in the U.S. are located in Fort Worth. *Hispanic Business, June 1999*

HOTELS & MOTELS

Hotels/Motels

Area	Hotels/ Motels	Rooms	Luxury-Level Hotels/Motels		Average Minimum Rates ($)		
			♦♦♦♦	♦♦♦♦♦	♦♦	♦♦♦	♦♦♦♦
City	39	4,718	0	0	59	99	n/a
Suburbs	46	5,831	0	0	n/a	n/a	n/a
Total	85	10,549	0	0	n/a	n/a	n/a

Note: n/a not available; classifications range from one diamond (budget properties with basic amenities) to five diamond (luxury properties with the finest service, rooms and facilities).
Source: OAG, Business Travel Planner, Winter 1998-99

CONVENTION CENTERS

Major Convention Centers

Center Name	Meeting Rooms	Exhibit Space (sq. ft.)
American Airlines Training & Conference Center	8	n/a
Tarrant County Convention Center	25	170,000
Will Rogers Memorial Center	6	124,000

Note: n/a not available
Source: Trade Shows Worldwide, 1998; Meetings & Conventions, 4/15/99; Sucessful Meetings, 3/31/98

Living Environment

COST OF LIVING

Cost of Living Index

Composite Index	Groceries	Housing	Utilities	Trans-portation	Health Care	Misc. Goods/ Services
92.9	102.3	75.4	102.4	94.6	99.4	99.3

Note: U.S. = 100
Source: ACCRA, Cost of Living Index, 1st Quarter 1999

HOUSING

Median Home Prices and Housing Affordability

Area	Median Price[2] 1st Qtr. 1999 ($)	HOI[3] 1st Qtr. 1999	Afford- ability Rank[4]
MSA[1]	106,000	77.0	81
U.S.	134,000	69.6	–

Note: (1) Metropolitan Statistical Area - see Appendix A for areas included; (2) U.S. figures calculated from the sales of 524,324 new and existing homes in 181 markets; (3) Housing Opportunity Index - percent of homes sold that were within the reach of the median income household at the prevailing mortgage interest rate; (4) Rank is from 1-181 with 1 being most affordable
Source: National Association of Home Builders, Housing Opportunity Index, 1st Quarter 1999

Median Home Price Projection

It is projected that the median price of existing single-family homes in the metro area will decrease by -1.0% in 1999. Nationwide, home prices are projected to increase 3.8%.
Kiplinger's Personal Finance Magazine, January 1999

Average New Home Price

Area	Price ($)
City	98,207
U.S.	142,735

Note: Figures are based on a new home with 1,800 sq. ft. of living area on an 8,000 sq. ft. lot.
Source: ACCRA, Cost of Living Index, 1st Quarter 1999

Average Apartment Rent

Area	Rent ($/mth)
City	662
U.S.	601

Note: Figures are based on an unfurnished two bedroom, 1-1/2 or 2 bath apartment, approximately 950 sq. ft. in size, excluding all utilities except water
Source: ACCRA, Cost of Living Index, 1st Quarter 1999

RESIDENTIAL UTILITIES

Average Residential Utility Costs

Area	All Electric ($/mth)	Part Electric ($/mth)	Other Energy ($/mth)	Phone ($/mth)
City	–	73.66	30.27	17.33
U.S.	100.02	55.73	43.33	19.71

Source: ACCRA, Cost of Living Index, 1st Quarter 1999

HEALTH CARE

Average Health Care Costs

Area	Hospital ($/day)	Doctor ($/visit)	Dentist ($/visit)
City	339.20	53.80	69.40
U.S.	430.43	52.45	66.35

Note: Hospital—based on a semi-private room; Doctor—based on a general practitioner's routine exam of an established patient; Dentist—based on adult teeth cleaning and periodic oral exam.
Source: ACCRA, Cost of Living Index, 1st Quarter 1999

Distribution of Office-Based Physicians

Area	Family/Gen. Practitioners	Specialists		
		Medical	Surgical	Other
MSA[1]	308	532	528	472

Note: Data as of 12/31/97; (1) Metropolitan Statistical Area - see Appendix A for areas included
Source: American Medical Assn., Physician Characteristics & Distribution in the U.S., 1999

Hospitals

Fort Worth has 7 general medical and surgical hospitals, 1 psychiatric, 2 rehabilitation, 1 other specialty, 1 children's general, 1 children's psychiatric. *AHA Guide to the Healthcare Field, 1998-99*

EDUCATION

Public School District Statistics

District Name	Num. Sch.	Enroll.	Classroom Teachers	Pupils per Teacher	Minority Pupils (%)	Current Exp.[1] ($/pupil)
Castleberry ISD	7	3,212	213	15.1	n/a	n/a
Eagle Mt-Saginaw ISD	10	5,605	333	16.8	n/a	n/a
Fort Worth ISD	132	76,901	n/a	n/a	74.9	4,967
Masonic Home ISD	1	73	15	4.9	n/a	n/a

Note: Data covers the 1997-1998 school year unless otherwise noted; (1) Data covers fiscal year 1996; SD = School District; ISD = Independent School District; n/a not available
Source: National Center for Education Statistics, Common Core of Data Public Education Agency Universe 1997-98; National Center for Education Statistics, Characteristics of the 100 Largest Public Elementary and Secondary School Districts in the United States: 1997-98, July 1999

Educational Quality

School District	Education Quotient[1]	Graduate Outcome[2]	Community Index[3]	Resource Index[4]
Fort Worth ISD	66.0	66.0	121.0	55.0

Note: Nearly 1,000 secondary school districts were rated in terms of educational quality. The scores range from a low of 50 to a high of 150; (1) Average of the Graduate Outcome, Community and Resource indexes; (2) Based on graduation rates and college board scores (SAT/ACT); (3) Based on the surrounding community's average level of education and the area's average income level; (4) Based on teacher salaries, per-pupil expenditures and student-teacher ratios.
Source: Expansion Management, Ratings Issue, 1998

Educational Attainment by Race

Area	High School Graduate (%)					Bachelor's Degree (%)				
	Total	White	Black	Other	Hisp.[2]	Total	White	Black	Other	Hisp.[2]
City	71.6	79.2	62.6	39.6	37.4	21.5	27.0	8.8	9.7	6.3
MSA[1]	79.1	82.4	69.4	52.9	47.9	22.6	24.2	12.8	16.1	9.3
U.S.	75.2	77.9	63.1	60.4	49.8	20.3	21.5	11.4	19.4	9.2

Note: Figures shown cover persons 25 years old and over; (1) Metropolitan Statistical Area - see Appendix A for areas included; (2) people of Hispanic origin can be of any race
Source: 1990 Census of Population and Housing, Summary Tape File 3C

School Enrollment by Type

Area	Preprimary				Elementary/High School			
	Public		Private		Public		Private	
	Enrollment	%	Enrollment	%	Enrollment	%	Enrollment	%
City	4,297	60.0	2,866	40.0	69,185	90.9	6,935	9.1
MSA[1]	13,513	55.4	10,874	44.6	216,997	92.6	17,279	7.4
U.S.	2,679,029	59.5	1,824,256	40.5	38,379,689	90.2	4,187,099	9.8

Note: Figures shown cover persons 3 years old and over;
(1) Metropolitan Statistical Area - see Appendix A for areas included
Source: 1990 Census of Population and Housing, Summary Tape File 3C

School Enrollment by Race

Area	Preprimary (%)				Elementary/High School (%)			
	White	Black	Other	Hisp.[1]	White	Black	Other	Hisp.[1]
City	66.5	23.3	10.3	14.9	50.6	28.9	20.5	27.9
MSA[2]	83.3	10.5	6.2	8.1	74.3	14.0	11.6	14.9
U.S.	80.4	12.5	7.1	7.8	74.1	15.6	10.3	12.5

Note: Figures shown cover persons 3 years old and over; (1) people of Hispanic origin can be of any race; (2) Metropolitan Statistical Area - see Appendix A for areas included
Source: 1990 Census of Population and Housing, Summary Tape File 3C

Classroom Teacher Salaries in Public Schools

District	B.A. Degree		M.A. Degree		Maximum	
	Min. ($)	Rank[1]	Max. ($)	Rank[1]	Max. ($)	Rank[1]
Fort Worth	28,200	28	47,406	36	49,697	56
Average	26,980	-	46,065	-	51,435	-

Note: Salaries are for 1997-1998; (1) Rank ranges from 1 to 100
Source: American Federation of Teachers, Survey & Analysis of Salary Trends, 1998

Higher Education

Two-Year Colleges		Four-Year Colleges		Medical Schools	Law Schools	Voc/ Tech
Public	Private	Public	Private			
1	1	0	1	0	0	13

Source: College Blue Book, Occupational Education, 1997; Medical School Admission Requirements, 1999-2000; Peterson's Guide to Two-Year Colleges, 1999; Peterson's Guide to Four-Year Colleges, 2000; Barron's Guide to Law Schools, 1999

MAJOR EMPLOYERS

Major Employers

AMR Corp. (air transportation)
American Airlines
APCI Inc. (plating & polishing)
Sabre Group (computer programming services)
Teleservice Resources
Con-Way Southern Express
Harris Methodist Fort Worth
Tarrant County Hospital District
Tandy Corp.
Union Pacific Resources (oil & gas)

Note: Companies listed are located in the city
Source: Dun's Business Rankings, 1999; Ward's Business Directory, 1998

PUBLIC SAFETY

Crime Rate

Area	All Crimes	Violent Crimes				Property Crimes		
		Murder	Forcible Rape	Robbery	Aggrav. Assault	Burglary	Larceny -Theft	Motor Vehicle Theft
City	7,317.8	15.5	55.5	293.4	538.2	1,375.4	4,187.1	852.9
Suburbs[1]	4,702.7	3.2	39.0	85.2	377.7	787.0	3,012.8	397.7
MSA[2]	5,461.3	6.8	43.8	145.6	424.2	957.7	3,353.5	529.7
U.S.	4,922.7	6.8	35.9	186.1	382.0	919.6	2,886.5	505.8

Note: Crime rate is the number of crimes per 100,000 pop.; (1) defined as all areas within the MSA but located outside the central city; (2) Metropolitan Statistical Area - see Appendix A for areas incl.
Source: FBI Uniform Crime Reports, 1997

RECREATION

Culture and Recreation

Museums	Symphony Orchestras	Opera Companies	Dance Companies	Professional Theatres	Zoos	Pro Sports Teams
8	1	1	2	3	1	0

Source: International Directory of the Performing Arts, 1997; Official Museum Directory, 1999; Stern's Performing Arts Directory, 1997; USA Today Four Sport Stadium Guide, 1997; Chamber of Commerce/Economic Development, 1999

Library System

The Ft. Worth Public Library has nine branches, holdings of 1,157,390 volumes, and a budget of $8,014,275 (1995-1996). *American Library Directory, 1998-1999*

MEDIA

Newspapers

Name	Type	Freq.	Distribution	Circulation
Benbrook News	General	1x/wk	Local	6,000
Fort Worth Star-Telegram	General	7x/wk	Area	240,136
Fort Worth Texas Times	General	1x/wk	Local	50,000
North Texas Catholic	Religious	1x/wk	Local	26,500
River Oaks News	General	1x/wk	Local	4,500
TCU Daily Skiff	n/a	4x/wk	Campus	4,600
White Settlement Bomber News	General	1x/wk	Local	7,060

Note: Includes newspapers with circulations of 1,000 or more located in the city; n/a not available
Source: Burrelle's Media Directory, 1999 Edition

Television Stations

Name	Ch.	Affiliation	Type	Owner
KXAS	n/a	NBCT	Commercial	General Electric Corporation
KTVT	11	CBST	Commercial	Gaylord Broadcasting Company

Note: Stations included broadcast in the Fort Worth metro area; n/a not available
Source: Burrelle's Media Directory, 1999 Edition

AM Radio Stations

Call Letters	Freq. (kHz)	Target Audience	Station Format	Music Format
KMKI	620	General	M/N/S	Adult Contemporary/Adult Standards/AOR/ Big Band/Easy Listening/Oldies
WBAP	820	General	E/N/S/T	n/a
KFJZ	870	Hispanic	M	n/a
KRLD	1080	General	N/S/T	n/a
KOOO	1190	General	S/T	n/a
KAHZ	1360	General	E/M/N/S/T	n/a
KIWF	1540	Hispanic	M/N/T	n/a

Note: Stations included broadcast in the Fort Worth metro area; n/a not available
Target Audience: A=Asian; B=Black; C=Christian; E=Ethnic; F=French; G=General; H=Hispanic; M=Men; N=Native American; R=Religious; S=Senior Citizen; W=Women; Y=Young Adult; Z=Children
Station Format: E=Educational; M=Music; N=News; S=Sports; T=Talk
Music Format: AOR=Album Oriented Rock; MOR=Middle-of-the-Road
Source: Burrelle's Media Directory, 1999 Edition

FM Radio Stations

Call Letters	Freq. (mHz)	Target Audience	Station Format	Music Format
KTCU	88.7	General	M/N/S	Adult Standards/Alternative
KCBI	90.9	G/R	M/N/S	Christian
KSYE	91.5	General	M/N/S	Christian/MOR
KSCS	96.3	General	M	Country

Note: Stations included broadcast in the Fort Worth metro area
Station Format: E=Educational; M=Music; N=News; S=Sports; T=Talk
Target Audience: A=Asian; B=Black; C=Christian; E=Ethnic; F=French; G=General; H=Hispanic; M=Men; N=Native American; R=Religious; S=Senior Citizen; W=Women; Y=Young Adult; Z=Children
Music Format: AOR=Album Oriented Rock; MOR=Middle-of-the-Road
Source: Burrelle's Media Directory, 1999 Edition

CLIMATE

Average and Extreme Temperatures

Temperature	Jan	Feb	Mar	Apr	May	Jun	Jul	Aug	Sep	Oct	Nov	Dec	Yr.
Extreme High (°F)	88	88	96	98	103	113	110	108	107	106	89	90	113
Average High (°F)	54	59	67	76	83	92	96	96	88	79	67	58	76
Average Temp. (°F)	44	49	57	66	73	81	85	85	78	68	56	47	66
Average Low (°F)	33	38	45	54	63	71	75	74	67	56	45	37	55
Extreme Low (°F)	4	6	11	29	41	51	59	56	43	29	19	-1	-1

Note: Figures cover the years 1953-1990
Source: National Climatic Data Center, International Station Meteorological Climate Summary, 3/95

Average Precipitation/Snowfall/Humidity

Precip./Humidity	Jan	Feb	Mar	Apr	May	Jun	Jul	Aug	Sep	Oct	Nov	Dec	Yr.
Avg. Precip. (in.)	1.8	2.2	2.6	3.7	4.9	2.8	2.1	1.9	3.0	3.3	2.1	1.7	32.3
Avg. Snowfall (in.)	1	1	Tr	0	0	0	0	0	0	0	Tr	Tr	3
Avg. Rel. Hum. 6am (%)	79	79	79	81	86	85	80	79	83	82	80	79	81
Avg. Rel. Hum. 3pm (%)	52	51	48	50	53	47	42	41	46	47	49	51	48

Note: Figures cover the years 1953-1990; Tr = Trace amounts (<0.05 in. of rain; <0.5 in. of snow)
Source: National Climatic Data Center, International Station Meteorological Climate Summary, 3/95

Weather Conditions

Temperature			Daytime Sky			Precipitation		
10°F & below	32°F & below	90°F & above	Clear	Partly cloudy	Cloudy	0.01 inch or more precip.	0.1 inch or more snow/ice	Thunder-storms
1	40	100	123	136	106	79	3	47

Note: Figures are average number of days per year and covers the years 1953-1990
Source: National Climatic Data Center, International Station Meteorological Climate Summary, 3/95

AIR & WATER QUALITY

Maximum Pollutant Concentrations

	Particulate Matter (ug/m³)	Carbon Monoxide (ppm)	Sulfur Dioxide (ppm)	Nitrogen Dioxide (ppm)	Ozone (ppm)	Lead (ug/m³)
MSA[1] Level	47	3	n/a	0.016	0.13	n/a
NAAQS[2]	150	9	0.140	0.053	0.12	1.50
Met NAAQS?	Yes	Yes	n/a	Yes	No	n/a

Note: (1) Metropolitan Statistical Area - see Appendix A for areas included; (2) National Ambient Air Quality Standards; ppm = parts per million; ug/m³ = micrograms per cubic meter; n/a not available
Source: EPA, National Air Quality and Emissions Trends Report, 1997

Pollutant Standards Index

In the Fort Worth MSA (see Appendix A for areas included), the Pollutant Standards Index (PSI) exceeded 100 on 14 days in 1997. A PSI value greater than 100 indicates that air quality would be in the unhealthful range on that day. *EPA, National Air Quality and Emissions Trends Report, 1997*

Drinking Water

Water System Name	Pop. Served	Primary Water Source Type	Number of Violations in 1998	Type of Violation/ Contaminants
City of Fort Worth	475,000	Surface	None	None

Note: Data as of July 10, 1999
Source: EPA, Office of Ground Water and Drinking Water, Safe Drinking Water Information System

Fort Worth tap water is alkaline, hard and fluoridated.
Editor & Publisher Market Guide, 1999

Houston, Texas

Background

Two brothers back in 1836, John K. and Augustus C. Allen, bought a 6,642 acre tract of marshy, mosquito-infested land 56 miles north of the Gulf of Mexico and named it Houston, after the hero of San Jacinto. From that moment on, Houston has experienced nothing but impressive economic and population growth.

By the end of its first year in the Republic of Texas, Houston claimed 1,500 residents, one theater, and interestingly, no churches. The first churches came three years later. By the end of its second year, Houston saw its first steamship, and its position as one of the top ranking ports in the country had been defined.

Certainly, Houston owes much to the Houston ship channel, the "golden strip" on which oil refineries, chemical plants, cement factories, and grain elevators conduct their bustling economic activity. The diversity of these industries is a testament to Houston's economy in general.

Houston, like Miami and Los Angeles, has been transformed by a trade economy that now accounts for about 10 percent of regional employment. Since 1986, tonnage through the Port of Houston has grown by one-third, helping the city recover the jobs lost during the "oil bust" of the early 1980s. *World Trade, 6/96*

As Texas' biggest city, Houston is also enjoying new manufacturing expansion in its diversified economy. A revitalized downtown will soon become Continental Airlines' relocated worldwide headquarters, bringing in over 3,000 jobs from the suburbs.

Not limited to being a manufacturing center, Houston boasts of being one of the major scientific research areas in the world. The presence of the Lyndon B. Johnson Space Center has spawned a number of related industries in medical and technological research. The Texas Medical Center oversees a network of medical institutions, including St. Luke's Episcopal Hospital, the Texas Children's Hospital, and the Methodist Hospital.

A city whose reputation lies upon advanced research will certainly be devoted to education and the arts. Rice University, for example, whose admission standards rank as one of the highest in the nation, is located in Houston, as are Dominican College and the University of St. Thomas.

Houston also plays patron to the Museum of Fine Arts, the Contemporary Arts Museum, and the Houston Ballet and Grand Opera. A host of smaller cultural institutions, such as the Gilbert and Sullivan Society, the Virtuoso Quartet, and the Houston Harpsichord Society enliven the scene. Two new privately funded museums, the Holocaust Museum Houston and the Museum of Health & Medical Science, opened last year. And a new baseball stadium was completed last April in the city's downtown.

Located in the flat Coastal Plains, Houston's climate is predominantly marine. The terrain includes many small streams and bayous which, together with the nearness to Galveston Bay, favor the development of fog. Temperatures are moderated by the influence of winds from the Gulf of Mexico, which is 50 miles away. Mild winters are the norm, as is abundant rainfall. Polar air penetrates the area frequently enough to provide variability in the weather.

General Rankings and Evaluative Comments

■ Houston was ranked #15 out of 19 large, southern metropolitan areas in *Money's* 1998 survey of "The Best Places to Live in America." The survey was conducted by first contacting 512 representative households nationwide and asking them to rank 37 quality-of-life factors on a scale of 1 to 10. Next, a demographic profile was compiled on the 300 largest metropolitan statistical areas in the U.S. The numbers were crunched together to arrive at an overall ranking (things Americans consider most important, like clean air and water, low crime and good schools, received extra weight). Unlike previous years, the 1998 rankings were broken down by region (northeast, midwest, south, west) and population size (100,000 to 249,999; 250,000 to 999,999; 1 million plus). The city had a nationwide ranking of #50 out of 300 in 1997 and #35 out of 300 in 1996. *Money, July 1998; Money, July 1997; Money, September 1996*

■ *Ladies Home Journal* ranked America's 200 largest cities based on the qualities women care about most. Houston ranked #171 out of 200. Criteria: low crime rate, well-paying jobs, quality health and child care, good public schools, the presence of women in government, size of the gender wage gap, number of sexual-harassment and discrimination complaints filed, unemployment and divorce rates, commute times, population density, number of houses of worship, parks and cultural offerings, number of women's health specialists, how well a community's women cared for themselves, complexion kindness index based on UV radiation levels, odds of finding affordable fashions, rental rates for romance movies, champagne sales and other matters of the heart. *Ladies Home Journal, November 1998*

■ Zero Population Growth ranked 229 cities in terms of children's health, safety, and economic well-being. Houston was ranked #15 out of 25 major cities (main city in a metro area with population of greater than 2 million) and was given a grade of C. Criteria: total population, percent of population under 18 years of age, household language, percent population change, percent of births to teens, infant mortality rate, percent of low birth weights, dropout rate, enrollment in preprimary school, violent and property crime rates, unemployment rate, percent of children in poverty, percent of owner occupied units, number of bad air days, percent of public transportation commuters, and average travel time to work. *Zero Population Growth, Children's Environmental Index, Fall 1999*

■ Houston was ranked #30 out of 59 metro areas in *The Regional Economist's* "Rational Livability Ranking of 59 Large Metro Areas." The rankings were based on the metro area's total population change over the period 1990-97 divided by the number of people moving in from elsewhere in the United States (net domestic in-migration). *St. Louis Federal Reserve Bank of St. Louis, The Regional Economist, April 1999*

■ Houston appeared on *Travel & Leisure's* list of the world's 100 best cities. It was ranked #42 in the U.S. Criteria: activities/attractions, culture/arts, people, restaurants/food, and value. *Travel & Leisure, 1998 World's Best Awards*

■ Houston was selected by *Yahoo! Internet Life* as one of "America's Most Wired Cities & Towns." The city ranked #26 out of 50. Criteria: home and work net use, domain density, hosts per capita, directory density and content quality. *Yahoo! Internet Life, March 1999*

■ Cognetics studied 273 metro areas in the United States, ranking them by entrepreneurial activity. Houston was ranked #27 out of the 50 largest metro areas. Criteria: Significant Starts (firms started in the last 10 years that still employ at least 5 people) and Young Growers (percent of firms 10 years old or less that grew significantly during the last 4 years). *Cognetics, "Entrepreneurial Hot Spots: The Best Places in America to Start and Grow a Company," 1998*

■ Houston appeared on *Forbes* list of "Best Places for Business Growth." Rank: #9 out of 162 metro areas. Criteria: average wage and salary increases, job growth rates, number of technology clusters (measures business activity in 13 different technology areas), overall concentration of technology activity relative to national average and technology output growth. *Forbes, May 31, 1999*

■ Houston was included among *Entrepreneur* magazine's listing of the "20 Best Cities for Small Business." It was ranked #14 among large metro areas and #3 among central metro areas. Criteria: entrepreneurial activity, small-business growth, economic growth, and risk of failure. *Entrepreneur, October 1999*

■ Houston was selected as one of the "Best American Cities to Start a Business" by *Point of View* magazine. Criteria: coolness, quality-of-life, and business concerns. The city was ranked #23 out of 75. *Point of View, November 1998*

■ Reliastar Financial Corp. ranked the 125 largest metropolitan areas according to the general financial security of residents. Houston was ranked #51 out of 125 with a score of 3.4. The score indicates the percentage a metropolitan area is above or below the metropolitan norm. A metro area with a score of 10.6 is 10.6% above the metro average. Criteria: Earnings and Wealth Potential (household income, education, net assets, cost of living); Safety Net (health insurance, retirement savings, life insurance, income support programs); Personal Threats (unemployment rate, low-income households, crime rate); Community Economic Vitality (cost of community services, job quality, job creation, housing costs). *Reliastar Financial Corp., "The Best Cities to Earn and Save Money," 1999 Edition*

Business Environment

STATE ECONOMY

State Economic Profile

"Economic growth in Texas has slowed as both its new and old economies are under pressure. Weak commodity prices and over-capacity have hurt TX's old economic powers, agriculture and oil. Soft global demand has slowed TX's new economic powers, semiconductors and computer sales. A slowing US economy in 1999 will also place a drag on TX's biotech and software companies. Despite the current slowdown, TX's long-term outlook is extremely bright, and its current problems will last no more than two years.

Weak commodity prices, over-capacity and soft foreign demand have all coincided to undermine TX's oil and farm sector. Despite OPEC cutbacks, the TX oil industry remains vulnerable because of its high costs, high inventories and high capacity. TX's farm sector is similarly positioned; commodity prices are expected to continue their long-term downward trend.

The TX economy is more diversified today than ever before. Growth in services and hi-tech employment have more than offset declines in TX's resource economy. Services employment in 1998 grew at 3.8%, adding some 93,000 jobs, while construction employment grew 4.9%, adding 22,700 jobs. Construction employment, along with home sales and starts, should contract in 1999 and 2000. TX's demographic situation is positive; the state continues to attract educated, young households. However, the current weakness in the state's semiconductor and computer industry has slowed job growth from its previous feverish pace. In the near-term, TX's growth should slow along with the US economy. Its long-term prospects are bright given its business friendly atmosphere and central location." *National Association of Realtors, Economic Profiles: The Fifty States and the District of Columbia, http://nar.realtor.com/databank/profiles.htm*

IMPORTS/EXPORTS

Total Export Sales

Area	1994 ($000)	1995 ($000)	1996 ($000)	1997 ($000)	% Chg. 1994-97	% Chg. 1996-97
MSA[1]	13,388,170	16,247,880	16,541,463	18,595,875	38.9	12.4
U.S.	512,415,609	583,030,524	622,827,063	687,597,999	34.2	10.4

Note: (1) Metropolitan Statistical Area - see Appendix A for areas included
Source: U.S. Department of Commerce, International Trade Association, Metropolitan Area Exports: An Export Performance Report on Over 250 U.S. Cities, November 10, 1998

CITY FINANCES

City Government Finances

Component	FY94 ($000)	FY94 (per capita $)
Revenue	2,022,210	1,174.84
Expenditure	2,055,402	1,194.12
Debt Outstanding	3,822,263	2,220.61
Cash & Securities	3,929,559	2,282.95

Source: U.S. Bureau of the Census, City Government Finances: 1993-94

City Government Revenue by Source

Source	FY94 ($000)	FY94 (per capita $)	FY94 (%)
From Federal Government	66,040	38.37	3.3
From State Governments	19,702	11.45	1.0
From Local Governments	10,152	5.90	0.5
Property Taxes	407,904	236.98	20.2
General Sales Taxes	226,361	131.51	11.2
Selective Sales Taxes	140,584	81.67	7.0
Income Taxes	0	0.00	0.0
Current Charges	434,987	252.71	21.5
Utility/Liquor Store	252,502	146.70	12.5
Employee Retirement[1]	283,521	164.72	14.0
Other	180,457	104.84	8.9

Note: (1) Excludes "city contributions," classified as "nonrevenue," intragovernmental transfers.
Source: U.S. Bureau of the Census, City Government Finances: 1993-94

City Government Expenditures by Function

Function	FY94 ($000)	FY94 (per capita $)	FY94 (%)
Educational Services	27,739	16.12	1.3
Employee Retirement[1]	83,418	48.46	4.1
Environment/Housing	404,820	235.19	19.7
Government Administration	84,816	49.28	4.1
Interest on General Debt	154,720	89.89	7.5
Public Safety	513,730	298.46	25.0
Social Services	68,504	39.80	3.3
Transportation	347,943	202.14	16.9
Utility/Liquor Store	274,054	159.22	13.3
Other	95,658	55.57	4.7

Note: (1) Payments to beneficiaries including withdrawal of contributions.
Source: U.S. Bureau of the Census, City Government Finances: 1993-94

Municipal Bond Ratings

Area	Moody's	S & P
Houston	Aaa	n/a

Note: n/a not available; n/r not rated
Source: Moody's Bond Record, 6/99

POPULATION

Population Growth

Area	1980	1990	% Chg. 1980-90	July 1998 Estimate	% Chg. 1990-98
City	1,595,167	1,630,672	2.2	1,786,691	9.6
MSA[1]	2,735,766	3,301,937	20.7	3,948,587	19.6
U.S.	226,545,805	248,765,170	9.8	270,299,000	8.7

Note: (1) Metropolitan Statistical Area - see Appendix A for areas included;
July 1998 MSA population estimate was calculated by the editors
Source: 1980/1990 Census of Housing and Population, Summary Tape File 3C;
Census Bureau Population Estimates 1998

Population Characteristics

Race	City 1980 Population	%	City 1990 Population	%	% Chg. 1980-90	MSA[1] 1990 Population	%
White	981,563	61.5	860,323	52.8	-12.4	2,191,107	66.4
Black	439,604	27.6	457,574	28.1	4.1	610,377	18.5
Amer Indian/Esk/Aleut	3,945	0.2	4,376	0.3	10.9	9,912	0.3
Asian/Pacific Islander	35,448	2.2	66,008	4.0	86.2	124,723	3.8
Other	134,607	8.4	242,391	14.9	80.1	365,818	11.1
Hispanic Origin[2]	281,331	17.6	442,943	27.2	57.4	696,208	21.1

Note: (1) Metropolitan Statistical Area - see Appendix A for areas included;
(2) people of Hispanic origin can be of any race
Source: 1980/1990 Census of Housing and Population, Summary Tape File 3C

Ancestry

Area	German	Irish	English	Italian	U.S.	French	Polish	Dutch
City	11.7	8.4	8.8	2.1	2.9	3.0	1.5	1.0
MSA[1]	17.0	12.5	11.4	2.6	4.1	3.9	2.0	1.5
U.S.	23.3	15.6	13.1	5.9	5.3	4.2	3.8	2.5

Note: Figures are percentages and include persons that reported multiple ancestry (eg. if a person reported being Irish and Italian, they were included in both columns); (1) Metropolitan Statistical Area - see Appendix A for areas included
Source: 1990 Census of Population and Housing, Summary Tape File 3C

Age

Area	Median Age (Years)	Age Distribution (%) Under 5	Under 18	18-24	25-44	45-64	65+	80+
City	30.3	8.3	26.7	11.6	36.4	17.1	8.2	1.6
MSA[1]	30.4	8.5	28.9	10.4	36.9	16.7	7.0	1.4
U.S.	32.9	7.3	25.6	10.5	32.6	18.7	12.5	2.8

Note: (1) Metropolitan Statistical Area - see Appendix A for areas included
Source: 1990 Census of Population and Housing, Summary Tape File 3C

Male/Female Ratio

Area	Number of males per 100 females (all ages)	Number of males per 100 females (18 years old+)
City	98.4	96.3
MSA[1]	98.8	96.6
U.S.	95.0	91.9

Note: (1) Metropolitan Statistical Area - see Appendix A for areas included
Source: 1990 Census of Population, General Population Characteristics

INCOME

Per Capita/Median/Average Income

Area	Per Capita ($)	Median Household ($)	Average Household ($)
City	14,261	26,261	37,296
MSA[1]	15,091	31,473	41,650
U.S.	14,420	30,056	38,453

Note: All figures are for 1989; (1) Metropolitan Statistical Area - see Appendix A for areas included
Source: 1990 Census of Population and Housing, Summary Tape File 3C

Household Income Distribution by Race

Income ($)	City (%)					U.S. (%)				
	Total	White	Black	Other	Hisp.[1]	Total	White	Black	Other	Hisp.[1]
Less than 5,000	8.9	5.2	16.4	10.6	9.7	6.2	4.8	15.2	8.6	8.8
5,000 - 9,999	9.1	6.9	13.2	10.7	11.1	9.3	8.6	14.2	9.9	11.1
10,000 - 14,999	9.9	8.1	12.2	13.3	14.5	8.8	8.5	11.0	9.8	11.0
15,000 - 24,999	19.7	17.9	21.5	24.0	25.4	17.5	17.3	18.9	18.5	20.5
25,000 - 34,999	15.8	16.2	14.9	15.8	16.8	15.8	16.1	14.2	15.4	16.4
35,000 - 49,999	15.2	16.9	12.3	13.4	12.8	17.9	18.6	13.3	16.1	16.0
50,000 - 74,999	12.1	15.2	7.1	8.1	6.7	15.0	15.8	9.3	13.4	11.1
75,000 - 99,999	4.5	6.3	1.6	2.3	1.7	5.1	5.5	2.6	4.7	3.1
100,000+	4.8	7.3	0.7	1.8	1.2	4.4	4.8	1.3	3.7	1.9

Note: All figures are for 1989; (1) people of Hispanic origin can be of any race
Source: 1990 Census of Population and Housing, Summary Tape File 3C

Effective Buying Income

Area	Per Capita ($)	Median Household ($)	Average Household ($)
City	17,300	32,961	46,019
MSA[1]	19,045	39,325	53,256
U.S.	16,803	34,536	45,243

Note: Data as of 1/1/99; (1) Metropolitan Statistical Area - see Appendix A for areas included
Source: Standard Rate & Data Service, Newspaper Advertising Source, 9/99

Effective Household Buying Income Distribution

Area	% of Households Earning						
	$10,000 -$19,999	$20,000 -$34,999	$35,000 -$49,999	$50,000 -$74,999	$75,000 -$99,000	$100,000 -$124,999	$125,000 and up
City	15.9	23.1	16.5	16.0	7.3	3.0	4.2
MSA[1]	13.4	20.8	17.1	19.8	9.8	3.8	4.5
U.S.	16.0	22.6	18.2	18.9	7.2	2.4	2.7

Note: Data as of 1/1/99; (1) Metropolitan Statistical Area - see Appendix A for areas included
Source: Standard Rate & Data Service, Newspaper Advertising Source, 9/99

Poverty Rates by Race and Age

Area	Total (%)	By Race (%)				By Age (%)		
		White	Black	Other	Hisp.[2]	Under 5 years old	Under 18 years old	65 years and over
City	20.7	12.4	30.7	29.3	30.7	31.4	30.0	17.8
MSA[1]	15.1	9.4	27.9	24.8	26.6	21.6	20.2	16.0
U.S.	13.1	9.8	29.5	23.1	25.3	20.1	18.3	12.8

Note: Figures show the percent of people living below the poverty line in 1989. The average poverty threshold was $12,674 for a family of four in 1989; (1) Metropolitan Statistical Area - see Appendix A for areas included; (2) people of Hispanic origin can be of any race
Source: 1990 Census of Population and Housing, Summary Tape File 3C

EMPLOYMENT

Labor Force and Employment

Area	Civilian Labor Force			Workers Employed		
	Jun. 1998	Jun. 1999	% Chg.	Jun. 1998	Jun. 1999	% Chg.
City	1,039,379	1,064,139	2.4	976,636	993,824	1.8
MSA[1]	2,163,969	2,212,962	2.3	2,056,977	2,093,177	1.8
U.S.	138,798,000	140,666,000	1.3	132,265,000	134,395,000	1.6

Note: Data is not seasonally adjusted and covers workers 16 years of age and older; (1) Metropolitan Statistical Area - see Appendix A for areas included
Source: Bureau of Labor Statistics, http://stats.bls.gov

Unemployment Rate

Area	1998						1999					
	Jul.	Aug.	Sep.	Oct.	Nov.	Dec.	Jan.	Feb.	Mar.	Apr.	May.	Jun.
City	5.5	5.1	4.9	4.5	4.7	4.5	5.4	5.1	4.8	5.1	5.6	6.6
MSA[1]	4.5	4.1	4.0	3.7	3.8	3.6	4.4	4.2	4.0	4.2	4.6	5.4
U.S.	4.7	4.5	4.4	4.2	4.1	4.0	4.8	4.7	4.4	4.1	4.0	4.5

Note: Data is not seasonally adjusted and covers workers 16 years of age and older; all figures are percentages; (1) Metropolitan Statistical Area - see Appendix A for areas included
Source: Bureau of Labor Statistics, http://stats.bls.gov

Employment by Industry

Sector	MSA[1]		U.S.
	Number of Employees	Percent of Total	Percent of Total
Services	634,700	31.2	30.4
Retail Trade	334,200	16.4	17.7
Government	253,100	12.4	15.6
Manufacturing	214,100	10.5	14.3
Finance/Insurance/Real Estate	110,600	5.4	5.9
Wholesale Trade	133,400	6.6	5.4
Transportation/Public Utilities	144,400	7.1	5.3
Construction	144,600	7.1	5.0
Mining	64,000	3.1	0.4

Note: Figures cover non-farm employment as of 6/99 and are not seasonally adjusted;
(1) Metropolitan Statistical Area - see Appendix A for areas included
Source: Bureau of Labor Statistics, http://stats.bls.gov

Employment by Occupation

Occupation Category	City (%)	MSA[1] (%)	U.S. (%)
White Collar	60.6	62.6	58.1
Executive/Admin./Management	13.0	14.0	12.3
Professional	14.8	14.8	14.1
Technical & Related Support	4.3	4.4	3.7
Sales	12.6	13.0	11.8
Administrative Support/Clerical	16.0	16.4	16.3
Blue Collar	23.5	23.8	26.2
Precision Production/Craft/Repair	10.4	11.6	11.3
Machine Operators/Assem./Insp.	4.6	4.3	6.8
Transportation/Material Movers	4.0	3.9	4.1
Cleaners/Helpers/Laborers	4.5	4.0	3.9
Services	14.8	12.5	13.2
Farming/Forestry/Fishing	1.1	1.1	2.5

Note: Figures cover employed persons 16 years old and over;
(1) Metropolitan Statistical Area - see Appendix A for areas included
Source: 1990 Census of Population and Housing, Summary Tape File 3C

Occupational Employment Projections: 1996 - 2006

Occupations Expected to Have the Largest Job Growth (ranked by numerical growth)	Fast-Growing Occupations[1] (ranked by percent growth)
1. Cashiers	1. Desktop publishers
2. Salespersons, retail	2. Systems analysts
3. General managers & top executives	3. Customer service representatives
4. Truck drivers, light	4. Physical therapy assistants and aides
5. Child care workers, private household	5. Computer engineers
6. General office clerks	6. Emergency medical technicians
7. Systems analysts	7. Medical assistants
8. Food preparation workers	8. Respiratory therapists
9. Food service workers	9. Telephone & cable TV line install & repair
10. Registered nurses	10. Physical therapists

Note: Projections cover Texas; (1) Excludes occupations with total job growth less than 300
Source: U.S. Department of Labor, Employment and Training Administration, America's Labor Market Information System (ALMIS)

TAXES

Major State and Local Tax Rates

State Corp. Income (%)	State Personal Income (%)	Residential Property (effective rate per $100)	Sales & Use		State Gasoline (cents/gallon)	State Cigarette (cents/pack)
			State (%)	Local (%)		
None[a]	None	2.70	6.25	2.0	20.0	41.0

Note: Personal/corporate income, sales, gasoline and cigarette tax rates as of January 1999. Property tax rates as of 1997; (a) Texas imposes a franchise tax of 4.5% of earned surplus
Source: Federation of Tax Administrators, www.taxadmin.org; Washington D.C. Department of Finance and Revenue, Tax Rates and Tax Burdens in the District of Columbia: A Nationwide Comparison, July 1998; Chamber of Commerce, 1999

Total Taxes Per Capita and as a Percent of Income

Area	Per Capita Income ($)	Per Capita Taxes ($)			Percent of Income (%)		
		Total	Federal	State/Local	Total	Federal	State/Local
Texas	25,563	8,741	6,051	2,690	34.2	23.7	10.5
U.S.	27,876	9,881	6,690	3,191	35.4	24.0	11.4

Note: Figures are for 1998
Source: Tax Foundation, www.taxfoundation.org

Estimated Tax Burden

Area	State Income	Local Income	Property	Sales	Total
Houston	0	0	5,500	804	6,304

Note: The numbers are estimates of taxes paid by a married couple with two children and annual earnings of $75,000. Sales tax estimates assume they spend average amounts on food, clothing, household goods and gasoline. Property tax estimates assume they live in a $250,000 home.
Source: Kiplinger's Personal Finance Magazine, October 1998

COMMERCIAL REAL ESTATE

Office Market

Class/ Location	Total Space (sq. ft.)	Vacant Space (sq. ft.)	Vac. Rate (%)	Under Constr. (sq. ft.)	Net Absorp. (sq. ft.)	Rental Rates ($/sq. ft./yr.)
Class A						
CBD	21,040,551	872,919	4.1	0	763,887	16.55-26.63
Outside CBD	25,223,238	1,125,418	4.5	3,369,364	1,218,272	10.00-28.00
Class B						
CBD	7,652,820	688,122	9.0	0	517,913	13.00-21.00
Outside CBD	49,702,293	4,581,786	9.2	0	552,986	8.00-26.00

Note: Data as of 10/98 and covers Houston; CBD = Central Business District; n/a not available;
Source: Society of Industrial and Office Realtors, 1999 Comparative Statistics of Industrial and Office Real Estate Markets

"Houston's tight office market will ease somewhat in 1999. Several buildings under construction are for users who will give up large blocks of leased space. By the third quarter of 1999, more than one million square feet will also become available through new construction. More will be ready by the end of the year. The growth of computer companies such as Compaq and BMC will boost Houston's economy; however, low oil prices could still have a negative impact, despite the economy's diversification over the past decade. Houston's SIOR reporter anticipates a six to 10 percent increase in sales prices outside the CBD; a one to five percent gain in absorption, construction and rental rates; and a one to five percent reduction in vacancy during 1999." *Society of Industrial and Office Realtors, 1999 Comparative Statistics of Industrial and Office Real Estate Markets*

Industrial Market

Location	Total Space (sq. ft.)	Vacant Space (sq. ft.)	Vac. Rate (%)	Under Constr. (sq. ft.)	Net Absorp. (sq. ft.)	Lease ($/sq.ft./yr.)
Central City	106,769,490	9,045,943	8.5	240,000	1,778,342	2.49-5.13
Suburban	126,660,534	9,742,087	7.7	3,877,340	5,058,670	2.89-6.04

Note: Data as of 10/98 and covers Houston; n/a not available
Source: Society of Industrial and Office Realtors, 1999 Comparative Statistics of Industrial and Office Real Estate Markets

"About 79,500 new jobs were created in Houston dining the past year, and the local economy is humming. Future plans for Houston include a $1.4 billion improvement package for the three airports and a new container terminal at the Port of Houston—things that will favorably affect the industrial market. Relocations to Houston also continue at a steady pace, with companies coming from Scotland, France, Japan, Taiwan, Australia, and England. Despite those optimistic signs, our SIOR reporter anticipates that the dollar volume of leases and sales, as well as construction, absorption, sales prices, and lease prices will all advance by only one to five percent during 1999. There is a moderate to substantial shortage for most types of industrial space, and capital for development is available—but developers are still cautious." *Society of Industrial and Office Realtors, 1999 Comparative Statistics of Industrial and Office Real Estate Markets*

Retail Market

Shopping Center Inventory (sq. ft.)	Shopping Center Construction (sq. ft.)	Construction as a Percent of Inventory (%)	Torto Wheaton Rent Index[1] ($/sq. ft.)
67,233,000	1,250,000	1.9	14.04

Note: Data as of 1997 and covers the Metropolitan Statistical Area - see Appendix A for areas included; (1) Index is based on a model that predicts what the average rent should be for leases with certain characteristics, in certain locations during certain years.
Source: National Association of Realtors, 1997-1998 Market Conditions Report

"Houston's rebounding economy has aided its retail sector. With the exception of 1995, the area's retail rent index has risen every year since 1991. Houston residents command relatively

high per capita incomes. In 1996, the MSA's per-capita income was $25,700 compared to $22,200 for Texas and $24,200 nationally. The return of the oil industry is expected to further boost the economy. 1996 and 1997 were strong years for retail development; however, the market seems to have settled into a sustainable pace. Most developers are expected to concentrate on grocery store-anchored centers and niche market centers. Shopping center completions are expected to average 1.4 million square feet over the next two years."
National Association of Realtors, 1997-1998 Market Conditions Report

COMMERCIAL UTILITIES

Typical Monthly Electric Bills

Area	Commercial Service ($/month)		Industrial Service ($/month)	
	12 kW demand 1,500 kWh	100 kW demand 30,000 kWh	1,000 kW demand 400,000 kWh	20,000 kW demand 10,000,000 kWh
City	132	2,198	24,139	311,297
U.S.	150	2,174	23,995	508,569

Note: Based on rates in effect January 1, 1999
Source: Edison Electric Institute, Typical Residential, Commercial and Industrial Bills, Winter 1999

TRANSPORTATION

Transportation Statistics

Average minutes to work	24.7
Interstate highways	I-10; I-45
Bus lines	
In-city	Metropolitan Transit Authority of Harris County, 1,427 vehicles
Inter-city	10
Passenger air service	
Airport	Ellington Field; Bush Intercontinental; William P. Hobby
Airlines	37
Aircraft departures	244,787 (1996)
Enplaned passengers	15,695,374 (1996)
Rail service	Amtrak
Motor freight carriers	170 local; 634 non-local truck lines
Major waterways/ports	Gulf of Mexico; Port of Houston

Source: Editor & Publisher Market Guide, 1999; FAA Airport Activity Statistics, 1997; Amtrak National Time Table, Northeast Timetable, Spring/Summer 1999; 1990 Census of Population and Housing, STF 3C; Chamber of Commerce/Economic Development 1999; Jane's Urban Transport Systems 1999-2000

Means of Transportation to Work

Area	Car/Truck/Van		Public Transportation			Bicycle	Walked	Other Means	Worked at Home
	Drove Alone	Car-pooled	Bus	Subway	Railroad				
City	71.7	15.5	6.3	0.0	0.0	0.4	3.0	1.2	2.0
MSA[1]	75.7	14.6	4.0	0.0	0.0	0.3	2.2	1.1	2.1
U.S.	73.2	13.4	3.0	1.5	0.5	0.4	3.9	1.2	3.0

Note: Figures shown are percentages and only include workers 16 years old and over;
(1) Metropolitan Statistical Area - see Appendix A for areas included
Source: 1990 Census of Population and Housing, Summary Tape File 3C

BUSINESSES

Major Business Headquarters

Company Name	1999 Rankings	
	Fortune 500	Forbes 500
American General	156	-
Baker Hughes	265	-
Browning-Ferris Industries	332	-
Coastal	235	-
Compaq Computer	28	-
Continental Airlines	207	-
Cooper Industries	317	-
David Weekley Homes	-	465
El Paso Energy	286	-
Enron	27	-
Enterprise Products	-	163
Fiesta Mart	-	303
Goodman Manufacturing	-	79
Grocers Supply Co	-	127
Gulf States Toyota	-	52
Houston Industries	147	-
Randall's Food Markets	-	58
Sysco	97	-
Texas Petrochemicals	-	455

Note: Companies listed are located in the city; dashes indicate no ranking
Fortune 500: Companies that produce a 10-K are ranked 1 to 500 based on 1998 revenue
Forbes 500: Private companies are ranked 1 to 500 based on 1997 revenue
Source: Forbes, November 30, 1998; Fortune, April 26, 1999

Best Companies to Work For

Continental Airlines, BMC Software and Enron (energy), headquartered in Houston, are among the "100 Best Companies to Work for in America." Criteria: trust in management, pride in work/company, camaraderie, company responses to the Hewitt People Practices Inventory, and employee responses to their Great Place to Work survey. The companies also had to be at least 10 years old and have a minimum of 500 employees. *Fortune, January 11, 1999*

Compaq Computer Corp. (computer hardware) and Continental Airlines (transportation), headquartered in Houston, are among the "100 Best Places to Work in IS." Criteria: compensation, turnover and training. *Computerworld, May 25, 1998*

Fast-Growing Businesses

According to *Inc.*, Houston is home to one of America's 100 fastest-growing private companies: Business Integrators. Criteria for inclusion: must be an independent, privately-held, U.S. corporation, proprietorship or partnership; sales of at least $200,000 in 1995; five-year operating/sales history; increase in 1999 sales over 1998 sales; holding companies, regulated banks, and utilities were excluded. *Inc. 500, 1999*

Houston is home to one of *Business Week's* "hot growth" companies: Metro Networks. Criteria: increase in sales and profits, return on capital and stock price. *Business Week, 5/31/99*

According to *Fortune*, Houston is home to four of America's 100 fastest-growing companies: Consolidated Graphics, Veritas DCG, El Paso Energy and Stewart Information Services. Companies were ranked based on earnings-per-share growth, revenue growth and total return over the previous three years. Criteria for inclusion: public companies with sales of least $50 million. Companies that lost money in the most recent quarter, or ended in the red for the past four quarters as a whole, were not eligible. Limited partnerships and REITs were also not considered. *Fortune, "America's Fastest-Growing Companies," 1999*

According to Deloitte & Touche LLP, Houston is home to two of America's 100 fastest-growing high-technology companies: Alpha Technologies Group and Texas

Biotechnology Corporation. Companies are ranked by percentage growth in revenue over a five-year period. Criteria for inclusion: must be a U.S. company developing and/or providing technology products or services; company must have been in business for five years with 1993 revenues of at least $50,000. *Deloitte & Touche LLP, November 17, 1998*

Women-Owned Firms: Number, Employment and Sales

Area	Number of Firms	Employ-ment	Sales ($000)	Rank[2]
MSA[1]	136,400	560,100	78,180,300	5

Note: (1) Metropolitan Statistical Area - see Appendix A for areas included;
(2) Calculated on an averaging of the number of businesses, employment and sales
Source: The National Foundation for Women Business Owners, 1999 Facts on Women-Owned Businesses: Trends in the Top 50 Metropolitan Areas

Women-Owned Firms: Growth

Area	% change from 1992 to 1999			Rank[2]
	Number of Firms	Employ-ment	Sales	
MSA[1]	43.6	208.8	224.3	4

Note: (1) Metropolitan Statistical Area - see Appendix A for areas included; (2) Calculated on an averaging of the percent growth of number of businesses, employment and sales
Source: The National Foundation for Women Business Owners, 1999 Facts on Women-Owned Businesses: Trends in the Top 50 Metropolitan Areas

Minority Business Opportunity

Houston is home to two companies which are on the Black Enterprise Industrial/Service 100 list (largest based on gross sales): Olajuwon Holdings (Denny's restaurants); Wilson Financial Group Inc. (death care industry) . Criteria: operational in previous calendar year, at least 51% black-owned and manufactures/owns the product it sells or provides industrial or consumer services. Brokerages, real estate firms and firms that provide professional services are not eligible. *Black Enterprise, www.blackenterprise.com*

Houston is home to two companies which are on the Black Enterprise Auto Dealer 100 list (largest based on gross sales): Northwood Lincoln-Mercury/JMC Auto Group (Lincoln-Mercury); Barnett Automotive Group (GMC, Pontiac) . Criteria: 1) operational in previous calendar year; 2) at least 51% black-owned. *Black Enterprise, www.blackenterprise.com*

20 of the 500 largest Hispanic-owned companies in the U.S. are located in Houston. *Hispanic Business, June 1999*

Houston is home to four companies which are on the Hispanic Business Fastest-Growing 100 list (greatest sales growth from 1994 to 1998): Plaza Group Inc. (petrochemicals distribution); Standard Glass & Mirror Inc. (glass & glazing contracting); Analytical Computer Services (computer sales and services); Trevino Group Inc. (general contracting). *Hispanic Business, July/August 1999*

Small Business Opportunity

According to *Forbes*, Houston is home to three of America's 200 best small companies: Cal Dive International, Dril Quip and Midcoast Energy Resources. Criteria: companies included must be publicly traded since November 1997 with a stock price of at least $5 per share and an average daily float of 1,000 shares. The company's latest 12-month sales must be between $5 and $350 million, return on equity (ROE) must be a minimum of 12% for both the past 5 years and the most recent four quarters, and five-year sales and EPS growth must average at least 10%. Companies with declining sales or earnings during the past year were dropped as well as businesses with debt/equity ratios over 1.25. Companies with negative operating cash flow in each of the past two years were also excluded. *Forbes, November 2, 1998*

HOTELS & MOTELS

Hotels/Motels

Area	Hotels/ Motels	Rooms	Luxury-Level Hotels/Motels		Average Minimum Rates ($)		
			♦♦♦♦	♦♦♦♦♦	♦♦	♦♦♦	♦♦♦♦
City	154	26,022	6	0	69	111	195
Airport	17	3,898	0	0	n/a	n/a	n/a
Suburbs	25	1,982	0	0	n/a	n/a	n/a
Total	196	31,902	6	0	n/a	n/a	n/a

Note: n/a not available; classifications range from one diamond (budget properties with basic amenities) to five diamond (luxury properties with the finest service, rooms and facilities).
Source: OAG, Business Travel Planner, Winter 1998-99

CONVENTION CENTERS

Major Convention Centers

Center Name	Meeting Rooms	Exhibit Space (sq. ft.)
Astrodome USA	28	1,150,000
George R. Brown Convention Center	41	451,500
INNOVA	5	19,138
Krystal Vallarta	5	13,000
The Summit	n/a	n/a
Westin Galleria	4	75,000

Note: n/a not available
Source: Trade Shows Worldwide, 1998; Meetings & Conventions, 4/15/99; Sucessful Meetings, 3/31/98

Living Environment

COST OF LIVING

Cost of Living Index

Composite Index	Groceries	Housing	Utilities	Trans-portation	Health Care	Misc. Goods/ Services
94.9	90.6	84.3	101.0	106.7	110.2	98.5

Note: U.S. = 100; Figures are for the Metropolitan Statistical Area - see Appendix A for areas included
Source: ACCRA, Cost of Living Index, 1st Quarter 1999

HOUSING

Median Home Prices and Housing Affordability

Area	Median Price[2] 1st Qtr. 1999 ($)	HOI[3] 1st Qtr. 1999	Afford-ability Rank[4]
MSA[1]	111,000	71.6	107
U.S.	134,000	69.6	–

Note: (1) Metropolitan Statistical Area - see Appendix A for areas included; (2) U.S. figures calculated from the sales of 524,324 new and existing homes in 181 markets; (3) Housing Opportunity Index - percent of homes sold that were within the reach of the median income household at the prevailing mortgage interest rate; (4) Rank is from 1-181 with 1 being most affordable
Source: National Association of Home Builders, Housing Opportunity Index, 1st Quarter 1999

Median Home Price Projection

It is projected that the median price of existing single-family homes in the metro area will increase by 5.0% in 1999. Nationwide, home prices are projected to increase 3.8%.
Kiplinger's Personal Finance Magazine, January 1999

Average New Home Price

Area	Price ($)
MSA[1]	113,422
U.S.	142,735

Note: Figures are based on a new home with 1,800 sq. ft. of living area on an 8,000 sq. ft. lot;
(1) Metropolitan Statistical Area - see Appendix A for areas included
Source: ACCRA, Cost of Living Index, 1st Quarter 1999

Average Apartment Rent

Area	Rent ($/mth)
MSA[1]	686
U.S.	601

Note: Figures are based on an unfurnished two bedroom, 1-1/2 or 2 bath apartment, approximately 950 sq. ft. in size, excluding all utilities except water; (1) Metropolitan Statistical Area - see Appendix A for areas included
Source: ACCRA, Cost of Living Index, 1st Quarter 1999

RESIDENTIAL UTILITIES

Average Residential Utility Costs

Area	All Electric ($/mth)	Part Electric ($/mth)	Other Energy ($/mth)	Phone ($/mth)
MSA[1]	–	76.14	26.12	17.50
U.S.	100.02	55.73	43.33	19.71

Note: (1) (1) Metropolitan Statistical Area - see Appendix A for areas included
Source: ACCRA, Cost of Living Index, 1st Quarter 1999

HEALTH CARE

Average Health Care Costs

Area	Hospital ($/day)	Doctor ($/visit)	Dentist ($/visit)
MSA[1]	445.41	61.50	71.08
U.S.	430.43	52.45	66.35

Note: Hospital—based on a semi-private room; Doctor—based on a general practitioner's routine exam of an established patient; Dentist—based on adult teeth cleaning and periodic oral exam; (1) Metropolitan Statistical Area - see Appendix A for areas included
Source: ACCRA, Cost of Living Index, 1st Quarter 1999

Distribution of Office-Based Physicians

Area	Family/Gen. Practitioners	Specialists		
		Medical	Surgical	Other
MSA[1]	853	2,215	1,821	1,939

Note: Data as of 12/31/97; (1) Metropolitan Statistical Area - see Appendix A for areas included
Source: American Medical Assn., Physician Characteristics & Distribution in the U.S., 1999

Hospitals

Houston has 24 general medical and surgical hospitals, 7 psychiatric, 1 obstetrics and gynecology, 3 rehabilitation, 1 orthopedic, 1 alcoholism and other chemical dependency, 5 other specialty, 1 children's general, 1 children's orthopedic. *AHA Guide to the Healthcare Field, 1998-99*

According to *U.S. News and World Report,* Houston has 6 of the best hospitals in the U.S.: **University of Texas, M.D. Anderson Cancer Center**, noted for cancer, gynecology, otolaryngology, urology; **Texas Heart Institute-St. Luke's Episcopal Hospital**, noted for cardiology; **Hermann Hospital**, noted for orthopedics, rheumatology; **TIRR (The Institute for Rehabilitation and Research)**, noted for rehabilitation; **Methodist Hospital**, noted for geriatrics, gynecology, neurology, ophthalmology, orthopedics, otolaryngology, rheumatology, urology; **Texas Children's Hospital**, noted for pediatrics. *U.S. News Online, "America's Best Hospitals," 10th Edition, www.usnews.com*

EDUCATION

Public School District Statistics

District Name	Num. Sch.	Enroll.	Classroom Teachers	Pupils per Teacher	Minority Pupils (%)	Current Exp.[1] ($/pupil)
Aldine ISD	51	48,585	3,192	15.2	84.6	5,147
Cypress-Fairbanks ISD	51	55,593	3,455	16.1	35.7	4,661
George I Sanchez Charter	2	398	20	19.9	n/a	n/a
Girls & Boys Prep Academy	1	340	26	13.1	n/a	n/a
Houston ISD	299	210,988	11,597	18.2	89.3	4,987
Medical Center Charter School	1	116	5	23.2	n/a	n/a
North Forest ISD	17	13,579	n/a	n/a	n/a	n/a
Raul Yzaguirre School For Succ	1	191	n/a	n/a	n/a	n/a
Ser-Ninos Charter School	1	219	9	24.3	n/a	n/a
Sheldon ISD	7	3,916	255	15.4	n/a	n/a
Spring Branch ISD	38	30,880	2,006	15.4	n/a	n/a
Spring ISD	25	21,537	n/a	n/a	n/a	n/a
Univ of Houston Charter Sch	1	40	4	10.0	n/a	n/a
West Houston Charter School	1	102	9	11.3	n/a	n/a

Note: Data covers the 1997-1998 school year unless otherwise noted; (1) Data covers fiscal year 1996; SD = School District; ISD = Independent School District; n/a not available
Source: National Center for Education Statistics, Common Core of Data Public Education Agency Universe 1997-98; National Center for Education Statistics, Characteristics of the 100 Largest Public Elementary and Secondary School Districts in the United States: 1997-98, July 1999

Educational Quality

School District	Education Quotient[1]	Graduate Outcome[2]	Community Index[3]	Resource Index[4]
Houston ISD	68.0	63.0	101.0	72.0

Note: Nearly 1,000 secondary school districts were rated in terms of educational quality. The scores range from a low of 50 to a high of 150; (1) Average of the Graduate Outcome, Community and Resource indexes; (2) Based on graduation rates and college board scores (SAT/ACT); (3) Based on the surrounding community's average level of education and the area's average income level; (4) Based on teacher salaries, per-pupil expenditures and student-teacher ratios.
Source: Expansion Management, Ratings Issue, 1998

Educational Attainment by Race

Area	High School Graduate (%)					Bachelor's Degree (%)				
	Total	White	Black	Other	Hisp.[2]	Total	White	Black	Other	Hisp.[2]
City	70.5	79.1	66.3	45.0	36.6	25.1	33.0	13.4	14.8	7.3
MSA[1]	75.1	81.1	68.9	50.2	41.6	25.1	29.0	15.1	16.3	7.9
U.S.	75.2	77.9	63.1	60.4	49.8	20.3	21.5	11.4	19.4	9.2

Note: Figures shown cover persons 25 years old and over; (1) Metropolitan Statistical Area - see Appendix A for areas included; (2) people of Hispanic origin can be of any race
Source: 1990 Census of Population and Housing, Summary Tape File 3C

School Enrollment by Type

Area	Preprimary				Elementary/High School			
	Public		Private		Public		Private	
	Enrollment	%	Enrollment	%	Enrollment	%	Enrollment	%
City	14,485	54.0	12,343	46.0	274,727	92.3	22,938	7.7
MSA[1]	34,923	52.8	31,273	47.2	607,238	93.9	39,303	6.1
U.S.	2,679,029	59.5	1,824,256	40.5	38,379,689	90.2	4,187,099	9.8

Note: Figures shown cover persons 3 years old and over; (1) Metropolitan Statistical Area - see Appendix A for areas included
Source: 1990 Census of Population and Housing, Summary Tape File 3C

School Enrollment by Race

Area	Preprimary (%)				Elementary/High School (%)			
	White	Black	Other	Hisp.[1]	White	Black	Other	Hisp.[1]
City	54.6	29.7	15.6	22.8	40.2	33.3	26.5	38.1
MSA[2]	71.3	17.7	11.0	16.0	58.6	21.4	20.1	28.5
U.S.	80.4	12.5	7.1	7.8	74.1	15.6	10.3	12.5

Note: Figures shown cover persons 3 years old and over; (1) people of Hispanic origin can be of any race; (2) Metropolitan Statistical Area - see Appendix A for areas included
Source: 1990 Census of Population and Housing, Summary Tape File 3C

Classroom Teacher Salaries in Public Schools

District	B.A. Degree		M.A. Degree		Maximum	
	Min. ($)	Rank[1]	Max. ($)	Rank[1]	Max. ($)	Rank[1]
Houston	27,754	34	46,214	44	48,723	63
Average	26,980	-	46,065	-	51,435	-

Note: Salaries are for 1997-1998; (1) Rank ranges from 1 to 100
Source: American Federation of Teachers, Survey & Analysis of Salary Trends, 1998

Higher Education

Two-Year Colleges		Four-Year Colleges		Medical Schools	Law Schools	Voc/ Tech
Public	Private	Public	Private			
4	4	5	3	2	3	40

Source: College Blue Book, Occupational Education, 1997; Medical School Admission Requirements, 1999-2000; Peterson's Guide to Two-Year Colleges, 1999; Peterson's Guide to Four-Year Colleges, 2000; Barron's Guide to Law Schools, 1999

MAJOR EMPLOYERS

Major Employers

United Space Alliance	Compaq Computer Corp.
Chase Bank of Texas	American Eco (construction)
Kellogg Brown & Root (heavy construction)	Cumberland Maritime Corp.
St. Luke's Episcopal Hospital	Texas Children's Hospital
U. of Texas MD Anderson Cancer Center	Diamond Offshore General

Note: Companies listed are located in the city
Source: Dun's Business Rankings, 1999; Ward's Business Directory, 1998

PUBLIC SAFETY

Crime Rate

Area	All Crimes	Violent Crimes				Property Crimes		
		Murder	Forcible Rape	Robbery	Aggrav. Assault	Burglary	Larceny -Theft	Motor Vehicle Theft
City	7,263.6	14.1	43.9	452.2	664.3	1,330.5	3,604.2	1,154.4
Suburbs[1]	3,994.4	4.7	30.7	108.8	363.2	823.4	2,263.1	400.6
MSA[2]	5,518.3	9.1	36.8	268.9	503.6	1,059.8	2,888.3	752.0
U.S.	4,922.7	6.8	35.9	186.1	382.0	919.6	2,886.5	505.8

Note: Crime rate is the number of crimes per 100,000 pop.; (1) defined as all areas within the MSA but located outside the central city; (2) Metropolitan Statistical Area - see Appendix A for areas incl.
Source: FBI Uniform Crime Reports, 1997

RECREATION

Culture and Recreation

Museums	Symphony Orchestras	Opera Companies	Dance Companies	Professional Theatres	Zoos	Pro Sports Teams
11	1	2	10	5	1	3

Source: International Directory of the Performing Arts, 1997; Official Museum Directory, 1999; Stern's Performing Arts Directory, 1997; USA Today Four Sport Stadium Guide, 1997; Chamber of Commerce/Economic Development, 1999

Library System

The Houston Public Library has 35 branches, holdings of 4,573,356 volumes, and a budget of $28,282,900 (1996-1997). *American Library Directory, 1998-1999*

MEDIA

Newspapers

Name	Type	Freq.	Distribution	Circulation
The Bay Area Sun	General	1x/wk	Area	35,000
The Citizen	General	1x/wk	Local	26,450
Houston Chronicle	General	7x/wk	Area	553,387
La Buena Suerte	Hispanic	1x/wk	Area	100,000
La Informacion	Hispanic	1x/wk	Local	78,000
La Subasta	Hispanic	3x/wk	State	185,000
The Leader	General	1x/wk	Local	77,160
The 1960 Sun	General	1x/wk	Area	81,000
Semana News	Hispanic	1x/wk	Local	125,000
Southern Chinese News	Asian	7x/wk	Local	25,000

Note: Includes newspapers with circulations of 25,000 or more located in the city;
Source: Burrelle's Media Directory, 1999 Edition

Television Stations

Name	Ch.	Affiliation	Type	Owner
KPRC	n/a	NBCT	Commercial	Post-Newsweek Business Information Inc.
KUHT	n/a	PBS	Public	University of Houston
KHOU	11	CBST	Commercial	A.H. Belo Corporation
KTRK	13	ABCT	Commercial	ABC Inc.
KTXH	20	UPN	Commercial	Paramount Communications Inc.
KLTJ	22	n/a	Non-comm.	GO Inc.
KRIV	26	FBC	Commercial	Fox Television Stations Inc.
KHTV	39	WB	Commercial	Tribune Broadcasting Company
KXLN	45	UNIN	Commercial	Univision Television Group
KTMD	48	TMUN	Commercial	Telemundo Group Inc.
KPXB	49	n/a	Commercial	Paxson Communications Corporation
KNWS	51	n/a	n/a	Johnson Broadcasting Corporation
KVVV	57	n/a	Commercial	ValueVision International Inc.
KHSH	67	n/a	Commercial	USA Networks Inc.

Note: Stations included broadcast in the Houston metro area; n/a not available
Source: Burrelle's Media Directory, 1999 Edition

AM Radio Stations

Call Letters	Freq. (kHz)	Target Audience	Station Format	Music Format
KILT	610	General	S/T	n/a
KIKK	650	General	M	Country
KSEV	700	General	M/N/S/T	Big Band/Oldies
KTRH	740	General	N/S	n/a
KBME	790	n/a	M/N	Adult Standards
KEYH	850	Hispanic	M	Latin
KJOJ	880	Religious	M/N/S/T	Christian
KYST	920	Hispanic	M	n/a
KPRC	950	General	N/S/T	n/a
KLAT	1010	Hispanic	M	Latin
KENR	1070	General	M/T	Adult Contemporary
KTEK	1110	Religious	M/N/S	Christian
KGOL	1180	A/G	E/M/N/S/T	n/a
KXYZ	1320	Hispanic	N/T	n/a
KHCB	1400	Hispanic	M/N/S	Christian/Latin
KYLR	1400	General	M/N/S/T	n/a
KCUL	1410	General	M/N/S/T	Oldies
KCOH	1430	Black	E/M/N/S/T	R&B/Urban Contemporary
KYOK	1590	General	M/S/T	Adult Contemporary/Christian

Note: Stations included broadcast in the Houston metro area; n/a not available
Target Audience: A=Asian; B=Black; C=Christian; E=Ethnic; F=French; G=General; H=Hispanic;
M=Men; N=Native American; R=Religious; S=Senior Citizen; W=Women; Y=Young Adult; Z=Children
Station Format: E=Educational; M=Music; N=News; S=Sports; T=Talk
Source: Burrelle's Media Directory, 1999 Edition

FM Radio Stations

Call Letters	Freq. (mHz)	Target Audience	Station Format	Music Format
KUHF	88.7	General	M/N	Classical
KSBJ	89.3	General	E/M/N/S	Christian
KPFT	90.1	General	M	Classic Rock/Jazz
KTSU	90.9	General	M	n/a
KBWC	91.1	General	E/M	Christian/Jazz/R&B
KTRU	91.7	General	E/M/N/S/T	Alternative
KRTS	92.1	General	M	Classical
KCUL	92.3	General	M/N/S	Oldies
KKBQ	92.9	General	M	Country
KKRW	93.7	General	M/N/T	Classic Rock
KLDE	94.5	General	M	Oldies
KIKK	95.7	General	M	Country
KHMX	96.5	General	M/N/S	Adult Contemporary
KBXX	97.9	Black	Hispanic	Men
KTJM	98.5	General	M/T	Oldies
KODA	99.1	General	M	Adult Contemporary/Jazz
KILT	100.3	General	M/N/T	Country
KLOL	101.1	G/M	M/N/S/T	AOR/Classic Rock
KMJQ	102.1	General	M	Urban Contemporary
KLTN	102.9	G/H	M	Latin
KLTN	102.9	General	M	Latin
KZEY	103.9	Black	Women	M
KRBE	104.1	General	M/N/T	Top 40
KRTX	104.9	G/H	M	Latin
KHCB	105.7	Religious	M/N/S	Christian
KQQK	106.5	Hispanic	M	Latin
KTBZ	107.5	General	M/N/T	Alternative

Note: Stations included broadcast in the Houston metro area; n/a not available
Station Format: E=Educational; M=Music; N=News; S=Sports; T=Talk
Target Audience: A=Asian; B=Black; C=Christian; E=Ethnic; F=French; G=General; H=Hispanic;
M=Men; N=Native American; R=Religious; S=Senior Citizen; W=Women; Y=Young Adult; Z=Children
Music Format: AOR=Album Oriented Rock; MOR=Middle-of-the-Road
Source: Burrelle's Media Directory, 1999 Edition

CLIMATE

Average and Extreme Temperatures

Temperature	Jan	Feb	Mar	Apr	May	Jun	Jul	Aug	Sep	Oct	Nov	Dec	Yr.
Extreme High (°F)	84	91	91	95	97	103	104	107	102	94	89	83	107
Average High (°F)	61	65	73	79	85	91	93	93	89	81	72	65	79
Average Temp. (°F)	51	54	62	69	75	81	83	83	79	70	61	54	69
Average Low (°F)	41	43	51	58	65	71	73	73	68	58	50	43	58
Extreme Low (°F)	12	20	22	31	44	52	62	62	48	32	19	7	7

Note: Figures cover the years 1969-1990
Source: National Climatic Data Center, International Station Meteorological Climate Summary, 3/95

Average Precipitation/Snowfall/Humidity

Precip./Humidity	Jan	Feb	Mar	Apr	May	Jun	Jul	Aug	Sep	Oct	Nov	Dec	Yr.
Avg. Precip. (in.)	3.3	2.7	3.3	3.3	5.6	4.9	3.7	3.7	4.8	4.7	3.7	3.3	46.9
Avg. Snowfall (in.)	Tr	Tr	0	0	0	0	0	0	0	0	Tr	Tr	Tr
Avg. Rel. Hum. 6am (%)	85	86	87	89	91	92	93	93	93	91	89	86	90
Avg. Rel. Hum. 3pm (%)	58	55	54	54	57	56	55	55	57	53	55	57	55

Note: Figures cover the years 1969-1990; Tr = Trace amounts (<0.05 in. of rain; <0.5 in. of snow)
Source: National Climatic Data Center, International Station Meteorological Climate Summary, 3/95

Weather Conditions

Temperature			Daytime Sky			Precipitation		
32°F & below	45°F & below	90°F & above	Clear	Partly cloudy	Cloudy	0.01 inch or more precip.	0.1 inch or more snow/ice	Thunder-storms
21	87	96	83	168	114	101	1	62

Note: Figures are average number of days per year and covers the years 1969-1990
Source: National Climatic Data Center, International Station Meteorological Climate Summary, 3/95

AIR & WATER QUALITY

Maximum Pollutant Concentrations

	Particulate Matter (ug/m³)	Carbon Monoxide (ppm)	Sulfur Dioxide (ppm)	Nitrogen Dioxide (ppm)	Ozone (ppm)	Lead (ug/m³)
MSA[1] Level	134	7	0.025	0.025	0.21	0.00
NAAQS[2]	150	9	0.140	0.053	0.12	1.50
Met NAAQS?	Yes	Yes	Yes	Yes	No	Yes

Note: (1) Metropolitan Statistical Area - see Appendix A for areas included; (2) National Ambient Air Quality Standards; ppm = parts per million; ug/m³ = micrograms per cubic meter; n/a not available
Source: EPA, National Air Quality and Emissions Trends Report, 1997

Pollutant Standards Index

In the Houston MSA (see Appendix A for areas included), the Pollutant Standards Index (PSI) exceeded 100 on 47 days in 1997. A PSI value greater than 100 indicates that air quality would be in the unhealthful range on that day. *EPA, National Air Quality and Emissions Trends Report, 1997*

Drinking Water

Water System Name	Pop. Served	Primary Water Source Type	Number of Violations in 1998	Type of Violation/ Contaminants
Houston Public Works Dept.	2,354,040	Surface	None	None

Note: Data as of July 10, 1999
Source: EPA, Office of Ground Water and Drinking Water, Safe Drinking Water Information System

Houston tap water is alkaline, hard.
Editor & Publisher Market Guide, 1999

Jackson, Mississippi

Background

In 1792, A French-Canadian, Louis LeFleur, established a trading post on a high bluff on the Pearl River, wanting to build a trade in furs with the local Choctaws. The settlement that grew up around the post was called Le Fleur's Bluff. In 1821 the Mississippi legislature decided to move the state capital from Natchez on the Mississippi to the center of the new State. It chose Le Fleur's Bluff and renamed it Jackson, to honor the hero of the Battle of New Orleans, General Andrew Jackson.

The city changed hands several times during the Civil War; at one point much of it was burned to the ground by the troops of William Tecumseh Sherman. The Yankees did not burn the City Hall, and rumors flew that Sherman, a Mason, spared it because the local lodge met there. After the war, Jackson became an important transportation center, as railroads increasingly crisscrossed the South. Thus the city earned its nickname of Crossroads of the South. In 1930, as the rest of the country spiraled downward in the midst of the Great Depression, Jackson received a boost with the serendipitous discovery of natural gas field nearby, which helped the growth of industry. The city fathers in the 1960s developed an economic plan to attract business. Dozens of factories were built in the next few years.

The result was a Jackson that has a diverse economy. Electrical products, processed foods, furniture, metal goods, and a variety of other items are produced in the metropolitan area. Assisting the city's business climate is the still important natural gas industry.

In recent years telecommunications have had significant impact on the city's commerce. A prime example is the recently merged MCI WorldCom, the second largest long distance communications company in the nation, which has its headquarters in the Jackson metropolitan area. Other important area companies in this field are Mobil Telecommunications Technology Corporation and LDDS Communications.

Jackson is still an important transportation hub in the South, equidistant from Memphis to the north and New Orleans to south; the same is true for Dallas to the west and Atlanta to the east. Jackson International Airport and Hawkins Field have eight major airlines that service them.

Being the State's capital, public employees make up a major segment of the area's workforce. The medical industry also has a significant presence in the city, the most famous of which is the University of Mississippi Medical Center. Other higher education institutions exist, including Jackson State University and Mississippi College.

Summers are long, hot, and humid in Jackson, with winds drifting up from the Gulf of Mexico to the south. Temperatures range from the sixties to the nineties. The winters are short, but unexpectedly cool, with Arctic air coming in from the north; temperatures during this time range from the thirties to the sixties. Most of the yearly rain of fifty-one inches falls in the winter, spring, and summer; autumns tend to be rather dry. Snowfall is negligible, usually slightly more than an inch per year.

General Rankings and Evaluative Comments

- Jackson was ranked #19 out of 44 mid-sized, southern metropolitan areas in *Money's* 1998 survey of "The Best Places to Live in America." The survey was conducted by first contacting 512 representative households nationwide and asking them to rank 37 quality-of-life factors on a scale of 1 to 10. Next, a demographic profile was compiled on the 300 largest metropolitan statistical areas in the U.S. The numbers were crunched together to arrive at an overall ranking (things Americans consider most important, like clean air and water, low crime and good schools, received extra weight). Unlike previous years, the 1998 rankings were broken down by region (northeast, midwest, south, west) and population size (100,000 to 249,999; 250,000 to 999,999; 1 million plus). The city had a nationwide ranking of #137 out of 300 in 1997 and #205 out of 300 in 1996. *Money, July 1998; Money, July 1997; Money, September 1996*

- *Ladies Home Journal* ranked America's 200 largest cities based on the qualities women care about most. Jackson ranked #176 out of 200. Criteria: low crime rate, well-paying jobs, quality health and child care, good public schools, the presence of women in government, size of the gender wage gap, number of sexual-harassment and discrimination complaints filed, unemployment and divorce rates, commute times, population density, number of houses of worship, parks and cultural offerings, number of women's health specialists, how well a community's women cared for themselves, complexion kindness index based on UV radiation levels, odds of finding affordable fashions, rental rates for romance movies, champagne sales and other matters of the heart. *Ladies Home Journal, November 1998*

- Zero Population Growth ranked 229 cities in terms of children's health, safety, and economic well-being. Jackson was ranked #82 out of 112 independent cities (cities with populations greater than 100,000 which were neither Major Cities nor Suburbs/Outer Cities) and was given a grade of D. Criteria: total population, percent of population under 18 years of age, household language, percent population change, percent of births to teens, infant mortality rate, percent of low birth weights, dropout rate, enrollment in preprimary school, violent and property crime rates, unemployment rate, percent of children in poverty, percent of owner occupied units, number of bad air days, percent of public transportation commuters, and average travel time to work. *Zero Population Growth, Children's Environmental Index, Fall 1999*

- Cognetics studied 273 metro areas in the United States, ranking them by entrepreneurial activity. Jackson was ranked #24 out of 134 smaller metro areas. Criteria: Significant Starts (firms started in the last 10 years that still employ at least 5 people) and Young Growers (percent of firms 10 years old or less that grew significantly during the last 4 years). *Cognetics, "Entrepreneurial Hot Spots: The Best Places in America to Start and Grow a Company," 1998*

- Jackson was selected as one of the "Best American Cities to Start a Business" by *Point of View* magazine. Criteria: coolness, quality-of-life, and business concerns. The city was ranked #18 out of 75. *Point of View, November 1998*

- Reliastar Financial Corp. ranked the 125 largest metropolitan areas according to the general financial security of residents. Jackson was ranked #19 out of 125 with a score of 8.6. The score indicates the percentage a metropolitan area is above or below the metropolitan norm. A metro area with a score of 10.6 is 10.6% above the metro average. Criteria: Earnings and Wealth Potential (household income, education, net assets, cost of living); Safety Net (health insurance, retirement savings, life insurance, income support programs); Personal Threats (unemployment rate, low-income households, crime rate); Community Economic Vitality (cost of community services, job quality, job creation, housing costs). *Reliastar Financial Corp., "The Best Cities to Earn and Save Money," 1999 Edition*

Business Environment

STATE ECONOMY

State Economic Profile

"Mississippi's economy continues to lag the nation and is projected to slow further in 1999 and 2000. MS's manufacturing sector continues to shed jobs, which are not being offset by the slow growth in the services sector. MS's healthiest sectors remain gaming and construction, neither of which is expected to provide significant long-term job growth.

The textiles and apparel industries have lost 35% of their employment base in the last five years. Falling trade barriers have allowed much of low-skilled manufacturing to shift offshore. The weakness in Asian currencies has made MS much less cost effective.

The damage inflicted by Hurricane George and the expansion of the gaming industry have resulted in a significant increase in construction activity. Construction employment increased almost 10% in 1998. Residential permits were up 28%, driven by a boom in multifamily construction activity. In addition highway projects in Tunica County and along the Gulf have added to construction employment. Most of this activity should taper off in 1999 and 2000.

Mississippi's growth engine has been the gaming industry. The $650 million Beau Rivage Resort recently opened in Biloxi. With its 1,780 hotel rooms and 25,000 sq. ft. retail complex, the development will boost tax revenues, employment and tourism dollars. Gaming, however, is very sensitive to the business cycle. A weakening US economy in 2000 will dampen gaming revenues.

Mississippi's dependence on gaming and construction does not leave it well positioned to weather the next downturn. MS's outlook for 1999 is one of slowing economic growth and housing markets." *National Association of Realtors, Economic Profiles: The Fifty States and the District of Columbia, http://nar.realtor.com/databank/profiles.htm*

IMPORTS/EXPORTS

Total Export Sales

Area	1994 ($000)	1995 ($000)	1996 ($000)	1997 ($000)	% Chg. 1994-97	% Chg. 1996-97
MSA[1]	154,261	203,013	231,401	318,106	106.2	37.5
U.S.	512,415,609	583,030,524	622,827,063	687,597,999	34.2	10.4

Note: (1) Metropolitan Statistical Area - see Appendix A for areas included
Source: U.S. Department of Commerce, International Trade Association, Metropolitan Area Exports: An Export Performance Report on Over 250 U.S. Cities, November 10, 1998

CITY FINANCES

City Government Finances

Component	FY92 ($000)	FY92 (per capita $)
Revenue	154,406	772.28
Expenditure	162,921	814.87
Debt Outstanding	326,600	1,633.54
Cash & Securities	213,934	1,070.02

Source: U.S. Bureau of the Census, City Government Finances: 1991-92

City Government Revenue by Source

Source	FY92 ($000)	FY92 (per capita $)	FY92 (%)
From Federal Government	10,884	54.44	7.0
From State Governments	27,598	138.04	17.9
From Local Governments	783	3.92	0.5
Property Taxes	42,746	213.80	27.7
General Sales Taxes	0	0.00	0.0
Selective Sales Taxes	4,391	21.96	2.8
Income Taxes	0	0.00	0.0
Current Charges	29,718	148.64	19.2
Utility/Liquor Store	17,858	89.32	11.6
Employee Retirement[1]	0	0.00	0.0
Other	20,428	102.17	13.2

Note: (1) Excludes "city contributions," classified as "nonrevenue," intragovernmental transfers.
Source: U.S. Bureau of the Census, City Government Finances: 1991-92

City Government Expenditures by Function

Function	FY92 ($000)	FY92 (per capita $)	FY92 (%)
Educational Services	0	0.00	0.0
Employee Retirement[1]	0	0.00	0.0
Environment/Housing	36,404	182.08	22.3
Government Administration	5,505	27.53	3.4
Interest on General Debt	11,225	56.14	6.9
Public Safety	33,803	169.07	20.7
Social Services	0	0.00	0.0
Transportation	29,140	145.75	17.9
Utility/Liquor Store	29,752	148.81	18.3
Other	17,092	85.49	10.5

Note: (1) Payments to beneficiaries including withdrawal of contributions.
Source: U.S. Bureau of the Census, City Government Finances: 1991-92

Municipal Bond Ratings

Area	Moody's	S & P
Jackson	Aaa	n/a

Note: n/a not available; n/r not rated
Source: Moody's Bond Record, 6/99

POPULATION

Population Growth

Area	1980	1990	% Chg. 1980-90	July 1998 Estimate	% Chg. 1990-98
City	202,893	196,594	-3.1	188,419	-4.2
MSA[1]	362,038	395,396	9.2	429,626	8.7
U.S.	226,545,805	248,765,170	9.8	270,299,000	8.7

Note: (1) Metropolitan Statistical Area - see Appendix A for areas included;
July 1998 MSA population estimate was calculated by the editors
Source: 1980/1990 Census of Housing and Population, Summary Tape File 3C;
Census Bureau Population Estimates 1998

Population Characteristics

Race	City 1980 Population	%	City 1990 Population	%	% Chg. 1980-90	MSA[1] 1990 Population	%
White	106,518	52.5	85,742	43.6	-19.5	224,894	56.9
Black	95,218	46.9	109,587	55.7	15.1	167,899	42.5
Amer Indian/Esk/Aleut	213	0.1	186	0.1	-12.7	350	0.1
Asian/Pacific Islander	733	0.4	949	0.5	29.5	1,872	0.5
Other	211	0.1	130	0.1	-38.4	381	0.1
Hispanic Origin[2]	1,497	0.7	732	0.4	-51.1	2,050	0.5

Note: (1) Metropolitan Statistical Area - see Appendix A for areas included;
(2) people of Hispanic origin can be of any race
Source: 1980/1990 Census of Housing and Population, Summary Tape File 3C

Ancestry

Area	German	Irish	English	Italian	U.S.	French	Polish	Dutch
City	7.1	10.0	9.6	0.9	5.5	2.2	0.3	0.9
MSA[1]	9.2	14.1	11.1	1.1	8.0	2.5	0.4	1.1
U.S.	23.3	15.6	13.1	5.9	5.3	4.2	3.8	2.5

Note: Figures are percentages and include persons that reported multiple ancestry (eg. if a person reported being Irish and Italian, they were included in both columns); (1) Metropolitan Statistical Area - see Appendix A for areas included
Source: 1990 Census of Population and Housing, Summary Tape File 3C

Age

Area	Median Age (Years)	Age Distribution (%) Under 5	Under 18	18-24	25-44	45-64	65+	80+
City	30.7	7.7	27.5	12.1	32.3	16.5	11.6	2.6
MSA[1]	31.0	7.6	28.0	11.1	33.0	17.4	10.6	2.3
U.S.	32.9	7.3	25.6	10.5	32.6	18.7	12.5	2.8

Note: (1) Metropolitan Statistical Area - see Appendix A for areas included
Source: 1990 Census of Population and Housing, Summary Tape File 3C

Male/Female Ratio

Area	Number of males per 100 females (all ages)	Number of males per 100 females (18 years old+)
City	86.5	81.3
MSA[1]	89.6	84.9
U.S.	95.0	91.9

Note: (1) Metropolitan Statistical Area - see Appendix A for areas included
Source: 1990 Census of Population, General Population Characteristics

INCOME

Per Capita/Median/Average Income

Area	Per Capita ($)	Median Household ($)	Average Household ($)
City	12,216	23,270	33,118
MSA[1]	12,311	26,365	34,434
U.S.	14,420	30,056	38,453

Note: All figures are for 1989; (1) Metropolitan Statistical Area - see Appendix A for areas included
Source: 1990 Census of Population and Housing, Summary Tape File 3C

Household Income Distribution by Race

Income ($)	City (%)					U.S. (%)				
	Total	White	Black	Other	Hisp.[1]	Total	White	Black	Other	Hisp.[1]
Less than 5,000	10.6	5.0	16.5	21.1	13.4	6.2	4.8	15.2	8.6	8.8
5,000 - 9,999	12.2	8.0	16.8	13.1	13.7	9.3	8.6	14.2	9.9	11.1
10,000 - 14,999	10.5	7.7	13.5	10.6	6.1	8.8	8.5	11.0	9.8	11.0
15,000 - 24,999	19.6	19.1	20.1	13.7	5.3	17.5	17.3	18.9	18.5	20.5
25,000 - 34,999	15.3	15.7	14.9	11.4	35.5	15.8	16.1	14.2	15.4	16.4
35,000 - 49,999	14.7	18.6	10.5	21.7	22.1	17.9	18.6	13.3	16.1	16.0
50,000 - 74,999	10.5	14.5	6.2	4.9	3.8	15.0	15.8	9.3	13.4	11.1
75,000 - 99,999	2.9	4.7	1.0	0.9	0.0	5.1	5.5	2.6	4.7	3.1
100,000+	3.7	6.7	0.5	2.6	0.0	4.4	4.8	1.3	3.7	1.9

Note: All figures are for 1989; (1) people of Hispanic origin can be of any race
Source: 1990 Census of Population and Housing, Summary Tape File 3C

Effective Buying Income

Area	Per Capita ($)	Median Household ($)	Average Household ($)
City	15,725	30,773	42,957
MSA[1]	16,394	33,854	45,823
U.S.	16,803	34,536	45,243

Note: Data as of 1/1/99; (1) Metropolitan Statistical Area - see Appendix A for areas included
Source: Standard Rate & Data Service, Newspaper Advertising Source, 9/99

Effective Household Buying Income Distribution

Area	% of Households Earning						
	$10,000 -$19,999	$20,000 -$34,999	$35,000 -$49,999	$50,000 -$74,999	$75,000 -$99,000	$100,000 -$124,999	$125,000 and up
City	17.3	22.5	16.2	15.8	6.5	2.1	3.6
MSA[1]	16.0	21.3	16.9	18.8	7.7	2.3	2.7
U.S.	16.0	22.6	18.2	18.9	7.2	2.4	2.7

Note: Data as of 1/1/99; (1) Metropolitan Statistical Area - see Appendix A for areas included
Source: Standard Rate & Data Service, Newspaper Advertising Source, 9/99

Poverty Rates by Race and Age

Area	Total (%)	By Race (%)				By Age (%)		
		White	Black	Other	Hisp.[2]	Under 5 years old	Under 18 years old	65 years and over
City	22.7	7.7	34.5	21.6	23.2	34.7	32.1	20.7
MSA[1]	19.3	6.8	36.3	17.3	22.1	29.3	26.8	23.3
U.S.	13.1	9.8	29.5	23.1	25.3	20.1	18.3	12.8

Note: Figures show the percent of people living below the poverty line in 1989. The average poverty threshold was $12,674 for a family of four in 1989; (1) Metropolitan Statistical Area - see Appendix A for areas included; (2) people of Hispanic origin can be of any race
Source: 1990 Census of Population and Housing, Summary Tape File 3C

EMPLOYMENT

Labor Force and Employment

Area	Civilian Labor Force			Workers Employed		
	Jun. 1998	Jun. 1999	% Chg.	Jun. 1998	Jun. 1999	% Chg.
City	100,923	102,043	1.1	95,454	96,994	1.6
MSA[1]	227,597	230,411	1.2	218,282	221,804	1.6
U.S.	138,798,000	140,666,000	1.3	132,265,000	134,395,000	1.6

Note: Data is not seasonally adjusted and covers workers 16 years of age and older;
(1) Metropolitan Statistical Area - see Appendix A for areas included
Source: Bureau of Labor Statistics, http://stats.bls.gov

Unemployment Rate

Area	1998						1999					
	Jul.	Aug.	Sep.	Oct.	Nov.	Dec.	Jan.	Feb.	Mar.	Apr.	May.	Jun.
City	4.8	5.2	4.7	4.6	4.0	3.6	4.7	3.5	4.1	3.4	4.3	4.9
MSA[1]	3.6	4.0	3.5	3.5	3.0	2.7	3.6	2.7	3.1	2.6	3.3	3.7
U.S.	4.7	4.5	4.4	4.2	4.1	4.0	4.8	4.7	4.4	4.1	4.0	4.5

Note: Data is not seasonally adjusted and covers workers 16 years of age and older; all figures are percentages; (1) Metropolitan Statistical Area - see Appendix A for areas included
Source: Bureau of Labor Statistics, http://stats.bls.gov

Employment by Industry

Sector	MSA[1]		U.S.
	Number of Employees	Percent of Total	Percent of Total
Services	60,900	26.5	30.4
Retail Trade	39,000	16.9	17.7
Government	47,500	20.6	15.6
Manufacturing	20,700	9.0	14.3
Finance/Insurance/Real Estate	16,500	7.2	5.9
Wholesale Trade	15,300	6.6	5.4
Transportation/Public Utilities	16,900	7.3	5.3
Construction	12,300	5.3	5.0
Mining	n/a	n/a	0.4

Note: Figures cover non-farm employment as of 6/99 and are not seasonally adjusted;
(1) Metropolitan Statistical Area - see Appendix A for areas included; n/a not available
Source: Bureau of Labor Statistics, http://stats.bls.gov

Employment by Occupation

Occupation Category	City (%)	MSA[1] (%)	U.S. (%)
White Collar	62.4	63.2	58.1
Executive/Admin./Management	10.9	12.3	12.3
Professional	17.1	15.7	14.1
Technical & Related Support	3.7	4.1	3.7
Sales	12.8	13.4	11.8
Administrative Support/Clerical	18.0	17.8	16.3
Blue Collar	21.1	22.5	26.2
Precision Production/Craft/Repair	8.6	9.8	11.3
Machine Operators/Assem./Insp.	5.1	5.4	6.8
Transportation/Material Movers	3.8	3.8	4.1
Cleaners/Helpers/Laborers	3.6	3.6	3.9
Services	15.2	12.7	13.2
Farming/Forestry/Fishing	1.2	1.6	2.5

Note: Figures cover employed persons 16 years old and over;
(1) Metropolitan Statistical Area - see Appendix A for areas included
Source: 1990 Census of Population and Housing, Summary Tape File 3C

Occupational Employment Projections: 1996 - 2006

Occupations Expected to Have the Largest Job Growth (ranked by numerical growth)	Fast-Growing Occupations[1] (ranked by percent growth)
1. Salespersons, retail	1. Database administrators
2. Cashiers	2. Paralegals
3. General managers & top executives	3. Systems analysts
4. Truck drivers, light	4. Home health aides
5. Teachers aides, clerical & paraprofess.	5. Physical therapy assistants and aides
6. Marketing & sales, supervisors	6. Medical assistants
7. Nursing aides/orderlies/attendants	7. Physical therapists
8. Registered nurses	8. Emergency medical technicians
9. Maintenance repairers, general utility	9. Teachers, special education
10. Home health aides	10. Medical records technicians

Note: Projections cover Mississippi; (1) Excludes occupations with total job growth less than 300
Source: U.S. Department of Labor, Employment and Training Administration, America's Labor Market Information System (ALMIS)

TAXES

Major State and Local Tax Rates

State Corp. Income (%)	State Personal Income (%)	Residential Property (effective rate per $100)	Sales & Use State (%)	Sales & Use Local (%)	State Gasoline (cents/ gallon)	State Cigarette (cents/ pack)
3.0 - 5.0	3.0 - 5.0	1.28	7.0	None	18.4[a]	18.0

Note: Personal/corporate income, sales, gasoline and cigarette tax rates as of January 1999.
Property tax rates as of 1997; (a) Rate is comprised of 18 cents excise and 0.4 cents motor carrier tax
Source: Federation of Tax Administrators, www.taxadmin.org; Washington D.C. Department of Finance and Revenue, Tax Rates and Tax Burdens in the District of Columbia: A Nationwide Comparison, July 1998; Chamber of Commerce, 1999

Total Taxes Per Capita and as a Percent of Income

Area	Per Capita Income ($)	Per Capita Taxes ($) Total	Per Capita Taxes ($) Federal	Per Capita Taxes ($) State/ Local	Percent of Income (%) Total	Percent of Income (%) Federal	Percent of Income (%) State/ Local
Mississippi	20,047	6,954	4,481	2,474	34.7	22.3	12.3
U.S.	27,876	9,881	6,690	3,191	35.4	24.0	11.4

Note: Figures are for 1998
Source: Tax Foundation, www.taxfoundation.org

Estimated Tax Burden

Area	State Income	Local Income	Property	Sales	Total
Jackson	2,350	0	3,250	1,047	6,647

Note: The numbers are estimates of taxes paid by a married couple with two children and annual earnings of $75,000. Sales tax estimates assume they spend average amounts on food, clothing, household goods and gasoline. Property tax estimates assume they live in a $250,000 home.
Source: Kiplinger's Personal Finance Magazine, October 1998

COMMERCIAL REAL ESTATE

Office Market

Class/ Location	Total Space (sq. ft.)	Vacant Space (sq. ft.)	Vac. Rate (%)	Under Constr. (sq. ft.)	Net Absorp. (sq. ft.)	Rental Rates ($/sq.ft./yr.)
Class A						
CBD	1,776,000	25,000	1.4	0	87,000	17.00-19.00
Outside CBD	2,743,000	75,000	2.7	136,000	569,000	17.00-22.00
Class B						
CBD	5,976,000	185,000	3.1	0	116,000	13.00-15.00
Outside CBD	6,957,000	200,000	2.9	0	200,000	12.00-16.00

Note: Data as of 10/98 and covers Jackson; CBD = Central Business District; n/a not available;
Source: Society of Industrial and Office Realtors, 1999 Comparative Statistics of Industrial and Office Real Estate Markets

"Pre-leased development will enter the market in 1999. Low unemployment is the prime constraint for area economic growth. Local plans for infrastructure improvement and growth will positively influence the market. Absorption should decrease after 1998's extraordinary performance. Construction will decrease as well. Financial incentives including the Rural Economic Development Program, income tax credits, sales tax exemptions, and development bonds will keep growth. Low costs of living and high quality of life will attract more relocations to the market. Tightening of the market should push effective rental rates higher. Development activity will be strong in the suburbs. More lease transactions comparable to those done in 1998 with Chemfirst, Allstate, AG. Edwards, and Primerica are expected to occur." Society of Industrial and Office Realtors, 1999 Comparative Statistics of Industrial and Office Real Estate Markets

Industrial Market

Location	Total Space (sq. ft.)	Vacant Space (sq. ft.)	Vac. Rate (%)	Under Constr. (sq. ft.)	Net Absorp. (sq. ft.)	Lease ($/sq.ft./yr.)
Central City	4,866,000	800,000	16.4	0	-150,000	1.50-5.00
Suburban	14,240,000	425,000	3.0	350,000	549,575	3.00-9.50

Note: Data as of 10/98 and covers Jackson; n/a not available
Source: Society of Industrial and Office Realtors, 1999 Comparative Statistics of Industrial and Office Real Estate Markets

"Incentives that are unmatched will continue to draw relocations to the metro-Jackson market. Hughes Aircraft Delco-remy and other manufacturers' high opinion of the workforce will encourage further local growth. Mississippi's 'right-to-work' status will continue to restrict mandatory membership in labor unions. With only 2.5 percent of the new industrial development in 1998 going to leased facilities, limited speculative construction will occur. Owner occupied build-to-suit space will dominate the market again with nearly all construction being of this nature. General Motors' 350,000 sq. ft. facility and HydroEllay's 40,000 sq. ft. building are examples of newcomer influence in the market. More large industrial companies are expected to move into Jackson in 1999. Overall activity in the market though is expected to slow slightly." *Society of Industrial and Office Realtors, 1999 Comparative Statistics of Industrial and Office Real Estate Markets*

COMMERCIAL UTILITIES

Typical Monthly Electric Bills

Area	Commercial Service ($/month)		Industrial Service ($/month)	
	12 kW demand 1,500 kWh	100 kW demand 30,000 kWh	1,000 kW demand 400,000 kWh	20,000 kW demand 10,000,000 kWh
City	152	1,999	19,870	283,966
U.S.	150	2,174	23,995	508,569

Note: Based on rates in effect January 1, 1999
Source: Edison Electric Institute, Typical Residential, Commercial and Industrial Bills, Winter 1999

TRANSPORTATION

Transportation Statistics

Average minutes to work	17.9
Interstate highways	I-20; I-55
Bus lines	
In-city	JATRAN, 42 buses; Steel Magnolia Trolley
Inter-city	1
Passenger air service	
Airport	Jackson International
Airlines	10
Aircraft departures	12,174 (1996)
Enplaned passengers	375,604 (1996)
Rail service	Amtrak
Motor freight carriers	n/a
Major waterways/ports	None

Source: Editor & Publisher Market Guide, 1999; FAA Airport Activity Statistics, 1997; Amtrak National Time Table, Northeast Timetable, Spring/Summer 1999; 1990 Census of Population and Housing, STF 3C; Chamber of Commerce/Economic Development 1999; Jane's Urban Transport Systems 1999-2000

Means of Transportation to Work

Area	Car/Truck/Van		Public Transportation			Bicycle	Walked	Other Means	Worked at Home
	Drove Alone	Car-pooled	Bus	Subway	Railroad				
City	78.6	15.0	1.8	0.0	0.0	0.1	2.1	0.9	1.6
MSA[1]	80.2	14.5	1.1	0.0	0.0	0.1	1.7	0.9	1.6
U.S.	73.2	13.4	3.0	1.5	0.5	0.4	3.9	1.2	3.0

Note: Figures shown are percentages and only include workers 16 years old and over; (1) Metropolitan Statistical Area - see Appendix A for areas included
Source: 1990 Census of Population and Housing, Summary Tape File 3C

BUSINESSES

Major Business Headquarters

Company Name	1999 Rankings	
	Fortune 500	Forbes 500
Jitney Jungle Stores of America	-	62
MCI Worldcom	80	-

Note: Companies listed are located in the city; dashes indicate no ranking
Fortune 500: Companies that produce a 10-K are ranked 1 to 500 based on 1998 revenue
Forbes 500: Private companies are ranked 1 to 500 based on 1997 revenue
Source: Forbes, November 30, 1998; Fortune, April 26, 1999

Fast-Growing Businesses

Jackson is home to one of *Business Week's* "hot growth" companies: Friede Goldman International. Criteria: increase in sales and profits, return on capital and stock price. *Business Week, 5/31/99*

HOTELS & MOTELS

Hotels/Motels

Area	Hotels/Motels	Rooms	Luxury-Level Hotels/Motels		Average Minimum Rates ($)		
			♦♦♦♦	♦♦♦♦♦	♦♦	♦♦♦	♦♦♦♦
City	31	4,315	0	0	60	67	n/a

Note: n/a not available; classifications range from one diamond (budget properties with basic amenities) to five diamond (luxury properties with the finest service, rooms and facilities).
Source: OAG, Business Travel Planner, Winter 1998-99

CONVENTION CENTERS

Major Convention Centers

Center Name	Meeting Rooms	Exhibit Space (sq. ft.)
Mississippi Trade Mart	3	64,000

Source: Trade Shows Worldwide, 1998; Meetings & Conventions, 4/15/99; Sucessful Meetings, 3/31/98

Living Environment

COST OF LIVING

Cost of Living Index

Composite Index	Groceries	Housing	Utilities	Trans- portation	Health Care	Misc. Goods/ Services
90.8	89.0	88.6	100.7	93.1	77.2	92.4

Note: U.S. = 100
Source: ACCRA, Cost of Living Index, 1st Quarter 1999

HOUSING

Median Home Prices and Housing Affordability

Area	Median Price[2] 1st Qtr. 1999 ($)	HOI[3] 1st Qtr. 1999	Afford- ability Rank[4]
MSA[1]	116,000	68.8	122
U.S.	134,000	69.6	—

Note: (1) Metropolitan Statistical Area - see Appendix A for areas included; (2) U.S. figures calculated from the sales of 524,324 new and existing homes in 181 markets; (3) Housing Opportunity Index - percent of homes sold that were within the reach of the median income household at the prevailing mortgage interest rate; (4) Rank is from 1-181 with 1 being most affordable
Source: National Association of Home Builders, Housing Opportunity Index, 1st Quarter 1999

Median Home Price Projection

It is projected that the median price of existing single-family homes in the metro area will increase by 0.8% in 1999. Nationwide, home prices are projected to increase 3.8%.
Kiplinger's Personal Finance Magazine, January 1999

Average New Home Price

Area	Price ($)
City	124,341
U.S.	142,735

Note: Figures are based on a new home with 1,800 sq. ft. of living area on an 8,000 sq. ft. lot.
Source: ACCRA, Cost of Living Index, 1st Quarter 1999

Average Apartment Rent

Area	Rent ($/mth)
City	578
U.S.	601

Note: Figures are based on an unfurnished two bedroom, 1-1/2 or 2 bath apartment, approximately 950 sq. ft. in size, excluding all utilities except water
Source: ACCRA, Cost of Living Index, 1st Quarter 1999

RESIDENTIAL UTILITIES

Average Residential Utility Costs

Area	All Electric ($/mth)	Part Electric ($/mth)	Other Energy ($/mth)	Phone ($/mth)
City	—	71.45	23.57	26.21
U.S.	100.02	55.73	43.33	19.71

Source: ACCRA, Cost of Living Index, 1st Quarter 1999

HEALTH CARE

Average Health Care Costs

Area	Hospital ($/day)	Doctor ($/visit)	Dentist ($/visit)
City	247.60	43.50	52.37
U.S.	430.43	52.45	66.35

Note: Hospital—based on a semi-private room; Doctor—based on a general practitioner's routine exam of an established patient; Dentist—based on adult teeth cleaning and periodic oral exam.
Source: ACCRA, Cost of Living Index, 1st Quarter 1999

Distribution of Office-Based Physicians

Area	Family/Gen. Practitioners	Specialists		
		Medical	Surgical	Other
MSA[1]	25	51	40	29

Note: Data as of 12/31/97; (1) Metropolitan Statistical Area - see Appendix A for areas included
Source: American Medical Assn., Physician Characteristics & Distribution in the U.S., 1999

Hospitals

Jackson has 6 general medical and surgical hospitals, 1 psychiatric, 1 obstetrics and gynecology, 1 rehabilitation, 1 other specialty. *AHA Guide to the Healthcare Field, 1998-99*

EDUCATION

Public School District Statistics

District Name	Num. Sch.	Enroll.	Classroom Teachers	Pupils per Teacher	Minority Pupils (%)	Current Exp.[1] ($/pupil)
Jackson Public School Dist	60	32,235	1,835	17.6	n/a	n/a
MDHS Division of Youth	2	487	33	14.8	n/a	n/a
MS Sch For The Blind	1	170	28	6.1	n/a	n/a
MS School For The Deaf	1	138	36	3.8	n/a	n/a

Note: Data covers the 1997-1998 school year unless otherwise noted; (1) Data covers fiscal year 1996; SD = School District; ISD = Independent School District; n/a not available
Source: National Center for Education Statistics, Common Core of Data Public Education Agency Universe 1997-98; National Center for Education Statistics, Characteristics of the 100 Largest Public Elementary and Secondary School Districts in the United States: 1997-98, July 1999

Educational Quality

School District	Education Quotient[1]	Graduate Outcome[2]	Community Index[3]	Resource Index[4]
Jackson Public	65.0	61.0	83.0	69.0

Note: Nearly 1,000 secondary school districts were rated in terms of educational quality. The scores range from a low of 50 to a high of 150; (1) Average of the Graduate Outcome, Community and Resource indexes; (2) Based on graduation rates and college board scores (SAT/ACT); (3) Based on the surrounding community's average level of education and the area's average income level; (4) Based on teacher salaries, per-pupil expenditures and student-teacher ratios.
Source: Expansion Management, Ratings Issue, 1998

Educational Attainment by Race

Area	High School Graduate (%)					Bachelor's Degree (%)				
	Total	White	Black	Other	Hisp.[2]	Total	White	Black	Other	Hisp.[2]
City	75.0	86.0	63.2	80.7	74.8	26.9	35.0	17.8	59.1	36.0
MSA[1]	74.4	83.8	58.2	79.1	71.5	25.1	30.8	14.8	53.5	25.4
U.S.	75.2	77.9	63.1	60.4	49.8	20.3	21.5	11.4	19.4	9.2

Note: Figures shown cover persons 25 years old and over; (1) Metropolitan Statistical Area - see Appendix A for areas included; (2) people of Hispanic origin can be of any race
Source: 1990 Census of Population and Housing, Summary Tape File 3C

School Enrollment by Type

Area	Preprimary				Elementary/High School			
	Public		Private		Public		Private	
	Enrollment	%	Enrollment	%	Enrollment	%	Enrollment	%
City	2,137	53.6	1,848	46.4	32,054	85.4	5,479	14.6
MSA[1]	4,230	52.6	3,807	47.4	67,006	87.0	10,043	13.0
U.S.	2,679,029	59.5	1,824,256	40.5	38,379,689	90.2	4,187,099	9.8

Note: Figures shown cover persons 3 years old and over;
(1) Metropolitan Statistical Area - see Appendix A for areas included
Source: 1990 Census of Population and Housing, Summary Tape File 3C

School Enrollment by Race

Area	Preprimary (%)				Elementary/High School (%)			
	White	Black	Other	Hisp.[1]	White	Black	Other	Hisp.[1]
City	40.5	58.4	1.1	0.0	29.5	70.0	0.6	0.3
MSA[2]	53.1	45.1	1.8	0.4	46.2	53.2	0.6	0.6
U.S.	80.4	12.5	7.1	7.8	74.1	15.6	10.3	12.5

Note: Figures shown cover persons 3 years old and over; (1) people of Hispanic origin can be of any race; (2) Metropolitan Statistical Area - see Appendix A for areas included
Source: 1990 Census of Population and Housing, Summary Tape File 3C

Classroom Teacher Salaries in Public Schools

District	B.A. Degree		M.A. Degree		Maximum	
	Min. ($)	Rank[1]	Max. ($)	Rank[1]	Max. ($)	Rank[1]
Jackson	22,249	97	37,183	90	43,227	86
Average	26,980	-	46,065	-	51,435	-

Note: Salaries are for 1997-1998; (1) Rank ranges from 1 to 100
Source: American Federation of Teachers, Survey & Analysis of Salary Trends, 1998

Higher Education

Two-Year Colleges		Four-Year Colleges		Medical Schools	Law Schools	Voc/ Tech
Public	Private	Public	Private			
0	0	2	2	1	1	3

Source: College Blue Book, Occupational Education, 1997; Medical School Admission Requirements, 1999-2000; Peterson's Guide to Two-Year Colleges, 1999; Peterson's Guide to Four-Year Colleges, 2000; Barron's Guide to Law Schools, 1999

MAJOR EMPLOYERS

Major Employers

St. Dominic Jackson Memorial Hospital	Trustmark National Bank
Methodist Healthcare Jackson Hospitals	Blue Cross & Blue Shield of Mississippi
Statewide Healthcare Services	River Oaks Hospital
Southern Farm Bureau Life Insurance	Tele-Fibernet Corp.
LDDS-Metro Communications	McCarthy-Holman Co. (groceries)

Note: Companies listed are located in the city
Source: Dun's Business Rankings, 1999; Ward's Business Directory, 1998

PUBLIC SAFETY

Crime Rate

Area	All Crimes	Violent Crimes				Property Crimes		
		Murder	Forcible Rape	Robbery	Aggrav. Assault	Burglary	Larceny -Theft	Motor Vehicle Theft
City	10,199.2	30.8	107.7	579.8	363.5	2,637.8	4,827.1	1,652.5
Suburbs[1]	3,969.5	8.0	23.2	72.4	151.9	864.9	2,601.0	248.0
MSA[2]	6,892.2	18.7	62.8	310.4	251.2	1,696.7	3,645.4	906.9
U.S.	4,922.7	6.8	35.9	186.1	382.0	919.6	2,886.5	505.8

Note: Crime rate is the number of crimes per 100,000 pop.; (1) defined as all areas within the MSA but located outside the central city; (2) Metropolitan Statistical Area - see Appendix A for areas incl.
Source: FBI Uniform Crime Reports, 1997

RECREATION

Culture and Recreation

Museums	Symphony Orchestras	Opera Companies	Dance Companies	Professional Theatres	Zoos	Pro Sports Teams
8	2	1	1	2	1	0

Source: International Directory of the Performing Arts, 1997; Official Museum Directory, 1999; Stern's Performing Arts Directory, 1997; USA Today Four Sport Stadium Guide, 1997; Chamber of Commerce/Economic Development, 1999

Library System

The Jackson-Hinds Library System has 15 branches, holdings of 506,495 volumes, and a budget of $2,875,052 (1996-1997). *American Library Directory, 1998-1999*

MEDIA

Newspapers

Name	Type	Freq.	Distribution	Circulation
The Clarion-Ledger	General	7x/wk	Area	109,395
Jackson Advocate	Black	1x/wk	State	26,000
Mississippi Today	Religious	1x/wk	State	13,500

Note: Includes newspapers with circulations of 1,000 or more located in the city;
Source: Burrelle's Media Directory, 1999 Edition

Television Stations

Name	Ch.	Affiliation	Type	Owner
WMAB	n/a	PBS	Public	Mississippi Authority for Educational TV
WLBT	n/a	NBCT	Commercial	Civic Communications
WJTV	12	CBST	Commercial	Media General Inc.
WMAE	12	PBS	Public	Mississippi Authority for Educational TV
WMAW	14	PBS	Public	Mississippi Authority for Educational TV
WAPT	16	ABCT	Commercial	Hearst Corporation
WMAU	17	PBS	Public	Mississippi Authority for Educational TV
WMAV	18	PBS	Public	Mississippi Authority for Educational TV
WMAH	19	PBS	Public	Mississippi Authority for Educational TV
WMAO	23	PBS	Public	Mississippi Authority for Educational TV
WMPN	29	n/a	Public	Mississippi Authority for Educational TV
WDBD	40	FBC	Commercial	Pegasus Broadcast Television Inc.

Note: Stations included broadcast in the Jackson metro area; n/a not available
Source: Burrelle's Media Directory, 1999 Edition

AM Radio Stations

Call Letters	Freq. (kHz)	Target Audience	Station Format	Music Format
WJDS	620	General	S	n/a
WSLI	930	General	S	n/a
WIIN	980	General	M	Oldies
WTWZ	1120	General	T	n/a
WJNT	1180	General	n/a	n/a
WKXI	1400	General	M/N/S	Christian/Oldies/R&B
WJXN	1450	General	M/N/T	Adult Contemporary/Christian

Note: Stations included broadcast in the Jackson metro area; n/a not available
Target Audience: A=Asian; B=Black; C=Christian; E=Ethnic; F=French; G=General; H=Hispanic; M=Men; N=Native American; R=Religious; S=Senior Citizen; W=Women; Y=Young Adult; Z=Children
Station Format: E=Educational; M=Music; N=News; S=Sports; T=Talk
Source: Burrelle's Media Directory, 1999 Edition

FM Radio Stations

Call Letters	Freq. (mHz)	Target Audience	Station Format	Music Format
WMAW	88.1	General	M/N/S	Classical
WJSU	88.5	General	M	Christian/Jazz
WMAU	88.9	General	E/M/N	Classical
WMAE	89.5	General	M/N	Classical
WMAB	89.9	General	M/N	Classical
WMPR	90.1	Black	M/N/S	Christian/Gospel/R&B
WMAH	90.3	General	M/N/S	Classical/Jazz
WMAV	90.3	General	M/N/S	Classical
WMAO	90.9	General	M/N/S	Classical
WMPN	91.3	General	M/N/S	Classical
WTYX	94.7	General	M	Classic Rock
WKTF	95.5	General	M/N/T	Adult Contemporary/Top 40
WJDX	96.3	General	M	Urban Contemporary
WRJH	97.7	Religious	M	Christian
WYOY	101.7	General	M/N	Adult Top 40
WMSI	102.9	General	M	Country
WSTZ	106.7	Men	M	Classic Rock
WKXI	107.5	Black	M/N/S/T	Adult Contemporary/Urban Contemporary

Note: Stations included broadcast in the Jackson metro area
Station Format: E=Educational; M=Music; N=News; S=Sports; T=Talk
Target Audience: A=Asian; B=Black; C=Christian; E=Ethnic; F=French; G=General; H=Hispanic;
M=Men; N=Native American; R=Religious; S=Senior Citizen; W=Women; Y=Young Adult; Z=Children
Source: Burrelle's Media Directory, 1999 Edition

CLIMATE

Average and Extreme Temperatures

Temperature	Jan	Feb	Mar	Apr	May	Jun	Jul	Aug	Sep	Oct	Nov	Dec	Yr.
Extreme High (°F)	82	85	89	94	99	105	106	102	104	95	88	84	106
Average High (°F)	56	60	69	77	84	90	92	92	87	78	68	59	76
Average Temp. (°F)	45	48	57	65	72	79	82	81	76	65	56	49	65
Average Low (°F)	34	36	44	52	60	68	71	70	65	52	44	37	53
Extreme Low (°F)	2	11	15	27	38	47	51	55	35	29	17	4	2

Note: Figures cover the years 1963-1990
Source: National Climatic Data Center, International Station Meteorological Climate Summary, 3/95

Average Precipitation/Snowfall/Humidity

Precip./Humidity	Jan	Feb	Mar	Apr	May	Jun	Jul	Aug	Sep	Oct	Nov	Dec	Yr.
Avg. Precip. (in.)	5.1	4.7	5.8	5.7	5.4	3.0	4.5	3.8	3.6	3.3	4.7	5.8	55.4
Avg. Snowfall (in.)	1	Tr	Tr	Tr	0	0	0	0	0	0	Tr	Tr	1
Avg. Rel. Hum. 6am (%)	87	87	88	90	92	92	93	94	94	93	90	87	91
Avg. Rel. Hum. 3pm (%)	59	54	51	50	53	52	56	56	55	49	52	58	54

Note: Figures cover the years 1963-1990; Tr = Trace amounts (<0.05 in. of rain; <0.5 in. of snow)
Source: National Climatic Data Center, International Station Meteorological Climate Summary, 3/95

Weather Conditions

Temperature			Daytime Sky			Precipitation		
10°F & below	32°F & below	90°F & above	Clear	Partly cloudy	Cloudy	0.01 inch or more precip.	0.1 inch or more snow/ice	Thunder-storms
1	50	84	103	144	118	106	2	68

Note: Figures are average number of days per year and covers the years 1963-1990
Source: National Climatic Data Center, International Station Meteorological Climate Summary, 3/95

AIR & WATER QUALITY

Maximum Pollutant Concentrations

	Particulate Matter (ug/m^3)	Carbon Monoxide (ppm)	Sulfur Dioxide (ppm)	Nitrogen Dioxide (ppm)	Ozone (ppm)	Lead (ug/m^3)
MSA[1] Level	111	4	0.007	n/a	0.10	n/a
NAAQS[2]	150	9	0.140	0.053	0.12	1.50
Met NAAQS?	Yes	Yes	Yes	n/a	Yes	n/a

Note: (1) Metropolitan Statistical Area - see Appendix A for areas included; (2) National Ambient Air Quality Standards; ppm = parts per million; ug/m^3 = micrograms per cubic meter; n/a not available
Source: EPA, National Air Quality and Emissions Trends Report, 1997

Drinking Water

Water System Name	Pop. Served	Primary Water Source Type	Number of Violations in 1998	Type of Violation/ Contaminants
City of Jackson	205,895	Ground	None	None

Note: Data as of July 10, 1999
Source: EPA, Office of Ground Water and Drinking Water, Safe Drinking Water Information System

Jackson tap water is alkaline, hard, fluoridated and chloromine disinfected.
Editor & Publisher Market Guide, 1999

Jacksonville, Florida

Background

The Jacksonville we see today is largely a product of the reconstruction that occurred during the 1940s, after a fire had razed 147 city blocks a few decades earlier. Lying under the modern structures, however, is a history that dates back earlier than the settlement of Plymouth Rock by the Pilgrims.

Located in the northeast part of Florida, on the St. John's River, Jacksonville was settled by English, Spanish, and French explorers from the Sixteenth through Eighteenth centuries. Sites commemorating their presence include: the Fort Caroline National Monument, marking the French settlement led by Rene de Laudonniere in 1564; Spanish Pond one quarter mile east of Fort Caroline, where Spanish forces led by Pedro Menendez, captured the Fort; and Fort George Island, from which General James Oglethorpe led English attacks against the Spanish during the Eighteenth century.

Jacksonville was attractive to these early settlers because of its easy access to the Atlantic Ocean, which meant a favorable port.

Today, Jacksonville is still a favorable port. In addition, it is the financial hub of Florida, with a branch of the Federal Reserve Bank located there. There also continues to be much economic activity in the transportation, machinery, paper, beer, and pulpwood industries, and nearly 5,000 new jobs have been created during the past 5 years by companies expanding or relocating here, including AT & T, Merrill Lynch, Sara Lee, and Johnson & Johnson.

Jacksonville also boasts the Children's Museum, the Jacksonville Symphony Orchestra, the Gator Bowl, and its beach facilities.

Summers are long, warm, and relatively humid. Winters are generally mild, although periodic invasions of cold northern air bring the temperature down. Temperatures along the beaches rarely rise above 90 degrees. Summer thunderstorms usually occur before noon along the beaches, and inland in the afternoons. The greatest rainfall, as localized thundershowers, occurs during the summer months. Although the area is in the Hurricane Belt, this section of the coast has been very fortunate in escaping hurricane-force winds.

General Rankings and Evaluative Comments

■ Jacksonville was ranked #5 out of 19 large, southern metropolitan areas in *Money's* 1998 survey of "The Best Places to Live in America." The survey was conducted by first contacting 512 representative households nationwide and asking them to rank 37 quality-of-life factors on a scale of 1 to 10. Next, a demographic profile was compiled on the 300 largest metropolitan statistical areas in the U.S. The numbers were crunched together to arrive at an overall ranking (things Americans consider most important, like clean air and water, low crime and good schools, received extra weight). Unlike previous years, the 1998 rankings were broken down by region (northeast, midwest, south, west) and population size (100,000 to 249,999; 250,000 to 999,999; 1 million plus). The city had a nationwide ranking of #9 out of 300 in 1997 and #20 out of 300 in 1996. *Money, July 1998; Money, July 1997; Money, September 1996*

■ *Ladies Home Journal* ranked America's 200 largest cities based on the qualities women care about most. Jacksonville ranked #89 out of 200. Criteria: low crime rate, well-paying jobs, quality health and child care, good public schools, the presence of women in government, size of the gender wage gap, number of sexual-harassment and discrimination complaints filed, unemployment and divorce rates, commute times, population density, number of houses of worship, parks and cultural offerings, number of women's health specialists, how well a community's women cared for themselves, complexion kindness index based on UV radiation levels, odds of finding affordable fashions, rental rates for romance movies, champagne sales and other matters of the heart. *Ladies Home Journal, November 1998*

■ Zero Population Growth ranked 229 cities in terms of children's health, safety, and economic well-being. Jacksonville was ranked #53 out of 112 independent cities (cities with populations greater than 100,000 which were neither Major Cities nor Suburbs/Outer Cities) and was given a grade of C. Criteria: total population, percent of population under 18 years of age, household language, percent population change, percent of births to teens, infant mortality rate, percent of low birth weights, dropout rate, enrollment in preprimary school, violent and property crime rates, unemployment rate, percent of children in poverty, percent of owner occupied units, number of bad air days, percent of public transportation commuters, and average travel time to work. *Zero Population Growth, Children's Environmental Index, Fall 1999*

■ Jacksonville was ranked #13 out of 59 metro areas in *The Regional Economist's* "Rational Livability Ranking of 59 Large Metro Areas." The rankings were based on the metro area's total population change over the period 1990-97 divided by the number of people moving in from elsewhere in the United States (net domestic in-migration). *St. Louis Federal Reserve Bank of St. Louis, The Regional Economist, April 1999*

■ Jacksonville was selected by *Yahoo! Internet Life* as one of "America's Most Wired Cities & Towns." The city ranked #47 out of 50. Criteria: home and work net use, domain density, hosts per capita, directory density and content quality. *Yahoo! Internet Life, March 1999*

■ Cognetics studied 273 metro areas in the United States, ranking them by entrepreneurial activity. Jacksonville was ranked #5 out of 134 smaller metro areas. Criteria: Significant Starts (firms started in the last 10 years that still employ at least 5 people) and Young Growers (percent of firms 10 years old or less that grew significantly during the last 4 years). *Cognetics, "Entrepreneurial Hot Spots: The Best Places in America to Start and Grow a Company," 1998*

■ Jacksonville was included among *Entrepreneur* magazine's listing of the "20 Best Cities for Small Business." It was ranked #12 among large metro areas. Criteria: entrepreneurial activity, small-business growth, economic growth, and risk of failure. *Entrepreneur, October 1999*

■ Jacksonville was selected as one of the "Best American Cities to Start a Business" by *Point of View* magazine. Criteria: coolness, quality-of-life, and business concerns. The city was ranked #10 out of 75. *Point of View, November 1998*

■ Reliastar Financial Corp. ranked the 125 largest metropolitan areas according to the general financial security of residents. Jacksonville was ranked #78 out of 125 with a score of -1.4. The score indicates the percentage a metropolitan area is above or below the metropolitan norm. A metro area with a score of 10.6 is 10.6% above the metro average. Criteria: Earnings and Wealth Potential (household income, education, net assets, cost of living); Safety Net (health insurance, retirement savings, life insurance, income support programs); Personal Threats (unemployment rate, low-income households, crime rate); Community Economic Vitality (cost of community services, job quality, job creation, housing costs).
Reliastar Financial Corp., "The Best Cities to Earn and Save Money," 1999 Edition

Business Environment

STATE ECONOMY

State Economic Profile

"Florida's economy has been among the nation's strongest in recent years. Job growth has outpaced the nation by a considerable amount since 1992.

While Florida has been able to avoid any significant fallout from the Asian crisis, the weakening of economies in Latin American will dampen both tourism and international trade. 1998 saw the decline in Latin tourism more than offset by domestic visitors. Domestic tourism is projected to soften as US growth cools in 1999, offering no offset against the expected decline in Latin tourism. Weaker tourism and trade with Latin American will slow growth in 1999; FL will still outpace the nation in job growth as Gross State Product growth (GSP) slows.

Over half of FL's 230,000 new jobs created in 1998 were in the services sector, which grew at 5.2%, more than offsetting a minor decline in manufacturing employment. Much of this growth is taking place in the finance and business services sector.

In spite of strong home sales and a slowing construction market, FL's price appreciation continued to lag the nation. Although residential permits per 1,000 residents stands at 5.1, well above the national average, this number is only slightly up from 1997 and will decline in 1999.

Growth in FL, while strong throughout, has been hottest in the Naples, Ft. Myers and Orlando areas. Construction and employment in the construction industry has begun to slow in South Florida. Projected employment and housing gains will be concentrated in Northern and Central Florida during 1999. Growing diversification of the economy into financial and business services promises a strong outlook for the years ahead." *National Association of Realtors, Economic Profiles: The Fifty States and the District of Columbia, http://nar.realtor.com/databank/profiles.htm*

IMPORTS/EXPORTS

Total Export Sales

Area	1994 ($000)	1995 ($000)	1996 ($000)	1997 ($000)	% Chg. 1994-97	% Chg. 1996-97
MSA[1]	500,396	604,066	676,985	721,337	44.2	6.6
U.S.	512,415,609	583,030,524	622,827,063	687,597,999	34.2	10.4

Note: (1) Metropolitan Statistical Area - see Appendix A for areas included
Source: U.S. Department of Commerce, International Trade Association, Metropolitan Area Exports: An Export Performance Report on Over 250 U.S. Cities, November 10, 1998

CITY FINANCES

City Government Finances

Component	FY94 ($000)	FY94 (per capita $)
Revenue	1,690,773	2,549.34
Expenditure	1,597,821	2,409.18
Debt Outstanding	4,797,598	7,233.78
Cash & Securities	3,766,545	5,679.17

Source: U.S. Bureau of the Census, City Government Finances: 1993-94

City Government Revenue by Source

Source	FY94 ($000)	FY94 (per capita $)	FY94 (%)
From Federal Government	69,842	105.31	4.1
From State Governments	63,624	95.93	3.8
From Local Governments	230	0.35	0.0
Property Taxes	207,022	312.15	12.2
General Sales Taxes	41,513	62.59	2.5
Selective Sales Taxes	66,418	100.14	3.9
Income Taxes	0	0.00	0.0
Current Charges	152,855	230.47	9.0
Utility/Liquor Store	752,009	1,133.87	44.5
Employee Retirement[1]	133,037	200.59	7.9
Other	204,223	307.93	12.1

Note: (1) Excludes "city contributions," classified as "nonrevenue," intragovernmental transfers.
Source: U.S. Bureau of the Census, City Government Finances: 1993-94

City Government Expenditures by Function

Function	FY94 ($000)	FY94 (per capita $)	FY94 (%)
Educational Services	10,588	15.96	0.7
Employee Retirement[1]	47,320	71.35	3.0
Environment/Housing	190,257	286.87	11.9
Government Administration	61,596	92.87	3.9
Interest on General Debt	185,035	278.99	11.6
Public Safety	194,520	293.30	12.2
Social Services	49,281	74.31	3.1
Transportation	88,850	133.97	5.6
Utility/Liquor Store	686,108	1,034.51	42.9
Other	84,266	127.06	5.3

Note: (1) Payments to beneficiaries including withdrawal of contributions.
Source: U.S. Bureau of the Census, City Government Finances: 1993-94

Municipal Bond Ratings

Area	Moody's	S & P
Jacksonville	Aa2	n/a

Note: n/a not available; n/r not rated
Source: Moody's Bond Record, 6/99

POPULATION

Population Growth

Area	1980	1990	% Chg. 1980-90	July 1998 Estimate	% Chg. 1990-98
City	540,920	635,230	17.4	693,630	9.2
MSA[1]	722,252	906,727	25.5	1,042,601	15.0
U.S.	226,545,805	248,765,170	9.8	270,299,000	8.7

Note: (1) Metropolitan Statistical Area - see Appendix A for areas included;
July 1998 MSA population estimate was calculated by the editors
Source: 1980/1990 Census of Housing and Population, Summary Tape File 3C;
Census Bureau Population Estimates 1998

Population Characteristics

Race	City 1980 Population	City 1980 %	City 1990 Population	City 1990 %	% Chg. 1980-90	MSA[1] 1990 Population	MSA[1] 1990 %
White	394,661	73.0	456,358	71.8	15.6	701,960	77.4
Black	137,150	25.4	160,421	25.3	17.0	181,026	20.0
Amer Indian/Esk/Aleut	1,950	0.4	2,270	0.4	16.4	3,182	0.4
Asian/Pacific Islander	5,485	1.0	11,791	1.9	115.0	14,873	1.6
Other	1,674	0.3	4,390	0.7	162.2	5,686	0.6
Hispanic Origin[2]	9,775	1.8	15,572	2.5	59.3	22,206	2.4

Note: (1) Metropolitan Statistical Area - see Appendix A for areas included;
(2) people of Hispanic origin can be of any race
Source: 1980/1990 Census of Housing and Population, Summary Tape File 3C

Ancestry

Area	German	Irish	English	Italian	U.S.	French	Polish	Dutch
City	16.7	15.4	14.1	3.3	6.4	3.6	1.7	1.9
MSA[1]	18.1	16.8	15.7	3.7	7.0	4.0	1.9	2.1
U.S.	23.3	15.6	13.1	5.9	5.3	4.2	3.8	2.5

Note: Figures are percentages and include persons that reported multiple ancestry (eg. if a person reported being Irish and Italian, they were included in both columns); (1) Metropolitan Statistical Area - see Appendix A for areas included
Source: 1990 Census of Population and Housing, Summary Tape File 3C

Age

Area	Median Age (Years)	Under 5	Under 18	18-24	25-44	45-64	65+	80+
City	31.2	8.1	26.1	11.1	34.6	17.5	10.6	2.1
MSA[1]	32.0	7.8	26.0	10.6	34.2	18.3	10.9	2.2
U.S.	32.9	7.3	25.6	10.5	32.6	18.7	12.5	2.8

Note: (1) Metropolitan Statistical Area - see Appendix A for areas included
Source: 1990 Census of Population and Housing, Summary Tape File 3C

Male/Female Ratio

Area	Number of males per 100 females (all ages)	Number of males per 100 females (18 years old+)
City	95.4	92.9
MSA[1]	95.5	93.1
U.S.	95.0	91.9

Note: (1) Metropolitan Statistical Area - see Appendix A for areas included
Source: 1990 Census of Population, General Population Characteristics

INCOME

Per Capita/Median/Average Income

Area	Per Capita ($)	Median Household ($)	Average Household ($)
City	13,661	28,305	35,281
MSA[1]	14,141	29,514	36,739
U.S.	14,420	30,056	38,453

Note: All figures are for 1989; (1) Metropolitan Statistical Area - see Appendix A for areas included
Source: 1990 Census of Population and Housing, Summary Tape File 3C

Household Income Distribution by Race

Income ($)	City (%)					U.S. (%)				
	Total	White	Black	Other	Hisp.[1]	Total	White	Black	Other	Hisp.[1]
Less than 5,000	6.9	4.2	16.1	5.2	9.0	6.2	4.8	15.2	8.6	8.8
5,000 - 9,999	8.3	6.7	14.0	5.9	6.3	9.3	8.6	14.2	9.9	11.1
10,000 - 14,999	9.1	7.8	13.4	10.6	12.1	8.8	8.5	11.0	9.8	11.0
15,000 - 24,999	19.3	19.1	20.0	19.8	19.7	17.5	17.3	18.9	18.5	20.5
25,000 - 34,999	17.3	18.2	14.3	17.6	19.0	15.8	16.1	14.2	15.4	16.4
35,000 - 49,999	18.9	20.7	12.9	18.7	16.9	17.9	18.6	13.3	16.1	16.0
50,000 - 74,999	13.4	15.2	7.2	16.0	12.1	15.0	15.8	9.3	13.4	11.1
75,000 - 99,999	4.0	4.7	1.7	2.8	3.1	5.1	5.5	2.6	4.7	3.1
100,000+	2.7	3.4	0.5	3.4	1.7	4.4	4.8	1.3	3.7	1.9

Note: All figures are for 1989; (1) people of Hispanic origin can be of any race
Source: 1990 Census of Population and Housing, Summary Tape File 3C

Effective Buying Income

Area	Per Capita ($)	Median Household ($)	Average Household ($)
City	16,175	34,044	42,710
MSA[1]	17,449	35,058	46,178
U.S.	16,803	34,536	45,243

Note: Data as of 1/1/99; (1) Metropolitan Statistical Area - see Appendix A for areas included
Source: Standard Rate & Data Service, Newspaper Advertising Source, 9/99

Effective Household Buying Income Distribution

Area	% of Households Earning						
	$10,000 -$19,999	$20,000 -$34,999	$35,000 -$49,999	$50,000 -$74,999	$75,000 -$99,000	$100,000 -$124,999	$125,000 and up
City	15.4	23.9	19.1	18.5	6.7	2.1	2.1
MSA[1]	15.2	23.6	19.3	19.0	7.1	2.2	2.5
U.S.	16.0	22.6	18.2	18.9	7.2	2.4	2.7

Note: Data as of 1/1/99; (1) Metropolitan Statistical Area - see Appendix A for areas included
Source: Standard Rate & Data Service, Newspaper Advertising Source, 9/99

Poverty Rates by Race and Age

Area	Total (%)	By Race (%)				By Age (%)		
		White	Black	Other	Hisp.[2]	Under 5 years old	Under 18 years old	65 years and over
City	13.0	7.5	28.6	12.3	15.0	19.9	18.6	16.1
MSA[1]	11.8	7.4	29.2	12.0	13.9	18.6	16.8	14.5
U.S.	13.1	9.8	29.5	23.1	25.3	20.1	18.3	12.8

Note: Figures show the percent of people living below the poverty line in 1989. The average poverty threshold was $12,674 for a family of four in 1989; (1) Metropolitan Statistical Area - see Appendix A for areas included; (2) people of Hispanic origin can be of any race
Source: 1990 Census of Population and Housing, Summary Tape File 3C

EMPLOYMENT

Labor Force and Employment

Area	Civilian Labor Force			Workers Employed		
	Jun. 1998	Jun. 1999	% Chg.	Jun. 1998	Jun. 1999	% Chg.
City	384,517	396,630	3.2	370,983	383,518	3.4
MSA[1]	540,295	557,693	3.2	522,227	539,871	3.4
U.S.	138,798,000	140,666,000	1.3	132,265,000	134,395,000	1.6

Note: Data is not seasonally adjusted and covers workers 16 years of age and older;
(1) Metropolitan Statistical Area - see Appendix A for areas included
Source: Bureau of Labor Statistics, http://stats.bls.gov

Unemployment Rate

Area	1998						1999					
	Jul.	Aug.	Sep.	Oct.	Nov.	Dec.	Jan.	Feb.	Mar.	Apr.	May.	Jun.
City	3.3	3.1	3.0	2.9	3.0	2.7	3.4	3.1	3.2	3.2	3.2	3.3
MSA[1]	3.1	2.9	2.9	2.8	2.9	2.7	3.3	3.1	3.1	3.1	3.2	3.2
U.S.	4.7	4.5	4.4	4.2	4.1	4.0	4.8	4.7	4.4	4.1	4.0	4.5

Note: Data is not seasonally adjusted and covers workers 16 years of age and older; all figures are percentages; (1) Metropolitan Statistical Area - see Appendix A for areas included
Source: Bureau of Labor Statistics, http://stats.bls.gov

Employment by Industry

Sector	MSA[1]		U.S.
	Number of Employees	Percent of Total	Percent of Total
Services	185,700	33.7	30.4
Retail Trade	101,300	18.4	17.7
Government	66,800	12.1	15.6
Manufacturing	40,900	7.4	14.3
Finance/Insurance/Real Estate	57,200	10.4	5.9
Wholesale Trade	30,100	5.5	5.4
Transportation/Public Utilities	38,300	7.0	5.3
Construction	29,700	5.4	5.0
Mining	n/a	n/a	0.4

Note: Figures cover non-farm employment as of 6/99 and are not seasonally adjusted; (1) Metropolitan Statistical Area - see Appendix A for areas included; n/a not available
Source: Bureau of Labor Statistics, http://stats.bls.gov

Employment by Occupation

Occupation Category	City (%)	MSA[1] (%)	U.S. (%)
White Collar	62.4	61.7	58.1
Executive/Admin./Management	13.1	13.2	12.3
Professional	11.7	12.0	14.1
Technical & Related Support	3.7	3.8	3.7
Sales	13.2	13.7	11.8
Administrative Support/Clerical	20.6	19.1	16.3
Blue Collar	23.9	24.0	26.2
Precision Production/Craft/Repair	11.2	11.5	11.3
Machine Operators/Assem./Insp.	4.1	4.0	6.8
Transportation/Material Movers	4.4	4.4	4.1
Cleaners/Helpers/Laborers	4.2	4.1	3.9
Services	12.6	12.8	13.2
Farming/Forestry/Fishing	1.1	1.5	2.5

Note: Figures cover employed persons 16 years old and over; (1) Metropolitan Statistical Area - see Appendix A for areas included
Source: 1990 Census of Population and Housing, Summary Tape File 3C

Occupational Employment Projections: 1996 - 2006

Occupations Expected to Have the Largest Job Growth (ranked by numerical growth)	Fast-Growing Occupations[1] (ranked by percent growth)
1. Cashiers	1. Systems analysts
2. Salespersons, retail	2. Physical therapy assistants and aides
3. General managers & top executives	3. Desktop publishers
4. Registered nurses	4. Home health aides
5. Waiters & waitresses	5. Computer engineers
6. Marketing & sales, supervisors	6. Medical assistants
7. Janitors/cleaners/maids, ex. priv. hshld.	7. Physical therapists
8. General office clerks	8. Paralegals
9. Food preparation workers	9. Emergency medical technicians
10. Hand packers & packagers	10. Occupational therapists

Note: Projections cover Florida; (1) Excludes occupations with total job growth less than 300
Source: U.S. Department of Labor, Employment and Training Administration, America's Labor Market Information System (ALMIS)

TAXES

Major State and Local Tax Rates

State Corp. Income (%)	State Personal Income (%)	Residential Property (effective rate per $100)	Sales & Use State (%)	Sales & Use Local (%)	State Gasoline (cents/ gallon)	State Cigarette (cents/ pack)
5.5[a]	None	1.11	6.0	0.5	13.1[b]	33.9

Note: Personal/corporate income, sales, gasoline and cigarette tax rates as of January 1999.
Property tax rates as of 1997; (a) 3.3% Alternative Minimum Tax. An exemption of $5,000 is allowed;
(b) Rate is comprised of 4 cents excise and 9.1 cents motor carrier tax
Source: Federation of Tax Administrators, www.taxadmin.org; Washington D.C. Department of Finance and Revenue, Tax Rates and Tax Burdens in the District of Columbia: A Nationwide Comparison, July 1998; Chamber of Commerce, 1999

Total Taxes Per Capita and as a Percent of Income

Area	Per Capita Income ($)	Per Capita Taxes ($) Total	Per Capita Taxes ($) Federal	Per Capita Taxes ($) State/ Local	Percent of Income (%) Total	Percent of Income (%) Federal	Percent of Income (%) State/ Local
Florida	27,655	9,768	6,824	2,944	35.3	24.7	10.6
U.S.	27,876	9,881	6,690	3,191	35.4	24.0	11.4

Note: Figures are for 1998
Source: Tax Foundation, www.taxfoundation.org

Estimated Tax Burden

Area	State Income	Local Income	Property	Sales	Total
Jacksonville	0	0	4,250	634	4,884

Note: The numbers are estimates of taxes paid by a married couple with two children and annual earnings of $75,000. Sales tax estimates assume they spend average amounts on food, clothing, household goods and gasoline. Property tax estimates assume they live in a $250,000 home.
Source: Kiplinger's Personal Finance Magazine, October 1998

COMMERCIAL REAL ESTATE

Office Market

Class/ Location	Total Space (sq. ft.)	Vacant Space (sq. ft.)	Vac. Rate (%)	Under Constr. (sq. ft.)	Net Absorp. (sq. ft.)	Rental Rates ($/sq. ft./yr.)
Class A						
CBD	5,834,277	726,951	12.5	0	-283,951	16.50-25.00
Outside CBD	8,179,380	666,619	8.1	1,260,619	1,444,712	12.50-20.00
Class B						
CBD	4,448,501	554,288	12.5	0	-156,083	7.00-17.50
Outside CBD	4,206,726	342,848	8.1	499,435	690,097	9.50-21.90

Note: Data as of 10/98 and covers Jacksonville; CBD = Central Business District; n/a not available; Source: Society of Industrial and Office Realtors, 1999 Comparative Statistics of Industrial and Office Real Estate Markets

"Jacksonville's accessibility via I-10 and I-95 and its population of 1.1 million people provide the office market with stable interest from businesses looking to expand or relocate. There are more than 700,000 sq. ft. of office space in the construction pipeline and construction is expected to increase over the next few years. As new product is brought to the market, vacancies are expected to increase by six to ten percent. The diverse economy should afford the market some staying power if global or financial fluctuations continue to 'scare' capital investments. Our SIOR reporter believes that rental rates will remain constant over the next year. The reporter also foresees decreases in sales prices for all but Class A CBD properties." *Society of Industrial and Office Realtors, 1999 Comparative Statistics of Industrial and Office Real Estate Markets*

Industrial Market

Location	Total Space (sq. ft.)	Vacant Space (sq. ft.)	Vac. Rate (%)	Under Constr. (sq. ft.)	Net Absorp. (sq. ft.)	Gross Lease ($/sq.ft./yr.)
Central City	n/a	n/a	n/a	n/a	n/a	n/a
Suburban	75,975,000	3,640,000	4.8	1,790,000	2,425,000	2.00-7.00

Note: Data as of 10/98 and covers Jacksonville; n/a not available
Source: Society of Industrial and Office Realtors, 1999 Comparative Statistics of Industrial and Office Real Estate Markets

"Our local SIOR reporter forecasts moderate increases in demand for industrial space in 1999. This increase will focus on bulk distribution centers and research and development facilities. Approximately 1.3 million sq. ft. of speculative buildings are planned to come on line in 1999, most will be located in the northwest and the southeast quadrants. More than 700,000 sq. ft. of distribution and manufacturing space is in the permit phase for the Westside and the Northside sub-markets. Plans for the redevelopment of a naval facility are currently under review by the local Port Authority. This base is expected to close in 1999. Our reporter's outlook for Jacksonville indicates no substantial changes in market conditions over the next year. The availability of labor and quality-of-life issues have kept Jacksonville a strong player in the industrial market." *Society of Industrial and Office Realtors, 1999 Comparative Statistics of Industrial and Office Real Estate Markets*

Retail Market

Shopping Center Inventory (sq. ft.)	Shopping Center Construction (sq. ft.)	Construction as a Percent of Inventory (%)	Torto Wheaton Rent Index[1] ($/sq. ft.)
24,723,000	989,000	4.0	11.99

Note: Data as of 1997 and covers the Metropolitan Statistical Area - see Appendix A for areas included; (1) Index is based on a model that predicts what the average rent should be for leases with certain characteristics, in certain locations during certain years.
Source: National Association of Realtors, 1997-1998 Market Conditions Report

"Jacksonville's retail market has been a virtual roller coaster in recent years. The area's retail rent index dropped over 20% in 1995, rebounded 36% in 1996, and fell 2% last year. The area has both positive and negative forces affecting the retail sector. Unlike Orlando and Fort Lauderdale, employment growth has been below the state average of 3.1%, and Jacksonville's per-capita income is among the lowest in the nation. Positively, the area has a diverse economic base and low business costs. New retail projects include: Sleiman Enterprises Timberlin Parc project (150,000 square feet) and a Publix-anchored Kernan Square on Beach Boulevard (80,000 square feet)." *National Association of Realtors, 1997-1998 Market Conditions Report*

COMMERCIAL UTILITIES

Typical Monthly Electric Bills

Area	Commercial Service ($/month)		Industrial Service ($/month)	
	12 kW demand 1,500 kWh	100 kW demand 30,000 kWh	1,000 kW demand 400,000 kWh	20,000 kW demand 10,000,000 kWh
City[1]	95	1,823[a]	20,450	450,200
U.S.[2]	150	2,174	23,995	508,569

Note: (1) Based on rates in effect January 1, 1998; (2) Based on rates in effect January 1, 1999; (a) Based on 120 kW demand and 30,000 kWh usage.
Source: Memphis Light, Gas and Water, 1998 Utility Bill Comparisons for Selected U.S. Cities; Edison Electric Institute, Typical Residential, Commercial and Industrial Bills, Winter 1999

TRANSPORTATION

Transportation Statistics

Average minutes to work	21.6
Interstate highways	I-10; I-95
Bus lines	
In-city	Jacksonville Transportation Authority, 184 vehicles
Inter-city	2
Passenger air service	
Airport	Jacksonville International
Airlines	12
Aircraft departures	26,240 (1996)
Enplaned passengers	1,660,738 (1996)
Rail service	Amtrak
Motor freight carriers	10
Major waterways/ports	St. Johns River

Source: Editor & Publisher Market Guide, 1999; FAA Airport Activity Statistics, 1997; Amtrak National Time Table, Northeast Timetable, Spring/Summer 1999; 1990 Census of Population and Housing, STF 3C; Chamber of Commerce/Economic Development 1999; Jane's Urban Transport Systems 1999-2000

Means of Transportation to Work

Area	Car/Truck/Van		Public Transportation			Bicycle	Walked	Other Means	Worked at Home
	Drove Alone	Car-pooled	Bus	Subway	Railroad				
City	75.5	14.2	2.5	0.0	0.0	0.6	2.7	1.7	2.7
MSA[1]	76.2	14.3	1.9	0.0	0.0	0.7	2.6	1.7	2.6
U.S.	73.2	13.4	3.0	1.5	0.5	0.4	3.9	1.2	3.0

Note: Figures shown are percentages and only include workers 16 years old and over; (1) Metropolitan Statistical Area - see Appendix A for areas included
Source: 1990 Census of Population and Housing, Summary Tape File 3C

BUSINESSES

Major Business Headquarters

Company Name	1999 Rankings	
	Fortune 500	Forbes 500
Winn-Dixie Stores	115	-

Note: Companies listed are located in the city; dashes indicate no ranking
Fortune 500: Companies that produce a 10-K are ranked 1 to 500 based on 1998 revenue
Forbes 500: Private companies are ranked 1 to 500 based on 1997 revenue
Source: Forbes, November 30, 1998; Fortune, April 26, 1999

Best Companies to Work For

Barnett Banks (banking), headquartered in Jacksonville, is among the "100 Best Places to Work in IS." Criteria: compensation, turnover and training. *Computerworld, May 25, 1998*

Barnett Banks Inc., FACS Management Inc. (management software) and Jacksonville Cardiovascular Clinic, headquartered in Jacksonville, are among the best companies for women. Criteria: salary, benefits, opportunities for advancement and work/family policies. *www.womenswire.com*

Fast-Growing Businesses

According to *Inc.*, Jacksonville is home to one of America's 100 fastest-growing private companies: Providence Construction. Criteria for inclusion: must be an independent, privately-held, U.S. corporation, proprietorship or partnership; sales of at least $200,000 in 1995; five-year operating/sales history; increase in 1999 sales over 1998 sales; holding companies, regulated banks, and utilities were excluded. *Inc. 500, 1999*

Jacksonville is home to one of *Business Week's* "hot growth" companies: Barnett. Criteria: increase in sales and profits, return on capital and stock price. *Business Week, 5/31/99*

According to *Fortune*, Jacksonville is home to one of America's 100 fastest-growing companies: Armor Holdings. Companies were ranked based on earnings-per-share growth, revenue growth and total return over the previous three years. Criteria for inclusion: public companies with sales of least $50 million. Companies that lost money in the most recent quarter, or ended in the red for the past four quarters as a whole, were not eligible. Limited partnerships and REITs were also not considered. *Fortune, "America's Fastest-Growing Companies," 1999*

Small Business Opportunity

According to *Forbes*, Jacksonville is home to three of America's 200 best small companies: Barnett, Computer Management Sciences and FPIC Insurance Group. Criteria: companies included must be publicly traded since November 1997 with a stock price of at least $5 per share and an average daily float of 1,000 shares. The company's latest 12-month sales must be between $5 and $350 million, return on equity (ROE) must be a minimum of 12% for both the past 5 years and the most recent four quarters, and five-year sales and EPS growth must average at least 10%. Companies with declining sales or earnings during the past year were dropped as well as businesses with debt/equity ratios over 1.25. Companies with negative operating cash flow in each of the past two years were also excluded. *Forbes, November 2, 1998*

HOTELS & MOTELS

Hotels/Motels

Area	Hotels/ Motels	Rooms	Luxury-Level Hotels/Motels		Average Minimum Rates ($)		
			♦♦♦♦	♦♦♦♦♦	♦♦	♦♦♦	♦♦♦♦
City	48	6,181	0	0	66	104	n/a
Airport	6	1,133	0	0	n/a	n/a	n/a
Suburbs	18	2,682	2	0	n/a	n/a	n/a
Total	72	9,996	2	0	n/a	n/a	n/a

Note: n/a not available; classifications range from one diamond (budget properties with basic amenities) to five diamond (luxury properties with the finest service, rooms and facilities). Source: OAG, Business Travel Planner, Winter 1998-99

CONVENTION CENTERS   **Major Convention Centers**

Center Name	Meeting Rooms	Exhibit Space (sq. ft.)
Civic Auditorium and Exposition Center	8	21,500
Greater Jacksonville Fairgrounds	1	91,458
Morroco Shrine Auditorium	12	32,000
Prime F. Osborn III Convention Center	22	100,000
Veterams Memorial Coliseum (Jacksonville)	1	48,000

Source: Trade Shows Worldwide, 1998; Meetings & Conventions, 4/15/99; Sucessful Meetings, 3/31/98

Living Environment

COST OF LIVING

Cost of Living Index

Composite Index	Groceries	Housing	Utilities	Trans-portation	Health Care	Misc. Goods/ Services
95.2	102.5	78.2	100.3	107.6	93.9	101.2

Note: U.S. = 100
Source: ACCRA, Cost of Living Index, 1st Quarter 1999

HOUSING

Median Home Prices and Housing Affordability

Area	Median Price[2] 1st Qtr. 1999 ($)	HOI[3] 1st Qtr. 1999	Afford-ability Rank[4]
MSA[1]	104,000	80.2	55
U.S.	134,000	69.6	—

Note: (1) Metropolitan Statistical Area - see Appendix A for areas included; (2) U.S. figures calculated from the sales of 524,324 new and existing homes in 181 markets; (3) Housing Opportunity Index - percent of homes sold that were within the reach of the median income household at the prevailing mortgage interest rate; (4) Rank is from 1-181 with 1 being most affordable
Source: National Association of Home Builders, Housing Opportunity Index, 1st Quarter 1999

Median Home Price Projection

It is projected that the median price of existing single-family homes in the metro area will increase by 5.5% in 1999. Nationwide, home prices are projected to increase 3.8%.
Kiplinger's Personal Finance Magazine, January 1999

Average New Home Price

Area	Price ($)
City	107,000
U.S.	142,735

Note: Figures are based on a new home with 1,800 sq. ft. of living area on an 8,000 sq. ft. lot.
Source: ACCRA, Cost of Living Index, 1st Quarter 1999

Average Apartment Rent

Area	Rent ($/mth)
City	628
U.S.	601

Note: Figures are based on an unfurnished two bedroom, 1-1/2 or 2 bath apartment, approximately 950 sq. ft. in size, excluding all utilities except water
Source: ACCRA, Cost of Living Index, 1st Quarter 1999

RESIDENTIAL UTILITIES

Average Residential Utility Costs

Area	All Electric ($/mth)	Part Electric ($/mth)	Other Energy ($/mth)	Phone ($/mth)
City	102.45	—	—	16.22
U.S.	100.02	55.73	43.33	19.71

Source: ACCRA, Cost of Living Index, 1st Quarter 1999

HEALTH CARE

Average Health Care Costs

Area	Hospital ($/day)	Doctor ($/visit)	Dentist ($/visit)
City	364.60	56.20	57.75
U.S.	430.43	52.45	66.35

Note: Hospital—based on a semi-private room; Doctor—based on a general practitioner's routine exam of an established patient; Dentist—based on adult teeth cleaning and periodic oral exam.
Source: ACCRA, Cost of Living Index, 1st Quarter 1999

Distribution of Office-Based Physicians

Area	Family/Gen. Practitioners	Specialists		
		Medical	Surgical	Other
MSA[1]	269	614	458	467

Note: Data as of 12/31/97; (1) Metropolitan Statistical Area - see Appendix A for areas included
Source: American Medical Assn., Physician Characteristics & Distribution in the U.S., 1999

Hospitals

Jacksonville has 7 general medical and surgical hospitals, 1 psychiatric, 1 rehabilitation, 1 other specialty. *AHA Guide to the Healthcare Field, 1998-99*

EDUCATION

Public School District Statistics

District Name	Num. Sch.	Enroll.	Classroom Teachers	Pupils per Teacher	Minority Pupils (%)	Current Exp.[1] ($/pupil)
Duval County Sch Dist	161	126,979	6,507	19.5	47.1	4,683

Note: Data covers the 1997-1998 school year unless otherwise noted; (1) Data covers fiscal year 1996; SD = School District; ISD = Independent School District; n/a not available
Source: National Center for Education Statistics, Common Core of Data Public Education Agency Universe 1997-98; National Center for Education Statistics, Characteristics of the 100 Largest Public Elementary and Secondary School Districts in the United States: 1997-98, July 1999

Educational Quality

School District	Education Quotient[1]	Graduate Outcome[2]	Community Index[3]	Resource Index[4]
Duval County	105.0	99.0	96.0	118.0

Note: Nearly 1,000 secondary school districts were rated in terms of educational quality. The scores range from a low of 50 to a high of 150; (1) Average of the Graduate Outcome, Community and Resource indexes; (2) Based on graduation rates and college board scores (SAT/ACT); (3) Based on the surrounding community's average level of education and the area's average income level; (4) Based on teacher salaries, per-pupil expenditures and student-teacher ratios.
Source: Expansion Management, Ratings Issue, 1998

Educational Attainment by Race

Area	High School Graduate (%)					Bachelor's Degree (%)				
	Total	White	Black	Other	Hisp.[2]	Total	White	Black	Other	Hisp.[2]
City	76.4	80.2	63.6	77.1	78.9	17.9	19.6	10.9	25.3	20.2
MSA[1]	77.4	80.6	62.5	76.6	78.5	18.6	20.1	10.8	25.0	20.3
U.S.	75.2	77.9	63.1	60.4	49.8	20.3	21.5	11.4	19.4	9.2

Note: Figures shown cover persons 25 years old and over; (1) Metropolitan Statistical Area - see Appendix A for areas included; (2) people of Hispanic origin can be of any race
Source: 1990 Census of Population and Housing, Summary Tape File 3C

School Enrollment by Type

Area	Preprimary				Elementary/High School			
	Public		Private		Public		Private	
	Enrollment	%	Enrollment	%	Enrollment	%	Enrollment	%
City	6,877	55.5	5,519	44.5	92,698	87.5	13,236	12.5
MSA[1]	9,288	54.2	7,843	45.8	135,736	88.8	17,193	11.2
U.S.	2,679,029	59.5	1,824,256	40.5	38,379,689	90.2	4,187,099	9.8

Note: Figures shown cover persons 3 years old and over;
(1) Metropolitan Statistical Area - see Appendix A for areas included
Source: 1990 Census of Population and Housing, Summary Tape File 3C

School Enrollment by Race

Area	Preprimary (%)				Elementary/High School (%)			
	White	Black	Other	Hisp.[1]	White	Black	Other	Hisp.[1]
City	71.3	26.7	2.0	2.1	62.4	33.6	4.0	2.8
MSA[2]	76.9	21.2	1.9	2.1	69.8	26.6	3.5	2.9
U.S.	80.4	12.5	7.1	7.8	74.1	15.6	10.3	12.5

Note: Figures shown cover persons 3 years old and over; (1) people of Hispanic origin can be of any race; (2) Metropolitan Statistical Area - see Appendix A for areas included
Source: 1990 Census of Population and Housing, Summary Tape File 3C

Classroom Teacher Salaries in Public Schools

District	B.A. Degree		M.A. Degree		Maximum	
	Min. ($)	Rank[1]	Max. ($)	Rank[1]	Max. ($)	Rank[1]
Jacksonville	24,782	68	44,662	54	47,475	73
Average	26,980	-	46,065	-	51,435	-

Note: Salaries are for 1997-1998; (1) Rank ranges from 1 to 100
Source: American Federation of Teachers, Survey & Analysis of Salary Trends, 1998

Higher Education

Two-Year Colleges		Four-Year Colleges		Medical Schools	Law Schools	Voc/ Tech
Public	Private	Public	Private			
1	2	1	4	0	1	15

Source: College Blue Book, Occupational Education, 1997; Medical School Admission Requirements, 1999-2000; Peterson's Guide to Two-Year Colleges, 1999; Peterson's Guide to Four-Year Colleges, 2000; Barron's Guide to Law Schools, 1999

MAJOR EMPLOYERS

Major Employers

Winn-Dixie Stores (groceries)	Blue Cross & Blue Shield of Florida
Baronial Transportation Corp.	St. Luke's Hospital Assn.
Memorial Healthcare Group	Southern Baptist Hospital of Florida
St. Vincent's Medical Center	University Medical Center
Mayo Clinic Jacksonville	Southeastern Resources (help supply services)

Note: Companies listed are located in the city
Source: Dun's Business Rankings, 1999; Ward's Business Directory, 1998

PUBLIC SAFETY

Crime Rate

Area	All Crimes	Violent Crimes				Property Crimes		
		Murder	Forcible Rape	Robbery	Aggrav. Assault	Burglary	Larceny -Theft	Motor Vehicle Theft
City	8,252.6	10.7	86.3	337.2	909.1	1,756.9	4,382.6	769.8
Suburbs[1]	4,597.3	4.1	54.9	103.3	512.5	891.3	2,808.3	223.1
MSA[2]	7,107.3	8.6	76.4	263.9	784.9	1,485.7	3,889.4	598.5
U.S.	4,922.7	6.8	35.9	186.1	382.0	919.6	2,886.5	505.8

Note: Crime rate is the number of crimes per 100,000 pop.; (1) defined as all areas within the MSA but located outside the central city; (2) Metropolitan Statistical Area - see Appendix A for areas incl.
Source: FBI Uniform Crime Reports, 1997

RECREATION

Culture and Recreation

Museums	Symphony Orchestras	Opera Companies	Dance Companies	Professional Theatres	Zoos	Pro Sports Teams
6	1	0	2	1	1	1

Source: International Directory of the Performing Arts, 1997; Official Museum Directory, 1999; Stern's Performing Arts Directory, 1997; USA Today Four Sport Stadium Guide, 1997; Chamber of Commerce/Economic Development, 1999

Library System

The Jacksonville Public Library has 16 branches, holdings of 2,721,590 volumes, and a budget of $13,975,644 (1995-1996). *American Library Directory, 1998-1999*

MEDIA

Newspapers

Name	Type	Freq.	Distribution	Circulation
The Beaches Leader	General	2x/wk	Area	22,500
The Florida Times-Union	General	7x/wk	Area	197,706
Jacksonville Advocate	Black	1x/wk	Area	36,000
Jacksonville Free Press	Black	1x/wk	Area	33,055
Northeast Florida Advocate	Black	1x/wk	U.S.	38,000
Sun Times Weekly	n/a	1x/wk	Local	11,000
The Veteran Voice	n/a	1x/mo	Regional	10,000

Note: Includes newspapers with circulations of 10,000 or more located in the city; n/a not available
Source: Burrelle's Media Directory, 1999 Edition

Television Stations

Name	Ch.	Affiliation	Type	Owner
WJXT	n/a	CBST	Commercial	Post-Newsweek Business Information Inc.
WJCT	n/a	PBS	Public	WJCT Inc.
WTLV	12	NBCT	Commercial	Gannett Broadcasting
WJWB	17	WB	Commercial	Media General Inc.
WJXX	25	ABCT	Commercial	Allbritton Communications Company
WAWS	30	FBC	Commercial	Clear Channel Broadcasting Inc.
WTEV	47	n/a	Commercial	RDS Communications
WJEB	59	n/a	Non-comm.	Jacksonville Educators Broadcasting Corp.

Note: Stations included broadcast in the Jacksonville metro area; n/a not available
Source: Burrelle's Media Directory, 1999 Edition

AM Radio Stations

Call Letters	Freq. (kHz)	Target Audience	Station Format	Music Format
WOKV	690	General	N/S/T	n/a
WNZS	930	General	S	n/a
WIOJ	1010	General	M/T	Christian
WROS	1050	General	E/M/T	Christian
WJAX	1220	General	M	Easy Listening
WJGR	1320	General	N/S/T	n/a
WCGL	1360	B/R	M/T	Christian/Gospel
WZAZ	1400	Religious	M	Christian
WZNZ	1460	General	N/S/T	n/a
WOBS	1530	H/R	M/N/T	Christian
WQOP	1600	n/a	n/a	n/a

Note: Stations included broadcast in the Jacksonville metro area; n/a not available
Target Audience: A=Asian; B=Black; C=Christian; E=Ethnic; F=French; G=General; H=Hispanic; M=Men; N=Native American; R=Religious; S=Senior Citizen; W=Women; Y=Young Adult; Z=Children
Station Format: E=Educational; M=Music; N=News; S=Sports; T=Talk
Source: Burrelle's Media Directory, 1999 Edition

FM Radio Stations

Call Letters	Freq. (mHz)	Target Audience	Station Format	Music Format
WJFR	88.7	General	E/M/N	Christian
WJCT	89.9	General	M/N	Classical
WKTZ	90.9	General	M	Easy Listening
WJBT	92.7	General	M/N/T	R&B/Urban Contemporary
WPLA	93.3	General	M/N	Alternative
WAPE	95.1	General	M	n/a
WEJZ	96.1	General	M	Adult Contemporary
WKQL	96.9	General	M	Oldies
WFSJ	97.9	General	M/N/S	Jazz
WQIK	99.1	General	M/N	Country
WSOL	101.5	Black	M/N/S	Urban Contemporary
WMXQ	102.9	General	M/N/S	Adult Contemporary
WFYV	104.5	General	M	AOR/Classic Rock/Modern Rock
WBGB	106.5	General	M	Classic Rock
WROO	107.3	General	E/M/N/S	Country

Note: Stations included broadcast in the Jacksonville metro area; n/a not available
Station Format: E=Educational; M=Music; N=News; S=Sports; T=Talk
Target Audience: A=Asian; B=Black; C=Christian; E=Ethnic; F=French; G=General; H=Hispanic;
M=Men; N=Native American; R=Religious; S=Senior Citizen; W=Women; Y=Young Adult; Z=Children
Music Format: AOR=Album Oriented Rock; MOR=Middle-of-the-Road
Source: Burrelle's Media Directory, 1999 Edition

CLIMATE

Average and Extreme Temperatures

Temperature	Jan	Feb	Mar	Apr	May	Jun	Jul	Aug	Sep	Oct	Nov	Dec	Yr.
Extreme High (°F)	84	88	91	95	100	103	103	102	98	96	88	84	103
Average High (°F)	65	68	74	80	86	90	92	91	87	80	73	67	79
Average Temp. (°F)	54	57	62	69	75	80	83	82	79	71	62	56	69
Average Low (°F)	43	45	51	57	64	70	73	73	70	61	51	44	58
Extreme Low (°F)	7	22	23	34	45	47	61	63	48	36	21	11	7

Note: Figures cover the years 1948-1990
Source: National Climatic Data Center, International Station Meteorological Climate Summary, 3/95

Average Precipitation/Snowfall/Humidity

Precip./Humidity	Jan	Feb	Mar	Apr	May	Jun	Jul	Aug	Sep	Oct	Nov	Dec	Yr.
Avg. Precip. (in.)	3.0	3.7	3.8	3.0	3.6	5.3	6.2	7.4	7.8	3.7	2.0	2.6	52.0
Avg. Snowfall (in.)	Tr	Tr	Tr	0	0	0	0	0	0	0	0	Tr	0
Avg. Rel. Hum. 7am (%)	86	86	87	86	86	88	89	91	92	91	89	88	88
Avg. Rel. Hum. 4pm (%)	56	53	50	49	54	61	64	65	66	62	58	58	58

Note: Figures cover the years 1948-1990; Tr = Trace amounts (<0.05 in. of rain; <0.5 in. of snow)
Source: National Climatic Data Center, International Station Meteorological Climate Summary, 3/95

Weather Conditions

Temperature			Daytime Sky			Precipitation		
10°F & below	32°F & below	90°F & above	Clear	Partly cloudy	Cloudy	0.01 inch or more precip.	0.1 inch or more snow/ice	Thunder-storms
< 1	16	83	86	181	98	114	1	65

Note: Figures are average number of days per year and covers the years 1948-1990
Source: National Climatic Data Center, International Station Meteorological Climate Summary, 3/95

AIR & WATER QUALITY

Maximum Pollutant Concentrations

	Particulate Matter (ug/m³)	Carbon Monoxide (ppm)	Sulfur Dioxide (ppm)	Nitrogen Dioxide (ppm)	Ozone (ppm)	Lead (ug/m³)
MSA[1] Level	62	3	0.035	0.014	0.12	0.02
NAAQS[2]	150	9	0.140	0.053	0.12	1.50
Met NAAQS?	Yes	Yes	Yes	Yes	Yes	Yes

Note: (1) Metropolitan Statistical Area - see Appendix A for areas included; (2) National Ambient Air Quality Standards; ppm = parts per million; ug/m³ = micrograms per cubic meter; n/a not available
Source: EPA, National Air Quality and Emissions Trends Report, 1997

Pollutant Standards Index

In the Jacksonville MSA (see Appendix A for areas included), the Pollutant Standards Index (PSI) exceeded 100 on 4 days in 1997. A PSI value greater than 100 indicates that air quality would be in the unhealthful range on that day. *EPA, National Air Quality and Emissions Trends Report, 1997*

Drinking Water

Water System Name	Pop. Served	Primary Water Source Type	Number of Violations in 1998	Type of Violation/ Contaminants
City of Jacksonville-North Grid	413,212	Ground	None	None
City of Jacksonville-South Grid	396,461	Ground	None	None

Note: Data as of July 10, 1999
Source: EPA, Office of Ground Water and Drinking Water, Safe Drinking Water Information System

Jacksonville tap water is alkaline, very hard and naturally fluoridated.
Editor & Publisher Market Guide, 1999

Knoxville, Tennessee

Background

Home of the Tennessee Valley Authority, "Bleak House" (Confederate Memorial Hall), and the 1982 World's Fair, Knoxville's central business district reflects every period of its history.

Knoxville was settled at the end of the 18th century when a flood of pioneers migrated to Tennessee. It soon established itself as the gateway to the west. In 1791, William Blount, its first territorial governor, chose James White's Fort as the capital of the territory, subsequently renaming it for Secretary of War, James Knox.

The city played an important part in the Civil War and was occupied by both the Confederate and Union Armies. Knoxville rapidly recovered during Reconstruction and became the business center of the east Tennessee Valley.

Metropolitan Knoxville is home to many widely diversified industries. Aluminum and clothing constitute the primary manufactured products. Chemicals, plastics, textiles, electronic components, electrical machinery, paper, railroad equipment, rubber goods, tobacco, and fertilizer are some of its other products.

The facility at Oak Ridge, which is close by, was built during World War II in order to develop the atomic bomb. Nuclear research is still carried on.

Through the years Knoxville has played host to numerous sports championships: 1988 National Chess Championship for elementary school children; 1993 A.A.U. Junior Olympic Games; 1996 National Gymnastics Championship; and the 1997 Super National Scholastic Chess Championships.The Chess Tournament was the largest ever held in the United States and possibly the world. *New York Times, April 27, 1997*

Pulitzer Prize-winner James Agee, is Knoxville's native son. The author fondly depicts his background in a number of his works.

The city is located where the Holston and French Broad rivers meet to create the Tennessee River, about 110 miles northeast of Chattanooga. It lies in a broad valley between the Cumberland Mountains to the northwest and the Great Smoky Mountains to the southeast. The Cumberland Mountains weaken the force of cold winter air which frequently moves south of Knoxville, and modifies the hot summer winds common to the plains to the west. The topography also creates winds that are generally light and encourages few tornadoes.

General Rankings and Evaluative Comments

- Knoxville was ranked #8 out of 44 mid-sized, southern metropolitan areas in *Money's* 1998 survey of "The Best Places to Live in America." The survey was conducted by first contacting 512 representative households nationwide and asking them to rank 37 quality-of-life factors on a scale of 1 to 10. Next, a demographic profile was compiled on the 300 largest metropolitan statistical areas in the U.S. The numbers were crunched together to arrive at an overall ranking (things Americans consider most important, like clean air and water, low crime and good schools, received extra weight). Unlike previous years, the 1998 rankings were broken down by region (northeast, midwest, south, west) and population size (100,000 to 249,999; 250,000 to 999,999; 1 million plus). The city had a nationwide ranking of #96 out of 300 in 1997 and #160 out of 300 in 1996. *Money, July 1998; Money, July 1997; Money, September 1996*

- *Ladies Home Journal* ranked America's 200 largest cities based on the qualities women care about most. Knoxville ranked #119 out of 200. Criteria: low crime rate, well-paying jobs, quality health and child care, good public schools, the presence of women in government, size of the gender wage gap, number of sexual-harassment and discrimination complaints filed, unemployment and divorce rates, commute times, population density, number of houses of worship, parks and cultural offerings, number of women's health specialists, how well a community's women cared for themselves, complexion kindness index based on UV radiation levels, odds of finding affordable fashions, rental rates for romance movies, champagne sales and other matters of the heart. *Ladies Home Journal, November 1998*

- Zero Population Growth ranked 229 cities in terms of children's health, safety, and economic well-being. Knoxville was ranked #67 out of 112 independent cities (cities with populations greater than 100,000 which were neither Major Cities nor Suburbs/Outer Cities) and was given a grade of C. Criteria: total population, percent of population under 18 years of age, household language, percent population change, percent of births to teens, infant mortality rate, percent of low birth weights, dropout rate, enrollment in preprimary school, violent and property crime rates, unemployment rate, percent of children in poverty, percent of owner occupied units, number of bad air days, percent of public transportation commuters, and average travel time to work. *Zero Population Growth, Children's Environmental Index, Fall 1999*

- Cognetics studied 273 metro areas in the United States, ranking them by entrepreneurial activity. Knoxville was ranked #40 out of 134 smaller metro areas. Criteria: Significant Starts (firms started in the last 10 years that still employ at least 5 people) and Young Growers (percent of firms 10 years old or less that grew significantly during the last 4 years). *Cognetics, "Entrepreneurial Hot Spots: The Best Places in America to Start and Grow a Company," 1998*

- Reliastar Financial Corp. ranked the 125 largest metropolitan areas according to the general financial security of residents. Knoxville was ranked #110 out of 125 with a score of -9.5. The score indicates the percentage a metropolitan area is above or below the metropolitan norm. A metro area with a score of 10.6 is 10.6% above the metro average. Criteria: Earnings and Wealth Potential (household income, education, net assets, cost of living); Safety Net (health insurance, retirement savings, life insurance, income support programs); Personal Threats (unemployment rate, low-income households, crime rate); Community Economic Vitality (cost of community services, job quality, job creation, housing costs). *Reliastar Financial Corp., "The Best Cities to Earn and Save Money," 1999 Edition*

Business Environment

STATE ECONOMY

State Economic Profile

"Tennessee's economy has been decelerating for almost three years now, a trend that should continue into 1999 and 2000. TN continues to shed jobs in its manufacturing sector, specifically textiles and apparels. In previous years, growth in other sectors was enough to offset these losses. Now growth in these other sectors has slowed. TN's demographics are still strong, and TN continues to have one of the lowest business costs in the country. The TN outlook is one of moderating growth.

TN's manufacturing employment shed some 11,500 jobs in 1998, a decline of 2.2%. Weak export demand and a strong dollar have undermined the apparel industry's competitive position. Soft commodity prices have also hurt TN's metals industry. Neither of these situations will reverse in 1999.

Job growth across TN has been mixed. Declines in manufacturing have hit central and eastern TN harder than the west. Memphis' distribution and transportation sectors, located along the Mississippi, have continued to provide job growth even as the manufacturing sector stumbles. Federal Express and United Parcel Service continue to expand operations. A slowing of the US economy in 1999 and 2000 will weaken the demand for distribution services, although less so than in most industries.

Nashville's economic outlook is less bright. Almost half of 1998's employment gains were in the construction industry. The city's tourism and convention industry remain strong, although it appears likely that commercial construction, especially hotel, has outpaced demand. Construction employment should contract in 1999. The slowing US economy will also place a drag on tourism." *National Association of Realtors, Economic Profiles: The Fifty States and the District of Columbia, http://nar.realtor.com/databank/profiles.htm*

IMPORTS/EXPORTS

Total Export Sales

Area	1994 ($000)	1995 ($000)	1996 ($000)	1997 ($000)	% Chg. 1994-97	% Chg. 1996-97
MSA[1]	689,179	633,188	764,137	884,213	28.3	15.7
U.S.	512,415,609	583,030,524	622,827,063	687,597,999	34.2	10.4

Note: (1) Metropolitan Statistical Area - see Appendix A for areas included
Source: U.S. Department of Commerce, International Trade Association, Metropolitan Area Exports: An Export Performance Report on Over 250 U.S. Cities, November 10, 1998

CITY FINANCES

City Government Finances

Component	FY92 ($000)	FY92 (per capita $)
Revenue	513,661	3,021.71
Expenditure	470,518	2,767.92
Debt Outstanding	297,959	1,752.80
Cash & Securities	444,569	2,615.27

Source: U.S. Bureau of the Census, City Government Finances: 1991-92

City Government Revenue by Source

Source	FY92 ($000)	FY92 (per capita $)	FY92 (%)
From Federal Government	5,981	35.18	1.2
From State Governments	17,132	100.78	3.3
From Local Governments	23,047	135.58	4.5
Property Taxes	46,846	275.58	9.1
General Sales Taxes	0	0.00	0.0
Selective Sales Taxes	9,236	54.33	1.8
Income Taxes	0	0.00	0.0
Current Charges	25,868	152.17	5.0
Utility/Liquor Store	323,431	1,902.65	63.0
Employee Retirement[1]	47,856	281.52	9.3
Other	14,264	83.91	2.8

Note: (1) Excludes "city contributions," classified as "nonrevenue," intragovernmental transfers.
Source: U.S. Bureau of the Census, City Government Finances: 1991-92

City Government Expenditures by Function

Function	FY92 ($000)	FY92 (per capita $)	FY92 (%)
Educational Services	4,464	26.26	0.9
Employee Retirement[1]	16,128	94.88	3.4
Environment/Housing	33,381	196.37	7.1
Government Administration	4,905	28.85	1.0
Interest on General Debt	11,240	66.12	2.4
Public Safety	36,905	217.10	7.8
Social Services	3,910	23.00	0.8
Transportation	4,606	27.10	1.0
Utility/Liquor Store	343,754	2,022.20	73.1
Other	11,225	66.03	2.4

Note: (1) Payments to beneficiaries including withdrawal of contributions.
Source: U.S. Bureau of the Census, City Government Finances: 1991-92

Municipal Bond Ratings

Area	Moody's	S & P
Knoxville	Aa3	n/a

Note: n/a not available; n/r not rated
Source: Moody's Bond Record, 6/99

POPULATION

Population Growth

Area	1980	1990	% Chg. 1980-90	July 1998 Estimate	% Chg. 1990-98
City	175,030	165,121	-5.7	165,540	0.3
MSA[1]	565,970	604,816	6.9	670,383	10.8
U.S.	226,545,805	248,765,170	9.8	270,299,000	8.7

Note: (1) Metropolitan Statistical Area - see Appendix A for areas included;
July 1998 MSA population estimate was calculated by the editors
Source: 1980/1990 Census of Housing and Population, Summary Tape File 3C;
Census Bureau Population Estimates 1998

Population Characteristics

Race	City 1980 Population	%	City 1990 Population	%	% Chg. 1980-90	MSA[1] 1990 Population	%
White	147,892	84.5	136,789	82.8	-7.5	562,156	92.9
Black	25,438	14.5	25,770	15.6	1.3	35,881	5.9
Amer Indian/Esk/Aleut	475	0.3	592	0.4	24.6	1,716	0.3
Asian/Pacific Islander	907	0.5	1,653	1.0	82.2	4,275	0.7
Other	318	0.2	317	0.2	-0.3	788	0.1
Hispanic Origin[2]	1,317	0.8	986	0.6	-25.1	3,444	0.6

Note: (1) Metropolitan Statistical Area - see Appendix A for areas included;
(2) people of Hispanic origin can be of any race
Source: 1980/1990 Census of Housing and Population, Summary Tape File 3C

Ancestry

Area	German	Irish	English	Italian	U.S.	French	Polish	Dutch
City	17.8	18.1	15.4	1.7	9.8	2.5	0.8	3.6
MSA[1]	19.6	19.7	16.9	1.5	12.3	2.5	0.8	4.1
U.S.	23.3	15.6	13.1	5.9	5.3	4.2	3.8	2.5

Note: Figures are percentages and include persons that reported multiple ancestry (eg. if a person reported being Irish and Italian, they were included in both columns); (1) Metropolitan Statistical Area - see Appendix A for areas included
Source: 1990 Census of Population and Housing, Summary Tape File 3C

Age

Area	Median Age (Years)	Age Distribution (%) Under 5	Under 18	18-24	25-44	45-64	65+	80+
City	32.4	5.9	19.8	16.5	31.1	17.2	15.4	3.8
MSA[1]	34.5	6.2	22.9	11.4	32.0	20.5	13.3	2.8
U.S.	32.9	7.3	25.6	10.5	32.6	18.7	12.5	2.8

Note: (1) Metropolitan Statistical Area - see Appendix A for areas included
Source: 1990 Census of Population and Housing, Summary Tape File 3C

Male/Female Ratio

Area	Number of males per 100 females (all ages)	Number of males per 100 females (18 years old+)
City	86.7	83.7
MSA[1]	92.2	88.9
U.S.	95.0	91.9

Note: (1) Metropolitan Statistical Area - see Appendix A for areas included
Source: 1990 Census of Population, General Population Characteristics

INCOME

Per Capita/Median/Average Income

Area	Per Capita ($)	Median Household ($)	Average Household ($)
City	12,108	19,923	27,960
MSA[1]	12,984	25,134	32,693
U.S.	14,420	30,056	38,453

Note: All figures are for 1989; (1) Metropolitan Statistical Area - see Appendix A for areas included
Source: 1990 Census of Population and Housing, Summary Tape File 3C

Household Income Distribution by Race

Income ($)	City (%)					U.S. (%)				
	Total	White	Black	Other	Hisp.[1]	Total	White	Black	Other	Hisp.[1]
Less than 5,000	11.7	9.5	25.6	12.8	10.0	6.2	4.8	15.2	8.6	8.8
5,000 - 9,999	14.7	14.0	17.9	21.3	16.4	9.3	8.6	14.2	9.9	11.1
10,000 - 14,999	12.8	12.7	13.8	13.9	10.6	8.8	8.5	11.0	9.8	11.0
15,000 - 24,999	20.4	20.7	17.9	21.4	29.4	17.5	17.3	18.9	18.5	20.5
25,000 - 34,999	15.0	15.7	10.5	17.3	12.1	15.8	16.1	14.2	15.4	16.4
35,000 - 49,999	13.1	13.8	9.1	6.5	8.2	17.9	18.6	13.3	16.1	16.0
50,000 - 74,999	8.0	8.7	3.7	4.5	10.9	15.0	15.8	9.3	13.4	11.1
75,000 - 99,999	2.0	2.1	1.2	1.0	0.0	5.1	5.5	2.6	4.7	3.1
100,000+	2.3	2.6	0.3	1.4	2.4	4.4	4.8	1.3	3.7	1.9

Note: All figures are for 1989; (1) people of Hispanic origin can be of any race
Source: 1990 Census of Population and Housing, Summary Tape File 3C

Effective Buying Income

Area	Per Capita ($)	Median Household ($)	Average Household ($)
City	15,639	25,537	36,271
MSA[1]	17,329	31,471	43,073
U.S.	16,803	34,536	45,243

Note: Data as of 1/1/99; (1) Metropolitan Statistical Area - see Appendix A for areas included
Source: Standard Rate & Data Service, Newspaper Advertising Source, 9/99

Effective Household Buying Income Distribution

Area	% of Households Earning						
	$10,000 -$19,999	$20,000 -$34,999	$35,000 -$49,999	$50,000 -$74,999	$75,000 -$99,000	$100,000 -$124,999	$125,000 and up
City	21.3	23.4	15.4	12.9	4.3	1.4	2.1
MSA[1]	17.8	23.0	17.2	16.8	6.6	2.1	2.4
U.S.	16.0	22.6	18.2	18.9	7.2	2.4	2.7

Note: Data as of 1/1/99; (1) Metropolitan Statistical Area - see Appendix A for areas included
Source: Standard Rate & Data Service, Newspaper Advertising Source, 9/99

Poverty Rates by Race and Age

Area	Total (%)	By Race (%)				By Age (%)		
		White	Black	Other	Hisp.[2]	Under 5 years old	Under 18 years old	65 years and over
City	20.8	17.4	38.6	25.3	34.4	32.0	29.8	16.2
MSA[1]	14.2	12.9	33.6	19.7	18.7	21.8	18.7	16.1
U.S.	13.1	9.8	29.5	23.1	25.3	20.1	18.3	12.8

Note: Figures show the percent of people living below the poverty line in 1989. The average poverty threshold was $12,674 for a family of four in 1989; (1) Metropolitan Statistical Area - see Appendix A for areas included; (2) people of Hispanic origin can be of any race
Source: 1990 Census of Population and Housing, Summary Tape File 3C

EMPLOYMENT

Labor Force and Employment

Area	Civilian Labor Force			Workers Employed		
	Jun. 1998	Jun. 1999	% Chg.	Jun. 1998	Jun. 1999	% Chg.
City	93,291	93,453	0.2	89,647	90,526	1.0
MSA[1]	350,525	351,858	0.4	339,193	342,520	1.0
U.S.	138,798,000	140,666,000	1.3	132,265,000	134,395,000	1.6

Note: Data is not seasonally adjusted and covers workers 16 years of age and older;
(1) Metropolitan Statistical Area - see Appendix A for areas included
Source: Bureau of Labor Statistics, http://stats.bls.gov

Unemployment Rate

Area	1998						1999					
	Jul.	Aug.	Sep.	Oct.	Nov.	Dec.	Jan.	Feb.	Mar.	Apr.	May.	Jun.
City	4.7	4.7	4.6	4.4	4.4	3.7	3.9	3.8	3.5	3.2	2.9	3.1
MSA[1]	3.4	3.5	3.3	3.3	3.5	3.1	4.8	4.6	4.2	3.2	2.6	2.7
U.S.	4.7	4.5	4.4	4.2	4.1	4.0	4.8	4.7	4.4	4.1	4.0	4.5

Note: Data is not seasonally adjusted and covers workers 16 years of age and older; all figures are percentages; (1) Metropolitan Statistical Area - see Appendix A for areas included
Source: Bureau of Labor Statistics, http://stats.bls.gov

Employment by Industry

Sector	MSA[1]		U.S.
	Number of Employees	Percent of Total	Percent of Total
Services	91,000	27.7	30.4
Retail Trade	71,900	21.9	17.7
Government	54,900	16.7	15.6
Manufacturing	46,700	14.2	14.3
Finance/Insurance/Real Estate	15,200	4.6	5.9
Wholesale Trade	17,300	5.3	5.4
Transportation/Public Utilities	14,200	4.3	5.3
Construction	16,700	5.1	5.0
Mining	600	0.2	0.4

Note: Figures cover non-farm employment as of 6/99 and are not seasonally adjusted; (1) Metropolitan Statistical Area - see Appendix A for areas included
Source: Bureau of Labor Statistics, http://stats.bls.gov

Employment by Occupation

Occupation Category	City (%)	MSA[1] (%)	U.S. (%)
White Collar	60.1	57.2	58.1
Executive/Admin./Management	11.0	11.4	12.3
Professional	16.6	14.5	14.1
Technical & Related Support	3.7	3.9	3.7
Sales	13.7	13.2	11.8
Administrative Support/Clerical	15.2	14.4	16.3
Blue Collar	22.7	28.4	26.2
Precision Production/Craft/Repair	8.4	12.1	11.3
Machine Operators/Assem./Insp.	6.1	7.9	6.8
Transportation/Material Movers	4.2	4.3	4.1
Cleaners/Helpers/Laborers	3.9	4.1	3.9
Services	16.2	12.8	13.2
Farming/Forestry/Fishing	1.0	1.6	2.5

Note: Figures cover employed persons 16 years old and over; (1) Metropolitan Statistical Area - see Appendix A for areas included
Source: 1990 Census of Population and Housing, Summary Tape File 3C

Occupational Employment Projections: 1996 - 2006

Occupations Expected to Have the Largest Job Growth (ranked by numerical growth)	Fast-Growing Occupations1 (ranked by percent growth)
1. Salespersons, retail	1. Personal and home care aides
2. Truck drivers, light	2. Systems analysts
3. Cashiers	3. Paralegals
4. General managers & top executives	4. Respiratory therapists
5. Janitors/cleaners/maids, ex. priv. hshld.	5. Home health aides
6. Food service workers	6. Directors, religious activities & educ.
7. Child care workers, private household	7. Computer engineers
8. Cooks, fast food and short order	8. Child care workers, private household
9. Registered nurses	9. Corrections officers & jailers
10. Waiters & waitresses	10. Emergency medical technicians

Note: Projections cover Tennessee; (1) Excludes occupations with total job growth less than 300
Source: U.S. Department of Labor, Employment and Training Administration, America's Labor Market Information System (ALMIS)

TAXES

Major State and Local Tax Rates

State Corp. Income (%)	State Personal Income (%)	Residential Property (effective rate per $100)	Sales & Use		State Gasoline (cents/ gallon)	State Cigarette (cents/ pack)
			State (%)	Local (%)		
6.0	6.0[a]	n/a	6.0	2.25	21.0[b]	13.0[c]

Note: Personal/corporate income, sales, gasoline and cigarette tax rates as of January 1999. Property tax rates as of 1997; (a) Applies to interest and dividend income only; (b) Rate is comprised of 20 cents excise and 1 cent motor carrier tax. Does not include a 1 cent local option tax; (c) Counties and cities may impose an additional tax of 1 cent per pack. Dealers pay a additional enforcement and admin. fee of 0.05 cent per pack
Source: Federation of Tax Administrators, www.taxadmin.org; Washington D.C. Department of Finance and Revenue, Tax Rates and Tax Burdens in the District of Columbia: A Nationwide Comparison, July 1998; Chamber of Commerce, 1999

Total Taxes Per Capita and as a Percent of Income

Area	Per Capita Income ($)	Per Capita Taxes ($)			Percent of Income (%)		
		Total	Federal	State/ Local	Total	Federal	State/ Local
Tennessee	24,591	8,048	5,930	2,118	32.7	24.1	8.6
U.S.	27,876	9,881	6,690	3,191	35.4	24.0	11.4

Note: Figures are for 1998
Source: Tax Foundation, www.taxfoundation.org

COMMERCIAL REAL ESTATE

Office Market

Class/ Location	Total Space (sq. ft.)	Vacant Space (sq. ft.)	Vac. Rate (%)	Under Constr. (sq. ft.)	Net Absorp. (sq. ft.)	Rental Rates ($/sq.ft./yr.)
Class A						
CBD	1,240,000	100,000	8.1	0	11,600	15.00-16.00
Outside CBD	475,000	20,000	4.2	160,000	3,750	15.50-17.00
Class B						
CBD	3,500,000	500,000	14.3	0	0	10.00-12.00
Outside CBD	4,500,000	250,000	5.6	10,000	65,000	12.50-14.00

Note: Data as of 10/98 and covers Knoxville; CBD = Central Business District; n/a not available;
Source: Society of Industrial and Office Realtors, 1999 Comparative Statistics of Industrial and Office Real Estate Markets

"Completion of several projects will allow tenants such as US Cellular to occupy their space before the year's end. Although a surface review will show a strong economy, our SIOR reporter believes that there will be a downturn after the first quarter. If the economy slows its pace, local tax incentives, such as the absence of a personal income tax and the availability of credits for corporate income tax, will lessen the impact of a recession. Oak Ridge may not fare well with its current vacancy rate of 30 percent. Construction of Ripley's new one million gallon aquarium in Gatlinburg, in addition to the existing national parks, Dollywood and musical theme venues, will attract new households looking for a high quality of life." *Society of Industrial and Office Realtors, 1999 Comparative Statistics of Industrial and Office Real Estate Markets*

Industrial Market

Location	Total Space (sq. ft.)	Vacant Space (sq. ft.)	Vac. Rate (%)	Under Constr. (sq. ft.)	Net Absorp. (sq. ft.)	Lease ($/sq.ft./yr.)
Central City	20,258,740	929,550	4.6	n/a	511,857	n/a
Suburban	13,189,283	605,175	4.6	n/a	108,984	n/a

Note: Data as of 10/98 and covers Knoxville; n/a not available
Source: Society of Industrial and Office Realtors, 1999 Comparative Statistics of Industrial and Office Real Estate Markets

"The local economy's diversity may help combat the effects of a potential economic slowdown. Continued interest in expansion and relocations will drive the market next year. New development will focus on the I-40/75 and Fellissippi Parkway interchange and on I-640's perimeter loop. Build-to-suit and pre-leased space will remain competitive. Continued improvements to the infrastructure will facilitate growth. Our local SIOR reporter indicates that sales and lease prices will increase over the next year. Site prices are expected to see increases between 11 and 15 percent. This is partially a result of a shortage of available space and the demand for build-to-suit facilities. Vacancy rates, already below five percent, are expected to remain fairly low. Knoxville's proximity to major south-central U.S. cities will help Knoxville remain a key distribution center for many corporations." *Society of Industrial and Office Realtors, 1999 Comparative Statistics of Industrial and Office Real Estate Markets*

COMMERCIAL UTILITIES

Typical Monthly Electric Bills

Area	Commercial Service ($/month)		Industrial Service ($/month)	
	12 kW demand 1,500 kWh	100 kW demand 30,000 kWh	1,000 kW demand 400,000 kWh	20,000 kW demand 10,000,000 kWh
City	n/a	n/a	n/a	n/a
U.S.	150	2,174	23,995	508,569

Note: Based on rates in effect January 1, 1999; n/a not available
Source: Edison Electric Institute, Typical Residential, Commercial and Industrial Bills, Winter 1999

TRANSPORTATION

Transportation Statistics

Average minutes to work	18.1
Interstate highways	I-40; I-75
Bus lines	
In-city	Knoxville Area Transit
Inter-city	1
Passenger air service	
Airport	McGhee-Tyson Airport
Airlines	13
Aircraft departures	11,222 (1996)
Enplaned passengers	601,472 (1996)
Rail service	No Amtrak service
Motor freight carriers	64
Major waterways/ports	Tennessee River; Port of Knoxville

Source: Editor & Publisher Market Guide, 1999; FAA Airport Activity Statistics, 1997; Amtrak National Time Table, Northeast Timetable, Spring/Summer 1999; 1990 Census of Population and Housing, STF 3C; Chamber of Commerce/Economic Development 1999; Jane's Urban Transport Systems 1999-2000

Means of Transportation to Work

Area	Car/Truck/Van		Public Transportation			Bicycle	Walked	Other Means	Worked at Home
	Drove Alone	Car-pooled	Bus	Subway	Railroad				
City	77.1	13.1	1.8	0.0	0.0	0.2	4.8	1.0	1.9
MSA[1]	80.5	13.2	0.6	0.0	0.0	0.1	2.3	0.8	2.5
U.S.	73.2	13.4	3.0	1.5	0.5	0.4	3.9	1.2	3.0

Note: Figures shown are percentages and only include workers 16 years old and over;
(1) Metropolitan Statistical Area - see Appendix A for areas included
Source: 1990 Census of Population and Housing, Summary Tape File 3C

BUSINESSES

Major Business Headquarters

Company Name	1999 Rankings	
	Fortune 500	Forbes 500
HT Hackney	-	99
Pilot	-	121
Regal Cinemas	-	490

Note: Companies listed are located in the city; dashes indicate no ranking
Fortune 500: Companies that produce a 10-K are ranked 1 to 500 based on 1998 revenue
Forbes 500: Private companies are ranked 1 to 500 based on 1997 revenue
Source: Forbes, November 30, 1998; Fortune, April 26, 1999

HOTELS & MOTELS

Hotels/Motels

Area	Hotels/ Motels	Rooms	Luxury-Level Hotels/Motels		Average Minimum Rates ($)		
			◆◆◆◆	◆◆◆◆◆	◆◆	◆◆◆	◆◆◆◆
City	50	5,656	0	0	58	90	n/a
Airport	6	664	0	0	n/a	n/a	n/a
Total	56	6,320	0	0	n/a	n/a	n/a

Note: n/a not available; classifications range from one diamond (budget properties with basic amenities) to five diamond (luxury properties with the finest service, rooms and facilities).
Source: OAG, Business Travel Planner, Winter 1998-99

CONVENTION CENTERS

Major Convention Centers

Center Name	Meeting Rooms	Exhibit Space (sq. ft.)
Civic Auditorium/Coliseum/Convention Center	15	67,000
Hyatt Regency Knoxville	13	15,378
Knoxville Convention/Exhibition Center	16	66,396
Tennessee Valley Fairgrounds	n/a	60,000
Thompson-Boling Assembly Center and Arena	n/a	22,000

Note: n/a not available
Source: Trade Shows Worldwide, 1998; Meetings & Conventions, 4/15/99;
Sucessful Meetings, 3/31/98

Living Environment

COST OF LIVING

Cost of Living Index

Composite Index	Groceries	Housing	Utilities	Trans-portation	Health Care	Misc. Goods/ Services
93.4	96.1	86.6	95.5	90.2	94.9	98.1

Note: U.S. = 100
Source: ACCRA, Cost of Living Index, 1st Quarter 1999

HOUSING

Median Home Prices and Housing Affordability

Area	Median Price[2] 1st Qtr. 1999 ($)	HOI[3] 1st Qtr. 1999	Afford-ability Rank[4]
MSA[1]	88,000	86.8	13
U.S.	134,000	69.6	–

Note: (1) Metropolitan Statistical Area - see Appendix A for areas included; (2) U.S. figures calculated from the sales of 524,324 new and existing homes in 181 markets; (3) Housing Opportunity Index - percent of homes sold that were within the reach of the median income household at the prevailing mortgage interest rate; (4) Rank is from 1-181 with 1 being most affordable
Source: National Association of Home Builders, Housing Opportunity Index, 1st Quarter 1999

Median Home Price Projection

It is projected that the median price of existing single-family homes in the metro area will increase by 3.6% in 1999. Nationwide, home prices are projected to increase 3.8%.
Kiplinger's Personal Finance Magazine, January 1999

Average New Home Price

Area	Price ($)
City	121,860
U.S.	142,735

Note: Figures are based on a new home with 1,800 sq. ft. of living area on an 8,000 sq. ft. lot.
Source: ACCRA, Cost of Living Index, 1st Quarter 1999

Average Apartment Rent

Area	Rent ($/mth)
City	576
U.S.	601

Note: Figures are based on an unfurnished two bedroom, 1-1/2 or 2 bath apartment, approximately 950 sq. ft. in size, excluding all utilities except water
Source: ACCRA, Cost of Living Index, 1st Quarter 1999

RESIDENTIAL UTILITIES

Average Residential Utility Costs

Area	All Electric ($/mth)	Part Electric ($/mth)	Other Energy ($/mth)	Phone ($/mth)
City	–	44.43	49.93	19.47
U.S.	100.02	55.73	43.33	19.71

Source: ACCRA, Cost of Living Index, 1st Quarter 1999

HEALTH CARE

Average Health Care Costs

Area	Hospital ($/day)	Doctor ($/visit)	Dentist ($/visit)
City	385.50	54.60	59.20
U.S.	430.43	52.45	66.35

Note: Hospital—based on a semi-private room; Doctor—based on a general practitioner's routine exam of an established patient; Dentist—based on adult teeth cleaning and periodic oral exam.
Source: ACCRA, Cost of Living Index, 1st Quarter 1999

Distribution of Office-Based Physicians

Area	Family/Gen. Practitioners	Specialists		
		Medical	Surgical	Other
MSA[1]	225	471	379	354

Note: Data as of 12/31/97; (1) Metropolitan Statistical Area - see Appendix A for areas included
Source: American Medical Assn., Physician Characteristics & Distribution in the U.S., 1999

Hospitals

Knoxville has 5 general medical and surgical hospitals, 1 psychiatric, 1 children's general.
AHA Guide to the Healthcare Field, 1998-99

EDUCATION

Public School District Statistics

District Name	Num. Sch.	Enroll.	Classroom Teachers	Pupils per Teacher	Minority Pupils (%)	Current Exp.[1] ($/pupil)
Knox County School District	85	51,152	n/a	n/a	14.5	4,284

Note: Data covers the 1997-1998 school year unless otherwise noted; (1) Data covers fiscal year 1996; SD = School District; ISD = Independent School District; n/a not available
Source: National Center for Education Statistics, Common Core of Data Public Education Agency Universe 1997-98; National Center for Education Statistics, Characteristics of the 100 Largest Public Elementary and Secondary School Districts in the United States: 1997-98, July 1999

Educational Quality

School District	Education Quotient[1]	Graduate Outcome[2]	Community Index[3]	Resource Index[4]
Knox County	107.0	123.0	83.0	80.0

Note: Nearly 1,000 secondary school districts were rated in terms of educational quality. The scores range from a low of 50 to a high of 150; (1) Average of the Graduate Outcome, Community and Resource indexes; (2) Based on graduation rates and college board scores (SAT/ACT); (3) Based on the surrounding community's average level of education and the area's average income level; (4) Based on teacher salaries, per-pupil expenditures and student-teacher ratios.
Source: Expansion Management, Ratings Issue, 1998

Educational Attainment by Race

Area	High School Graduate (%)					Bachelor's Degree (%)				
	Total	White	Black	Other	Hisp.[2]	Total	White	Black	Other	Hisp.[2]
City	70.8	71.5	64.9	82.7	89.6	21.7	22.9	11.0	48.2	49.3
MSA[1]	70.3	70.3	66.8	80.1	80.8	19.2	19.2	13.5	42.5	33.7
U.S.	75.2	77.9	63.1	60.4	49.8	20.3	21.5	11.4	19.4	9.2

Note: Figures shown cover persons 25 years old and over; (1) Metropolitan Statistical Area - see Appendix A for areas included; (2) people of Hispanic origin can be of any race
Source: 1990 Census of Population and Housing, Summary Tape File 3C

School Enrollment by Type

Area	Preprimary				Elementary/High School			
	Public		Private		Public		Private	
	Enrollment	%	Enrollment	%	Enrollment	%	Enrollment	%
City	1,461	68.5	673	31.5	19,991	94.3	1,216	5.7
MSA[1]	5,577	65.8	2,903	34.2	89,754	95.4	4,299	4.6
U.S.	2,679,029	59.5	1,824,256	40.5	38,379,689	90.2	4,187,099	9.8

Note: Figures shown cover persons 3 years old and over;
(1) Metropolitan Statistical Area - see Appendix A for areas included
Source: 1990 Census of Population and Housing, Summary Tape File 3C

School Enrollment by Race

Area	Preprimary (%)				Elementary/High School (%)			
	White	Black	Other	Hisp.[1]	White	Black	Other	Hisp.[1]
City	78.3	19.2	2.5	0.4	71.8	26.4	1.8	0.9
MSA[2]	91.3	6.5	2.2	0.8	90.4	8.2	1.4	0.8
U.S.	80.4	12.5	7.1	7.8	74.1	15.6	10.3	12.5

Note: Figures shown cover persons 3 years old and over; (1) people of Hispanic origin can be of any race; (2) Metropolitan Statistical Area - see Appendix A for areas included
Source: 1990 Census of Population and Housing, Summary Tape File 3C

Classroom Teacher Salaries in Public Schools

District	B.A. Degree		M.A. Degree		Maximum	
	Min. ($)	Rank[1]	Max. ($)	Rank[1]	Max. ($)	Rank[1]
	n/a	n/a	n/a	n/a	n/a	n/a
Average	26,980	-	46,065	-	51,435	-

Note: Salaries are for 1997-1998; (1) Rank ranges from 1 to 100; n/a not available
Source: American Federation of Teachers, Survey & Analysis of Salary Trends, 1998

Higher Education

Two-Year Colleges		Four-Year Colleges		Medical Schools	Law Schools	Voc/Tech
Public	Private	Public	Private			
1	4	1	3	0	1	7

Source: College Blue Book, Occupational Education, 1997; Medical School Admission Requirements, 1999-2000; Peterson's Guide to Two-Year Colleges, 1999; Peterson's Guide to Four-Year Colleges, 2000; Barron's Guide to Law Schools, 1999

MAJOR EMPLOYERS

Major Employers

Baptist Hospital of East Tennessee
East Tennessee Children's Hospital Assn.
Fort Sanders Regional Medical Center
Fort Sanders Parkwest Medical Center
Tennessee Valley Authority
Matsushita Electronic Components
SNK Corp. (newspapers)
Goody's Family Cothing
St. Mary's Health System
KTPJ Inc. (eating places)

Note: Companies listed are located in the city
Source: Dun's Business Rankings, 1999; Ward's Business Directory, 1998

PUBLIC SAFETY

Crime Rate

Area	All Crimes	Violent Crimes				Property Crimes		
		Murder	Forcible Rape	Robbery	Aggrav. Assault	Burglary	Larceny-Theft	Motor Vehicle Theft
City	6,356.8	10.8	55.2	310.3	480.6	1,161.0	3,463.7	875.2
Suburbs[1]	n/a	n/a	n/a	n/a	n/a	n/a	n/a	n/a
MSA[2]	n/a	n/a	n/a	n/a	n/a	n/a	n/a	n/a
U.S.	4,922.7	6.8	35.9	186.1	382.0	919.6	2,886.5	505.8

Note: Crime rate is the number of crimes per 100,000 pop.; (1) defined as all areas within the MSA but located outside the central city; (2) Metropolitan Statistical Area - see Appendix A for areas incl.
Source: FBI Uniform Crime Reports, 1997

RECREATION

Culture and Recreation

Museums	Symphony Orchestras	Opera Companies	Dance Companies	Professional Theatres	Zoos	Pro Sports Teams
7	1	1	3	2	1	0

Source: International Directory of the Performing Arts, 1997; Official Museum Directory, 1999; Stern's Performing Arts Directory, 1997; USA Today Four Sport Stadium Guide, 1997; Chamber of Commerce/Economic Development, 1999

Library System

The Knox County Public Library System has 17 branches, holdings of 783,565 volumes, and a budget of $6,567,350 (1996-1997). *American Library Directory, 1998-1999*

MEDIA

Newspapers

Name	Type	Freq.	Distribution	Circulation
The Daily Beacon	General	5x/wk	Camp/Comm	16,500
The Knoxville News-Sentinel	General	7x/wk	Area	119,529

Note: Includes newspapers with circulations of 1,000 or more located in the city;
Source: Burrelle's Media Directory, 1999 Edition

Television Stations

Name	Ch.	Affiliation	Type	Owner
WSJK	n/a	PBS	Public	East Tennessee Public Communications Corp.
WATE	n/a	ABCT	Commercial	Young Broadcasting Inc.
WVLT	n/a	CBST	Commercial	Gray Communications Inc.
WBIR	10	NBCT	Commercial	Gannett Broadcasting
WKOP	15	PBS	Public	East Tennessee Public Communications Corp.
WBXX	20	n/a	Commercial	WINT-TV
WTNZ	43	FBC	Commercial	Raycom Media Inc.
WPXK	54	n/a	Commercial	Paxson Communications Corporation

Note: Stations included broadcast in the Knoxville metro area; n/a not available
Source: Burrelle's Media Directory, 1999 Edition

AM Radio Stations

Call Letters	Freq. (kHz)	Target Audience	Station Format	Music Format
WRJZ	620	Religious	E/M/N/T	Christian
WMEN	760	n/a	T	n/a
WKXV	900	General	M/T	n/a
WNOX	990	General	N/T	n/a
WQBB	1040	General	M/N	Adult Standards/Big Band/Christian/Easy Listening
WHJM	1180	Religious	M	Christian
WIMZ	1240	General	S	n/a
WITA	1490	General	M/T	Christian

Note: Stations included broadcast in the Knoxville metro area; n/a not available
Target Audience: A=Asian; B=Black; C=Christian; E=Ethnic; F=French; G=General; H=Hispanic; M=Men; N=Native American; R=Religious; S=Senior Citizen; W=Women; Y=Young Adult; Z=Children
Station Format: E=Educational; M=Music; N=News; S=Sports; T=Talk
Source: Burrelle's Media Directory, 1999 Edition

FM Radio Stations

Call Letters	Freq. (mHz)	Target Audience	Station Format	Music Format
WUTK	90.3	General	M	Alternative/Christian/Country/Jazz/Oldies/R&B
WKCS	91.1	General	M	Adult Contemporary/Country
WUOT	91.9	General	M	Classical/Jazz
WWST	93.1	General	M	Top 40
WNFZ	94.3	General	M	Modern Rock
WJXB	97.5	General	M	Adult Contemporary
WXVO	98.7	Young Adult	M/N/T	Jazz
WNOX	99.1	General	M/T	Adult Contemporary/Urban Contemporary
WOKI	100.3	General	M/N	Country
WMYU	102.1	General	M	Oldies
WIMZ	103.5	General	M/N/S	Classic Rock
WQBB	104.5	General	M/N	Country
WIVK	107.7	General	M/N/S	Country

Note: Stations included broadcast in the Knoxville metro area
Station Format: E=Educational; M=Music; N=News; S=Sports; T=Talk
Target Audience: A=Asian; B=Black; C=Christian; E=Ethnic; F=French; G=General; H=Hispanic; M=Men; N=Native American; R=Religious; S=Senior Citizen; W=Women; Y=Young Adult; Z=Children
Source: Burrelle's Media Directory, 1999 Edition

CLIMATE

Average and Extreme Temperatures

Temperature	Jan	Feb	Mar	Apr	May	Jun	Jul	Aug	Sep	Oct	Nov	Dec	Yr.
Extreme High (°F)	77	83	86	91	94	102	103	102	103	91	84	80	103
Average High (°F)	47	52	61	71	78	85	88	87	82	71	59	50	69
Average Temp. (°F)	38	42	50	59	67	75	78	77	71	60	49	41	59
Average Low (°F)	29	32	39	47	56	64	68	67	61	48	38	32	48
Extreme Low (°F)	-24	-2	1	22	32	43	49	53	36	25	5	-6	-24

Note: Figures cover the years 1948-1990
Source: National Climatic Data Center, International Station Meteorological Climate Summary, 3/95

Average Precipitation/Snowfall/Humidity

Precip./Humidity	Jan	Feb	Mar	Apr	May	Jun	Jul	Aug	Sep	Oct	Nov	Dec	Yr.
Avg. Precip. (in.)	4.5	4.3	5.0	3.6	3.9	3.8	4.5	3.1	2.9	2.8	3.8	4.5	46.7
Avg. Snowfall (in.)	5	4	2	1	0	0	0	0	0	Tr	1	2	13
Avg. Rel. Hum. 7am (%)	81	80	79	80	85	86	89	91	91	89	84	82	85
Avg. Rel. Hum. 4pm (%)	60	54	50	46	52	54	56	55	54	51	54	59	54

Note: Figures cover the years 1948-1990; Tr = Trace amounts (<0.05 in. of rain; <0.5 in. of snow)
Source: National Climatic Data Center, International Station Meteorological Climate Summary, 3/95

Weather Conditions

Temperature			Daytime Sky			Precipitation		
10°F & below	32°F & below	90°F & above	Clear	Partly cloudy	Cloudy	0.01 inch or more precip.	0.1 inch or more snow/ice	Thunder-storms
3	73	33	85	142	138	125	8	47

Note: Figures are average number of days per year and covers the years 1948-1990
Source: National Climatic Data Center, International Station Meteorological Climate Summary, 3/95

AIR & WATER QUALITY

Maximum Pollutant Concentrations

	Particulate Matter (ug/m³)	Carbon Monoxide (ppm)	Sulfur Dioxide (ppm)	Nitrogen Dioxide (ppm)	Ozone (ppm)	Lead (ug/m³)
MSA[1] Level	141	5	0.048	n/a	0.12	0.00
NAAQS[2]	150	9	0.140	0.053	0.12	1.50
Met NAAQS?	Yes	Yes	Yes	n/a	Yes	Yes

Note: (1) Metropolitan Statistical Area - see Appendix A for areas included; (2) National Ambient Air Quality Standards; ppm = parts per million; ug/m³ = micrograms per cubic meter; n/a not available
Source: EPA, National Air Quality and Emissions Trends Report, 1997

Pollutant Standards Index

In the Knoxville MSA (see Appendix A for areas included), the Pollutant Standards Index (PSI) exceeded 100 on 38 days in 1997. A PSI value greater than 100 indicates that air quality would be in the unhealthful range on that day. *EPA, National Air Quality and Emissions Trends Report, 1997*

Drinking Water

Water System Name	Pop. Served	Primary Water Source Type	Number of Violations in 1998	Type of Violation/ Contaminants
Knoxville UB#1 Whitaker Plant	161,709	Surface	None	None

Note: Data as of July 10, 1999
Source: EPA, Office of Ground Water and Drinking Water, Safe Drinking Water Information System

Knoxville tap water is alkaline, hard and fluoridated.
Editor & Publisher Market Guide, 1999

Memphis, Tennessee

Background

Memphis, named after the ancient city in Egypt, has had a long and illustrious history. Inhabited for centuries by the Chickasaws it came to the attention of early white explorers, and was visited by Hernado de Soto in 1541. French explorers followed. By the Treaty of Paris of 1783 the western lands up to the Mississippi claimed by the British crown passed to the newly independent United States, and the Chickasaws gave up their claim to the area of Memphis in 1818. The next year a trio of American citizens, James Winchester, John Overton, and General Andrew Jackson, the latter fresh from his laurels as the victor of the Battle of New Orleans, in 1815, organized a settlement.

In the years before the Civil War, Memphis flourished, serving as a natural inland port because of advantageous location on the Mississippi. At the opening of the Civil War it was a prize of both northern and southern armies. As the war lengthened and the North drew a cordon around its southern foes, Memphis fell. In later years, suffering under the economic malaise that affected so much of the South, Memphis came on hard times, exacerbated by a series of devastating epidemics of yellow fever. But the city survived and by the end of the nineteenth century was clearly flourishing. In the next century Memphis took its place as the virtual economic capital of Tennessee and the state's largest city.

The driving force in the early expansion of Memphis was cotton, and, by the end of the nineteenth century, the rapidly expanding lumber trade. After World War II the city's industry saw a rapid expansion, including foodstuffs, chemicals, and electrical goods. Livestock and meatpacking have proved highly profitable, and the city has attracted such agricultural products from across the Upper South, earning the sobriquet America's Distribution Center.

Medical care has been a principal occupation of the city's residents, with a large hospital complex, the Memphis Medical Center. The center includes the famous St. Jude Children's Research Hospital.

The recording industry, too, has flourished in Memphis, for music has been of long importance. The composer W.C. Handy developed the blues in Memphis, and of course the late rock-and-roll idol Elvis Presley had brought renown to the city.

For a while the city seemed to be decaying at its core, in that buildings were being vacated or even razed. But in the late 1970s the city fathers undertook to revive the core area, and launched a project that, by the 1990s, had spent three quarters of a billion dollars in reviving buildings and in new construction. A convention center and theme park (Mud Island Park) have been built, the latter connected by monorail to the downtown area. In the course of renovation the Orpheum Theater and the Peabody Hotel, both once landmarks, have been restored to their one-time grandeur. In the hotel there is a ritual whereby ducks march through the lobby each day, as of old. In the mid-1990s city leaders developed a new economic development plan called Memphis 2005. The effort includes attracting new businesses, upgrading the workforce, and finding new outlets for Memphis products in world markets. By the late 1990s, general prosperity brought another downtown building boom, including the construction of a baseball stadium.

The climate of Memphis is mild, averaging yearly 238 clear days, with mean temperatures ranging from eighty degrees in summers to forty-three degrees in winters. Average yearly precipitation is forty-nine inches. The city experiences a yearly average of five inches of snow. Memphis lies in a portion of the state that is warmer than other regions of not only Tennessee but of the Upper South, another indication that the city, with its advantageous river location, has been favored by nature.

General Rankings and Evaluative Comments

- Memphis was ranked #18 out of 19 large, southern metropolitan areas in *Money's* 1998 survey of "The Best Places to Live in America." The survey was conducted by first contacting 512 representative households nationwide and asking them to rank 37 quality-of-life factors on a scale of 1 to 10. Next, a demographic profile was compiled on the 300 largest metropolitan statistical areas in the U.S. The numbers were crunched together to arrive at an overall ranking (things Americans consider most important, like clean air and water, low crime and good schools, received extra weight). Unlike previous years, the 1998 rankings were broken down by region (northeast, midwest, south, west) and population size (100,000 to 249,999; 250,000 to 999,999; 1 million plus). The city had a nationwide ranking of #202 out of 300 in 1997 and #183 out of 300 in 1996. *Money, July 1998; Money, July 1997; Money, September 1996*

- *Ladies Home Journal* ranked America's 200 largest cities based on the qualities women care about most. Memphis ranked #189 out of 200. Criteria: low crime rate, well-paying jobs, quality health and child care, good public schools, the presence of women in government, size of the gender wage gap, number of sexual-harassment and discrimination complaints filed, unemployment and divorce rates, commute times, population density, number of houses of worship, parks and cultural offerings, number of women's health specialists, how well a community's women cared for themselves, complexion kindness index based on UV radiation levels, odds of finding affordable fashions, rental rates for romance movies, champagne sales and other matters of the heart. *Ladies Home Journal, November 1998*

- Zero Population Growth ranked 229 cities in terms of children's health, safety, and economic well-being. Memphis was ranked #106 out of 112 independent cities (cities with populations greater than 100,000 which were neither Major Cities nor Suburbs/Outer Cities) and was given a grade of F. Criteria: total population, percent of population under 18 years of age, household language, percent population change, percent of births to teens, infant mortality rate, percent of low birth weights, dropout rate, enrollment in preprimary school, violent and property crime rates, unemployment rate, percent of children in poverty, percent of owner occupied units, number of bad air days, percent of public transportation commuters, and average travel time to work. *Zero Population Growth, Children's Environmental Index, Fall 1999*

- Memphis was ranked #32 out of 59 metro areas in *The Regional Economist's* "Rational Livability Ranking of 59 Large Metro Areas." The rankings were based on the metro area's total population change over the period 1990-97 divided by the number of people moving in from elsewhere in the United States (net domestic in-migration). *St. Louis Federal Reserve Bank of St. Louis, The Regional Economist, April 1999*

- Cognetics studied 273 metro areas in the United States, ranking them by entrepreneurial activity. Memphis was ranked #20 out of the 50 largest metro areas. Criteria: Significant Starts (firms started in the last 10 years that still employ at least 5 people) and Young Growers (percent of firms 10 years old or less that grew significantly during the last 4 years). *Cognetics, "Entrepreneurial Hot Spots: The Best Places in America to Start and Grow a Company," 1998*

- Memphis was selected as one of the "Best American Cities to Start a Business" by *Point of View* magazine. Criteria: coolness, quality-of-life, and business concerns. The city was ranked #41 out of 75. *Point of View, November 1998*

- Reliastar Financial Corp. ranked the 125 largest metropolitan areas according to the general financial security of residents. Memphis was ranked #103 out of 125 with a score of -6.9. The score indicates the percentage a metropolitan area is above or below the metropolitan norm. A metro area with a score of 10.6 is 10.6% above the metro average. Criteria: Earnings and Wealth Potential (household income, education, net assets, cost of living); Safety Net (health insurance, retirement savings, life insurance, income support programs); Personal Threats (unemployment rate, low-income households, crime rate); Community Economic Vitality (cost of community services, job quality, job creation, housing costs). *Reliastar Financial Corp., "The Best Cities to Earn and Save Money," 1999 Edition*

Business Environment

STATE ECONOMY

State Economic Profile

"Tennessee's economy has been decelerating for almost three years now, a trend that should continue into 1999 and 2000. TN continues to shed jobs in its manufacturing sector, specifically textiles and apparels. In previous years, growth in other sectors was enough to offset these losses. Now growth in these other sectors has slowed. TN's demographics are still strong, and TN continues to have one of the lowest business costs in the country. The TN outlook is one of moderating growth.

TN's manufacturing employment shed some 11,500 jobs in 1998, a decline of 2.2%. Weak export demand and a strong dollar have undermined the apparel industry's competitive position. Soft commodity prices have also hurt TN's metals industry. Neither of these situations will reverse in 1999.

Job growth across TN has been mixed. Declines in manufacturing have hit central and eastern TN harder than the west. Memphis' distribution and transportation sectors, located along the Mississippi, have continued to provide job growth even as the manufacturing sector stumbles. Federal Express and United Parcel Service continue to expand operations. A slowing of the US economy in 1999 and 2000 will weaken the demand for distribution services, although less so than in most industries.

Nashville's economic outlook is less bright. Almost half of 1998's employment gains were in the construction industry. The city's tourism and convention industry remain strong, although it appears likely that commercial construction, especially hotel, has outpaced demand. Construction employment should contract in 1999. The slowing US economy will also place a drag on tourism." *National Association of Realtors, Economic Profiles: The Fifty States and the District of Columbia, http://nar.realtor.com/databank/profiles.htm*

IMPORTS/EXPORTS

Total Export Sales

Area	1994 ($000)	1995 ($000)	1996 ($000)	1997 ($000)	% Chg. 1994-97	% Chg. 1996-97
MSA[1]	2,729,489	4,163,838	3,786,080	3,636,922	33.2	-3.9
U.S.	512,415,609	583,030,524	622,827,063	687,597,999	34.2	10.4

Note: (1) Metropolitan Statistical Area - see Appendix A for areas included
Source: U.S. Department of Commerce, International Trade Association, Metropolitan Area Exports: An Export Performance Report on Over 250 U.S. Cities, November 10, 1998

CITY FINANCES

City Government Finances

Component	FY94 ($000)	FY94 (per capita $)
Revenue	2,103,376	3,466.24
Expenditure	1,915,346	3,156.38
Debt Outstanding	840,087	1,384.41
Cash & Securities	1,822,111	3,002.73

Source: U.S. Bureau of the Census, City Government Finances: 1993-94

City Government Revenue by Source

Source	FY94 ($000)	FY94 (per capita $)	FY94 (%)
From Federal Government	30,792	50.74	1.5
From State Governments	339,017	558.68	16.1
From Local Governments	258,717	426.35	12.3
Property Taxes	178,705	294.50	8.5
General Sales Taxes	0	0.00	0.0
Selective Sales Taxes	30,488	50.24	1.4
Income Taxes	0	0.00	0.0
Current Charges	104,899	172.87	5.0
Utility/Liquor Store	932,477	1,536.67	44.3
Employee Retirement[1]	173,780	286.38	8.3
Other	54,501	89.81	2.6

Note: (1) Excludes "city contributions," classified as "nonrevenue," intragovernmental transfers.
Source: U.S. Bureau of the Census, City Government Finances: 1993-94

City Government Expenditures by Function

Function	FY94 ($000)	FY94 (per capita $)	FY94 (%)
Educational Services	520,039	856.99	27.2
Employee Retirement[1]	75,281	124.06	3.9
Environment/Housing	173,850	286.49	9.1
Government Administration	17,071	28.13	0.9
Interest on General Debt	20,063	33.06	1.0
Public Safety	157,054	258.82	8.2
Social Services	6,674	11.00	0.3
Transportation	34,486	56.83	1.8
Utility/Liquor Store	854,216	1,407.70	44.6
Other	56,612	93.29	3.0

Note: (1) Payments to beneficiaries including withdrawal of contributions.
Source: U.S. Bureau of the Census, City Government Finances: 1993-94

Municipal Bond Ratings

Area	Moody's	S & P
Memphis	n/a	n/a

Note: n/a not available; n/r not rated
Source: Moody's Bond Record, 6/99

POPULATION

Population Growth

Area	1980	1990	% Chg. 1980-90	July 1998 Estimate	% Chg. 1990-98
City	646,356	610,337	-5.6	603,507	-1.1
MSA[1]	913,472	981,747	7.5	1,101,767	12.2
U.S.	226,545,805	248,765,170	9.8	270,299,000	8.7

Note: (1) Metropolitan Statistical Area - see Appendix A for areas included;
July 1998 MSA population estimate was calculated by the editors
Source: 1980/1990 Census of Housing and Population, Summary Tape File 3C;
Census Bureau Population Estimates 1998

Population Characteristics

Race	City 1980 Population	%	City 1990 Population	%	% Chg. 1980-90	MSA[1] 1990 Population	%
White	334,363	51.7	268,420	44.0	-19.7	569,959	58.1
Black	307,573	47.6	334,981	54.9	8.9	399,325	40.7
Amer Indian/Esk/Aleut	680	0.1	1,146	0.2	68.5	2,170	0.2
Asian/Pacific Islander	2,864	0.4	4,589	0.8	60.2	8,072	0.8
Other	876	0.1	1,201	0.2	37.1	2,221	0.2
Hispanic Origin[2]	5,225	0.8	4,011	0.7	-23.2	7,316	0.7

Note: (1) Metropolitan Statistical Area - see Appendix A for areas included;
(2) people of Hispanic origin can be of any race
Source: 1980/1990 Census of Housing and Population, Summary Tape File 3C

Ancestry

Area	German	Irish	English	Italian	U.S.	French	Polish	Dutch
City	8.3	10.7	9.0	1.9	5.6	2.0	0.6	1.2
MSA[1]	11.4	14.2	11.2	2.3	7.7	2.5	0.9	1.6
U.S.	23.3	15.6	13.1	5.9	5.3	4.2	3.8	2.5

Note: Figures are percentages and include persons that reported multiple ancestry (eg. if a person reported being Irish and Italian, they were included in both columns); (1) Metropolitan Statistical Area - see Appendix A for areas included
Source: 1990 Census of Population and Housing, Summary Tape File 3C

Age

Area	Median Age (Years)	Age Distribution (%) Under 5	Under 18	18-24	25-44	45-64	65+	80+
City	31.4	8.1	26.9	11.2	32.2	17.5	12.2	2.7
MSA[1]	31.2	8.1	27.9	10.9	33.5	17.5	10.3	2.2
U.S.	32.9	7.3	25.6	10.5	32.6	18.7	12.5	2.8

Note: (1) Metropolitan Statistical Area - see Appendix A for areas included
Source: 1990 Census of Population and Housing, Summary Tape File 3C

Male/Female Ratio

Area	Number of males per 100 females (all ages)	Number of males per 100 females (18 years old+)
City	87.4	82.2
MSA[1]	91.3	86.8
U.S.	95.0	91.9

Note: (1) Metropolitan Statistical Area - see Appendix A for areas included
Source: 1990 Census of Population, General Population Characteristics

INCOME

Per Capita/Median/Average Income

Area	Per Capita ($)	Median Household ($)	Average Household ($)
City	11,682	22,674	30,656
MSA[1]	12,935	26,994	35,139
U.S.	14,420	30,056	38,453

Note: All figures are for 1989; (1) Metropolitan Statistical Area - see Appendix A for areas included
Source: 1990 Census of Population and Housing, Summary Tape File 3C

Household Income Distribution by Race

Income ($)	City (%)					U.S. (%)				
	Total	White	Black	Other	Hisp.[1]	Total	White	Black	Other	Hisp.[1]
Less than 5,000	11.7	5.2	18.7	8.9	11.1	6.2	4.8	15.2	8.6	8.8
5,000 - 9,999	11.5	8.2	15.1	10.4	8.9	9.3	8.6	14.2	9.9	11.1
10,000 - 14,999	10.7	8.7	12.8	14.3	17.8	8.8	8.5	11.0	9.8	11.0
15,000 - 24,999	20.0	19.4	20.7	19.8	19.7	17.5	17.3	18.9	18.5	20.5
25,000 - 34,999	15.8	17.3	14.1	14.0	9.1	15.8	16.1	14.2	15.4	16.4
35,000 - 49,999	14.7	18.2	10.9	15.0	22.5	17.9	18.6	13.3	16.1	16.0
50,000 - 74,999	10.0	13.6	6.1	9.8	6.9	15.0	15.8	9.3	13.4	11.1
75,000 - 99,999	2.7	4.1	1.1	3.8	1.3	5.1	5.5	2.6	4.7	3.1
100,000+	2.9	5.2	0.4	4.1	2.7	4.4	4.8	1.3	3.7	1.9

Note: All figures are for 1989; (1) people of Hispanic origin can be of any race
Source: 1990 Census of Population and Housing, Summary Tape File 3C

Effective Buying Income

Area	Per Capita ($)	Median Household ($)	Average Household ($)
City	14,711	28,988	38,844
MSA[1]	16,785	33,719	45,668
U.S.	16,803	34,536	45,243

Note: Data as of 1/1/99; (1) Metropolitan Statistical Area - see Appendix A for areas included
Source: Standard Rate & Data Service, Newspaper Advertising Source, 9/99

Effective Household Buying Income Distribution

Area	% of Households Earning						
	$10,000 -$19,999	$20,000 -$34,999	$35,000 -$49,999	$50,000 -$74,999	$75,000 -$99,000	$100,000 -$124,999	$125,000 and up
City	17.7	23.1	16.5	15.3	5.2	1.8	2.6
MSA[1]	15.5	21.5	17.3	18.4	7.3	2.4	3.0
U.S.	16.0	22.6	18.2	18.9	7.2	2.4	2.7

Note: Data as of 1/1/99; (1) Metropolitan Statistical Area - see Appendix A for areas included
Source: Standard Rate & Data Service, Newspaper Advertising Source, 9/99

Poverty Rates by Race and Age

Area	Total (%)	By Race (%)				By Age (%)		
		White	Black	Other	Hisp.[2]	Under 5 years old	Under 18 years old	65 years and over
City	23.0	8.1	34.8	23.1	24.0	38.4	34.9	21.8
MSA[1]	18.3	6.7	34.9	17.8	20.2	29.6	26.6	21.4
U.S.	13.1	9.8	29.5	23.1	25.3	20.1	18.3	12.8

Note: Figures show the percent of people living below the poverty line in 1989. The average poverty threshold was $12,674 for a family of four in 1989; (1) Metropolitan Statistical Area - see Appendix A for areas included; (2) people of Hispanic origin can be of any race
Source: 1990 Census of Population and Housing, Summary Tape File 3C

EMPLOYMENT

Labor Force and Employment

Area	Civilian Labor Force			Workers Employed		
	Jun. 1998	Jun. 1999	% Chg.	Jun. 1998	Jun. 1999	% Chg.
City	319,989	330,604	3.3	303,635	316,737	4.3
MSA[1]	556,726	576,204	3.5	533,433	556,625	4.3
U.S.	138,798,000	140,666,000	1.3	132,265,000	134,395,000	1.6

Note: Data is not seasonally adjusted and covers workers 16 years of age and older;
(1) Metropolitan Statistical Area - see Appendix A for areas included
Source: Bureau of Labor Statistics, http://stats.bls.gov

Unemployment Rate

Area	1998						1999					
	Jul.	Aug.	Sep.	Oct.	Nov.	Dec.	Jan.	Feb.	Mar.	Apr.	May.	Jun.
City	4.6	4.7	4.8	4.1	4.0	3.4	4.4	4.3	4.3	4.1	3.8	4.2
MSA[1]	3.8	3.9	4.0	3.4	3.3	2.8	3.6	3.5	3.4	3.2	3.1	3.4
U.S.	4.7	4.5	4.4	4.2	4.1	4.0	4.8	4.7	4.4	4.1	4.0	4.5

Note: Data is not seasonally adjusted and covers workers 16 years of age and older; all figures are percentages; (1) Metropolitan Statistical Area - see Appendix A for areas included
Source: Bureau of Labor Statistics, http://stats.bls.gov

Employment by Industry

Sector	MSA[1]		U.S.
	Number of Employees	Percent of Total	Percent of Total
Services	173,700	29.2	30.4
Retail Trade	106,700	17.9	17.7
Government	79,200	13.3	15.6
Manufacturing	63,400	10.7	14.3
Finance/Insurance/Real Estate	29,200	4.9	5.9
Wholesale Trade	40,900	6.9	5.4
Transportation/Public Utilities	73,900	12.4	5.3
Construction	n/a	n/a	5.0
Mining	n/a	n/a	0.4

Note: Figures cover non-farm employment as of 6/99 and are not seasonally adjusted; (1) Metropolitan Statistical Area - see Appendix A for areas included; n/a not available
Source: Bureau of Labor Statistics, http://stats.bls.gov

Employment by Occupation

Occupation Category	City (%)	MSA[1] (%)	U.S. (%)
White Collar	58.1	60.8	58.1
Executive/Admin./Management	10.8	12.4	12.3
Professional	13.2	12.9	14.1
Technical & Related Support	3.7	4.0	3.7
Sales	11.9	13.2	11.8
Administrative Support/Clerical	18.5	18.3	16.3
Blue Collar	25.1	24.7	26.2
Precision Production/Craft/Repair	8.8	9.7	11.3
Machine Operators/Assem./Insp.	6.2	5.8	6.8
Transportation/Material Movers	4.6	4.4	4.1
Cleaners/Helpers/Laborers	5.5	4.8	3.9
Services	15.8	13.3	13.2
Farming/Forestry/Fishing	1.0	1.2	2.5

Note: Figures cover employed persons 16 years old and over; (1) Metropolitan Statistical Area - see Appendix A for areas included
Source: 1990 Census of Population and Housing, Summary Tape File 3C

Occupational Employment Projections: 1996 - 2006

Occupations Expected to Have the Largest Job Growth (ranked by numerical growth)	Fast-Growing Occupations[1] (ranked by percent growth)
1. Salespersons, retail	1. Personal and home care aides
2. Truck drivers, light	2. Systems analysts
3. Cashiers	3. Paralegals
4. General managers & top executives	4. Respiratory therapists
5. Janitors/cleaners/maids, ex. priv. hshld.	5. Home health aides
6. Food service workers	6. Directors, religious activities & educ.
7. Child care workers, private household	7. Computer engineers
8. Cooks, fast food and short order	8. Child care workers, private household
9. Registered nurses	9. Corrections officers & jailers
10. Waiters & waitresses	10. Emergency medical technicians

Note: Projections cover Tennessee; (1) Excludes occupations with total job growth less than 300
Source: U.S. Department of Labor, Employment and Training Administration, America's Labor Market Information System (ALMIS)

TAXES

Major State and Local Tax Rates

State Corp. Income (%)	State Personal Income (%)	Residential Property (effective rate per $100)	Sales & Use		State Gasoline (cents/ gallon)	State Cigarette (cents/ pack)
			State (%)	Local (%)		
6.0	6.0[a]	1.42	6.0	2.25	21.0[b]	13.0[c]

Note: Personal/corporate income, sales, gasoline and cigarette tax rates as of January 1999. Property tax rates as of 1997; (a) Applies to interest and dividend income only; (b) Rate is comprised of 20 cents excise and 1 cent motor carrier tax. Does not include a 1 cent local option tax; (c) Counties and cities may impose an additional tax of 1 cent per pack. Dealers pay a additional enforcement and admin. fee of 0.05 cent per pack
Source: Federation of Tax Administrators, www.taxadmin.org; Washington D.C. Department of Finance and Revenue, Tax Rates and Tax Burdens in the District of Columbia: A Nationwide Comparison, July 1998; Chamber of Commerce, 1999

Total Taxes Per Capita and as a Percent of Income

Area	Per Capita Income ($)	Per Capita Taxes ($)			Percent of Income (%)		
		Total	Federal	State/ Local	Total	Federal	State/ Local
Tennessee	24,591	8,048	5,930	2,118	32.7	24.1	8.6
U.S.	27,876	9,881	6,690	3,191	35.4	24.0	11.4

Note: Figures are for 1998
Source: Tax Foundation, www.taxfoundation.org

Estimated Tax Burden

Area	State Income	Local Income	Property	Sales	Total
Memphis	0	0	3,000	1,233	4,233

Note: The numbers are estimates of taxes paid by a married couple with two children and annual earnings of $75,000. Sales tax estimates assume they spend average amounts on food, clothing, household goods and gasoline. Property tax estimates assume they live in a $250,000 home.
Source: Kiplinger's Personal Finance Magazine, October 1998

**COMMERCIAL
REAL ESTATE**

Office Market

Class/ Location	Total Space (sq. ft.)	Vacant Space (sq. ft.)	Vac. Rate (%)	Under Constr. (sq. ft.)	Net Absorp. (sq. ft.)	Rental Rates ($/sq.ft./yr.)
Class A						
CBD	2,489,470	341,345	13.7	0	19,834	12.00-19.50
Outside CBD	10,453,760	444,894	4.3	846,400	321,540	14.00-22.50
Class B						
CBD	3,258,000	458,585	14.1	0	-290,295	9.00-14.50
Outside CBD	4,231,200	191,520	4.5	0	25,796	10.00-17.00

Note: Data as of 10/98 and covers Memphis; CBD = Central Business District; n/a not available;
Source: Society of Industrial and Office Realtors, 1999 Comparative Statistics of Industrial and Office
Real Estate Markets

"More than one-half of nearly one million sq. ft. of new space announced is currently under construction. A substantial portion of this is pre-leased, larger Class A suburban offices, a trend not expected to change. Demand for smaller user space is expected to be unsatisfied. The completion of the parallel runway at the airport will allow United Parcel Service to open their new hub by second quarter 1999. This is expected to moderately increase absorption as ancillary services benefit from the hub. The local SIOR reporter forecasts a year very similar to 1998. A healthy increase in absorption and a moderate decrease in vacancies is foreseen. Landlord concessions are expected to decrease moderately as vacancies fall in the suburban markets." *Society of Industrial and Office Realtors, 1999 Comparative Statistics of Industrial and Office Real Estate Markets*

Industrial Market

Location	Total Space (sq. ft.)	Vacant Space (sq. ft.)	Vac. Rate (%)	Under Constr. (sq. ft.)	Net Absorp. (sq. ft.)	Gross Lease ($/sq.ft./yr.)
Central City	45,300,000	8,127,000	17.9	0	946,000	2.15-3.50
Suburban	94,467,000	9,905,000	10.5	4,954,000	4,578,000	3.00-6.00

Note: Data as of 10/98 and covers Memphis; n/a not available
Source: Society of Industrial and Office Realtors, 1999 Comparative Statistics of Industrial and Office
Real Estate Markets

"Speculative development will remain alive under the watch of seasoned, yet optimistic, developers. More than 3.5 million sq. ft. of build-to-suit property is expected in 1999. Several sites already prepared for building are located in the southeastern area of Shelby County. Construction has begun on build-to-suit properties in DeSoto County, Mississippi, where the land is less expensive and more easily developed. The Metro Memphis area is one of the nation's primary distribution centers and offers important logistics savings to large distributors. If an economic slump occurs as the result of market fluctuations, local absorption may suffer. The dollar volume of sales is predicted to decrease by 50 percent from 1998. Lease prices and site prices are expected to see little change." *Society of Industrial and Office Realtors, 1999 Comparative Statistics of Industrial and Office Real Estate Markets*

COMMERCIAL UTILITIES

Typical Monthly Electric Bills

Area	Commercial Service ($/month)		Industrial Service ($/month)	
	12 kW demand 1,500 kWh	100 kW demand 30,000 kWh	1,000 kW demand 400,000 kWh	20,000 kW demand 10,000,000 kWh
City[1]	110	2,221[a]	23,278	490,800
U.S.[2]	150	2,174	23,995	508,569

Note: (1) Based on rates in effect January 1, 1998; (2) Based on rates in effect January 1, 1999;
(a) Based on 120 kW demand and 30,000 kWh usage.
Source: Memphis Light, Gas and Water, 1998 Utility Bill Comparisons for Selected U.S. Cities;
Edison Electric Institute, Typical Residential, Commercial and Industrial Bills, Winter 1999

TRANSPORTATION

Transportation Statistics

Average minutes to work	20.8
Interstate highways	I-40; I-55
Bus lines	
In-city	Memphia Area TA, 230 vehicles
Inter-city	1
Passenger air service	
Airport	Memphis International
Airlines	7
Aircraft departures	97,606 (1996)
Enplaned passengers	3,943,809 (1996)
Rail service	Amtrak
Motor freight carriers	200
Major waterways/ports	Mississippi River

Source: Editor & Publisher Market Guide, 1999; FAA Airport Activity Statistics, 1997; Amtrak National Time Table, Northeast Timetable, Spring/Summer 1999; 1990 Census of Population and Housing, STF 3C; Chamber of Commerce/Economic Development 1999; Jane's Urban Transport Systems 1999-2000

Means of Transportation to Work

Area	Car/Truck/Van		Public Transportation			Bicycle	Walked	Other Means	Worked at Home
	Drove Alone	Car-pooled	Bus	Subway	Railroad				
City	75.4	15.1	4.5	0.0	0.0	0.1	2.5	1.0	1.3
MSA[1]	78.2	13.6	2.7	0.0	0.0	0.1	3.0	1.0	1.5
U.S.	73.2	13.4	3.0	1.5	0.5	0.4	3.9	1.2	3.0

Note: Figures shown are percentages and only include workers 16 years old and over;
(1) Metropolitan Statistical Area - see Appendix A for areas included
Source: 1990 Census of Population and Housing, Summary Tape File 3C

BUSINESSES

Major Business Headquarters

Company Name	1999 Rankings	
	Fortune 500	Forbes 500
Autozone	456	-
Dunavant Enterprises	-	146
FDX	94	-

Note: Companies listed are located in the city; dashes indicate no ranking
Fortune 500: Companies that produce a 10-K are ranked 1 to 500 based on 1998 revenue
Forbes 500: Private companies are ranked 1 to 500 based on 1997 revenue
Source: Forbes, November 30, 1998; Fortune, April 26, 1999

Best Companies to Work For

First Tennessee Bank and Federal Express, headquartered in Memphis, are among the " 100 Best Companies to Work for in America." Criteria: trust in management, pride in work/company, camaraderie, company responses to the Hewitt People Practices Inventory, and employee responses to their Great Place to Work survey. The companies also had to be at least 10 years old and have a minimum of 500 employees. *Fortune, January 11, 1999*

Federal Express and First Tennessee Bank, headquartered in Memphis, are among the " 100 Best Companies for Working Mothers." Criteria: fair wages, opportunities for women to advance, support for child care, flexible work schedules, family-friendly benefits, and work/life supports. *Working Mother, October 1998*

Federal Express Corp. (transportation), headquartered in Memphis, is among the " 100 Best Places to Work in IS." Criteria: compensation, turnover and training. *Computerworld, May 25, 1998*

Fast-Growing Businesses

According to *Fortune*, Memphis is home to one of America's 100 fastest-growing companies: Concord EFS. Companies were ranked based on earnings-per-share growth, revenue growth and total return over the previous three years. Criteria for inclusion: public companies with sales of least $50 million. Companies that lost money in the most recent quarter, or ended in the red for the past four quarters as a whole, were not eligible. Limited partnerships and REITs were also not considered. *Fortune, "America's Fastest-Growing Companies," 1999*

Minority Business Opportunity

Memphis is home to one company which is on the Black Enterprise Auto Dealer 100 list (largest based on gross sales): Covington Pike Lincoln-Mercury/JMC Auto Group (Lincoln-Mercury) . Criteria: 1) operational in previous calendar year; 2) at least 51% black-owned. *Black Enterprise, www.blackenterprise.com*

Small Business Opportunity

According to *Forbes*, Memphis is home to two of America's 200 best small companies: Concord EFS and SCB Computer Technology. Criteria: companies included must be publicly traded since November 1997 with a stock price of at least $5 per share and an average daily float of 1,000 shares. The company's latest 12-month sales must be between $5 and $350 million, return on equity (ROE) must be a minimum of 12% for both the past 5 years and the most recent four quarters, and five-year sales and EPS growth must average at least 10%. Companies with declining sales or earnings during the past year were dropped as well as businesses with debt/equity ratios over 1.25. Companies with negative operating cash flow in each of the past two years were also excluded. *Forbes, November 2, 1998*

HOTELS & MOTELS

Hotels/Motels

Area	Hotels/ Motels	Rooms	Luxury-Level Hotels/Motels		Average Minimum Rates ($)		
			♦♦♦♦	♦♦♦♦♦	♦♦	♦♦♦	♦♦♦♦
City	52	7,657	1	0	69	104	140
Airport	14	2,371	0	0	n/a	n/a	n/a
Suburbs	24	2,320	0	0	n/a	n/a	n/a
Total	90	12,348	1	0	n/a	n/a	n/a

Note: n/a not available; classifications range from one diamond (budget properties with basic amenities) to five diamond (luxury properties with the finest service, rooms and facilities).
Source: OAG, Business Travel Planner, Winter 1998-99

CONVENTION CENTERS

Major Convention Centers

Center Name	Meeting Rooms	Exhibit Space (sq. ft.)
Memphis Cook Convention Center	26	150,000
Peabody Memphis	32	83,700
The Fogelman Executive Center	16	n/a

Note: n/a not available
Source: Trade Shows Worldwide, 1998; Meetings & Conventions, 4/15/99; Sucessful Meetings, 3/31/98

Living Environment

COST OF LIVING

Cost of Living Index

Composite Index	Groceries	Housing	Utilities	Trans-portation	Health Care	Misc. Goods/ Services
92.3	94.9	90.1	83.2	99.2	94.4	92.7

Note: U.S. = 100
Source: ACCRA, Cost of Living Index, 1st Quarter 1999

HOUSING

Median Home Prices and Housing Affordability

Area	Median Price[2] 1st Qtr. 1999 ($)	HOI[3] 1st Qtr. 1999	Afford-ability Rank[4]
MSA[1]	105,000	74.7	94
U.S.	134,000	69.6	–

Note: (1) Metropolitan Statistical Area - see Appendix A for areas included; (2) U.S. figures calculated from the sales of 524,324 new and existing homes in 181 markets; (3) Housing Opportunity Index - percent of homes sold that were within the reach of the median income household at the prevailing mortgage interest rate; (4) Rank is from 1-181 with 1 being most affordable
Source: National Association of Home Builders, Housing Opportunity Index, 1st Quarter 1999

Median Home Price Projection

It is projected that the median price of existing single-family homes in the metro area will increase by 3.2% in 1999. Nationwide, home prices are projected to increase 3.8%.
Kiplinger's Personal Finance Magazine, January 1999

Average New Home Price

Area	Price ($)
City	124,121
U.S.	142,735

Note: Figures are based on a new home with 1,800 sq. ft. of living area on an 8,000 sq. ft. lot.
Source: ACCRA, Cost of Living Index, 1st Quarter 1999

Average Apartment Rent

Area	Rent ($/mth)
City	625
U.S.	601

Note: Figures are based on an unfurnished two bedroom, 1-1/2 or 2 bath apartment, approximately 950 sq. ft. in size, excluding all utilities except water
Source: ACCRA, Cost of Living Index, 1st Quarter 1999

RESIDENTIAL UTILITIES

Average Residential Utility Costs

Area	All Electric ($/mth)	Part Electric ($/mth)	Other Energy ($/mth)	Phone ($/mth)
City	–	51.62	27.97	20.34
U.S.	100.02	55.73	43.33	19.71

Source: ACCRA, Cost of Living Index, 1st Quarter 1999

HEALTH CARE

Average Health Care Costs

Area	Hospital ($/day)	Doctor ($/visit)	Dentist ($/visit)
City	272.60	54.60	67.40
U.S.	430.43	52.45	66.35

Note: Hospital—based on a semi-private room; Doctor—based on a general practitioner's routine exam of an established patient; Dentist—based on adult teeth cleaning and periodic oral exam.
Source: ACCRA, Cost of Living Index, 1st Quarter 1999

Distribution of Office-Based Physicians

Area	Family/Gen. Practitioners	Specialists		
		Medical	Surgical	Other
MSA[1]	205	739	583	554

Note: Data as of 12/31/97; (1) Metropolitan Statistical Area - see Appendix A for areas included
Source: American Medical Assn., Physician Characteristics & Distribution in the U.S., 1999

Hospitals

Memphis has 8 general medical and surgical hospitals, 3 psychiatric, 1 rehabilitation, 1 other specialty. *AHA Guide to the Healthcare Field, 1998-99*

According to *U.S. News and World Report,* Memphis has 1 of the best hospitals in the U.S.: **Baptist Memorial Hospital**, noted for neurology. *U.S. News Online, "America's Best Hospitals," 10th Edition, www.usnews.com*

EDUCATION

Public School District Statistics

District Name	Num. Sch.	Enroll.	Classroom Teachers	Pupils per Teacher	Minority Pupils (%)	Current Exp.[1] ($/pupil)
Memphis City School District	163	111,227	n/a	n/a	85.4	4,787
Shelby County School District	46	45,899	n/a	n/a	n/a	n/a

Note: Data covers the 1997-1998 school year unless otherwise noted; (1) Data covers fiscal year 1996; SD = School District; ISD = Independent School District; n/a not available
Source: National Center for Education Statistics, Common Core of Data Public Education Agency Universe 1997-98; National Center for Education Statistics, Characteristics of the 100 Largest Public Elementary and Secondary School Districts in the United States: 1997-98, July 1999

Educational Quality

School District	Education Quotient[1]	Graduate Outcome[2]	Community Index[3]	Resource Index[4]
Memphis City	102.0	103.0	89.0	104.0

Note: Nearly 1,000 secondary school districts were rated in terms of educational quality. The scores range from a low of 50 to a high of 150; (1) Average of the Graduate Outcome, Community and Resource indexes; (2) Based on graduation rates and college board scores (SAT/ACT); (3) Based on the surrounding community's average level of education and the area's average income level; (4) Based on teacher salaries, per-pupil expenditures and student-teacher ratios.
Source: Expansion Management, Ratings Issue, 1998

Educational Attainment by Race

Area	High School Graduate (%)					Bachelor's Degree (%)				
	Total	White	Black	Other	Hisp.[2]	Total	White	Black	Other	Hisp.[2]
City	70.4	81.1	59.2	70.8	63.3	17.5	25.2	9.0	32.4	17.4
MSA[1]	73.5	82.2	58.1	76.6	69.5	19.0	24.2	9.2	34.5	21.0
U.S.	75.2	77.9	63.1	60.4	49.8	20.3	21.5	11.4	19.4	9.2

Note: Figures shown cover persons 25 years old and over; (1) Metropolitan Statistical Area - see Appendix A for areas included; (2) people of Hispanic origin can be of any race
Source: 1990 Census of Population and Housing, Summary Tape File 3C

School Enrollment by Type

Area	Preprimary				Elementary/High School			
	Public		Private		Public		Private	
	Enrollment	%	Enrollment	%	Enrollment	%	Enrollment	%
City	5,573	59.5	3,792	40.5	95,610	89.3	11,422	10.7
MSA[1]	9,081	54.6	7,545	45.4	160,890	88.9	19,987	11.1
U.S.	2,679,029	59.5	1,824,256	40.5	38,379,689	90.2	4,187,099	9.8

Note: Figures shown cover persons 3 years old and over;
(1) Metropolitan Statistical Area - see Appendix A for areas included
Source: 1990 Census of Population and Housing, Summary Tape File 3C

School Enrollment by Race

Area	Preprimary (%)				Elementary/High School (%)			
	White	Black	Other	Hisp.[1]	White	Black	Other	Hisp.[1]
City	41.7	57.2	1.1	0.4	27.4	71.4	1.2	0.7
MSA[2]	60.8	37.9	1.4	0.6	47.2	51.4	1.4	0.7
U.S.	80.4	12.5	7.1	7.8	74.1	15.6	10.3	12.5

Note: Figures shown cover persons 3 years old and over; (1) people of Hispanic origin can be of any race; (2) Metropolitan Statistical Area - see Appendix A for areas included
Source: 1990 Census of Population and Housing, Summary Tape File 3C

Classroom Teacher Salaries in Public Schools

District	B.A. Degree		M.A. Degree		Maximum	
	Min. ($)	Rank[1]	Max. ($)	Rank[1]	Max. ($)	Rank[1]
Memphis	28,977	23	43,885	60	50,144	52
Average	26,980	-	46,065	-	51,435	-

Note: Salaries are for 1997-1998; (1) Rank ranges from 1 to 100
Source: American Federation of Teachers, Survey & Analysis of Salary Trends, 1998

Higher Education

Two-Year Colleges		Four-Year Colleges		Medical Schools	Law Schools	Voc/ Tech
Public	Private	Public	Private			
2	1	2	5	1	1	22

Source: College Blue Book, Occupational Education, 1997; Medical School Admission Requirements, 1999-2000; Peterson's Guide to Two-Year Colleges, 1999; Peterson's Guide to Four-Year Colleges, 2000; Barron's Guide to Law Schools, 1999

MAJOR EMPLOYERS

Major Employers

Federal Express	Methodist Health Care Methodist Hospitals
Baptist Memorial Hospital	St. Francis Hospital
Autozone	St. Jude Children's Research Hospital
Memphis Publishing	Promus Hotel Corp.
Resortquest International	First Tennessee Bank National Assn.

Note: Companies listed are located in the city
Source: Dun's Business Rankings, 1999; Ward's Business Directory, 1998

PUBLIC SAFETY

Crime Rate

Area	All Crimes	Violent Crimes				Property Crimes		
		Murder	Forcible Rape	Robbery	Aggrav. Assault	Burglary	Larceny -Theft	Motor Vehicle Theft
City	10,041.7	21.6	147.1	822.0	865.9	2,426.9	3,961.0	1,797.2
Suburbs[1]	4,764.5	7.9	51.9	151.7	326.3	1,036.4	2,665.3	525.1
MSA[2]	7,839.1	15.9	107.4	542.2	640.7	1,846.5	3,420.2	1,266.2
U.S.	4,922.7	6.8	35.9	186.1	382.0	919.6	2,886.5	505.8

Note: Crime rate is the number of crimes per 100,000 pop.; (1) defined as all areas within the MSA but located outside the central city; (2) Metropolitan Statistical Area - see Appendix A for areas incl.
Source: FBI Uniform Crime Reports, 1997

RECREATION

Culture and Recreation

Museums	Symphony Orchestras	Opera Companies	Dance Companies	Professional Theatres	Zoos	Pro Sports Teams
10	1	1	0	2	1	0

Source: International Directory of the Performing Arts, 1997; Official Museum Directory, 1999; Stern's Performing Arts Directory, 1997; USA Today Four Sport Stadium Guide, 1997; Chamber of Commerce/Economic Development, 1999

Library System

The Memphis-Shelby County Public Library has 21 branches and holdings of 1,726,329 volumes. *American Library Directory, 1998-1999*

MEDIA

Newspapers

Name	Type	Freq.	Distribution	Circulation
The Commercial Appeal	General	7x/wk	Area	210,000
The Daily Helmsman	n/a	4x/wk	Campus	9,500
Daily News	n/a	5x/wk	Area	50,000
Hebrew Watchman	Religious	1x/wk	Local	3,000
Silver Star News	Black	1x/wk	Local	28,000
West Tennessee Catholic	Religious	1x/wk	Regional	17,100

Note: Includes newspapers with circulations of 1,000 or more located in the city; n/a not available
Source: Burrelle's Media Directory, 1999 Edition

Television Stations

Name	Ch.	Affiliation	Type	Owner
WREG	n/a	CBST	Commercial	New York Times Company
WMC	n/a	NBCT	Commercial	Raycom Media Inc.
WHBQ	13	FBC	Commercial	Fox Television Stations Inc.
WPTY	24	ABCT	Commercial	Clear Channel Broadcasting Inc.
WLMT	30	UPN	Commercial	Max Media Properties L.L.C.

Note: Stations included broadcast in the Memphis metro area; n/a not available
Source: Burrelle's Media Directory, 1999 Edition

FM Radio Stations

Call Letters	Freq. (mHz)	Target Audience	Station Format	Music Format
WKNA	88.9	General	E/M/N/T	Classical
WEVL	89.9	General	E/M	Alternative/Big Band/Country/Jazz/Oldies
WKNP	90.1	General	M/N/T	Classical
WKNQ	90.7	General	M/N	Classical
WKNO	91.1	General	M/N/T	Classical
WUMR	91.7	General	E/M/N/S/T	Jazz
WMFS	92.9	General	M	AOR
WOGY	94.1	General	M/N/S	Country
WOTO	95.7	General	M/N/T	Oldies
WHRK	97.1	General	M	Urban Contemporary
WSRR	98.1	General	M	Classic Rock/Oldies
WMC	99.7	General	M	Adult Contemporary
KJMS	101.1	General	M	Adult Contemporary
WEGR	102.7	General	M/N/S/T	Classic Rock
WRBO	103.5	General	M	Oldies/R&B
WRVR	104.5	General	M	Adult Contemporary
WGKX	105.9	General	M	Country
KXHT	107.1	Black	Young Adult M/N/S	
WKSL	107.5	n/a	n/a	n/a

Note: Stations included broadcast in the Memphis metro area; n/a not available
Station Format: E=Educational; M=Music; N=News; S=Sports; T=Talk
Target Audience: A=Asian; B=Black; C=Christian; E=Ethnic; F=French; G=General; H=Hispanic;
M=Men; N=Native American; R=Religious; S=Senior Citizen; W=Women; Y=Young Adult; Z=Children
Music Format: AOR=Album Oriented Rock; MOR=Middle-of-the-Road
Source: Burrelle's Media Directory, 1999 Edition

AM Radio Stations

Call Letters	Freq. (kHz)	Target Audience	Station Format	Music Format
WHBQ	560	General	S	n/a
WREC	600	General	N/S/T	n/a
WCRV	640	General	M/T	Christian
WJCE	680	General	M/N/S	R&B
WMC	790	General	N/S/T	n/a
WSFZ	1030	Men	N/S/T	n/a
WDIA	1070	Black	M	Adult Contemporary
WGSF	1210	H/M	M/N/S	Christian/Latin
WLOK	1340	B/C	T	n/a
WBBP	1480	General	M/N/S	Christian

Note: Stations included broadcast in the Memphis metro area; n/a not available
Target Audience: A=Asian; B=Black; C=Christian; E=Ethnic; F=French; G=General; H=Hispanic; M=Men; N=Native American; R=Religious; S=Senior Citizen; W=Women; Y=Young Adult; Z=Children
Station Format: E=Educational; M=Music; N=News; S=Sports; T=Talk
Source: Burrelle's Media Directory, 1999 Edition

CLIMATE

Average and Extreme Temperatures

Temperature	Jan	Feb	Mar	Apr	May	Jun	Jul	Aug	Sep	Oct	Nov	Dec	Yr.
Extreme High (°F)	83	85	90	95	99	104	107	104	105	97	86	82	107
Average High (°F)	57	62	69	78	84	90	92	92	87	78	68	60	77
Average Temp. (°F)	46	50	57	65	72	79	81	81	76	65	55	48	65
Average Low (°F)	34	37	44	51	59	67	70	69	64	51	42	36	52
Extreme Low (°F)	0	8	15	28	38	42	55	53	34	24	16	2	0

Note: Figures cover the years 1948-1990
Source: National Climatic Data Center, International Station Meteorological Climate Summary, 3/95

Average Precipitation/Snowfall/Humidity

Precip./Humidity	Jan	Feb	Mar	Apr	May	Jun	Jul	Aug	Sep	Oct	Nov	Dec	Yr.
Avg. Precip. (in.)	4.9	5.1	6.6	5.2	4.3	3.7	5.3	3.5	3.6	2.7	4.2	5.6	54.8
Avg. Snowfall (in.)	1	Tr	Tr	Tr	0	0	0	0	0	0	Tr	Tr	1
Avg. Rel. Hum. 6am (%)	87	86	87	90	91	91	93	93	92	91	88	87	90
Avg. Rel. Hum. 3pm (%)	56	51	47	46	50	52	57	54	54	48	49	54	51

Note: Figures cover the years 1948-1990; Tr = Trace amounts (<0.05 in. of rain; <0.5 in. of snow)
Source: National Climatic Data Center, International Station Meteorological Climate Summary, 3/95

Weather Conditions

Temperature			Daytime Sky			Precipitation		
10°F & below	32°F & below	90°F & above	Clear	Partly cloudy	Cloudy	0.01 inch or more precip.	0.1 inch or more snow/ice	Thunder-storms
1	53	86	101	152	112	104	2	59

Note: Figures are average number of days per year and covers the years 1948-1990
Source: National Climatic Data Center, International Station Meteorological Climate Summary, 3/95

AIR & WATER QUALITY

Maximum Pollutant Concentrations

	Particulate Matter (ug/m^3)	Carbon Monoxide (ppm)	Sulfur Dioxide (ppm)	Nitrogen Dioxide (ppm)	Ozone (ppm)	Lead (ug/m^3)
MSA[1] Level	76	6	0.033	0.028	0.12	0.03
NAAQS[2]	150	9	0.140	0.053	0.12	1.50
Met NAAQS?	Yes	Yes	Yes	Yes	Yes	Yes

Note: (1) Metropolitan Statistical Area - see Appendix A for areas included; (2) National Ambient Air Quality Standards; ppm = parts per million; ug/m^3 = micrograms per cubic meter; n/a not available
Source: EPA, National Air Quality and Emissions Trends Report, 1997

Pollutant Standards Index

In the Memphis MSA (see Appendix A for areas included), the Pollutant Standards Index (PSI) exceeded 100 on 17 days in 1997. A PSI value greater than 100 indicates that air quality would be in the unhealthful range on that day. *EPA, National Air Quality and Emissions Trends Report, 1997*

Drinking Water

Water System Name	Pop. Served	Primary Water Source Type	Number of Violations in 1998	Type of Violation/ Contaminants
MLG&W	644,275	Ground	None	None

Note: Data as of July 10, 1999
Source: EPA, Office of Ground Water and Drinking Water, Safe Drinking Water Information System

Memphis tap water is neutral, hardness 46ppm and fluoridated.
Editor & Publisher Market Guide, 1999

Miami, Florida

Background

While the majority of Miami's residents are Caucasian of European descent, a growing number are of Cuban, Puerto Rican, and Haitian descent. Given this flavorful mix, Miami is the city with a hot international setting, with a Latin American accent.

Thanks to early pioneer Julia Tuttle, railroad magnate Henry Flagler extended the East Coast Railroad beyond Palm Beach. Within 15 years of that decision, Miami became known as the "Gold Coast." The land boom of the 1920s brought wealthy socialites, as well as African-Americans in search of work. Pink and aquamarine hued Art Deco hotels were squeezed onto a tiny tract of land called Miami Beach, and the population of the Miami metro area swelled from 1,681 in 1900 to 1,934,014 in 1990.

Given Miami's origins in a tourist-oriented economy, many of the activities in which residents engage are "leisurely" including swimming, scuba diving, golf, tennis, and boating. Due to the increasing number of citizens retiring to the Miami area, shuffle board is popular as well.

For those who enjoy professional sports, the city is host to the following teams: Miami Dolphin football; Florida Marlins baseball; Miami Heat basketball; Florida Panther hockey. Cultural activities range from the Miami City Ballet and the Coconut Grove Playhouse to numerous art galleries and museums, including the Bass Museum of Art. A visit to the Villa Vizcaya, a gorgeous palazzo in the Italian Renaissance style built by industrialist James Deering, or the Miami MetroZoo are popular past times.

Miami's prime location on Biscayne Bay in the southeastern United States makes it a perfect nexus for travel and trade. The Port of Miami is a bustling center for many cruise and cargo ships. The Port is also a base of the National Oceanic and Atmospheric Administration. The Miami International Airport is a busy destination point to and from many Latin American and Caribbean countries.

Even with Miami's social and financial problems, local economists viewing the situation from an economic development standpoint, do not see these as indicators of market weakness. Miami is still at the trading crossroads of the Western Hemisphere as the chief shipment point for exports and imports with Latin America and the Caribbean. The Port of Miami alone handles 42 percent of all U.S. Caribbean nations and 36 percent of all U.S. trade with Central and South America. In 1996, the port handled nearly 6 million tons of cargo valued at $15 billion and 1997 saw a 6 percent increase in cargo tonnage.

The sultry, sub-tropical climate against a backdrop of Spanish, Art Deco, and modern architecture makes Miami a uniquely cosmopolitan city. The Art Deco Historic District, known as South Beach and located on the tip of Miami Beach, has recently developed an international reputation in the fashion, film, and music industries. Greater Miami and the Beaches is now the third-largest center for film, television, and print production in the country.

Long, warm summers are typical of this subtropical area, as are mild, dry winters. The marine influence is evidenced by the narrow daily range of temperature and the rapid warming of cold air masses. During the summer months, rainfall occurs in early morning near the ocean and in early afternoon further inland.

Hurricanes occasionally affect the Miami area, usually in September and October. Destructive tornadoes are quite rare. Funnel clouds are occasionally sighted and a few touch the ground briefly, but significant destruction is unusual. Waterspouts are visible from the beaches during the summer months but seldom cause any damage. During June, July, and August, there are numerous beautiful, but dangerous, lightning events.

General Rankings and Evaluative Comments

- Miami was ranked #19 out of 19 large, southern metropolitan areas in *Money's* 1998 survey of "The Best Places to Live in America." The survey was conducted by first contacting 512 representative households nationwide and asking them to rank 37 quality-of-life factors on a scale of 1 to 10. Next, a demographic profile was compiled on the 300 largest metropolitan statistical areas in the U.S. The numbers were crunched together to arrive at an overall ranking (things Americans consider most important, like clean air and water, low crime and good schools, received extra weight). Unlike previous years, the 1998 rankings were broken down by region (northeast, midwest, south, west) and population size (100,000 to 249,999; 250,000 to 999,999; 1 million plus). The city had a nationwide ranking of #56 out of 300 in 1997 and #22 out of 300 in 1996. *Money, July 1998; Money, July 1997; Money, September 1996*

- *Ladies Home Journal* ranked America's 200 largest cities based on the qualities women care about most. Miami ranked #152 out of 200. Criteria: low crime rate, well-paying jobs, quality health and child care, good public schools, the presence of women in government, size of the gender wage gap, number of sexual-harassment and discrimination complaints filed, unemployment and divorce rates, commute times, population density, number of houses of worship, parks and cultural offerings, number of women's health specialists, how well a community's women cared for themselves, complexion kindness index based on UV radiation levels, odds of finding affordable fashions, rental rates for romance movies, champagne sales and other matters of the heart. *Ladies Home Journal, November 1998*

- Zero Population Growth ranked 229 cities in terms of children's health, safety, and economic well-being. Miami was ranked #20 out of 25 major cities (main city in a metro area with population of greater than 2 million) and was given a grade of D. Criteria: total population, percent of population under 18 years of age, household language, percent population change, percent of births to teens, infant mortality rate, percent of low birth weights, dropout rate, enrollment in preprimary school, violent and property crime rates, unemployment rate, percent of children in poverty, percent of owner occupied units, number of bad air days, percent of public transportation commuters, and average travel time to work. *Zero Population Growth, Children's Environmental Index, Fall 1999*

- Miami was ranked #56 out of 59 metro areas in *The Regional Economist's* "Rational Livability Ranking of 59 Large Metro Areas." The rankings were based on the metro area's total population change over the period 1990-97 divided by the number of people moving in from elsewhere in the United States (net domestic in-migration). *St. Louis Federal Reserve Bank of St. Louis, The Regional Economist, April 1999*

- Miami was ranked #10 out of 100 in a study titled "Quality of Life in U.S. Cities: A New Ranking." The study showed a statistical model that associated the quality of life with housing prices and wage rates. In the model, high housing prices, low wages rates, or a combination of the two are "signals" of a high quality of life. *Pension Real Estate Association Quarterly, "Quality of Life in U.S. Cities: A New Ranking," Winter 1999*

- Miami appeared on *Travel & Leisure's* list of the world's 100 best cities. It was ranked #48 in the U.S. Criteria: activities/attractions, culture/arts, people, restaurants/food, and value. *Travel & Leisure, 1998 World's Best Awards*

- Miami was selected by *Yahoo! Internet Life* as one of "America's Most Wired Cities & Towns." The city ranked #28 out of 50. Criteria: home and work net use, domain density, hosts per capita, directory density and content quality. *Yahoo! Internet Life, March 1999*

- Cognetics studied 273 metro areas in the United States, ranking them by entrepreneurial activity. Miami was ranked #25 out of the 50 largest metro areas. Criteria: Significant Starts (firms started in the last 10 years that still employ at least 5 people) and Young Growers (percent of firms 10 years old or less that grew significantly during the last 4 years). *Cognetics, "Entrepreneurial Hot Spots: The Best Places in America to Start and Grow a Company," 1998*

- Miami was selected as one of the "Best American Cities to Start a Business" by *Point of View* magazine. Criteria: coolness, quality-of-life, and business concerns. The city was ranked #48 out of 75. *Point of View, November 1998*

- Reliastar Financial Corp. ranked the 125 largest metropolitan areas according to the general financial security of residents. Miami was ranked #116 out of 125 with a score of -15.3. The score indicates the percentage a metropolitan area is above or below the metropolitan norm. A metro area with a score of 10.6 is 10.6% above the metro average. Criteria: Earnings and Wealth Potential (household income, education, net assets, cost of living); Safety Net (health insurance, retirement savings, life insurance, income support programs); Personal Threats (unemployment rate, low-income households, crime rate); Community Economic Vitality (cost of community services, job quality, job creation, housing costs).
  Reliastar Financial Corp., "The Best Cities to Earn and Save Money," 1999 Edition

Business Environment

STATE ECONOMY

State Economic Profile

"Florida's economy has been among the nation's strongest in recent years. Job growth has outpaced the nation by a considerable amount since 1992.

While Florida has been able to avoid any significant fallout from the Asian crisis, the weakening of economies in Latin American will dampen both tourism and international trade. 1998 saw the decline in Latin tourism more than offset by domestic visitors. Domestic tourism is projected to soften as US growth cools in 1999, offering no offset against the expected decline in Latin tourism. Weaker tourism and trade with Latin American will slow growth in 1999; FL will still outpace the nation in job growth as Gross State Product growth (GSP) slows.

Over half of FL's 230,000 new jobs created in 1998 were in the services sector, which grew at 5.2%, more than offsetting a minor decline in manufacturing employment. Much of this growth is taking place in the finance and business services sector.

In spite of strong home sales and a slowing construction market, FL's price appreciation continued to lag the nation. Although residential permits per 1,000 residents stands at 5.1, well above the national average, this number is only slightly up from 1997 and will decline in 1999.

Growth in FL, while strong throughout, has been hottest in the Naples, Ft. Myers and Orlando areas. Construction and employment in the construction industry has begun to slow in South Florida. Projected employment and housing gains will be concentrated in Northern and Central Florida during 1999. Growing diversification of the economy into financial and business services promises a strong outlook for the years ahead." *National Association of Realtors, Economic Profiles: The Fifty States and the District of Columbia, http://nar.realtor.com/databank/profiles.htm*

IMPORTS/EXPORTS

Total Export Sales

Area	1994 ($000)	1995 ($000)	1996 ($000)	1997 ($000)	% Chg. 1994-97	% Chg. 1996-97
MSA[1]	9,266,746	10,200,815	10,681,236	12,692,289	37.0	18.8
U.S.	512,415,609	583,030,524	622,827,063	687,597,999	34.2	10.4

Note: (1) Metropolitan Statistical Area - see Appendix A for areas included
Source: U.S. Department of Commerce, International Trade Association, Metropolitan Area Exports: An Export Performance Report on Over 250 U.S. Cities, November 10, 1998

CITY FINANCES

City Government Finances

Component	FY92 ($000)	FY92 (per capita $)
Revenue	380,926	1,051.68
Expenditure	358,865	990.77
Debt Outstanding	564,770	1,559.25
Cash & Securities	888,982	2,454.35

Source: U.S. Bureau of the Census, City Government Finances: 1991-92

City Government Revenue by Source

Source	FY92 ($000)	FY92 (per capita $)	FY92 (%)
From Federal Government	13,931	38.46	3.7
From State Governments	27,921	77.09	7.3
From Local Governments	6,608	18.24	1.7
Property Taxes	126,851	350.22	33.3
General Sales Taxes	0	0.00	0.0
Selective Sales Taxes	34,681	95.75	9.1
Income Taxes	0	0.00	0.0
Current Charges	56,342	155.55	14.8
Utility/Liquor Store	0	0.00	0.0
Employee Retirement[1]	74,743	206.35	19.6
Other	39,849	110.02	10.5

Note: (1) Excludes "city contributions," classified as "nonrevenue," intragovernmental transfers.
Source: U.S. Bureau of the Census, City Government Finances: 1991-92

City Government Expenditures by Function

Function	FY92 ($000)	FY92 (per capita $)	FY92 (%)
Educational Services	0	0.00	0.0
Employee Retirement[1]	35,004	96.64	9.8
Environment/Housing	95,188	262.80	26.5
Government Administration	24,610	67.94	6.9
Interest on General Debt	33,189	91.63	9.2
Public Safety	136,733	377.50	38.1
Social Services	1,125	3.11	0.3
Transportation	16,117	44.50	4.5
Utility/Liquor Store	0	0.00	0.0
Other	16,899	46.66	4.7

Note: (1) Payments to beneficiaries including withdrawal of contributions.
Source: U.S. Bureau of the Census, City Government Finances: 1991-92

Municipal Bond Ratings

Area	Moody's	S & P
Miami	Ba1	n/a

Note: n/a not available; n/r not rated
Source: Moody's Bond Record, 6/99

POPULATION

Population Growth

Area	1980	1990	% Chg. 1980-90	July 1998 Estimate	% Chg. 1990-98
City	346,865	358,548	3.4	368,624	2.8
MSA[1]	1,625,781	1,937,094	19.1	2,122,503	9.6
U.S.	226,545,805	248,765,170	9.8	270,299,000	8.7

Note: (1) Metropolitan Statistical Area - see Appendix A for areas included;
July 1998 MSA population estimate was calculated by the editors
Source: 1980/1990 Census of Housing and Population, Summary Tape File 3C;
Census Bureau Population Estimates 1998

Population Characteristics

Race	City 1980 Population	%	City 1990 Population	%	% Chg. 1980-90	MSA[1] 1990 Population	%
White	225,200	64.9	236,040	65.8	4.8	1,415,346	73.1
Black	87,018	25.1	97,822	27.3	12.4	398,424	20.6
Amer Indian/Esk/Aleut	334	0.1	526	0.1	57.5	2,889	0.1
Asian/Pacific Islander	2,050	0.6	2,151	0.6	4.9	24,773	1.3
Other	32,263	9.3	22,009	6.1	-31.8	95,662	4.9
Hispanic Origin[2]	194,037	55.9	223,438	62.3	15.2	949,700	49.0

Note: (1) Metropolitan Statistical Area - see Appendix A for areas included;
(2) people of Hispanic origin can be of any race
Source: 1980/1990 Census of Housing and Population, Summary Tape File 3C

Ancestry

Area	German	Irish	English	Italian	U.S.	French	Polish	Dutch
City	1.9	1.6	1.9	1.0	2.2	0.9	0.7	0.2
MSA[1]	5.9	4.5	4.6	2.9	3.1	1.5	2.1	0.6
U.S.	23.3	15.6	13.1	5.9	5.3	4.2	3.8	2.5

Note: Figures are percentages and include persons that reported multiple ancestry (eg. if a person reported being Irish and Italian, they were included in both columns); (1) Metropolitan Statistical Area - see Appendix A for areas included
Source: 1990 Census of Population and Housing, Summary Tape File 3C

Age

Area	Median Age (Years)	Age Distribution (%) Under 5	Under 18	18-24	25-44	45-64	65+	80+
City	35.9	7.1	23.0	9.1	29.6	21.6	16.7	4.1
MSA[1]	34.2	7.1	24.2	9.7	31.6	20.5	14.0	3.5
U.S.	32.9	7.3	25.6	10.5	32.6	18.7	12.5	2.8

Note: (1) Metropolitan Statistical Area - see Appendix A for areas included
Source: 1990 Census of Population and Housing, Summary Tape File 3C

Male/Female Ratio

Area	Number of males per 100 females (all ages)	Number of males per 100 females (18 years old+)
City	92.6	90.1
MSA[1]	91.6	88.1
U.S.	95.0	91.9

Note: (1) Metropolitan Statistical Area - see Appendix A for areas included
Source: 1990 Census of Population, General Population Characteristics

INCOME

Per Capita/Median/Average Income

Area	Per Capita ($)	Median Household ($)	Average Household ($)
City	9,799	16,925	26,507
MSA[1]	13,686	26,909	37,903
U.S.	14,420	30,056	38,453

Note: All figures are for 1989; (1) Metropolitan Statistical Area - see Appendix A for areas included
Source: 1990 Census of Population and Housing, Summary Tape File 3C

Household Income Distribution by Race

Income ($)	City (%)					U.S. (%)				
	Total	White	Black	Other	Hisp.[1]	Total	White	Black	Other	Hisp.[1]
Less than 5,000	17.1	15.2	22.6	16.1	17.5	6.2	4.8	15.2	8.6	8.8
5,000 - 9,999	15.0	14.1	18.3	13.5	15.4	9.3	8.6	14.2	9.9	11.1
10,000 - 14,999	13.3	12.5	15.3	13.8	13.7	8.8	8.5	11.0	9.8	11.0
15,000 - 24,999	19.5	19.3	19.5	22.2	20.9	17.5	17.3	18.9	18.5	20.5
25,000 - 34,999	12.7	12.6	11.6	17.4	12.8	15.8	16.1	14.2	15.4	16.4
35,000 - 49,999	10.6	11.6	7.9	9.2	10.2	17.9	18.6	13.3	16.1	16.0
50,000 - 74,999	6.9	8.3	3.4	5.2	6.3	15.0	15.8	9.3	13.4	11.1
75,000 - 99,999	2.4	2.9	0.9	2.2	1.8	5.1	5.5	2.6	4.7	3.1
100,000+	2.6	3.4	0.6	0.4	1.5	4.4	4.8	1.3	3.7	1.9

Note: All figures are for 1989; (1) people of Hispanic origin can be of any race
Source: 1990 Census of Population and Housing, Summary Tape File 3C

Effective Buying Income

Area	Per Capita ($)	Median Household ($)	Average Household ($)
City	10,686	19,318	29,699
MSA[1]	15,030	29,383	42,550
U.S.	16,803	34,536	45,243

Note: Data as of 1/1/99; (1) Metropolitan Statistical Area - see Appendix A for areas included
Source: Standard Rate & Data Service, Newspaper Advertising Source, 9/99

Effective Household Buying Income Distribution

Area	% of Households Earning						
	$10,000 -$19,999	$20,000 -$34,999	$35,000 -$49,999	$50,000 -$74,999	$75,000 -$99,000	$100,000 -$124,999	$125,000 and up
City	23.4	21.9	11.7	8.8	3.2	1.2	1.8
MSA[1]	17.9	22.5	16.0	15.4	5.7	2.2	3.2
U.S.	16.0	22.6	18.2	18.9	7.2	2.4	2.7

Note: Data as of 1/1/99; (1) Metropolitan Statistical Area - see Appendix A for areas included
Source: Standard Rate & Data Service, Newspaper Advertising Source, 9/99

Poverty Rates by Race and Age

Area	Total (%)	By Race (%)				By Age (%)		
		White	Black	Other	Hisp.[2]	Under 5 years old	Under 18 years old	65 years and over
City	31.2	25.0	46.0	32.0	28.5	46.9	44.1	32.2
MSA[1]	17.9	14.2	30.3	21.5	19.5	24.9	24.3	20.0
U.S.	13.1	9.8	29.5	23.1	25.3	20.1	18.3	12.8

Note: Figures show the percent of people living below the poverty line in 1989. The average poverty threshold was $12,674 for a family of four in 1989; (1) Metropolitan Statistical Area - see Appendix A for areas included; (2) people of Hispanic origin can be of any race
Source: 1990 Census of Population and Housing, Summary Tape File 3C

EMPLOYMENT

Labor Force and Employment

Area	Civilian Labor Force			Workers Employed		
	Jun. 1998	Jun. 1999	% Chg.	Jun. 1998	Jun. 1999	% Chg.
City	180,863	183,684	1.6	162,814	166,762	2.4
MSA[1]	1,041,525	1,060,538	1.8	969,523	993,032	2.4
U.S.	138,798,000	140,666,000	1.3	132,265,000	134,395,000	1.6

Note: Data is not seasonally adjusted and covers workers 16 years of age and older;
(1) Metropolitan Statistical Area - see Appendix A for areas included
Source: Bureau of Labor Statistics, http://stats.bls.gov

Unemployment Rate

Area	1998						1999					
	Jul.	Aug.	Sep.	Oct.	Nov.	Dec.	Jan.	Feb.	Mar.	Apr.	May.	Jun.
City	9.0	8.8	9.2	9.2	9.5	8.8	10.2	9.2	9.0	9.5	9.3	9.2
MSA[1]	6.2	6.1	6.4	6.4	6.6	6.1	7.1	6.3	6.2	6.6	6.4	6.4
U.S.	4.7	4.5	4.4	4.2	4.1	4.0	4.8	4.7	4.4	4.1	4.0	4.5

Note: Data is not seasonally adjusted and covers workers 16 years of age and older; all figures are percentages; (1) Metropolitan Statistical Area - see Appendix A for areas included
Source: Bureau of Labor Statistics, http://stats.bls.gov

Employment by Industry

Sector	MSA[1]		U.S.
	Number of Employees	Percent of Total	Percent of Total
Services	329,200	33.0	30.4
Retail Trade	176,300	17.7	17.7
Government	139,900	14.0	15.6
Manufacturing	75,700	7.6	14.3
Finance/Insurance/Real Estate	66,700	6.7	5.9
Wholesale Trade	82,700	8.3	5.4
Transportation/Public Utilities	89,500	9.0	5.3
Construction	36,400	3.7	5.0
Mining	300	<0.1	0.4

Note: Figures cover non-farm employment as of 6/99 and are not seasonally adjusted;
(1) Metropolitan Statistical Area - see Appendix A for areas included
Source: Bureau of Labor Statistics, http://stats.bls.gov

Employment by Occupation

Occupation Category	City (%)	MSA[1] (%)	U.S. (%)
White Collar	46.1	59.3	58.1
Executive/Admin./Management	8.7	12.4	12.3
Professional	8.6	12.1	14.1
Technical & Related Support	2.4	3.3	3.7
Sales	11.5	13.5	11.8
Administrative Support/Clerical	14.9	17.9	16.3
Blue Collar	31.6	24.2	26.2
Precision Production/Craft/Repair	12.2	10.7	11.3
Machine Operators/Assem./Insp.	8.9	5.6	6.8
Transportation/Material Movers	4.6	4.0	4.1
Cleaners/Helpers/Laborers	6.0	4.0	3.9
Services	20.4	14.9	13.2
Farming/Forestry/Fishing	1.9	1.7	2.5

Note: Figures cover employed persons 16 years old and over;
(1) Metropolitan Statistical Area - see Appendix A for areas included
Source: 1990 Census of Population and Housing, Summary Tape File 3C

Occupational Employment Projections: 1996 - 2006

Occupations Expected to Have the Largest Job Growth (ranked by numerical growth)	Fast-Growing Occupations[1] (ranked by percent growth)
1. Cashiers	1. Systems analysts
2. Salespersons, retail	2. Physical therapy assistants and aides
3. General managers & top executives	3. Desktop publishers
4. Registered nurses	4. Home health aides
5. Waiters & waitresses	5. Computer engineers
6. Marketing & sales, supervisors	6. Medical assistants
7. Janitors/cleaners/maids, ex. priv. hshld.	7. Physical therapists
8. General office clerks	8. Paralegals
9. Food preparation workers	9. Emergency medical technicians
10. Hand packers & packagers	10. Occupational therapists

Note: Projections cover Florida; (1) Excludes occupations with total job growth less than 300
Source: U.S. Department of Labor, Employment and Training Administration, America's Labor Market Information System (ALMIS)

TAXES

Major State and Local Tax Rates

State Corp. Income (%)	State Personal Income (%)	Residential Property (effective rate per $100)	Sales & Use State (%)	Sales & Use Local (%)	State Gasoline (cents/ gallon)	State Cigarette (cents/ pack)
5.5[a]	None	n/a	6.0	0.5	13.1[b]	33.9

Note: Personal/corporate income, sales, gasoline and cigarette tax rates as of January 1999.
Property tax rates as of 1997; (a) 3.3% Alternative Minimum Tax. An exemption of $5,000 is allowed;
(b) Rate is comprised of 4 cents excise and 9.1 cents motor carrier tax
Source: Federation of Tax Administrators, www.taxadmin.org; Washington D.C. Department of Finance and Revenue, Tax Rates and Tax Burdens in the District of Columbia: A Nationwide Comparison, July 1998; Chamber of Commerce, 1999

Total Taxes Per Capita and as a Percent of Income

Area	Per Capita Income ($)	Per Capita Taxes ($) Total	Per Capita Taxes ($) Federal	Per Capita Taxes ($) State/ Local	Percent of Income (%) Total	Percent of Income (%) Federal	Percent of Income (%) State/ Local
Florida	27,655	9,768	6,824	2,944	35.3	24.7	10.6
U.S.	27,876	9,881	6,690	3,191	35.4	24.0	11.4

Note: Figures are for 1998
Source: Tax Foundation, www.taxfoundation.org

Estimated Tax Burden

Area	State Income	Local Income	Property	Sales	Total
Miami	0	0	4,750	634	5,384

Note: The numbers are estimates of taxes paid by a married couple with two children and annual earnings of $75,000. Sales tax estimates assume they spend average amounts on food, clothing, household goods and gasoline. Property tax estimates assume they live in a $250,000 home.
Source: Kiplinger's Personal Finance Magazine, October 1998

**COMMERCIAL
REAL ESTATE**

Office Market

Class/ Location	Total Space (sq. ft.)	Vacant Space (sq. ft.)	Vac. Rate (%)	Under Constr. (sq. ft.)	Net Absorp. (sq. ft.)	Rental Rates ($/sq.ft./yr.)
Class A						
CBD	5,410,916	503,592	9.3	525,000	230,203	20.00-32.00
Outside CBD	4,612,278	244,038	5.3	770,703	346,153	10.45-40.00
Class B						
CBD	4,114,182	651,859	15.8	n/a	111,283	15.00-28.50
Outside CBD	14,591,219	1,358,959	9.3	n/a	285,194	10.00-31.56

Note: Data as of 10/98 and covers Miami; CBD = Central Business District; n/a not available;
Source: Society of Industrial and Office Realtors, 1999 Comparative Statistics of Industrial and Office Real Estate Markets

"Absorption will be maintained near one million sq. ft. in the coming year. Speculative development will increase as we move into the next decade. Increases in international trade will encourage international businesses to locate offices in Miami. A careful eye will be kept on the international financial markets and the economic conditions of Latin American countries. The regional economy is expected to grow at a rate of two percent annually or greater over the next few years. Many of the sub-markets will experience growth greater than that of Miami's CBD, as Dade County's growth trends toward areas west and north of the city itself." *Society of Industrial and Office Realtors, 1999 Comparative Statistics of Industrial and Office Real Estate Markets*

Industrial Market

Location	Total Space (sq. ft.)	Vacant Space (sq. ft.)	Vac. Rate (%)	Under Constr. (sq. ft.)	Net Absorp. (sq. ft.)	Gross Lease ($/sq.ft./yr.)
Central City	62,500,000	4,687,500	7.5	0	-917,500	2.35-3.35
Suburban	94,800,000	4,929,600	5.2	1,950,000	1,770,400	5.65-7.65

Note: Data as of 10/98 and covers Miami/Dade County; n/a not available
Source: Society of Industrial and Office Realtors, 1999 Comparative Statistics of Industrial and Office Real Estate Markets

"New construction is expected to decrease in 1999 by one to five percent. This will be a timely respite from the nearly two million sq. ft. of additions noted in 1998. However, the shortage of buildings sized 100,000 sq. ft. and larger may encourage new construction in that market segment. Many organizations unable to locate such space in 1998 are still shopping in 1999. Increases in site prices will make it more difficult to locate 'ready to go' land. Residential development in the West Airport area may start to border office and industrial products, as districts boundaries blur. Increases in warehouse/distribution prices are anticipated by our local SIOR reporter. These increases may be in the amount of five percent. Lease prices for this space is also expected to increase by up to five percent. Absorption levels are expected to remain constant." *Society of Industrial and Office Realtors, 1999 Comparative Statistics of Industrial and Office Real Estate Markets*

Retail Market

Shopping Center Inventory (sq. ft.)	Shopping Center Construction (sq. ft.)	Construction as a Percent of Inventory (%)	Torto Wheaton Rent Index[1] ($/sq. ft.)
32,943,000	853,000	2.6	14.37

Note: Data as of 1997 and covers the Metropolitan Statistical Area - see Appendix A for areas included; (1) Index is based on a model that predicts what the average rent should be for leases with certain characteristics, in certain locations during certain years.
Source: National Association of Realtors, 1997-1998 Market Conditions Report

"Retail trade is indeed one of Miami's most important sectors. Retail accounts for 27% of the area's jobs, buoyed by the strength of the tourism industry. The economic impact of tourism is estimated to be $13.5 billion. The demographics of Miami's millions of visitors have been changing. In 1989, 61% of the area's tourists were Americans; in 1996, an estimated 61% were foreign. Miami's retail vacancy rate has stabilized, while the rent index rose 4% last year. Shopping center completions remained robust at 850,000 square feet, with that rate expected to continue through 2000." *National Association of Realtors, 1997-1998 Market Conditions Report*

COMMERCIAL UTILITIES

Typical Monthly Electric Bills

Area	Commercial Service ($/month)		Industrial Service ($/month)	
	12 kW demand 1,500 kWh	100 kW demand 30,000 kWh	1,000 kW demand 400,000 kWh	20,000 kW demand 10,000,000 kWh
City	118	1,993	23,247	387,510
U.S.	150	2,174	23,995	508,569

Note: Based on rates in effect January 1, 1999
Source: Edison Electric Institute, Typical Residential, Commercial and Industrial Bills, Winter 1999

TRANSPORTATION

Transportation Statistics

Average minutes to work	23.8
Interstate highways	I-95
Bus lines	
In-city	Metro Dade Transit Agency, 795 vehicles
Inter-city	1
Passenger air service	
Airport	Miami International
Airlines	85 scheduled airlines
Aircraft departures	127,880 (1996)
Enplaned passengers	11,905,703 (1996)
Rail service	Amtrak; Tri-Rail; Metro Rail
Motor freight carriers	57
Major waterways/ports	Port of Miami; Atlantic Intracoastal Waterway

Source: Editor & Publisher Market Guide, 1999; FAA Airport Activity Statistics, 1997; Amtrak National Time Table, Northeast Timetable, Spring/Summer 1999; 1990 Census of Population and Housing, STF 3C; Chamber of Commerce/Economic Development 1999; Jane's Urban Transport Systems 1999-2000

Means of Transportation to Work

Area	Car/Truck/Van		Public Transportation			Bicycle	Walked	Other Means	Worked at Home
	Drove Alone	Car-pooled	Bus	Subway	Railroad				
City	60.9	18.0	11.8	0.6	0.2	0.6	4.2	1.8	1.9
MSA[1]	72.4	15.6	4.8	0.7	0.1	0.5	2.5	1.3	2.0
U.S.	73.2	13.4	3.0	1.5	0.5	0.4	3.9	1.2	3.0

Note: Figures shown are percentages and only include workers 16 years old and over;
(1) Metropolitan Statistical Area - see Appendix A for areas included
Source: 1990 Census of Population and Housing, Summary Tape File 3C

BUSINESSES

Major Business Headquarters

Company Name	1999 Rankings	
	Fortune 500	Forbes 500
Braman Enterprises	-	424
CHS Electronics	189	-
Potamkin Cos	-	119
Ryder System	312	-
Southern Wine & Spirits	-	56

Note: Companies listed are located in the city; dashes indicate no ranking
Fortune 500: Companies that produce a 10-K are ranked 1 to 500 based on 1998 revenue
Forbes 500: Private companies are ranked 1 to 500 based on 1997 revenue
Source: Forbes, November 30, 1998; Fortune, April 26, 1999

Fast-Growing Businesses

According to *Inc.*, Miami is home to one of America's 100 fastest-growing private companies: Let's Talk Cellular & Wireless. Criteria for inclusion: must be an independent, privately-held, U.S. corporation, proprietorship or partnership; sales of at least $200,000 in 1995; five-year operating/sales history; increase in 1999 sales over 1998 sales; holding companies, regulated banks, and utilities were excluded. *Inc. 500, 1999*

Miami is home to one of *Business Week's* "hot growth" companies: Vitech America. Criteria: increase in sales and profits, return on capital and stock price. *Business Week, 5/31/99*

Women-Owned Firms: Number, Employment and Sales

Area	Number of Firms	Employ-ment	Sales ($000)	Rank[2]
MSA[1]	91,900	397,900	51,018,000	15

Note: (1) Metropolitan Statistical Area - see Appendix A for areas included;
(2) Calculated on an averaging of the number of businesses, employment and sales
Source: The National Foundation for Women Business Owners, 1999 Facts on Women-Owned Businesses: Trends in the Top 50 Metropolitan Areas

Women-Owned Firms: Growth

Area	% change from 1992 to 1999			Rank[2]
	Number of Firms	Employ-ment	Sales	
MSA[1]	55.2	141.7	161.1	6

Note: (1) Metropolitan Statistical Area - see Appendix A for areas included; (2) Calculated on an averaging of the percent growth of number of businesses, employment and sales
Source: The National Foundation for Women Business Owners, 1999 Facts on Women-Owned Businesses: Trends in the Top 50 Metropolitan Areas

Minority Business Opportunity

71 of the 500 largest Hispanic-owned companies in the U.S. are located in Miami. *Hispanic Business, June 1999*

Miami is home to four companies which are on the Hispanic Business Fastest-Growing 100 list (greatest sales growth from 1994 to 1998): Paez-Fletcher Co. (electronic security wholesale); Petro Hydro Inc. (environmental engineering svcs.); Perishable Express Inc. (customs brokerage svcs.); International Music Distribution Inc. (Latin music CDs wholesale). *Hispanic Business, July/August 1999*

Small Business Opportunity

According to *Forbes*, Miami is home to two of America's 200 best small companies: Quipp and Supreme International. Criteria: companies included must be publicly traded since November 1997 with a stock price of at least $5 per share and an average daily float of 1,000 shares. The company's latest 12-month sales must be between $5 and $350 million, return on equity (ROE) must be a minimum of 12% for both the past 5 years and the most recent four quarters, and five-year sales and EPS growth must average at least 10%. Companies with declining sales or earnings during the past year were dropped as well as businesses with debt/equity ratios over 1.25. Companies with negative operating cash flow in each of the past two years were also excluded. *Forbes, November 2, 1998*

HOTELS & MOTELS

Hotels/Motels

Area	Hotels/ Motels	Rooms	Luxury-Level Hotels/Motels		Average Minimum Rates ($)		
			♦♦♦♦	♦♦♦♦♦	♦♦	♦♦♦	♦♦♦♦
City	36	9,229	1	0	80	131	175
Airport	28	5,728	0	0	n/a	n/a	n/a
Suburbs	125	17,656	3	0	n/a	n/a	n/a
Total	189	32,613	4	0	n/a	n/a	n/a

Note: n/a not available; classifications range from one diamond (budget properties with basic amenities) to five diamond (luxury properties with the finest service, rooms and facilities).
Source: OAG, Business Travel Planner, Winter 1998-99

CONVENTION CENTERS

Major Convention Centers

Center Name	Meeting Rooms	Exhibit Space (sq. ft.)
Coconut Grove Convention Center	10	150,000
Dade County Youth Fair & Exposition Center	9	10,000
Miami Convention Center	37	28,000
Radisson Centre/Radisson Mart Plaza Hotel	32	137,600

Source: Trade Shows Worldwide, 1998; Meetings & Conventions, 4/15/99; Sucessful Meetings, 3/31/98

Living Environment

COST OF LIVING

Cost of Living Index

Composite Index	Groceries	Housing	Utilities	Trans-portation	Health Care	Misc. Goods/Services
107.7	102.9	113.0	103.0	106.8	101.6	108.0

Note: U.S. = 100; Figures are for the Metropolitan Statistical Area - see Appendix A for areas included
Source: ACCRA, Cost of Living Index, 4th Quarter 1998

HOUSING

Median Home Prices and Housing Affordability

Area	Median Price[2] 1st Qtr. 1999 ($)	HOI[3] 1st Qtr. 1999	Afford-ability Rank[4]
MSA[1]	110,000	65.4	138
U.S.	134,000	69.6	–

Note: (1) Metropolitan Statistical Area - see Appendix A for areas included; (2) U.S. figures calculated from the sales of 524,324 new and existing homes in 181 markets; (3) Housing Opportunity Index - percent of homes sold that were within the reach of the median income household at the prevailing mortgage interest rate; (4) Rank is from 1-181 with 1 being most affordable
Source: National Association of Home Builders, Housing Opportunity Index, 1st Quarter 1999

Median Home Price Projection

It is projected that the median price of existing single-family homes in the metro area will increase by 3.4% in 1999. Nationwide, home prices are projected to increase 3.8%.
Kiplinger's Personal Finance Magazine, January 1999

Average New Home Price

Area	Price ($)
MSA[1]	155,544
U.S.	141,438

Note: Figures are based on a new home with 1,800 sq. ft. of living area on an 8,000 sq. ft. lot; (1) Metropolitan Statistical Area - see Appendix A for areas included
Source: ACCRA, Cost of Living Index, 4th Quarter 1998

Average Apartment Rent

Area	Rent ($/mth)
MSA[1]	775
U.S.	593

Note: Figures are based on an unfurnished two bedroom, 1-1/2 or 2 bath apartment, approximately 950 sq. ft. in size, excluding all utilities except water; (1) Metropolitan Statistical Area - see Appendix A for areas included
Source: ACCRA, Cost of Living Index, 4th Quarter 1998

RESIDENTIAL UTILITIES

Average Residential Utility Costs

Area	All Electric ($/mth)	Part Electric ($/mth)	Other Energy ($/mth)	Phone ($/mth)
MSA[1]	106.04	–	–	16.27
U.S.	101.64	55.45	43.56	19.81

Note: (1) (1) Metropolitan Statistical Area - see Appendix A for areas included
Source: ACCRA, Cost of Living Index, 4th Quarter 1998

HEALTH CARE

Average Health Care Costs

Area	Hospital ($/day)	Doctor ($/visit)	Dentist ($/visit)
MSA[1]	558.40	53.00	59.00
U.S.	417.46	51.94	64.89

Note: Hospital—based on a semi-private room; Doctor—based on a general practitioner's routine exam of an established patient; Dentist—based on adult teeth cleaning and periodic oral exam; (1) Metropolitan Statistical Area - see Appendix A for areas included
Source: ACCRA, Cost of Living Index, 4th Quarter 1998

Distribution of Office-Based Physicians

Area	Family/Gen. Practitioners	Specialists		
		Medical	Surgical	Other
MSA[1]	739	1,857	1,246	1,248

Note: Data as of 12/31/97; (1) Metropolitan Statistical Area - see Appendix A for areas included
Source: American Medical Assn., Physician Characteristics & Distribution in the U.S., 1999

Hospitals

Miami has 1 general medical and surgical hospital, 3 psychiatric, 1 eye, ear, nose and throat, 1 rehabilitation, 1 other specialty, 1 children's general. *AHA Guide to the Healthcare Field, 1998-99*

According to *U.S. News and World Report,* Miami has 1 of the best hospitals in the U.S.: **University of Miami, Jackson Memorial Hospital**, noted for gastroenterology, geriatrics, gynecology, ophthalmology, otolaryngology, pediatrics. *U.S. News Online, "America's Best Hospitals," 10th Edition, www.usnews.com*

EDUCATION

Public School District Statistics

District Name	Num. Sch.	Enroll.	Classroom Teachers	Pupils per Teacher	Minority Pupils (%)	Current Exp.[1] ($/pupil)
Dade County Sch Dist	321	345,958	17,149	20.2	86.9	5,745

Note: Data covers the 1997-1998 school year unless otherwise noted; (1) Data covers fiscal year 1996; SD = School District; ISD = Independent School District; n/a not available
Source: National Center for Education Statistics, Common Core of Data Public Education Agency Universe 1997-98; National Center for Education Statistics, Characteristics of the 100 Largest Public Elementary and Secondary School Districts in the United States: 1997-98, July 1999

Educational Quality

School District	Education Quotient[1]	Graduate Outcome[2]	Community Index[3]	Resource Index[4]
Dade County	91.0	79.0	55.0	123.0

Note: Nearly 1,000 secondary school districts were rated in terms of educational quality. The scores range from a low of 50 to a high of 150; (1) Average of the Graduate Outcome, Community and Resource indexes; (2) Based on graduation rates and college board scores (SAT/ACT); (3) Based on the surrounding community's average level of education and the area's average income level; (4) Based on teacher salaries, per-pupil expenditures and student-teacher ratios.
Source: Expansion Management, Ratings Issue, 1998

Educational Attainment by Race

Area	High School Graduate (%)					Bachelor's Degree (%)				
	Total	White	Black	Other	Hisp.[2]	Total	White	Black	Other	Hisp.[2]
City	47.6	50.6	39.7	42.6	43.0	12.8	15.5	4.9	10.7	10.5
MSA[1]	65.0	67.6	56.0	57.0	55.1	18.8	20.8	9.9	17.1	14.1
U.S.	75.2	77.9	63.1	60.4	49.8	20.3	21.5	11.4	19.4	9.2

Note: Figures shown cover persons 25 years old and over; (1) Metropolitan Statistical Area - see Appendix A for areas included; (2) people of Hispanic origin can be of any race
Source: 1990 Census of Population and Housing, Summary Tape File 3C

School Enrollment by Type

Area	Preprimary				Elementary/High School			
	Public		Private		Public		Private	
	Enrollment	%	Enrollment	%	Enrollment	%	Enrollment	%
City	2,688	61.0	1,720	39.0	53,740	90.3	5,750	9.7
MSA[1]	14,892	43.9	19,029	56.1	281,730	86.5	44,139	13.5
U.S.	2,679,029	59.5	1,824,256	40.5	38,379,689	90.2	4,187,099	9.8

Note: Figures shown cover persons 3 years old and over;
(1) Metropolitan Statistical Area - see Appendix A for areas included
Source: 1990 Census of Population and Housing, Summary Tape File 3C

School Enrollment by Race

Area	Preprimary (%)				Elementary/High School (%)			
	White	Black	Other	Hisp.[1]	White	Black	Other	Hisp.[1]
City	48.8	46.8	4.4	40.9	51.7	40.5	7.8	53.5
MSA[2]	66.7	28.6	4.6	35.5	62.4	30.2	7.4	47.6
U.S.	80.4	12.5	7.1	7.8	74.1	15.6	10.3	12.5

Note: Figures shown cover persons 3 years old and over; (1) people of Hispanic origin can be of any race; (2) Metropolitan Statistical Area - see Appendix A for areas included
Source: 1990 Census of Population and Housing, Summary Tape File 3C

Classroom Teacher Salaries in Public Schools

District	B.A. Degree		M.A. Degree		Maximum	
	Min. ($)	Rank[1]	Max. ($)	Rank[1]	Max. ($)	Rank[1]
Miami	28,150	30	54,300	9	58,300	11
Average	26,980	-	46,065	-	51,435	-

Note: Salaries are for 1997-1998; (1) Rank ranges from 1 to 100
Source: American Federation of Teachers, Survey & Analysis of Salary Trends, 1998

Higher Education

Two-Year Colleges		Four-Year Colleges		Medical Schools	Law Schools	Voc/ Tech
Public	Private	Public	Private			
1	3	1	7	1	1	26

Source: College Blue Book, Occupational Education, 1997; Medical School Admission Requirements, 1999-2000; Peterson's Guide to Two-Year Colleges, 1999; Peterson's Guide to Four-Year Colleges, 2000; Barron's Guide to Law Schools, 1999

MAJOR EMPLOYERS

Major Employers

American Bankers Insurance Group
Carnival Corp.
Mount Sinai Medical Center of Greater Miami
Ryder Truck Rental
Variety Children's Hospital

Baptist Hospital of Miami
Mercy Hospital
Royal Caribbean Cruise Line
South Miami Hospital
Worldex Travel Center

Note: Companies listed are located in the city
Source: Dun's Business Rankings, 1999; Ward's Business Directory, 1998

PUBLIC SAFETY

Crime Rate

Area	All Crimes	Violent Crimes				Property Crimes		
		Murder	Forcible Rape	Robbery	Aggrav. Assault	Burglary	Larceny -Theft	Motor Vehicle Theft
City	12,828.8	26.3	48.2	1,153.0	1,586.2	2,283.5	5,771.0	1,960.6
Suburbs[1]	10,332.5	12.0	62.5	477.8	886.1	1,756.9	5,622.3	1,514.8
MSA[2]	10,792.3	14.7	59.9	602.2	1,015.1	1,853.9	5,649.7	1,596.9
U.S.	4,922.7	6.8	35.9	186.1	382.0	919.6	2,886.5	505.8

Note: Crime rate is the number of crimes per 100,000 pop.; (1) defined as all areas within the MSA but located outside the central city; (2) Metropolitan Statistical Area - see Appendix A for areas incl.
Source: FBI Uniform Crime Reports, 1997

RECREATION

Culture and Recreation

Museums	Symphony Orchestras	Opera Companies	Dance Companies	Professional Theatres	Zoos	Pro Sports Teams
10	2	1	4	3	1	4

Source: International Directory of the Performing Arts, 1997; Official Museum Directory, 1999; Stern's Performing Arts Directory, 1997; USA Today Four Sport Stadium Guide, 1997; Chamber of Commerce/Economic Development, 1999

Library System

The Miami-Dade Public Library has 32 branches, holdings of 3,983,968 volumes, and a budget of $32,194,685 (1996-1997). *American Library Directory, 1998-1999*

MEDIA

Newspapers

Name	Type	Freq.	Distribution	Circulation
Coral Gables News	General	2x/wk	Local	15,000
Daily Business Review	n/a	5x/wk	Area	10,000
Diario las Americas	Hispanic	6x/wk	Local	68,374
El Nuevo Herald	Hispanic	7x/wk	Area	104,000
The Flyer	n/a	1x/wk	Area	1,030,000
Hialeah/Opa-Locka News	General	2x/wk	Local	15,000
Kendall Gazette	General	1x/wk	Local	18,000
Miami Beach News	General	2x/wk	Local	4,000
Miami Herald	General	7x/wk	Area	419,187
Miami Laker	General	1x/mo	Local	27,000
The Miami Times	Black	1x/wk	Area	28,170
North Bay Village News	General	2x/wk	Local	6,000
North Miami Beach News	General	2x/wk	Local	90,000
North Miami News	General	2x/wk	Local	15,000
South Miami News	General	2x/wk	Local	7,500
The Weekly News - TWN	Alternative	1x/wk	Area	22,500
The Wire	Alternative	1x/wk	Local	13,000

Note: Includes newspapers with circulations of 1,000 or more located in the city; n/a not available
Source: Burrelle's Media Directory, 1999 Edition

Television Stations

Name	Ch.	Affiliation	Type	Owner
WPBT	n/a	PBS	Public	Community TV Foundation of South Florida Inc.
WFOR	n/a	CBST	Commercial	Westinghouse Broadcasting Company
WTVJ	n/a	NBCT	Commercial	General Electric Corporation
WSVN	n/a	n/a	Commercial	Edmund N. Ansin
WWFD	n/a	n/a	Commercial	Hispanic Keys Broadcasting
WPLG	10	ABCT	Commercial	Post-Newsweek Business Information Inc.
WLRN	17	n/a	Public	School Board of Dade County
WLTV	23	UNIN	Commercial	Univision Communications Inc.
WBFS	33	n/a	Commercial	United Paramount Network
WPXM	35	n/a	Commercial	Paxson Communications Corporation
WSCV	51	TMUN	Commercial	Telemundo Group Inc.
WAMI	69	n/a	Commercial	n/a

Note: Stations included broadcast in the Miami metro area; n/a not available
Source: Burrelle's Media Directory, 1999 Edition

AM Radio Stations

Call Letters	Freq. (kHz)	Target Audience	Station Format	Music Format
WIOD	610	General	N	n/a
WWFE	670	G/H	M/N/S/T	Latin
WAQI	710	G/H	N/T	n/a
WAXY	790	General	M/T	n/a
WINZ	940	General	T	n/a
WVCG	1080	n/a	M/N/T	n/a
WQBA	1140	Hispanic	N/S/T	n/a
WNMA	1210	General	N/S/T	n/a
WCMQ	1210	Hispanic	N/S/T	n/a
WSUA	1260	Hispanic	M/N/S/T	Adult Contemporary/Latin
WKAT	1360	Hispanic	M/N/S/T	Latin
WOCN	1450	General	N/S/T	n/a
WMBM	1490	General	E/M/N/S/T	Christian
WRHC	1550	G/H	N/S/T	n/a

Note: Stations included broadcast in the Miami metro area; n/a not available
Target Audience: A=Asian; B=Black; C=Christian; E=Ethnic; F=French; G=General; H=Hispanic; M=Men; N=Native American; R=Religious; S=Senior Citizen; W=Women; Y=Young Adult; Z=Children
Station Format: E=Educational; M=Music; N=News; S=Sports; T=Talk
Source: Burrelle's Media Directory, 1999 Edition

FM Radio Stations

Call Letters	Freq. (mHz)	Target Audience	Station Format	Music Format
WDNA	88.9	G/M	M	Jazz
WMCU	89.7	Religious	M/N/S	Adult Contemporary/Christian
WVUM	90.5	Religious	M/N/S	n/a
WLRN	91.3	General	E/M/N	Alternative/Big Band/Classical/Jazz/R&B
WCMQ	92.3	Hispanic	M/N	Adult Top 40/Latin/Oldies
WTMI	93.1	General	M	Classical/Jazz
WLVE	93.9	General	M/N/T	Jazz
WZTA	94.9	General	M/N/S	AOR
WXDJ	95.7	Hispanic	M	Latin
WPOW	96.5	General	M	n/a
WFLC	97.3	General	M/N	Adult Contemporary
WRTO	98.3	G/H	M	Latin
WEDR	99.1	Black	M	R&B
WLYF	101.5	G/W	M	Adult Contemporary/Easy Listening
WMXJ	102.7	General	M	Oldies
WHQT	105.1	General	M	Urban Contemporary
WBGG	105.9	General	M/N/S	Oldies
WRMA	106.7	Hispanic	M	Adult Contemporary
WAMR	107.5	Hispanic	M	Latin

Note: Stations included broadcast in the Miami metro area; n/a not available
Station Format: E=Educational; M=Music; N=News; S=Sports; T=Talk
Target Audience: A=Asian; B=Black; C=Christian; E=Ethnic; F=French; G=General; H=Hispanic; M=Men; N=Native American; R=Religious; S=Senior Citizen; W=Women; Y=Young Adult; Z=Children
Music Format: AOR=Album Oriented Rock; MOR=Middle-of-the-Road
Source: Burrelle's Media Directory, 1999 Edition

CLIMATE

Average and Extreme Temperatures

Temperature	Jan	Feb	Mar	Apr	May	Jun	Jul	Aug	Sep	Oct	Nov	Dec	Yr.
Extreme High (°F)	88	89	92	96	95	98	98	98	97	95	89	87	98
Average High (°F)	75	77	79	82	85	88	89	90	88	85	80	77	83
Average Temp. (°F)	68	69	72	75	79	82	83	83	82	78	73	69	76
Average Low (°F)	59	60	64	68	72	75	76	76	76	72	66	61	69
Extreme Low (°F)	30	35	32	42	55	60	69	68	68	53	39	30	30

Note: Figures cover the years 1948-1990
Source: National Climatic Data Center, International Station Meteorological Climate Summary, 3/95

Average Precipitation/Snowfall/Humidity

Precip./Humidity	Jan	Feb	Mar	Apr	May	Jun	Jul	Aug	Sep	Oct	Nov	Dec	Yr.
Avg. Precip. (in.)	1.9	2.0	2.3	3.0	6.2	8.7	6.1	7.5	8.2	6.6	2.7	1.8	57.1
Avg. Snowfall (in.)	0	0	0	0	0	0	0	0	0	0	0	0	0
Avg. Rel. Hum. 7am (%)	84	84	82	80	81	84	84	86	88	87	85	84	84
Avg. Rel. Hum. 4pm (%)	59	57	57	57	62	68	66	67	69	65	63	60	63

Note: Figures cover the years 1948-1990; Tr = Trace amounts (<0.05 in. of rain; <0.5 in. of snow)
Source: National Climatic Data Center, International Station Meteorological Climate Summary, 3/95

Weather Conditions

Temperature			Daytime Sky			Precipitation		
32°F & below	45°F & below	90°F & above	Clear	Partly cloudy	Cloudy	0.01 inch or more precip.	0.1 inch or more snow/ice	Thunder-storms
< 1	7	55	48	263	54	128	0	74

Note: Figures are average number of days per year and covers the years 1948-1990
Source: National Climatic Data Center, International Station Meteorological Climate Summary, 3/95

AIR & WATER QUALITY

Maximum Pollutant Concentrations

	Particulate Matter (ug/m^3)	Carbon Monoxide (ppm)	Sulfur Dioxide (ppm)	Nitrogen Dioxide (ppm)	Ozone (ppm)	Lead (ug/m^3)
MSA[1] Level	52	4	0.004	0.017	0.11	n/a
NAAQS[2]	150	9	0.140	0.053	0.12	1.50
Met NAAQS?	Yes	Yes	Yes	Yes	Yes	n/a

Note: (1) Metropolitan Statistical Area - see Appendix A for areas included; (2) National Ambient Air Quality Standards; ppm = parts per million; ug/m^3 = micrograms per cubic meter; n/a not available
Source: EPA, National Air Quality and Emissions Trends Report, 1997

Pollutant Standards Index

In the Miami MSA (see Appendix A for areas included), the Pollutant Standards Index (PSI) exceeded 100 on 3 days in 1997. A PSI value greater than 100 indicates that air quality would be in the unhealthful range on that day. *EPA, National Air Quality and Emissions Trends Report, 1997*

Drinking Water

Water System Name	Pop. Served	Primary Water Source Type	Number of Violations in 1998	Type of Violation/Contaminants
MDWASA - Main System	1,705,156	Ground	None	None

Note: Data as of July 10, 1999
Source: EPA, Office of Ground Water and Drinking Water, Safe Drinking Water Information System

Miami tap water is alkaline, soft and fluoridated.
Editor & Publisher Market Guide, 1999

Nashville, Tennessee

Background

Nashville, the capital of Tennessee, was founded on Christmas Day in 1779 by James Robertson and John Donelson, and sits in the minds of millions as the country music capital of the world. This is the place to record, if you want to make it into the country music industry, and where the Grand Ole Opry—the longest running radio show in the country—still captures the hearts of millions of devoted listeners. It is no wonder, given how profoundly this industry has touched people, names like Dolly, Chet, Loretta, Hank, and Johnny are more familiar than the city's true native sons: Andrew, James, and Sam . . . Jackson, Polk, and Houston, that is.

According to the Country Music Association, over half of the single records produced in the United States come from Nashville. This puts the city on a par with Los Angeles and New York in music recording, publishing, distribution, and production. Luckily for Nashville, its recording industry has spawned opportunities in the related fields of the television and motion picture industries as well.

The magnitude of Nashville's recording industry is impressive, but other industries are important to the city, such as health care management, automobile production, and printing and publishing. And, Nashville is a devoted patron of the arts and education. The Davidson Academy, forerunner of the George Peabody College for Teachers, was founded in Nashville, as were Vanderbilt and Fisk Universities. Fisk was the first private black university in the United States. In addition, the citizens take pride in their numerous art galleries, prize-winning national parks, historical mansions, and special-interest museums.

Located on the Cumberland River in central Tennessee, Nashville's weather is moderate with great temperature extremes a rarity. The average relative humidity is moderate. The city is not in the most common path of storms that cross the country, but is in a zone of moderate frequency for thunderstorms.

General Rankings and Evaluative Comments

- Nashville was ranked #7 out of 19 large, southern metropolitan areas in *Money's* 1998 survey of "The Best Places to Live in America." The survey was conducted by first contacting 512 representative households nationwide and asking them to rank 37 quality-of-life factors on a scale of 1 to 10. Next, a demographic profile was compiled on the 300 largest metropolitan statistical areas in the U.S. The numbers were crunched together to arrive at an overall ranking (things Americans consider most important, like clean air and water, low crime and good schools, received extra weight). Unlike previous years, the 1998 rankings were broken down by region (northeast, midwest, south, west) and population size (100,000 to 249,999; 250,000 to 999,999; 1 million plus). The city had a nationwide ranking of #116 out of 300 in 1997 and #101 out of 300 in 1996. *Money, July 1998; Money, July 1997; Money, September 1996*

- *Ladies Home Journal* ranked America's 200 largest cities based on the qualities women care about most. Nashville ranked #88 out of 200. Criteria: low crime rate, well-paying jobs, quality health and child care, good public schools, the presence of women in government, size of the gender wage gap, number of sexual-harassment and discrimination complaints filed, unemployment and divorce rates, commute times, population density, number of houses of worship, parks and cultural offerings, number of women's health specialists, how well a community's women cared for themselves, complexion kindness index based on UV radiation levels, odds of finding affordable fashions, rental rates for romance movies, champagne sales and other matters of the heart. Ladies Home Journal, November 1998

- Zero Population Growth ranked 229 cities in terms of children's health, safety, and economic well-being. Nashville was ranked #80 out of 112 independent cities (cities with populations greater than 100,000 which were neither Major Cities nor Suburbs/Outer Cities) and was given a grade of C-. Criteria: total population, percent of population under 18 years of age, household language, percent population change, percent of births to teens, infant mortality rate, percent of low birth weights, dropout rate, enrollment in preprimary school, violent and property crime rates, unemployment rate, percent of children in poverty, percent of owner occupied units, number of bad air days, percent of public transportation commuters, and average travel time to work. *Zero Population Growth, Children's Environmental Index, Fall 1999*

- Nashville was ranked #11 out of 59 metro areas in *The Regional Economist's* "Rational Livability Ranking of 59 Large Metro Areas." The rankings were based on the metro area's total population change over the period 1990-97 divided by the number of people moving in from elsewhere in the United States (net domestic in-migration). *St. Louis Federal Reserve Bank of St. Louis, The Regional Economist, April 1999*

- Nashville appeared on *Travel & Leisure's* list of the world's 100 best cities. It was ranked #37 in the U.S. Criteria: activities/attractions, culture/arts, people, restaurants/food, and value. *Travel & Leisure, 1998 World's Best Awards*

- Nashville was selected by *Yahoo! Internet Life* as one of "America's Most Wired Cities & Towns." The city ranked #17 out of 50. Criteria: home and work net use, domain density, hosts per capita, directory density and content quality. *Yahoo! Internet Life, March 1999*

- Cognetics studied 273 metro areas in the United States, ranking them by entrepreneurial activity. Nashville was ranked #7 out of the 50 largest metro areas. Criteria: Significant Starts (firms started in the last 10 years that still employ at least 5 people) and Young Growers (percent of firms 10 years old or less that grew significantly during the last 4 years). *Cognetics, "Entrepreneurial Hot Spots: The Best Places in America to Start and Grow a Company," 1998*

- Nashville was selected as one of the "Best American Cities to Start a Business" by *Point of View* magazine. Criteria: coolness, quality-of-life, and business concerns. The city was ranked #17 out of 75. *Point of View, November 1998*

- Reliastar Financial Corp. ranked the 125 largest metropolitan areas according to the general financial security of residents. Nashville was ranked #74 (tie) out of 125 with a score of -1.0. The score indicates the percentage a metropolitan area is above or below the metropolitan norm. A metro area with a score of 10.6 is 10.6% above the metro average. Criteria: Earnings and Wealth Potential (household income, education, net assets, cost of living); Safety Net (health insurance, retirement savings, life insurance, income support programs); Personal Threats (unemployment rate, low-income households, crime rate); Community Economic Vitality (cost of community services, job quality, job creation, housing costs).
Reliastar Financial Corp., "The Best Cities to Earn and Save Money," 1999 Edition

Business Environment

STATE ECONOMY

State Economic Profile

"Tennessee's economy has been decelerating for almost three years now, a trend that should continue into 1999 and 2000. TN continues to shed jobs in its manufacturing sector, specifically textiles and apparels. In previous years, growth in other sectors was enough to offset these losses. Now growth in these other sectors has slowed. TN's demographics are still strong, and TN continues to have one of the lowest business costs in the country. The TN outlook is one of moderating growth.

TN's manufacturing employment shed some 11,500 jobs in 1998, a decline of 2.2%. Weak export demand and a strong dollar have undermined the apparel industry's competitive position. Soft commodity prices have also hurt TN's metals industry. Neither of these situations will reverse in 1999.

Job growth across TN has been mixed. Declines in manufacturing have hit central and eastern TN harder than the west. Memphis' distribution and transportation sectors, located along the Mississippi, have continued to provide job growth even as the manufacturing sector stumbles. Federal Express and United Parcel Service continue to expand operations. A slowing of the US economy in 1999 and 2000 will weaken the demand for distribution services, although less so than in most industries.

Nashville's economic outlook is less bright. Almost half of 1998's employment gains were in the construction industry. The city's tourism and convention industry remain strong, although it appears likely that commercial construction, especially hotel, has outpaced demand. Construction employment should contract in 1999. The slowing US economy will also place a drag on tourism." *National Association of Realtors, Economic Profiles: The Fifty States and the District of Columbia, http://nar.realtor.com/databank/profiles.htm*

IMPORTS/EXPORTS

Total Export Sales

Area	1994 ($000)	1995 ($000)	1996 ($000)	1997 ($000)	% Chg. 1994-97	% Chg. 1996-97
MSA[1]	1,310,492	1,412,348	1,445,492	1,767,089	34.8	22.2
U.S.	512,415,609	583,030,524	622,827,063	687,597,999	34.2	10.4

Note: (1) Metropolitan Statistical Area - see Appendix A for areas included
Source: U.S. Department of Commerce, International Trade Association, Metropolitan Area Exports: An Export Performance Report on Over 250 U.S. Cities, November 10, 1998

CITY FINANCES

City Government Finances

Component	FY92 ($000)	FY92 (per capita $)
Revenue	1,636,251	3,309.15
Expenditure	1,525,110	3,084.38
Debt Outstanding	2,215,909	4,481.45
Cash & Securities	2,084,832	4,216.36

Source: U.S. Bureau of the Census, City Government Finances: 1991-92

City Government Revenue by Source

Source	FY92 ($000)	FY92 (per capita $)	FY92 (%)
From Federal Government	12,614	25.51	0.8
From State Governments	244,750	494.98	15.0
From Local Governments	779	1.58	0.0
Property Taxes	263,324	532.55	16.1
General Sales Taxes	145,263	293.78	8.9
Selective Sales Taxes	27,793	56.21	1.7
Income Taxes	0	0.00	0.0
Current Charges	135,850	274.74	8.3
Utility/Liquor Store	604,657	1,222.86	37.0
Employee Retirement[1]	42,154	85.25	2.6
Other	159,067	321.70	9.7

Note: (1) Excludes "city contributions," classified as "nonrevenue," intragovernmental transfers.
Source: U.S. Bureau of the Census, City Government Finances: 1991-92

City Government Expenditures by Function

Function	FY92 ($000)	FY92 (per capita $)	FY92 (%)
Educational Services	280,035	566.34	18.4
Employee Retirement[1]	39,648	80.18	2.6
Environment/Housing	114,342	231.25	7.5
Government Administration	44,535	90.07	2.9
Interest on General Debt	115,288	233.16	7.6
Public Safety	137,297	277.67	9.0
Social Services	91,165	184.37	6.0
Transportation	35,672	72.14	2.3
Utility/Liquor Store	628,504	1,271.09	41.2
Other	38,624	78.11	2.5

Note: (1) Payments to beneficiaries including withdrawal of contributions.
Source: U.S. Bureau of the Census, City Government Finances: 1991-92

Municipal Bond Ratings

Area	Moody's	S & P
Nashville	n/a	n/a

Note: n/a not available; n/r not rated
Source: Moody's Bond Record, 6/99

POPULATION

Population Growth

Area	1980	1990	% Chg. 1980-90	July 1998 Estimate	% Chg. 1990-98
City	455,663	488,518	7.2	510,274	4.5
MSA[1]	850,505	985,026	15.8	1,161,228	17.9
U.S.	226,545,805	248,765,170	9.8	270,299,000	8.7

Note: (1) Metropolitan Statistical Area - see Appendix A for areas included;
July 1998 MSA population estimate was calculated by the editors
Source: 1980/1990 Census of Housing and Population, Summary Tape File 3C;
Census Bureau Population Estimates 1998

Population Characteristics

Race	City 1980 Population	%	City 1990 Population	%	% Chg. 1980-90	MSA[1] 1990 Population	%
White	345,766	75.9	360,795	73.9	4.3	818,848	83.1
Black	105,869	23.2	118,802	24.3	12.2	152,302	15.5
Amer Indian/Esk/Aleut	743	0.2	1,439	0.3	93.7	2,663	0.3
Asian/Pacific Islander	2,418	0.5	6,220	1.3	157.2	9,349	0.9
Other	867	0.2	1,262	0.3	45.6	1,864	0.2
Hispanic Origin[2]	3,627	0.8	4,131	0.8	13.9	7,250	0.7

Note: (1) Metropolitan Statistical Area - see Appendix A for areas included;
(2) people of Hispanic origin can be of any race
Source: 1980/1990 Census of Housing and Population, Summary Tape File 3C

Ancestry

Area	German	Irish	English	Italian	U.S.	French	Polish	Dutch
City	14.9	16.5	15.2	1.9	9.3	3.0	0.9	1.9
MSA[1]	16.2	18.3	16.5	1.9	11.9	3.0	0.9	2.2
U.S.	23.3	15.6	13.1	5.9	5.3	4.2	3.8	2.5

Note: Figures are percentages and include persons that reported multiple ancestry (eg. if a person
reported being Irish and Italian, they were included in both columns); (1) Metropolitan Statistical Area -
see Appendix A for areas included
Source: 1990 Census of Population and Housing, Summary Tape File 3C

Age

Area	Median Age (Years)	Age Distribution (%) Under 5	Under 18	18-24	25-44	45-64	65+	80+
City	32.2	7.0	22.9	11.6	36.2	17.9	11.4	2.6
MSA[1]	32.4	7.1	25.1	10.7	35.0	18.5	10.6	2.3
U.S.	32.9	7.3	25.6	10.5	32.6	18.7	12.5	2.8

Note: (1) Metropolitan Statistical Area - see Appendix A for areas included
Source: 1990 Census of Population and Housing, Summary Tape File 3C

Male/Female Ratio

Area	Number of males per 100 females (all ages)	Number of males per 100 females (18 years old+)
City	90.2	86.5
MSA[1]	93.2	89.5
U.S.	95.0	91.9

Note: (1) Metropolitan Statistical Area - see Appendix A for areas included
Source: 1990 Census of Population, General Population Characteristics

INCOME

Per Capita/Median/Average Income

Area	Per Capita ($)	Median Household ($)	Average Household ($)
City	14,490	27,821	35,188
MSA[1]	14,567	30,223	37,811
U.S.	14,420	30,056	38,453

Note: All figures are for 1989; (1) Metropolitan Statistical Area - see Appendix A for areas included
Source: 1990 Census of Population and Housing, Summary Tape File 3C

Household Income Distribution by Race

Income ($)	City (%)					U.S. (%)				
	Total	White	Black	Other	Hisp.[1]	Total	White	Black	Other	Hisp.[1]
Less than 5,000	7.6	4.8	17.9	8.2	3.2	6.2	4.8	15.2	8.6	8.8
5,000 - 9,999	8.3	7.2	12.1	8.9	7.1	9.3	8.6	14.2	9.9	11.1
10,000 - 14,999	9.0	8.2	11.7	9.2	8.6	8.8	8.5	11.0	9.8	11.0
15,000 - 24,999	19.6	19.4	20.4	18.7	23.3	17.5	17.3	18.9	18.5	20.5
25,000 - 34,999	17.3	18.1	14.3	21.9	21.6	15.8	16.1	14.2	15.4	16.4
35,000 - 49,999	17.9	19.5	12.3	17.0	17.6	17.9	18.6	13.3	16.1	16.0
50,000 - 74,999	13.5	14.9	8.6	11.2	14.3	15.0	15.8	9.3	13.4	11.1
75,000 - 99,999	3.7	4.2	2.0	2.7	2.5	5.1	5.5	2.6	4.7	3.1
100,000+	3.1	3.8	0.7	2.1	1.8	4.4	4.8	1.3	3.7	1.9

Note: All figures are for 1989; (1) people of Hispanic origin can be of any race
Source: 1990 Census of Population and Housing, Summary Tape File 3C

Effective Buying Income

Area	Per Capita ($)	Median Household ($)	Average Household ($)
City	19,588	37,587	47,297
MSA[1]	20,167	39,453	52,094
U.S.	16,803	34,536	45,243

Note: Data as of 1/1/99; (1) Metropolitan Statistical Area - see Appendix A for areas included
Source: Standard Rate & Data Service, Newspaper Advertising Source, 9/99

Effective Household Buying Income Distribution

Area	% of Households Earning						
	$10,000 -$19,999	$20,000 -$34,999	$35,000 -$49,999	$50,000 -$74,999	$75,000 -$99,000	$100,000 -$124,999	$125,000 and up
City	13.4	22.1	18.3	20.1	8.7	3.0	3.3
MSA[1]	13.0	20.9	18.6	21.1	9.1	3.2	3.7
U.S.	16.0	22.6	18.2	18.9	7.2	2.4	2.7

Note: Data as of 1/1/99; (1) Metropolitan Statistical Area - see Appendix A for areas included
Source: Standard Rate & Data Service, Newspaper Advertising Source, 9/99

Poverty Rates by Race and Age

Area	Total (%)	By Race (%)				By Age (%)		
		White	Black	Other	Hisp.[2]	Under 5 years old	Under 18 years old	65 years and over
City	13.4	8.6	27.9	18.1	14.3	22.5	20.4	15.1
MSA[1]	11.3	8.4	27.2	16.1	12.1	17.1	15.0	16.6
U.S.	13.1	9.8	29.5	23.1	25.3	20.1	18.3	12.8

Note: Figures show the percent of people living below the poverty line in 1989. The average poverty threshold was $12,674 for a family of four in 1989; (1) Metropolitan Statistical Area - see Appendix A for areas included; (2) people of Hispanic origin can be of any race
Source: 1990 Census of Population and Housing, Summary Tape File 3C

EMPLOYMENT

Labor Force and Employment

Area	Civilian Labor Force			Workers Employed		
	Jun. 1998	Jun. 1999	% Chg.	Jun. 1998	Jun. 1999	% Chg.
City	309,438	317,633	2.6	300,617	309,512	3.0
MSA[1]	647,559	662,228	2.3	627,615	646,186	3.0
U.S.	138,798,000	140,666,000	1.3	132,265,000	134,395,000	1.6

Note: Data is not seasonally adjusted and covers workers 16 years of age and older;
(1) Metropolitan Statistical Area - see Appendix A for areas included
Source: Bureau of Labor Statistics, http://stats.bls.gov

Unemployment Rate

Area	1998						1999					
	Jul.	Aug.	Sep.	Oct.	Nov.	Dec.	Jan.	Feb.	Mar.	Apr.	May.	Jun.
City	2.4	2.5	2.5	2.6	2.6	2.1	2.7	2.6	2.7	2.6	2.4	2.6
MSA[1]	2.7	2.8	2.6	2.7	2.6	2.1	2.9	2.8	2.7	2.6	2.3	2.4
U.S.	4.7	4.5	4.4	4.2	4.1	4.0	4.8	4.7	4.4	4.1	4.0	4.5

Note: Data is not seasonally adjusted and covers workers 16 years of age and older; all figures are percentages; (1) Metropolitan Statistical Area - see Appendix A for areas included
Source: Bureau of Labor Statistics, http://stats.bls.gov

Employment by Industry

Sector	MSA[1]		U.S.
	Number of Employees	Percent of Total	Percent of Total
Services	209,600	31.8	30.4
Retail Trade	122,600	18.6	17.7
Government	82,200	12.5	15.6
Manufacturing	95,600	14.5	14.3
Finance/Insurance/Real Estate	42,600	6.5	5.9
Wholesale Trade	39,000	5.9	5.4
Transportation/Public Utilities	33,000	5.0	5.3
Construction	n/a	n/a	5.0
Mining	n/a	n/a	0.4

Note: Figures cover non-farm employment as of 6/99 and are not seasonally adjusted; (1) Metropolitan Statistical Area - see Appendix A for areas included; n/a not available
Source: Bureau of Labor Statistics, http://stats.bls.gov

Employment by Occupation

Occupation Category	City (%)	MSA[1] (%)	U.S. (%)
White Collar	64.7	60.9	58.1
Executive/Admin./Management	13.5	13.1	12.3
Professional	15.4	13.7	14.1
Technical & Related Support	4.0	3.6	3.7
Sales	13.3	13.3	11.8
Administrative Support/Clerical	18.5	17.1	16.3
Blue Collar	20.8	25.5	26.2
Precision Production/Craft/Repair	8.7	10.8	11.3
Machine Operators/Assem./Insp.	5.0	6.7	6.8
Transportation/Material Movers	3.7	4.1	4.1
Cleaners/Helpers/Laborers	3.5	3.9	3.9
Services	13.6	12.1	13.2
Farming/Forestry/Fishing	0.8	1.5	2.5

Note: Figures cover employed persons 16 years old and over; (1) Metropolitan Statistical Area - see Appendix A for areas included
Source: 1990 Census of Population and Housing, Summary Tape File 3C

Occupational Employment Projections: 1996 - 2006

Occupations Expected to Have the Largest Job Growth (ranked by numerical growth)	Fast-Growing Occupations[1] (ranked by percent growth)
1. Salespersons, retail	1. Personal and home care aides
2. Truck drivers, light	2. Systems analysts
3. Cashiers	3. Paralegals
4. General managers & top executives	4. Respiratory therapists
5. Janitors/cleaners/maids, ex. priv. hshld.	5. Home health aides
6. Food service workers	6. Directors, religious activities & educ.
7. Child care workers, private household	7. Computer engineers
8. Cooks, fast food and short order	8. Child care workers, private household
9. Registered nurses	9. Corrections officers & jailers
10. Waiters & waitresses	10. Emergency medical technicians

Note: Projections cover Tennessee; (1) Excludes occupations with total job growth less than 300
Source: U.S. Department of Labor, Employment and Training Administration, America's Labor Market Information System (ALMIS)

TAXES

Major State and Local Tax Rates

State Corp. Income (%)	State Personal Income (%)	Residential Property (effective rate per $100)	Sales & Use		State Gasoline (cents/ gallon)	State Cigarette (cents/ pack)
			State (%)	Local (%)		
6.0	6.0[a]	n/a	6.0	2.25	21.0[b]	13.0[c]

Note: Personal/corporate income, sales, gasoline and cigarette tax rates as of January 1999.
Property tax rates as of 1997; (a) Applies to interest and dividend income only; (b) Rate is comprised of 20 cents excise and 1 cent motor carrier tax. Does not include a 1 cent local option tax; (c) Counties and cities may impose an additional tax of 1 cent per pack. Dealers pay a additional enforcement and admin. fee of 0.05 cent per pack
Source: Federation of Tax Administrators, www.taxadmin.org; Washington D.C. Department of Finance and Revenue, Tax Rates and Tax Burdens in the District of Columbia: A Nationwide Comparison, July 1998; Chamber of Commerce, 1999

Total Taxes Per Capita and as a Percent of Income

Area	Per Capita Income ($)	Per Capita Taxes ($)			Percent of Income (%)		
		Total	Federal	State/ Local	Total	Federal	State/ Local
Tennessee	24,591	8,048	5,930	2,118	32.7	24.1	8.6
U.S.	27,876	9,881	6,690	3,191	35.4	24.0	11.4

Note: Figures are for 1998
Source: Tax Foundation, www.taxfoundation.org

Estimated Tax Burden

Area	State Income	Local Income	Property	Sales	Total
Nashville	0	0	2,250	1,233	3,483

Note: The numbers are estimates of taxes paid by a married couple with two children and annual earnings of $75,000. Sales tax estimates assume they spend average amounts on food, clothing, household goods and gasoline. Property tax estimates assume they live in a $250,000 home.
Source: Kiplinger's Personal Finance Magazine, October 1998

**COMMERCIAL
REAL ESTATE**

Office Market

Class/ Location	Total Space (sq. ft.)	Vacant Space (sq. ft.)	Vac. Rate (%)	Under Constr. (sq. ft.)	Net Absorp. (sq. ft.)	Rental Rates ($/sq.ft./yr.)
Class A						
CBD	2,853,680	221,147	7.7	225,000	-7,440	16.00-20.00
Outside CBD	7,262,695	361,284	5.0	2,094,362	434,236	18.00-24.00
Class B						
CBD	1,607,042	172,075	10.7	n/a	51,738	11.00-16.00
Outside CBD	3,677,658	241,023	6.6	n/a	64,854	14.00-18.00

Note: Data as of 10/98 and covers Nashville; CBD = Central Business District; n/a not available;
Source: Society of Industrial and Office Realtors, 1999 Comparative Statistics of Industrial and Office Real Estate Markets

"Brentwood/Cool Springs experienced 39 percent of total area construction during 1998. This trend is expected to persist in 1999. Thirty-three percent of the currently proposed office space is in this sub-market. Within the airport sub-market there are proposals to increase Lakeview Plaza with a third phase of construction, and Gaedeke Landers' 285,000 sq. ft. building is expected to come to market during the summer. Our SIOR correspondent forecasts no change in sales prices for existing structures in both Class A and Class B space in all locations. With the potential for corporate downsizing and the entry of new space to the market, vacancies may increase slightly." *Society of Industrial and Office Realtors, 1999 Comparative Statistics of Industrial and Office Real Estate Markets*

Industrial Market

Location	Total Space (sq. ft.)	Vacant Space (sq. ft.)	Vac. Rate (%)	Under Constr. (sq. ft.)	Net Absorp. (sq. ft.)	Gross Lease ($/sq.ft./yr.)
Central City	9,000,000	427,000	4.7	0	-185,000	3.20-4.75
Suburban	171,177,000	5,050,000	3.0	730,000	1,369,000	2.85-4.25

Note: Data as of 10/98 and covers Nashville; n/a not available
Source: Society of Industrial and Office Realtors, 1999 Comparative Statistics of Industrial and Office Real Estate Markets

"Many of the 1998 projects that were placed on hold will break ground in 1999. Labor constraints will be the biggest challenge facing the Nashville market. This constraint is one of the factors that led our local SIOR reporter to predict steady growth for the market as opposed to 'boom-like' growth. With several users having moved into their own space in 1998, it is predicted that many of the larger spaces will need the year to lease out. This situation may postpone some new development. The strong trend of rapid leasing will help to absorb existing space. Vacancies in the suburban markets are expected to remain low. Our reporter forecasts reductions in the total amount of construction in warehouse and distribution space. This will be coupled with increases in the construction of High-Tech/R&D space." *Society of Industrial and Office Realtors, 1999 Comparative Statistics of Industrial and Office Real Estate Markets*

Retail Market

Shopping Center Inventory (sq. ft.)	Shopping Center Construction (sq. ft.)	Construction as a Percent of Inventory (%)	Torto Wheaton Rent Index[1] ($/sq. ft.)
23,502,000	2,000	0.0	12.56

Note: Data as of 1997 and covers the Metropolitan Statistical Area - see Appendix A for areas included; (1) Index is based on a model that predicts what the average rent should be for leases with certain characteristics, in certain locations during certain years.
Source: National Association of Realtors, 1997-1998 Market Conditions Report

"After experiencing vigorous growth in 1994, 1995 and 1996, Nashville's economy has slowed somewhat to a more sustainable pace. However, the area's retail market continues to surge behind a burgeoning tourism industry that contributes an estimated $8 billion to the state's economy and strong personal income growth. The number of shopping center completions slowed in 1997, which allowed the retail rent index to increase 8.1%. Big-box retailers have accounted for a large portion of demand, which is expected to continue at a robust pace in the near future. Nashville's retail rent index is expected to climb to near $15.00 per square foot by 2000." *National Association of Realtors, 1997-1998 Market Conditions Report*

COMMERCIAL UTILITIES

Typical Monthly Electric Bills

Area	Commercial Service ($/month)		Industrial Service ($/month)	
	12 kW demand 1,500 kWh	100 kW demand 30,000 kWh	1,000 kW demand 400,000 kWh	20,000 kW demand 10,000,000 kWh
City	n/a	n/a	n/a	n/a
U.S.	150	2,174	23,995	508,569

Note: Based on rates in effect January 1, 1999; n/a not available
Source: Edison Electric Institute, Typical Residential, Commercial and Industrial Bills, Winter 1999

TRANSPORTATION

Transportation Statistics

Average minutes to work	20.3
Interstate highways	I-24; I-40; I-65
Bus lines	
In-city	Metropolitan TA, 170 vehicles
Inter-city	2
Passenger air service	
Airport	Nashville International
Airlines	8
Aircraft departures	47,770 (1996)
Enplaned passengers	3,254,956 (1996)
Rail service	Amtrak Thruway Motorcoach Connections
Motor freight carriers	140+
Major waterways/ports	Cumberland River; Port of Nashville

Source: Editor & Publisher Market Guide, 1999; FAA Airport Activity Statistics, 1997; Amtrak National Time Table, Northeast Timetable, Spring/Summer 1999; 1990 Census of Population and Housing, STF 3C; Chamber of Commerce/Economic Development 1999; Jane's Urban Transport Systems 1999-2000

Means of Transportation to Work

Area	Car/Truck/Van		Public Transportation			Bicycle	Walked	Other Means	Worked at Home
	Drove Alone	Car-pooled	Bus	Subway	Railroad				
City	78.1	13.4	2.8	0.0	0.0	0.1	2.6	0.8	2.2
MSA[1]	79.1	13.8	1.6	0.0	0.0	0.1	1.9	0.9	2.6
U.S.	73.2	13.4	3.0	1.5	0.5	0.4	3.9	1.2	3.0

Note: Figures shown are percentages and only include workers 16 years old and over;
(1) Metropolitan Statistical Area - see Appendix A for areas included
Source: 1990 Census of Population and Housing, Summary Tape File 3C

BUSINESSES

Major Business Headquarters

Company Name	1999 Rankings	
	Fortune 500	Forbes 500
Columbia/HCA Healthcare	74	-
Dollar General	459	-
Ingram Industries	-	90

Note: Companies listed are located in the city; dashes indicate no ranking
Fortune 500: Companies that produce a 10-K are ranked 1 to 500 based on 1998 revenue
Forbes 500: Private companies are ranked 1 to 500 based on 1997 revenue
Source: Forbes, November 30, 1998; Fortune, April 26, 1999

Fast-Growing Businesses

According to *Fortune*, Nashville is home to one of America's 100 fastest-growing companies: Renal Care Group. Companies were ranked based on earnings-per-share growth, revenue growth and total return over the previous three years. Criteria for inclusion: public companies with sales of least $50 million. Companies that lost money in the most recent quarter, or ended in the red for the past four quarters as a whole, were not eligible. Limited partnerships and REITs were also not considered. *Fortune, "America's Fastest-Growing Companies," 1999*

Women-Owned Firms: Number, Employment and Sales

Area	Number of Firms	Employ- ment	Sales ($000)	Rank[2]
MSA[1]	42,700	139,300	17,323,700	41

Note: (1) Metropolitan Statistical Area - see Appendix A for areas included;
(2) Calculated on an averaging of the number of businesses, employment and sales
Source: The National Foundation for Women Business Owners, 1999 Facts on Women-Owned Businesses: Trends in the Top 50 Metropolitan Areas

Women-Owned Firms: Growth

Area	% change from 1992 to 1999			Rank[2]
	Number of Firms	Employ- ment	Sales	
MSA[1]	48.0	155.3	169.2	5

Note: (1) Metropolitan Statistical Area - see Appendix A for areas included; (2) Calculated on an averaging of the percent growth of number of businesses, employment and sales
Source: The National Foundation for Women Business Owners, 1999 Facts on Women-Owned Businesses: Trends in the Top 50 Metropolitan Areas

Small Business Opportunity

According to *Forbes*, Nashville is home to two of America's 200 best small companies: Central Parking and Renal Care Group. Criteria: companies included must be publicly traded since November 1997 with a stock price of at least $5 per share and an average daily float of 1,000 shares. The company's latest 12-month sales must be between $5 and $350 million, return on equity (ROE) must be a minimum of 12% for both the past 5 years and the most recent four quarters, and five-year sales and EPS growth must average at least 10%. Companies with declining sales or earnings during the past year were dropped as well as businesses with debt/equity ratios over 1.25. Companies with negative operating cash flow in each of the past two years were also excluded. Forbes, November 2, 1998

HOTELS & MOTELS

Hotels/Motels

Area	Hotels/ Motels	Rooms	Luxury-Level Hotels/Motels		Average Minimum Rates ($)		
			♦♦♦♦	♦♦♦♦♦	♦♦	♦♦♦	♦♦♦♦
City	68	12,136	1	0	62	107	164
Airport	28	4,976	0	0	n/a	n/a	n/a
Suburbs	34	3,351	0	0	n/a	n/a	n/a
Total	130	20,463	1	0	n/a	n/a	n/a

Note: n/a not available; classifications range from one diamond (budget properties with basic amenities) to five diamond (luxury properties with the finest service, rooms and facilities).
Source: OAG, Business Travel Planner, Winter 1998-99

CONVENTION CENTERS

Major Convention Centers

Center Name	Meeting Rooms	Exhibit Space (sq. ft.)
Holiday Inn Crowne Plaza	15	15,748
Nashville Convention Center	36	118,675
Nashville Municipal Auditorium	4	63,000
Opryland Hotel Convention Center	74	500,000
Stouffer Nashville Hotel	14	25,054
Tennessee State Fairgrounds	n/a	243,014
Willis Corroon Confernce Center	17	n/a

Note: n/a not available
Source: Trade Shows Worldwide, 1998; Meetings & Conventions, 4/15/99;
Sucessful Meetings, 3/31/98

Living Environment

COST OF LIVING

Cost of Living Index

Composite Index	Groceries	Housing	Utilities	Trans-portation	Health Care	Misc. Goods/ Services
96.1	96.5	94.4	93.9	99.8	89.1	97.8

Note: U.S. = 100
Source: ACCRA, Cost of Living Index, 1st Quarter 1999

HOUSING

Median Home Prices and Housing Affordability

Area	Median Price[2] 1st Qtr. 1999 ($)	HOI[3] 1st Qtr. 1999	Afford-ability Rank[4]
MSA[1]	116,000	84.0	26
U.S.	134,000	69.6	–

Note: (1) Metropolitan Statistical Area - see Appendix A for areas included; (2) U.S. figures calculated from the sales of 524,324 new and existing homes in 181 markets; (3) Housing Opportunity Index - percent of homes sold that were within the reach of the median income household at the prevailing mortgage interest rate; (4) Rank is from 1-181 with 1 being most affordable
Source: National Association of Home Builders, Housing Opportunity Index, 1st Quarter 1999

Median Home Price Projection

It is projected that the median price of existing single-family homes in the metro area will increase by 3.0% in 1999. Nationwide, home prices are projected to increase 3.8%.
Kiplinger's Personal Finance Magazine, January 1999

Average New Home Price

Area	Price ($)
City	131,550
U.S.	142,735

Note: Figures are based on a new home with 1,800 sq. ft. of living area on an 8,000 sq. ft. lot.
Source: ACCRA, Cost of Living Index, 1st Quarter 1999

Average Apartment Rent

Area	Rent ($/mth)
City	625
U.S.	601

Note: Figures are based on an unfurnished two bedroom, 1-1/2 or 2 bath apartment, approximately 950 sq. ft. in size, excluding all utilities except water
Source: ACCRA, Cost of Living Index, 1st Quarter 1999

RESIDENTIAL UTILITIES

Average Residential Utility Costs

Area	All Electric ($/mth)	Part Electric ($/mth)	Other Energy ($/mth)	Phone ($/mth)
City	–	47.23	47.35	16.85
U.S.	100.02	55.73	43.33	19.71

Source: ACCRA, Cost of Living Index, 1st Quarter 1999

HEALTH CARE

Average Health Care Costs

Area	Hospital ($/day)	Doctor ($/visit)	Dentist ($/visit)
City	275.60	53.14	57.40
U.S.	430.43	52.45	66.35

Note: Hospital—based on a semi-private room; Doctor—based on a general practitioner's routine exam of an established patient; Dentist—based on adult teeth cleaning and periodic oral exam.
Source: ACCRA, Cost of Living Index, 1st Quarter 1999

Distribution of Office-Based Physicians

Area	Family/Gen. Practitioners	Specialists		
		Medical	Surgical	Other
MSA[1]	205	893	721	744

Note: Data as of 12/31/97; (1) Metropolitan Statistical Area - see Appendix A for areas included
Source: American Medical Assn., Physician Characteristics & Distribution in the U.S., 1999

Hospitals

Nashville has 7 general medical and surgical hospitals, 2 psychiatric, 1 rehabilitation, 1 chronic disease. *AHA Guide to the Healthcare Field, 1998-99*

According to *U.S. News and World Report,* Nashville has 2 of the best hospitals in the U.S.: **Vanderbilt University Hospital and Clinic**, noted for cancer, cardiology, endocrinology, gastroenterology, gynecology, orthopedics, otolaryngology, pulmonology, urology; **St. Thomas Hospital**, noted for cardiology, endocrinology, urology. *U.S. News Online, "America's Best Hospitals," 10th Edition, www.usnews.com*

EDUCATION

Public School District Statistics

District Name	Num. Sch.	Enroll.	Classroom Teachers	Pupils per Teacher	Minority Pupils (%)	Current Exp.[1] ($/pupil)
Nashville-Davidson County SD	124	67,558	n/a	n/a	48.0	5,078

Note: Data covers the 1997-1998 school year unless otherwise noted; (1) Data covers fiscal year 1996; SD = School District; ISD = Independent School District; n/a not available
Source: National Center for Education Statistics, Common Core of Data Public Education Agency Universe 1997-98; National Center for Education Statistics, Characteristics of the 100 Largest Public Elementary and Secondary School Districts in the United States: 1997-98, July 1999

Educational Quality

School District	Education Quotient[1]	Graduate Outcome[2]	Community Index[3]	Resource Index[4]
Nashville-Davidson Co.	109.0	112.0	106.0	104.0

Note: Nearly 1,000 secondary school districts were rated in terms of educational quality. The scores range from a low of 50 to a high of 150; (1) Average of the Graduate Outcome, Community and Resource indexes; (2) Based on graduation rates and college board scores (SAT/ACT); (3) Based on the surrounding community's average level of education and the area's average income level; (4) Based on teacher salaries, per-pupil expenditures and student-teacher ratios.
Source: Expansion Management, Ratings Issue, 1998

Educational Attainment by Race

Area	High School Graduate (%)					Bachelor's Degree (%)				
	Total	White	Black	Other	Hisp.[2]	Total	White	Black	Other	Hisp.[2]
City	75.4	77.7	66.7	73.8	73.5	23.6	25.4	16.6	32.3	24.7
MSA[1]	74.0	75.6	64.4	75.2	74.2	21.4	22.3	15.1	31.2	23.4
U.S.	75.2	77.9	63.1	60.4	49.8	20.3	21.5	11.4	19.4	9.2

Note: Figures shown cover persons 25 years old and over; (1) Metropolitan Statistical Area - see Appendix A for areas included; (2) people of Hispanic origin can be of any race
Source: 1990 Census of Population and Housing, Summary Tape File 3C

School Enrollment by Type

Area	Preprimary				Elementary/High School			
	Public		Private		Public		Private	
	Enrollment	%	Enrollment	%	Enrollment	%	Enrollment	%
City	3,671	51.4	3,472	48.6	61,254	84.7	11,083	15.3
MSA[1]	9,119	56.1	7,129	43.9	143,901	88.2	19,299	11.8
U.S.	2,679,029	59.5	1,824,256	40.5	38,379,689	90.2	4,187,099	9.8

Note: Figures shown cover persons 3 years old and over;
(1) Metropolitan Statistical Area - see Appendix A for areas included
Source: 1990 Census of Population and Housing, Summary Tape File 3C

School Enrollment by Race

Area	Preprimary (%)				Elementary/High School (%)			
	White	Black	Other	Hisp.[1]	White	Black	Other	Hisp.[1]
City	73.3	24.3	2.4	0.8	63.8	34.0	2.2	1.1
MSA[2]	83.9	14.4	1.7	1.0	79.0	19.3	1.7	1.0
U.S.	80.4	12.5	7.1	7.8	74.1	15.6	10.3	12.5

Note: Figures shown cover persons 3 years old and over; (1) people of Hispanic origin can be of any race; (2) Metropolitan Statistical Area - see Appendix A for areas included
Source: 1990 Census of Population and Housing, Summary Tape File 3C

Classroom Teacher Salaries in Public Schools

District	B.A. Degree		M.A. Degree		Maximum	
	Min. ($)	Rank[1]	Max. ($)	Rank[1]	Max. ($)	Rank[1]
Nashville	24,720	69	42,580	74	50,429	51
Average	26,980	-	46,065	-	51,435	-

Note: Salaries are for 1997-1998; (1) Rank ranges from 1 to 100
Source: American Federation of Teachers, Survey & Analysis of Salary Trends, 1998

Higher Education

Two-Year Colleges		Four-Year Colleges		Medical Schools	Law Schools	Voc/ Tech
Public	Private	Public	Private			
1	6	1	9	2	2	13

Source: College Blue Book, Occupational Education, 1997; Medical School Admission Requirements, 1999-2000; Peterson's Guide to Two-Year Colleges, 1999; Peterson's Guide to Four-Year Colleges, 2000; Barron's Guide to Law Schools, 1999

MAJOR EMPLOYERS

Major Employers

AGC Life Insurance
Baptist Hospital
Gaylord Entertainment
Columbia/HCA Information Services
American General Life & Accident

Aladdin Manufacturing
Columbia Healthcare of Central Virginia
Intermedia Management (electrical work)
SunTrust Bank of Tennessee
Willis Corroon Corp. (insurance)

Note: Companies listed are located in the city
Source: Dun's Business Rankings, 1999; Ward's Business Directory, 1998

PUBLIC SAFETY

Crime Rate

Area	All Crimes	Violent Crimes				Property Crimes		
		Murder	Forcible Rape	Robbery	Aggrav. Assault	Burglary	Larceny -Theft	Motor Vehicle Theft
City	11,091.4	21.1	103.4	485.6	1,136.7	1,660.8	6,147.3	1,536.5
Suburbs[1]	4,214.3	3.8	37.2	65.6	369.4	822.6	2,625.2	290.5
MSA[2]	7,510.3	12.1	68.9	266.9	737.1	1,224.3	4,313.2	887.7
U.S.	4,922.7	6.8	35.9	186.1	382.0	919.6	2,886.5	505.8

Note: Crime rate is the number of crimes per 100,000 pop.; (1) defined as all areas within the MSA but located outside the central city; (2) Metropolitan Statistical Area - see Appendix A for areas incl.
Source: FBI Uniform Crime Reports, 1997

RECREATION

Culture and Recreation

Museums	Symphony Orchestras	Opera Companies	Dance Companies	Professional Theatres	Zoos	Pro Sports Teams
12	2	1	2	3	0	1

Source: International Directory of the Performing Arts, 1997; Official Museum Directory, 1999; Stern's Performing Arts Directory, 1997; USA Today Four Sport Stadium Guide, 1997; Chamber of Commerce/Economic Development, 1999

Library System

The Public Library of Nashville & Davidson County has 18 branches, holdings of 781,800 volumes, and a budget of $12,051,260 (1996-1997). *American Library Directory, 1998-1999*

MEDIA

Newspapers

Name	Type	Freq.	Distribution	Circulation
Belle Meade News	General	1x/wk	Local	23,487
Green Hills News	General	1x/wk	Local	23,487
Nashville Scene	General	1x/wk	Area	153,000
Nashville Today	General	1x/wk	Local	23,487
Observer	Religious	23x/yr	Area	3,200
The Tennessean	General	7x/wk	Area	148,000
West Meade News	General	1x/wk	Local	20,000
West Side News	General	1x/wk	Local	23,487

Note: Includes newspapers with circulations of 1,000 or more located in the city;
Source: Burrelle's Media Directory, 1999 Edition

Television Stations

Name	Ch.	Affiliation	Type	Owner
WKRN	n/a	ABCT	Commercial	Young Broadcasting Inc.
WSMV	n/a	NBCT	Commercial	Meredith Corporation
WTVF	n/a	CBST	Commercial	Landmark Television of Tennessee Inc.
WDCN	n/a	PBS	Public	Metro Board of Public Education
WZTV	17	FBC	Commercial	Sinclair Communications Inc.
WUXP	30	UPN	Commercial	Sinclair Communications Inc.
WHTN	39	n/a	Commercial	Christian Television Network
WNAB	58	WB	n/a	Speer Communications Holding Company

Note: Stations included broadcast in the Nashville metro area; n/a not available
Source: Burrelle's Media Directory, 1999 Edition

AM Radio Stations

Call Letters	Freq. (kHz)	Target Audience	Station Format	Music Format
WSM	650	General	M/N/S	Country
WENO	760	Religious	M/T	Christian
WMDB	880	Z/G	M/N	Adult Contemp./Christian/Jazz/R&B/Urban Contemp.
WYFN	980	General	M	Christian
WAMB	1160	Hispanic	M/N/S	Big Band/Easy Listening/Jazz/MOR
WKDA	1240	General	N/T	n/a
WNQM	1300	H/R	M/N/T	Christian/Latin
WNAH	1360	General	M	Christian
WVOL	1470	General	M	Classic Rock/Oldies
WLAC	1510	General	N/T	n/a

Note: Stations included broadcast in the Nashville metro area; n/a not available
Target Audience: A=Asian; B=Black; C=Christian; E=Ethnic; F=French; G=General; H=Hispanic;
M=Men; N=Native American; R=Religious; S=Senior Citizen; W=Women; Y=Young Adult; Z=Children
Station Format: E=Educational; M=Music; N=News; S=Sports; T=Talk
Music Format: AOR=Album Oriented Rock; MOR=Middle-of-the-Road
Source: Burrelle's Media Directory, 1999 Edition

FM Radio Stations

Call Letters	Freq. (mHz)	Target Audience	Station Format	Music Format
WFSK	88.1	B/G/R	E/M/N/T	Blues/Gospel/Jazz/Latin/Oldies/Reggae/R&B/ Urban Contemporary/World Music
WNAZ	89.1	Religious	M	Christian
WPLN	90.3	General	M/N	Classical
WRVU	91.1	General	M/N/S	AOR/Big Band/Jazz/R&B/Urban Contemporary
WHRS	91.7	General	M	Classical
WQQK	92.1	General	M	n/a
WJXA	92.9	General	M/N	Adult Contemporary
WYYB	93.7	General	M/N/S	Alternative
WRLG	94.1	General	M	Alternative
WSM	95.5	General	M/N/S	Country
WRMX	96.3	General	M/N	Oldies
WSIX	97.9	General	M	Country
WAMB	98.7	General	M/N/S	Adult Standards/Easy Listening/Jazz/Latin
WWTN	99.7	General	N/S/T	n/a
WRLT	100.1	General	M	Alternative/Jazz
WJZC	101.1	General	M	Jazz
WQZQ	102.5	General	M	Adult Contemporary/Top 40
WZPC	102.9	General	M/N/T	Alternative
WKDF	103.3	Alternative	M/N/S	Country
WGFX	104.5	General	M/N/S/T	Classic Rock
WVRY	105.1	General	M/N/S	Christian
WNRQ	105.9	General	M	Classic Rock
WNPL	106.7	General	n/a	n/a
WRVW	107.5	General	M	n/a

Note: Stations included broadcast in the Nashville metro area; n/a not available
Station Format: E=Educational; M=Music; N=News; S=Sports; T=Talk
Target Audience: A=Asian; B=Black; C=Christian; E=Ethnic; F=French; G=General; H=Hispanic;
M=Men; N=Native American; R=Religious; S=Senior Citizen; W=Women; Y=Young Adult; Z=Children
Music Format: AOR=Album Oriented Rock; MOR=Middle-of-the-Road
Source: Burrelle's Media Directory, 1999 Edition

CLIMATE

Average and Extreme Temperatures

Temperature	Jan	Feb	Mar	Apr	May	Jun	Jul	Aug	Sep	Oct	Nov	Dec	Yr.
Extreme High (°F)	78	84	86	91	95	106	107	104	105	94	84	79	107
Average High (°F)	47	51	60	71	79	87	90	89	83	72	60	50	70
Average Temp. (°F)	38	41	50	60	68	76	80	79	72	61	49	41	60
Average Low (°F)	28	31	39	48	57	65	69	68	61	48	39	31	49
Extreme Low (°F)	-17	-13	2	23	34	42	54	49	36	26	-1	-10	-17

Note: Figures cover the years 1948-1990
Source: National Climatic Data Center, International Station Meteorological Climate Summary, 3/95

Average Precipitation/Snowfall/Humidity

Precip./Humidity	Jan	Feb	Mar	Apr	May	Jun	Jul	Aug	Sep	Oct	Nov	Dec	Yr.
Avg. Precip. (in.)	4.4	4.2	5.0	4.1	4.6	3.7	3.8	3.3	3.2	2.6	3.9	4.6	47.4
Avg. Snowfall (in.)	4	3	1	Tr	0	0	0	0	0	Tr	1	1	11
Avg. Rel. Hum. 6am (%)	81	81	80	81	86	86	88	90	90	87	83	82	85
Avg. Rel. Hum. 3pm (%)	61	57	51	48	52	52	54	53	52	49	55	59	54

Note: Figures cover the years 1948-1990; Tr = Trace amounts (<0.05 in. of rain; <0.5 in. of snow)
Source: National Climatic Data Center, International Station Meteorological Climate Summary, 3/95

Weather Conditions

Temperature			Daytime Sky			Precipitation		
10°F & below	32°F & below	90°F & above	Clear	Partly cloudy	Cloudy	0.01 inch or more precip.	0.1 inch or more snow/ice	Thunder-storms
5	76	51	98	135	132	119	8	54

Note: Figures are average number of days per year and covers the years 1948-1990
Source: National Climatic Data Center, International Station Meteorological Climate Summary, 3/95

AIR & WATER QUALITY

Maximum Pollutant Concentrations

	Particulate Matter (ug/m³)	Carbon Monoxide (ppm)	Sulfur Dioxide (ppm)	Nitrogen Dioxide (ppm)	Ozone (ppm)	Lead (ug/m3)
MSA[1] Level	69	6	0.086	0.012	0.13	0.08
NAAQS[2]	150	9	0.140	0.053	0.12	1.50
Met NAAQS?	Yes	Yes	Yes	Yes	No	Yes

Note: (1) Metropolitan Statistical Area - see Appendix A for areas included; (2) National Ambient Air Quality Standards; ppm = parts per million; ug/m³ = micrograms per cubic meter; n/a not available
Source: EPA, National Air Quality and Emissions Trends Report, 1997

Pollutant Standards Index

In the Nashville MSA (see Appendix A for areas included), the Pollutant Standards Index (PSI) exceeded 100 on 24 days in 1997. A PSI value greater than 100 indicates that air quality would be in the unhealthful range on that day. *EPA, National Air Quality and Emissions Trends Report, 1997*

Drinking Water

Water System Name	Pop. Served	Primary Water Source Type	Number of Violations in 1998	Type of Violation/ Contaminants
Nashville Water Dept. #1	414,209	Surface	None	None

Note: Data as of July 10, 1999
Source: EPA, Office of Ground Water and Drinking Water, Safe Drinking Water Information System

Nashville tap water is alkaline, soft.
Editor & Publisher Market Guide, 1999

New Orleans, Louisiana

Background

Many people agree that New Orleans, the largest city in Louisiana, sits on a pedestal with San Francisco and New York City as one of the most colorful cities in the United States. Indeed, like her cosmopolitan sisters to the East and West, New Orleans is rich in unique local history, colorful "debauched" areas, and most importantly, an individual character that separates her from any city in the world.

New Orleans was founded by the brothers Le Moyne, Sieurs d'Iberville, and de Bienville, in 1718. Despite early obstacles such as disease, starvation, and an unwilling working class, New Orleans nevertheless emerged as a genteel antebellum, slave society, fashioning itself after the rigid social hierarchy of Versailles. Even after New Orleans fell under Spanish hands, this unequal, however gracious, lifestyle, continued.

The transfer of control from Spain to the United States in the Louisiana Purchase changed New Orleans's Old World isolation. The newly arrived American settlers introduced aggressive business acumen to the area, as well as the idea of respect for the self-made man. As trade opened up with countries around the world, this made for a very happy union. New Orleans became "Queen City of the South," growing prosperous from adventurous riverboat traders and speculators.

The highly popular musical form, Dixieland Jazz, was born in New Orleans, and during the city's popular Mardi Gras festival, Dixieland musicians parade through the streets in joyous rhythm.

Today, despite a changing skyline, much of New Orlean's Old World charm still remains. It is a city resulting from a polyglot of Southern, Cajun, African-American, and European cultures.

Greater New Orleans is one of the 10 U.S. winners of the 1996 National Civic League's All-America City and Community Award. The program recognized 10 communities for addressing problems such as racial and ethnic discord, crime, neighborhood blight, and joblessness. Greater New Orleans was singled out for its "forward-thinking" Career Academies which have helped prepare students to move from school into the workplace.

The New Orleans metro area is virtually surrounded by water which influences its climate. Although quite humid, the adjacent lakes and Gulf of Mexico help to modify the temperatures. Between mid-June and September the temperatures do not rise above 90 degrees due to the near-daily sporadic thunderstorms. Cold spells, which sometimes reach the area in the winter, seldom last for more than three or four days.

The nearby lakes and marshes contribute to the formation of fogs which do not seriously affect automobile traffic, but do suspend air travel between New Orleans and the Gulf for several days at a time.

Frequent and sometimes heavy rains are typical, but thunderstorms with damaging winds are infrequent. Tornadoes are extremely rare, although waterspouts are more common. Hurricanes have been known to cause destruction in the area.

General Rankings and Evaluative Comments

- New Orleans was ranked #17 out of 19 large, southern metropolitan areas in *Money's* 1998 survey of "The Best Places to Live in America." The survey was conducted by first contacting 512 representative households nationwide and asking them to rank 37 quality-of-life factors on a scale of 1 to 10. Next, a demographic profile was compiled on the 300 largest metropolitan statistical areas in the U.S. The numbers were crunched together to arrive at an overall ranking (things Americans consider most important, like clean air and water, low crime and good schools, received extra weight). Unlike previous years, the 1998 rankings were broken down by region (northeast, midwest, south, west) and population size (100,000 to 249,999; 250,000 to 999,999; 1 million plus). The city had a nationwide ranking of #111 out of 300 in 1997 and #105 out of 300 in 1996. *Money, July 1998; Money, July 1997; Money, September 1996*

- *Ladies Home Journal* ranked America's 200 largest cities based on the qualities women care about most. New Orleans ranked #175 out of 200. Criteria: low crime rate, well-paying jobs, quality health and child care, good public schools, the presence of women in government, size of the gender wage gap, number of sexual-harassment and discrimination complaints filed, unemployment and divorce rates, commute times, population density, number of houses of worship, parks and cultural offerings, number of women's health specialists, how well a community's women cared for themselves, complexion kindness index based on UV radiation levels, odds of finding affordable fashions, rental rates for romance movies, champagne sales and other matters of the heart. *Ladies Home Journal, November 1998*

- Zero Population Growth ranked 229 cities in terms of children's health, safety, and economic well-being. New Orleans was ranked #104 out of 112 independent cities (cities with populations greater than 100,000 which were neither Major Cities nor Suburbs/Outer Cities) and was given a grade of F. Criteria: total population, percent of population under 18 years of age, household language, percent population change, percent of births to teens, infant mortality rate, percent of low birth weights, dropout rate, enrollment in preprimary school, violent and property crime rates, unemployment rate, percent of children in poverty, percent of owner occupied units, number of bad air days, percent of public transportation commuters, and average travel time to work. *Zero Population Growth, Children's Environmental Index, Fall 1999*

- New Orleans was ranked #46 out of 59 metro areas in *The Regional Economist's* "Rational Livability Ranking of 59 Large Metro Areas." The rankings were based on the metro area's total population change over the period 1990-97 divided by the number of people moving in from elsewhere in the United States (net domestic in-migration). *St. Louis Federal Reserve Bank of St. Louis, The Regional Economist, April 1999*

- New Orleans appeared on *Travel & Leisure's* list of the world's 100 best cities. It was ranked #8 in the U.S. and #19 in the world. Criteria: activities/attractions, culture/arts, people, restaurants/food, and value. *Travel & Leisure, 1998 World's Best Awards*

- *Conde Nast Traveler* polled 37,293 readers for travel satisfaction. Cities were ranked based on the following criteria: people/friendliness, environment/ambiance, cultural enrichment, restaurants and fun/energy. New Orleans appeared in the top 25, ranking number 4, with an overall rating of 73.8 out of 100. *Conde Nast Traveler, Readers' Choice Poll 1998*

- New Orleans was selected by *Yahoo! Internet Life* as one of "America's Most Wired Cities & Towns." The city ranked #43 out of 50. Criteria: home and work net use, domain density, hosts per capita, directory density and content quality. *Yahoo! Internet Life, March 1999*

- Cognetics studied 273 metro areas in the United States, ranking them by entrepreneurial activity. New Orleans was ranked #41 out of the 50 largest metro areas. Criteria: Significant Starts (firms started in the last 10 years that still employ at least 5 people) and Young Growers (percent of firms 10 years old or less that grew significantly during the last 4 years). *Cognetics, "Entrepreneurial Hot Spots: The Best Places in America to Start and Grow a Company," 1998*

■ New Orleans was selected as one of the "Best American Cities to Start a Business" by *Point of View* magazine. Criteria: coolness, quality-of-life, and business concerns. The city was ranked #28 out of 75. *Point of View, November 1998*

■ Reliastar Financial Corp. ranked the 125 largest metropolitan areas according to the general financial security of residents. New Orleans was ranked #102 out of 125 with a score of -6.5. The score indicates the percentage a metropolitan area is above or below the metropolitan norm. A metro area with a score of 10.6 is 10.6% above the metro average. Criteria: Earnings and Wealth Potential (household income, education, net assets, cost of living); Safety Net (health insurance, retirement savings, life insurance, income support programs); Personal Threats (unemployment rate, low-income households, crime rate); Community Economic Vitality (cost of community services, job quality, job creation, housing costs). *Reliastar Financial Corp., "The Best Cities to Earn and Save Money," 1999 Edition*

Business Environment

STATE ECONOMY

State Economic Profile

"Louisiana experienced fairly stable growth and kept pace with the nation, in spite of depressed energy prices. A surge in construction and transportation employment offset declines in manufacturing. The almost 7% increase in construction employment is, however, unsustainable. Accordingly, employment growth in 1999 should slow from its already low level of 1.2%.

New Orleans has traditionally proven an engine for state growth. In 1998, however, New Orleans had an employment growth rate of only 0.4% below the paltry 1.2% for the state as a whole. The small metro areas bordering Texas, Shreveport and Lake Charles, have offset some employment losses with gains in gambling employment. New Orleans' gaming industry has not been able to serve as an engine of growth for the city. Current talks of Amoco and/or Shell moving their offices out of New Orleans only darken the outlook.

The strongest sector of LA's economy has been construction, which added over 8,000 jobs in 1998, almost 40% of total state job gains. Much of this has been in the commercial real estate sector. The slow growth in the economy and continued weak population outlook, especially the high rate of loss of young households, will result in a decline in construction employment in 1999 along with softer property markets.

The upside is that Louisiana's transportation industry is providing significant employment growth and is poised to expand when European and Asian markets come out of the current woes. In addition, LA's transportation, infrastructure, and low business and living costs leave it in a good position to attract future business." *National Association of Realtors, Economic Profiles: The Fifty States and the District of Columbia, http://nar.realtor.com/databank/profiles.htm*

IMPORTS/EXPORTS

Total Export Sales

Area	1994 ($000)	1995 ($000)	1996 ($000)	1997 ($000)	% Chg. 1994-97	% Chg. 1996-97
MSA[1]	2,326,231	3,037,819	3,316,761	2,770,835	19.1	-16.5
U.S.	512,415,609	583,030,524	622,827,063	687,597,999	34.2	10.4

Note: (1) Metropolitan Statistical Area - see Appendix A for areas included
Source: U.S. Department of Commerce, International Trade Association, Metropolitan Area Exports: An Export Performance Report on Over 250 U.S. Cities, November 10, 1998

CITY FINANCES

City Government Finances

Component	FY92 ($000)	FY92 (per capita $)
Revenue	746,656	1,523.19
Expenditure	772,877	1,576.68
Debt Outstanding	1,125,844	2,296.74
Cash & Securities	1,107,565	2,259.45

Source: U.S. Bureau of the Census, City Government Finances: 1991-92

City Government Revenue by Source

Source	FY92 ($000)	FY92 (per capita $)	FY92 (%)
From Federal Government	77,804	158.72	10.4
From State Governments	44,968	91.74	6.0
From Local Governments	10	0.02	0.0
Property Taxes	137,619	280.74	18.4
General Sales Taxes	88,445	180.43	11.8
Selective Sales Taxes	48,641	99.23	6.5
Income Taxes	0	0.00	0.0
Current Charges	147,538	300.98	19.8
Utility/Liquor Store	55,727	113.68	7.5
Employee Retirement[1]	33,255	67.84	4.5
Other	112,649	229.81	15.1

Note: (1) Excludes "city contributions," classified as "nonrevenue," intragovernmental transfers.
Source: U.S. Bureau of the Census, City Government Finances: 1991-92

City Government Expenditures by Function

Function	FY92 ($000)	FY92 (per capita $)	FY92 (%)
Educational Services	7,520	15.34	1.0
Employee Retirement[1]	34,782	70.96	4.5
Environment/Housing	198,822	405.60	25.7
Government Administration	80,607	164.44	10.4
Interest on General Debt	93,950	191.66	12.2
Public Safety	167,735	342.18	21.7
Social Services	19,923	40.64	2.6
Transportation	90,392	184.40	11.7
Utility/Liquor Store	54,473	111.13	7.0
Other	24,673	50.33	3.2

Note: (1) Payments to beneficiaries including withdrawal of contributions.
Source: U.S. Bureau of the Census, City Government Finances: 1991-92

Municipal Bond Ratings

Area	Moody's	S & P
New Orleans	Aaa	n/a

Note: n/a not available; n/r not rated
Source: Moody's Bond Record, 6/99

POPULATION

Population Growth

Area	1980	1990	% Chg. 1980-90	July 1998 Estimate	% Chg. 1990-98
City	557,515	496,938	-10.9	465,538	-6.3
MSA[1]	1,256,256	1,238,816	-1.4	1,322,100	6.7
U.S.	226,545,805	248,765,170	9.8	270,299,000	8.7

Note: (1) Metropolitan Statistical Area - see Appendix A for areas included;
July 1998 MSA population estimate was calculated by the editors
Source: 1980/1990 Census of Housing and Population, Summary Tape File 3C;
Census Bureau Population Estimates 1998

Population Characteristics

Race	City 1980 Population	%	City 1990 Population	%	% Chg. 1980-90	MSA[1] 1990 Population	%
White	238,192	42.7	173,305	34.9	-27.2	770,363	62.2
Black	308,039	55.3	308,364	62.1	0.1	430,894	34.8
Amer Indian/Esk/Aleut	623	0.1	815	0.2	30.8	3,838	0.3
Asian/Pacific Islander	7,458	1.3	9,295	1.9	24.6	20,976	1.7
Other	3,203	0.6	5,159	1.0	61.1	12,745	1.0
Hispanic Origin[2]	19,226	3.4	15,900	3.2	-17.3	51,574	4.2

Note: (1) Metropolitan Statistical Area - see Appendix A for areas included;
(2) people of Hispanic origin can be of any race
Source: 1980/1990 Census of Housing and Population, Summary Tape File 3C

Ancestry

Area	German	Irish	English	Italian	U.S.	French	Polish	Dutch
City	9.8	6.8	5.3	4.3	2.5	8.4	0.6	0.5
MSA[1]	17.0	11.9	7.2	9.0	3.5	17.3	0.8	0.8
U.S.	23.3	15.6	13.1	5.9	5.3	4.2	3.8	2.5

Note: Figures are percentages and include persons that reported multiple ancestry (eg. if a person reported being Irish and Italian, they were included in both columns); (1) Metropolitan Statistical Area - see Appendix A for areas included
Source: 1990 Census of Population and Housing, Summary Tape File 3C

Age

Area	Median Age (Years)	Under 5	Under 18	18-24	25-44	45-64	65+	80+
City	31.5	7.7	27.6	11.1	31.4	16.9	13.0	3.0
MSA[1]	31.8	7.7	27.9	10.1	32.8	18.1	11.0	2.2
U.S.	32.9	7.3	25.6	10.5	32.6	18.7	12.5	2.8

Note: (1) Metropolitan Statistical Area - see Appendix A for areas included
Source: 1990 Census of Population and Housing, Summary Tape File 3C

Male/Female Ratio

Area	Number of males per 100 females (all ages)	Number of males per 100 females (18 years old+)
City	86.6	81.6
MSA[1]	90.5	86.3
U.S.	95.0	91.9

Note: (1) Metropolitan Statistical Area - see Appendix A for areas included
Source: 1990 Census of Population, General Population Characteristics

INCOME

Per Capita/Median/Average Income

Area	Per Capita ($)	Median Household ($)	Average Household ($)
City	11,372	18,477	29,283
MSA[1]	12,108	24,442	32,569
U.S.	14,420	30,056	38,453

Note: All figures are for 1989; (1) Metropolitan Statistical Area - see Appendix A for areas included
Source: 1990 Census of Population and Housing, Summary Tape File 3C

Household Income Distribution by Race

Income ($)	City (%) Total	White	Black	Other	Hisp.[1]	U.S. (%) Total	White	Black	Other	Hisp.[1]
Less than 5,000	18.0	8.4	25.4	17.5	13.3	6.2	4.8	15.2	8.6	8.8
5,000 - 9,999	13.4	10.2	15.9	12.4	14.0	9.3	8.6	14.2	9.9	11.1
10,000 - 14,999	11.9	10.1	13.2	13.5	14.1	8.8	8.5	11.0	9.8	11.0
15,000 - 24,999	17.9	17.6	17.9	22.9	20.8	17.5	17.3	18.9	18.5	20.5
25,000 - 34,999	12.6	13.8	11.6	12.2	13.1	15.8	16.1	14.2	15.4	16.4
35,000 - 49,999	11.4	14.3	9.2	9.3	12.7	17.9	18.6	13.3	16.1	16.0
50,000 - 74,999	8.6	13.0	5.2	8.4	7.8	15.0	15.8	9.3	13.4	11.1
75,000 - 99,999	2.8	5.2	1.0	1.9	2.5	5.1	5.5	2.6	4.7	3.1
100,000+	3.6	7.5	0.6	1.9	1.7	4.4	4.8	1.3	3.7	1.9

Note: All figures are for 1989; (1) people of Hispanic origin can be of any race
Source: 1990 Census of Population and Housing, Summary Tape File 3C

Effective Buying Income

Area	Per Capita ($)	Median Household ($)	Average Household ($)
City	14,252	23,748	37,349
MSA[1]	15,361	30,139	41,297
U.S.	16,803	34,536	45,243

Note: Data as of 1/1/99; (1) Metropolitan Statistical Area - see Appendix A for areas included
Source: Standard Rate & Data Service, Newspaper Advertising Source, 9/99

Effective Household Buying Income Distribution

Area	$10,000-$19,999	$20,000-$34,999	$35,000-$49,999	$50,000-$74,999	$75,000-$99,999	$100,000-$124,999	$125,000 and up
City	19.6	20.8	12.8	12.0	5.0	1.9	3.2
MSA[1]	17.1	22.0	16.3	16.5	6.2	2.0	2.5
U.S.	16.0	22.6	18.2	18.9	7.2	2.4	2.7

Note: Data as of 1/1/99; (1) Metropolitan Statistical Area - see Appendix A for areas included
Source: Standard Rate & Data Service, Newspaper Advertising Source, 9/99

Poverty Rates by Race and Age

Area	Total (%)	White	Black	Other	Hisp.[2]	Under 5 years old	Under 18 years old	65 years and over
City	31.6	11.8	42.2	37.4	26.1	48.8	46.3	24.6
MSA[1]	21.2	10.1	40.8	25.9	18.7	31.5	30.3	19.2
U.S.	13.1	9.8	29.5	23.1	25.3	20.1	18.3	12.8

Note: Figures show the percent of people living below the poverty line in 1989. The average poverty threshold was $12,674 for a family of four in 1989; (1) Metropolitan Statistical Area - see Appendix A for areas included; (2) people of Hispanic origin can be of any race
Source: 1990 Census of Population and Housing, Summary Tape File 3C

EMPLOYMENT

Labor Force and Employment

Area	Civilian Labor Force Jun. 1998	Jun. 1999	% Chg.	Workers Employed Jun. 1998	Jun. 1999	% Chg.
City	208,725	202,476	-3.0	193,475	191,807	-0.9
MSA[1]	638,166	623,538	-2.3	600,137	594,963	-0.9
U.S.	138,798,000	140,666,000	1.3	132,265,000	134,395,000	1.6

Note: Data is not seasonally adjusted and covers workers 16 years of age and older; (1) Metropolitan Statistical Area - see Appendix A for areas included
Source: Bureau of Labor Statistics, http://stats.bls.gov

Unemployment Rate

Area	1998						1999					
	Jul.	Aug.	Sep.	Oct.	Nov.	Dec.	Jan.	Feb.	Mar.	Apr.	May.	Jun.
City	6.8	6.8	6.0	5.2	4.9	4.6	5.5	4.8	4.4	4.5	3.8	5.3
MSA[1]	5.6	5.5	4.9	4.4	4.1	4.0	4.7	4.3	3.9	3.9	3.3	4.6
U.S.	4.7	4.5	4.4	4.2	4.1	4.0	4.8	4.7	4.4	4.1	4.0	4.5

Note: Data is not seasonally adjusted and covers workers 16 years of age and older; all figures are percentages; (1) Metropolitan Statistical Area - see Appendix A for areas included
Source: Bureau of Labor Statistics, http://stats.bls.gov

Employment by Industry

Sector	MSA[1]		U.S.
	Number of Employees	Percent of Total	Percent of Total
Services	191,400	30.7	30.4
Retail Trade	116,800	18.7	17.7
Government	105,900	17.0	15.6
Manufacturing	50,000	8.0	14.3
Finance/Insurance/Real Estate	32,100	5.1	5.9
Wholesale Trade	36,300	5.8	5.4
Transportation/Public Utilities	41,500	6.7	5.3
Construction	35,900	5.8	5.0
Mining	14,100	2.3	0.4

Note: Figures cover non-farm employment as of 6/99 and are not seasonally adjusted;
(1) Metropolitan Statistical Area - see Appendix A for areas included
Source: Bureau of Labor Statistics, http://stats.bls.gov

Employment by Occupation

Occupation Category	City (%)	MSA[1] (%)	U.S. (%)
White Collar	61.6	62.5	58.1
Executive/Admin./Management	11.2	11.9	12.3
Professional	19.4	15.8	14.1
Technical & Related Support	3.5	3.9	3.7
Sales	10.7	13.2	11.8
Administrative Support/Clerical	16.8	17.7	16.3
Blue Collar	18.2	21.8	26.2
Precision Production/Craft/Repair	7.0	10.3	11.3
Machine Operators/Assem./Insp.	3.2	3.6	6.8
Transportation/Material Movers	4.5	4.6	4.1
Cleaners/Helpers/Laborers	3.5	3.4	3.9
Services	19.2	14.6	13.2
Farming/Forestry/Fishing	1.0	1.1	2.5

Note: Figures cover employed persons 16 years old and over;
(1) Metropolitan Statistical Area - see Appendix A for areas included
Source: 1990 Census of Population and Housing, Summary Tape File 3C

Occupational Employment Projections: 1996 - 2006

Occupations Expected to Have the Largest Job Growth (ranked by numerical growth)	Fast-Growing Occupations[1] (ranked by percent growth)
1. Cashiers	1. Database administrators
2. Salespersons, retail	2. Systems analysts
3. Registered nurses	3. Physical therapy assistants and aides
4. Truck drivers, light	4. Home health aides
5. General managers & top executives	5. Emergency medical technicians
6. Cooks, fast food and short order	6. Computer engineers
7. Home health aides	7. Medical assistants
8. Marketing & sales, supervisors	8. Engineering/science/computer sys. mgrs.
9. Maintenance repairers, general utility	9. Data processing equipment repairers
10. Nursing aides/orderlies/attendants	10. Physical therapists

Note: Projections cover Louisiana; (1) Excludes occupations with total job growth less than 300
Source: U.S. Department of Labor, Employment and Training Administration, America's Labor Market Information System (ALMIS)

TAXES

Major State and Local Tax Rates

State Corp. Income (%)	State Personal Income (%)	Residential Property (effective rate per $100)	Sales & Use		State Gasoline (cents/gallon)	State Cigarette (cents/pack)
			State (%)	Local (%)		
4.0 - 8.0	2.0 - 6.0	1.65	4.0	5.0	20.0	20.0

Note: Personal/corporate income, sales, gasoline and cigarette tax rates as of January 1999.
Property tax rates as of 1997.
Source: Federation of Tax Administrators, www.taxadmin.org; Washington D.C. Department of Finance and Revenue, Tax Rates and Tax Burdens in the District of Columbia: A Nationwide Comparison, July 1998; Chamber of Commerce, 1999

Total Taxes Per Capita and as a Percent of Income

Area	Per Capita Income ($)	Per Capita Taxes ($)			Percent of Income (%)		
		Total	Federal	State/Local	Total	Federal	State/Local
Louisiana	22,128	7,241	4,984	2,257	32.7	22.5	9.8
U.S.	27,876	9,881	6,690	3,191	35.4	24.0	11.4

Note: Figures are for 1998
Source: Tax Foundation, www.taxfoundation.org

Estimated Tax Burden

Area	State Income	Local Income	Property	Sales	Total
New Orleans	1,486	0	1,500	1,034	4,020

Note: The numbers are estimates of taxes paid by a married couple with two children and annual earnings of $75,000. Sales tax estimates assume they spend average amounts on food, clothing, household goods and gasoline. Property tax estimates assume they live in a $250,000 home.
Source: Kiplinger's Personal Finance Magazine, October 1998

**COMMERCIAL
REAL ESTATE**

Office Market

Class/ Location	Total Space (sq. ft.)	Vacant Space (sq. ft.)	Vac. Rate (%)	Under Constr. (sq. ft.)	Net Absorp. (sq. ft.)	Rental Rates ($/sq. ft./yr.)
Class A						
CBD	7,578,639	1,391,516	18.4	n/a	-34,462	14.00-19.00
Outside CBD	2,178,359	90,098	4.1	n/a	-22,943	19.50-25.00
Class B						
CBD	5,323,308	1,272,358	23.9	n/a	220,944	9.00-12.00
Outside CBD	2,742,151	60,186	2.2	n/a	-23,951	12.00-17.00

*Note: Data as of 10/98 and covers New Orleans; CBD = Central Business District; n/a not available;
Source: Society of Industrial and Office Realtors, 1999 Comparative Statistics of Industrial and Office
Real Estate Markets*

"Slow growth is expected in the New Orleans office market during 1999. Although the oil and gas industry in Louisiana may lose as many as 2,000 jobs before mid-1999, other factors are favorable. Tim Ryan, dean of the College of Business Administration at the University of New Orleans, expects the region to add 13,000 jobs in the next two years. The lack of new construction, rising demand for office space, and purchase prices equal to 70 percent of the cost of new construction will produce an attractive acquisition environment. SIOR's reporter expects the price of both Class A and B properties to increase by 11 to 15 percent. Rental rates are also expected to rise from six to 10 percent in 1999 as vacancy rates tighten." *Society of Industrial and Office Realtors, 1999 Comparative Statistics of Industrial and Office Real Estate Markets*

Industrial Market

Location	Total Space (sq. ft.)	Vacant Space (sq. ft.)	Vac. Rate (%)	Under Constr. (sq. ft.)	Net Absorp. (sq. ft.)	Net Lease ($/sq. ft./yr.)
Central City	17,164,311	1,288,857	7.5	10,000	-68,785	1.45-3.00
Suburban	36,257,659	4,156,073	11.5	300,000	465,677	2.65-4.75

*Note: Data as of 10/98 and covers New Orleans; n/a not available
Source: Society of Industrial and Office Realtors, 1999 Comparative Statistics of Industrial and Office
Real Estate Markets*

"Economists at Southeastern Louisiana University and Louisiana Stale University have predicted the addition of 67,400 new, nonagricultural jobs across Louisiana during the next two years. New Orleans is expected to claim 19,000 of these—producing a possible 3.1 percent job growth rate for the city. Chemical manufacturing, construction, shipbuilding, and the service sectors are expected to expand the most. Thus, the industrial community should remain active, despite low prices for oil and gas. SIOR's reporters predict an extension of current trends in 1999. Sales prices for warehouse/distribution facilities and High Tech/R&D products could rise as much as five percent. Lease prices for warehouses are expected go up by six to 10 percent due to limited supply. The remaining market factors, including construction levels, should remain the same." *Society of Industrial and Office Realtors, 1999 Comparative Statistics of Industrial and Office Real Estate Markets*

COMMERCIAL UTILITIES

Typical Monthly Electric Bills

Area	Commercial Service ($/month)		Industrial Service ($/month)	
	12 kW demand 1,500 kWh	100 kW demand 30,000 kWh	1,000 kW demand 400,000 kWh	20,000 kW demand 10,000,000 kWh
City	146	2,047	21,777	n/a
U.S.	150	2,174	23,995	508,569

*Note: Based on rates in effect January 1, 1999; n/a not available
Source: Edison Electric Institute, Typical Residential, Commercial and Industrial Bills, Winter 1999*

TRANSPORTATION

Transportation Statistics

Average minutes to work	23.7
Interstate highways	I-10; I-59
Bus lines	
In-city	New Orleans Regional TA, 553 vehicles
Inter-city	3
Passenger air service	
Airport	New Orleans International
Airlines	13
Aircraft departures	58,493 (1996)
Enplaned passengers	4,179,901 (1996)
Rail service	Amtrak; Light Rail
Motor freight carriers	85
Major waterways/ports	Port of New Orleans; Mississippi River

Source: Editor & Publisher Market Guide, 1999; FAA Airport Activity Statistics, 1997; Amtrak National Time Table, Northeast Timetable, Spring/Summer 1999; 1990 Census of Population and Housing, STF 3C; Chamber of Commerce/Economic Development 1999; Jane's Urban Transport Systems 1999-2000

Means of Transportation to Work

Area	Car/Truck/Van		Public Transportation			Bicycle	Walked	Other Means	Worked at Home
	Drove Alone	Car-pooled	Bus	Subway	Railroad				
City	58.6	15.4	15.6	0.0	0.0	0.9	5.2	2.3	1.9
MSA[1]	70.9	15.3	6.6	0.0	0.0	0.5	3.1	1.8	1.7
U.S.	73.2	13.4	3.0	1.5	0.5	0.4	3.9	1.2	3.0

Note: Figures shown are percentages and only include workers 16 years old and over;
(1) Metropolitan Statistical Area - see Appendix A for areas included
Source: 1990 Census of Population and Housing, Summary Tape File 3C

BUSINESSES

Major Business Headquarters

Company Name	1999 Rankings	
	Fortune 500	Forbes 500
Entergy	146	-

Note: Companies listed are located in the city; dashes indicate no ranking
Fortune 500: Companies that produce a 10-K are ranked 1 to 500 based on 1998 revenue
Forbes 500: Private companies are ranked 1 to 500 based on 1997 revenue
Source: Forbes, November 30, 1998; Fortune, April 26, 1999

Best Companies to Work For

Entergy Corp. (utilities), headquartered in New Orleans, is among the " 100 Best Places to Work in IS." Criteria: compensation, turnover and training. *Computerworld, May 25, 1998*

Women-Owned Firms: Number, Employment and Sales

Area	Number of Firms	Employ-ment	Sales ($000)	Rank[2]
MSA[1]	39,800	218,300	23,747,800	36

Note: (1) Metropolitan Statistical Area - see Appendix A for areas included;
(2) Calculated on an averaging of the number of businesses, employment and sales
Source: The National Foundation for Women Business Owners, 1999 Facts on Women-Owned Businesses: Trends in the Top 50 Metropolitan Areas

Women-Owned Firms: Growth

Area	% change from 1992 to 1999			Rank[2]
	Number of Firms	Employment	Sales	
MSA[1]	40.5	165.9	189.5	13

Note: (1) Metropolitan Statistical Area - see Appendix A for areas included; (2) Calculated on an averaging of the percent growth of number of businesses, employment and sales
Source: The National Foundation for Women Business Owners, 1999 Facts on Women-Owned Businesses: Trends in the Top 50 Metropolitan Areas

Minority Business Opportunity

New Orleans is home to two companies which are on the Black Enterprise Industrial/Service 100 list (largest based on gross sales): Belle of Orleans dba Bally's Casino Lakeshore (gaming entertainment); Lundy Enterprises, LLC (food services) . Criteria: operational in previous calendar year, at least 51% black-owned and manufactures/owns the product it sells or provides industrial or consumer services. Brokerages, real estate firms and firms that provide professional services are not eligible. *Black Enterprise, www.blackenterprise.com*

HOTELS & MOTELS

Hotels/Motels

Area	Hotels/ Motels	Rooms	Luxury-Level Hotels/Motels		Average Minimum Rates ($)		
			◆◆◆◆	◆◆◆◆◆	◆◆	◆◆◆	◆◆◆◆
City	97	19,148	4	1	82	127	194
Airport	21	3,458	0	0	n/a	n/a	n/a
Suburbs	12	1,588	0	0	n/a	n/a	n/a
Total	130	24,194	4	1	n/a	n/a	n/a

Note: n/a not available; classifications range from one diamond (budget properties with basic amenities) to five diamond (luxury properties with the finest service, rooms and facilities).
Source: OAG, Business Travel Planner, Winter 1998-99

New Orleans is home to one of the top 100 hotels in the world according to Travel & Leisure: Windsor Court (#53) . Criteria: value, rooms/ambience, location, facilities/activities and service. Travel & Leisure, 1998 World's Best Awards, Best Hotels and Resorts

CONVENTION CENTERS

Major Convention Centers

Center Name	Meeting Rooms	Exhibit Space (sq. ft.)
Fairmont Hotel of New Orleans	21	n/a
Louisiana Superdome	52	269,975
Morial Convention Center	83	700,000
New Orleans Cultural Center	6	242,250
Pontchartraim Center	6	34,704
Waterbury Conference Center	8	n/a

Note: n/a not available
Source: Trade Shows Worldwide, 1998; Meetings & Conventions, 4/15/99;
Sucessful Meetings, 3/31/98

Living Environment

COST OF LIVING

Cost of Living Index

Composite Index	Groceries	Housing	Utilities	Trans-portation	Health Care	Misc. Goods/ Services
96.8	98.1	88.2	126.8	111.6	86.6	93.3

Note: U.S. = 100
Source: ACCRA, Cost of Living Index, 1st Quarter 1999

HOUSING

Median Home Prices and Housing Affordability

Area	Median Price[2] 1st Qtr. 1999 ($)	HOI[3] 1st Qtr. 1999	Afford-ability Rank[4]
MSA[1]	102,000	73.5	100
U.S.	134,000	69.6	–

Note: (1) Metropolitan Statistical Area - see Appendix A for areas included; (2) U.S. figures calculated from the sales of 524,324 new and existing homes in 181 markets; (3) Housing Opportunity Index - percent of homes sold that were within the reach of the median income household at the prevailing mortgage interest rate; (4) Rank is from 1-181 with 1 being most affordable
Source: National Association of Home Builders, Housing Opportunity Index, 1st Quarter 1999

Median Home Price Projection

It is projected that the median price of existing single-family homes in the metro area will increase by 3.0% in 1999. Nationwide, home prices are projected to increase 3.8%.
Kiplinger's Personal Finance Magazine, January 1999

Average New Home Price

Area	Price ($)
City	123,800
U.S.	142,735

Note: Figures are based on a new home with 1,800 sq. ft. of living area on an 8,000 sq. ft. lot.
Source: ACCRA, Cost of Living Index, 1st Quarter 1999

Average Apartment Rent

Area	Rent ($/mth)
City	578
U.S.	601

Note: Figures are based on an unfurnished two bedroom, 1-1/2 or 2 bath apartment, approximately 950 sq. ft. in size, excluding all utilities except water
Source: ACCRA, Cost of Living Index, 1st Quarter 1999

RESIDENTIAL UTILITIES

Average Residential Utility Costs

Area	All Electric ($/mth)	Part Electric ($/mth)	Other Energy ($/mth)	Phone ($/mth)
City	130.90	–	–	18.63
U.S.	100.02	55.73	43.33	19.71

Source: ACCRA, Cost of Living Index, 1st Quarter 1999

HEALTH CARE

Average Health Care Costs

Area	Hospital ($/day)	Doctor ($/visit)	Dentist ($/visit)
City	412.20	42.50	57.50
U.S.	430.43	52.45	66.35

Note: Hospital—based on a semi-private room; Doctor—based on a general practitioner's routine exam of an established patient; Dentist—based on adult teeth cleaning and periodic oral exam.
Source: ACCRA, Cost of Living Index, 1st Quarter 1999

Distribution of Office-Based Physicians

Area	Family/Gen. Practitioners	Specialists		
		Medical	Surgical	Other
MSA[1]	210	1,113	911	917

Note: Data as of 12/31/97; (1) Metropolitan Statistical Area - see Appendix A for areas included
Source: American Medical Assn., Physician Characteristics & Distribution in the U.S., 1999

Hospitals

New Orleans has 1 general medical and surgical hospital, 4 psychiatric, 1 children's general, 1 children's psychiatric. *AHA Guide to the Healthcare Field, 1998-99*

According to *U.S. News and World Report,* New Orleans has 2 of the best hospitals in the U.S.:
Ocshner Foundation Hospital, noted for cardiology; **Memorial Medical Center**, noted for endocrinology. *U.S. News Online, "America's Best Hospitals," 10th Edition, www.usnews.com*

EDUCATION

Public School District Statistics

District Name	Num. Sch.	Enroll.	Classroom Teachers	Pupils per Teacher	Minority Pupils (%)	Current Exp.[1] ($/pupil)
Orleans Parish School Board	122	83,175	4,418	18.8	94.9	4,436

Note: Data covers the 1997-1998 school year unless otherwise noted; (1) Data covers fiscal year 1996; SD = School District; ISD = Independent School District; n/a not available
Source: National Center for Education Statistics, Common Core of Data Public Education Agency Universe 1997-98; National Center for Education Statistics, Characteristics of the 100 Largest Public Elementary and Secondary School Districts in the United States: 1997-98, July 1999

Educational Quality

School District	Education Quotient[1]	Graduate Outcome[2]	Community Index[3]	Resource Index[4]
Orleans Parish	68.0	53.0	57.0	99.0

Note: Nearly 1,000 secondary school districts were rated in terms of educational quality. The scores range from a low of 50 to a high of 150; (1) Average of the Graduate Outcome, Community and Resource indexes; (2) Based on graduation rates and college board scores (SAT/ACT); (3) Based on the surrounding community's average level of education and the area's average income level; (4) Based on teacher salaries, per-pupil expenditures and student-teacher ratios.
Source: Expansion Management, Ratings Issue, 1998

Educational Attainment by Race

Area	High School Graduate (%)					Bachelor's Degree (%)				
	Total	White	Black	Other	Hisp.[2]	Total	White	Black	Other	Hisp.[2]
City	68.1	81.4	58.4	57.6	60.3	22.4	36.6	11.6	20.4	18.7
MSA[1]	72.3	78.8	58.4	64.5	68.3	19.7	23.6	10.8	21.3	17.5
U.S.	75.2	77.9	63.1	60.4	49.8	20.3	21.5	11.4	19.4	9.2

Note: Figures shown cover persons 25 years old and over; (1) Metropolitan Statistical Area - see Appendix A for areas included; (2) people of Hispanic origin can be of any race
Source: 1990 Census of Population and Housing, Summary Tape File 3C

School Enrollment by Type

Area	Preprimary				Elementary/High School			
	Public		Private		Public		Private	
	Enrollment	%	Enrollment	%	Enrollment	%	Enrollment	%
City	4,980	53.7	4,290	46.3	75,984	79.7	19,309	20.3
MSA[1]	10,527	42.0	14,557	58.0	178,094	75.0	59,271	25.0
U.S.	2,679,029	59.5	1,824,256	40.5	38,379,689	90.2	4,187,099	9.8

Note: Figures shown cover persons 3 years old and over;
(1) Metropolitan Statistical Area - see Appendix A for areas included
Source: 1990 Census of Population and Housing, Summary Tape File 3C

School Enrollment by Race

Area	Preprimary (%)				Elementary/High School (%)			
	White	Black	Other	Hisp.[1]	White	Black	Other	Hisp.[1]
City	30.5	67.4	2.1	2.2	17.6	78.5	3.8	3.0
MSA[2]	63.6	34.1	2.3	3.1	51.1	45.3	3.6	4.2
U.S.	80.4	12.5	7.1	7.8	74.1	15.6	10.3	12.5

Note: Figures shown cover persons 3 years old and over; (1) people of Hispanic origin can be of any race; (2) Metropolitan Statistical Area - see Appendix A for areas included
Source: 1990 Census of Population and Housing, Summary Tape File 3C

Classroom Teacher Salaries in Public Schools

District	B.A. Degree		M.A. Degree		Maximum	
	Min. ($)	Rank[1]	Max. ($)	Rank[1]	Max. ($)	Rank[1]
New Orleans	22,605	91	38,579	88	39,955	95
Average	26,980	-	46,065	-	51,435	-

Note: Salaries are for 1997-1998; (1) Rank ranges from 1 to 100
Source: American Federation of Teachers, Survey & Analysis of Salary Trends, 1998

Higher Education

Two-Year Colleges		Four-Year Colleges		Medical Schools	Law Schools	Voc/ Tech
Public	Private	Public	Private			
1	0	3	7	2	2	13

Source: College Blue Book, Occupational Education, 1997; Medical School Admission Requirements, 1999-2000; Peterson's Guide to Two-Year Colleges, 1999; Peterson's Guide to Four-Year Colleges, 2000; Barron's Guide to Law Schools, 1999

MAJOR EMPLOYERS

Major Employers

Children's Hospital
Louisana Stadium & Exposition District
Pan American Life Insurance
Great River Transportation Co.
Touro Infirmary

Shell Offshore
Regional Transit Authority
Ochsner Clinic Health Services Corp.
Tidewater Marine
University Health Care System

Note: Companies listed are located in the city
Source: Dun's Business Rankings, 1999; Ward's Business Directory, 1998

PUBLIC SAFETY

Crime Rate

Area	All Crimes	Violent Crimes				Property Crimes		
		Murder	Forcible Rape	Robbery	Aggrav. Assault	Burglary	Larceny -Theft	Motor Vehicle Theft
City	9,355.8	54.7	78.8	813.1	773.8	1,659.5	4,055.8	1,920.1
Suburbs[1]	6,265.2	7.7	32.7	185.9	498.2	1,014.1	3,847.8	678.9
MSA[2]	7,408.7	25.1	49.8	417.9	600.2	1,252.9	3,924.8	1,138.1
U.S.	4,922.7	6.8	35.9	186.1	382.0	919.6	2,886.5	505.8

Note: Crime rate is the number of crimes per 100,000 pop.; (1) defined as all areas within the MSA but located outside the central city; (2) Metropolitan Statistical Area - see Appendix A for areas incl.
Source: FBI Uniform Crime Reports, 1997

RECREATION

Culture and Recreation

Museums	Symphony Orchestras	Opera Companies	Dance Companies	Professional Theatres	Zoos	Pro Sports Teams
11	1	1	1	3	1	1

Source: International Directory of the Performing Arts, 1997; Official Museum Directory, 1999; Stern's Performing Arts Directory, 1997; USA Today Four Sport Stadium Guide, 1997; Chamber of Commerce/Economic Development, 1999

Library System

The New Orleans Public Library has 14 branches and holdings of 957,472 volumes.
American Library Directory, 1998-1999

MEDIA

Newspapers

Name	Type	Freq.	Distribution	Circulation
Jewish Civic Press	Religious	1x/mo	Regional	15,000
Louisiana Weekly	Black	1x/wk	Local	8,000
New Orleans Data Newsweekly	Black	1x/wk	Local	20,000
New Orleans Tribune	n/a	1x/mo	Local	25,000
The Times-Picayune	General	7x/wk	Area	265,820

Note: Includes newspapers with circulations of 1,000 or more located in the city; n/a not available
Source: Burrelle's Media Directory, 1999 Edition

Television Stations

Name	Ch.	Affiliation	Type	Owner
WWL	n/a	CBST	Commercial	A.H. Belo Corporation
WDSU	n/a	NBCT	Commercial	Pulitzer Broadcasting Company
WVUE	n/a	FBC	Commercial	Emmis Broadcasting Corporation
WYES	12	PBS	Public	Greater New Orleans Educational TV Foundation
WHNO	20	n/a	Commercial	Lesea Broadcasting Corporation
WGNO	26	ABCT	Commercial	Tribune Broadcasting Company
WLAE	32	PBS	Public	Educational Broadcasting Foundation
WNOL	38	WB	Commercial	Qwest Broadcasting

Note: Stations included broadcast in the New Orleans metro area; n/a not available
Source: Burrelle's Media Directory, 1999 Edition

FM Radio Stations

Call Letters	Freq. (mHz)	Target Audience	Station Format	Music Format
WBSN	89.1	Religious	M	Adult Contemporary/Christian
WWNO	89.9	General	M/N	Classical/Jazz
KTLN	90.5	General	M/N	Classical/Jazz
WWOZ	90.7	General	E/M/N	Big Band/Jazz/Oldies/R&B
WTUL	91.5	General	M	Alternative/Classical/Jazz
WQUE	93.3	General	M/N	Urban Contemporary
WTKL	95.7	General	M	Oldies
WYLD	98.5	General	M/N/T	Urban Contemporary
WRNO	99.5	General	M/T	Classic Rock
WNOE	101.1	General	M	Country
WLMG	101.9	General	M/N	Adult Contemporary
KMEZ	102.9	General	M	Oldies/R&B/Urban Contemporary
KUMX	104.1	Women	M	Top 40
KKND	106.7	General	M	Alternative

Note: Stations included broadcast in the New Orleans metro area
Station Format: E=Educational; M=Music; N=News; S=Sports; T=Talk
Target Audience: A=Asian; B=Black; C=Christian; E=Ethnic; F=French; G=General; H=Hispanic;
M=Men; N=Native American; R=Religious; S=Senior Citizen; W=Women; Y=Young Adult; Z=Children
Source: Burrelle's Media Directory, 1999 Edition

AM Radio Stations

Call Letters	Freq. (kHz)	Target Audience	Station Format	Music Format
WVOG	600	Religious	M/T	Christian
WSHO	800	Religious	M/N/S/T	Christian
WWL	870	General	N/S/T	n/a
WYLD	940	General	M/N/S	Christian
WBOK	1230	General	M	Gospel
WODT	1280	General	M/N	n/a
WSMB	1350	General	T	n/a
WBYU	1450	General	M/N/S/T	Oldies

Note: Stations included broadcast in the New Orleans metro area; n/a not available
Target Audience: A=Asian; B=Black; C=Christian; E=Ethnic; F=French; G=General; H=Hispanic;
M=Men; N=Native American; R=Religious; S=Senior Citizen; W=Women; Y=Young Adult; Z=Children
Station Format: E=Educational; M=Music; N=News; S=Sports; T=Talk
Source: Burrelle's Media Directory, 1999 Edition

CLIMATE

Average and Extreme Temperatures

Temperature	Jan	Feb	Mar	Apr	May	Jun	Jul	Aug	Sep	Oct	Nov	Dec	Yr.
Extreme High (°F)	83	85	89	92	96	100	101	102	101	92	87	84	102
Average High (°F)	62	65	71	78	85	89	91	90	87	80	71	64	78
Average Temp. (°F)	53	56	62	69	75	81	82	82	79	70	61	55	69
Average Low (°F)	43	46	52	59	66	71	73	73	70	59	51	45	59
Extreme Low (°F)	14	19	25	32	41	50	60	60	42	35	24	11	11

Note: Figures cover the years 1948-1990
Source: National Climatic Data Center, International Station Meteorological Climate Summary, 3/95

Average Precipitation/Snowfall/Humidity

Precip./Humidity	Jan	Feb	Mar	Apr	May	Jun	Jul	Aug	Sep	Oct	Nov	Dec	Yr.
Avg. Precip. (in.)	4.7	5.6	5.2	4.7	4.4	5.4	6.4	5.9	5.5	2.8	4.4	5.5	60.6
Avg. Snowfall (in.)	Tr	Tr	Tr	0	0	0	0	0	0	0	0	Tr	Tr
Avg. Rel. Hum. 6am (%)	85	84	84	88	89	89	91	91	89	87	86	85	88
Avg. Rel. Hum. 3pm (%)	62	59	57	57	58	61	66	65	63	56	59	62	60

Note: Figures cover the years 1948-1990; Tr = Trace amounts (<0.05 in. of rain; <0.5 in. of snow)
Source: National Climatic Data Center, International Station Meteorological Climate Summary, 3/95

Weather Conditions

Temperature			Daytime Sky			Precipitation		
10°F & below	32°F & below	90°F & above	Clear	Partly cloudy	Cloudy	0.01 inch or more precip.	0.1 inch or more snow/ice	Thunder-storms
0	13	70	90	169	106	114	1	69

Note: Figures are average number of days per year and covers the years 1948-1990
Source: National Climatic Data Center, International Station Meteorological Climate Summary, 3/95

AIR & WATER QUALITY

Maximum Pollutant Concentrations

	Particulate Matter (ug/m³)	Carbon Monoxide (ppm)	Sulfur Dioxide (ppm)	Nitrogen Dioxide (ppm)	Ozone (ppm)	Lead (ug/m³)
MSA[1] Level	94	3	0.017	0.018	0.11	0.05
NAAQS[2]	150	9	0.140	0.053	0.12	1.50
Met NAAQS?	Yes	Yes	Yes	Yes	Yes	Yes

Note: (1) Metropolitan Statistical Area - see Appendix A for areas included; (2) National Ambient Air
Quality Standards; ppm = parts per million; ug/m³ = micrograms per cubic meter; n/a not available
Source: EPA, National Air Quality and Emissions Trends Report, 1997

Pollutant Standards Index

In the New Orleans MSA (see Appendix A for areas included), the Pollutant Standards Index (PSI) exceeded 100 on 7 days in 1997. A PSI value greater than 100 indicates that air quality would be in the unhealthful range on that day. *EPA, National Air Quality and Emissions Trends Report, 1997*

Drinking Water

Water System Name	Pop. Served	Primary Water Source Type	Number of Violations in 1998	Type of Violation/ Contaminants
New Orleans-Carrolton WW	440,229	Surface	None	None

Note: Data as of July 10, 1999
Source: EPA, Office of Ground Water and Drinking Water, Safe Drinking Water Information System

New Orleans tap water is alkaline, soft and fluoridated.
Editor & Publisher Market Guide, 1999

Orlando, Florida

Background

The city of Orlando can hold the viewer aghast with its rampant tourism. Not only is it home to the worldwide tourist attractions of Disney World, Epcot Center, and Sea World, but Orlando, and its surrounding area, also hosts such institutions as Medieval Times Dinner Tournament, Tupperware Exhibit and Museum, Wet-N-Wild, Watermania, and Sleuth's Mystery Dinner Theatre, as well as thousands of T-shirt, citrus, and shell vendor shacks.

Orlando has its own high-tech corridor called "Laser Lane" because of the University of Central Florida Center for Research and Education in Optics and Lasers. The research facility is now home to 80 companies, including Sprint and Bell South, and is ranked #8 out of the top 10 research parks in the U.S.

Aside from the glitz that pumps most of the money into Orlando's economy, Orlando is also called "The City Beautiful." The warm climate and abundant rains produce a variety of lush flora and fauna. This provides an attractive setting for the many young people who settle in the area, spending their nights in the numerous jazz clubs, restaurants, and pubs along Orange Avenue and Church Street. Stereotypically the land of orange juice and sunshine, Orlando may be the up and coming city for young job seekers and professionals.

This genteel setting is a far cry from Orlando's rough and tumble origins. The city started out as a makeshift campsite in the middle of a cotton plantation. The Civil War and devastating rains brought an end to the cotton trade, and its settlers turned to raising livestock.

The transition to a new livelihood did not insure any peace and serenity. Rustling, chaotic brawls, and senseless shootings were an everyday occurrence. Martial law had to be imposed by a few large ranch families.

The greatest impetus toward modernity came from the installation of Cape Canaveral, 50 miles away, which brought missile assembly and electronic component production to the area, and Walt Disney World, created out of 27,000 acres of unexplored swampland, which set the tone for Orlando as a tourist-oriented economy.

Recently, Orlando has become a major film production site. Nickelodeon, the world's largest teleproduction studio dedicated to children's television programming, is headquartered there, as are the Gold Channel, America's Health Network and an increasing number of other cable networks.

Orlando is surrounded by many lakes. Its relative humidity remains high year round. In winter the humidity may drop. June through September is the rainy season. During this time, scattered afternoon thunderstorms are an almost daily occurrence. During the winter months rainfall is light and the afternoons are most pleasant. Hurricanes are not usually considered a threat to the area.

General Rankings and Evaluative Comments

■ Orlando was ranked #3 out of 19 large, southern metropolitan areas in *Money's* 1998 survey of "The Best Places to Live in America." The survey was conducted by first contacting 512 representative households nationwide and asking them to rank 37 quality-of-life factors on a scale of 1 to 10. Next, a demographic profile was compiled on the 300 largest metropolitan statistical areas in the U.S. The numbers were crunched together to arrive at an overall ranking (things Americans consider most important, like clean air and water, low crime and good schools, received extra weight). Unlike previous years, the 1998 rankings were broken down by region (northeast, midwest, south, west) and population size (100,000 to 249,999; 250,000 to 999,999; 1 million plus). The city had a nationwide ranking of #18 out of 300 in 1997 and #12 out of 300 in 1996. *Money, July 1998; Money, July 1997; Money, September 1996*

■ *Ladies Home Journal* ranked America's 200 largest cities based on the qualities women care about most. Orlando ranked #22 out of 200. Criteria: low crime rate, well-paying jobs, quality health and child care, good public schools, the presence of women in government, size of the gender wage gap, number of sexual-harassment and discrimination complaints filed, unemployment and divorce rates, commute times, population density, number of houses of worship, parks and cultural offerings, number of women's health specialists, how well a community's women cared for themselves, complexion kindness index based on UV radiation levels, odds of finding affordable fashions, rental rates for romance movies, champagne sales and other matters of the heart. *Ladies Home Journal, November 1998*

■ Zero Population Growth ranked 229 cities in terms of children's health, safety, and economic well-being. Orlando was ranked #89 out of 112 independent cities (cities with populations greater than 100,000 which were neither Major Cities nor Suburbs/Outer Cities) and was given a grade of D. Criteria: total population, percent of population under 18 years of age, household language, percent population change, percent of births to teens, infant mortality rate, percent of low birth weights, dropout rate, enrollment in preprimary school, violent and property crime rates, unemployment rate, percent of children in poverty, percent of owner occupied units, number of bad air days, percent of public transportation commuters, and average travel time to work. *Zero Population Growth, Children's Environmental Index, Fall 1999*

■ Orlando was ranked #7 out of 59 metro areas in *The Regional Economist's* "Rational Livability Ranking of 59 Large Metro Areas." The rankings were based on the metro area's total population change over the period 1990-97 divided by the number of people moving in from elsewhere in the United States (net domestic in-migration). *St. Louis Federal Reserve Bank of St. Louis, The Regional Economist, April 1999*

■ Orlando appeared on *Travel & Leisure's* list of the world's 100 best cities. It was ranked #32 in the U.S. and #89 in the world. Criteria: activities/attractions, culture/arts, people, restaurants/food, and value. *Travel & Leisure, 1998 World's Best Awards*

■ *Conde Nast Traveler* polled 37,293 readers for travel satisfaction. Cities were ranked based on the following criteria: people/friendliness, environment/ambiance, cultural enrichment, restaurants and fun/energy. Orlando appeared in the top 25, ranking number 25, with an overall rating of 52.8 out of 100. *Conde Nast Traveler, Readers' Choice Poll 1998*

■ Orlando was selected by *Yahoo! Internet Life* as one of "America's Most Wired Cities & Towns." The city ranked #33 out of 50. Criteria: home and work net use, domain density, hosts per capita, directory density and content quality. *Yahoo! Internet Life, March 1999*

■ Cognetics studied 273 metro areas in the United States, ranking them by entrepreneurial activity. Orlando was ranked #6 out of the 50 largest metro areas. Criteria: Significant Starts (firms started in the last 10 years that still employ at least 5 people) and Young Growers (percent of firms 10 years old or less that grew significantly during the last 4 years). *Cognetics, "Entrepreneurial Hot Spots: The Best Places in America to Start and Grow a Company," 1998*

- Orlando was included among *Entrepreneur* magazine's listing of the "20 Best Cities for Small Business." It was ranked #5 among large metro areas and #4 among southern metro areas. Criteria: entrepreneurial activity, small-business growth, economic growth, and risk of failure. *Entrepreneur, October 1999*

- Orlando was selected as one of the "Best American Cities to Start a Business" by *Point of View* magazine. Criteria: coolness, quality-of-life, and business concerns. The city was ranked #8 out of 75. *Point of View, November 1998*

- Reliastar Financial Corp. ranked the 125 largest metropolitan areas according to the general financial security of residents. Orlando was ranked #63 out of 125 with a score of 1.9. The score indicates the percentage a metropolitan area is above or below the metropolitan norm. A metro area with a score of 10.6 is 10.6% above the metro average. Criteria: Earnings and Wealth Potential (household income, education, net assets, cost of living); Safety Net (health insurance, retirement savings, life insurance, income support programs); Personal Threats (unemployment rate, low-income households, crime rate); Community Economic Vitality (cost of community services, job quality, job creation, housing costs). *Reliastar Financial Corp., "The Best Cities to Earn and Save Money," 1999 Edition*

Business Environment

STATE ECONOMY

State Economic Profile

"Florida's economy has been among the nation's strongest in recent years. Job growth has outpaced the nation by a considerable amount since 1992.

While Florida has been able to avoid any significant fallout from the Asian crisis, the weakening of economies in Latin American will dampen both tourism and international trade. 1998 saw the decline in Latin tourism more than offset by domestic visitors. Domestic tourism is projected to soften as US growth cools in 1999, offering no offset against the expected decline in Latin tourism. Weaker tourism and trade with Latin American will slow growth in 1999; FL will still outpace the nation in job growth as Gross State Product growth (GSP) slows.

Over half of FL's 230,000 new jobs created in 1998 were in the services sector, which grew at 5.2%, more than offsetting a minor decline in manufacturing employment. Much of this growth is taking place in the finance and business services sector.

In spite of strong home sales and a slowing construction market, FL's price appreciation continued to lag the nation. Although residential permits per 1,000 residents stands at 5.1, well above the national average, this number is only slightly up from 1997 and will decline in 1999.

Growth in FL, while strong throughout, has been hottest in the Naples, Ft. Myers and Orlando areas. Construction and employment in the construction industry has begun to slow in South Florida. Projected employment and housing gains will be concentrated in Northern and Central Florida during 1999. Growing diversification of the economy into financial and business services promises a strong outlook for the years ahead." *National Association of Realtors, Economic Profiles: The Fifty States and the District of Columbia, http://nar.realtor.com/databank/profiles.htm*

IMPORTS/EXPORTS

Total Export Sales

Area	1994 ($000)	1995 ($000)	1996 ($000)	1997 ($000)	% Chg. 1994-97	% Chg. 1996-97
MSA[1]	848,512	968,816	1,218,957	1,662,795	96.0	36.4
U.S.	512,415,609	583,030,524	622,827,063	687,597,999	34.2	10.4

Note: (1) Metropolitan Statistical Area - see Appendix A for areas included
Source: U.S. Department of Commerce, International Trade Association, Metropolitan Area Exports: An Export Performance Report on Over 250 U.S. Cities, November 10, 1998

CITY FINANCES

City Government Finances

Component	FY92 ($000)	FY92 (per capita $)
Revenue	344,245	2,002.34
Expenditure	294,755	1,714.48
Debt Outstanding	513,908	2,989.21
Cash & Securities	556,615	3,237.62

Source: U.S. Bureau of the Census, City Government Finances: 1991-92

City Government Revenue by Source

Source	FY92 ($000)	FY92 (per capita $)	FY92 (%)
From Federal Government	36,530	212.48	10.6
From State Governments	25,510	148.38	7.4
From Local Governments	26,005	151.26	7.6
Property Taxes	41,157	239.39	12.0
General Sales Taxes	0	0.00	0.0
Selective Sales Taxes	37,622	218.83	10.9
Income Taxes	0	0.00	0.0
Current Charges	98,752	574.40	28.7
Utility/Liquor Store	0	0.00	0.0
Employee Retirement[1]	14,716	85.60	4.3
Other	63,953	371.99	18.6

Note: (1) Excludes "city contributions," classified as "nonrevenue," intragovernmental transfers.
Source: U.S. Bureau of the Census, City Government Finances: 1991-92

City Government Expenditures by Function

Function	FY92 ($000)	FY92 (per capita $)	FY92 (%)
Educational Services	80	0.47	0.0
Employee Retirement[1]	5,258	30.58	1.8
Environment/Housing	92,816	539.88	31.5
Government Administration	20,138	117.14	6.8
Interest on General Debt	24,168	140.58	8.2
Public Safety	58,487	340.20	19.8
Social Services	0	0.00	0.0
Transportation	37,676	219.15	12.8
Utility/Liquor Store	800	4.65	0.3
Other	55,332	321.85	18.8

Note: (1) Payments to beneficiaries including withdrawal of contributions.
Source: U.S. Bureau of the Census, City Government Finances: 1991-92

Municipal Bond Ratings

Area	Moody's	S & P
Orlando	Aaa	n/a

Note: n/a not available; n/r not rated
Source: Moody's Bond Record, 6/99

POPULATION

Population Growth

Area	1980	1990	% Chg. 1980-90	July 1998 Estimate	% Chg. 1990-98
City	128,291	164,693	28.4	181,175	10.0
MSA[1]	700,055	1,072,748	53.2	1,481,441	38.1
U.S.	226,545,805	248,765,170	9.8	270,299,000	8.7

Note: (1) Metropolitan Statistical Area - see Appendix A for areas included;
July 1998 MSA population estimate was calculated by the editors
Source: 1980/1990 Census of Housing and Population, Summary Tape File 3C;
Census Bureau Population Estimates 1998

Population Characteristics

Race	City 1980 Population	%	City 1990 Population	%	% Chg. 1980-90	MSA[1] 1990 Population	%
White	87,751	68.4	112,933	68.6	28.7	888,648	82.8
Black	38,380	29.9	44,342	26.9	15.5	132,796	12.4
Amer Indian/Esk/Aleut	300	0.2	510	0.3	70.0	3,704	0.3
Asian/Pacific Islander	782	0.6	2,516	1.5	221.7	20,332	1.9
Other	1,078	0.8	4,392	2.7	307.4	27,268	2.5
Hispanic Origin[2]	5,024	3.9	14,121	8.6	181.1	94,658	8.8

Note: (1) Metropolitan Statistical Area - see Appendix A for areas included;
(2) people of Hispanic origin can be of any race
Source: 1980/1990 Census of Housing and Population, Summary Tape File 3C

Ancestry

Area	German	Irish	English	Italian	U.S.	French	Polish	Dutch
City	18.2	13.3	13.1	4.8	4.3	3.7	2.2	1.9
MSA[1]	22.0	16.4	15.9	6.1	5.4	4.4	3.0	2.5
U.S.	23.3	15.6	13.1	5.9	5.3	4.2	3.8	2.5

Note: Figures are percentages and include persons that reported multiple ancestry (eg. if a person reported being Irish and Italian, they were included in both columns); (1) Metropolitan Statistical Area - see Appendix A for areas included
Source: 1990 Census of Population and Housing, Summary Tape File 3C

Age

Area	Median Age (Years)	Age Distribution (%) Under 5	Under 18	18-24	25-44	45-64	65+	80+
City	30.2	6.8	21.0	16.1	36.4	15.2	11.4	2.9
MSA[1]	32.1	7.2	24.3	11.3	35.2	18.3	10.9	2.2
U.S.	32.9	7.3	25.6	10.5	32.6	18.7	12.5	2.8

Note: (1) Metropolitan Statistical Area - see Appendix A for areas included
Source: 1990 Census of Population and Housing, Summary Tape File 3C

Male/Female Ratio

Area	Number of males per 100 females (all ages)	Number of males per 100 females (18 years old+)
City	101.0	101.0
MSA[1]	97.3	95.3
U.S.	95.0	91.9

Note: (1) Metropolitan Statistical Area - see Appendix A for areas included
Source: 1990 Census of Population, General Population Characteristics

INCOME

Per Capita/Median/Average Income

Area	Per Capita ($)	Median Household ($)	Average Household ($)
City	13,879	26,119	33,136
MSA[1]	14,895	31,230	39,069
U.S.	14,420	30,056	38,453

Note: All figures are for 1989; (1) Metropolitan Statistical Area - see Appendix A for areas included
Source: 1990 Census of Population and Housing, Summary Tape File 3C

Household Income Distribution by Race

Income ($)	City (%)					U.S. (%)				
	Total	White	Black	Other	Hisp.[1]	Total	White	Black	Other	Hisp.[1]
Less than 5,000	6.8	4.3	15.7	8.4	9.1	6.2	4.8	15.2	8.6	8.8
5,000 - 9,999	8.5	7.1	13.1	11.4	11.8	9.3	8.6	14.2	9.9	11.1
10,000 - 14,999	10.2	9.0	13.6	15.1	14.0	8.8	8.5	11.0	9.8	11.0
15,000 - 24,999	21.9	21.2	24.5	23.1	23.9	17.5	17.3	18.9	18.5	20.5
25,000 - 34,999	17.6	18.7	12.9	22.5	16.6	15.8	16.1	14.2	15.4	16.4
35,000 - 49,999	17.1	18.9	12.2	8.8	13.2	17.9	18.6	13.3	16.1	16.0
50,000 - 74,999	11.9	13.6	6.7	7.6	7.3	15.0	15.8	9.3	13.4	11.1
75,000 - 99,999	3.1	3.8	0.9	2.0	2.3	5.1	5.5	2.6	4.7	3.1
100,000+	2.7	3.4	0.5	1.2	1.9	4.4	4.8	1.3	3.7	1.9

Note: All figures are for 1989; (1) people of Hispanic origin can be of any race
Source: 1990 Census of Population and Housing, Summary Tape File 3C

Effective Buying Income

Area	Per Capita ($)	Median Household ($)	Average Household ($)
City	16,369	30,680	40,447
MSA[1]	17,461	34,560	45,696
U.S.	16,803	34,536	45,243

Note: Data as of 1/1/99; (1) Metropolitan Statistical Area - see Appendix A for areas included
Source: Standard Rate & Data Service, Newspaper Advertising Source, 9/99

Effective Household Buying Income Distribution

Area	% of Households Earning						
	$10,000 -$19,999	$20,000 -$34,999	$35,000 -$49,999	$50,000 -$74,999	$75,000 -$99,000	$100,000 -$124,999	$125,000 and up
City	17.5	26.9	18.5	16.0	5.1	1.2	1.9
MSA[1]	16.1	25.2	19.3	18.3	7.0	2.2	2.6
U.S.	16.0	22.6	18.2	18.9	7.2	2.4	2.7

Note: Data as of 1/1/99; (1) Metropolitan Statistical Area - see Appendix A for areas included
Source: Standard Rate & Data Service, Newspaper Advertising Source, 9/99

Poverty Rates by Race and Age

Area	Total (%)	By Race (%)				By Age (%)		
		White	Black	Other	Hisp.[2]	Under 5 years old	Under 18 years old	65 years and over
City	15.8	8.2	33.9	20.6	21.6	29.0	27.1	16.1
MSA[1]	10.0	7.3	26.4	15.0	15.9	14.8	14.0	10.7
U.S.	13.1	9.8	29.5	23.1	25.3	20.1	18.3	12.8

Note: Figures show the percent of people living below the poverty line in 1989. The average poverty threshold was $12,674 for a family of four in 1989; (1) Metropolitan Statistical Area - see Appendix A for areas included; (2) people of Hispanic origin can be of any race
Source: 1990 Census of Population and Housing, Summary Tape File 3C

EMPLOYMENT

Labor Force and Employment

Area	Civilian Labor Force			Workers Employed		
	Jun. 1998	Jun. 1999	% Chg.	Jun. 1998	Jun. 1999	% Chg.
City	110,687	115,963	4.8	106,808	112,122	5.0
MSA[1]	849,096	889,215	4.7	821,730	862,611	5.0
U.S.	138,798,000	140,666,000	1.3	132,265,000	134,395,000	1.6

Note: Data is not seasonally adjusted and covers workers 16 years of age and older;
(1) Metropolitan Statistical Area - see Appendix A for areas included
Source: Bureau of Labor Statistics, http://stats.bls.gov

Unemployment Rate

Area	1998						1999					
	Jul.	Aug.	Sep.	Oct.	Nov.	Dec.	Jan.	Feb.	Mar.	Apr.	May.	Jun.
City	3.3	3.1	3.3	3.1	3.2	2.9	3.6	3.2	3.0	3.1	3.2	3.3
MSA[1]	3.1	2.9	3.1	2.9	2.9	2.6	3.3	2.9	2.8	2.8	2.8	3.0
U.S.	4.7	4.5	4.4	4.2	4.1	4.0	4.8	4.7	4.4	4.1	4.0	4.5

Note: Data is not seasonally adjusted and covers workers 16 years of age and older; all figures are percentages; (1) Metropolitan Statistical Area - see Appendix A for areas included
Source: Bureau of Labor Statistics, http://stats.bls.gov

Employment by Industry

Sector	MSA[1]		U.S.
	Number of Employees	Percent of Total	Percent of Total
Services	376,000	42.7	30.4
Retail Trade	164,600	18.7	17.7
Government	89,700	10.2	15.6
Manufacturing	54,500	6.2	14.3
Finance/Insurance/Real Estate	52,000	5.9	5.9
Wholesale Trade	48,000	5.5	5.4
Transportation/Public Utilities	45,000	5.1	5.3
Construction	50,000	5.7	5.0
Mining	n/a	n/a	0.4

Note: Figures cover non-farm employment as of 6/99 and are not seasonally adjusted; (1) Metropolitan Statistical Area - see Appendix A for areas included; n/a not available
Source: Bureau of Labor Statistics, http://stats.bls.gov

Employment by Occupation

Occupation Category	City (%)	MSA[1] (%)	U.S. (%)
White Collar	60.3	61.0	58.1
Executive/Admin./Management	13.4	13.7	12.3
Professional	13.9	12.9	14.1
Technical & Related Support	3.6	3.4	3.7
Sales	12.8	14.4	11.8
Administrative Support/Clerical	16.5	16.6	16.3
Blue Collar	19.5	21.4	26.2
Precision Production/Craft/Repair	8.9	10.6	11.3
Machine Operators/Assem./Insp.	3.1	3.4	6.8
Transportation/Material Movers	3.6	3.9	4.1
Cleaners/Helpers/Laborers	3.9	3.5	3.9
Services	18.7	15.6	13.2
Farming/Forestry/Fishing	1.6	1.9	2.5

Note: Figures cover employed persons 16 years old and over; (1) Metropolitan Statistical Area - see Appendix A for areas included
Source: 1990 Census of Population and Housing, Summary Tape File 3C

Occupational Employment Projections: 1996 - 2006

Occupations Expected to Have the Largest Job Growth (ranked by numerical growth)	Fast-Growing Occupations[1] (ranked by percent growth)
1. Cashiers	1. Systems analysts
2. Salespersons, retail	2. Physical therapy assistants and aides
3. General managers & top executives	3. Desktop publishers
4. Registered nurses	4. Home health aides
5. Waiters & waitresses	5. Computer engineers
6. Marketing & sales, supervisors	6. Medical assistants
7. Janitors/cleaners/maids, ex. priv. hshld.	7. Physical therapists
8. General office clerks	8. Paralegals
9. Food preparation workers	9. Emergency medical technicians
10. Hand packers & packagers	10. Occupational therapists

Note: Projections cover Florida; (1) Excludes occupations with total job growth less than 300
Source: U.S. Department of Labor, Employment and Training Administration, America's Labor Market Information System (ALMIS)

TAXES

Major State and Local Tax Rates

State Corp. Income (%)	State Personal Income (%)	Residential Property (effective rate per $100)	Sales & Use State (%)	Sales & Use Local (%)	State Gasoline (cents/ gallon)	State Cigarette (cents/ pack)
5.5[a]	None	n/a	6.0	None	13.1[b]	33.9

Note: Personal/corporate income, sales, gasoline and cigarette tax rates as of January 1999.
Property tax rates as of 1997; (a) 3.3% Alternative Minimum Tax. An exemption of $5,000 is allowed;
(b) Rate is comprised of 4 cents excise and 9.1 cents motor carrier tax
Source: Federation of Tax Administrators, www.taxadmin.org; Washington D.C. Department of Finance and Revenue, Tax Rates and Tax Burdens in the District of Columbia: A Nationwide Comparison, July 1998; Chamber of Commerce, 1999

Total Taxes Per Capita and as a Percent of Income

Area	Per Capita Income ($)	Per Capita Taxes ($) Total	Per Capita Taxes ($) Federal	Per Capita Taxes ($) State/ Local	Percent of Income (%) Total	Percent of Income (%) Federal	Percent of Income (%) State/ Local
Florida	27,655	9,768	6,824	2,944	35.3	24.7	10.6
U.S.	27,876	9,881	6,690	3,191	35.4	24.0	11.4

Note: Figures are for 1998
Source: Tax Foundation, www.taxfoundation.org

COMMERCIAL REAL ESTATE

Office Market

Class/ Location	Total Space (sq. ft.)	Vacant Space (sq. ft.)	Vac. Rate (%)	Under Constr. (sq. ft.)	Net Absorp. (sq. ft.)	Rental Rates ($/sq.ft./yr.)
Class A						
CBD	4,097,418	204,870	5.0	854,650	2,292	15.00-28.00
Outside CBD	8,860,282	443,014	5.0	626,000	636,899	12.00-22.00
Class B						
CBD	1,306,354	143,699	11.0	0	-71,781	8.00-21.00
Outside CBD	10,141,162	1,115,528	11.0	129,806	-462,438	7.25-18.00

Note: Data as of 10/98 and covers Orlando; CBD = Central Business District; n/a not available;
Source: Society of Industrial and Office Realtors, 1999 Comparative Statistics of Industrial and Office Real Estate Markets

"Development is expected in both the CBD and suburban markets, but it is not expected to significantly outpace demand. With completion of the new courthouse in the CBD, a considerable amount of Class A and B space was vacated. This will dampen 1999 downtown construction. Nevertheless, CNL/St. Joe will continue building the first new office tower downtown in 10 years. Maitland Center will likely see 700,000 sq. ft. of construction. In the Winter Park office sub-market, the redevelopment of the Orlando Naval Training Center will include 1.5 million sq. ft. of office space. In the Seminole sub-market, Pizzuti Company, Crescent Resources, and Weeks Corporation are likely to compete for speculative and build-to-suit projects." *Society of Industrial and Office Realtors, 1999 Comparative Statistics of Industrial and Office Real Estate Markets*

Industrial Market

Location	Total Space (sq. ft.)	Vacant Space (sq. ft.)	Vac. Rate (%)	Under Constr. (sq. ft.)	Net Absorp. (sq. ft.)	Net Lease ($/sq.ft./yr.)
Central City	n/a	n/a	n/a	n/a	n/a	n/a
Suburban	73,635,645	5,007,224	6.8	1,834,236	2,342,589	3.50-6.50

Note: Data as of 10/98 and covers Orlando; n/a not available
Source: Society of Industrial and Office Realtors, 1999 Comparative Statistics of Industrial and Office Real Estate Markets

"Absorption will maintain its strong pace in 1999, with between 1.2 million sq. ft. and 1.4 million sq. ft. likely. Development should exceed 1998 levels with three new developers that entered the market in 1998. Efforts from the local Economic Development Agency will attract business into the target areas. Plans to improve the area's transportation network will also facilitate growth. A proposed intermodal system is expected to include construction of a light rail system and improvements to both the expressway and highway. Forecasts by our SIOR reporter indicate increases in sales and lease prices for industrial space. Shortages in all industrial sectors will encourage a moderate increase in new construction. Site prices should see increases in value between six and 10 percent." *Society of Industrial and Office Realtors, 1999 Comparative Statistics of Industrial and Office Real Estate Markets*

Retail Market

Shopping Center Inventory (sq. ft.)	Shopping Center Construction (sq. ft.)	Construction as a Percent of Inventory (%)	Torto Wheaton Rent Index[1] ($/sq. ft.)
35,281,000	872,000	2.5	14.17

Note: Data as of 1997 and covers the Metropolitan Statistical Area - see Appendix A for areas included; (1) Index is based on a model that predicts what the average rent should be for leases with certain characteristics, in certain locations during certain years.
Source: National Association of Realtors, 1997-1998 Market Conditions Report

"Orlando's economy revolves around tourism. The most recent tourism numbers are up, which has bolstered the retail trade sector. Indeed, retail trade is Orlando's second-largest employer and its largest source of tax revenue. Shopping, especially at outlet malls, has been brisk. Orlando's Belz Factory hosted an estimated 12 million visitors in 1996. The area's retail market has been robust, with strong demand outpacing new construction. The retail rent index jumped 20% in 1997 after an 18% increase the year before. Several community-sized shopping centers were constructed last year, anchored by Publix and Winn-Dixie, Orlando's rent index should continue to climb over the next two years." *National Association of Realtors, 1997-1998 Market Conditions Report*

COMMERCIAL UTILITIES ## Typical Monthly Electric Bills

Area	Commercial Service ($/month)		Industrial Service ($/month)	
	12 kW demand 1,500 kWh	100 kW demand 30,000 kWh	1,000 kW demand 400,000 kWh	20,000 kW demand 10,000,000 kWh
City	118	1,993	23,247	387,510
U.S.	150	2,174	23,995	508,569

Note: Based on rates in effect January 1, 1999
Source: Edison Electric Institute, Typical Residential, Commercial and Industrial Bills, Winter 1999

TRANSPORTATION

Transportation Statistics

Average minutes to work	20.1
Interstate highways	I-4
Bus lines	
In-city	LYNX (Central Florida RTA), 240 vehicles
Inter-city	5
Passenger air service	
Airport	Orlando International
Airlines	16
Aircraft departures	107,987 (1996)
Enplaned passengers	10,827,876 (1996)
Rail service	Amtrak
Motor freight carriers	34
Major waterways/ports	None

Source: Editor & Publisher Market Guide, 1999; FAA Airport Activity Statistics, 1997; Amtrak National Time Table, Northeast Timetable, Spring/Summer 1999; 1990 Census of Population and Housing, STF 3C; Chamber of Commerce/Economic Development 1999; Jane's Urban Transport Systems 1999-2000

Means of Transportation to Work

Area	Car/Truck/Van		Public Transportation			Bicycle	Walked	Other Means	Worked at Home
	Drove Alone	Car-pooled	Bus	Subway	Railroad				
City	68.3	12.6	3.5	0.0	0.0	0.8	11.9	1.5	1.3
MSA[1]	78.1	13.3	1.4	0.0	0.0	0.6	3.5	1.2	2.0
U.S.	73.2	13.4	3.0	1.5	0.5	0.4	3.9	1.2	3.0

Note: Figures shown are percentages and only include workers 16 years old and over;
(1) Metropolitan Statistical Area - see Appendix A for areas included
Source: 1990 Census of Population and Housing, Summary Tape File 3C

BUSINESSES

Major Business Headquarters

Company Name	1999 Rankings	
	Fortune 500	Forbes 500
Darden Restaurants	448	-

Note: Companies listed are located in the city; dashes indicate no ranking
Fortune 500: Companies that produce a 10-K are ranked 1 to 500 based on 1998 revenue
Forbes 500: Private companies are ranked 1 to 500 based on 1997 revenue
Source: Forbes, November 30, 1998; Fortune, April 26, 1999

Fast-Growing Businesses

According to *Inc.*, Orlando is home to one of America's 100 fastest-growing private companies: Construct Two Group. Criteria for inclusion: must be an independent, privately-held, U.S. corporation, proprietorship or partnership; sales of at least $200,000 in 1995; five-year operating/sales history; increase in 1999 sales over 1998 sales; holding companies, regulated banks, and utilities were excluded. *Inc. 500, 1999*

According to Deloitte & Touche LLP, Orlando is home to one of America's 100 fastest-growing high-technology companies: LaserSight Inc.. Companies are ranked by percentage growth in revenue over a five-year period. Criteria for inclusion: must be a U.S. company developing and/or providing technology products or services; company must have been in business for five years with 1993 revenues of at least $50,000. *Deloitte & Touche LLP, November 17, 1998*

Women-Owned Firms: Number, Employment and Sales

Area	Number of Firms	Employment	Sales ($000)	Rank[2]
MSA[1]	59,000	182,900	23,897,400	33

Note: (1) Metropolitan Statistical Area - see Appendix A for areas included;
(2) Calculated on an averaging of the number of businesses, employment and sales
Source: The National Foundation for Women Business Owners, 1999 Facts on Women-Owned Businesses: Trends in the Top 50 Metropolitan Areas

Women-Owned Firms: Growth

Area	% change from 1992 to 1999			Rank[2]
	Number of Firms	Employment	Sales	
MSA[1]	59.0	129.5	155.5	9

Note: (1) Metropolitan Statistical Area - see Appendix A for areas included; (2) Calculated on an averaging of the percent growth of number of businesses, employment and sales
Source: The National Foundation for Women Business Owners, 1999 Facts on Women-Owned Businesses: Trends in the Top 50 Metropolitan Areas

Minority Business Opportunity

Orlando is home to one company which is on the Black Enterprise Auto Dealer 100 list (largest based on gross sales): Tropical Ford Inc. (Ford) . Criteria: 1) operational in previous calendar year; 2) at least 51% black-owned. *Black Enterprise, www.blackenterprise.com*

Four of the 500 largest Hispanic-owned companies in the U.S. are located in Orlando. *Hispanic Business, June 1999*

Orlando is home to two companies which are on the Hispanic Business Fastest-Growing 100 list (greatest sales growth from 1994 to 1998): Kid's Prep School Inc. (child care svcs.); Cafe Homes (building contractor). *Hispanic Business, July/August 1999*

HOTELS & MOTELS

Hotels/Motels

Area	Hotels/ Motels	Rooms	Luxury-Level Hotels/Motels		Average Minimum Rates ($)		
			♦♦♦♦	♦♦♦♦♦	♦♦	♦♦♦	♦♦♦♦
City	105	34,419	5	0	62	119	202
Airport	16	4,246	0	0	n/a	n/a	n/a
Suburbs	149	52,527	4	0	n/a	n/a	n/a
Total	270	91,192	9	0	n/a	n/a	n/a

Note: n/a not available; classifications range from one diamond (budget properties with basic amenities) to five diamond (luxury properties with the finest service, rooms and facilities).
Source: OAG, Business Travel Planner, Winter 1998-99

Orlando is home to two of the top 100 hotels in the world according to *Travel & Leisure*: Disney's Yacht & Beach Club Resort (#22) and Disney's Grand Floridian (#49) . Criteria: value, rooms/ambience, location, facilities/activities and service. *Travel & Leisure, 1998 World's Best Awards, Best Hotels and Resorts*

CONVENTION CENTERS

Major Convention Centers

Center Name	Meeting Rooms	Exhibit Space (sq. ft.)
Buena Vista Palace	40	88,000
Centroplex Expo Centre	7	65,000
Orange County Convention Center	41	35,000
Stouffer Orlando Resort	45	180,000
The Peabody Orlando	32	54,000
Tupperware Convention Center	3	23,600
Twin Towers Hotel and Convention Center	n/a	n/a

Note: n/a not available
Source: Trade Shows Worldwide, 1998; Meetings & Conventions, 4/15/99;
Sucessful Meetings, 3/31/98

Living Environment

COST OF LIVING

Cost of Living Index

Composite Index	Groceries	Housing	Utilities	Trans-portation	Health Care	Misc. Goods/Services
100.5	98.6	95.4	102.3	96.6	112.5	104.6

Note: U.S. = 100
Source: ACCRA, Cost of Living Index, 1st Quarter 1999

HOUSING

Median Home Prices and Housing Affordability

Area	Median Price[2] 1st Qtr. 1999 ($)	HOI[3] 1st Qtr. 1999	Afford-ability Rank[4]
MSA[1]	107,000	79.5	62
U.S.	134,000	69.6	–

Note: (1) Metropolitan Statistical Area - see Appendix A for areas included; (2) U.S. figures calculated from the sales of 524,324 new and existing homes in 181 markets; (3) Housing Opportunity Index - percent of homes sold that were within the reach of the median income household at the prevailing mortgage interest rate; (4) Rank is from 1-181 with 1 being most affordable
Source: National Association of Home Builders, Housing Opportunity Index, 1st Quarter 1999

Median Home Price Projection

It is projected that the median price of existing single-family homes in the metro area will increase by 4.6% in 1999. Nationwide, home prices are projected to increase 3.8%.
Kiplinger's Personal Finance Magazine, January 1999

Average New Home Price

Area	Price ($)
City	133,713
U.S.	142,735

Note: Figures are based on a new home with 1,800 sq. ft. of living area on an 8,000 sq. ft. lot.
Source: ACCRA, Cost of Living Index, 1st Quarter 1999

Average Apartment Rent

Area	Rent ($/mth)
City	655
U.S.	601

Note: Figures are based on an unfurnished two bedroom, 1-1/2 or 2 bath apartment, approximately 950 sq. ft. in size, excluding all utilities except water
Source: ACCRA, Cost of Living Index, 1st Quarter 1999

RESIDENTIAL UTILITIES

Average Residential Utility Costs

Area	All Electric ($/mth)	Part Electric ($/mth)	Other Energy ($/mth)	Phone ($/mth)
City	100.63	–	–	21.41
U.S.	100.02	55.73	43.33	19.71

Source: ACCRA, Cost of Living Index, 1st Quarter 1999

HEALTH CARE

Average Health Care Costs

Area	Hospital ($/day)	Doctor ($/visit)	Dentist ($/visit)
City	515.50	61.10	73.90
U.S.	430.43	52.45	66.35

Note: Hospital—based on a semi-private room; Doctor—based on a general practitioner's routine exam of an established patient; Dentist—based on adult teeth cleaning and periodic oral exam.
Source: ACCRA, Cost of Living Index, 1st Quarter 1999

Distribution of Office-Based Physicians

Area	Family/Gen. Practitioners	Specialists Medical	Specialists Surgical	Specialists Other
MSA[1]	332	748	647	549

Note: Data as of 12/31/97; (1) Metropolitan Statistical Area - see Appendix A for areas included
Source: American Medical Assn., Physician Characteristics & Distribution in the U.S., 1999

Hospitals

Orlando has 4 general medical and surgical hospitals, 1 psychiatric, 1 children's psychiatric. *AHA Guide to the Healthcare Field, 1998-99*

According to *U.S. News and World Report,* Orlando has 1 of the best hospitals in the U.S.: **Florida Hospital Medical Center,** noted for endocrinology. *U.S. News Online, "America's Best Hospitals," 10th Edition, www.usnews.com*

EDUCATION

Public School District Statistics

District Name	Num. Sch.	Enroll.	Classroom Teachers	Pupils per Teacher	Minority Pupils (%)	Current Exp.[1] ($/pupil)
Orange County Sch Dist	160	133,826	7,754	17.3	50.8	4,997

Note: Data covers the 1997-1998 school year unless otherwise noted; (1) Data covers fiscal year 1996; SD = School District; ISD = Independent School District; n/a not available
Source: National Center for Education Statistics, Common Core of Data Public Education Agency Universe 1997-98; National Center for Education Statistics, Characteristics of the 100 Largest Public Elementary and Secondary School Districts in the United States: 1997-98, July 1999

Educational Quality

School District	Education Quotient[1]	Graduate Outcome[2]	Community Index[3]	Resource Index[4]
Orange County	104.0	101.0	101.0	111.0

Note: Nearly 1,000 secondary school districts were rated in terms of educational quality. The scores range from a low of 50 to a high of 150; (1) Average of the Graduate Outcome, Community and Resource indexes; (2) Based on graduation rates and college board scores (SAT/ACT); (3) Based on the surrounding community's average level of education and the area's average income level; (4) Based on teacher salaries, per-pupil expenditures and student-teacher ratios.
Source: Expansion Management, Ratings Issue, 1998

Educational Attainment by Race

Area	High School Graduate (%) Total	White	Black	Other	Hisp.[2]	Bachelor's Degree (%) Total	White	Black	Other	Hisp.[2]
City	78.1	85.2	56.5	69.3	67.0	22.6	26.6	9.8	21.2	17.0
MSA[1]	79.9	82.6	60.3	72.0	68.9	21.6	22.8	11.5	21.4	16.0
U.S.	75.2	77.9	63.1	60.4	49.8	20.3	21.5	11.4	19.4	9.2

Note: Figures shown cover persons 25 years old and over; (1) Metropolitan Statistical Area - see Appendix A for areas included; (2) people of Hispanic origin can be of any race
Source: 1990 Census of Population and Housing, Summary Tape File 3C

School Enrollment by Type

Area	Preprimary Public Enrollment	%	Preprimary Private Enrollment	%	Elementary/High School Public Enrollment	%	Elementary/High School Private Enrollment	%
City	1,419	60.7	918	39.3	19,932	92.8	1,549	7.2
MSA[1]	9,698	49.2	9,997	50.8	154,434	91.4	14,467	8.6
U.S.	2,679,029	59.5	1,824,256	40.5	38,379,689	90.2	4,187,099	9.8

Note: Figures shown cover persons 3 years old and over;
(1) Metropolitan Statistical Area - see Appendix A for areas included
Source: 1990 Census of Population and Housing, Summary Tape File 3C

School Enrollment by Race

Area	Preprimary (%)				Elementary/High School (%)			
	White	Black	Other	Hisp.[1]	White	Black	Other	Hisp.[1]
City	60.2	37.5	2.3	10.9	49.0	44.6	6.4	11.9
MSA[2]	82.3	14.2	3.5	7.5	74.8	18.7	6.5	11.8
U.S.	80.4	12.5	7.1	7.8	74.1	15.6	10.3	12.5

Note: Figures shown cover persons 3 years old and over; (1) people of Hispanic origin can be of any race; (2) Metropolitan Statistical Area - see Appendix A for areas included
Source: 1990 Census of Population and Housing, Summary Tape File 3C

Classroom Teacher Salaries in Public Schools

District	B.A. Degree		M.A. Degree		Maximum	
	Min. ($)	Rank[1]	Max. ($)	Rank[1]	Max. ($)	Rank[1]
	n/a	n/a	n/a	n/a	n/a	n/a
Average	26,980	-	46,065	-	51,435	-

Note: Salaries are for 1997-1998; (1) Rank ranges from 1 to 100; n/a not available
Source: American Federation of Teachers, Survey & Analysis of Salary Trends, 1998

Higher Education

Two-Year Colleges		Four-Year Colleges		Medical Schools	Law Schools	Voc/ Tech
Public	Private	Public	Private			
1	3	1	1	0	1	15

Source: College Blue Book, Occupational Education, 1997; Medical School Admission Requirements, 1999-2000; Peterson's Guide to Two-Year Colleges, 1999; Peterson's Guide to Four-Year Colleges, 2000; Barron's Guide to Law Schools, 1999

MAJOR EMPLOYERS

Major Employers

Darden Restaurants	CFI Resorts Management
Harcourt Brace & Co.	Orlando Regional Healthcare System
Sea World of Florida	Sentinel Communications
Service America	Universal City Florida
Tamar Inns	Walt Disney World

Note: Companies listed are located in the city
Source: Dun's Business Rankings, 1999; Ward's Business Directory, 1998

PUBLIC SAFETY

Crime Rate

Area	All Crimes	Violent Crimes				Property Crimes		
		Murder	Forcible Rape	Robbery	Aggrav. Assault	Burglary	Larceny -Theft	Motor Vehicle Theft
City	13,626.5	7.5	93.6	679.1	1,501.3	2,380.6	7,658.9	1,305.4
Suburbs[1]	6,766.4	3.5	47.3	206.0	629.0	1,403.8	3,901.3	575.4
MSA[2]	7,658.0	4.1	53.4	267.5	742.4	1,530.8	4,389.6	670.3
U.S.	4,922.7	6.8	35.9	186.1	382.0	919.6	2,886.5	505.8

Note: Crime rate is the number of crimes per 100,000 pop.; (1) defined as all areas within the MSA but located outside the central city; (2) Metropolitan Statistical Area - see Appendix A for areas incl.
Source: FBI Uniform Crime Reports, 1997

RECREATION

Culture and Recreation

Museums	Symphony Orchestras	Opera Companies	Dance Companies	Professional Theatres	Zoos	Pro Sports Teams
3	1	1	1	2	1	1

Source: International Directory of the Performing Arts, 1997; Official Museum Directory, 1999; Stern's Performing Arts Directory, 1997; USA Today Four Sport Stadium Guide, 1997; Chamber of Commerce/Economic Development, 1999

Library System

The Orange County Library System has 11 branches, holdings of 1,739,300 volumes, and a budget of $16,846,314 (1995-1996). *American Library Directory, 1998-1999*

MEDIA

Newspapers

Name	Type	Freq.	Distribution	Circulation
The Orlando Sentinel	General	7x/wk	Regional	250,887
Orlando Sun Review	General	1x/wk	Local	16,000

Note: Includes newspapers with circulations of 1,000 or more located in the city;
Source: Burrelle's Media Directory, 1999 Edition

Television Stations

Name	Ch.	Affiliation	Type	Owner
WESH	n/a	NBCT	Commercial	Pulitzer Broadcasting Company
WKMG	n/a	CBST	Commercial	Post-Newsweek Business Information Inc.
WFTV	n/a	ABCT	Commercial	Cox Communications Inc.
WMFE	24	PBS	Public	Community Communications Inc.
WACX	55	n/a	Commercial	Associated Christian Television System
WOPX	56	n/a	Commercial	Paxson Communications Corporation
WRBW	65	UPN	Commercial	Rainbow Broadcasting Ltd.

Note: Stations included broadcast in the Orlando metro area; n/a not available
Source: Burrelle's Media Directory, 1999 Edition

FM Radio Stations

Call Letters	Freq. (mHz)	Target Audience	Station Format	Music Format
WLAZ	88.7	G/H	E/M	Latin
WUCF	89.9	General	M/N	Jazz
WMFE	90.7	General	E/M/N	Classical
WPRK	91.5	General	E/M	Alternative/Classical/Jazz/Latin/Urban Contemporary
WWKA	92.3	General	M/N/S	Country
WCFB	94.5	General	M/N/S	Urban Contemporary
WPYO	95.3	General	M	Adult Top 40
WHTQ	96.5	General	M/N/S	Classic Rock
WMMO	98.9	General	M	Adult Contemporary
WSHE	100.3	General	M	Oldies
WJRR	101.1	General	M	AOR
WJHM	101.9	General	M/N/T	R&B/Urban Contemporary
WLOQ	103.1	General	M	Jazz
WTKS	104.1	General	M/T	Adult Contemporary/Modern Rock
WOMX	105.1	General	M/N	Adult Contemporary
WOCL	105.9	General	M/N/T	Oldies/R&B
WXXL	106.7	General	M/N/T	Top 40
WMGF	107.7	General	M/N	Adult Contemporary

Note: Stations included broadcast in the Orlando metro area
Station Format: E=Educational; M=Music; N=News; S=Sports; T=Talk
Target Audience: A=Asian; B=Black; C=Christian; E=Ethnic; F=French; G=General; H=Hispanic;
M=Men; N=Native American; R=Religious; S=Senior Citizen; W=Women; Y=Young Adult; Z=Children
Music Format: AOR=Album Oriented Rock; MOR=Middle-of-the-Road
Source: Burrelle's Media Directory, 1999 Edition

AM Radio Stations

Call Letters	Freq. (kHz)	Target Audience	Station Format	Music Format
WQTM	540	Men	S	n/a
WDBO	580	General	N/T	n/a
WWNZ	740	General	N/S	n/a
WHOO	990	General	M/N/S	Oldies
WONQ	1030	Hispanic	M/N/S	Adult Contemporary/Latin
WAJL	1190	General	E/M/N/T	Gospel/Reggae
WPRD	1440	A/H/R	M/N/S/T	Latin
WUNA	1480	Hispanic	M	Latin
WOKB	1600	General	M/T	Christian

Note: Stations included broadcast in the Orlando metro area; n/a not available
Target Audience: A=Asian; B=Black; C=Christian; E=Ethnic; F=French; G=General; H=Hispanic; M=Men; N=Native American; R=Religious; S=Senior Citizen; W=Women; Y=Young Adult; Z=Children
Station Format: E=Educational; M=Music; N=News; S=Sports; T=Talk
Source: Burrelle's Media Directory, 1999 Edition

CLIMATE

Average and Extreme Temperatures

Temperature	Jan	Feb	Mar	Apr	May	Jun	Jul	Aug	Sep	Oct	Nov	Dec	Yr.
Extreme High (°F)	86	89	90	95	100	100	99	100	98	95	89	90	100
Average High (°F)	70	72	77	82	87	90	91	91	89	83	78	72	82
Average Temp. (°F)	59	62	67	72	77	81	82	82	81	75	68	62	72
Average Low (°F)	48	51	56	60	66	71	73	74	72	66	58	51	62
Extreme Low (°F)	19	29	25	38	51	53	64	65	57	44	32	20	19

Note: Figures cover the years 1952-1990
Source: National Climatic Data Center, International Station Meteorological Climate Summary, 3/95

Average Precipitation/Snowfall/Humidity

Precip./Humidity	Jan	Feb	Mar	Apr	May	Jun	Jul	Aug	Sep	Oct	Nov	Dec	Yr.
Avg. Precip. (in.)	2.3	2.8	3.4	2.0	3.2	7.0	7.2	5.8	5.8	2.7	3.5	2.0	47.7
Avg. Snowfall (in.)	Tr	0	0	0	0	0	0	0	0	0	0	0	Tr
Avg. Rel. Hum. 7am (%)	87	87	88	87	88	89	90	92	92	89	89	87	89
Avg. Rel. Hum. 4pm (%)	53	51	49	47	51	61	65	66	66	59	56	55	57

Note: Figures cover the years 1952-1990; Tr = Trace amounts (<0.05 in. of rain; <0.5 in. of snow)
Source: National Climatic Data Center, International Station Meteorological Climate Summary, 3/95

Weather Conditions

Temperature			Daytime Sky			Precipitation		
32°F & below	45°F & below	90°F & above	Clear	Partly cloudy	Cloudy	0.01 inch or more precip.	0.1 inch or more snow/ice	Thunder-storms
3	35	90	76	208	81	115	0	80

Note: Figures are average number of days per year and covers the years 1952-1990
Source: National Climatic Data Center, International Station Meteorological Climate Summary, 3/95

AIR & WATER QUALITY

Maximum Pollutant Concentrations

	Particulate Matter (ug/m³)	Carbon Monoxide (ppm)	Sulfur Dioxide (ppm)	Nitrogen Dioxide (ppm)	Ozone (ppm)	Lead (ug/m³)
MSA[1] Level	52	4	0.006	0.013	0.11	n/a
NAAQS[2]	150	9	0.140	0.053	0.12	1.50
Met NAAQS?	Yes	Yes	Yes	Yes	Yes	n/a

Note: (1) Metropolitan Statistical Area - see Appendix A for areas included; (2) National Ambient Air Quality Standards; ppm = parts per million; ug/m³ = micrograms per cubic meter; n/a not available
Source: EPA, National Air Quality and Emissions Trends Report, 1997

Pollutant Standards Index

In the Orlando MSA (see Appendix A for areas included), the Pollutant Standards Index (PSI) exceeded 100 on 5 days in 1997. A PSI value greater than 100 indicates that air quality would be in the unhealthful range on that day. *EPA, National Air Quality and Emissions Trends Report, 1997*

Drinking Water

Water System Name	Pop. Served	Primary Water Source Type	Number of Violations in 1998	Type of Violation/ Contaminants
Orlando Utilities Commission	356,041	Ground	None	None

Note: Data as of July 10, 1999
Source: EPA, Office of Ground Water and Drinking Water, Safe Drinking Water Information System

Orlando tap water is alkaline, hard and fluoridated.
Editor & Publisher Market Guide, 1999

San Antonio, Texas

Background

San Antonio is a charming preservation of its Mexican-Spanish heritage. Walking along its famous Paseo Del Rio at night, with cream colored stucco structures, seashell ornamented facades, and gently illuminating tiny lights is very romantic.

Emotional intensity is nothing new to San Antonio. The city began in the early 18th century as a cohesion of different Spanish missions, whose zealous aim was to convert the Coahuiltecan natives to Christianity and European ways of farming. A debilitating epidemic, however, killed most of the natives, as well as the missions' goal, causing the city to be abandoned.

In 1836, San Antonio became the site of interest again, when a small band of American soldiers were unable to successfully defend themselves against an army of 4,000 Mexican soldiers, led by General Antonio de Lopez Santa Anna. Fighting desperately from within the walls of the Mission San Antonio de Valero, or The Alamo, all 183 men were killed. This commendable act of courage inspired the cry "Remember the Alamo," from the throats of every American soldier led by General Sam Houston, who were determined to wrest Texas territory and independence from Mexico.

Despite the Anglo victory over the Mexicans more than 150 years ago, the Mexican culture and its influence remains strong. We see the evidence of this in the architecture, the Franciscan educational system, the variety of Spanish-language media, and the racial composition of the population, in which over half the city's residents are Latino.

This picturesque and practical blend of old and new makes San Antonio unique among American cities. One will see this not only in the lifestyle, but in the types of jobs available as well—particularly in the military sector.

The city also has diversified growth sectors which continue to build on its core tourism and trade strengths. The city's Kelly Air Force Base is becoming a city-run industrial and warehouse complex and much of the nearly 5,000-acre base will be available for economic development. The city is also investing $12 million in a new downtown International Center that will be home to the North American Development Bank. Completed projects include a $22 million plant expansion by Frito Lay, and a new San Antonio call center by Southwestern Bell that employs 1,000. *Site Selection, December 1997/January 1998*

San Antonio's location on the edge of the Gulf Coastal Plains exposes it to a modified subtropical climate. Summers are hot with temperatures above 90 degrees 80 percent of the time, although extremely high temperatures are rare. Winters are mild.

Since the city is only 140 miles from the Gulf of Mexico, tropical storms occasionally occur, bringing strong winds and heavy rains. Relative humidity is above 80 percent during the early morning hours, dropping to near 50 percent in the late afternoon.

General Rankings and Evaluative Comments

- San Antonio was ranked #13 out of 19 large, southern metropolitan areas in *Money's* 1998 survey of "The Best Places to Live in America." The survey was conducted by first contacting 512 representative households nationwide and asking them to rank 37 quality-of-life factors on a scale of 1 to 10. Next, a demographic profile was compiled on the 300 largest metropolitan statistical areas in the U.S. The numbers were crunched together to arrive at an overall ranking (things Americans consider most important, like clean air and water, low crime and good schools, received extra weight). Unlike previous years, the 1998 rankings were broken down by region (northeast, midwest, south, west) and population size (100,000 to 249,999; 250,000 to 999,999; 1 million plus). The city had a nationwide ranking of #53 out of 300 in 1997 and #17 out of 300 in 1996. *Money, July 1998; Money, July 1997; Money, September 1996*

- *Ladies Home Journal* ranked America's 200 largest cities based on the qualities women care about most. San Antonio ranked #147 out of 200. Criteria: low crime rate, well-paying jobs, quality health and child care, good public schools, the presence of women in government, size of the gender wage gap, number of sexual-harassment and discrimination complaints filed, unemployment and divorce rates, commute times, population density, number of houses of worship, parks and cultural offerings, number of women's health specialists, how well a community's women cared for themselves, complexion kindness index based on UV radiation levels, odds of finding affordable fashions, rental rates for romance movies, champagne sales and other matters of the heart. *Ladies Home Journal, November 1998*

- Zero Population Growth ranked 229 cities in terms of children's health, safety, and economic well-being. San Antonio was ranked #68 out of 112 independent cities (cities with populations greater than 100,000 which were neither Major Cities nor Suburbs/Outer Cities) and was given a grade of C. Criteria: total population, percent of population under 18 years of age, household language, percent population change, percent of births to teens, infant mortality rate, percent of low birth weights, dropout rate, enrollment in preprimary school, violent and property crime rates, unemployment rate, percent of children in poverty, percent of owner occupied units, number of bad air days, percent of public transportation commuters, and average travel time to work. *Zero Population Growth, Children's Environmental Index, Fall 1999*

- San Antonio was ranked #21 out of 59 metro areas in *The Regional Economist's* "Rational Livability Ranking of 59 Large Metro Areas." The rankings were based on the metro area's total population change over the period 1990-97 divided by the number of people moving in from elsewhere in the United States (net domestic in-migration). *St. Louis Federal Reserve Bank of St. Louis, The Regional Economist, April 1999*

- San Antonio appeared on *Travel & Leisure's* list of the world's 100 best cities. It was ranked #11 in the U.S. and #28 in the world. Criteria: activities/attractions, culture/arts, people, restaurants/food, and value. *Travel & Leisure, 1998 World's Best Awards*

- *Conde Nast Traveler* polled 37,293 readers for travel satisfaction. Cities were ranked based on the following criteria: people/friendliness, environment/ambiance, cultural enrichment, restaurants and fun/energy. San Antonio appeared in the top 25, ranking number 12, with an overall rating of 67.5 out of 100. *Conde Nast Traveler, Readers' Choice Poll 1998*

- Cognetics studied 273 metro areas in the United States, ranking them by entrepreneurial activity. San Antonio was ranked #17 out of the 50 largest metro areas. Criteria: Significant Starts (firms started in the last 10 years that still employ at least 5 people) and Young Growers (percent of firms 10 years old or less that grew significantly during the last 4 years). Cognetics, "Entrepreneurial Hot Spots: The Best Places in America to Start and Grow a Company," 1998

- San Antonio was selected as one of the "Best American Cities to Start a Business" by *Point of View* magazine. Criteria: coolness, quality-of-life, and business concerns. The city was ranked #47 out of 75. *Point of View, November 1998*

- Reliastar Financial Corp. ranked the 125 largest metropolitan areas according to the general financial security of residents. San Antonio was ranked #32 out of 125 with a score of 6.1. The score indicates the percentage a metropolitan area is above or below the metropolitan norm. A metro area with a score of 10.6 is 10.6% above the metro average. Criteria: Earnings and Wealth Potential (household income, education, net assets, cost of living); Safety Net (health insurance, retirement savings, life insurance, income support programs); Personal Threats (unemployment rate, low-income households, crime rate); Community Economic Vitality (cost of community services, job quality, job creation, housing costs).
  Reliastar Financial Corp., "The Best Cities to Earn and Save Money," 1999 Edition

Business Environment

STATE ECONOMY

State Economic Profile

"Economic growth in Texas has slowed as both its new and old economies are under pressure. Weak commodity prices and over-capacity have hurt TX's old economic powers, agriculture and oil. Soft global demand has slowed TX's new economic powers, semiconductors and computer sales. A slowing US economy in 1999 will also place a drag on TX's biotech and software companies. Despite the current slowdown, TX's long-term outlook is extremely bright, and its current problems will last no more than two years.

Weak commodity prices, over-capacity and soft foreign demand have all coincided to undermine TX's oil and farm sector. Despite OPEC cutbacks, the TX oil industry remains vulnerable because of its high costs, high inventories and high capacity. TX's farm sector is similarly positioned; commodity prices are expected to continue their long-term downward trend.

The TX economy is more diversified today than ever before. Growth in services and hi-tech employment have more than offset declines in TX's resource economy. Services employment in 1998 grew at 3.8%, adding some 93,000 jobs, while construction employment grew 4.9%, adding 22,700 jobs. Construction employment, along with home sales and starts, should contract in 1999 and 2000. TX's demographic situation is positive; the state continues to attract educated, young households. However, the current weakness in the state's semiconductor and computer industry has slowed job growth from its previous feverish pace. In the near-term, TX's growth should slow along with the US economy. Its long-term prospects are bright given its business friendly atmosphere and central location." *National Association of Realtors, Economic Profiles: The Fifty States and the District of Columbia, http://nar.realtor.com/databank/profiles.htm*

IMPORTS/EXPORTS

Total Export Sales

Area	1994 ($000)	1995 ($000)	1996 ($000)	1997 ($000)	% Chg. 1994-97	% Chg. 1996-97
MSA[1]	656,276	771,089	1,049,965	1,342,822	104.6	27.9
U.S.	512,415,609	583,030,524	622,827,063	687,597,999	34.2	10.4

Note: (1) Metropolitan Statistical Area - see Appendix A for areas included
Source: U.S. Department of Commerce, International Trade Association, Metropolitan Area Exports: An Export Performance Report on Over 250 U.S. Cities, November 10, 1998

CITY FINANCES

City Government Finances

Component	FY94 ($000)	FY94 (per capita $)
Revenue	1,677,193	1,622.08
Expenditure	1,685,100	1,629.72
Debt Outstanding	4,274,074	4,133.62
Cash & Securities	1,257,491	1,216.17

Source: U.S. Bureau of the Census, City Government Finances: 1993-94

City Government Revenue by Source

Source	FY94 ($000)	FY94 (per capita $)	FY94 (%)
From Federal Government	24,556	23.75	1.5
From State Governments	74,339	71.90	4.4
From Local Governments	52,142	50.43	3.1
Property Taxes	131,262	126.95	7.8
General Sales Taxes	80,683	78.03	4.8
Selective Sales Taxes	33,386	32.29	2.0
Income Taxes	0	0.00	0.0
Current Charges	192,260	185.94	11.5
Utility/Liquor Store	975,098	943.05	58.1
Employee Retirement[1]	33,295	32.20	2.0
Other	80,172	77.54	4.8

Note: (1) Excludes "city contributions," classified as "nonrevenue," intragovernmental transfers.
Source: U.S. Bureau of the Census, City Government Finances: 1993-94

City Government Expenditures by Function

Function	FY94 ($000)	FY94 (per capita $)	FY94 (%)
Educational Services	27,126	26.23	1.6
Employee Retirement[1]	13,918	13.46	0.8
Environment/Housing	249,846	241.64	14.8
Government Administration	31,553	30.52	1.9
Interest on General Debt	56,321	54.47	3.3
Public Safety	194,829	188.43	11.6
Social Services	46,703	45.17	2.8
Transportation	99,377	96.11	5.9
Utility/Liquor Store	908,336	878.49	53.9
Other	57,091	55.21	3.4

Note: (1) Payments to beneficiaries including withdrawal of contributions.
Source: U.S. Bureau of the Census, City Government Finances: 1993-94

Municipal Bond Ratings

Area	Moody's	S & P
San Antonio	n/a	n/a

Note: n/a not available; n/r not rated
Source: Moody's Bond Record, 6/99

POPULATION

Population Growth

Area	1980	1990	% Chg. 1980-90	July 1998 Estimate	% Chg. 1990-98
City	785,809	935,927	19.1	1,114,130	19.0
MSA[1]	1,072,125	1,302,099	21.5	1,545,231	18.7
U.S.	226,545,805	248,765,170	9.8	270,299,000	8.7

Note: (1) Metropolitan Statistical Area - see Appendix A for areas included;
July 1998 MSA population estimate was calculated by the editors
Source: 1980/1990 Census of Housing and Population, Summary Tape File 3C;
Census Bureau Population Estimates 1998

Population Characteristics

Race	City 1980 Population	%	City 1990 Population	%	% Chg. 1980-90	MSA[1] 1990 Population	%
White	621,679	79.1	676,464	72.3	8.8	979,319	75.2
Black	57,566	7.3	65,852	7.0	14.4	88,709	6.8
Amer Indian/Esk/Aleut	2,375	0.3	3,447	0.4	45.1	4,673	0.4
Asian/Pacific Islander	5,821	0.7	10,625	1.1	82.5	16,020	1.2
Other	98,368	12.5	179,539	19.2	82.5	213,378	16.4
Hispanic Origin[2]	421,954	53.7	517,974	55.3	22.8	616,878	47.4

Note: (1) Metropolitan Statistical Area - see Appendix A for areas included;
(2) people of Hispanic origin can be of any race
Source: 1980/1990 Census of Housing and Population, Summary Tape File 3C

Ancestry

Area	German	Irish	English	Italian	U.S.	French	Polish	Dutch
City	14.0	8.2	7.7	1.7	2.1	2.4	1.6	0.9
MSA[1]	17.9	9.8	9.2	1.9	2.4	2.8	2.0	1.1
U.S.	23.3	15.6	13.1	5.9	5.3	4.2	3.8	2.5

Note: Figures are percentages and include persons that reported multiple ancestry (eg. if a person reported being Irish and Italian, they were included in both columns); (1) Metropolitan Statistical Area - see Appendix A for areas included
Source: 1990 Census of Population and Housing, Summary Tape File 3C

Age

Area	Median Age (Years)	Age Distribution (%) Under 5	Under 18	18-24	25-44	45-64	65+	80+
City	29.8	8.4	29.1	11.5	32.4	16.7	10.4	2.2
MSA[1]	30.3	8.3	29.0	11.0	32.7	17.2	10.2	2.1
U.S.	32.9	7.3	25.6	10.5	32.6	18.7	12.5	2.8

Note: (1) Metropolitan Statistical Area - see Appendix A for areas included
Source: 1990 Census of Population and Housing, Summary Tape File 3C

Male/Female Ratio

Area	Number of males per 100 females (all ages)	Number of males per 100 females (18 years old+)
City	93.0	88.7
MSA[1]	94.6	90.7
U.S.	95.0	91.9

Note: (1) Metropolitan Statistical Area - see Appendix A for areas included
Source: 1990 Census of Population, General Population Characteristics

INCOME

Per Capita/Median/Average Income

Area	Per Capita ($)	Median Household ($)	Average Household ($)
City	10,884	23,584	30,622
MSA[1]	11,865	26,092	33,646
U.S.	14,420	30,056	38,453

Note: All figures are for 1989; (1) Metropolitan Statistical Area - see Appendix A for areas included
Source: 1990 Census of Population and Housing, Summary Tape File 3C

Household Income Distribution by Race

Income ($)	City (%)					U.S. (%)				
	Total	White	Black	Other	Hisp.[1]	Total	White	Black	Other	Hisp.[1]
Less than 5,000	9.8	8.2	17.9	13.7	13.2	6.2	4.8	15.2	8.6	8.8
5,000 - 9,999	10.1	9.3	12.9	12.5	12.6	9.3	8.6	14.2	9.9	11.1
10,000 - 14,999	11.2	10.5	13.0	13.8	13.2	8.8	8.5	11.0	9.8	11.0
15,000 - 24,999	21.3	20.7	22.0	23.8	23.1	17.5	17.3	18.9	18.5	20.5
25,000 - 34,999	16.3	16.3	14.4	16.9	15.9	15.8	16.1	14.2	15.4	16.4
35,000 - 49,999	15.1	16.1	11.2	12.4	13.2	17.9	18.6	13.3	16.1	16.0
50,000 - 74,999	10.5	12.1	6.5	5.4	6.6	15.0	15.8	9.3	13.4	11.1
75,000 - 99,999	3.1	3.8	1.4	1.0	1.3	5.1	5.5	2.6	4.7	3.1
100,000+	2.4	2.9	0.8	0.6	0.8	4.4	4.8	1.3	3.7	1.9

Note: All figures are for 1989; (1) people of Hispanic origin can be of any race
Source: 1990 Census of Population and Housing, Summary Tape File 3C

Effective Buying Income

Area	Per Capita ($)	Median Household ($)	Average Household ($)
City	13,207	28,830	37,511
MSA[1]	14,764	31,311	42,249
U.S.	16,803	34,536	45,243

Note: Data as of 1/1/99; (1) Metropolitan Statistical Area - see Appendix A for areas included
Source: Standard Rate & Data Service, Newspaper Advertising Source, 9/99

Effective Household Buying Income Distribution

Area	% of Households Earning						
	$10,000 -$19,999	$20,000 -$34,999	$35,000 -$49,999	$50,000 -$74,999	$75,000 -$99,000	$100,000 -$124,999	$125,000 and up
City	18.5	25.0	16.7	14.8	5.6	1.8	1.9
MSA[1]	17.2	24.1	17.5	16.7	6.2	2.0	2.2
U.S.	16.0	22.6	18.2	18.9	7.2	2.4	2.7

Note: Data as of 1/1/99; (1) Metropolitan Statistical Area - see Appendix A for areas included
Source: Standard Rate & Data Service, Newspaper Advertising Source, 9/99

Poverty Rates by Race and Age

Area	Total (%)	By Race (%)				By Age (%)		
		White	Black	Other	Hisp.[2]	Under 5 years old	Under 18 years old	65 years and over
City	22.6	19.1	30.3	32.3	30.8	35.4	32.5	19.1
MSA[1]	19.5	16.2	26.4	30.5	29.3	30.3	27.7	17.2
U.S.	13.1	9.8	29.5	23.1	25.3	20.1	18.3	12.8

Note: Figures show the percent of people living below the poverty line in 1989. The average poverty threshold was $12,674 for a family of four in 1989; (1) Metropolitan Statistical Area - see Appendix A for areas included; (2) people of Hispanic origin can be of any race
Source: 1990 Census of Population and Housing, Summary Tape File 3C

EMPLOYMENT

Labor Force and Employment

Area	Civilian Labor Force			Workers Employed		
	Jun. 1998	Jun. 1999	% Chg.	Jun. 1998	Jun. 1999	% Chg.
City	531,687	543,082	2.1	504,016	521,309	3.4
MSA[1]	769,922	787,806	2.3	734,308	759,502	3.4
U.S.	138,798,000	140,666,000	1.3	132,265,000	134,395,000	1.6

Note: Data is not seasonally adjusted and covers workers 16 years of age and older;
(1) Metropolitan Statistical Area - see Appendix A for areas included
Source: Bureau of Labor Statistics, http://stats.bls.gov

Unemployment Rate

Area	1998						1999					
	Jul.	Aug.	Sep.	Oct.	Nov.	Dec.	Jan.	Feb.	Mar.	Apr.	May.	Jun.
City	4.7	4.4	4.2	3.7	3.6	3.3	3.7	3.3	3.1	2.9	3.2	4.0
MSA[1]	4.2	3.9	3.7	3.3	3.3	2.9	3.3	3.0	2.8	2.6	2.8	3.6
U.S.	4.7	4.5	4.4	4.2	4.1	4.0	4.8	4.7	4.4	4.1	4.0	4.5

Note: Data is not seasonally adjusted and covers workers 16 years of age and older; all figures are percentages; (1) Metropolitan Statistical Area - see Appendix A for areas included
Source: Bureau of Labor Statistics, http://stats.bls.gov

Employment by Industry

Sector	MSA[1]		U.S.
	Number of Employees	Percent of Total	Percent of Total
Services	233,400	33.0	30.4
Retail Trade	138,800	19.6	17.7
Government	131,900	18.7	15.6
Manufacturing	52,800	7.5	14.3
Finance/Insurance/Real Estate	47,200	6.7	5.9
Wholesale Trade	30,600	4.3	5.4
Transportation/Public Utilities	32,400	4.6	5.3
Construction	37,500	5.3	5.0
Mining	1,800	0.3	0.4

Note: Figures cover non-farm employment as of 6/99 and are not seasonally adjusted;
(1) Metropolitan Statistical Area - see Appendix A for areas included
Source: Bureau of Labor Statistics, http://stats.bls.gov

Employment by Occupation

Occupation Category	City (%)	MSA[1] (%)	U.S. (%)
White Collar	59.7	60.9	58.1
Executive/Admin./Management	11.7	12.3	12.3
Professional	13.3	14.0	14.1
Technical & Related Support	4.0	4.1	3.7
Sales	13.0	13.1	11.8
Administrative Support/Clerical	17.7	17.4	16.3
Blue Collar	23.1	22.8	26.2
Precision Production/Craft/Repair	10.7	10.9	11.3
Machine Operators/Assem./Insp.	4.4	4.3	6.8
Transportation/Material Movers	3.9	3.9	4.1
Cleaners/Helpers/Laborers	4.0	3.7	3.9
Services	16.2	15.0	13.2
Farming/Forestry/Fishing	1.0	1.3	2.5

Note: Figures cover employed persons 16 years old and over;
(1) Metropolitan Statistical Area - see Appendix A for areas included
Source: 1990 Census of Population and Housing, Summary Tape File 3C

Occupational Employment Projections: 1996 - 2006

Occupations Expected to Have the Largest Job Growth (ranked by numerical growth)	Fast-Growing Occupations[1] (ranked by percent growth)
1. Cashiers	1. Desktop publishers
2. Salespersons, retail	2. Systems analysts
3. General managers & top executives	3. Customer service representatives
4. Truck drivers, light	4. Physical therapy assistants and aides
5. Child care workers, private household	5. Computer engineers
6. General office clerks	6. Emergency medical technicians
7. Systems analysts	7. Medical assistants
8. Food preparation workers	8. Respiratory therapists
9. Food service workers	9. Telephone & cable TV line install & repair
10. Registered nurses	10. Physical therapists

Note: Projections cover Texas; (1) Excludes occupations with total job growth less than 300
Source: U.S. Department of Labor, Employment and Training Administration, America's Labor Market Information System (ALMIS)

TAXES

Major State and Local Tax Rates

State Corp. Income (%)	State Personal Income (%)	Residential Property (effective rate per $100)	Sales & Use State (%)	Sales & Use Local (%)	State Gasoline (cents/gallon)	State Cigarette (cents/pack)
None[a]	None	n/a	6.25	1.5	20.0	41.0

Note: Personal/corporate income, sales, gasoline and cigarette tax rates as of January 1999. Property tax rates as of 1997; (a) Texas imposes a franchise tax of 4.5% of earned surplus
Source: Federation of Tax Administrators, www.taxadmin.org; Washington D.C. Department of Finance and Revenue, Tax Rates and Tax Burdens in the District of Columbia: A Nationwide Comparison, July 1998; Chamber of Commerce, 1999

Total Taxes Per Capita and as a Percent of Income

Area	Per Capita Income ($)	Per Capita Taxes ($) Total	Federal	State/Local	Percent of Income (%) Total	Federal	State/Local
Texas	25,563	8,741	6,051	2,690	34.2	23.7	10.5
U.S.	27,876	9,881	6,690	3,191	35.4	24.0	11.4

Note: Figures are for 1998
Source: Tax Foundation, www.taxfoundation.org

Estimated Tax Burden

Area	State Income	Local Income	Property	Sales	Total
San Antonio	0	0	6,250	756	7,006

Note: The numbers are estimates of taxes paid by a married couple with two children and annual earnings of $75,000. Sales tax estimates assume they spend average amounts on food, clothing, household goods and gasoline. Property tax estimates assume they live in a $250,000 home.
Source: Kiplinger's Personal Finance Magazine, October 1998

**COMMERCIAL
REAL ESTATE**

Office Market

Class/ Location	Total Space (sq. ft.)	Vacant Space (sq. ft.)	Vac. Rate (%)	Under Constr. (sq. ft.)	Net Absorp. (sq. ft.)	Rental Rates ($/sq.ft./yr.)
Class A						
CBD	1,983,233	126,996	6.4	0	-1,865	15.00-21.94
Outside CBD	4,993,590	431,302	8.6	291,033	-230,856	14.75-24.00
Class B						
CBD	2,817,578	495,512	17.6	0	158,035	10.80-15.00
Outside CBD	7,038,837	902,423	12.8	154,679	121,551	10.20-20.00

Note: Data as of 10/98 and covers San Antonio; CBD = Central Business District; n/a not available;
Source: Society of Industrial and Office Realtors, 1999 Comparative Statistics of Industrial and Office
Real Estate Markets

"At least four major office projects will be completed in San Antonio during 1999, and several others are proposed. All tolled, an increase of six to 10 percent is expected in new construction, relieving the constraint in Class A vacancy. The new development will occur primarily in the north central and northwest markets. SIOR's reporters also expect rental rates and sales prices to gain as much as 10 percent in 1999. San Antonio's economy is based on industries that are expected to grow in the future. Above-average population growth and a young, bilingual work force will support this growth. The city will also benefit from additional NAFTA-related business, as the Mexican economy gains strength. Thus, another good year is likely for the San Antonio office market." *Society of Industrial and Office Realtors, 1999 Comparative Statistics of Industrial and Office Real Estate Markets*

Industrial Market

Location	Total Space (sq. ft.)	Vacant Space (sq. ft.)	Vac. Rate (%)	Under Constr. (sq. ft.)	Net Absorp. (sq. ft.)	Net Lease ($/sq.ft./yr.)
Central City	12,500,000	281,343	2.3	n/a	180,000	2.64-3.60
Suburban	47,442,970	3,551,157	7.5	1,152,508	1,100,000	3.12-7.44

Note: Data as of 10/98 and covers San Antonio; n/a not available
Source: Society of Industrial and Office Realtors, 1999 Comparative Statistics of Industrial and Office
Real Estate Markets

"The outlook for San Antonio is favorable. Continued population growth and rates of employment above national levels are expected. San Antonio's economy will be fueled by a stronger Mexican economy (NAFTA trade), thriving tourism, and the development of telecommunications, health care, and back office financial operations. Nevertheless, record levels of construction should fall by six to 10 percent in 1999. One reason for the downturn in construction may be the six million sq. ft. of inventory that will he released into the private sector when Kelly Air Force Base is redeveloped. Another is a moderate money supply. Our SIOR reporters expect sales prices to remain above replacement costs for a broad range of property sizes in 1999, and lease prices to remain flat. Speculative bulk distribution development will be concentrated in the northeast quadrant of the MSA with High Tech/R&D development in north central and northwest areas." *Society of Industrial and Office Realtors, 1999 Comparative Statistics of Industrial and Office Real Estate Markets*

COMMERCIAL UTILITIES

Typical Monthly Electric Bills

Area	Commercial Service ($/month)		Industrial Service ($/month)	
	12 kW demand 1,500 kWh	100 kW demand 30,000 kWh	1,000 kW demand 400,000 kWh	20,000 kW demand 10,000,000 kWh
City[1]	92	1,699[a]	17,068	288,200
U.S.[2]	150	2,174	23,995	508,569

Note: (1) Based on rates in effect January 1, 1998; (2) Based on rates in effect January 1, 1999;
(a) Based on 120 kW demand and 30,000 kWh usage.
Source: Memphis Light, Gas and Water, 1998 Utility Bill Comparisons for Selected U.S. Cities;
Edison Electric Institute, Typical Residential, Commercial and Industrial Bills, Winter 1999

TRANSPORTATION

Transportation Statistics

Average minutes to work	21.7
Interstate highways	I-10; I-35; I-37
Bus lines	
In-city	Via Metropolitan TA, 522 vehicles
Inter-city	3
Passenger air service	
Airport	San Antonio International
Airlines	13
Aircraft departures	45,301 (1996)
Enplaned passengers	3,319,410 (1996)
Rail service	Amtrak
Motor freight carriers	40
Major waterways/ports	None

Source: Editor & Publisher Market Guide, 1999; FAA Airport Activity Statistics, 1997; Amtrak National Time Table, Northeast Timetable, Spring/Summer 1999; 1990 Census of Population and Housing, STF 3C; Chamber of Commerce/Economic Development 1999; Jane's Urban Transport Systems 1999-2000

Means of Transportation to Work

Area	Car/Truck/Van Drove Alone	Car-pooled	Bus	Subway	Railroad	Bicycle	Walked	Other Means	Worked at Home
City	73.4	15.5	4.8	0.0	0.0	0.1	3.1	1.1	1.9
MSA[1]	74.6	14.8	3.6	0.0	0.0	0.2	3.6	1.0	2.3
U.S.	73.2	13.4	3.0	1.5	0.5	0.4	3.9	1.2	3.0

Note: Figures shown are percentages and only include workers 16 years old and over;
(1) Metropolitan Statistical Area - see Appendix A for areas included
Source: 1990 Census of Population and Housing, Summary Tape File 3C

BUSINESSES

Major Business Headquarters

Company Name	1999 Rankings Fortune 500	Forbes 500
HB Zachry	-	348
HE Butt Grocery	-	16
McCombs Enterprises	-	330
SBC Communications	35	-
USAA	214	-
Ultramar Diamond Shamrock	196	-
Valero Energy	294	-

Note: Companies listed are located in the city; dashes indicate no ranking
Fortune 500: Companies that produce a 10-K are ranked 1 to 500 based on 1998 revenue
Forbes 500: Private companies are ranked 1 to 500 based on 1997 revenue
Source: Forbes, November 30, 1998; Fortune, April 26, 1999

Best Companies to Work For

USAA (insurance), headquartered in San Antonio, is among the "100 Best Companies to Work for in America." Criteria: trust in management, pride in work/company, camaraderie, company responses to the Hewitt People Practices Inventory, and employee responses to their Great Place to Work survey. The companies also had to be at least 10 years old and have a minimum of 500 employees. *Fortune, January 11, 1999*

USAA (insurance), headquartered in San Antonio, is among the "100 Best Companies for Working Mothers." Criteria: fair wages, opportunities for women to advance, support for child care, flexible work schedules, family-friendly benefits, and work/life supports. Working Mother, October 1998

USAA (insurance), headquartered in San Antonio, is among the "100 Best Places to Work in IS." Criteria: compensation, turnover and training. *Computerworld, May 25, 1998*

Women-Owned Firms: Number, Employment and Sales

Area	Number of Firms	Employment	Sales ($000)	Rank[2]
MSA[1]	42,200	138,800	11,560,100	42

*Note: (1) Metropolitan Statistical Area - see Appendix A for areas included;
(2) Calculated on an averaging of the number of businesses, employment and sales
Source: The National Foundation for Women Business Owners, 1999 Facts on Women-Owned
Businesses: Trends in the Top 50 Metropolitan Areas*

Women-Owned Firms: Growth

Area	% change from 1992 to 1999			Rank[2]
	Number of Firms	Employment	Sales	
MSA[1]	39.3	126.4	125.4	33

*Note: (1) Metropolitan Statistical Area - see Appendix A for areas included; (2) Calculated on an
averaging of the percent growth of number of businesses, employment and sales
Source: The National Foundation for Women Business Owners, 1999 Facts on Women-Owned
Businesses: Trends in the Top 50 Metropolitan Areas*

Minority Business Opportunity

16 of the 500 largest Hispanic-owned companies in the U.S. are located in San Antonio.
Hispanic Business, June 1999

San Antonio is home to three companies which are on the Hispanic Business Fastest-Growing
100 list (greatest sales growth from 1994 to 1998): Davila Plumbing (plumbing & general
contracting); Madrid Properties Inc. (residential construction); Professional Performance
Development Group Inc. (medical log and management svcs.). *Hispanic Business,
July/August 1999*

Small Business Opportunity

According to *Forbes*, San Antonio is home to one of America's 200 best small companies:
Lancer. Criteria: companies included must be publicly traded since November 1997 with a
stock price of at least $5 per share and an average daily float of 1,000 shares. The company's
latest 12-month sales must be between $5 and $350 million, return on equity (ROE) must be a
minimum of 12% for both the past 5 years and the most recent four quarters, and five-year
sales and EPS growth must average at least 10%. Companies with declining sales or earnings
during the past year were dropped as well as businesses with debt/equity ratios over 1.25.
Companies with negative operating cash flow in each of the past two years were also
excluded. *Forbes, November 2, 1998*

HOTELS & MOTELS

Hotels/Motels

Area	Hotels/ Motels	Rooms	Luxury-Level Hotels/Motels		Average Minimum Rates ($)		
			♦♦♦♦	♦♦♦♦♦	♦♦	♦♦♦	♦♦♦♦
City	128	18,236	5	0	62	107	184
Airport	14	2,327	0	0	n/a	n/a	n/a
Suburbs	2	160	0	0	n/a	n/a	n/a
Total	144	20,723	5	0	n/a	n/a	n/a

*Note: n/a not available; classifications range from one diamond (budget properties with basic
amenities) to five diamond (luxury properties with the finest service, rooms and facilities).
Source: OAG, Business Travel Planner, Winter 1998-99*

CONVENTION CENTERS

Major Convention Centers

Center Name	Meeting Rooms	Exhibit Space (sq. ft.)
Alamodome	16	160,000
Henry B. Gonzalez Convention Center	46	240,000
Joe Freeman Coliseum	n/a	155,964
San Antonio Convention	43	240,000
San Antonio Municipal Auditorium	8	23,000
Villita Assembly Building	3	12,880

Note: n/a not available
Source: Trade Shows Worldwide, 1998; Meetings & Conventions, 4/15/99;
Sucessful Meetings, 3/31/98

Living Environment

COST OF LIVING

Cost of Living Index

Composite Index	Groceries	Housing	Utilities	Trans-portation	Health Care	Misc. Goods/ Services
89.9	83.7	84.0	77.1	98.7	89.0	98.5

Note: U.S. = 100
Source: ACCRA, Cost of Living Index, 1st Quarter 1999

HOUSING

Median Home Prices and Housing Affordability

Area	Median Price[2] 1st Qtr. 1999 ($)	HOI[3] 1st Qtr. 1999	Afford-ability Rank[4]
MSA[1]	94,000	71.4	108
U.S.	134,000	69.6	–

Note: (1) Metropolitan Statistical Area - see Appendix A for areas included; (2) U.S. figures calculated from the sales of 524,324 new and existing homes in 181 markets; (3) Housing Opportunity Index - percent of homes sold that were within the reach of the median income household at the prevailing mortgage interest rate; (4) Rank is from 1-181 with 1 being most affordable
Source: National Association of Home Builders, Housing Opportunity Index, 1st Quarter 1999

Median Home Price Projection

It is projected that the median price of existing single-family homes in the metro area will increase by 4.4% in 1999. Nationwide, home prices are projected to increase 3.8%.
Kiplinger's Personal Finance Magazine, January 1999

Average New Home Price

Area	Price ($)
City	119,181
U.S.	142,735

Note: Figures are based on a new home with 1,800 sq. ft. of living area on an 8,000 sq. ft. lot.
Source: ACCRA, Cost of Living Index, 1st Quarter 1999

Average Apartment Rent

Area	Rent ($/mth)
City	587
U.S.	601

Note: Figures are based on an unfurnished two bedroom, 1-1/2 or 2 bath apartment, approximately 950 sq. ft. in size, excluding all utilities except water
Source: ACCRA, Cost of Living Index, 1st Quarter 1999

RESIDENTIAL UTILITIES

Average Residential Utility Costs

Area	All Electric ($/mth)	Part Electric ($/mth)	Other Energy ($/mth)	Phone ($/mth)
City	–	54.80	20.83	16.38
U.S.	100.02	55.73	43.33	19.71

Source: ACCRA, Cost of Living Index, 1st Quarter 1999

HEALTH CARE

Average Health Care Costs

Area	Hospital ($/day)	Doctor ($/visit)	Dentist ($/visit)
City	405.40	49.40	53.80
U.S.	430.43	52.45	66.35

Note: Hospital—based on a semi-private room; Doctor—based on a general practitioner's routine exam of an established patient; Dentist—based on adult teeth cleaning and periodic oral exam.
Source: ACCRA, Cost of Living Index, 1st Quarter 1999

Distribution of Office-Based Physicians

Area	Family/Gen. Practitioners	Specialists		
		Medical	Surgical	Other
MSA[1]	359	798	635	747

Note: Data as of 12/31/97; (1) Metropolitan Statistical Area - see Appendix A for areas included
Source: American Medical Assn., Physician Characteristics & Distribution in the U.S., 1999

Hospitals

San Antonio has 1 general medical and surgical hospital, 3 psychiatric, 1 tuberculosis and other respiratory disease, 2 rehabilitation, 1 other specialty, 1 children's psychiatric. *AHA Guide to the Healthcare Field, 1998-99*

EDUCATION

Public School District Statistics

District Name	Num. Sch.	Enroll.	Classroom Teachers	Pupils per Teacher	Minority Pupils (%)	Current Exp.[1] ($/pupil)
Alamo Heights ISD	6	4,282	295	14.5	n/a	n/a
Blessed Sacrament Acad Charter	1	152	11	13.8	n/a	n/a
Building Alternative Charter	1	189	10	18.9	n/a	n/a
East Central ISD	11	7,102	445	16.0	n/a	n/a
Edgewood ISD	26	14,142	n/a	n/a	n/a	n/a
Ft Sam Houston ISD	3	1,318	117	11.3	n/a	n/a
Harlandale ISD	25	15,143	959	15.8	n/a	n/a
Judson ISD	20	15,828	1,048	15.1	n/a	n/a
Lackland ISD	2	956	73	13.1	n/a	n/a
North East ISD	59	46,550	3,052	15.3	47.3	5,075
Northside ISD	79	60,083	n/a	n/a	60.0	4,724
San Antonio ISD	108	61,112	n/a	n/a	94.9	5,628
South San Antonio ISD	19	10,338	700	14.8	n/a	n/a
Southside ISD	5	3,833	248	15.5	n/a	n/a
Southwest ISD	14	9,417	657	14.3	n/a	n/a

Note: Data covers the 1997-1998 school year unless otherwise noted; (1) Data covers fiscal year 1996; SD = School District; ISD = Independent School District; n/a not available
Source: National Center for Education Statistics, Common Core of Data Public Education Agency Universe 1997-98; National Center for Education Statistics, Characteristics of the 100 Largest Public Elementary and Secondary School Districts in the United States: 1997-98, July 1999

Educational Quality

School District	Education Quotient[1]	Graduate Outcome[2]	Community Index[3]	Resource Index[4]
San Antonio N.E. ISD	96.0	114.0	74.0	63.0

Note: Nearly 1,000 secondary school districts were rated in terms of educational quality. The scores range from a low of 50 to a high of 150; (1) Average of the Graduate Outcome, Community and Resource indexes; (2) Based on graduation rates and college board scores (SAT/ACT); (3) Based on the surrounding community's average level of education and the area's average income level; (4) Based on teacher salaries, per-pupil expenditures and student-teacher ratios.
Source: Expansion Management, Ratings Issue, 1998

Educational Attainment by Race

Area	High School Graduate (%)					Bachelor's Degree (%)				
	Total	White	Black	Other	Hisp.[2]	Total	White	Black	Other	Hisp.[2]
City	69.1	72.5	72.8	53.4	52.8	17.8	20.6	13.0	7.8	7.1
MSA[1]	72.7	75.8	75.9	55.4	54.4	19.4	22.0	14.4	8.2	7.7
U.S.	75.2	77.9	63.1	60.4	49.8	20.3	21.5	11.4	19.4	9.2

Note: Figures shown cover persons 25 years old and over; (1) Metropolitan Statistical Area - see Appendix A for areas included; (2) people of Hispanic origin can be of any race
Source: 1990 Census of Population and Housing, Summary Tape File 3C

School Enrollment by Type

Area	Preprimary Public Enrollment	%	Preprimary Private Enrollment	%	Elementary/High School Public Enrollment	%	Elementary/High School Private Enrollment	%
City	9,035	61.2	5,735	38.8	173,354	92.5	14,116	7.5
MSA[1]	12,989	59.1	8,978	40.9	240,288	92.4	19,686	7.6
U.S.	2,679,029	59.5	1,824,256	40.5	38,379,689	90.2	4,187,099	9.8

Note: Figures shown cover persons 3 years old and over;
(1) Metropolitan Statistical Area - see Appendix A for areas included
Source: 1990 Census of Population and Housing, Summary Tape File 3C

School Enrollment by Race

Area	Preprimary (%) White	Black	Other	Hisp.[1]	Elementary/High School (%) White	Black	Other	Hisp.[1]
City	71.9	7.5	20.6	51.9	67.0	6.8	26.2	68.2
MSA[2]	75.1	7.9	17.0	42.9	70.1	7.0	22.8	59.1
U.S.	80.4	12.5	7.1	7.8	74.1	15.6	10.3	12.5

Note: Figures shown cover persons 3 years old and over; (1) people of Hispanic origin can be of any race; (2) Metropolitan Statistical Area - see Appendix A for areas included
Source: 1990 Census of Population and Housing, Summary Tape File 3C

Classroom Teacher Salaries in Public Schools

District	B.A. Degree Min. ($)	Rank[1]	M.A. Degree Max. ($)	Rank[1]	Maximum Max. ($)	Rank[1]
San Antonio	26,500	49	47,673	34	47,673	70
Average	26,980	-	46,065	-	51,435	-

Note: Salaries are for 1997-1998; (1) Rank ranges from 1 to 100
Source: American Federation of Teachers, Survey & Analysis of Salary Trends, 1998

Higher Education

Two-Year Colleges Public	Private	Four-Year Colleges Public	Private	Medical Schools	Law Schools	Voc/Tech
3	2	2	4	1	1	21

Source: College Blue Book, Occupational Education, 1997; Medical School Admission Requirements, 1999-2000; Peterson's Guide to Two-Year Colleges, 1999; Peterson's Guide to Four-Year Colleges, 2000; Barron's Guide to Law Schools, 1999

MAJOR EMPLOYERS

Major Employers

Baptist Memorial Healthcare System
West Telemarketing Group
QVC San Antonio (mail order)
United Services Automobile Assn.
Southwest Research Institute
Bexar County Hospital District
Six Flags San Antonio
Pacific Telesis Group
Via Metropolitan Transit
International Business Benefits Corp.

Note: Companies listed are located in the city
Source: Dun's Business Rankings, 1999; Ward's Business Directory, 1998

PUBLIC SAFETY

Crime Rate

Area	All Crimes	Violent Crimes Murder	Forcible Rape	Robbery	Aggrav. Assault	Property Crimes Burglary	Larceny-Theft	Motor Vehicle Theft
City	8,050.5	9.2	59.5	196.1	136.9	1,274.5	5,544.3	830.0
Suburbs[1]	3,671.2	3.5	24.1	49.6	290.6	701.6	2,403.3	198.5
MSA[2]	6,661.5	7.4	48.3	149.6	185.6	1,092.8	4,548.1	629.7
U.S.	4,922.7	6.8	35.9	186.1	382.0	919.6	2,886.5	505.8

Note: Crime rate is the number of crimes per 100,000 pop.; (1) defined as all areas within the MSA but located outside the central city; (2) Metropolitan Statistical Area - see Appendix A for areas incl.
Source: FBI Uniform Crime Reports, 1997

RECREATION

Culture and Recreation

Museums	Symphony Orchestras	Opera Companies	Dance Companies	Professional Theatres	Zoos	Pro Sports Teams
14	1	0	2	2	1	1

Source: International Directory of the Performing Arts, 1997; Official Museum Directory, 1999; Stern's Performing Arts Directory, 1997; USA Today Four Sport Stadium Guide, 1997; Chamber of Commerce/Economic Development, 1999

Library System

The San Antonio Public Library has 18 branches, holdings of 1,754,291 volumes, and a budget of $17,096,937 (1996-1997). *American Library Directory, 1998-1999*

MEDIA

FM Radio Stations

Call Letters	Freq. (mHz)	Target Audience	Station Format	Music Format
KPAC	88.3	General	E/M	Classical
KSTX	89.1	General	E/M/N/T	Alternative/Jazz/R&B
KTXI	90.1	General	E/M/N	Classical/Country
KSYM	90.1	Alternative	M	Alternative/Blues/Country/Jazz/Latin/Reggae/Urban Contemporary
KRTU	91.7	General	M	Big Band/Classical/Jazz/R&B
KXXM	92.5	Black	M	Urban Contemporary
KROM	92.9	Hispanic	M	Latin
KRIO	94.1	Hispanic	M/N/S	Latin
KAJA	97.3	General	M/N/S	Country
KBUC	98.3	n/a	M	Country
KISS	99.5	General	M/N/S/T	Alternative/AOR
KCYY	100.3	General	M	Country
KONO	101.1	General	M/N/S	Oldies
KQXT	101.9	General	M	Adult Contemporary/Easy Listening
KTFM	102.7	General	M	Adult Contemporary
KZEP	104.5	General	M/N/T	Classic Rock
KSMG	105.3	General	M	Adult Contemporary
KCJZ	106.7	General	M	Jazz
KXTN	107.5	Hispanic	M	Latin

Note: Stations included broadcast in the San Antonio metro area; n/a not available
Station Format: E=Educational; M=Music; N=News; S=Sports; T=Talk
Target Audience: A=Asian; B=Black; C=Christian; E=Ethnic; F=French; G=General; H=Hispanic; M=Men; N=Native American; R=Religious; S=Senior Citizen; W=Women; Y=Young Adult; Z=Children
Music Format: AOR=Album Oriented Rock; MOR=Middle-of-the-Road
Source: Burrelle's Media Directory, 1999 Edition

AM Radio Stations

Call Letters	Freq. (kHz)	Target Audience	Station Format	Music Format
KTSA	550	General	N/T	n/a
KSLR	630	G/M	M/N/T	Christian
KKYX	680	n/a	M/N/S	Country
KSAH	720	Hispanic	M/N/S	Latin
KTKR	760	General	S	n/a
KCHG	810	General	M/N/S/T	Adult Contemporary/Christian
KONO	860	General	M	Oldies
KLUP	930	General	M/N	Adult Standards
KBIB	1000	H/R	M	Christian
KDRY	1100	Religious	M/T	Christian
KENS	1160	General	N/T	n/a
WOAI	1200	General	N/S/T	n/a
KZDC	1250	General	M/N	Classic Rock
KCOR	1350	Hispanic	M/N/S	Latin
KEDA	1540	Hispanic	M/N/S	Latin

Note: Stations included broadcast in the San Antonio metro area; n/a not available
Target Audience: A=Asian; B=Black; C=Christian; E=Ethnic; F=French; G=General; H=Hispanic;
M=Men; N=Native American; R=Religious; S=Senior Citizen; W=Women; Y=Young Adult; Z=Children
Station Format: E=Educational; M=Music; N=News; S=Sports; T=Talk
Source: Burrelle's Media Directory, 1999 Edition

Newspapers

Name	Type	Freq.	Distribution	Circulation
La Prensa de San Antonio	Hispanic	2x/wk	Regional	162,000
North San Antonio Times	General	1x/wk	Local	10,000
The Recorder Times	General	1x/wk	Local	90,600
San Antonio Express-News	General	7x/wk	Area	235,002
San Antonio Register	Black	1x/wk	U.S.	10,000
Southside Reporter	General	1x/wk	Local	68,000
Southside Sun	General	1x/wk	Local	31,000
Visitante	Hispanic	1x/wk	U.S.	16,500
Westside Sun	General	1x/wk	Local	50,000

Note: Includes newspapers with circulations of 10,000 or more located in the city;
Source: Burrelle's Media Directory, 1999 Edition

Television Stations

Name	Ch.	Affiliation	Type	Owner
KMOL	n/a	NBCT	Commercial	Chris Craft Inc.
KENS	n/a	CBST	Commercial	A.H. Belo Corporation
KLRN	n/a	PBS	Public	Alamo Public Telecommunications Council
KSAT	12	ABCT	Commercial	Post-Newsweek Business Information Inc.
KABB	29	FBC	Commercial	Sinclair Communications Inc.
KRRT	35	WB	Commercial	Glencairn Communications
KWEX	41	UNIN	Commercial	Univision Television Group
KVDA	60	TMUN	Commercial	Telemundo Group Inc.

Note: Stations included broadcast in the San Antonio metro area; n/a not available
Source: Burrelle's Media Directory, 1999 Edition

CLIMATE

Average and Extreme Temperatures

Temperature	Jan	Feb	Mar	Apr	May	Jun	Jul	Aug	Sep	Oct	Nov	Dec	Yr.
Extreme High (°F)	89	97	100	100	103	105	106	108	103	98	94	90	108
Average High (°F)	62	66	74	80	86	92	95	95	90	82	71	64	80
Average Temp. (°F)	51	55	62	70	76	82	85	85	80	71	60	53	69
Average Low (°F)	39	43	50	58	66	72	74	74	69	59	49	41	58
Extreme Low (°F)	0	6	19	31	43	53	62	61	46	33	21	6	0

Note: Figures cover the years 1948-1990
Source: National Climatic Data Center, International Station Meteorological Climate Summary, 3/95

Average Precipitation/Snowfall/Humidity

Precip./Humidity	Jan	Feb	Mar	Apr	May	Jun	Jul	Aug	Sep	Oct	Nov	Dec	Yr.
Avg. Precip. (in.)	1.5	1.8	1.5	2.6	3.8	3.6	2.0	2.5	3.3	3.2	2.3	1.4	29.6
Avg. Snowfall (in.)	1	Tr	Tr	0	0	0	0	0	0	0	Tr	Tr	1
Avg. Rel. Hum. 6am (%)	79	80	79	82	87	87	87	86	85	83	81	79	83
Avg. Rel. Hum. 3pm (%)	51	48	45	48	51	48	43	42	47	46	48	49	47

Note: Figures cover the years 1948-1990; Tr = Trace amounts (<0.05 in. of rain; <0.5 in. of snow)
Source: National Climatic Data Center, International Station Meteorological Climate Summary, 3/95

Weather Conditions

Temperature			Daytime Sky			Precipitation		
32°F & below	45°F & below	90°F & above	Clear	Partly cloudy	Cloudy	0.01 inch or more precip.	0.1 inch or more snow/ice	Thunder-storms
23	91	112	97	153	115	81	1	36

Note: Figures are average number of days per year and covers the years 1948-1990
Source: National Climatic Data Center, International Station Meteorological Climate Summary, 3/95

AIR & WATER QUALITY

Maximum Pollutant Concentrations

	Particulate Matter (ug/m^3)	Carbon Monoxide (ppm)	Sulfur Dioxide (ppm)	Nitrogen Dioxide (ppm)	Ozone (ppm)	Lead (ug/m^3)
MSA[1] Level	41	4	n/a	0.022	0.10	n/a
NAAQS[2]	150	9	0.140	0.053	0.12	1.50
Met NAAQS?	Yes	Yes	n/a	Yes	Yes	n/a

Note: (1) Metropolitan Statistical Area - see Appendix A for areas included; (2) National Ambient Air Quality Standards; ppm = parts per million; ug/m^3 = micrograms per cubic meter; n/a not available
Source: EPA, National Air Quality and Emissions Trends Report, 1997

Pollutant Standards Index

In the San Antonio MSA (see Appendix A for areas included), the Pollutant Standards Index (PSI) exceeded 100 on 3 days in 1997. A PSI value greater than 100 indicates that air quality would be in the unhealthful range on that day. *EPA, National Air Quality and Emissions Trends Report, 1997*

Drinking Water

Water System Name	Pop. Served	Primary Water Source Type	Number of Violations in 1998	Type of Violation/ Contaminants
San Antonio Water System	1,150,338	Ground	None	None

Note: Data as of July 10, 1999
Source: EPA, Office of Ground Water and Drinking Water, Safe Drinking Water Information System

San Antonio tap water is not fluoridated and has moderate mineral content, chiefly sodium bicarbonate. *Editor & Publisher Market Guide, 1999*

Tampa, Florida

Background

Although Tampa was visited by Spanish explorers, such as Ponce de Leon and Hernando De Soto as early as 1521, this city, located on the mouth of the Hillsborough River on Tampa Bay, did not see significant growth until the mid-nineteenth century.

Like many cities of northern Florida, such as Jacksonville, Tampa was a fort during the Seminole War, and during the Civil War, captured by Union Armies. Like many Florida cities, Tampa enjoyed prosperity and development when the railroad transported tourists from up north to enjoy the warmth and sunshine of Florida.

Two historical events in the late nineteenth century set Tampa apart from other Florida cities. First, Tampa played a significant role during the Spanish-American War in 1898, as a chief port of embarkation for American troops to Cuba. During that time, Col. Theodore Roosevelt occupied a Tampa hotel as his military headquarters. Second, a cigar factory in nearby Ybor City, named after owner Vicente Martinez Ybor, was the site where Jose Marti—the George Washington of Cuba—exhorted workers to take up arms against the tyranny of Spanish rule in the late 1800s.

Today, Tampa enjoys its role as the 11th largest port in the United States. Industries as varied as phosphate export, shrimp fishing, citrus canning, electronic equipment, and cigar, beer, and paint manufacturing comprise the chief income-earning sectors. Although Tampa struggles with rapid growth, it remains a relaxed city of sunshine and beachgoers.

Chase Manhattan Bank has announced a major relocation and expansion in Tampa and Hillsborough County, and User Technology Association Group recently selected Tampa for its newest software center. UTA Group will produce high level software applications for business and government clients, and could employ up to 50 developers within a year.

Winters are mild. Summers are long, warm, and humid. Freezing temperatures occur on one or two mornings per year during December, January, and February. A dramatic feature of the Tampa climate is the summer thunderstorm season. Most occur during the late afternoon, sometimes causing temperature to drop 20 degrees. The area is vulnerable to tidal surges as the land has an elevation less than 15 feet above sea level.

General Rankings and Evaluative Comments

- Tampa was ranked #4 out of 19 large, southern metropolitan areas in *Money's* 1998 survey of "The Best Places to Live in America." The survey was conducted by first contacting 512 representative households nationwide and asking them to rank 37 quality-of-life factors on a scale of 1 to 10. Next, a demographic profile was compiled on the 300 largest metropolitan statistical areas in the U.S. The numbers were crunched together to arrive at an overall ranking (things Americans consider most important, like clean air and water, low crime and good schools, received extra weight). Unlike previous years, the 1998 rankings were broken down by region (northeast, midwest, south, west) and population size (100,000 to 249,999; 250,000 to 999,999; 1 million plus). The city had a nationwide ranking of #31 out of 300 in 1997 and #11 out of 300 in 1996. *Money, July 1998; Money, July 1997; Money, September 1996*

- *Ladies Home Journal* ranked America's 200 largest cities based on the qualities women care about most. Tampa ranked #91 out of 200. Criteria: low crime rate, well-paying jobs, quality health and child care, good public schools, the presence of women in government, size of the gender wage gap, number of sexual-harassment and discrimination complaints filed, unemployment and divorce rates, commute times, population density, number of houses of worship, parks and cultural offerings, number of women's health specialists, how well a community's women cared for themselves, complexion kindness index based on UV radiation levels, odds of finding affordable fashions, rental rates for romance movies, champagne sales and other matters of the heart. *Ladies Home Journal, November 1998*

- Zero Population Growth ranked 229 cities in terms of children's health, safety, and economic well-being. Tampa was ranked #13 out of 25 major cities (main city in a metro area with population of greater than 2 million) and was given a grade of C. Criteria: total population, percent of population under 18 years of age, household language, percent population change, percent of births to teens, infant mortality rate, percent of low birth weights, dropout rate, enrollment in preprimary school, violent and property crime rates, unemployment rate, percent of children in poverty, percent of owner occupied units, number of bad air days, percent of public transportation commuters, and average travel time to work. *Zero Population Growth, Children's Environmental Index, Fall 1999*

- Tampa was ranked #15 out of 59 metro areas in *The Regional Economist's* "Rational Livability Ranking of 59 Large Metro Areas." The rankings were based on the metro area's total population change over the period 1990-97 divided by the number of people moving in from elsewhere in the United States (net domestic in-migration). *St. Louis Federal Reserve Bank of St. Louis, The Regional Economist, April 1999*

- Tampa was selected by *Yahoo! Internet Life* as one of "America's Most Wired Cities & Towns." The city ranked #37 out of 50. Criteria: home and work net use, domain density, hosts per capita, directory density and content quality. *Yahoo! Internet Life, March 1999*

- Cognetics studied 273 metro areas in the United States, ranking them by entrepreneurial activity. Tampa was ranked #26 out of the 50 largest metro areas. Criteria: Significant Starts (firms started in the last 10 years that still employ at least 5 people) and Young Growers (percent of firms 10 years old or less that grew significantly during the last 4 years). *Cognetics, "Entrepreneurial Hot Spots: The Best Places in America to Start and Grow a Company," 1998*

- Tampa appeared on *Forbes* list of "Best Places for Business Growth." Rank: #15 out of 162 metro areas. Criteria: average wage and salary increases, job growth rates, number of technology clusters (measures business activity in 13 different technology areas), overall concentration of technology activity relative to national average and technology output growth. *Forbes, May 31, 1999*

- Tampa was selected as one of the "Best American Cities to Start a Business" by *Point of View* magazine. Criteria: coolness, quality-of-life, and business concerns. The city was ranked #39 out of 75. *Point of View, November 1998*

- Tampa appeared on *Sales & Marketing Management's* list of the "20 Hottest Cities for Selling." Rank: #20 out of 20. *S&MM* editors looked at Metropolitan Statistical Areas with populations of more than 150,000. The areas were ranked based on population increases, retail sales increases, effective buying income, increase in both residential and commercial building permits issued, unemployment rates, job growth, mix of industries, tax rates, number of corporate relocations, and the number of new corporations.
  Sales & Marketing Management, April 1999

- Reliastar Financial Corp. ranked the 125 largest metropolitan areas according to the general financial security of residents. Tampa was ranked #67 out of 125 with a score of 1.1. The score indicates the percentage a metropolitan area is above or below the metropolitan norm. A metro area with a score of 10.6 is 10.6% above the metro average. Criteria: Earnings and Wealth Potential (household income, education, net assets, cost of living); Safety Net (health insurance, retirement savings, life insurance, income support programs); Personal Threats (unemployment rate, low-income households, crime rate); Community Economic Vitality (cost of community services, job quality, job creation, housing costs).
  Reliastar Financial Corp., "The Best Cities to Earn and Save Money," 1999 Edition

Business Environment

STATE ECONOMY

State Economic Profile

"Florida's economy has been among the nation's strongest in recent years. Job growth has outpaced the nation by a considerable amount since 1992.

While Florida has been able to avoid any significant fallout from the Asian crisis, the weakening of economies in Latin American will dampen both tourism and international trade. 1998 saw the decline in Latin tourism more than offset by domestic visitors. Domestic tourism is projected to soften as US growth cools in 1999, offering no offset against the expected decline in Latin tourism. Weaker tourism and trade with Latin American will slow growth in 1999; FL will still outpace the nation in job growth as Gross State Product growth (GSP) slows.

Over half of FL's 230,000 new jobs created in 1998 were in the services sector, which grew at 5.2%, more than offsetting a minor decline in manufacturing employment. Much of this growth is taking place in the finance and business services sector.

In spite of strong home sales and a slowing construction market, FL's price appreciation continued to lag the nation. Although residential permits per 1,000 residents stands at 5.1, well above the national average, this number is only slightly up from 1997 and will decline in 1999.

Growth in FL, while strong throughout, has been hottest in the Naples, Ft. Myers and Orlando areas. Construction and employment in the construction industry has begun to slow in South Florida. Projected employment and housing gains will be concentrated in Northern and Central Florida during 1999. Growing diversification of the economy into financial and business services promises a strong outlook for the years ahead." *National Association of Realtors, Economic Profiles: The Fifty States and the District of Columbia, http://nar.realtor.com/databank/profiles.htm*

IMPORTS/EXPORTS

Total Export Sales

Area	1994 ($000)	1995 ($000)	1996 ($000)	1997 ($000)	% Chg. 1994-97	% Chg. 1996-97
MSA[1]	1,835,814	2,116,050	1,921,833	2,273,787	23.9	18.3
U.S.	512,415,609	583,030,524	622,827,063	687,597,999	34.2	10.4

Note: (1) Metropolitan Statistical Area - see Appendix A for areas included
Source: U.S. Department of Commerce, International Trade Association, Metropolitan Area Exports: An Export Performance Report on Over 250 U.S. Cities, November 10, 1998

CITY FINANCES

City Government Finances

Component	FY92 ($000)	FY92 (per capita $)
Revenue	382,821	1,358.02
Expenditure	407,824	1,446.72
Debt Outstanding	682,771	2,422.07
Cash & Securities	752,383	2,669.01

Source: U.S. Bureau of the Census, City Government Finances: 1991-92

City Government Revenue by Source

Source	FY92 ($000)	FY92 (per capita $)	FY92 (%)
From Federal Government	12,098	42.92	3.2
From State Governments	25,261	89.61	6.6
From Local Governments	12,446	44.15	3.3
Property Taxes	57,829	205.14	15.1
General Sales Taxes	0	0.00	0.0
Selective Sales Taxes	58,813	208.63	15.4
Income Taxes	0	0.00	0.0
Current Charges	96,723	343.12	25.3
Utility/Liquor Store	30,377	107.76	7.9
Employee Retirement[1]	46,069	163.43	12.0
Other	43,205	153.27	11.3

Note: (1) Excludes "city contributions," classified as "nonrevenue," intragovernmental transfers.
Source: U.S. Bureau of the Census, City Government Finances: 1991-92

City Government Expenditures by Function

Function	FY92 ($000)	FY92 (per capita $)	FY92 (%)
Educational Services	0	0.00	0.0
Employee Retirement[1]	26,792	95.04	6.6
Environment/Housing	153,717	545.30	37.7
Government Administration	10,622	37.68	2.6
Interest on General Debt	38,694	137.26	9.5
Public Safety	79,323	281.39	19.5
Social Services	3,873	13.74	0.9
Transportation	31,301	111.04	7.7
Utility/Liquor Store	53,634	190.26	13.2
Other	9,868	35.01	2.4

Note: (1) Payments to beneficiaries including withdrawal of contributions.
Source: U.S. Bureau of the Census, City Government Finances: 1991-92

Municipal Bond Ratings

Area	Moody's	S & P
Tampa	Aaa	n/a

Note: n/a not available; n/r not rated
Source: Moody's Bond Record, 6/99

POPULATION

Population Growth

Area	1980	1990	% Chg. 1980-90	July 1998 Estimate	% Chg. 1990-98
City	271,523	280,015	3.1	289,156	3.3
MSA[1]	1,613,621	2,067,959	28.2	2,242,989	8.5
U.S.	226,545,805	248,765,170	9.8	270,299,000	8.7

Note: (1) Metropolitan Statistical Area - see Appendix A for areas included;
July 1998 MSA population estimate was calculated by the editors
Source: 1980/1990 Census of Housing and Population, Summary Tape File 3C;
Census Bureau Population Estimates 1998

Population Characteristics

Race	City 1980 Population	%	City 1990 Population	%	% Chg. 1980-90	MSA[1] 1990 Population	%
White	202,507	74.6	198,756	71.0	-1.9	1,828,737	88.4
Black	63,578	23.4	69,871	25.0	9.9	184,087	8.9
Amer Indian/Esk/Aleut	607	0.2	997	0.4	64.3	6,752	0.3
Asian/Pacific Islander	1,894	0.7	3,948	1.4	108.4	22,860	1.1
Other	2,937	1.1	6,443	2.3	119.4	25,523	1.2
Hispanic Origin[2]	35,982	13.3	41,247	14.7	14.6	136,027	6.6

Note: (1) Metropolitan Statistical Area - see Appendix A for areas included;
(2) people of Hispanic origin can be of any race
Source: 1980/1990 Census of Housing and Population, Summary Tape File 3C

Ancestry

Area	German	Irish	English	Italian	U.S.	French	Polish	Dutch
City	15.2	12.3	12.5	6.2	4.7	3.2	1.8	1.8
MSA[1]	23.5	17.3	16.9	7.8	5.0	4.8	3.7	2.6
U.S.	23.3	15.6	13.1	5.9	5.3	4.2	3.8	2.5

Note: Figures are percentages and include persons that reported multiple ancestry (eg. if a person reported being Irish and Italian, they were included in both columns); (1) Metropolitan Statistical Area - see Appendix A for areas included
Source: 1990 Census of Population and Housing, Summary Tape File 3C

Age

Area	Median Age (Years)	Age Distribution (%) Under 5	Under 18	18-24	25-44	45-64	65+	80+
City	33.2	7.4	22.9	10.8	33.0	18.7	14.6	3.4
MSA[1]	38.5	6.0	20.4	8.4	29.7	20.0	21.5	4.9
U.S.	32.9	7.3	25.6	10.5	32.6	18.7	12.5	2.8

Note: (1) Metropolitan Statistical Area - see Appendix A for areas included
Source: 1990 Census of Population and Housing, Summary Tape File 3C

Male/Female Ratio

Area	Number of males per 100 females (all ages)	Number of males per 100 females (18 years old+)
City	92.8	88.7
MSA[1]	91.0	87.8
U.S.	95.0	91.9

Note: (1) Metropolitan Statistical Area - see Appendix A for areas included
Source: 1990 Census of Population, General Population Characteristics

INCOME

Per Capita/Median/Average Income

Area	Per Capita ($)	Median Household ($)	Average Household ($)
City	13,277	22,772	31,813
MSA[1]	14,374	26,036	33,685
U.S.	14,420	30,056	38,453

Note: All figures are for 1989; (1) Metropolitan Statistical Area - see Appendix A for areas included
Source: 1990 Census of Population and Housing, Summary Tape File 3C

Household Income Distribution by Race

Income ($)	City (%)					U.S. (%)				
	Total	White	Black	Other	Hisp.[1]	Total	White	Black	Other	Hisp.[1]
Less than 5,000	9.7	6.6	20.4	12.1	13.0	6.2	4.8	15.2	8.6	8.8
5,000 - 9,999	11.7	10.2	17.2	10.7	11.7	9.3	8.6	14.2	9.9	11.1
10,000 - 14,999	11.5	10.9	13.8	13.3	13.7	8.8	8.5	11.0	9.8	11.0
15,000 - 24,999	21.0	21.0	20.2	25.6	20.9	17.5	17.3	18.9	18.5	20.5
25,000 - 34,999	16.1	17.0	12.4	17.6	16.2	15.8	16.1	14.2	15.4	16.4
35,000 - 49,999	14.6	16.0	9.8	12.0	13.3	17.9	18.6	13.3	16.1	16.0
50,000 - 74,999	9.2	10.5	4.9	6.2	7.9	15.0	15.8	9.3	13.4	11.1
75,000 - 99,999	2.9	3.5	0.9	1.3	1.7	5.1	5.5	2.6	4.7	3.1
100,000+	3.4	4.3	0.5	1.3	1.7	4.4	4.8	1.3	3.7	1.9

Note: All figures are for 1989; (1) people of Hispanic origin can be of any race
Source: 1990 Census of Population and Housing, Summary Tape File 3C

Effective Buying Income

Area	Per Capita ($)	Median Household ($)	Average Household ($)
City	15,967	28,011	38,804
MSA[1]	17,489	30,719	41,747
U.S.	16,803	34,536	45,243

Note: Data as of 1/1/99; (1) Metropolitan Statistical Area - see Appendix A for areas included
Source: Standard Rate & Data Service, Newspaper Advertising Source, 9/99

Effective Household Buying Income Distribution

Area	% of Households Earning						
	$10,000 -$19,999	$20,000 -$34,999	$35,000 -$49,999	$50,000 -$74,999	$75,000 -$99,000	$100,000 -$124,999	$125,000 and up
City	19.4	24.4	16.5	13.8	4.8	1.8	2.8
MSA[1]	18.9	26.0	17.9	15.8	5.6	1.9	2.2
U.S.	16.0	22.6	18.2	18.9	7.2	2.4	2.7

Note: Data as of 1/1/99; (1) Metropolitan Statistical Area - see Appendix A for areas included
Source: Standard Rate & Data Service, Newspaper Advertising Source, 9/99

Poverty Rates by Race and Age

Area	Total (%)	By Race (%)				By Age (%)		
		White	Black	Other	Hisp.[2]	Under 5 years old	Under 18 years old	65 years and over
City	19.4	12.2	39.8	21.0	20.6	35.0	30.9	19.4
MSA[1]	11.4	9.0	33.1	20.4	19.4	20.2	17.6	9.4
U.S.	13.1	9.8	29.5	23.1	25.3	20.1	18.3	12.8

Note: Figures show the percent of people living below the poverty line in 1989. The average poverty threshold was $12,674 for a family of four in 1989; (1) Metropolitan Statistical Area - see Appendix A for areas included; (2) people of Hispanic origin can be of any race
Source: 1990 Census of Population and Housing, Summary Tape File 3C

EMPLOYMENT

Labor Force and Employment

Area	Civilian Labor Force			Workers Employed		
	Jun. 1998	Jun. 1999	% Chg.	Jun. 1998	Jun. 1999	% Chg.
City	168,389	177,555	5.4	162,313	171,614	5.7
MSA[1]	1,173,939	1,235,670	5.3	1,136,410	1,201,527	5.7
U.S.	138,798,000	140,666,000	1.3	132,265,000	134,395,000	1.6

Note: Data is not seasonally adjusted and covers workers 16 years of age and older;
(1) Metropolitan Statistical Area - see Appendix A for areas included
Source: Bureau of Labor Statistics, http://stats.bls.gov

Unemployment Rate

Area	1998						1999					
	Jul.	Aug.	Sep.	Oct.	Nov.	Dec.	Jan.	Feb.	Mar.	Apr.	May.	Jun.
City	3.6	3.4	3.4	3.1	3.2	2.9	3.7	3.3	3.3	3.4	3.4	3.3
MSA[1]	3.0	2.9	3.0	2.9	2.9	2.7	3.2	2.9	2.8	2.9	2.8	2.8
U.S.	4.7	4.5	4.4	4.2	4.1	4.0	4.8	4.7	4.4	4.1	4.0	4.5

Note: Data is not seasonally adjusted and covers workers 16 years of age and older; all figures are percentages; (1) Metropolitan Statistical Area - see Appendix A for areas included
Source: Bureau of Labor Statistics, http://stats.bls.gov

Employment by Industry

Sector	MSA[1]		U.S.
	Number of Employees	Percent of Total	Percent of Total
Services	490,000	41.5	30.4
Retail Trade	199,500	16.9	17.7
Government	138,000	11.7	15.6
Manufacturing	90,200	7.6	14.3
Finance/Insurance/Real Estate	87,700	7.4	5.9
Wholesale Trade	63,100	5.3	5.4
Transportation/Public Utilities	53,000	4.5	5.3
Construction	58,300	4.9	5.0
Mining	500	<0.1	0.4

Note: Figures cover non-farm employment as of 6/99 and are not seasonally adjusted;
(1) Metropolitan Statistical Area - see Appendix A for areas included
Source: Bureau of Labor Statistics, http://stats.bls.gov

Employment by Occupation

Occupation Category	City (%)	MSA[1] (%)	U.S. (%)
White Collar	59.8	61.2	58.1
Executive/Admin./Management	12.3	12.9	12.3
Professional	13.4	12.6	14.1
Technical & Related Support	3.5	3.9	3.7
Sales	12.6	14.8	11.8
Administrative Support/Clerical	18.0	17.1	16.3
Blue Collar	23.2	22.6	26.2
Precision Production/Craft/Repair	9.8	11.0	11.3
Machine Operators/Assem./Insp.	4.8	4.2	6.8
Transportation/Material Movers	4.2	3.8	4.1
Cleaners/Helpers/Laborers	4.5	3.6	3.9
Services	15.3	13.9	13.2
Farming/Forestry/Fishing	1.7	2.4	2.5

Note: Figures cover employed persons 16 years old and over;
(1) Metropolitan Statistical Area - see Appendix A for areas included
Source: 1990 Census of Population and Housing, Summary Tape File 3C

Occupational Employment Projections: 1996 - 2006

Occupations Expected to Have the Largest Job Growth (ranked by numerical growth)	Fast-Growing Occupations[1] (ranked by percent growth)
1. Cashiers	1. Systems analysts
2. Salespersons, retail	2. Physical therapy assistants and aides
3. General managers & top executives	3. Desktop publishers
4. Registered nurses	4. Home health aides
5. Waiters & waitresses	5. Computer engineers
6. Marketing & sales, supervisors	6. Medical assistants
7. Janitors/cleaners/maids, ex. priv. hshld.	7. Physical therapists
8. General office clerks	8. Paralegals
9. Food preparation workers	9. Emergency medical technicians
10. Hand packers & packagers	10. Occupational therapists

Note: Projections cover Florida; (1) Excludes occupations with total job growth less than 300
Source: U.S. Department of Labor, Employment and Training Administration, America's Labor Market
Information System (ALMIS)

TAXES

Major State and Local Tax Rates

State Corp. Income (%)	State Personal Income (%)	Residential Property (effective rate per $100)	Sales & Use		State Gasoline (cents/gallon)	State Cigarette (cents/pack)
			State (%)	Local (%)		
5.5[a]	None	n/a	6.0	1.0	13.1[b]	33.9

Note: Personal/corporate income, sales, gasoline and cigarette tax rates as of January 1999.
Property tax rates as of 1997; (a) 3.3% Alternative Minimum Tax. An exemption of $5,000 is allowed;
(b) Rate is comprised of 4 cents excise and 9.1 cents motor carrier tax
Source: Federation of Tax Administrators, www.taxadmin.org; Washington D.C. Department of
Finance and Revenue, Tax Rates and Tax Burdens in the District of Columbia: A Nationwide
Comparison, July 1998; Chamber of Commerce, 1999

Total Taxes Per Capita and as a Percent of Income

Area	Per Capita Income ($)	Per Capita Taxes ($)			Percent of Income (%)		
		Total	Federal	State/Local	Total	Federal	State/Local
Florida	27,655	9,768	6,824	2,944	35.3	24.7	10.6
U.S.	27,876	9,881	6,690	3,191	35.4	24.0	11.4

Note: Figures are for 1998
Source: Tax Foundation, www.taxfoundation.org

COMMERCIAL REAL ESTATE

Office Market

Class/Location	Total Space (sq. ft.)	Vacant Space (sq. ft.)	Vac. Rate (%)	Under Constr. (sq. ft.)	Net Absorp. (sq. ft.)	Rental Rates ($/sq.ft./yr.)
Class A						
CBD	4,687,212	389,600	8.3	90,000	162,884	15.50-25.00
Outside CBD	8,017,657	565,528	7.1	947,579	377,816	14.50-26.00
Class B						
CBD	896,974	141,609	15.8	0	108,820	11.00-19.00
Outside CBD	8,559,107	951,470	11.1	40,800	160,539	10.00-23.00

Note: Data as of 10/98 and covers Tampa; CBD = Central Business District; n/a not available;
Source: Society of Industrial and Office Realtors, 1999 Comparative Statistics of Industrial and Office
Real Estate Markets

"There is one million sq. ft. of speculative new office development planned for 1999. More than half of this space is in Pinellas County. This new inventory will likely lead to an increase in vacancy rates. In spite of this scenario, rental rates are expected to rise one to five percent. Conversely, sales prices are expected to decline in all markets and geographic areas. Although absorption is expected to increase, SIOR's local reporter expects new construction to relieve some of the pressure on the market. Further volatility in the foreign markets is expected to have a negative impact on the sale of institutional properties." *Society of Industrial and Office Realtors, 1999 Comparative Statistics of Industrial and Office Real Estate Markets*

Industrial Market

Location	Total Space (sq. ft.)	Vacant Space (sq. ft.)	Vac. Rate (%)	Under Constr. (sq. ft.)	Net Absorp. (sq. ft.)	Net Lease ($/sq.ft./yr.)
Central City	n/a	n/a	n/a	n/a	n/a	n/a
Suburban	64,621,252	4,529,609	7.0	446,612	1,100,411	n/a

Note: Data as of 10/98 and covers Tampa; n/a not available
Source: Society of Industrial and Office Realtors, 1999 Comparative Statistics of Industrial and Office Real Estate Markets

"The local Tampa economy will outperform the national economy during 1998. Demand is expected to remain moderate and become particularly strong for larger spaces of 50,000 sq. ft. or more. REITs will pull back from speculative construction in the Tampa market. As traditional investors fill the need for speculative space, a much slower pace of development is likely. Currently there are approximately two million sq. ft. planned. The Tampa economy has a strong manufacturing sector but a stronger back office sector. The trend of converting industrial space to office space will help deplete the inventory of buildings in the suburban markets." Society of Industrial and Office Realtors, 1999 Comparative Statistics of Industrial and Office Real Estate Markets

Retail Market

Shopping Center Inventory (sq. ft.)	Shopping Center Construction (sq. ft.)	Construction as a Percent of Inventory (%)	Torto Wheaton Rent Index[1] ($/sq. ft.)
45,090,000	396,000	0.9	11.13

Note: Data as of 1997 and covers the Metropolitan Statistical Area - see Appendix A for areas included; (1) Index is based on a model that predicts what the average rent should be for leases with certain characteristics, in certain locations during certain years.
Source: National Association of Realtors, 1997-1998 Market Conditions Report

"Money magazine recently ranked Tampa as the nation's most solid economy out of more than 300 metro areas. The area's retail rent index has been rising since 1994, buoyed by strong demand. The 980,000 square foot Brandon TownCenter at the intersection of Interstate 75 and Route 60 currently has a 94% occupancy rate. Its success has prompted the construction of the 1.2 million square foot Citrus Park Mall, due to open in early 1999. The mall will be located in northwest Hillsborough County, with Dillards, Burdines, Sears and J.C. Penney as anchors. Strong economic and population growth in the Tampa area, particularly Hillsborough, will bolster the retail market over the next few years." *National Association of Realtors, 1997-1998 Market Conditions Report*

COMMERCIAL UTILITIES

Typical Monthly Electric Bills

Area	Commercial Service ($/month)		Industrial Service ($/month)	
	12 kW demand 1,500 kWh	100 kW demand 30,000 kWh	1,000 kW demand 400,000 kWh	20,000 kW demand 10,000,000 kWh
City	115	1,972	23,433	384,639
U.S.	150	2,174	23,995	508,569

Note: Based on rates in effect January 1, 1999
Source: Edison Electric Institute, Typical Residential, Commercial and Industrial Bills, Winter 1999

TRANSPORTATION

Transportation Statistics

Average minutes to work	19.2
Interstate highways	I-4; I-75
Bus lines	
In-city	Hillsborough Area Regional TA, 300 vehicles
Inter-city	3
Passenger air service	
Airport	Tampa International
Airlines	22
Aircraft departures	67,088 (1996)
Enplaned passengers	5,712,015 (1996)
Rail service	Amtrak
Motor freight carriers	46
Major waterways/ports	Port of Tampa

Source: Editor & Publisher Market Guide, 1999; FAA Airport Activity Statistics, 1997; Amtrak National Time Table, Northeast Timetable, Spring/Summer 1999; 1990 Census of Population and Housing, STF 3C; Chamber of Commerce/Economic Development 1999; Jane's Urban Transport Systems 1999-2000

Means of Transportation to Work

Area	Car/Truck/Van		Public Transportation			Bicycle	Walked	Other Means	Worked at Home
	Drove Alone	Car-pooled	Bus	Subway	Railroad				
City	74.8	14.3	3.2	0.0	0.0	0.9	3.4	1.5	1.9
MSA[1]	78.8	13.3	1.3	0.0	0.0	0.7	2.3	1.3	2.3
U.S.	73.2	13.4	3.0	1.5	0.5	0.4	3.9	1.2	3.0

Note: Figures shown are percentages and only include workers 16 years old and over; (1) Metropolitan Statistical Area - see Appendix A for areas included
Source: 1990 Census of Population and Housing, Summary Tape File 3C

BUSINESSES

Major Business Headquarters

Company Name	1999 Rankings	
	Fortune 500	Forbes 500
Celotex	-	328
Lykes Bros	-	184

Note: Companies listed are located in the city; dashes indicate no ranking
Fortune 500: Companies that produce a 10-K are ranked 1 to 500 based on 1998 revenue
Forbes 500: Private companies are ranked 1 to 500 based on 1997 revenue
Source: Forbes, November 30, 1998; Fortune, April 26, 1999

Best Companies to Work For

Teco Energy (utilities), headquartered in Tampa, is among the " 100 Best Places to Work in IS." Criteria: compensation, turnover and training. *Computerworld, May 25, 1998*

Fast-Growing Businesses

According to *Inc.*, Tampa is home to one of America's 100 fastest-growing private companies: Physicians Healthcare Plans. Criteria for inclusion: must be an independent, privately-held, U.S. corporation, proprietorship or partnership; sales of at least $200,000 in 1995; five-year operating/sales history; increase in 1999 sales over 1998 sales; holding companies, regulated banks, and utilities were excluded. *Inc. 500, 1999*

Tampa is home to one of *Business Week's* "hot growth" companies: Coast Dental Services. Criteria: increase in sales and profits, return on capital and stock price. *Business Week, 5/31/99*

Women-Owned Firms: Number, Employment and Sales

Area	Number of Firms	Employ-ment	Sales ($000)	Rank[2]
MSA[1]	83,800	368,600	25,863,400	22

Note: (1) Metropolitan Statistical Area - see Appendix A for areas included;
(2) Calculated on an averaging of the number of businesses, employment and sales
Source: The National Foundation for Women Business Owners, 1999 Facts on Women-Owned
Businesses: Trends in the Top 50 Metropolitan Areas

Women-Owned Firms: Growth

Area	% change from 1992 to 1999			Rank[2]
	Number of Firms	Employ-ment	Sales	
MSA[1]	46.3	140.2	102.1	24

Note: (1) Metropolitan Statistical Area - see Appendix A for areas included; (2) Calculated on an averaging of the percent growth of number of businesses, employment and sales
Source: The National Foundation for Women Business Owners, 1999 Facts on Women-Owned
Businesses: Trends in the Top 50 Metropolitan Areas

Minority Business Opportunity

Tampa is home to one company which is on the Black Enterprise Auto Dealer 100 list (largest based on gross sales): Brandon Dodge Inc. (Dodge, Toyota) . Criteria: 1) operational in previous calendar year; 2) at least 51% black-owned. *Black Enterprise, www.blackenterprise.com*

Seven of the 500 largest Hispanic-owned companies in the U.S. are located in Tampa. *Hispanic Business, June 1999*

Tampa is home to three companies which are on the Hispanic Business Fastest-Growing 100 list (greatest sales growth from 1994 to 1998): THL Enterprises Inc. (roof contractors); Aero Simulation Inc. (flight simulator svcs.); Electric Machinery Enterprises Inc. (electrical contracting and modular construction mfg.). *Hispanic Business, July/August 1999*

HOTELS & MOTELS

Hotels/Motels

Area	Hotels/Motels	Rooms	Luxury-Level Hotels/Motels		Average Minimum Rates ($)		
			♦♦♦♦	♦♦♦♦♦	♦♦	♦♦♦	♦♦♦♦
City	50	7,121	0	0	58	119	n/a
Airport	18	4,674	1	0	n/a	n/a	n/a
Suburbs	11	1,547	0	0	n/a	n/a	n/a
Total	79	13,342	1	0	n/a	n/a	n/a

Note: n/a not available; classifications range from one diamond (budget properties with basic amenities) to five diamond (luxury properties with the finest service, rooms and facilities).
Source: OAG, Business Travel Planner, Winter 1998-99

CONVENTION CENTERS

Major Convention Centers

Center Name	Meeting Rooms	Exhibit Space (sq. ft.)
Florida State Fair and Expo Park	n/a	168,000
Phyllis P. Marshall Center/Univ. of South Florida	n/a	n/a
Tampa Convention Center	18	200,000

Note: n/a not available
Source: Trade Shows Worldwide, 1998; Meetings & Conventions, 4/15/99;
Sucessful Meetings, 3/31/98

Living Environment

COST OF LIVING

Cost of Living Index

Composite Index	Groceries	Housing	Utilities	Trans-portation	Health Care	Misc. Goods/ Services
103.8	102.2	108.5	88.2	102.9	113.4	103.3

Note: U.S. = 100
Source: ACCRA, Cost of Living Index, 1st Quarter 1999

HOUSING

Median Home Prices and Housing Affordability

Area	Median Price[2] 1st Qtr. 1999 ($)	HOI[3] 1st Qtr. 1999	Afford-ability Rank[4]
MSA[1]	90,000	81.1	42
U.S.	134,000	69.6	–

Note: (1) Metropolitan Statistical Area - see Appendix A for areas included; (2) U.S. figures calculated from the sales of 524,324 new and existing homes in 181 markets; (3) Housing Opportunity Index - percent of homes sold that were within the reach of the median income household at the prevailing mortgage interest rate; (4) Rank is from 1-181 with 1 being most affordable
Source: National Association of Home Builders, Housing Opportunity Index, 1st Quarter 1999

Median Home Price Projection

It is projected that the median price of existing single-family homes in the metro area will increase by 5.1% in 1999. Nationwide, home prices are projected to increase 3.8%.
Kiplinger's Personal Finance Magazine, January 1999

Average New Home Price

Area	Price ($)
City	149,649
U.S.	142,735

Note: Figures are based on a new home with 1,800 sq. ft. of living area on an 8,000 sq. ft. lot.
Source: ACCRA, Cost of Living Index, 1st Quarter 1999

Average Apartment Rent

Area	Rent ($/mth)
City	837
U.S.	601

Note: Figures are based on an unfurnished two bedroom, 1-1/2 or 2 bath apartment, approximately 950 sq. ft. in size, excluding all utilities except water
Source: ACCRA, Cost of Living Index, 1st Quarter 1999

RESIDENTIAL UTILITIES

Average Residential Utility Costs

Area	All Electric ($/mth)	Part Electric ($/mth)	Other Energy ($/mth)	Phone ($/mth)
City	82.93	–	–	23.44
U.S.	100.02	55.73	43.33	19.71

Source: ACCRA, Cost of Living Index, 1st Quarter 1999

HEALTH CARE

Average Health Care Costs

Area	Hospital ($/day)	Doctor ($/visit)	Dentist ($/visit)
City	489.85	52.90	82.20
U.S.	430.43	52.45	66.35

Note: Hospital—based on a semi-private room; Doctor—based on a general practitioner's routine exam of an established patient; Dentist—based on adult teeth cleaning and periodic oral exam.
Source: ACCRA, Cost of Living Index, 1st Quarter 1999

Distribution of Office-Based Physicians

Area	Family/Gen. Practitioners	Specialists		
		Medical	Surgical	Other
MSA[1]	459	1,502	1,035	1,080

Note: Data as of 12/31/97; (1) Metropolitan Statistical Area - see Appendix A for areas included
Source: American Medical Assn., Physician Characteristics & Distribution in the U.S., 1999

Hospitals

Tampa has 7 general medical and surgical hospitals, 1 psychiatric, 2 other specialty, 1 children's orthopedic. *AHA Guide to the Healthcare Field, 1998-99*

According to *U.S. News and World Report,* Tampa has 1 of the best hospitals in the U.S.: **H. Lee Moffitt Cancer Center**, noted for cancer. *U.S. News Online, "America's Best Hospitals," 10th Edition, www.usnews.com*

EDUCATION

Public School District Statistics

District Name	Num. Sch.	Enroll.	Classroom Teachers	Pupils per Teacher	Minority Pupils (%)	Current Exp.[1] ($/pupil)
Hillsborough County Sch Dist	169	152,781	8,897	17.2	44.7	5,217

Note: Data covers the 1997-1998 school year unless otherwise noted; (1) Data covers fiscal year 1996; SD = School District; ISD = Independent School District; n/a not available
Source: National Center for Education Statistics, Common Core of Data Public Education Agency Universe 1997-98; National Center for Education Statistics, Characteristics of the 100 Largest Public Elementary and Secondary School Districts in the United States: 1997-98, July 1999

Educational Quality

School District	Education Quotient[1]	Graduate Outcome[2]	Community Index[3]	Resource Index[4]
Hillsborough County	123.0	123.0	92.0	130.0

Note: Nearly 1,000 secondary school districts were rated in terms of educational quality. The scores range from a low of 50 to a high of 150; (1) Average of the Graduate Outcome, Community and Resource indexes; (2) Based on graduation rates and college board scores (SAT/ACT); (3) Based on the surrounding community's average level of education and the area's average income level; (4) Based on teacher salaries, per-pupil expenditures and student-teacher ratios.
Source: Expansion Management, Ratings Issue, 1998

Educational Attainment by Race

Area	High School Graduate (%)					Bachelor's Degree (%)				
	Total	White	Black	Other	Hisp.[2]	Total	White	Black	Other	Hisp.[2]
City	70.6	74.7	57.1	61.5	54.4	18.7	21.7	8.0	15.1	11.3
MSA[1]	75.1	76.5	60.4	64.4	59.9	17.3	17.7	10.8	18.4	14.2
U.S.	75.2	77.9	63.1	60.4	49.8	20.3	21.5	11.4	19.4	9.2

Note: Figures shown cover persons 25 years old and over; (1) Metropolitan Statistical Area - see Appendix A for areas included; (2) people of Hispanic origin can be of any race
Source: 1990 Census of Population and Housing, Summary Tape File 3C

School Enrollment by Type

Area	Preprimary				Elementary/High School			
	Public		Private		Public		Private	
	Enrollment	%	Enrollment	%	Enrollment	%	Enrollment	%
City	3,016	59.3	2,068	40.7	35,768	88.4	4,676	11.6
MSA[1]	17,848	52.0	16,451	48.0	244,416	89.0	30,326	11.0
U.S.	2,679,029	59.5	1,824,256	40.5	38,379,689	90.2	4,187,099	9.8

Note: Figures shown cover persons 3 years old and over;
(1) Metropolitan Statistical Area - see Appendix A for areas included
Source: 1990 Census of Population and Housing, Summary Tape File 3C

School Enrollment by Race

Area	Preprimary (%)				Elementary/High School (%)			
	White	Black	Other	Hisp.[1]	White	Black	Other	Hisp.[1]
City	60.0	37.3	2.8	10.9	55.2	40.0	4.7	14.9
MSA[2]	82.6	14.6	2.8	6.4	80.0	16.0	4.0	8.9
U.S.	80.4	12.5	7.1	7.8	74.1	15.6	10.3	12.5

Note: Figures shown cover persons 3 years old and over; (1) people of Hispanic origin can be of any race; (2) Metropolitan Statistical Area - see Appendix A for areas included
Source: 1990 Census of Population and Housing, Summary Tape File 3C

Classroom Teacher Salaries in Public Schools

District	B.A. Degree		M.A. Degree		Maximum	
	Min. ($)	Rank[1]	Max. ($)	Rank[1]	Max. ($)	Rank[1]
Tampa	25,002	66	44,702	53	47,201	75
Average	26,980	-	46,065	-	51,435	-

Note: Salaries are for 1997-1998; (1) Rank ranges from 1 to 100
Source: American Federation of Teachers, Survey & Analysis of Salary Trends, 1998

Higher Education

Two-Year Colleges		Four-Year Colleges		Medical Schools	Law Schools	Voc/Tech
Public	Private	Public	Private			
1	2	1	6	1	0	16

Source: College Blue Book, Occupational Education, 1997; Medical School Admission Requirements, 1999-2000; Peterson's Guide to Two-Year Colleges, 1999; Peterson's Guide to Four-Year Colleges, 2000; Barron's Guide to Law Schools, 1999

MAJOR EMPLOYERS

Major Employers

Staffing Concepts	Southeastern Staffing
GTE Data Services	Florida Health Sciences Center
Inter-Link Financial Networks	Nutmeg Mills
Tribune Co.	St. Joseph's Hospital
Kash n' Karry Food Stores	Total Employment

Note: Companies listed are located in the city
Source: Dun's Business Rankings, 1999; Ward's Business Directory, 1998

PUBLIC SAFETY

Crime Rate

Area	All Crimes	Violent Crimes				Property Crimes		
		Murder	Forcible Rape	Robbery	Aggrav. Assault	Burglary	Larceny-Theft	Motor Vehicle Theft
City	12,260.1	11.7	88.4	846.7	1,717.1	2,202.6	5,983.7	1,410.0
Suburbs[1]	5,567.2	4.5	41.6	162.5	564.7	1,064.0	3,318.9	411.0
MSA[2]	6,453.4	5.5	47.8	253.1	717.3	1,214.7	3,671.7	543.3
U.S.	4,922.7	6.8	35.9	186.1	382.0	919.6	2,886.5	505.8

Note: Crime rate is the number of crimes per 100,000 pop.; (1) defined as all areas within the MSA but located outside the central city; (2) Metropolitan Statistical Area - see Appendix A for areas incl.
Source: FBI Uniform Crime Reports, 1997

RECREATION

Culture and Recreation

Museums	Symphony Orchestras	Opera Companies	Dance Companies	Professional Theatres	Zoos	Pro Sports Teams
7	1	0	0	3	1	3

Source: International Directory of the Performing Arts, 1997; Official Museum Directory, 1999; Stern's Performing Arts Directory, 1997; USA Today Four Sport Stadium Guide, 1997; Chamber of Commerce/Economic Development, 1999

Library System

The Tampa-Hillsborough County Public Library System has 18 branches, holdings of 2,271,226 volumes, and a budget of $18,136,821 (1998). *American Library Directory, 1998-1999*

MEDIA

Newspapers

Name	Type	Freq.	Distribution	Circulation
Carrollwood News	General	1x/wk	Local	45,000
The Florida Dollar Stretcher	Black	1x/wk	State	8,000
Florida Sentinel-Bulletin	General	2x/wk	Local	30,000
Lake Area News	n/a	1x/wk	Area	30,000
The Laker	n/a	1x/wk	Area	21,300
Lutz Community News	General	1x/wk	Local	10,000
Nuevo Siglo	Hispanic	1x/wk	Area	22,000
Pennysaver Weekly News	General	1x/wk	Local	8,000
Tampa Tribune	General	7x/wk	Area	268,876
Temple Terrace Beacon	General	1x/wk	Local	22,000
Town 'n Country News	General	1x/wk	Area	23,000
USF Oracle	n/a	5x/wk	Camp/Comm	15,000

Note: Includes newspapers with circulations of 1,000 or more located in the city; n/a not available
Source: Burrelle's Media Directory, 1999 Edition

Television Stations

Name	Ch.	Affiliation	Type	Owner
WEDU	n/a	PBS	Public	Florida West Coast Public Broadcasting
WFLA	n/a	NBCT	Commercial	Media General/Sun Belt Newspapers
WTVT	13	FBC	Commercial	Fox Television Stations Inc.
WUSF	16	n/a	Public	University of South Florida
WFTS	28	ABCT	Commercial	Scripps Howard Broadcasting
WWWB	32	WB	Commercial	WWWB-TV Company, Hearst Broadcasting
WTTA	38	n/a	Commercial	Bay TV
WRMD	57	TMUN	Commercial	Telemundo Group Inc.
WVEA	61	UNIN	Commercial	Latin Communications Group Television

Note: Stations included broadcast in the Tampa metro area; n/a not available
Source: Burrelle's Media Directory, 1999 Edition

AM Radio Stations

Call Letters	Freq. (kHz)	Target Audience	Station Format	Music Format
WRMD	680	Hispanic	M	Latin
WBDN	760	General	T	n/a
WFLA	970	General	N/T	n/a
WMTX	1040	General	M/N/S	Adult Contemporary
WTMP	1150	Black	M/N/S	Adult Contemporary/Christian/Oldies/R&B/ Urban Contemporary
WDAE	1250	General	M	Adult Contemporary
WQBN	1300	Hispanic	M/N	Latin
WRBQ	1380	Children	M	Top 40
WTBL	1470	General	M	n/a
WAMA	1550	Hispanic	M	Adult Contemporary/Latin

Note: Stations included broadcast in the Tampa metro area; n/a not available
Target Audience: A=Asian; B=Black; C=Christian; E=Ethnic; F=French; G=General; H=Hispanic; M=Men; N=Native American; R=Religious; S=Senior Citizen; W=Women; Y=Young Adult; Z=Children
Station Format: E=Educational; M=Music; N=News; S=Sports; T=Talk
Source: Burrelle's Media Directory, 1999 Edition

FM Radio Stations

Call Letters	Freq. (mHz)	Target Audience	Station Format	Music Format
WMNF	88.5	Z/G	M/N/S	Jazz/R&B
WUSF	89.7	General	M/N	Classical/Jazz
WBVM	90.5	G/H	M/N/T	Christian/Classical
WFLZ	93.3	General	M	n/a
WSSR	95.7	General	M	Adult Contemporary
WAKS	100.7	General	M/N	Adult Contemporary/Oldies
WDUV	103.5	General	M	Easy Listening
WRBQ	104.7	General	M/N/S	Country

Note: Stations included broadcast in the Tampa metro area; n/a not available
Station Format: E=Educational; M=Music; N=News; S=Sports; T=Talk
Target Audience: A=Asian; B=Black; C=Christian; E=Ethnic; F=French; G=General; H=Hispanic;
M=Men; N=Native American; R=Religious; S=Senior Citizen; W=Women; Y=Young Adult; Z=Children
Source: Burrelle's Media Directory, 1999 Edition

CLIMATE

Average and Extreme Temperatures

Temperature	Jan	Feb	Mar	Apr	May	Jun	Jul	Aug	Sep	Oct	Nov	Dec	Yr.
Extreme High (°F)	85	88	91	93	98	99	97	98	96	94	90	86	99
Average High (°F)	70	72	76	82	87	90	90	90	89	84	77	72	82
Average Temp. (°F)	60	62	67	72	78	81	82	83	81	75	68	62	73
Average Low (°F)	50	52	56	61	67	73	74	74	73	66	57	52	63
Extreme Low (°F)	21	24	29	40	49	53	63	67	57	40	23	18	18

Note: Figures cover the years 1948-1990
Source: National Climatic Data Center, International Station Meteorological Climate Summary, 3/95

Average Precipitation/Snowfall/Humidity

Precip./Humidity	Jan	Feb	Mar	Apr	May	Jun	Jul	Aug	Sep	Oct	Nov	Dec	Yr.
Avg. Precip. (in.)	2.1	2.8	3.5	1.8	3.0	5.6	7.3	7.9	6.5	2.3	1.8	2.1	46.7
Avg. Snowfall (in.)	Tr	Tr	Tr	0	0	0	0	0	0	0	0	Tr	Tr
Avg. Rel. Hum. 7am (%)	87	87	86	86	85	86	88	90	91	89	88	87	88
Avg. Rel. Hum. 4pm (%)	56	55	54	51	52	60	65	66	64	57	56	57	58

Note: Figures cover the years 1948-1990; Tr = Trace amounts (<0.05 in. of rain; <0.5 in. of snow)
Source: National Climatic Data Center, International Station Meteorological Climate Summary, 3/95

Weather Conditions

Temperature			Daytime Sky			Precipitation		
32°F & below	45°F & below	90°F & above	Clear	Partly cloudy	Cloudy	0.01 inch or more precip.	0.1 inch or more snow/ice	Thunder-storms
3	35	85	81	204	80	107	< 1	87

Note: Figures are average number of days per year and covers the years 1948-1990
Source: National Climatic Data Center, International Station Meteorological Climate Summary, 3/95

AIR & WATER QUALITY

Maximum Pollutant Concentrations

	Particulate Matter (ug/m³)	Carbon Monoxide (ppm)	Sulfur Dioxide (ppm)	Nitrogen Dioxide (ppm)	Ozone (ppm)	Lead (ug/m³)
MSA[1] Level	87	4	0.038	0.012	0.11	n/a
NAAQS[2]	150	9	0.140	0.053	0.12	1.50
Met NAAQS?	Yes	Yes	Yes	Yes	Yes	n/a

Note: (1) Metropolitan Statistical Area - see Appendix A for areas included; (2) National Ambient Air
Quality Standards; ppm = parts per million; ug/m³ = micrograms per cubic meter; n/a not available
Source: EPA, National Air Quality and Emissions Trends Report, 1997

Pollutant Standards Index

In the Tampa MSA (see Appendix A for areas included), the Pollutant Standards Index (PSI) exceeded 100 on 4 days in 1997. A PSI value greater than 100 indicates that air quality would be in the unhealthful range on that day. *EPA, National Air Quality and Emissions Trends Report, 1997*

Drinking Water

Water System Name	Pop. Served	Primary Water Source Type	Number of Violations in 1998	Type of Violation/ Contaminants
City of Tampa-Water Dept	475,000	Surface	None	None

Note: Data as of July 10, 1999
Source: EPA, Office of Ground Water and Drinking Water, Safe Drinking Water Information System

Tampa tap water is alkaline, moderately hard and not fluoridated.
Editor & Publisher Market Guide, 1999

Comparative Statistics

Population Growth: City

City	Population			% Change	
	1980	1990	1998[1]	1980-90	1990-98
Atlanta	425,022	394,017	403,819	-7.3	2.5
Austin	345,544	465,577	552,434	34.7	18.7
Birmingham	284,413	265,852	252,997	-6.5	-4.8
Chattanooga	169,550	152,488	147,790	-10.1	-3.1
Columbia	101,208	98,052	110,840	-3.1	13.0
Dallas	904,074	1,006,831	1,075,894	11.4	6.9
Ft. Lauderdale	153,279	149,377	153,728	-2.5	2.9
Ft. Worth	385,166	447,619	491,801	16.2	9.9
Houston	1,595,167	1,630,672	1,786,691	2.2	9.6
Jackson	202,893	196,594	188,419	-3.1	-4.2
Jacksonville	540,920	635,230	693,630	17.4	9.2
Knoxville	175,030	165,121	165,540	-5.7	0.3
Memphis	646,356	610,337	603,507	-5.6	-1.1
Miami	346,865	358,548	368,624	3.4	2.8
Nashville	455,663	488,518	510,274	7.2	4.5
New Orleans	557,515	496,938	465,538	-10.9	-6.3
Orlando	128,291	164,693	181,175	28.4	10.0
San Antonio	785,809	935,927	1,114,130	19.1	19.0
Tampa	271,523	280,015	289,156	3.1	3.3
U.S.	**226,545,805**	**248,765,170**	**270,299,000**	**9.8**	**8.7**

Note: (1) Census Bureau estimate as of 7/98
Source: 1980 Census; 1990 Census of Population and Housing, Summary Tape File 3C

Population Growth: Metro Area

MSA[1]	Population			% Change	
	1980	1990	1998[2]	1980-90	1990-98
Atlanta	2,138,231	2,833,511	3,735,140	32.5	31.8
Austin	536,688	781,572	1,106,364	45.6	41.6
Birmingham	883,946	907,810	912,956	2.7	0.6
Chattanooga	426,540	433,210	453,346	1.6	4.6
Columbia	410,088	453,331	499,633	10.5	10.2
Dallas	1,957,378	2,553,362	3,171,895	30.4	24.2
Ft. Lauderdale	1,018,200	1,255,488	1,499,128	23.3	19.4
Ft. Worth	(a)	1,332,053	1,581,760	(a)	18.7
Houston	2,735,766	3,301,937	3,948,587	20.7	19.6
Jackson	362,038	395,396	429,626	9.2	8.7
Jacksonville	722,252	906,727	1,042,601	25.5	15.0
Knoxville	565,970	604,816	670,383	6.9	10.8
Memphis	913,472	981,747	1,101,767	7.5	12.2
Miami	1,625,781	1,937,094	2,122,503	19.1	9.6
Nashville	850,505	985,026	1,161,228	15.8	17.9
New Orleans	1,256,256	1,238,816	1,322,100	-1.4	6.7
Orlando	700,055	1,072,748	1,481,441	53.2	38.1
San Antonio	1,072,125	1,302,099	1,545,231	21.5	18.7
Tampa	1,613,621	2,067,959	2,242,989	28.2	8.5
U.S.	**226,545,805**	**248,765,170**	**270,299,000**	**9.8**	**8.7**

Note: (1) Metropolitan Statistical Area - see Appendix A for areas included; (2) Pop. estimates calculated by the editors;
(a) Ft. Worth was part of the Dallas-Ft. Worth MSA in 1980
Source: 1980 Census; 1990 Census of Population and Housing, Summary Tape File 3C

Population Characteristics: City

City	1990 Percent of Total (%)					
	White	Black	American Indian/ Esk./Aleut.	Asian/ Pacific Islander	Other	Hispanic Origin[1]
Atlanta	31.1	67.1	0.2	0.8	0.9	1.9
Austin	70.7	12.4	0.4	3.0	13.5	22.6
Birmingham	35.7	63.4	0.2	0.7	0.1	0.4
Chattanooga	64.9	33.7	0.4	0.9	0.2	0.6
Columbia	53.8	43.6	0.3	1.4	0.9	2.1
Dallas	55.4	29.5	0.5	2.1	12.5	20.3
Ft. Lauderdale	69.6	28.1	0.3	0.8	1.2	7.1
Ft. Worth	63.9	22.0	0.4	1.9	11.7	19.2
Houston	52.8	28.1	0.3	4.0	14.9	27.2
Jackson	43.6	55.7	0.1	0.5	0.1	0.4
Jacksonville	71.8	25.3	0.4	1.9	0.7	2.5
Knoxville	82.8	15.6	0.4	1.0	0.2	0.6
Memphis	44.0	54.9	0.2	0.8	0.2	0.7
Miami	65.8	27.3	0.1	0.6	6.1	62.3
Nashville	73.9	24.3	0.3	1.3	0.3	0.8
New Orleans	34.9	62.1	0.2	1.9	1.0	3.2
Orlando	68.6	26.9	0.3	1.5	2.7	8.6
San Antonio	72.3	7.0	0.4	1.1	19.2	55.3
Tampa	71.0	25.0	0.4	1.4	2.3	14.7
U.S.	**80.3**	**12.0**	**0.8**	**2.9**	**3.9**	**8.8**

Note: (1) People of Hispanic origin can be of any race
Source: 1990 Census of Population and Housing, Summary Tape File 3C

Population Characteristics: Metro Area

MSA[1]	1990 Percent of Total (%)					
	White	Black	American Indian/ Esk./Aleut.	Asian/ Pacific Islander	Other	Hispanic Origin[2]
Atlanta	71.3	26.0	0.2	1.8	0.7	1.9
Austin	76.9	9.2	0.4	2.3	11.2	20.2
Birmingham	72.2	27.0	0.2	0.5	0.1	0.4
Chattanooga	85.6	13.4	0.3	0.6	0.2	0.6
Columbia	67.9	30.4	0.2	1.0	0.5	1.3
Dallas	72.7	16.1	0.5	2.6	8.1	14.1
Ft. Lauderdale	81.8	15.4	0.2	1.3	1.2	8.4
Ft. Worth	80.4	10.8	0.5	2.2	6.1	11.0
Houston	66.4	18.5	0.3	3.8	11.1	21.1
Jackson	56.9	42.5	0.1	0.5	0.1	0.5
Jacksonville	77.4	20.0	0.4	1.6	0.6	2.4
Knoxville	92.9	5.9	0.3	0.7	0.1	0.6
Memphis	58.1	40.7	0.2	0.8	0.2	0.7
Miami	73.1	20.6	0.1	1.3	4.9	49.0
Nashville	83.1	15.5	0.3	0.9	0.2	0.7
New Orleans	62.2	34.8	0.3	1.7	1.0	4.2
Orlando	82.8	12.4	0.3	1.9	2.5	8.8
San Antonio	75.2	6.8	0.4	1.2	16.4	47.4
Tampa	88.4	8.9	0.3	1.1	1.2	6.6
U.S.	**80.3**	**12.0**	**0.8**	**2.9**	**3.9**	**8.8**

Note: (1) Metropolitan Statistical Area - see Appendix A for areas included;
(2) People of Hispanic origin can be of any race
Source: 1990 Census of Population and Housing, Summary Tape File 3C

Age: City

City	Median Age (Years)	Age Distribution (%)						
		Under 5	Under 18	18-24	25-44	45-64	65+	80+
Atlanta	31.4	7.6	24.1	13.0	34.7	16.8	11.3	2.9
Austin	28.9	7.5	23.1	17.2	38.7	13.6	7.4	1.8
Birmingham	32.9	7.4	25.4	10.5	32.2	17.0	14.8	3.7
Chattanooga	34.6	6.8	23.3	10.8	30.6	20.1	15.2	3.9
Columbia	28.5	6.1	19.9	22.7	32.9	12.9	11.6	2.9
Dallas	30.5	8.0	25.0	11.4	37.6	16.4	9.7	2.2
Ft. Lauderdale	37.1	6.0	18.8	8.1	34.8	20.4	17.9	5.0
Ft. Worth	30.3	8.6	26.6	11.7	34.7	15.9	11.2	2.6
Houston	30.3	8.3	26.7	11.6	36.4	17.1	8.2	1.6
Jackson	30.7	7.7	27.5	12.1	32.3	16.5	11.6	2.6
Jacksonville	31.2	8.1	26.1	11.1	34.6	17.5	10.6	2.1
Knoxville	32.4	5.9	19.8	16.5	31.1	17.2	15.4	3.8
Memphis	31.4	8.1	26.9	11.2	32.2	17.5	12.2	2.7
Miami	35.9	7.1	23.0	9.1	29.6	21.6	16.7	4.1
Nashville	32.2	7.0	22.9	11.6	36.2	17.9	11.4	2.6
New Orleans	31.5	7.7	27.6	11.1	31.4	16.9	13.0	3.0
Orlando	30.2	6.8	21.0	16.1	36.4	15.2	11.4	2.9
San Antonio	29.8	8.4	29.1	11.5	32.4	16.7	10.4	2.2
Tampa	33.2	7.4	22.9	10.8	33.0	18.7	14.6	3.4
U.S.	**32.9**	**7.3**	**25.6**	**10.5**	**32.6**	**18.7**	**12.5**	**2.8**

Source: 1990 Census of Population and Housing, Summary Tape File 3C

Age: Metro Area

MSA[1]	Median Age (Years)	Age Distribution (%)						
		Under 5	Under 18	18-24	25-44	45-64	65+	80+
Atlanta	31.4	7.7	25.9	10.7	37.8	17.7	7.9	1.6
Austin	29.4	7.7	25.3	14.9	38.1	14.4	7.3	1.7
Birmingham	33.8	7.0	25.4	9.8	32.4	19.2	13.2	3.0
Chattanooga	34.5	6.6	24.8	10.0	31.4	20.9	13.0	2.9
Columbia	31.2	7.0	25.0	13.0	35.3	17.6	9.2	1.7
Dallas	30.4	8.4	27.2	10.7	37.7	16.7	7.7	1.7
Ft. Lauderdale	37.6	6.2	20.4	8.0	32.0	18.9	20.7	5.1
Ft. Worth	30.6	8.4	27.3	10.7	36.3	17.1	8.6	1.8
Houston	30.4	8.5	28.9	10.4	36.9	16.7	7.0	1.4
Jackson	31.0	7.6	28.0	11.1	33.0	17.4	10.6	2.3
Jacksonville	32.0	7.8	26.0	10.6	34.2	18.3	10.9	2.2
Knoxville	34.5	6.2	22.9	11.4	32.0	20.5	13.3	2.8
Memphis	31.2	8.1	27.9	10.9	33.5	17.5	10.3	2.2
Miami	34.2	7.1	24.2	9.7	31.6	20.5	14.0	3.5
Nashville	32.4	7.1	25.1	10.7	35.0	18.5	10.6	2.3
New Orleans	31.8	7.7	27.9	10.1	32.8	18.1	11.0	2.2
Orlando	32.1	7.2	24.3	11.3	35.2	18.3	10.9	2.2
San Antonio	30.3	8.3	29.0	11.0	32.7	17.2	10.2	2.1
Tampa	38.5	6.0	20.4	8.4	29.7	20.0	21.5	4.9
U.S.	**32.9**	**7.3**	**25.6**	**10.5**	**32.6**	**18.7**	**12.5**	**2.8**

Note: (1) Metropolitan Statistical Area - see Appendix A for areas included
Source: 1990 Census of Population and Housing, Summary Tape File 3C

Male/Female Ratio: City

City	Number of males per 100 females (all ages)	Number of males per 100 females (18 years old+)
Atlanta	91.0	87.8
Austin	99.9	98.4
Birmingham	83.2	78.8
Chattanooga	85.2	81.1
Columbia	95.4	93.7
Dallas	97.0	94.5
Ft. Lauderdale	100.9	101.6
Ft. Worth	96.3	94.3
Houston	98.4	96.3
Jackson	86.5	81.3
Jacksonville	95.4	92.9
Knoxville	86.7	83.7
Memphis	87.4	82.2
Miami	92.6	90.1
Nashville	90.2	86.5
New Orleans	86.6	81.6
Orlando	101.0	101.0
San Antonio	93.0	88.7
Tampa	92.8	88.7
U.S.	**95.0**	**91.9**

Source: 1990 Census of Population, General Population Characteristics

Male/Female Ratio: Metro Area

MSA[1]	Number of males per 100 females (all ages)	Number of males per 100 females (18 years old+)
Atlanta	94.7	91.5
Austin	99.8	97.8
Birmingham	89.7	85.6
Chattanooga	90.9	86.8
Columbia	94.4	91.7
Dallas	97.2	94.5
Ft. Lauderdale	91.7	88.8
Ft. Worth	97.8	95.4
Houston	98.8	96.6
Jackson	89.6	84.9
Jacksonville	95.5	93.1
Knoxville	92.2	88.9
Memphis	91.3	86.8
Miami	91.6	88.1
Nashville	93.2	89.5
New Orleans	90.5	86.3
Orlando	97.3	95.3
San Antonio	94.6	90.7
Tampa	91.0	87.8
U.S.	**95.0**	**91.9**

Note: (1) Metropolitan Statistical Area - see Appendix A for areas included
Source: 1990 Census of Population, General Population Characteristics

Educational Attainment by Race: City

City	High School Graduate (%)					Bachelor's Degree (%)				
	Total	White	Black	Other	Hisp.[1]	Total	White	Black	Other	Hisp.[1]
Atlanta	69.9	86.7	59.8	62.1	54.4	26.6	51.9	11.1	34.6	21.7
Austin	82.3	88.7	69.6	58.4	57.9	34.4	40.0	16.5	18.4	13.8
Birmingham	69.3	76.7	63.9	73.8	79.9	16.2	23.2	10.7	43.1	32.2
Chattanooga	69.0	73.6	57.6	76.6	79.7	18.2	22.0	8.6	37.9	28.9
Columbia	76.0	86.2	61.0	89.0	80.7	31.7	45.1	11.4	53.9	29.6
Dallas	73.5	82.5	67.2	38.6	33.9	27.1	36.9	10.9	10.9	7.0
Ft. Lauderdale	74.2	83.1	41.6	68.0	61.3	21.9	26.5	4.7	21.2	14.6
Ft. Worth	71.6	79.2	62.6	39.6	37.4	21.5	27.0	8.8	9.7	6.3
Houston	70.5	79.1	66.3	45.0	36.6	25.1	33.0	13.4	14.8	7.3
Jackson	75.0	86.0	63.2	80.7	74.8	26.9	35.0	17.8	59.1	36.0
Jacksonville	76.4	80.2	63.6	77.1	78.9	17.9	19.6	10.9	25.3	20.2
Knoxville	70.8	71.5	64.9	82.7	89.6	21.7	22.9	11.0	48.2	49.3
Memphis	70.4	81.1	59.2	70.8	63.3	17.5	25.2	9.0	32.4	17.4
Miami	47.6	50.6	39.7	42.6	43.0	12.8	15.5	4.9	10.7	10.5
Nashville	75.4	77.7	66.7	73.8	73.5	23.6	25.4	16.6	32.3	24.7
New Orleans	68.1	81.4	58.4	57.6	60.3	22.4	36.6	11.6	20.4	18.7
Orlando	78.1	85.2	56.5	69.3	67.0	22.6	26.6	9.8	21.2	17.0
San Antonio	69.1	72.5	72.8	53.4	52.8	17.8	20.6	13.0	7.8	7.1
Tampa	70.6	74.7	57.1	61.5	54.4	18.7	21.7	8.0	15.1	11.3
U.S.	**75.2**	**77.9**	**63.1**	**60.4**	**49.8**	**20.3**	**21.5**	**11.4**	**19.4**	**9.2**

Note: Figures shown cover persons 25 years old and over; (1) people of Hispanic origin can be of any race
Source: 1990 Census of Population and Housing, Summary Tape File 3C

Educational Attainment by Race: Metro Area

MSA[1]	High School Graduate (%)					Bachelor's Degree (%)				
	Total	White	Black	Other	Hisp.[2]	Total	White	Black	Other	Hisp.[2]
Atlanta	79.5	82.6	70.3	72.7	69.8	26.8	29.7	16.6	32.3	24.5
Austin	82.5	87.3	70.0	58.5	56.8	32.2	35.9	16.9	17.8	13.1
Birmingham	71.7	74.5	63.1	74.1	77.3	18.7	21.0	11.1	36.1	27.2
Chattanooga	67.7	69.0	57.9	72.5	76.4	15.7	16.5	9.1	32.2	23.0
Columbia	78.6	83.0	66.8	80.5	77.9	25.3	29.7	13.2	35.6	22.2
Dallas	79.0	84.1	70.1	50.0	41.7	27.6	31.5	13.5	16.5	8.9
Ft. Lauderdale	76.8	79.9	55.5	71.5	68.2	18.8	19.9	10.1	21.4	15.7
Ft. Worth	79.1	82.4	69.4	52.9	47.9	22.6	24.2	12.8	16.1	9.3
Houston	75.1	81.1	68.9	50.2	41.6	25.1	29.0	15.1	16.3	7.9
Jackson	74.4	83.8	58.2	79.1	71.5	25.1	30.8	14.8	53.5	25.4
Jacksonville	77.4	80.6	62.5	76.6	78.5	18.6	20.1	10.8	25.0	20.3
Knoxville	70.3	70.3	66.8	80.1	80.8	19.2	19.2	13.5	42.5	33.7
Memphis	73.5	82.2	58.1	76.6	69.5	19.0	24.2	9.2	34.5	21.0
Miami	65.0	67.6	56.0	57.0	55.1	18.8	20.8	9.9	17.1	14.1
Nashville	74.0	75.6	64.4	75.2	74.2	21.4	22.3	15.1	31.2	23.4
New Orleans	72.3	78.8	58.4	64.5	68.3	19.7	23.6	10.8	21.3	17.5
Orlando	79.9	82.6	60.3	72.0	68.9	21.6	22.8	11.5	21.4	16.0
San Antonio	72.7	75.8	75.9	55.4	54.4	19.4	22.0	14.4	8.2	7.7
Tampa	75.1	76.5	60.4	64.4	59.9	17.3	17.7	10.8	18.4	14.2
U.S.	**75.2**	**77.9**	**63.1**	**60.4**	**49.8**	**20.3**	**21.5**	**11.4**	**19.4**	**9.2**

Note: Figures shown cover persons 25 years old and over; (1) Metropolitan Statistical Area - see Appendix A for areas included; (2) people of Hispanic origin can be of any race
Source: 1990 Census of Population and Housing, Summary Tape File 3C

Per Capita/Median/Average Income: City

City	Per Capita ($)	Median Household ($)	Average Household ($)
Atlanta	15,279	22,275	37,882
Austin	14,295	25,414	33,947
Birmingham	10,127	19,193	25,313
Chattanooga	12,332	22,197	29,933
Columbia	12,210	23,216	31,826
Dallas	16,300	27,489	40,299
Ft. Lauderdale	19,814	27,239	43,756
Ft. Worth	13,162	26,547	34,359
Houston	14,261	26,261	37,296
Jackson	12,216	23,270	33,118
Jacksonville	13,661	28,305	35,281
Knoxville	12,108	19,923	27,960
Memphis	11,682	22,674	30,656
Miami	9,799	16,925	26,507
Nashville	14,490	27,821	35,188
New Orleans	11,372	18,477	29,283
Orlando	13,879	26,119	33,136
San Antonio	10,884	23,584	30,622
Tampa	13,277	22,772	31,813
U.S.	**14,420**	**30,056**	**38,453**

Note: Figures are for 1989
Source: 1990 Census of Population and Housing, Summary Tape File 3C

Per Capita/Median/Average Income: Metro Area

MSA[1]	Per Capita ($)	Median Household ($)	Average Household ($)
Atlanta	16,897	36,051	44,968
Austin	14,521	28,474	36,754
Birmingham	13,082	26,151	34,240
Chattanooga	12,493	25,475	32,334
Columbia	13,618	30,474	36,727
Dallas	16,455	33,277	43,582
Ft. Lauderdale	16,883	30,571	39,823
Ft. Worth	14,842	32,121	39,560
Houston	15,091	31,473	41,650
Jackson	12,311	26,365	34,434
Jacksonville	14,141	29,514	36,739
Knoxville	12,984	25,134	32,693
Memphis	12,935	26,994	35,139
Miami	13,686	26,909	37,903
Nashville	14,567	30,223	37,811
New Orleans	12,108	24,442	32,569
Orlando	14,895	31,230	39,069
San Antonio	11,865	26,092	33,646
Tampa	14,374	26,036	33,685
U.S.	**14,420**	**30,056**	**38,453**

Note: Figures are for 1989; (1) Metropolitan Statistical Area - see Appendix A for areas included
Source: 1990 Census of Population and Housing, Summary Tape File 3C

Household Income Distribution: City

City	Less than $5,000	$5,000 -$9,999	$10,000 -$14,999	$15,000 -$24,999	$25,000 -$34,999	$35,000 -$49,999	$50,000 -$74,999	$75,000 -$99,999	$100,000 and up
				% of Households Earning					
Atlanta	14.8	11.6	9.9	17.8	13.1	12.5	10.1	3.9	6.3
Austin	8.9	9.5	10.6	20.3	16.1	15.6	11.6	4.0	3.5
Birmingham	13.6	14.6	12.1	20.7	15.3	12.5	7.9	1.8	1.4
Chattanooga	10.6	12.9	11.2	20.2	15.7	14.1	10.1	2.6	2.7
Columbia	10.1	11.6	11.3	20.0	15.7	13.9	10.3	3.3	3.8
Dallas	7.3	8.2	9.2	20.2	16.7	15.7	11.8	4.6	6.2
Ft. Lauderdale	7.5	8.9	9.7	19.9	14.9	14.7	12.7	4.6	7.1
Ft. Worth	7.7	9.4	10.1	19.7	17.1	16.7	12.5	3.6	3.2
Houston	8.9	9.1	9.9	19.7	15.8	15.2	12.1	4.5	4.8
Jackson	10.6	12.2	10.5	19.6	15.3	14.7	10.5	2.9	3.7
Jacksonville	6.9	8.3	9.1	19.3	17.3	18.9	13.4	4.0	2.7
Knoxville	11.7	14.7	12.8	20.4	15.0	13.1	8.0	2.0	2.3
Memphis	11.7	11.5	10.7	20.0	15.8	14.7	10.0	2.7	2.9
Miami	17.1	15.0	13.3	19.5	12.7	10.6	6.9	2.4	2.6
Nashville	7.6	8.3	9.0	19.6	17.3	17.9	13.5	3.7	3.1
New Orleans	18.0	13.4	11.9	17.9	12.6	11.4	8.6	2.8	3.6
Orlando	6.8	8.5	10.2	21.9	17.6	17.1	11.9	3.1	2.7
San Antonio	9.8	10.1	11.2	21.3	16.3	15.1	10.5	3.1	2.4
Tampa	9.7	11.7	11.5	21.0	16.1	14.6	9.2	2.9	3.4
U.S.	**6.2**	**9.3**	**8.8**	**17.5**	**15.8**	**17.9**	**15.0**	**5.1**	**4.4**

Note: Figures are for 1989
Source: 1990 Census of Population and Housing, Summary Tape File 3C

Household Income Distribution: Metro Area

MSA[1]	Less than $5,000	$5,000 -$9,999	$10,000 -$14,999	$15,000 -$24,999	$25,000 -$34,999	$35,000 -$49,999	$50,000 -$74,999	$75,000 -$99,999	$100,000 and up
				% of Households Earning					
Atlanta	5.3	5.8	6.2	15.2	15.9	19.9	19.0	6.9	5.9
Austin	7.7	8.4	9.5	18.6	15.8	17.2	14.1	4.8	3.9
Birmingham	8.8	10.8	9.8	18.6	15.7	16.4	12.8	3.8	3.4
Chattanooga	7.8	11.1	10.4	19.7	16.7	16.5	12.0	3.0	2.7
Columbia	5.7	7.6	8.4	18.3	17.8	19.0	15.5	4.5	3.1
Dallas	5.3	6.4	7.4	17.1	16.2	18.6	16.9	6.3	5.9
Ft. Lauderdale	5.2	8.2	8.8	18.6	16.0	17.8	15.4	5.3	4.7
Ft. Worth	5.1	6.9	8.0	17.6	16.6	19.3	17.0	5.5	4.0
Houston	6.7	7.3	8.2	17.2	15.5	17.5	16.1	6.0	5.5
Jackson	9.2	10.3	9.8	18.3	15.3	17.1	13.1	3.7	3.2
Jacksonville	6.2	7.9	8.8	19.0	17.3	18.9	14.4	4.3	3.2
Knoxville	7.9	11.4	10.8	19.7	16.3	15.9	12.1	3.3	2.7
Memphis	9.4	9.6	9.2	18.2	15.6	17.0	13.4	3.9	3.6
Miami	9.4	9.9	9.6	17.7	15.0	15.7	13.0	4.7	4.9
Nashville	6.7	7.8	8.3	18.1	17.1	19.0	14.9	4.4	3.7
New Orleans	11.6	10.7	10.4	18.2	15.1	15.5	11.8	3.5	3.3
Orlando	4.2	6.6	8.4	19.1	18.1	19.5	15.6	4.7	3.8
San Antonio	8.5	9.0	10.2	20.2	16.5	16.7	12.3	3.6	3.0
Tampa	5.5	9.7	11.0	21.6	17.3	16.8	11.5	3.5	3.0
U.S.	**6.2**	**9.3**	**8.8**	**17.5**	**15.8**	**17.9**	**15.0**	**5.1**	**4.4**

Note: Figures are for 1989; (1) Metropolitan Statistical Area - see Appendix A for areas included
Source: 1990 Census of Population and Housing, Summary Tape File 3C

Effective Buying Income: City

City	Per Capita ($)	Median Household ($)	Average Household ($)
Atlanta	17,521	27,204	44,150
Austin	18,999	33,690	45,417
Birmingham	13,125	24,971	32,690
Chattanooga	15,943	28,919	38,764
Columbia	14,489	27,766	41,283
Dallas	19,949	34,730	50,071
Ft. Lauderdale	21,311	29,969	47,958
Ft. Worth	15,833	32,448	42,121
Houston	17,300	32,961	46,019
Jackson	15,725	30,773	42,957
Jacksonville	16,175	34,044	42,710
Knoxville	15,639	25,537	36,271
Memphis	14,711	28,988	38,844
Miami	10,686	19,318	29,699
Nashville	19,588	37,587	47,297
New Orleans	14,252	23,748	37,349
Orlando	16,369	30,680	40,447
San Antonio	13,207	28,830	37,511
Tampa	15,967	28,011	38,804
U.S.	**16,803**	**34,536**	**45,243**

Note: Data as of 1/1/99
Source: Standard Rate & Data Service, Newspaper Advertising Source, 9/99

Effective Buying Income: Metro Area

MSA[1]	Per Capita ($)	Median Household ($)	Average Household ($)
Atlanta	18,461	39,355	49,367
Austin	19,332	36,486	49,623
Birmingham	17,533	33,719	45,282
Chattanooga	16,163	30,705	41,414
Columbia	16,106	34,476	43,549
Dallas	20,448	41,000	54,713
Ft. Lauderdale	19,008	33,637	45,067
Ft. Worth	18,447	39,080	49,289
Houston	19,045	39,325	53,256
Jackson	16,394	33,854	45,823
Jacksonville	17,449	35,058	46,178
Knoxville	17,329	31,471	43,073
Memphis	16,785	33,719	45,668
Miami	15,030	29,383	42,550
Nashville	20,167	39,453	52,094
New Orleans	15,361	30,139	41,297
Orlando	17,461	34,560	45,696
San Antonio	14,764	31,311	42,249
Tampa	17,489	30,719	41,747
U.S.	**16,803**	**34,536**	**45,243**

Note: Data as of 1/1/99; (1) Metropolitan Statistical Area - see Appendix A for areas included
Source: Standard Rate & Data Service, Newspaper Advertising Source, 9/99

Effective Household Buying Income Distribution: City

City	% of Households Earning						
	$10,000 -$19,999	$20,000 -$34,999	$35,000 -$49,999	$50,000 -$74,999	$75,000 -$99,000	$100,000 -$124,999	$125,000 and up
Atlanta	17.6	21.7	13.6	12.6	5.7	2.5	5.0
Austin	15.7	23.0	16.8	17.1	7.4	3.1	3.6
Birmingham	20.5	24.1	15.3	12.9	4.2	1.2	1.2
Chattanooga	18.6	23.4	16.2	14.8	5.7	1.9	2.5
Columbia	19.5	24.5	15.5	13.8	5.1	2.0	2.5
Dallas	14.8	24.0	17.2	16.3	7.2	3.4	5.6
Ft. Lauderdale	17.8	24.1	15.3	14.9	5.9	2.7	5.1
Ft. Worth	16.7	23.8	17.7	17.1	6.7	2.1	2.6
Houston	15.9	23.1	16.5	16.0	7.3	3.0	4.2
Jackson	17.3	22.5	16.2	15.8	6.5	2.1	3.6
Jacksonville	15.4	23.9	19.1	18.5	6.7	2.1	2.1
Knoxville	21.3	23.4	15.4	12.9	4.3	1.4	2.1
Memphis	17.7	23.1	16.5	15.3	5.2	1.8	2.6
Miami	23.4	21.9	11.7	8.8	3.2	1.2	1.8
Nashville	13.4	22.1	18.3	20.1	8.7	3.0	3.3
New Orleans	19.6	20.8	12.8	12.0	5.0	1.9	3.2
Orlando	17.5	26.9	18.5	16.0	5.1	1.2	1.9
San Antonio	18.5	25.0	16.7	14.8	5.6	1.8	1.9
Tampa	19.4	24.4	16.5	13.8	4.8	1.8	2.8
U.S.	**16.0**	**22.6**	**18.2**	**18.9**	**7.2**	**2.4**	**2.7**

Note: Data as of 1/1/99
Source: Standard Rate & Data Service, Newspaper Advertising Source, 9/99

Effective Household Buying Income Distribution: Metro Area

MSA[1]	% of Households Earning						
	$10,000 -$19,999	$20,000 -$34,999	$35,000 -$49,999	$50,000 -$74,999	$75,000 -$99,000	$100,000 -$124,999	$125,000 and up
Atlanta	12.4	22.3	19.9	21.8	8.4	2.8	3.1
Austin	14.8	21.5	17.1	19.2	8.7	3.2	3.5
Birmingham	16.0	21.9	17.3	18.3	7.4	2.4	2.8
Chattanooga	18.1	23.8	17.7	16.2	5.8	1.8	2.3
Columbia	15.6	24.6	20.0	19.3	6.3	1.8	1.7
Dallas	12.4	21.0	18.0	21.1	9.9	3.8	4.6
Ft. Lauderdale	16.8	23.7	17.9	18.1	6.8	2.4	2.9
Ft. Worth	13.6	21.8	18.6	21.1	9.3	3.2	3.0
Houston	13.4	20.8	17.1	19.8	9.8	3.8	4.5
Jackson	16.0	21.3	16.9	18.8	7.7	2.3	2.7
Jacksonville	15.2	23.6	19.3	19.0	7.1	2.2	2.5
Knoxville	17.8	23.0	17.2	16.8	6.6	2.1	2.4
Memphis	15.5	21.5	17.3	18.4	7.3	2.4	3.0
Miami	17.9	22.5	16.0	15.4	5.7	2.2	3.2
Nashville	13.0	20.9	18.6	21.1	9.1	3.2	3.7
New Orleans	17.1	22.0	16.3	16.5	6.2	2.0	2.5
Orlando	16.1	25.2	19.3	18.3	7.0	2.2	2.6
San Antonio	17.2	24.1	17.5	16.7	6.2	2.0	2.2
Tampa	18.9	26.0	17.9	15.8	5.6	1.9	2.2
U.S.	**16.0**	**22.6**	**18.2**	**18.9**	**7.2**	**2.4**	**2.7**

Note: Data as of 1/1/99; (1) Metropolitan Statistical Area - see Appendix A for areas included
Source: Standard Rate & Data Service, Newspaper Advertising Source, 9/99

Poverty Rates by Race and Age: City

City	Total (%)	By Race (%)				By Age (%)		
		White	Black	Other	Hisp.[1]	Under 5 years old	Under 18 years old	65 years and over
Atlanta	27.3	9.8	35.0	35.5	30.5	47.1	42.9	25.1
Austin	17.9	13.5	26.5	30.2	27.4	23.4	21.5	11.7
Birmingham	24.8	11.4	32.2	22.8	21.0	38.3	35.9	22.2
Chattanooga	18.2	11.0	32.2	12.5	11.5	33.1	28.1	17.5
Columbia	21.2	11.8	32.4	26.3	22.5	29.9	28.7	16.7
Dallas	18.0	9.5	29.1	27.2	27.8	27.8	27.3	14.6
Ft. Lauderdale	17.1	8.8	38.1	17.3	21.0	33.2	31.0	10.8
Ft. Worth	17.4	10.8	31.3	25.4	25.9	26.0	24.9	14.4
Houston	20.7	12.4	30.7	29.3	30.7	31.4	30.0	17.8
Jackson	22.7	7.7	34.5	21.6	23.2	34.7	32.1	20.7
Jacksonville	13.0	7.5	28.6	12.3	15.0	19.9	18.6	16.1
Knoxville	20.8	17.4	38.6	25.3	34.4	32.0	29.8	16.2
Memphis	23.0	8.1	34.8	23.1	24.0	38.4	34.9	21.8
Miami	31.2	25.0	46.0	32.0	28.5	46.9	44.1	32.2
Nashville	13.4	8.6	27.9	18.1	14.3	22.5	20.4	15.1
New Orleans	31.6	11.8	42.2	37.4	26.1	48.8	46.3	24.6
Orlando	15.8	8.2	33.9	20.6	21.6	29.0	27.1	16.1
San Antonio	22.6	19.1	30.3	32.3	30.8	35.4	32.5	19.1
Tampa	19.4	12.2	39.8	21.0	20.6	35.0	30.9	19.4
U.S.	**13.1**	**9.8**	**29.5**	**23.1**	**25.3**	**20.1**	**18.3**	**12.8**

Note: Figures show the percent of people living below the poverty line in 1989. The average poverty threshold was $12,674 for a family of four in 1989; (1) People of Hispanic origin can be of any race
Source: 1990 Census of Population and Housing, Summary Tape File 3C

Poverty Rates by Race and Age: Metro Area

MSA[1]	Total (%)	By Race (%)				By Age (%)		
		White	Black	Other	Hisp.[2]	Under 5 years old	Under 18 years old	65 years and over
Atlanta	10.0	5.4	22.4	14.4	16.2	15.5	13.9	14.3
Austin	15.3	11.8	26.2	27.7	26.3	19.1	17.4	13.0
Birmingham	15.3	9.2	31.4	18.4	16.2	21.7	20.4	18.3
Chattanooga	13.6	10.8	31.3	12.3	14.2	21.5	18.3	17.5
Columbia	11.7	6.9	22.6	17.0	13.3	16.8	15.3	14.8
Dallas	12.0	7.2	26.7	22.7	24.0	17.2	16.2	13.1
Ft. Lauderdale	10.2	7.0	26.8	13.2	13.7	15.5	15.0	9.0
Ft. Worth	11.0	7.7	27.0	21.8	22.2	16.5	14.7	12.2
Houston	15.1	9.4	27.9	24.8	26.6	21.6	20.2	16.0
Jackson	19.3	6.8	36.3	17.3	22.1	29.3	26.8	23.3
Jacksonville	11.8	7.4	29.2	12.0	13.9	18.6	16.8	14.5
Knoxville	14.2	12.9	33.6	19.7	18.7	21.8	18.7	16.1
Memphis	18.3	6.7	34.9	17.8	20.2	29.6	26.6	21.4
Miami	17.9	14.2	30.3	21.5	19.5	24.9	24.3	20.0
Nashville	11.3	8.4	27.2	16.1	12.1	17.1	15.0	16.6
New Orleans	21.2	10.1	40.8	25.9	18.7	31.5	30.3	19.2
Orlando	10.0	7.3	26.4	15.0	15.9	14.8	14.0	10.7
San Antonio	19.5	16.2	26.4	30.5	29.3	30.3	27.7	17.2
Tampa	11.4	9.0	33.1	20.4	19.4	20.2	17.6	9.4
U.S.	**13.1**	**9.8**	**29.5**	**23.1**	**25.3**	**20.1**	**18.3**	**12.8**

Note: Figures show the percent of people living below the poverty line in 1989. The average poverty threshold was $12,674 for a family of four in 1989; (1) Metropolitan Statistical Area - see Appendix A for areas included; (2) People of Hispanic origin can be of any race
Source: 1990 Census of Population and Housing, Summary Tape File 3C

Major State and Local Tax Rates

City	State Corp. Income (%)	State Personal Income (%)	Residential Property (effective rate per $100)	Sales & Use		State Gasoline (cents/ gallon)	State Cigarette (cents/ pack)
				State (%)	Local (%)		
Atlanta	6.0	1.0 - 6.0	2.05	4.0	3.0	7.5	12.0
Austin	None[i]	None	n/a	6.25	2.0	20.0	41.0
Birmingham	5.0	2.0 - 5.0	0.79	4.0	4.0	18.0[a]	16.5[b]
Chattanooga	6.0	6.0[f]	n/a	6.0	2.25	21.0[g]	13.0[h]
Columbia	5.0	2.5 - 7.0	1.42	5.0	None	16.0	7.0
Dallas	None[i]	None	n/a	6.25	2.0	20.0	41.0
Fort Lauderdale	5.5[c]	None	n/a	6.0	None	13.1[d]	33.9
Fort Worth	None[i]	None	n/a	6.25	2.0	20.0	41.0
Houston	None[i]	None	2.70	6.25	2.0	20.0	41.0
Jackson	3.0 - 5.0	3.0 - 5.0	1.28	7.0	None	18.4[e]	18.0
Jacksonville	5.5[c]	None	1.11	6.0	0.5	13.1[d]	33.9
Knoxville	6.0	6.0[f]	n/a	6.0	2.25	21.0[g]	13.0[h]
Memphis	6.0	6.0[f]	1.42	6.0	2.25	21.0[g]	13.0[h]
Miami	5.5[c]	None	n/a	6.0	0.5	13.1[d]	33.9
Nashville	6.0	6.0[f]	n/a	6.0	2.25	21.0[g]	13.0[h]
New Orleans	4.0 - 8.0	2.0 - 6.0	1.65	4.0	5.0	20.0	20.0
Orlando	5.5[c]	None	n/a	6.0	None	13.1[d]	33.9
San Antonio	None[i]	None	n/a	6.25	1.5	20.0	41.0
Tampa	5.5[c]	None	n/a	6.0	1.0	13.1[d]	33.9

Note: (a) Rate is comprised of 16 cents excise plus 2 cents motor carrier tax. Rate does not include 1 - 3 cents local option tax; (b) Counties and cities may impose an additional tax of 1 - 6 cents per pack; (c) 3.3% Alternative Minimum Tax. An exemption of $5,000 is allowed; (d) Rate is comprised of 4 cents excise and 9.1 cents motor carrier tax; (e) Rate is comprised of 18 cents excise and 0.4 cents motor carrier tax; (f) Applies to interest and dividend income only; (g) Rate is comprised of 20 cents excise and 1 cent motor carrier tax. Does not include a 1 cent local option tax; (h) Counties and cities may impose an additional tax of 1 cent per pack. Dealers pay a additional enforcement and admin. fee of 0.05 cent per pack; (i) Texas imposes a franchise tax of 4.5% of earned surplus
Source: Source: Federation of Tax Administrators, www.taxadmin.org; Washington D.C. Department of Finance and Revenue, Tax Rates and Tax Burdens in the District of Columbia: A Nationwide Comparison, July 1999; Chambers of Commerce, 1999

Employment by Industry

MSA[1]	Services	Retail	Gov't.	Manuf.	Finance/ Ins./R.E.	Whole-sale	Transp./ Utilities	Constr.	Mining
Atlanta	30.6	17.6	12.3	10.5	6.7	8.4	8.6	5.2	0.1
Austin	29.5	17.4	20.3	13.6	5.3	4.5	3.4	5.9	0.2
Birmingham	29.7	17.4	13.9	10.9	7.6	7.0	6.6	6.3	0.6
Chattanooga	26.3	17.6	14.4	20.2	7.3	4.5	5.3	n/a	n/a
Columbia	25.6	17.2	25.0	8.8	7.5	5.5	4.5	n/a	n/a
Dallas	30.9	16.2	10.7	13.4	8.3	7.9	6.8	5.2	0.6
Ft. Lauderdale	35.2	21.7	13.1	5.9	7.6	6.4	4.6	5.5	<0.1
Ft. Worth	27.5	19.5	12.3	14.7	4.7	5.5	9.5	5.6	0.6
Houston	31.2	16.4	12.4	10.5	5.4	6.6	7.1	7.1	3.1
Jackson	26.5	16.9	20.6	9.0	7.2	6.6	7.3	5.3	n/a
Jacksonville	33.7	18.4	12.1	7.4	10.4	5.5	7.0	5.4	n/a
Knoxville	27.7	21.9	16.7	14.2	4.6	5.3	4.3	5.1	0.2
Memphis	29.2	17.9	13.3	10.7	4.9	6.9	12.4	n/a	n/a
Miami	33.0	17.7	14.0	7.6	6.7	8.3	9.0	3.7	<0.1
Nashville	31.8	18.6	12.5	14.5	6.5	5.9	5.0	n/a	n/a
New Orleans	30.7	18.7	17.0	8.0	5.1	5.8	6.7	5.8	2.3
Orlando	42.7	18.7	10.2	6.2	5.9	5.5	5.1	5.7	n/a
San Antonio	33.0	19.6	18.7	7.5	6.7	4.3	4.6	5.3	0.3
Tampa	41.5	16.9	11.7	7.6	7.4	5.3	4.5	4.9	<0.1
U.S.	**30.4**	**17.7**	**15.6**	**14.3**	**5.9**	**5.4**	**5.3**	**5.0**	**0.4**

Note: All figures are percentages covering non-farm employment as of 6/99 and are not seasonally adjusted; (1) Metropolitan Statistical Area - see Appendix A for areas included; n/a not available
Source: Bureau of Labor Statistics, http://stats.bls.gov

Labor Force, Employment and Job Growth: City

Area	Civilian Labor Force			Workers Employed		
	Jun. 1998	Jun. 1999	% Chg.	Jun. 1998	Jun. 1999	% Chg.
Atlanta	222,446	220,622	-0.8	208,028	208,425	0.2
Austin	369,091	381,934	3.5	356,377	371,152	4.1
Birmingham	133,369	134,573	0.9	126,198	127,314	0.9
Chattanooga	74,836	74,814	0.0	71,020	71,813	1.1
Columbia	48,970	50,878	3.9	47,221	48,941	3.6
Dallas	671,346	688,777	2.6	637,052	656,954	3.1
Ft. Lauderdale	93,747	95,911	2.3	88,170	90,732	2.9
Ft. Worth	271,479	279,786	3.1	257,658	266,665	3.5
Houston	1,039,379	1,064,139	2.4	976,636	993,824	1.8
Jackson	100,923	102,043	1.1	95,454	96,994	1.6
Jacksonville	384,517	396,630	3.2	370,983	383,518	3.4
Knoxville	93,291	93,453	0.2	89,647	90,526	1.0
Memphis	319,989	330,604	3.3	303,635	316,737	4.3
Miami	180,863	183,684	1.6	162,814	166,762	2.4
Nashville	309,438	317,633	2.6	300,617	309,512	3.0
New Orleans	208,725	202,476	-3.0	193,475	191,807	-0.9
Orlando	110,687	115,963	4.8	106,808	112,122	5.0
San Antonio	531,687	543,082	2.1	504,016	521,309	3.4
Tampa	168,389	177,555	5.4	162,313	171,614	5.7
U.S.	**138,798,000**	**140,666,000**	**1.3**	**132,265,000**	**134,395,000**	**1.6**

Note: Data is not seasonally adjusted and covers workers 16 years of age and older
Source: Bureau of Labor Statistics, http://stats.bls.gov

Labor Force, Employment and Job Growth: Metro Area

Area	Civilian Labor Force			Workers Employed		
	Jun. '98	Jun. '99	% Chg.	Jun. '98	Jun. '99	% Chg.
Atlanta	2,133,463	2,126,262	-0.3	2,052,330	2,056,258	0.2
Austin	683,165	707,903	3.6	661,832	689,270	4.1
Birmingham	478,093	482,423	0.9	461,747	465,830	0.9
Chattanooga	222,203	219,205	-1.3	211,901	211,387	-0.2
Columbia	283,326	293,735	3.7	276,484	286,555	3.6
Dallas	1,896,137	1,948,107	2.7	1,821,731	1,878,643	3.1
Ft. Lauderdale	763,483	782,027	2.4	727,176	748,309	2.9
Ft. Worth	893,824	922,233	3.2	859,054	889,085	3.5
Houston	2,163,969	2,212,962	2.3	2,056,977	2,093,177	1.8
Jackson	227,597	230,411	1.2	218,282	221,804	1.6
Jacksonville	540,295	557,693	3.2	522,227	539,871	3.4
Knoxville	350,525	351,858	0.4	339,193	342,520	1.0
Memphis	556,726	576,204	3.5	533,433	556,625	4.3
Miami	1,041,525	1,060,538	1.8	969,523	993,032	2.4
Nashville	647,559	662,228	2.3	627,615	646,186	3.0
New Orleans	638,166	623,538	-2.3	600,137	594,963	-0.9
Orlando	849,096	889,215	4.7	821,730	862,611	5.0
San Antonio	769,922	787,806	2.3	734,308	759,502	3.4
Tampa	1,173,939	1,235,670	5.3	1,136,410	1,201,527	5.7
U.S.	**138,798,000**	**140,666,000**	**1.3**	**132,265,000**	**134,395,000**	**1.6**

Note: Data is not seasonally adjusted and covers workers 16 years of age and older;
(1) Metropolitan Statistical Area - see Appendix A for areas included
Source: Bureau of Labor Statistics, http://stats.bls.gov

Unemployment Rate: City

Area	1998						1999					
	Jul.	Aug.	Sep.	Oct.	Nov.	Dec.	Jan.	Feb.	Mar.	Apr.	May.	Jun.
Atlanta	6.3	5.7	5.7	5.6	5.1	4.9	4.8	5.5	5.5	4.8	4.7	5.5
Austin	3.2	3.1	3.1	2.7	2.7	2.6	2.9	2.6	2.3	2.2	2.4	2.8
Birmingham	4.8	4.9	4.6	4.8	4.2	3.5	3.7	4.1	3.9	4.4	4.4	5.4
Chattanooga	4.3	4.5	4.1	3.9	4.0	3.4	4.4	4.3	4.1	3.9	3.7	4.0
Columbia	3.8	3.1	3.3	3.3	2.7	2.6	3.0	3.4	3.0	2.8	3.3	3.8
Dallas	4.6	4.4	4.2	3.9	4.0	3.6	4.2	3.9	3.6	3.6	3.9	4.6
Ft. Lauderdale	5.4	5.3	5.5	5.5	5.6	5.2	6.1	5.5	5.4	5.7	5.6	5.4
Ft. Worth	5.4	4.4	4.3	3.9	4.0	3.6	4.5	4.1	3.8	3.7	4.0	4.7
Houston	5.5	5.1	4.9	4.5	4.7	4.5	5.4	5.1	4.8	5.1	5.6	6.6
Jackson	4.8	5.2	4.7	4.6	4.0	3.6	4.7	3.5	4.1	3.4	4.3	4.9
Jacksonville	3.3	3.1	3.0	2.9	3.0	2.7	3.4	3.1	3.2	3.2	3.2	3.3
Knoxville	4.7	4.7	4.6	4.4	4.4	3.7	3.9	3.8	3.5	3.2	2.9	3.1
Memphis	4.6	4.7	4.8	4.1	4.0	3.4	4.4	4.3	4.3	4.1	3.8	4.2
Miami	9.0	8.8	9.2	9.2	9.5	8.8	10.2	9.2	9.0	9.5	9.3	9.2
Nashville	2.4	2.5	2.5	2.6	2.6	2.1	2.7	2.6	2.7	2.6	2.4	2.6
New Orleans	6.8	6.8	6.0	5.2	4.9	4.6	5.5	4.8	4.4	4.5	3.8	5.3
Orlando	3.3	3.1	3.3	3.1	3.2	2.9	3.6	3.2	3.0	3.1	3.2	3.3
San Antonio	4.7	4.4	4.2	3.7	3.6	3.3	3.7	3.3	3.1	2.9	3.2	4.0
Tampa	3.6	3.4	3.4	3.1	3.2	2.9	3.7	3.3	3.3	3.4	3.4	3.3
U.S.	**4.7**	**4.5**	**4.4**	**4.2**	**4.1**	**4.0**	**4.8**	**4.7**	**4.4**	**4.1**	**4.0**	**4.5**

Note: All figures are percentages, are not seasonally adjusted and covers workers 16 years of age and older
Source: Bureau of Labor Statistics, http://stats.bls.gov

Unemployment Rate: Metro Area

Area	1998						1999					
	Jul.	Aug.	Sep.	Oct.	Nov.	Dec.	Jan.	Feb.	Mar.	Apr.	May.	Jun.
Atlanta	3.9	3.3	3.5	3.3	3.0	2.8	2.9	3.2	3.4	2.8	2.8	3.3
Austin	2.9	2.8	2.7	2.4	2.5	2.3	2.7	2.4	2.1	2.0	2.2	2.6
Birmingham	3.0	3.1	2.9	3.1	2.6	2.2	2.4	2.7	2.5	2.9	2.8	3.4
Chattanooga	4.0	4.0	3.7	3.6	3.4	3.0	3.9	3.9	3.7	3.3	3.2	3.6
Columbia	2.5	2.1	2.2	2.2	1.8	1.7	2.0	2.2	1.8	1.8	2.2	2.4
Dallas	3.5	3.3	3.2	2.9	3.0	2.7	3.2	3.0	2.8	2.8	3.0	3.6
Ft. Lauderdale	4.3	4.3	4.4	4.4	4.5	4.1	4.9	4.4	4.3	4.6	4.5	4.3
Ft. Worth	4.1	3.3	3.3	3.0	3.0	2.7	3.4	3.1	2.9	2.8	3.1	3.6
Houston	4.5	4.1	4.0	3.7	3.8	3.6	4.4	4.2	4.0	4.2	4.6	5.4
Jackson	3.6	4.0	3.5	3.5	3.0	2.7	3.6	2.7	3.1	2.6	3.3	3.7
Jacksonville	3.1	2.9	2.9	2.8	2.9	2.7	3.3	3.1	3.1	3.1	3.2	3.2
Knoxville	3.4	3.5	3.3	3.3	3.5	3.1	4.8	4.6	4.2	3.2	2.6	2.7
Memphis	3.8	3.9	4.0	3.4	3.3	2.8	3.6	3.5	3.4	3.2	3.1	3.4
Miami	6.2	6.1	6.4	6.4	6.6	6.1	7.1	6.3	6.2	6.6	6.4	6.4
Nashville	2.7	2.8	2.6	2.7	2.6	2.1	2.9	2.8	2.7	2.6	2.3	2.4
New Orleans	5.6	5.5	4.9	4.4	4.1	4.0	4.7	4.3	3.9	3.9	3.3	4.6
Orlando	3.1	2.9	3.1	2.9	2.9	2.6	3.3	2.9	2.8	2.8	2.8	3.0
San Antonio	4.2	3.9	3.7	3.3	3.3	2.9	3.3	3.0	2.8	2.6	2.8	3.6
Tampa	3.0	2.9	3.0	2.9	2.9	2.7	3.2	2.9	2.8	2.9	2.8	2.8
U.S.	**4.7**	**4.5**	**4.4**	**4.2**	**4.1**	**4.0**	**4.8**	**4.7**	**4.4**	**4.1**	**4.0**	**4.5**

Note: All figures are percentages, are not seasonally adjusted and covers workers 16 years of age and older
(1) Metropolitan Statistical Area - see Appendix A for areas included
Source: Bureau of Labor Statistics, http://stats.bls.gov

Average Hourly Wages: Occupations A - C

MSA[1]	Accountants/ Auditors	Assemblers/ Fabricators	Automotive Mechanics	Book- keepers	Carpenters	Cashiers	Clerks, Gen. Office
Atlanta	18.89	9.30	14.76	11.49	12.98	6.69	9.45
Austin	17.40	7.84	14.27	10.66	14.06	7.06	8.49
Birmingham	17.97	9.29	12.68	10.80	11.59	6.20	8.76
Chattanooga	18.32	11.40	13.89	10.31	13.48	6.16	11.09
Columbia	16.88	8.22	12.44	9.94	12.01	6.21	8.82
Dallas	19.32	9.62	15.08	11.58	12.67	6.75	10.05
Ft. Lauderdale	23.23	8.57	13.03	11.75	12.94	6.70	9.38
Ft. Worth	19.81	8.28	14.03	11.19	12.55	6.60	8.96
Houston	19.74	8.75	14.40	11.72	12.29	6.57	9.80
Jackson	19.78	6.36	12.40	10.61	10.49	6.36	8.73
Jacksonville	17.75	8.62	12.78	10.63	11.21	6.67	9.45
Knoxville	17.43	9.40	11.69	10.58	11.89	6.74	9.97
Memphis	17.05	8.42	13.74	10.99	12.34	6.73	9.53
Miami	22.94	7.84	14.84	11.39	11.82	6.62	9.65
Nashville	17.40	15.74	15.34	11.29	11.93	6.84	9.74
New Orleans	16.73	10.08	12.73	10.56	12.40	6.18	8.88
Orlando	18.15	8.19	12.88	10.60	12.65	6.60	9.03
San Antonio	19.20	7.72	12.86	10.34	9.91	6.60	8.71
Tampa	19.60	8.31	13.63	10.48	10.84	6.50	8.74

Notes: Wage data is for 1997 and covers the Metropolitan Statistical Area - see Appendix A for areas included; dashes indicate that data was not available
Source: Bureau of Labor Statistics, 1997 Metro Area Occupational Employment and Wage Estimates

Average Hourly Wages: Occupations C - F

MSA[1]	Clerks, Ship./Rec.	Computer Program.	Computer Support Specialists	Cooks, Restaurant	Electricians	Financial Managers	First-Line Supervisor/ Mgr., Sales
Atlanta	11.30	23.41	18.37	9.13	15.67	27.28	18.02
Austin	9.79	20.04	17.14	7.48	15.30	27.31	16.14
Birmingham	10.41	25.27	16.19	7.30	13.53	27.84	14.45
Chattanooga	11.29	21.14	16.46	7.41	15.09	22.82	13.92
Columbia	10.70	19.25	14.64	7.35	13.52	23.85	15.29
Dallas	10.99	24.41	19.97	7.69	14.72	27.48	17.30
Ft. Lauderdale	11.27	22.36	19.12	8.63	12.90	26.80	19.08
Ft. Worth	10.75	22.93	17.30	7.48	14.35	28.93	15.66
Houston	10.86	25.64	19.04	7.23	15.53	30.24	17.29
Jackson	10.53	19.07	16.75	7.43	13.70	26.80	16.15
Jacksonville	11.53	20.98	15.44	7.87	13.99	24.96	15.40
Knoxville	10.05	21.34	15.19	7.26	13.56	24.19	15.08
Memphis	10.97	22.32	18.14	8.12	14.48	26.63	15.09
Miami	10.64	22.53	16.13	8.92	14.33	27.43	17.02
Nashville	10.58	22.51	17.01	8.30	14.06	26.36	16.05
New Orleans	11.86	19.44	16.16	7.38	14.35	22.68	14.62
Orlando	11.15	22.44	14.95	8.92	11.56	24.96	15.38
San Antonio	9.81	21.51	17.19	7.41	13.50	26.42	14.82
Tampa	10.39	21.84	15.24	7.84	12.43	26.19	15.38

Notes: Wage data is for 1997 and covers the Metropolitan Statistical Area - see Appendix A for areas included; dashes indicate that data was not available
Source: Bureau of Labor Statistics, 1997 Metro Area Occupational Employment and Wage Estimates

Average Hourly Wages: Occupations F - L

MSA[1]	Food Preparation Worker	General Managers/ Top Exec.	Guards	Hand Packers	Janitors/ Cleaners	Laborers, Land- scaping	Lawyers
Atlanta	6.85	31.36	7.70	7.27	7.58	8.51	35.50
Austin	6.60	26.91	8.34	6.72	7.09	7.44	33.29
Birmingham	6.55	29.29	7.57	6.30	6.24	7.79	32.93
Chattanooga	6.41	26.76	7.40	8.03	6.67	8.77	32.41
Columbia	6.66	27.53	8.00	6.56	7.20	7.91	30.31
Dallas	7.31	31.74	7.78	6.69	6.71	7.60	36.97
Ft. Lauderdale	6.90	29.50	7.25	6.28	6.73	8.33	39.09
Ft. Worth	6.80	27.78	-	7.15	7.11	7.72	40.67
Houston	7.14	30.46	8.26	6.83	7.10	8.06	40.99
Jackson	6.53	26.92	6.86	6.91	6.69	7.72	31.25
Jacksonville	6.62	27.01	8.31	6.82	6.93	7.81	38.62
Knoxville	7.06	26.26	7.63	6.98	7.41	8.24	35.55
Memphis	7.02	29.56	7.81	8.22	7.08	7.57	29.97
Miami	6.86	29.01	7.25	6.72	6.94	7.55	37.35
Nashville	7.10	29.33	8.41	7.51	7.60	8.19	32.97
New Orleans	6.20	26.05	6.96	6.33	7.16	7.73	34.52
Orlando	7.43	27.35	7.43	6.13	7.41	7.85	36.82
San Antonio	6.28	25.14	7.41	6.49	6.92	7.52	35.13
Tampa	6.97	27.98	8.01	6.60	7.47	7.65	33.97

Notes: Wage data is for 1997 and covers the Metropolitan Statistical Area - see Appendix A for areas included; dashes indicate that data was not available
Source: Bureau of Labor Statistics, 1997 Metro Area Occupational Employment and Wage Estimates

Average Hourly Wages: Occupations M - P

MSA[1]	Maids/ House- keepers	Main- tenance Repairers	Marketing/ Advertising/ P.R. Mgrs.	Nurses, Licensed Practical	Nurses, Registered	Nursing Aides/ Orderlies/ Attendants	Physicians/ Surgeons
Atlanta	6.60	12.01	27.66	12.40	18.32	7.80	46.74
Austin	6.60	9.74	29.38	12.82	19.51	7.37	53.84
Birmingham	6.43	10.49	25.96	11.14	19.63	7.26	47.00
Chattanooga	6.45	10.66	21.70	11.34	18.09	7.27	53.71
Columbia	6.56	10.59	21.67	11.45	17.34	8.28	45.93
Dallas	6.21	10.98	30.30	15.23	20.34	7.56	-
Ft. Lauderdale	6.91	10.13	23.43	13.67	24.47	7.89	53.05
Ft. Worth	6.28	10.73	24.85	14.27	18.93	6.81	55.88
Houston	6.10	11.76	30.35	13.25	21.84	6.62	-
Jackson	6.05	10.13	22.80	11.43	19.06	7.33	37.87
Jacksonville	6.44	10.06	27.03	14.55	19.51	7.57	56.89
Knoxville	7.12	10.74	26.80	11.16	18.02	7.59	55.24
Memphis	6.56	11.91	27.01	12.20	18.18	7.54	49.92
Miami	6.63	9.96	23.76	15.61	20.78	8.00	46.86
Nashville	7.15	11.14	23.13	12.47	18.80	7.80	44.82
New Orleans	6.35	10.79	23.59	11.88	21.33	6.38	42.28
Orlando	7.35	10.19	21.98	12.92	18.39	7.51	55.32
San Antonio	6.12	9.15	24.19	12.51	18.52	6.42	48.36
Tampa	6.48	9.87	23.51	12.67	19.10	8.01	51.71

Notes: Wage data is for 1997 and covers the Metropolitan Statistical Area - see Appendix A for areas included; dashes indicate that data was not available
Source: Bureau of Labor Statistics, 1997 Metro Area Occupational Employment and Wage Estimates

Average Hourly Wages: Occupations R - S

MSA[1]	Receptionists/ Info. Clerks	Sales Reps., Except Scien./Retail	Sales Reps., Scientific/ Exc. Retail	Sales- persons, Retail	Secretaries, Except Leg./Med.	Stock Clerk, Sales Floor	Systems Analysts
Atlanta	9.33	19.31	22.43	9.16	11.36	7.70	25.83
Austin	8.79	16.35	20.09	8.90	11.16	6.39	24.92
Birmingham	8.21	19.41	23.64	8.75	9.94	6.96	22.80
Chattanooga	8.28	17.38	19.54	7.98	9.80	7.37	22.54
Columbia	8.61	16.91	16.69	9.47	10.44	7.35	23.28
Dallas	9.16	21.16	24.11	9.19	12.49	7.71	24.60
Ft. Lauderdale	9.25	17.44	18.21	8.81	11.32	7.21	24.05
Ft. Worth	8.55	20.01	24.25	8.80	11.44	7.80	22.52
Houston	9.33	19.87	26.17	8.69	12.29	7.56	24.74
Jackson	8.33	17.07	24.09	8.87	10.16	7.19	21.57
Jacksonville	8.35	16.23	18.74	8.50	10.56	7.06	24.32
Knoxville	8.42	17.29	22.28	8.65	9.99	7.06	20.62
Memphis	8.37	18.19	20.21	9.24	10.74	7.10	20.40
Miami	8.99	15.74	20.36	8.87	11.58	7.10	21.35
Nashville	8.82	17.41	20.24	9.21	10.99	7.15	21.34
New Orleans	7.84	16.37	18.44	8.11	9.99	6.64	22.66
Orlando	8.50	17.63	22.85	8.60	10.47	7.18	21.91
San Antonio	8.18	17.11	19.06	7.89	10.33	6.28	24.21
Tampa	8.54	16.55	15.62	8.92	10.68	6.95	25.22

Notes: Wage data is for 1997 and covers the Metropolitan Statistical Area - see Appendix A for areas included; dashes indicate that data was not available
Source: Bureau of Labor Statistics, 1997 Metro Area Occupational Employment and Wage Estimates

Average Hourly Wages: Occupations T - Z

MSA[1]	Teacher Aides	Teachers, Elementary School	Teachers, Secondary School	Telemar- keters	Truck Driv., Heavy/ Trac. Trail.	Truck Drivers, Light	Waiters/ Waitresses
Atlanta	6.81	18.41	19.74	11.00	14.31	10.79	6.20
Austin	6.84	15.52	16.07	8.48	11.30	9.56	5.76
Birmingham	6.79	15.71	16.36	8.15	12.85	8.88	5.49
Chattanooga	7.16	15.22	16.65	7.65	13.03	12.61	5.62
Columbia	6.81	15.56	16.85	9.06	12.62	9.71	5.49
Dallas	7.20	18.97	16.17	9.02	14.74	9.56	5.64
Ft. Lauderdale	7.76	15.82	16.60	10.67	13.08	9.01	5.56
Ft. Worth	6.30	16.03	16.34	8.51	11.72	9.59	5.46
Houston	7.58	18.75	19.36	8.37	12.50	9.72	5.89
Jackson	6.29	14.00	14.23	7.59	14.49	9.75	5.57
Jacksonville	8.98	15.05	15.77	8.18	14.15	10.00	5.45
Knoxville	6.93	15.89	17.55	9.26	11.73	10.15	5.83
Memphis	-	15.43	15.88	10.70	15.36	10.81	5.50
Miami	8.54	14.35	18.98	11.10	11.67	8.62	5.86
Nashville	6.04	16.10	-	8.57	15.01	11.53	5.84
New Orleans	-	16.20	16.15	8.20	12.10	9.03	5.86
Orlando	6.31	11.41	12.54	8.32	11.70	10.62	5.74
San Antonio	6.38	16.54	17.24	7.37	11.72	8.35	5.93
Tampa	8.93	17.78	19.90	10.46	11.53	9.03	5.58

Notes: Wage data is for 1997 and covers the Metropolitan Statistical Area - see Appendix A for areas included; hourly wages for elementary and secondary school teachers were calculated by the editors from annual wage data assuming a 40 hour work week; dashes indicate that data was not available
Source: Bureau of Labor Statistics, 1997 Metro Area Occupational Employment and Wage Estimates

Means of Transportation to Work: City

City	Car/Truck/Van		Public Transportation			Bicycle	Walked	Other Means	Worked at Home
	Drove Alone	Car-pooled	Bus	Subway	Railroad				
Atlanta	61.2	11.6	16.7	2.9	0.1	0.3	3.8	1.2	2.4
Austin	73.6	13.3	4.8	0.0	0.0	0.8	3.3	1.3	2.8
Birmingham	76.2	16.1	3.5	0.0	0.0	0.2	2.3	0.8	1.0
Chattanooga	78.0	13.4	2.9	0.0	0.0	0.0	2.6	1.3	1.7
Columbia	61.5	11.8	4.6	0.0	0.0	0.8	17.8	1.9	1.7
Dallas	72.5	15.2	6.4	0.0	0.0	0.2	2.4	1.2	2.2
Ft. Lauderdale	73.6	13.3	4.4	0.0	0.2	1.1	3.3	1.6	2.6
Ft. Worth	76.7	16.3	1.6	0.0	0.0	0.2	2.3	1.2	1.8
Houston	71.7	15.5	6.3	0.0	0.0	0.4	3.0	1.2	2.0
Jackson	78.6	15.0	1.8	0.0	0.0	0.1	2.1	0.9	1.6
Jacksonville	75.5	14.2	2.5	0.0	0.0	0.6	2.7	1.7	2.7
Knoxville	77.1	13.1	1.8	0.0	0.0	0.2	4.8	1.0	1.9
Memphis	75.4	15.1	4.5	0.0	0.0	0.1	2.5	1.0	1.3
Miami	60.9	18.0	11.8	0.6	0.2	0.6	4.2	1.8	1.9
Nashville	78.1	13.4	2.8	0.0	0.0	0.1	2.6	0.8	2.2
New Orleans	58.6	15.4	15.6	0.0	0.0	0.9	5.2	2.3	1.9
Orlando	68.3	12.6	3.5	0.0	0.0	0.8	11.9	1.5	1.3
San Antonio	73.4	15.5	4.8	0.0	0.0	0.1	3.1	1.1	1.9
Tampa	74.8	14.3	3.2	0.0	0.0	0.9	3.4	1.5	1.9
U.S.	**73.2**	**13.4**	**3.0**	**1.5**	**0.5**	**0.4**	**3.9**	**1.2**	**3.0**

Note: Figures shown are percentages and only include workers 16 years old and over
Source: 1990 Census of Population and Housing, Summary Tape File 3C

Means of Transportation to Work: Metro Area

MSA[1]	Car/Truck/Van		Public Transportation			Bicycle	Walked	Other Means	Worked at Home
	Drove Alone	Car-pooled	Bus	Subway	Railroad				
Atlanta	78.0	12.7	3.5	1.0	0.1	0.1	1.5	1.0	2.2
Austin	75.3	13.9	3.2	0.0	0.0	0.5	2.9	1.2	3.0
Birmingham	81.2	14.0	1.2	0.0	0.0	0.1	1.4	0.6	1.6
Chattanooga	79.4	14.7	1.2	0.0	0.0	0.0	1.9	0.9	1.9
Columbia	76.4	14.3	1.6	0.0	0.0	0.2	4.6	1.1	1.8
Dallas	77.6	14.0	3.1	0.0	0.0	0.1	1.9	1.0	2.3
Ft. Lauderdale	79.7	12.8	1.8	0.0	0.1	0.7	1.8	1.2	1.9
Ft. Worth	80.9	13.5	0.6	0.0	0.0	0.1	1.7	0.9	2.2
Houston	75.7	14.6	4.0	0.0	0.0	0.3	2.2	1.1	2.1
Jackson	80.2	14.5	1.1	0.0	0.0	0.1	1.7	0.9	1.6
Jacksonville	76.2	14.3	1.9	0.0	0.0	0.7	2.6	1.7	2.6
Knoxville	80.5	13.2	0.6	0.0	0.0	0.1	2.3	0.8	2.5
Memphis	78.2	13.6	2.7	0.0	0.0	0.1	3.0	1.0	1.5
Miami	72.4	15.6	4.8	0.7	0.1	0.5	2.5	1.3	2.0
Nashville	79.1	13.8	1.6	0.0	0.0	0.1	1.9	0.9	2.6
New Orleans	70.9	15.3	6.6	0.0	0.0	0.5	3.1	1.8	1.7
Orlando	78.1	13.3	1.4	0.0	0.0	0.6	3.5	1.2	2.0
San Antonio	74.6	14.8	3.6	0.0	0.0	0.2	3.6	1.0	2.3
Tampa	78.8	13.3	1.3	0.0	0.0	0.7	2.3	1.3	2.3
U.S.	**73.2**	**13.4**	**3.0**	**1.5**	**0.5**	**0.4**	**3.9**	**1.2**	**3.0**

Note: Figures shown are percentages and only include workers 16 years old and over;
(1) Metropolitan Statistical Area - see Appendix A for areas included
Source: 1990 Census of Population and Housing, Summary Tape File 3C

Cost of Living Index

Area	Composite	Groceries	Housing	Utilities	Transp.	Health	Misc.
Atlanta	103.3	103.3	102.9	102.3	101.5	118.5	102.0
Austin	98.4	92.9	89.0	90.7	100.3	105.6	109.1
Birmingham[1]	97.8	98.2	94.5	101.8	97.5	95.1	99.8
Chattanooga	97.1	98.7	95.7	90.7	91.1	92.9	101.4
Columbia	97.3	98.5	90.3	121.8	87.1	94.1	100.2
Dallas[1]	100.4	98.5	95.2	101.8	105.1	109.6	102.5
Fort Lauderdale[1,3]	107.7	104.2	112.0	109.0	99.8	111.8	107.3
Fort Worth	92.9	102.3	75.4	102.4	94.6	99.4	99.3
Houston[1]	94.9	90.6	84.3	101.0	106.7	110.2	98.5
Jackson	90.8	89.0	88.6	100.7	93.1	77.2	92.4
Jacksonville	95.2	102.5	78.2	100.3	107.6	93.9	101.2
Knoxville	93.4	96.1	86.6	95.5	90.2	94.9	98.1
Memphis	92.3	94.9	90.1	83.2	99.2	94.4	92.7
Miami[1,3]	107.7	102.9	113.0	103.0	106.8	101.6	108.0
Nashville[2]	96.1	96.5	94.4	93.9	99.8	89.1	97.8
New Orleans	96.8	98.1	88.2	126.8	111.6	86.6	93.3
Orlando	100.5	98.6	95.4	102.3	96.6	112.5	104.6
San Antonio	89.9	83.7	84.0	77.1	98.7	89.0	98.5
Tampa	103.8	102.2	108.5	88.2	102.9	113.4	103.3
U.S.	**100.0**	**100.0**	**100.0**	**100.0**	**100.0**	**100.0**	**100.0**

Note: n/a not available; (1) Metropolitan Statistical Area (MSA) - see Appendix A for areas included;
(2) Nashville-Davidson; (3) 4th Quarter 1998
Source: ACCRA, Cost of Living Index, 1st Quarter 1999 unless otherwise noted

Median Home Prices and Housing Affordability

MSA[1]	Median Price[2] 1st Qtr. 1999 ($)	HOI[3] 1st Qtr. 1999	Affordability Rank[4]
Atlanta	130,000	80.7	47
Austin	137,000	66.9	132
Birmingham	105,000	79.6	60
Chattanooga	n/a	n/a	n/a
Columbia	105,000	80.5	50
Dallas	135,000	68.5	125
Ft. Lauderdale	113,000	79.2	63
Ft. Worth	106,000	77.0	81
Houston	111,000	71.6	107
Jackson	116,000	68.8	122
Jacksonville	104,000	80.2	55
Knoxville	88,000	86.8	13
Memphis	105,000	74.7	94
Miami	110,000	65.4	138
Nashville	116,000	84.0	26
New Orleans	102,000	73.5	100
Orlando	107,000	79.5	62
San Antonio	94,000	71.4	108
Tampa	90,000	81.1	42
U.S.	**134,000**	**69.6**	–

Note: (1) Metropolitan Statistical Area - see Appendix A for areas included; (2) U.S. figures calculated from the sales of 524,324 new and existing homes in 181 markets; (3) Housing Opportunity Index - percent of homes sold that were within the reach of the median income household at the prevailing mortgage interest rate; (4) Rank is from 1-181 with 1 being most affordable; n/a not available
Source: National Association of Home Builders, Housing News Service, 1st Quarter 1999

Average Home Prices

Area	Price ($)
Atlanta	144,634
Austin	110,500
Birmingham[1]	134,895
Chattanooga	136,520
Columbia	127,197
Dallas[1]	125,580
Fort Lauderdale[1,3]	149,400
Fort Worth	98,207
Houston[1]	113,422
Jackson	124,341
Jacksonville	107,000
Knoxville	121,860
Memphis	124,121
Miami[1,3]	155,544
Nashville[2]	131,550
New Orleans	123,800
Orlando	133,713
San Antonio	119,181
Tampa	149,649
U.S.	**142,735**

Note: Figures are based on a new home with 1,800 sq. ft. of living area on an 8,000 sq. ft. lot; n/a not available; (1) Metropolitan Statistical Area (MSA) - see Appendix A for areas included; (2) Nashville-Davidson; (3) 4th Quarter 1998
Source: ACCRA, Cost of Living Index, 1st Quarter 1999 unless otherwise noted

Average Apartment Rent

Area	Rent ($/mth)
Atlanta	728
Austin	872
Birmingham[1]	573
Chattanooga	605
Columbia	617
Dallas[1]	799
Fort Lauderdale[1,3]	921
Fort Worth	662
Houston[1]	686
Jackson	578
Jacksonville	628
Knoxville	576
Memphis	625
Miami[1,3]	775
Nashville[2]	625
New Orleans	578
Orlando	655
San Antonio	587
Tampa	837
U.S.	**601**

Note: Figures are based on an unfurnished two bedroom, 1-1/2 or 2 bath apartment, approximately 950 sq. ft. in size, excluding all utilities except water; n/a not available; (1) Metropolitan Statistical Area (MSA) - see Appendix A for areas included; (2) Nashville-Davidson; (3) 4th Quarter 1998
Source: ACCRA, Cost of Living Index, 1st Quarter 1999 unless otherwise noted

Average Residential Utility Costs

Area	All Electric ($/mth)	Part Electric ($/mth)	Other Energy ($/mth)	Phone ($/mth)
Atlanta	99.60	-	-	22.75
Austin	-	63.49	28.32	15.62
Birmingham[1]	-	57.94	40.89	22.98
Chattanooga	-	48.84	39.03	20.74
Columbia	121.38	-	-	23.50
Dallas[1]	-	75.66	28.38	16.33
Fort Lauderdale[1,3]	112.24	-	-	17.22
Fort Worth	-	73.66	30.27	17.33
Houston[1]	-	76.14	26.12	17.50
Jackson	-	71.45	23.57	26.21
Jacksonville	102.45	-	-	16.22
Knoxville	-	44.43	49.93	19.47
Memphis	-	51.62	27.97	20.34
Miami[1,3]	106.04	-	-	16.27
Nashville[2]	-	47.23	47.35	16.85
New Orleans	130.90	-	-	18.63
Orlando	100.63	-	-	21.41
San Antonio	-	54.80	20.83	16.38
Tampa	82.93	-	-	23.44
U.S.	**100.02**	**55.73**	**43.33**	**19.71**

Note: Dashes indicate data not applicable; n/a not available;
(1) Metropolitan Statistical Area (MSA) - see Appendix A for areas included; (2) Nashville-Davidson; (3) 4th Quarter 1998
Source: ACCRA, Cost of Living Index, 1st Quarter 1999 unless otherwise noted

Average Health Care Costs

Area	Hospital ($/day)	Doctor ($/visit)	Dentist ($/visit)
Atlanta	340.10	70.62	87.21
Austin	423.33	53.80	76.00
Birmingham[1]	467.00	53.00	55.40
Chattanooga	371.00	53.00	58.20
Columbia	374.75	55.80	58.20
Dallas[1]	503.00	52.50	76.91
Fort Lauderdale[1,3]	405.00	60.00	73.40
Fort Worth	339.20	53.80	69.40
Houston[1]	445.41	61.50	71.08
Jackson	247.60	43.50	52.37
Jacksonville	364.60	56.20	57.75
Knoxville	385.50	54.60	59.20
Memphis	272.60	54.60	67.40
Miami[1,3]	558.40	53.00	59.00
Nashville[2]	275.60	53.14	57.40
New Orleans	412.20	42.50	57.50
Orlando	515.50	61.10	73.90
San Antonio	405.40	49.40	53.80
Tampa	489.85	52.90	82.20
U.S.	**430.43**	**52.45**	**66.35**

Note: n/a not available; Hospital—based on a semi-private room; Doctor—based on a general practitioner's routine exam of an established patient; Dentist—based on adult teeth cleaning and periodic oral exam; (1) Metropolitan Statistical Area (MSA) - see Appendix A for areas included; (2) Nashville-Davidson; (3) 4th Quarter 1998
Source: ACCRA, Cost of Living Index, 1st Quarter 1999 unless otherwise noted

Distribution of Office-Based Physicians

MSA[1]	General Practitioners	Specialists		
		Medical	Surgical	Other
Atlanta	557	2,223	1,784	1,727
Austin	296	513	456	482
Birmingham	172	793	601	557
Chattanooga	89	269	249	217
Columbia	138	292	274	300
Dallas	514	1,545	1,402	1,461
Ft. Lauderdale	245	1,116	703	632
Ft. Worth	308	532	528	472
Houston	853	2,215	1,821	1,939
Jackson	25	51	40	29
Jacksonville	269	614	458	467
Knoxville	225	471	379	354
Memphis	205	739	583	554
Miami	739	1,857	1,246	1,248
Nashville	205	893	721	744
New Orleans	210	1,113	911	917
Orlando	332	748	647	549
San Antonio	359	798	635	747
Tampa	459	1,502	1,035	1,080

Note: Data as of 12/31/97; (1) Metropolitan Statistical Area - see Appendix A for areas included
Source: Physician Characteristics & Distribution in the U.S., 1999

Educational Quality

City	School District	Education Quotient[1]	Graduate Outcome[2]	Community Index[3]	Resource Index[4]
Atlanta	Atlanta City	82.0	51.0	119.0	135.0
Austin	Austin ISD	93.0	108.0	119.0	58.0
Birmingham	Birmingham City	58.0	58.0	78.0	54.0
Chattanooga	Chattanooga City	92.0	88.0	60.0	107.0
Columbia	Richland County	79.0	65.0	112.0	99.0
Dallas	Dallas ISD	62.0	55.0	109.0	66.0
Fort Lauderdale	Broward County	103.0	97.0	84.0	118.0
Fort Worth	Fort Worth ISD	66.0	66.0	121.0	55.0
Houston	Houston ISD	68.0	63.0	101.0	72.0
Jackson	Jackson Public	65.0	61.0	83.0	69.0
Jacksonville	Duval County	105.0	99.0	96.0	118.0
Knoxville	Knox County	107.0	123.0	83.0	80.0
Memphis	Memphis City	102.0	103.0	89.0	104.0
Miami	Dade County	91.0	79.0	55.0	123.0
Nashville	Nashville-Davidson Co.	109.0	112.0	106.0	104.0
New Orleans	Orleans Parish	68.0	53.0	57.0	99.0
Orlando	Orange County	104.0	101.0	101.0	111.0
San Antonio	San Antonio N.E. ISD	96.0	114.0	74.0	63.0
Tampa	Hillsborough County	123.0	123.0	92.0	130.0

Note: Nearly 1,000 secondary school districts were rated in terms of educational quality. The scores range from a low of 50 to a high of 150; (1) Average of the Graduate Outcome, Community and Resource indexes; (2) Based on graduation rates and college board scores (SAT/ACT); (3) Based on the surrounding community's average level of education and the area's average income level; (4) Based on teacher salaries, per-pupil expenditures and student-teacher ratios.
Source: Expansion Management, Ratings Issue 1998

School Enrollment by Type: City

City	Preprimary Public Enrollment	%	Private Enrollment	%	Elementary/High School Public Enrollment	%	Private Enrollment	%
Atlanta	3,898	59.8	2,621	40.2	55,393	90.3	5,935	9.7
Austin	4,815	52.7	4,328	47.3	62,838	93.4	4,472	6.6
Birmingham	2,439	64.8	1,323	35.2	41,586	90.5	4,349	9.5
Chattanooga	1,244	53.9	1,065	46.1	20,393	86.5	3,185	13.5
Columbia	742	52.0	684	48.0	11,931	89.9	1,334	10.1
Dallas	8,029	52.2	7,349	47.8	147,967	90.2	16,105	9.8
Ft. Lauderdale	946	46.1	1,108	53.9	15,660	84.4	2,903	15.6
Ft. Worth	4,297	60.0	2,866	40.0	69,185	90.9	6,935	9.1
Houston	14,485	54.0	12,343	46.0	274,727	92.3	22,938	7.7
Jackson	2,137	53.6	1,848	46.4	32,054	85.4	5,479	14.6
Jacksonville	6,877	55.5	5,519	44.5	92,698	87.5	13,236	12.5
Knoxville	1,461	68.5	673	31.5	19,991	94.3	1,216	5.7
Memphis	5,573	59.5	3,792	40.5	95,610	89.3	11,422	10.7
Miami	2,688	61.0	1,720	39.0	53,740	90.3	5,750	9.7
Nashville	3,671	51.4	3,472	48.6	61,254	84.7	11,083	15.3
New Orleans	4,980	53.7	4,290	46.3	75,984	79.7	19,309	20.3
Orlando	1,419	60.7	918	39.3	19,932	92.8	1,549	7.2
San Antonio	9,035	61.2	5,735	38.8	173,354	92.5	14,116	7.5
Tampa	3,016	59.3	2,068	40.7	35,768	88.4	4,676	11.6
U.S.	**2,679,029**	**59.5**	**1,824,256**	**40.5**	**38,379,689**	**90.2**	**4,187,099**	**9.8**

Note: Figures shown cover persons 3 years old and over
Source: 1990 Census of Population and Housing, Summary Tape File 3C

School Enrollment by Type: Metro Area

MSA[1]	Preprimary Public Enrollment	%	Private Enrollment	%	Elementary/High School Public Enrollment	%	Private Enrollment	%
Atlanta	28,793	49.6	29,303	50.4	437,891	92.0	37,989	8.0
Austin	8,688	52.4	7,888	47.6	119,826	94.2	7,318	5.8
Birmingham	7,796	52.9	6,946	47.1	143,764	91.0	14,224	9.0
Chattanooga	3,872	59.6	2,625	40.4	64,955	88.9	8,140	11.1
Columbia	4,221	53.5	3,664	46.5	73,368	93.4	5,155	6.6
Dallas	24,235	49.1	25,151	50.9	413,238	92.3	34,313	7.7
Ft. Lauderdale	9,740	43.6	12,606	56.4	146,453	87.1	21,625	12.9
Ft. Worth	13,513	55.4	10,874	44.6	216,997	92.6	17,279	7.4
Houston	34,923	52.8	31,273	47.2	607,238	93.9	39,303	6.1
Jackson	4,230	52.6	3,807	47.4	67,006	87.0	10,043	13.0
Jacksonville	9,288	54.2	7,843	45.8	135,736	88.8	17,193	11.2
Knoxville	5,577	65.8	2,903	34.2	89,754	95.4	4,299	4.6
Memphis	9,081	54.6	7,545	45.4	160,890	88.9	19,987	11.1
Miami	14,892	43.9	19,029	56.1	281,730	86.5	44,139	13.5
Nashville	9,119	56.1	7,129	43.9	143,901	88.2	19,299	11.8
New Orleans	10,527	42.0	14,557	58.0	178,094	75.0	59,271	25.0
Orlando	9,698	49.2	9,997	50.8	154,434	91.4	14,467	8.6
San Antonio	12,989	59.1	8,978	40.9	240,288	92.4	19,686	7.6
Tampa	17,848	52.0	16,451	48.0	244,416	89.0	30,326	11.0
U.S.	**2,679,029**	**59.5**	**1,824,256**	**40.5**	**38,379,689**	**90.2**	**4,187,099**	**9.8**

Note: Figures shown cover persons 3 years old and over;
(1) Metropolitan Statistical Area - see Appendix A for areas included
Source: 1990 Census of Population and Housing, Summary Tape File 3C

School Enrollment by Race: City

City	Preprimary (%)				Elementary/High School (%)			
	White	Black	Other	Hisp.[1]	White	Black	Other	Hisp.[1]
Atlanta	26.6	71.9	1.5	1.5	13.8	84.6	1.6	1.9
Austin	73.9	11.0	15.1	20.9	58.1	18.2	23.8	33.8
Birmingham	27.5	71.2	1.3	0.9	19.0	80.3	0.7	0.3
Chattanooga	59.5	39.2	1.3	0.2	51.0	47.0	2.0	0.8
Columbia	40.2	59.0	0.8	0.9	32.9	64.8	2.2	2.3
Dallas	56.1	31.5	12.4	16.8	38.2	39.7	22.2	30.3
Ft. Lauderdale	59.2	39.5	1.3	3.0	41.2	55.4	3.4	8.8
Ft. Worth	66.5	23.3	10.3	14.9	50.6	28.9	20.5	27.9
Houston	54.6	29.7	15.6	22.8	40.2	33.3	26.5	38.1
Jackson	40.5	58.4	1.1	0.0	29.5	70.0	0.6	0.3
Jacksonville	71.3	26.7	2.0	2.1	62.4	33.6	4.0	2.8
Knoxville	78.3	19.2	2.5	0.4	71.8	26.4	1.8	0.9
Memphis	41.7	57.2	1.1	0.4	27.4	71.4	1.2	0.7
Miami	48.8	46.8	4.4	40.9	51.7	40.5	7.8	53.5
Nashville	73.3	24.3	2.4	0.8	63.8	34.0	2.2	1.1
New Orleans	30.5	67.4	2.1	2.2	17.6	78.5	3.8	3.0
Orlando	60.2	37.5	2.3	10.9	49.0	44.6	6.4	11.9
San Antonio	71.9	7.5	20.6	51.9	67.0	6.8	26.2	68.2
Tampa	60.0	37.3	2.8	10.9	55.2	40.0	4.7	14.9
U.S.	**80.4**	**12.5**	**7.1**	**7.8**	**74.1**	**15.6**	**10.3**	**12.5**

Note: Figures shown cover persons 3 years old and over; (1) People of Hispanic origin can be of any race
Source: 1990 Census of Population and Housing, Summary Tape File 3C

School Enrollment by Race: Metro Area

MSA[1]	Preprimary (%)				Elementary/High School (%)			
	White	Black	Other	Hisp.[2]	White	Black	Other	Hisp.[2]
Atlanta	72.8	25.3	1.9	1.5	64.8	32.0	3.2	2.0
Austin	80.3	7.7	12.0	18.3	69.7	12.2	18.2	28.3
Birmingham	70.7	28.0	1.3	0.7	64.7	34.4	0.9	0.4
Chattanooga	83.9	14.9	1.2	0.3	81.4	17.2	1.5	0.7
Columbia	63.6	35.1	1.3	1.2	59.0	39.5	1.5	1.4
Dallas	76.1	15.8	8.2	10.6	64.7	20.3	15.0	19.3
Ft. Lauderdale	77.7	19.9	2.4	7.8	67.7	28.3	4.0	11.4
Ft. Worth	83.3	10.5	6.2	8.1	74.3	14.0	11.6	14.9
Houston	71.3	17.7	11.0	16.0	58.6	21.4	20.1	28.5
Jackson	53.1	45.1	1.8	0.4	46.2	53.2	0.6	0.6
Jacksonville	76.9	21.2	1.9	2.1	69.8	26.6	3.5	2.9
Knoxville	91.3	6.5	2.2	0.8	90.4	8.2	1.4	0.8
Memphis	60.8	37.9	1.4	0.6	47.2	51.4	1.4	0.7
Miami	66.7	28.6	4.6	35.5	62.4	30.2	7.4	47.6
Nashville	83.9	14.4	1.7	1.0	79.0	19.3	1.7	1.0
New Orleans	63.6	34.1	2.3	3.1	51.1	45.3	3.6	4.2
Orlando	82.3	14.2	3.5	7.5	74.8	18.7	6.5	11.8
San Antonio	75.1	7.9	17.0	42.9	70.1	7.0	22.8	59.1
Tampa	82.6	14.6	2.8	6.4	80.0	16.0	4.0	8.9
U.S.	**80.4**	**12.5**	**7.1**	**7.8**	**74.1**	**15.6**	**10.3**	**12.5**

Note: Figures shown cover persons 3 years old and over; (1) Metropolitan Statistical Area - see Appendix A for areas included; (2) People of Hispanic origin can be of any race
Source: 1990 Census of Population and Housing, Summary Tape File 3C

Crime Rate: City

| City | All Crimes | Violent Crimes | | | | Property Crimes | | |
		Murder	Forcible Rape	Robbery	Aggrav. Assault	Burglary	Larceny -Theft	Motor Vehicle Theft
Atlanta	13,921.6	35.6	87.0	1,128.9	1,797.0	2,181.9	6,821.4	1,869.7
Austin	7,870.0	7.3	51.8	235.1	351.5	1,375.1	5,031.8	817.4
Birmingham	9,590.0	39.2	80.7	485.8	769.5	1,884.2	5,110.9	1,219.7
Chattanooga	9,836.3	22.8	54.5	379.3	1,218.9	1,765.9	5,558.6	836.4
Columbia	11,291.2	11.2	59.7	473.0	1,009.5	1,514.3	7,450.0	773.5
Dallas	9,335.8	19.4	69.0	522.0	773.4	1,647.3	4,693.3	1,611.4
Ft. Lauderdale	12,084.3	9.9	58.5	760.7	635.6	2,297.9	6,236.6	2,085.1
Ft. Worth	7,317.8	15.5	55.5	293.4	538.2	1,375.4	4,187.1	852.9
Houston	7,263.6	14.1	43.9	452.2	664.3	1,330.5	3,604.2	1,154.4
Jackson	10,199.2	30.8	107.7	579.8	363.5	2,637.8	4,827.1	1,652.5
Jacksonville	8,252.6	10.7	86.3	337.2	909.1	1,756.9	4,382.6	769.8
Knoxville	6,356.8	10.8	55.2	310.3	480.6	1,161.0	3,463.7	875.2
Memphis	10,041.7	21.6	147.1	822.0	865.9	2,426.9	3,961.0	1,797.2
Miami	12,828.8	26.3	48.2	1,153.0	1,586.2	2,283.5	5,771.0	1,960.6
Nashville	11,091.4	21.1	103.4	485.6	1,136.7	1,660.8	6,147.3	1,536.5
New Orleans	9,355.8	54.7	78.8	813.1	773.8	1,659.5	4,055.8	1,920.1
Orlando	13,626.5	7.5	93.6	679.1	1,501.3	2,380.6	7,658.9	1,305.4
San Antonio	8,050.5	9.2	59.5	196.1	136.9	1,274.5	5,544.3	830.0
Tampa	12,260.1	11.7	88.4	846.7	1,717.1	2,202.6	5,983.7	1,410.0
U.S.	**4,922.7**	**6.8**	**35.9**	**186.1**	**382.0**	**919.6**	**2,886.5**	**505.8**

Note: Crime rate is the number of crimes per 100,000 population; n/a not available;
Source: FBI Uniform Crime Reports 1997

Crime Rate: Suburbs

| Suburbs[1] | All Crimes | Violent Crimes | | | | Property Crimes | | |
		Murder	Forcible Rape	Robbery	Aggrav. Assault	Burglary	Larceny -Theft	Motor Vehicle Theft
Atlanta	5,737.1	4.9	28.6	183.7	224.7	1,045.9	3,511.4	737.9
Austin	3,637.9	4.0	38.7	39.5	230.1	835.7	2,323.7	166.3
Birmingham	3,883.9	6.1	23.7	132.6	244.3	680.9	2,444.6	351.7
Chattanooga	n/a	n/a	n/a	n/a	n/a	n/a	n/a	n/a
Columbia	5,474.5	6.6	53.7	190.7	596.6	1,115.4	3,105.5	405.9
Dallas	4,384.4	3.3	29.9	65.8	236.9	801.7	2,911.7	335.1
Ft. Lauderdale	6,655.5	3.9	31.6	225.4	431.2	1,253.7	3,885.5	824.2
Ft. Worth	4,702.7	3.2	39.0	85.2	377.7	787.0	3,012.8	397.7
Houston	3,994.4	4.7	30.7	108.8	363.2	823.4	2,263.1	400.6
Jackson	3,969.5	8.0	23.2	72.4	151.9	864.9	2,601.0	248.0
Jacksonville	4,597.3	4.1	54.9	103.3	512.5	891.3	2,808.3	223.1
Knoxville	n/a	n/a	n/a	n/a	n/a	n/a	n/a	n/a
Memphis	4,764.5	7.9	51.9	151.7	326.3	1,036.4	2,665.3	525.1
Miami	10,332.5	12.0	62.5	477.8	886.1	1,756.9	5,622.3	1,514.8
Nashville	4,214.3	3.8	37.2	65.6	369.4	822.6	2,625.2	290.5
New Orleans	6,265.2	7.7	32.7	185.9	498.2	1,014.1	3,847.8	678.9
Orlando	6,766.4	3.5	47.3	206.0	629.0	1,403.8	3,901.3	575.4
San Antonio	3,671.2	3.5	24.1	49.6	290.6	701.6	2,403.3	198.5
Tampa	5,567.2	4.5	41.6	162.5	564.7	1,064.0	3,318.9	411.0
U.S.	**4,922.7**	**6.8**	**35.9**	**186.1**	**382.0**	**919.6**	**2,886.5**	**505.8**

Note: Crime rate is the number of crimes per 100,000 population; n/a not available; (1) Defined as all areas within the MSA but located outside the central city
Source: FBI Uniform Crime Reports 1997

Crime Rate: Metro Area

MSA[1]	All Crimes	Violent Crimes				Property Crimes		
		Murder	Forcible Rape	Robbery	Aggrav. Assault	Burglary	Larceny -Theft	Motor Vehicle Theft
Atlanta	6,711.5	8.6	35.5	296.2	411.9	1,181.2	3,905.5	872.6
Austin	5,905.2	5.8	45.7	144.3	295.1	1,124.7	3,774.5	515.1
Birmingham	5,639.6	16.3	41.3	241.2	405.9	1,051.2	3,265.0	618.8
Chattanooga	n/a	n/a	n/a	n/a	n/a	n/a	n/a	n/a
Columbia	6,721.7	7.6	55.0	251.3	685.2	1,200.9	4,037.0	484.7
Dallas	6,188.3	9.2	44.1	232.0	432.4	1,109.8	3,560.8	800.1
Ft. Lauderdale	7,294.7	4.6	34.8	288.4	455.2	1,376.6	4,162.4	972.7
Ft. Worth	5,461.3	6.8	43.8	145.6	424.2	957.7	3,353.5	529.7
Houston	5,518.3	9.1	36.8	268.9	503.6	1,059.8	2,888.3	752.0
Jackson	6,892.2	18.7	62.8	310.4	251.2	1,696.7	3,645.4	906.9
Jacksonville	7,107.3	8.6	76.4	263.9	784.9	1,485.7	3,889.4	598.5
Knoxville	n/a	n/a	n/a	n/a	n/a	n/a	n/a	n/a
Memphis	7,839.1	15.9	107.4	542.2	640.7	1,846.5	3,420.2	1,266.2
Miami	10,792.3	14.7	59.9	602.2	1,015.1	1,853.9	5,649.7	1,596.9
Nashville	7,510.3	12.1	68.9	266.9	737.1	1,224.3	4,313.2	887.7
New Orleans	7,408.7	25.1	49.8	417.9	600.2	1,252.9	3,924.8	1,138.1
Orlando	7,658.0	4.1	53.4	267.5	742.4	1,530.8	4,389.6	670.3
San Antonio	6,661.5	7.4	48.3	149.6	185.6	1,092.8	4,548.1	629.7
Tampa	6,453.4	5.5	47.8	253.1	717.3	1,214.7	3,671.7	543.3
U.S.	**4,922.7**	**6.8**	**35.9**	**186.1**	**382.0**	**919.6**	**2,886.5**	**505.8**

Note: Crime rate is the number of crimes per 100,000 population; n/a not available;
(1) Metropolitan Statistical Area - see Appendix A for areas included
Source: FBI Uniform Crime Reports 1997

Temperature & Precipitation: Yearly Averages and Extremes

City	Extreme Low (°F)	Average Low (°F)	Average Temp. (°F)	Average High (°F)	Extreme High (°F)	Average Precip. (in.)	Average Snow (in.)
Atlanta	-8	52	62	72	105	49.8	2
Austin	-2	58	69	79	109	31.1	1
Birmingham	-6	51	63	73	106	53.6	1
Chattanooga	-10	49	60	71	106	53.3	4
Columbia	-1	51	64	75	107	48.3	2
Dallas	-2	56	67	77	112	33.9	3
Ft. Lauderdale	30	69	76	83	98	57.1	0
Ft. Worth	-1	55	66	76	113	32.3	3
Houston	7	58	69	79	107	46.9	Tr
Jackson	2	53	65	76	106	55.4	1
Jacksonville	7	58	69	79	103	52.0	0
Knoxville	-24	48	59	69	103	46.7	13
Memphis	0	52	65	77	107	54.8	1
Miami	30	69	76	83	98	57.1	0
Nashville	-17	49	60	70	107	47.4	11
New Orleans	11	59	69	78	102	60.6	Tr
Orlando	19	62	72	82	100	47.7	Tr
San Antonio	0	58	69	80	108	29.6	1
Tampa	18	63	73	82	99	46.7	Tr

Note: Tr = Trace
Source: National Climatic Data Center, International Station Meteorological Climate Summary, 3/95

Weather Conditions

City	Temperature			Daytime Sky			Precipitation		
	10°F & below	32°F & below	90°F & above	Clear	Partly cloudy	Cloudy	.01 inch or more precip.	1.0 inch or more snow/ice	Thunder-storms
Atlanta	1	49	38	98	147	120	116	3	48
Austin	< 1	20	111	105	148	112	83	1	41
Birmingham	(a)	57	261	92	157	116	116	3	57
Chattanooga	2	73	48	88	141	136	120	3	55
Columbia	< 1	58	77	97	149	119	110	1	53
Dallas	1	34	102	108	160	97	78	2	49
Ft. Lauderdale	(a)	(b)	55	48	263	54	128	0	74
Ft. Worth	1	40	100	123	136	106	79	3	47
Houston	(a)	(b)	96	83	168	114	101	1	62
Jackson	1	50	84	103	144	118	106	2	68
Jacksonville	< 1	16	83	86	181	98	114	1	65
Knoxville	3	73	33	85	142	138	125	8	47
Memphis	1	53	86	101	152	112	104	2	59
Miami	(a)	(b)	55	48	263	54	128	0	74
Nashville	5	76	51	98	135	132	119	8	54
New Orleans	0	13	70	90	169	106	114	1	69
Orlando	(a)	(b)	90	76	208	81	115	0	80
San Antonio	(a)	(b)	112	97	153	115	81	1	36
Tampa	(a)	(b)	85	81	204	80	107	< 1	87

Note: Figures are average number of days per year; (a) Figures for 10 degrees and below are not available; (b) Figures for 32 degrees and below are not available
Source: National Climatic Data Center, International Station Meteorological Climate Summary, 3/95

Air Quality

MSA[1]	PSI>100[2] (days)	Ozone (ppm)	Carbon Monoxide (ppm)	Sulfur Dioxide (ppm)	Nitrogen Dioxide (ppm)	Particulate Matter (ug/m3)	Lead (ug/m3)
Atlanta	36	0.14	4	0.027	0.025	75	0.34
Austin	6	0.11	1	n/a	n/a	n/a	n/a
Birmingham	8	0.12	6	0.018	0.010	111	n/a
Chattanooga	n/a	0.11	n/a	n/a	n/a	63	n/a
Columbia	n/a	0.11	3	0.020	0.011	130	0.01
Dallas	32	0.14	5	0.022	0.018	104	0.04
Fort Lauderdale	0	0.09	5	0.011	0.010	39	0.04
Fort Worth	14	0.13	3	n/a	0.016	47	n/a
Houston	47	0.21	7	0.025	0.025	134	0.00
Jackson	n/a	0.10	4	0.007	n/a	111	n/a
Jacksonville	4	0.12	3	0.035	0.014	62	0.02
Knoxville	38	0.12	5	0.048	n/a	141	0.00
Memphis	17	0.12	6	0.033	0.028	76	0.03
Miami	3	0.11	4	0.004	0.017	52	n/a
Nashville	24	0.13	6	0.086	0.012	69	0.08
New Orleans	7	0.11	3	0.017	0.018	94	0.05
Orlando	5	0.11	4	0.006	0.013	52	n/a
San Antonio	3	0.10	4	n/a	0.022	41	n/a
Tampa	4	0.11	4	0.038	0.012	87	n/a
NAAQS[3]	-	0.12	9	0.140	0.053	150	1.50

Note: (1) Metropolitan Statistical Area - see Appendix A for areas included; (2) Number of days the Pollutant Standards Index (PSI) exceeded 100 in 1997. A PSI value greater than 100 indicates that air quality would be in the unhealthful range on that day; (3) National Ambient Air Quality Standard; ppm = parts per million; ug/m³ = micrograms per cubic meter; n/a not available
Source: EPA, National Air Quality and Emissions Trends Report, 1997

Water Quality

City	Tap Water
Atlanta	Neutral, soft
Austin	Alkaline, soft and fluoridated
Birmingham	Alkaline, soft
Chattanooga	Slightly alkaline, moderately hard and fluoridated
Columbia	Alkaline, very soft and fluoridated
Dallas	Moderately hard and fluoridated
Fort Lauderdale	Alkaline, very soft and fluoridated
Fort Worth	Alkaline, hard and fluoridated
Houston	Alkaline, hard
Jackson	Alkaline, hard, fluoridated and chloromine disinfected
Jacksonville	Alkaline, very hard and naturally fluoridated
Knoxville	Alkaline, hard and fluoridated
Memphis	Neutral, hardness 46ppm and fluoridated
Miami	Alkaline, soft and fluoridated
Nashville	Alkaline, soft
New Orleans	Alkaline, soft and fluoridated
Orlando	Alkaline, hard and fluoridated
San Antonio	Not fluoridated and has moderate mineral content, chiefly sodium bicarbonate
Tampa	Alkaline, moderately hard and not fluoridated

Source: Editor & Publisher Market Guide 1999

Appendix B

Metropolitan Statistical Areas

Atlanta, GA

Includes Barrow, Bartow, Carroll, Cherokee, Clayton, Cobb, Coweta, DeKalb, Douglas, Fayette, Forsyth, Fulton, Gwinnett, Henry, Newton, Paulding, Pickens, Rockdale, Spalding, and Walton Counties (as of 6/30/93)

Includes Barrow, Butts, Cherokee, Clayton, Cobb, Coweta, DeKalb, Douglas, Fayette, Forsyth, Fulton, Gwinnett, Henry, Newton, Paulding, Rockdale, Spalding, and Walton Counties (prior to 6/30/93)

Austin-San Marcos, TX

Includes Bastrop, Caldwell, Hays, Travis and Williamson Counties (as of 6/30/93)

Includes Hays, Travis and Williamson Counties (prior to 6/30/93)

Birmingham, AL

Includes Blount, Jefferson, St. Clair and Shelby Counties

Chattanooga, TN

Includes Catoosa, Dade and Walker Counties, GA; Hamilton and Marion Counties, TN

Columbia, SC

Includes Lexington and Richland Counties

Dallas, TX

Includes Collin, Dallas, Denton, Ellis, Henderson, Hunt, Kaufman and Rockwall Counties (as of 6/30/93)

Includes Collin, Dallas, Denton, Ellis, Kaufman and Rockwall Counties (prior to 6/30/93)

Ft. Lauderdale, FL

Includes Broward County

Ft. Worth-Arlington, TX

Includes Hood, Johnson, Parker and Tarrant Counties (as of 6/30/93)

Includes Johnson, Parker and Tarrant Counties (prior to 6/30/93)

Houston, TX

Includes Chambers, Fort Bend, Harris, Liberty, Montgomery and Waller Counties (as of 6/30/93)

Includes Fort Bend, Harris, Liberty, Montgomery and Waller Counties (prior to 6/30/93)

Jackson, MS

Includes Hinds, Madison and Rankin Counties

Jacksonville, FL

Includes Clay, Duval, Nassau and St. Johns Counties

Knoxville, TN

Includes Anderson, Blount, Knox, Loudon, Sevier and Union Counties (as of 6/30/93)

Includes Anderson, Blount, Grainger, Jefferson, Knox, Sevier and Union Counties (prior to 6/30/93)

Memphis, TN

Includes Crittenden County, AR; Desoto County, MS; Fayette, Shelby and Tipton Counties, TN

Miami, FL

Includes Dade County

Nashville, TN

Includes Cheatham, Davidson, Dickson, Robertson, Rutherford, Sumner, Williamson and Wilson Counties

New Orleans, LA

Includes Jefferson, Orleans, Plaquemines, St. Bernard, St. Charles, St. James, St. John the Baptist and St. Tammany Parishes (as of 6/30/93)

Includes Jefferson, Orleans, St. Bernard, St. Charles, St. John the Baptist and St. Tammany Parishes (prior to 6/30/93)

Orlando, FL

Includes Lake, Orange, Osceola and Seminole Counties (as of 6/30/93)

Includes Orange, Osceola and Seminole Counties (prior to 6/30/93)

San Antonio, TX

Includes Bexar, Comal, Guadalupe and Wilson Counties (as of 6/30/93)

Includes Bexar, Comal and Guadalupe Counties (prior to 6/30/93)

Tampa-St. Petersburg-Clearwater, FL

Includes Hernando, Hillsborough, Pasco and Pinellas Counties

Appendix C

Chambers of Commerce and Economic Development Organizations

Atlanta

Atlanta Chamber of Commerce
235 International Boulevard, NW
P.O. Box 1740
Atlanta, GA 30301
Phone: (404) 880-9000
Fax: (404) 586-8469

Atlanta Economic Development Corporation
230 Peachtree Street
Suite 210
Atlanta, GA 30303
Phone: (404) 658-7000
Fax: (404) 658-7734

Austin

Greater Austin Chamber of Commerce
111 Congress Avenue
Plaza Level
P.O. Box 1967
Phone: (512) 478-9383
Fax: (512) 578-6389

Birmingham

Birmingham Austin Chamber of Commerce
2027 First Avenue North
Birmingham, AL 35203
Phone: (205) 323-5461
Fax: (205) 250-7669

Chattanooga

Chattanooga Chamber of Commerce
1001 Market Street
Chattanooga, TN 37402
Phone: (423) 756-2121
Fax: (423) 267-7242

Columbia

Columbia Chamber of Commerce
P.O. Box 1360
Columbia, SC 29202
Phone: (803) 733-1110
Fax: (803) 733-1149

Dallas

City of Dallas
Economic Development Department
1500 Marilla Street
Room 5C South
Dallas, TX 75201
Phone: (214) 670-1685
Fax: (214) 670-0158

Greater Dallas Chamber of Commerce
1201 Elm Street
Suite 2000
Dallas, TX 75270
Phone: (214) 746-6600
Fax: (214) 746-6799

Fort Lauderdale

Fort Lauderdale Chamber of Commerce
512 NE 3rd Avenue
P.O. Box 14516
Phone: (954) 462-6000
Fax: (954) 527-8766

Fort Worth

City of Forth Worth
Economic Development Municipal Building
1000 Throckmorton Street
Phone: (817) 871-6103
Fax: (817) 871-6134

Fort Worth Chamber of Commerce
777 Taylor Street
Suite 900
Fort Worth, TX 76102-4997
Phone: (817) 336-2491
Fax: (817) 877-4034

Houston

Greater Houston Partnership
1200 Smith Street
Suite 700
Houston, TX 77002-4309
Phone: (713) 651-2100
Fax: (713) 844-3600

Jackson

Jackson Chamber of Commerce
P.O. Box 22548
Jackson, MI 29335-2548
Phone: (601) 948-7575
Fax: (601) 352-5553

Jacksonville

Jacksonville Chamber of Commerce
3 Independent Drive
Jacksonville, FL 32202
Phone: (904) 366-6600
Fax: (904) 632-0617

Knoxville

Greater Knoxville Chamber of Commerce
601 West Summit Hill Drive
Suite 300
Knoxville, TN 37915-2572
Phone: (423) 637-4550
Fax: (423) 523-2071

Memphis

Memphis Chamber of Commerce
19 North Riverside Drive
Memphis, TN 38103
Phone: (901) 543-5333
Fax: (901) 543-5335

Miami

Greater Miami Chamber of Commerce
Omni Complex
1601 Biscayne Boulevard
Miami, FL 33132-1260
Phone: (305) 350-7700
Fax: (305) 394-6902

The Beacon Council
One World Trade Plaza
Suite 2400
80 Southwest 8th Street
Miami, FL 33130
Phone: (305) 579-1300
Fax: (305) 375-0271

Nashville

Nashville Area Chamber of Commerce
161 4th Avenue, North
Nashville, TN 37219
Phone: (615) 259-4755
Fax: (615) 256-3074

New Orleans

City of New Orleans Partnership
Office of the Mayor
1300 Perdido Street
Room 2E04
New Orleans, LA 70112
Phone: (504) 565-6400

Orlando

Greater Orlando Chamber of Commerce
75 East Ivanhoe Boulevard
P.O. Box 1234
Orlando, FL 32802
Phone: (407) 425-1234
Fax: (407) 839-5020

Metro Orlando Economic Development
Commerce of Mid-Florida
200 East Robinson Street
Suite 600
Orlando, FL 32801
Phone: (407) 422-7159
Fax: (407) 843-9514

San Antonio

San Antonio Economic Development
Department
P.O. Box 839966
San Antonio, TX 78296
Phone: (210) 207-8080
Fax: (210) 207-8151

The Greater San Antonio Chamber of Commerce
P.O. Box 1628
San Antonio, TX 78296
Phone: (210) 229-2100
Fax: (210) 229-1600

Tampa

Greater Tampa Chamber of Commerce
P.O. Box 420
Tampa, FL 33601-0420
Phone: (813) 228-7777
Fax: (813) 223-7899

Appendix D

State Departments of Labor and Employment

Alabama

Department of Industrial Relations
649 Monroe Street
Montgomery, AL 36131
Phone: (334) 242-8055

Florida

Florida Department of State & Employment
Security Bureau of Labor Market Information
Suite 2000, Hartman Building
2012 Capitol Circle, Southeast
Tallahassee, FL 32399-2151
Phone: (850) 561-0032

Georgia

Georgia Department of Labor
Commissioners Office
148 International Boulevard, Northeast
Atlanta, GA 30303-1751
Phone: (404) 656-3011

Louisiana

Louisiana Department of
Employment & Training
Research & Statistics
P.O. Box 94094
Baton Rouge, LA
Phone: (225) 342-3141

Mississippi

Mississippi Department of Labor
Market Labor Information
P.O. Box 1699
Jackson, MI 39215
Phone: (601) 961-7424

South Carolina

South Carolina Department of Labor
Employment Security Commission
631 Hampton Street
Columbia, SC 29202
Phone: (803) 737-2660

Tennessee

Tennesee Department of Employment Security
Research & Statistics Division
500 James Robertson Parkway
Nashville, TN 37245-1000
Phone: (615) 741-2116

Texas

Texas Employment Commission Economic
Research & Analysis
101 East 15th Street
Austin, TX 78778-0001
Phone: (512) 463-2222